THE BORDERLANDS OF CULTURE

For Felicia
with great
admiration for
your developing
work and in
friendship,

Ramón S____

NEW AMERICANISTS *A Series Edited by Donald E. Pease*

Ramón Saldívar

THE BORDERLANDS OF CULTURE

Américo Paredes and the Transnational

Imaginary

DUKE UNIVERSITY PRESS   DURHAM & LONDON   2006

© 2006 Duke University Press

All rights reserved

Printed in the United States of America

on acid-free paper ∞

Designed by C. H. Westmoreland

Typeset in Adobe Garamond

by Tseng Information Systems, Inc.

Library of Congress Cataloging-in-

Publication Data appear on the last

printed page of this book.

TO DENISE

Amor, cuántos caminos hasta llegar a un beso

CONTENTS

ACKNOWLEDGMENTS

Many friends and colleagues have read and commented on portions of this book, and I am grateful to all of them. None was more important than Denise Boulangé, to whom I dedicate it with love. *Amor, nuestras almas se acercaron tanto así que yo guardo tú sabor.*

I am pleased to acknowledge the work of graduate and undergraduate research assistants, especially Alicia Schmidt Camacho, Marcial González, Raúl Coronado, Diana Vizcarra, and Lisa Coffey. The initial portion of the writing and research was completed during a sabbatical year provided by Stanford University and generous research funding from the dean of the School of Humanities and Sciences. I completed the last part of the research on Japan in the summer of 2003, after attending the Japanese American Studies Association meeting in Kobe as one of the representatives of the American Studies Association. Comments and questions posed by faculty and students at Ritsumeikan University (Kyoto), Aichi Prefectural University (Nagoya), Tokyo University, and Tsuda College (Tokyo) proved instrumental in determining the final shape of my argument. In particular, I would like to thank Professors Maskao Iino of Tsuda College, Masako Notoji and Yujin Yaguchi of the Center for Pacific and American Studies at Tokyo University, and Keiichi Tanaka of the Aichi Prefectural University for their gracious hospitality and their many helpful questions and observations. Professors Carla Kaplan of the University of Southern California, Min-Jung Kim of Ewha Womans University in Seoul, and Stephen Sumida of the University of Washington posed important questions that helped me clarify the nature of my project.

For their patience with numerous drafts and their many encouraging suggestions over the years that I have been talking and writing about this project, I am especially grateful to José David Saldívar, Sonia Saldivar-Hull, Mary Pratt, Renato Rosaldo, Paula Moya, Héctor Calderón, and Regenia Gagnier, brothers and sisters all. Walter Mignolo read the manuscript and offered many important suggestions. My ideas have also been significantly formed by responses I have received to papers presented at the University of Michigan, Cornell

University, Hampshire College, the University of Texas at Austin, the University of Texas at San Antonio, the Universidad de la Habana, Cuba, Harvard University, the Humanities Center at Stanford University, the University of Southern California, the University of Chicago, Dartmouth College, the American Studies Association, and the Modern Language Association. Alan and Vincent Paredes graciously shared time, memories, and photographs. My thanks also to Américo Paredes Jr. for his willingness to be interviewed for this project. Alejandro Rivera Leal created an original painting, *La pared de Paredes*, as the cover illustration, for which I am profoundly grateful. At Duke University Press, I am deeply indebted to J. Reynolds Smith, Kate Lothman, Katie Courtland, and Katharine Baker, whose meticulous care made the experience of publishing this book a joy.

Finally, I also gratefully acknowledge permission to use materials from the Américo Paredes Papers at the Benson Latin American Collection, General Libraries, the University of Texas at Austin; from the University of Texas at San Antonio Institute of Texan Cultures; the Norman Rockwell Museum and the Norman Rockwell Family Agency; the City College of San Francisco; the Ohio State University Japanese Collections; the Stanford University Libraries, Cambridge University Press, and *Stars and Stripes*.

Portions of part 2, chapters 3, 6, and 7 have been published in shorter and earlier versions. I am grateful to the editors and publishers of *American Literary History*, *Narrative*, and the *Stanford Humanities Review*, respectively, for permission to reprint this material.

Américo Paredes

SEPTEMBER 3, 1915 – MAY 5, 1999

1 Américo Paredes with guitar, 1997. © Tino (Valentino) Mauricio. Reprinted with the permission of Tino Mauricio.

In Memoriam

Instante tan corto que encierra una vida;
Es hilo de seda que al alma guardó.
—Américo Paredes, "In Memoriam,"
Cantos de adolescencia

So word by word, and line by line,
The dead man touched me from the past,
And all at once it seemed at last
The living soul was flashed on mine.
—Alfred, Lord Tennyson,
"In Memoriam A.H.H."

In November 1998, I accompanied Américo Paredes on what turned out to be his final visit to south Texas, the border, and the lower Rio Grande Valley city of Brownsville, where he had been born in 1915. Fragile from years of fighting numerous debilitating maladies, he nonetheless looked forward with great anticipation to the opportunity to feel once again the austere beauty of his homeland on the border coastal plains. It had been nearly a decade since his previous trip to Brownsville, and it was my good fortune to go along with him on what proved to be a farewell tour of the border and a deeply sentimental journey.

As we left his home in Austin for the three hundred–plus mile trip to Brownsville, Don Américo was dressed much as he usually was: soft leather shoes, brown cotton twill slacks, and a long-sleeved white *guayabera*, the shirt of choice for the soft humidity and mild semi-tropical temperatures of late fall in south Texas. A bit incongruously, and only as a precaution against the early morning falling damp, he wore a soft gray flannel beret. With his walking cane crooked in his arm, the ensemble effect was one of graceful informality.

At the age of eighty-three, Paredes had a face that resembled one of Picasso's sketches of Don Quixote. The angular lines of his forehead around his deep-set, hooded eyes forming a double parenthetical frame at the edges of his thin mouth were no longer mere wrinkles but deep strokes of definition engraved into the flesh of his long face. A defining goatee set off his brown eyes, aquiline nose, and thin lips. As he closed the door behind him, he waved one final time to his wife, Doña Amelia. Given that Don Américo tended to be overconfident about his stable but hardly robust health, Doña Amelia was wary of his tendency, as she put it, "to overdo things." She was anxious about his ability to handle the rigors of the trip from Austin to the border and was concerned that his companions for the trip to south Texas would be unable to contain his exuberance.

Mrs. Paredes had reason for concern. We arrived in south Texas to its typically glorious autumn weather, with rare white strands of clouds arcing high and slowly across a pure blue sky. The breeze was just strong enough to quaver the bright green fronds of the graceful royal palms that dot the landscapes of the lower Rio Grande Valley, making them click softly against one another; its warmth had a soothing effect on us, coming from the harsh hi-tech frenzy of Silicon Valley and Austin, Texas. For the next week, Don Américo was up every day before dawn, invigorated and eager to see old friends and family, including cousins, nieces and nephews, and his lone surviving elder brother, Lorenzo. He wanted to visit long-remembered places along the Rio Grande, in downtown Brownsville, and on the neighborhood street on which his boyhood home still stood. He wished to stand on Elizabeth Street in front of the old US Post Office as memories from his youth and stories from before his time crowded around him, urging themselves on him. He was enthusiastic to speak with young people at the schools he was scheduled to visit, and he seemed always ready for a rich south Texas Mexican dinner and a cold beer as a nightcap.

Everywhere he went—from Brownsville to Harlingen, San Benito, Weslaco, Mercedes, Relampago, Los Indios, Edcouch, and Elsa, all the high spots of south Texas—when people heard he was coming, they crowded around him to shake his hand, speak with him, and touch the legendary man. This was true at the planned receptions on the campuses of the University of Texas at Brownsville and at Texas Southmost College. But it also happened spontaneously at the airport in Harlingen, at the Luby's Cafeteria in Weslaco, and at the high school in Edcouch-Elsa. I came to think of the five days in the Rio Grande Valley as the Américo Paredes Adoration Tour. For me it offered a glimpse of what it must be like to serve as a roadie for a rock star—a traveler in the shadow of fame.

That part of south Texas is overwhelmingly Mexican American. The three counties that make up the region—Cameron, Hidalgo, and Willacy—are as much as 85 percent Mexican American and more. Consistently, these counties rank among the poorest in the nation. Only in the last generation or so, at the end of the twentieth century, have Mexican Americans regained control of some of the civic, social, and educational institutions of the region that they lost after 1848. To that generation of the late twentieth century, Paredes represented the efforts of a previous generation of the early twentieth century to establish the legitimacy of social and political self-determination in the region. His scholarly work focused on the folklore and vernacular arts of the United States–Mexico border region, a dialogic space between two worlds that he came to call "Greater Mexico" to indicate the Mexican labor diasporas north from the border, as well as the social, economic, political, and symbolic overlap between those contiguous worlds. His work served as a backstop to historical memory in a period of official collective amnesia about their interrelationship. It was for those reasons that he was being honored at the Edcouch-Elsa High School.

At the high school, Don Américo spoke with passion to the students about the importance of education. One could see in their eyes the depth of the inspiration his words aroused. It is not often that you get to see a legend in the flesh, and these young Chicanos and Chicanas, thanks to the work of their teachers, themselves formed during an era of activism in education, knew they found themselves in the presence of one. It was evident in the ways that they asked him, with awe and respect, to talk about the writing of *"With His Pistol in His Hand"* and *George Washington Gómez*. Plainly, he delighted in the role of storyteller and teacher, and it was evident that the students understood how words and ideas marshaled by courage and insisted on by will affect history.

At the conclusion of a brief and beautiful performance by the student *concertina*, a traditional Mexican music performance group, in this case entirely comprised of so-called at risk students, Don Américo congratulated each of the student musicians for their music and their academic success with a firm handshake and a soft *abrazo* (hug). When two of the young women at the head of the group burst into tears as he greeted them, he was flustered and moved by their sensitivity. For the remainder of the week, he kept returning to that moment, with a bemused self-mocking tone and a deliciously mischievous laugh, as he relished returning to Austin to declare to Mrs. Paredes that, even now in his eighties, he "could still make young women weep." Irony aside, he was also touched by the fact that not a few young men had wept as well. Later that same evening, at a dinner in his honor that my numerous Saldívar cousins had arranged, he picked up a guitar and sang the ballad of Gregorio Cortez. It had been a long time since he had played and sung outside his home and, as it turned out, it was to be among the very last.

Arriving in Brownsville, at Don Américo's request one of our first stops had been to the north bank of the Rio Grande. As we worked our way carefully down from the embankment to the river's verge, looking across the river to Mexico, I remembered that the first poem of Paredes's collection of poetry, *Between Two Worlds*, was a piece entitled "The Rio Grande," written in 1934 when he was eighteen years old. The verses displayed even then his intense focus on the geographic specificity of the south Texas border region and its connection to what Raymond Williams called individual "structures of feeling," those vitally human experiences to which official fixed forms of consciousness and knowledge do not speak at all (*Marxism and Literature* 130). In the poem, the river has both personal and political significance. I quote it in its entirety:

Muddy river, muddy river,
Moving slowly down your track,
With your swirls and counter-currents,
As though wanting to turn back,
As though wanting to turn back,
Towards the place where you were born,
While your currents swirl and eddy,
While you whisper, whimper, mourn;

So you wander down your channel
Always on, since it must be,
Till you die so very gently
By the margin of the sea.
All my pain and all my trouble
In your bosom let me hide,
Drain my soul of all its sorrow
As you drain the countryside,
For I was born beside your waters,
And since very young I knew
That my soul had hidden currents,
That my soul resembled you,
Troubled, dark, its bottom hidden
While its surface mocks the sun,
With its sighs and its rebellions,
Yet compelled to travel on.
When the soul must leave the body,
When the wasted flesh must die,
I shall trickle forth to join you,
In your bosom I shall lie;
We shall wander through the country
Where your banks in green are clad,
Past the shanties of *rancheros*,
By the ruins of old Bagdad,
Till at last your dying waters,
Will release their hold on me,
And my soul will sleep forever
By the margin of the sea.

The swirls and countercurrents of the river reflected in this poem are like the articulations of history and locale joined as one with the young poet. Like the chronotope of the river itself, he found them mesmerizing and compelling as figures for the alienation running deep in the hidden currents of the soul. He would return to them repeatedly throughout the course of his imaginative life as images of the contradictory coursing of history and human events.

Reflecting on the nature of history and its relation to human events, Walter Benjamin has argued that "to articulate the past historically does not mean to recognize it 'the way it really was' (Ranke). It means to seize hold of a memory as it flashes up at a moment of danger. . . . Only that historian will have the gift of fanning the spark of hope in the past who is firmly convinced that *even the dead* will not be safe from the enemy if he wins" ("Theses" 255). In this essay, Benjamin counters the newly supposedly scientific sense of nineteenth-century historiography represented by Leopold von Ranke (1795–1886), which strove for objectivity grounded in source material. Benjamin proposes an alternative function for the historian: the role of collector of communal wisdom. The historian's task, Benjamin suggests, is to ground the continuity of knowledge in legend and tradition, those deep repositories of historical understanding ("Eduard Fuchs" 288 n. 10). Only in this manner will he (or she) be able to resist the destruction of the past, the devastation of the social mechanisms that link one's contemporary experience to that of earlier generations.

In the earliest of his lyrical works, as in all of his later writings, Américo Paredes, too, much like Benjamin, wrestled with historical memory and the destruction of the past. He contended with all that was at stake in the attempt to keep social remembrance alive as what Benjamin called "an afterlife of that which has been understood and whose pulse can be felt in the present" ("Eduard Fuchs" 262). In his ethnographic and literary writings Paredes endeavored to remind us of the hold of places and times on our social selves and to liberate the forces within history that always make it something originary for the present. This held true for all of Paredes's writings, but especially for his literary creations, as works of mnemonic art. In a poem like "The Rio Grande," Paredes seizes just such an instant of historical memory as it flashes in a moment of danger, the danger of cultural eradication, and makes it concrete by grounding it on the reality of regional local space. Already, he realizes that even the dead are not safe from an enemy who is wholly determined to obliterate the social history of the region from the narrative of American history. (Indeed, by the time I was growing up in Brownsville in the 1950s and 1960s, attending the same schools that Paredes had attended four decades earlier, Paredes's fears proved all too well founded. References to Mexican American history and the patterns of its relations to American enculturation had been altogether erased from our Texas and American history lessons. Even the dead had not remained safe from this enemy.)

Raymond Williams reminds us that "perhaps the dead can be reduced to fixed forms, though their surviving records are against it. But the living will not be reduced" (*Marxism and Literature* 129). Paredes's work is always concerned with the surviving records of community, with the sense of place, and most important, with the hope of freedom associated with the structures of feeling tied to place, underwriting the value of social geographies as fields of care. As he does in this earliest of his poems, a version of which he also published in Spanish ("El Río Bravo"), Paredes habitually contends that social beings are embedded in the world of nature through the body's social sensorium. No political understanding could afford abstractions that did not take this embeddedness and the particularity of the border locale into consideration. It was his feeling that one's sense of identity is drawn from the long past, the deep kinships, the longitudinal prerogatives that denote identity and tradition and constitute the very essence of geopolitical change.

In considering the nature of social identity, Paredes requires us to interrogate what historical frames of mind mean and what kinds of knowledge they might produce. That his formulations of these prerogatives were cast in masculinist ideologies and were linked to unrelentingly obdurate patriarchal hierarchies made for limitations that his work could neither wholly articulate nor fully escape. Yet if we are to see Paredes's literary works as what Doris Sommer has in another Latin American context termed "foundational fictions" (*Foundational Fictions* 6), that is, as thought experiments with nation-building templates serving to play out the possibilities of class consciousness and cultural nationalism, or simply as real alternatives to American modernity, then we should understand the nature of those limits. Paredes attains them precisely through his internalization of the community of impulses that originate from that world in that time, contradictions and all. In their moments of most lucid insight, his writings grapple with these, his own, contradictions as well.

Paredes's work frequently exhibits those contradictions as a tension between national and transnational perspectives, a tension that makes his analysis of the Western hemisphere's different national formations and their intrahemispheric relations exceptionally significant for how we think about "America" today. His overlapping identities as a scholar of regional nationalist culture and as a transnational journalist and writer taught him to see the struggle for Mexican American social justice as part of a much larger and more elaborate geopolitical puzzle. For this reason, Paredes ordinarily sees the national culture or political event as a local inflection of a transnational phenomenon that can only be read according to a hemispheric dialectic of similarity and difference.

A strong reading of Paredes would see him as the "proto-Chicano" that he once labeled himself (*Between Two Worlds* 11), albeit with the same degree of irony and skepticism that he used as his customary mode of analysis. (Large doses of self-irony and the well-placed tongue-in-cheek served Paredes well from Texas to Asia and back again for nearly seven decades of critical writing.) But such a reading would also distinguish him as a precursor of the new American cultural studies in his persistent rearticulations of the triangulated cultural and political relationships between North and South America and their various and unexpected points of convergence in cold war Asia. Paredes is important because he negotiated the tension between the national and transnational forces at work in the Americas measuredly and by design. His extended experience with and deep understanding of the Latin American intellectual world provided him with a comparative perspective on the political, cultural, and social dynamics of the various forms of American nation-states that few other writers of his era shared.

Supplementing his understanding of the Americas with special insight into the particularities of Euro-African societies like Cuba and with experience in Euro-Indian societies like Mexico and Guatemala, Paredes's experiences in post–World War II Asia gave him yet something more. His years in Asia exposed him in a crucially formative way to the differing ethno-cultural complexities that imperialism and modernization in their multiple varieties had bequeathed to both the Americas and the Far East. In particular, his travels in Japan, China, and Korea disabused him of any naive faith that the mere shift from colonial to postcolonial status would in and of itself necessarily produce a just society. In addition, they taught him about the imbricated relations of dependence and independence between an occupying and occupied peoples in the wake of the global calamities that followed at the tail end of the classical age of empires.

The historian Eric Hobsbawm begins his magisterial study of the age of empires with questions similar to those Paredes posed in his own work. Hobsbawm cites as epigraph the words of French *Annales* historian Pierre Nora:

> Memory is life. It is always carried by groups of living people, and therefore it is in permanent evolution. It is subject to the dialectics of remem-

bering and forgetting, unaware of its successive deformations, open to all kinds of use and manipulation. . . . History is the always incomplete and problematic reconstruction of what is no longer there. Memory always belongs to our time and forms a lived bond with the eternal present; history is a representation of the past. (Hobsbawm 1)

Elsewhere Nora had argued that history was evanescent, amorphous, and hard to grasp. Events as such, the stuff of history, he claimed, merely "prick holes in the night without illuminating it" (427). To Nora's marvelous formulation about the nocturnal relationship between events and history, Hobsbawm adds the recognition that "for all of us there is a twilight zone between history and memory" (3). This holds true for individuals as well as for societies. That "twilight zone" between the past as "a generalized record accessible to inspection" and the past "as a remembered part of, or background to, one's own life" is for Hobsbawm the fabulous no-man's-land of time and of the obscurities and complexities with which it marks the course of events that characterize an epoch (3–4).

Recording the evanescent complexities and fabulous obscurities of events in history in both imaginative and analytical modes, Paredes understood that the crucial question the writer must ask is what particular emotional needs and desires are fulfilled in remembering and recording a specific history in a distinguishable way. It was a question that Paredes pursued as a social and a political aesthetic project of remembrance for the entirety of his intellectual life. Thus Paredes would later claim of both history itself and of historiography: "History (oral and written) is a dynamic process that is always open to change; . . . it tends to reshape itself according to the half-conscious desires and yearnings of those who behold it, changing a detail here, a name there, making itself less what probably was and more what it should have been" ("The Undying Love" 261). "Memories are like that," he would add; "with the passing of the years they change a bit. But the memory is all that matters" (261). Certainly, a stark opposition between the two oversimplifies the relationship between history and memory. As the historian Dominick LaCapra has observed, the relation may vary over time, as memory may serve as a source for history and history may test memory (19–20). Paredes is crucially aware of this variable relation and of the possibility that the test may work in the other direction as well, with memory serving in critical fashion against documentary sources. Implicit in the literary writings, the ethnographic and the folkloric texts, and in his autobiographical statements are ideas on how impulses of memory originating from local histories are transformed into critical structures of feeling that link them to transnational designs. In the "half-conscious desire and yearnings" tentatively articulated as memory in the folk wisdom of a community, one may find implicitly the matters that organize the course of history. Repeatedly, those texts of collective wisdom suggest why the recognitions of those designs persist as a memory that matters.

Paredes understood that the linking of those structures of feeling to transnational designs was continually being worked out dialectically through both cultural and socioeconomic forms. The historian E. P. Thompson has argued that what changes as economic relations change is the experience of living men and women in their everyday lives. He believed that this experience is "sorted out in social life and consciousness, in the complex matrix of the assent, the resistance, and the choices of historical men and women" (265). Remembering these changes in socioeconomic and cultural form in history, literature, and folklore was for Paredes, as an engaged intellectual of color on the periphery of modernism, tantamount to political agency itself. For this reason, history, memory, and poetics are for Paredes vitally connected. In fact, the connection proves so critical that memory actually becomes both his theory of history and his poetics as *anamnesis*, a praxis against forgetting. History as an act of remembrance is thus not obviously an objective reality; it is also a performance. History is not the official documents and records of the deeds of an age only; it is also the emplotment of those deeds as story in official and unofficial forms, conveying the conscious and unconscious desires, hopes, and prejudices of the story's emplotter. As Hayden White has shown, history cannot be simply the representation of what "really is," since as stories, histories "are linguistic entities and belong to the order of discourse." It follows necessarily that the emplotments of history cannot remain innocent. As a consequence, there is, argues White, "an unexpungeable relativity in every representation of historical phenomenon" (*Figural Realism* 27, 28). "Is it not possible," White challenges elsewhere, "that the question of narrative in any discussion of historical theory is always finally about the function of the imagination in the production of a specifically human truth?" (*Content of Form* 57). If history must ultimately claim a material basis, surely it must also rely on memory to shape our relationship to the past.

For all of these reasons having to do with the preserve of the imagination and the narrative arts in the service of human truth, memory is not just Paredes's subject; it is his methodology as well as his theory of history. From his earliest writings, he is aware that poetry, too, constitutes memory. This was the grand insight of "The Rio Grande," namely, that the projects of history and poetry were inevitably the same, to concoct *anamnesis*, a loss of forgetting. To be sure, this is the standpoint of classical rhetoric itself, connecting memory, history, and poetics in song, the space where the justice of memory holds sway. It is what allows Benjamin to propose that "memory brings about the convergence of imagination and thought" ("Central Park" 171). In *Cantos de adolescencia* (1937), assembling his first efforts in verse, Paredes had signaled as much when he chose at the beginning of his poetic career the path of mnemonics by rewriting in Spanish one of Tennyson's most elegiac of poems, "Crossing the Bar" (1889). He turns to Tennyson also for the title of one of the central sections of the volume, alluding to Tennyson's supreme poem of remembrance, "In Memoriam A. H. H." (1850). Attempting in this noble poem to recollect the essence of his departed dear friend Arthur Henry Hallam's soul, Tennyson feels the "dead man" touch him "from the past" in the climactic moment of the poem: "So word by word, and line by line, / The dead man touched me from the past, / And all at once it seemed at last / The living soul was flashed on mine." Subtitled "The Way of the Soul," Tennyson's poem momentarily admits Hallam's enormously influential lead in developing an aesthetic of sensation, which Hallam in an essay of 1831 had credited to Keats and Shelley alone among nineteenth-century poets (Hallam 182–98). T. S. Eliot would later join Hallam in celebration of this "poetry of sensation" as having attained "direct sensuous apprehension of thought" (Eliot 246), in contrast to the Wordsworthian aesthetic of discursive reflection, which had not. At issue in Tennyson's poem is whether the poet can apprehend directly and sensuously the "living soul" through the force of the imagination or whether the poet succeeds only in conjuring its phantasm from cold, reflective incertitude, fabricating it from desire through the "opposite disposition of purely intellectual contemplation" (Hallam 186).

Loss also motivates Paredes's *Cantos de adolescencia*. The special and immediate poignancy of Paredes's early poems written in memoriam stems from his grief over the tragic early death of his sister Blanca. As an eighteen-year-old apprentice in poetry looking forward over the course of his poetic life, Paredes, too, seeks assurances of faith from the experience of loss and imagines what Hallam called "a life of immediate sympathy with the external universe" (Hallam 186), a memory in touch with the living soul. Like Tennyson memorializing Hallam, Paredes uses the occasion of profound grief as an attempt to shape "thought into feeling" (Eliot 246) and to fortify the conviction that the spirit of the dead will one day truly rise up again to touch our living soul. Unlike Tennyson, however, Paredes does not encounter faith in the midst of doubt, nor does he seek solely a private solace. Instead, the act of remembrance itself becomes the critical category and the linchpin trope of his writings. Remembrance substitutes for faith in a passionate desire to memorialize personal history in social life and public space as defining elements of an aestheticized public sphere. Working under the sign of memory from the beginning of his poetic career onward, Paredes privileges a critical aesthetic based on a socially grounded sensorium that ultimately yields nothing less than an uncompromisingly radical historical critique fired by the functioning of what I am calling, following the work of the philosopher Charles Taylor, the social imaginary, that is, a level of understanding of the workings of society given expression on the symbolic level, even if it is not yet formulated as doctrinal knowledge (Taylor, "Two Theories" 189–90).

Echoes of another of Tennyson's most sublime poems, "Ulysses" (1833), also run through many of Paredes's later lyrics, stories, and nonfiction prose. Tennyson writes: "I am a part of all I have met; / Yet all experience is an arch wherethro' / Gleams that untravell'd world whose margin fades / For ever and for ever when I move" (ll. 18–21). In all of his writings, the mode of remembrance is crucial for who Américo Paredes is, for what he does, and for what he writes. The course of his biography, his individual life pattern—from the pan-American borderlands to Asia and back again, from vernacular journalist to social historian, from creative author to revisionary folklorist—displays a communal historical pattern of an epoch that forms, as Tennyson says, "a part of all I have met." Contained in this encounter with daily life and all experience are those complex emotions, reflections, and sensations which give rise to a peculiarly poetic organization, responsive to the demands of history, that I am calling Paredes's social aesthetic.

In this special context, then, Paredes made history, but only such history as it was possible for him to make, and under conditions not of his own creation. He made the world of all experience the arch through which gleamed that untraveled world whose margin fades beyond vision. Like Baudelaire and Benjamin, his immediate predecessors in mnemonic art, Paredes sought to articulate what Benjamin called a "theory of remembrance," (Benjamin "Remembrance" 137) adequate to forestalling the erasures of history. At the outset of this work, I wish to clarify that I am not presenting the life of a "great man," although Américo Paredes was surely a most remarkable man. Instead, I wish to *de*personalize that life by seeing it in context as a life pattern, a social aesthetic, and an act of remembrance. I wish to represent that life as Paredes lived it, in his words and in his work, as a methodology in performance for "fanning the spark of hope in the past."

In memoriam.

The various parts of this work should be read as layers and strata, superimpositions, or palimpsests, all of which reinforce one another while resisting one unified point of view. Part 1, "History and Remembrance as Social Aesthetics," presents an introductory chapter, ' "The Memory Is All That Matters," ' in which I take up in more detail the guiding concepts from which I derive the title of my book, namely, the borderlands and the transnational imaginary. I argue in the introduction that the transnational imaginary is an epistemically valuable way of describing our place in the world and understanding the meanings we ascribe to it and perform on it. When coupled with the notion of social aesthetics, it provides a suitable context for interpreting the complex dialectics of political, racial, and gender forms on the border as reflected in much of the best writing, folklore, popular performance, and music of borderland dwellers. It constitutes an interpretive framework that links the North and South Americas instead of the old and new Englands. A literary historiography that ignores those hemispheric relations effectively obscures certain historical events and makes opaque various political interests. It has the effect of devaluing several kinds of American literature—literatures that look from West to East and South to North, literatures not written in English, literatures written in unofficial vernaculars, literatures that advance a polemical use over an aesthetical form.

The ideas of memory, history, and their relationship to the notion of a borderland interspace of Greater Mexico serve as the guideposts for the second chapter of this section, "A Life in the Borderlands." It offers Américo Paredes narrating in his own voice a story that he called "a family autobiography." I have opted to give Paredes the first say before proceeding to the critical and analytical discussion of his life and works. In this self-presentation, Paredes focused on the social history of the border and the communal fates of his ancestors in order to make sense of the unusual circuits and surprising contours of his personal life. His narrative displays a remarkable instance of his constant fusion of aesthetics and politics into one voice of cultural advocacy.

In the chapters that follow in part II, "Fictions of the Transnational Imaginary," I take Paredes's life story and his interpretation of it as a general paradigm for the relationship of two conflicting yet dialogically interacting cultural traditions—"American" and "Mexican," to use for the moment an inadequate shorthand—that together have produced the richly imbricated multicultural heritage of the United States–Mexico borderlands. Paredes's own writings in fiction and nonfiction, poetry and prose, serve as the bases for the discussion. My project in this book is to interpret those literary and journalistic works of Paredes, one of the great border intellectuals of the twentieth century, in the context of transnational modernism. I wish to show how Paredes's work as a poet, novelist, prose writer, and journalist in the 1930s and 1940s prefigured his later work as a folklorist and ethnographer and set its political and aesthetic base.

My book started out as a study of comparative forms of modernism, focusing on the United States–Mexico borderlands as a site of convergence for European, North American, and Latin American modernisms. In the earliest versions of my work, modernism served as the guiding rationale for the argument. Paredes's writings were to serve in an exemplary capacity, representing the issues of modernity in a bicultural and bilingual context. This organizational measure is still discernable in this final version, but the experience of modernity rendered here stands now not in isolation as a motif in itself, but as a motive in relation to the world-historical events of the Great Depression, the Second World War, and the immediate postwar era as Paredes lived and described these experiences in the borderlands.

Chapter 3, "The Checkerboard of Consciousness in *George Washington Gómez*," concerning Paredes's first novel, set in the decades of the 1920s and 1930s, serves as the historical background to the later texts of full-fledged transnational modernity. Focusing on the narrative of personal emergence into history, Paredes's novel reinterprets the issues of the traditional bildungsroman in the context of race, ethnicity, and gender formation under conditions of colonial dominance and at the dawn of America's emergence as a global power.

Chapter 4, "Transnational Modernisms: Paredes, Roosevelt, Rockwell, Bulosan, and the Four Freedoms," takes the issues of nationalism and modernity as expressed in the political rhetoric and cultural aesthetics of the early 1940s as its theme. Franklin Delano Roosevelt and Norman Rockwell provide the two best-known instances of American modernity in relation to the nationalist ideology of freedom in their renditions of "The Four Freedoms." Paredes's reflections in verse on these categories serve as counterpoints both to the mainstream versions expressed by Roosevelt and Rockwell and to the oppositional ones voiced by other border intellectuals such as George I. Sánchez and Emma Tenayuca in chapter 5, "Paredes and the Modernist Vernacular Intellectuals."

Chapters 6, "The Borders of Modernity," and 7, "Bilingual Aesthetics and the Law of the Heart," turn to Paredes's alternative version of modernity, which I describe as a "subaltern modernity," as another way of describing the pathways of modern thought and the rhythms of sensibility that an evolving transnational world will require. In his most evocative lyrics from this period of his prewar writings, Paredes provides an aesthetics of the borderlands that turns, ultimately, on the bilingual and bicultural aspects of vernacular borderland culture.

Chapters 8, "Border Subjects and Transnational Sites: *The Hammon and the Beans and Other Stories*," and 9, "Narrative and the Idioms of Race, Nation, and Identity," serve as the transitional moments from Paredes's prewar to postwar writings. The stories from the first half of the short story collection elaborate what I term "the prosaics of everyday life" as they critically evaluate gender relations, the construction of race, and the nature of romance in a transnational context. The second half of the collection represents the crucial turn in Paredes's experience as a writer and thinker, namely, his extraordinarily consequential five-year sojourn in Asia as a participant in the US army of occupation of Japan, as a correspondent for the US Army newspaper *Pacific Stars and Stripes*, and as a special features columnist for the Mexico City daily *El Universal*. While furthering his exploration of the power of irony to represent the bewildering ambiguities of modern life, Paredes's stories exhibit scenes from the Asian Pacific war and the US occupation of Japan. The issues of transnationality and social aesthetics so centrally present in his earlier writings characterizing American modernity on the border are here exponentially activated as Paredes now writes from a vantage point that attempts to see from East to West, as well as from South to North.

I take the question of the transnational imaginary as the encompassing and illuminating issue of chapter 10, "The Postwar Borderlands and the Origins of the Transnational Imaginary: The Occupation-Era Writings in *Pacific Stars and Stripes* and *El Universal*," which describes Paredes's postwar journalism from Japan, China, and Korea. Paredes's newspaper articles in English and in Spanish are presented here in detail for the first time. Covering topics as diverse as the meaning of democracy, gender equality, political identity, and the function of popular music and film in the new postwar Japan, all as apprehended under conditions of military and political occupation, Paredes's articles offer an astonishingly prescient chronicle of subaltern modernity.

After his experiences in Asia from 1945 to 1950, Paredes returned home to pursue an academic career and scholarly work as an ethnographer and folklorist, the basis for his fame during his mature years as a professor at the University of Texas at Austin. Before he turned to academic scholarship for the remainder of his productive years, however, he had one more literary project to complete, a second novel entitled *The Shadow*, the subject of chapter 11, "*The Shadow* and the Imaginary Functioning of Institutions." In this final chapter of his literary life, Paredes turned once again to the familiar locale of Greater Mexico for his imaginative work. But this time, Paredes wrote from the perspective of south looking north, from Mexico to Texas. Returning as well to the prewar years of the 1920s and 1930s, Paredes now tells the story of the emergence of the borderlands into modernity from a hemispheric perspective. Fresh from the years of his Asian experiences, and with full understanding of the complexities and ambiguities of race and ethnicity as dialectically intertwined and dialogically complicit notions whose parameters were difficult to pin down, Paredes now looked again at the ways that principles of freedom, liberty, and self-determination had been wrenchingly betrayed in the flawed social and political revolutions of the early twentieth century.

In the conclusion, "A Transsentimental Journey," I attempt to account for Paredes's astonishingly perceptive analyses of modernity and the borderlands in a transnational context and to suggest how his invention of Greater Mexico encompasses issues that political and cultural theorists are addressing in the twenty-first century under terms such as *communities of fate*, *politics in the vernacular*, and *multicultural citizenship*.

In each of these chapters, I tell the same story, albeit in different ways and using different discourses. Readers might well ask, "Why don't we just get to the matter itself? Why do we have to hear the same story repeated?" I answer that the very incompleteness of the project reflects the nature of the process that I describe. Walter Benjamin, theorist of memory and remembrance par excellence, responds implicitly to questions of this sort when he writes, "the 'matter itself' is no more than the strata which yield their long-sought secrets only to the most meticulous investigation." He adds that

> in this sense, for authentic memories, it is far less important that the investigator report on them than that he mark, quite precisely, the site where he gained possession of them. Epic and rhapsodic in the strictest sense, genuine memory must therefore yield an image of the person who remembers, in the same way a good archaeological report not only informs us about the strata from which its findings originate, but also gives an account of the strata which first had to be broken through. ("Excavation and Memory" 574)

This is the reason that Paredes described his first novel, *George Washington Gómez*, as an "archeological piece" in his acknowledgments, or the poetry of *Between Two Worlds* as "the scribblings of a proto-Chicano of a half-century ago" in the prologue to that volume. His writings on the folktales, legends, proverbs, jests, ballads, and other vernacular arts of the borderlands together with his own literary creations attempt to account in epic, rhapsodic, and prosaic form for the strata of history inscribed in a community's social memory. In all these instances, Paredes's verbal art of memory never moved far from the social life of discourse in the open spaces of public squares, in the streets, in cities and villages of social groups, and in the generations and epochs of the borderlands of culture.

I

HISTORY AND REMEMBRANCE

AS SOCIAL AESTHETICS

1

"THE MEMORY IS ALL THAT MATTERS"

> Language has unmistakably made plain that
> memory is not an instrument for exploring
> the past, but rather a medium. It is the
> medium of that which is experienced, just
> as the earth is the medium in which ancient
> cities lie buried. He who seeks to approach his
> own buried past must conduct himself like a
> man digging. — Walter Benjamin,
> "Excavation and Writing"

In the spring of 1986, I received a telephone call from Américo Paredes, asking me if I could take the time to read the manuscript of a literary piece he had written some fifty years earlier. Presumed lost, but in fact in storage for half a century at his family home in Brownsville, Texas, the manuscript and other materials had only recently been recovered from among personal papers and boxes that had just been returned to him. A request of this sort from someone as legendary as Paredes, who in his retirement was one of the most esteemed intellectuals of the day, brings with it a set of conflicting responses. Of course I would read it; but what was it that I had agreed to read? And what might I be able to say about it? A few days later, Paredes delivered to my office a copy of a 451-page manuscript of a novel entitled "George Washington Gómez: A Mexicotexan novel." He also showed me the original typescript, a mass of sheets of yellowed, crumbling newsprint paper. Caught in the middle of the chaos of an academic semester, it took me several weeks to clear a weekend to begin reading the manuscript. Once I started reading the piece, I devoured it and regretted not having started sooner. I found the novel to be, in the language of reviewers, a spellbinding page-turner. Marked as it was by the idioms, styles, and forms of a realist bildungsroman, formed by the impulses of early twentieth-century American and Mexican modernism, and shaped by the social history of the United States–Mexico borderlands, the novel proved both aesthetically accomplished and historically impressive. Over the following two years, Paredes showed me the manuscripts of more work, including two volumes of poetry, a collection of short stories, another novel, a miscellany of prose, and snippets of memoirs and other personal writings that he himself described as "a family autobiography." He had composed all of these works between the mid-1930s and the mid-1950s. Along with others who urged Paredes to publish immediately this fabulous amount of fortuitously recovered literary material, I realized that an enormously significant literary historical record had just become available with the retrieval of these manuscripts.

Working in song, story, and tale, Paredes first elaborated in the realm of the imaginary the social scientific analytical themes, topics, and problematics of what we now refer to as "borderland theory," "border studies," and the "anthropology of borderlands."[1] For Paredes, history and the remembrance of history were categorically matters of social aesthetics, formalized as folklore, as vernacular local knowledge, and in the stories, legends, songs, customs, and beliefs of a particular place and time. In this project, I wish to contribute to an understanding of Paredes's place in the writing of the cultural history of the American western and southwestern borderlands and, more broadly, to the remapping of the field of American studies from a transnational perspective.[2] Paredes's work represents this transnationality by urging a vantage point beyond the typical North-South axis of most border histories. More significant, it illustrates the experiential realities of living spaces beyond the nation, supplementing and sometimes even superceding both Mexican and American national imperatives.

Forging a Fatherland

The forces that gave rise to the cultural forms of the border region that concerned Paredes in both his literary and folkloric writings date from the sixteenth century. Spanish explorers and their indigenous and mestizo retinues moved north from the interior of Mexico and began the colonization of what is now northern Mexico, Texas, and the rest of the southwestern United States. These settlers brought with them their cultural traditions, religion, folklore, literature, and language. In one part of that broader colonial endeavor, with the establishment of the province of Nuevo Santander by José de Escandón in 1749, the present Texas–Mexico border region became a place where the cultural traditions of the old and the new worlds collided and created new social realities.

In this region, from 1749 to 1821, new forms of nation building were enacted as the founding Spanish American colonials learned first how to retain loyalty to a far-off European sovereign, and then later to shift allegiance as subjects of the Spanish monarchy to the newly proclaimed constitutional Mexican monarchy after independence in 1821. When their attempt to keep Mexico within the fold of a pro-Spanish monarchy failed after 1824, they experienced what it meant to become citizens of the early Republic of Mexico.[3] In historian Manuel Gamio's celebrated phrase, Mexico was now deeply engaged in the project of *forjando patria*, or, "forging a fatherland."[4] First imagining then enacting the political institutions required that the people there transform themselves from subjects of a monarchy to citizens of a republic; the Spanish American inhabitants of the borderlands in effect were also working out the cultural idioms and practical implications of citizenship. As colonial subjects of the Spanish monarchy, they found themselves under the authority of the monarch and were governed by his laws. As republican citizens, they now had a share in the power of the sovereign and the authority to formulate their own laws. Following from this substantial transformation, would their newly constructed political forms allow them to retain a notion of blood heritage as Spanish (not Mexican) subjects while simultaneously combining it with a new, freely chosen political allegiance as citizens of a Mexican (and mestizo) nation? Who was and who was not a subject citizen?[5]

In the course of these transformations from monarchy to liberal democracy, after 1824 the former pro-monarchists now became centralist republicans. The republican opponents of monarchy became federalists (Bazant 8). Mexican sociologist Fernando Escalante has shown that despite these real differences between monarchists and federalists, liberals and conservatives, the imperative to consolidate state power was far more urgent for both than the need to create an effective citizenry and led to a high degree of accord on matters of law and sociability (372).[6] As a consequence, while early Mexican constitutions created "a broadly based nationality that included all people who were born in Mexico or who resided in the country, were members of the Catholic Church, and were willing to follow Mexico's laws," the category *citizen*, and its "access to public office and the public sphere," was restricted to independent male property holders (Lomnitz 306). This difference between Mexican nationality and Mexican citizenship proved crucial. With unique access to what Jürgen Habermas has called the public sphere, that strange new kind of liberal modern space between civil society and the state in which discussion of matters of public concern could occur, the citizen not only superseded nationality and the individual Mexican national but also now represented the nation as a whole (Lomnitz 307).[7] Moreover, if as Alexander Kluge and Oskar Negt have maintained, "the public sphere is the site where struggles are decided by other means than war," (Negt and Kluge 1–2) then access to the social sites, institutional forms, and political practices on the part of the polity is fundamental to nation building.[8] This is the sense in which Escalante refers to the project of Mexican nation building as the work of *ciudadanos imaginarios*, imaginary citizens (5–10). The creation of a new national identity required the complementary imagining for the citizen of a new role in the polity and new forms of action in the public sphere. All the while, and certainly by the mid-nineteenth century, especially among the intellectuals of this early republican period, many of these newly formed imaginary citizens also felt themselves becoming Americans, *americanos*.[9]

In the northern tier of Mexican provinces, the frontier periphery of the new nation, isolated from "the nascent projects of national integration and state building unfolding in central Mexico," the residents of the region "became Mexican" nationals and citizens, at least nominally (D. Gutiérrez, "Migration" 484–85).[10] However, because of the huge distances from the central seat of power in Mexico City, the people of northern Mexico remained isolated and acquired a fiercely independent sense of local autonomy. Thus, rather than identifying with the grand nation-building strategies of the ruling elites in central Mexico and their notion of an imagined integrated nation-state of Mexico proper, they acquired alternative forms of identity. Writing in the 1930s, the Mexican historian Manuel Gamio noted that "many inhabitants of rural districts in Mexico have little notion of their nationality or their country" (*Mexican Immigration* 128). What was true in remote rural Mexico was even truer in the borderlands, where the traditional power of the nation-state to regulate the flow of people, goods, and ideas remained relatively weak until the early part of the twentieth century.[11] For this reason, David Gutiérrez argues, the inhabitants of these remote borderlands districts constituted themselves as a separate people, residing in a "third space," and "most probably . . . identified themselves first as Catholics or Christians, second as members of intricate local networks of familial or kinship association," and only "last with their *patrias chicas* (their localities or regions)" ("Migration" 485).

To see the national allegiances of the inhabitants of the borderlands in exclusively Mexican, or American, terms is therefore misleading. Throughout the nineteenth century, but especially after midcentury, the inhabitants experienced the borderlands as a relatively coherent in-between region, a third space separate in many ways from Mexico and the United States (E. Young 5–11).[12] As historians Samuel Truett and Elliott Young note, "Ever since the border was mapped in 1854, the borderlands have supported a complex web of historical relationships that transcended—even as they emerged in tandem with—the U.S. and Mexican nations" (2). Borders are political and ideological boundaries that produce differences used to forge unique national identities. In the United States–Mexico borderlands, however, "cultural and ethnoracial" communities came into being that gainsaid these differences and remained unified across the national boundary lines: while borders divided, the borderlands united the region (E. Young 7). By understanding the forces that impelled these contradictory divisions and unities of the borderlands, we can begin to have a sense of how transnationalism profoundly shaped the lives of those who lived on the border and forged the historical structures that continue to affect the contemporary world.

These transnational forces first emerged early in the nineteenth century, when the central government in Mexico City licensed Anglo-American colonists to settle the sparsely populated northern territories of Mexico, hoping to use them as a dividing buffer between Mexico proper to the south and the encroaching United States to the north and east. The northeastern Mexican state of Coahuila y Tejas quickly attracted the most US immigrants, and soon they outnumbered the Mexican inhabitants (Holden and Zolov, "Manifest Destiny" 21). These Anglo-American settler colonials brought their own cultural traditions and political forms. Increasingly, however, they, too, saw themselves as Texans and joined in the larger Mexican national push for US-style federalism and greater control over local affairs. By 1835, the disputes between monarchist and republican Mexicans over whether to establish a centralist or a federalist regime eventually led beyond struggles in the public sphere to armed insurrection in the northern province of Texas.[13]

Allied with their Mexican Texan neighbors, Anglo Texans rose in rebellion to drive out the centralist garrisons in the Texas region. Immediately, centralist forces led by General Antonio López de Santa Anna embarked on a punitive expedition to quell the uprising and keep Texas within the Mexican fold (Bazant 15). The expedition began brilliantly for Santa Anna when after thirteen days of siege, his forces annihilated the joint Anglo-Mexican Texan garrison at the Alamo in San Antonio, killing all of the men under arms in the final attack of March 6, 1836. Final victory eluded Santa Anna, however, as the campaign ended in disaster. Defeated and captured by an army of rebellious Texans commanded by Sam Houston on April 21, 1836, in exchange for his life and freedom, "Santa Anna signed a treaty granting Texas its independence and recognizing the Rio Grande as the boundary" between the newly independent Republic of Texas and Mexico proper (Bazant 16). This provision of the battlefield treaty establishing a border between the Republics of Texas and Mexico remained a fiercely contested matter, however, as Mexico subsequently rejected the agreement as having been made under duress and therefore invalid. Instead, Mexico claimed the Nueces River in central Texas as the boundary between the two republics. Texans regarded the Rio Grande, two hundred miles farther south, as the border.

In the aftermath of these nation-forging affairs, the present characteristic feature of the United States–Mexico borderlands was firmly established. With equal measures of ambition and idealism, enthusiasm and violence, hope and faithlessness, the region became an intricately refractory zone where different cultures met and clashed. A newly independent Protestant Anglo-Texan republic came up against a Catholic Spanish-Mexican mestizo nation, each thinking of itself as uniquely "American." Particularly after the United States–Mexico war of 1846–48—with the annexation of the northern territories of

Mexico by the United States and the Treaty of Guadalupe-Hidalgo ending hostilities—former Spanish colonials and republican Mexicans residing in the conquered Mexican territories from the western border of Texas to the Pacific Ocean now became the first US Mexicans.[14] No longer citizens of Mexico and with their citizenship contested and denied by many Americans, they were left without the juridical protection of either nation (Griswold del Castillo 68). They were the first of many generations of Mexicans to become US citizens in name but not in fact (see figure 2). For many of these border people, as Truett and Young explain, events of the mid-nineteenth century "marked the beginning of years of negotiation between colonial, national, regional, and global coordinates that were—despite the U.S. annexation of land and people—anything but fixed" (6).

Folklore and the Social Base

Isolated from the main cultural centers to the south, north, and east, the Texas-Mexico border communities that emerged from this history developed a way of life based on economic self-sufficiency, social interdependency, and formal family ties. Strict hierarchies of gender, kinship, caste, and class created a dynamic, internally complex world. Jovita González, one of the first Mexican American folklorists and historians of the twentieth century to investigate the social structures of these colonial border communities, points out that their isolation retarded their political development, fostered a spirit of conservatism, and created a patriarchal life structured as in serfdom ("Social Life" 47–48).

Eighteenth-century customs, traditions, and beliefs brought by the first colonists still prevailed at the beginning of the nineteenth century in many of these communities. Rural life was pastoral in its simplicity, the necessities of life were few, and the government constituted a paternal hierarchy: "In his fortress-like home, built more for protection than comfort, the landowner lived like a feudal lord; he was master not only of the land, which he possessed, but also of the *peones* who worked the soil" (J. González, "Social Life" 48). The landowner class was served by a highly stratified workforce of mestizo or criollo vaqueros (cowboys) and Mexican Indian *peones* (peasants). And while a "social, racial, and economic gulf separated the *peón* from the land-

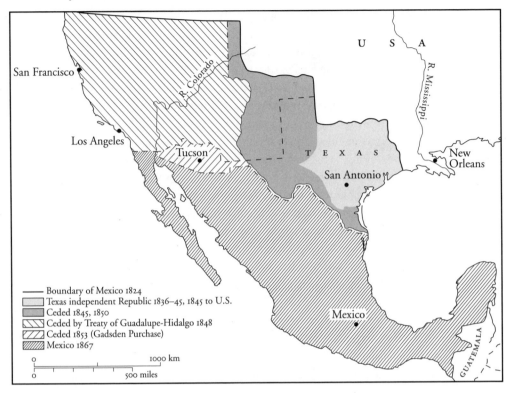

San Francisco

Los Angeles

Tucson

R. Colorado

U   S   A

R. Mississippi

T E X A S

San Antonio

New Orleans

Boundary of Mexico 1824
Texas independent Republic 1836–45, 1845 to U.S.
Ceded 1845, 1850
Ceded by Treaty of Guadalupe-Hidalgo 1848
Ceded 1853 (Gadsden Purchase)
Mexico 1867

Mexico

GUATEMALA

0   1000 km

0   500 miles

2 Map of the Mexican Territories ceded to the United States, 1848.
From Leslie Bethell, ed. *Mexico since Independence*. Reprinted with
the permission of Cambridge University Press.

owner," the difference between the vaquero, whether of mixed or cre-
ole descent, and the landowner was not as great (49–50). The *peón*
lived in virtual serfdom to the *amo* (master) of the ranch, while the
vaquero, often the son of a small-landowning rancher, lived an inter-
mediary existence (51–52).

Despite the powerful inherent contradictions occasioned by these
hierarchies of power and race that constantly threatened to overwhelm it, the social structure of these colonial communities provided
cultural stability and economic viability in the daily life of the people
of the region for nearly a century before they were violently incorporated into the expanding American empire after 1848. While the social
structure of the border communities remained in place until the early

twentieth century, the internal stresses caused by their rigidly hierarchical class, race, and gender relations were deepened by the massive political transformations warranted by the signing of the Treaty of Guadalupe-Hidalgo in 1848.

Under the terms of the treaty, former Mexican nationals residing in the conquered territories of what was now the "American" Southwest, including all of California and parts of Arizona, New Mexico, and Colorado, had one year to "elect" preference for Mexican citizenship or to remain in the conquered territories as US citizens and be admitted "to the enjoyment of all the rights of citizens of the United States, according to the principles of the Constitution" (Griswold del Castillo 62).[15] Legislative action and judicial interpretation from 1848 to 1910 dramatically altered the spirit of the treaty and forestalled the hopes of those Mexicans who elected to participate as citizen-subjects of the United States. Full participation in the construction of a new borderlands public sphere proved elusive. Citizenship rights were not respected; property rights remained fragile. As a result, "Within a generation the Mexican Americans who had been under the ostensible protection of the treaty became a disenfranchised, poverty-stricken minority" (Griswold del Castillo 86).

Paredes's own ancestral family belonged to the elite, educated, landowning classes of this ranching society who suffered the forfeitures of lands, disenfranchisement, and the frustration of their hopes for justice. Writing as a folklorist and historian of the region, Paredes would later state of this first generation of subjugated former Mexican nationals:

> The first Mexicans to become permanent residents of the United States—with the exception of a few political refugees—were the inhabitants of the Mexican territories ceded to the United States in 1848. This was the origin of the regional folk groups, and these were the first Mexican Americans—the majority of them very much against their will. They were at once involved in a long–drawn-out struggle with the North Americans and their culture. Cultural differences were aggravated by the opportunism of many North American adventurers, who in their desire for riches treated the new citizens from the start as a conquered people. Names like Juan Nepomuceno Cortina, Aniceto Pizaña, Gregorio Cortez, and Elfego Baca—all men who, as a *corrido* (narrative folksong) puts it, "defendieron su derecho" (defended their right)—were immortalized in songs and legends. This was the birth—ten years after the war between Mexico

and the United States—of the first examples of Mexican American folk-lore. Some of these rebels against the government of the United States were killed or taken prisoner by the North American authorities, who naturally treated them as bandits and lawbreakers. Others escaped into Mexico, where they lived out their lives as symbols of Anglo-American injustice. (Paredes, "Folklore of Groups" 9)

The "songs and legends" of everyday life of the people in these subjugated communities were "the first examples of Mexican American folklore" (Paredes, "Folklore of Groups" 9). These narratives have come down to us in a variety of Spanish-language vernacular forms, including ballads, proverbs, legends, fables, jokes, and other folk genres. In particular, however, the *corrido* form, dignified folk ballads in Spanish chronicling events from daily life that have taken on some special historical significance, has proven important in this regard in its representation of the male "warrior hero" fighting for social justice (McDowell; R. Saldívar, *Chicano Narrative*; Limón, *Mexican Ballads*). "The pacification and final Americanization of this area," writes Paredes, "is an important chapter in the history of the United States."

But, with few exceptions, documents available for study of the region are in English, being for the most part reports made by officials who were, to put it mildly, prejudiced against the people they were trying to "pacify." Where it is possible to check their reports with other existing data, it can be seen that their bias often led them to exaggerate or even to falsify the facts. The Texas-Mexican version does not exist in documents. It can be found in *corridos* and in prose narratives passed from father to son. It is folklore, and as such unreliable. But no history of the Rio Grande border that ignores this folklore can be complete. ("Folklore and History" 62–63)

The unofficial texts of this history in oral narrative, song, and other vernacular verbal genres passed not only from father to son but also from mother to daughter offer a conception of the world that is less than systematic and may even be confused or contradictory. Nevertheless, these texts prove at least as important as the newspapers, official records, and other documents of more modernized segments of society because they offer the only surviving evidence of conditions of life as experienced in the subaltern strata. As a far-reaching genre of long historical trajectory, the *corrido* will in time serve as the foundation for other literary and artistic creations. At one point preserved and distributed as loose-leafed broadsheets by small local printing presses and transmitted orally by popular word of mouth at community gatherings, by the end of the nineteenth century, the *corrido* served another function. It attained intense consumption and widespread distribution throughout Greater Mexico as the chief source of news and information for unlettered segments of the Mexican population on both sides of the border. For this reason, the *corrido* remained for Paredes extremely important for understanding the thought and sensibility of the nonelite sectors of the region. Taken as a whole, Paredes would argue, the folkloric material of these eighteenth- and nineteenth-century settlers, together with their more formalized documentary histories, constitute a philosophical folklore, a critical vernacular history of the region and of the early making of a US borderlands culture from out of the Spanish colonial and Mexican republican past.

Social Life on the Border

Given the symbolically historical importance of these folkloric forms, it is not surprising to find that folklore studies have formed the basis for a great deal of the twentieth-century cultural studies of the region and of the historical interpretation of its development into a modern American economy. John Gregory Bourke and J. Frank Dobie were two of the earliest folklorists who came to the borderlands in the early twentieth century and whose work helped define it.[16] If as a humorist and raconteur Dobie's intent was to provide an entertaining aspect of local color, Bourke, as a former US Army officer who had fought to secure the border, had something else in mind. His project clearly was meant to deliver the kind of useful information that would aid in the ongoing pacification, colonization, and Americanization of the region.[17]

A few natives of the area were also active in creating the early ethnographic record of the border region. I have already mentioned one, Jovita González: born near the Texas-Mexico border in 1903, she was descended from the first settlers of the area. In an autobiographical sketch, González wrote that in 1925 she had "the far reaching experience" of meeting Dobie ("Jovita González" xii).[18] Under his mentorship, she conducted important early research that helped set the stage for more comprehensive ethnographic and literary historical studies of the cultural life of the borderlands (Cotera, "Native Speakers" 253–56). Her master's thesis is based in great part on interviews she conducted in the 1920s with friends, relatives, and other local informants who reminisced about the social and economic life of their communities in the mid-nineteenth century and shared family documents from that era. With Dobie's sponsorship, the young González in 1930 became the first Mexican American to serve as president of the Texas Folklore Society until Paredes in 1961 (Limón, *Dancing with the Devil* 60–75).[19] Her folklore scholarship and her own creative fiction tell the story of nineteenth- and early twentieth-century Texas from the Texas-Mexican perspective and stand as records of an alternate history to the official one forged by Anglo scholars such as Dobie, the historian Walter Prescott Webb, the folklorist John Lomax, and a generation of their students.[20]

Following the early pattern set by González, Paredes drew directly from his experiences of border life for his ethnographic writings and literary works. Born in Brownsville, Texas, in 1915—and like González, a descendant of colonial border settlers—Paredes received his undergraduate and graduate degrees and then taught at the University of Texas at Austin from 1956 to 1984. In addition to his numerous scholarly writings, Paredes's works include two novels, collections of poetry, short fiction, and journalistic pieces in English and Spanish.[21] These works celebrate, with gentle irony and a haunting sense of the transformation of a culture, the vitality of life on the border. They set the stage for his later scholarly work, most famously *"With His Pistol in His Hand": A Border Ballad and Its Hero*, Paredes's study of a ballad cycle focused on the figure of Gregorio Cortez, an early twentieth-century Texas-Mexican defender of social justice. Following on this seminal work, Paredes's subsequent academic scholarship helped establish a critical and analytical tradition for doing ethnographic work among minority groups.

In 1989, Paredes was honored as one of the five inaugural recipients of the Charles Frankel Prize of the National Endowment for the Humanities for lifelong achievement in the humanities. In 1991, he was named as one of the first Mexican American recipients of the Orden Mexicana del Aguila Azteca, Mexico's highest award given for efforts in human rights and the preservation of Mexican culture. Later that year, the Texas Historical Association also honored Paredes for his exemplary contributions to the understanding of the western and southwestern frontier experience. Over the next few years, research centers and public schools were being named in his honor. Even the state legislature of Texas, on Paredes's death in 1999, recognized his achievements by passing a resolution marking his contributions to the intellectual life of the region. Having devoted his scholarly life to researching the folk life and popular culture of Greater Mexico and the American Southwest, Paredes's ethnographic and literary critical work is today arguably the definitive founding statement on the folk poetry, folktales, folk theater, proverbs, jests, legends, and riddles of the Mexican American people.[22]

The Social Imaginary and the Border *Corrido*

His first and most important scholarly work, *"With His Pistol in His Hand,"* is as much about the borderlands of south Texas and the traditions associated with the identity of its Mexican American communities as about the historical personage of Gregorio Cortez and the songs and stories recounting his legendary exploits of 1901. Cortez, a peaceful farmer unjustly persecuted by the law, having his brother murdered and his wife and children imprisoned, rises courageously in righteous wrath from the anonymity of history to defend himself and the rights of his community "with his pistol in his hand." Exultantly, the ballad tells us that "trying to overtake Cortez / was like overtaking a star" (alcanzar a Cortez / era alcanzar a una estrella).[23] But in the end, his star proves meteoric; his defeat and capture are inevitable. When as one man alone ("un solo mexicano"), against overwhelming odds and at the flood tide of successful escape into Mexico, Cortez learns that innocents are being punished for his spectacular evasions of his enemies, he surrenders the fight and thereby enters the realms of balladry and legend. Examining these ballads and legends, Paredes offered a history of the US-Mexican border, an analysis of poetic form, and an aesthetics of social action. In the introduction to *"With His Pistol in His Hand,"* Paredes writes:

> *El Corrido de Gregorio Cortez* . . . is a Border Mexican ballad, "Mexican" being understood in a cultural sense, without reference to citizenship or "blood." But we must stress "Border" too. It is as a border that the Lower Rio Grande has made its mark: in legend, in song, and in those documented old men's tales called histories.

Borders and ballads seem to go together, and their heroes are all cast in the same mold. During the Middle Ages there lived in some parts of Europe, especially in the border areas, a certain type of men whose fame has come down to us in legend and in song. On the Scottish-English border there were the heroes like Wallace, the rebel against English domination, like Jock o the Side, Hobie Noble, Willie Armstrong, and other Liddesdale and Teviotdale raiders, whose favorite occupation was defying the power of England.

Spain had its popular heroes too, as did Russia, during the periods when each of those countries held a border against the warlike tribes of the East. (xii–xiii)

It is crucial that Paredes at the beginning of his scholarly career links the struggles of the "Border people" of south Texas with the struggles of other peoples at the peripheries of power globally and historically. He does so specifically by referring, first, on *aesthetic* grounds to the forms of Spanish romance and the traditions of the European and English border ballad, and second, on *social* terms to the differences between citizenship based on blood heritage and that based on political allegiance. Writing about a similar border country tradition, Raymond Williams sought to preserve the history of the agency of the Welsh, Irish, and Scottish folk within the history of imperial Britain. As a border intellectual, Williams argued that in attempting to understand the land, its people, and their history, one needed to feel the materiality of their presence in the cultural geography of the landscape because that was where the significance of their history would reside (Williams, *People of the Black Mountains* 1–2). Like Williams, Paredes proposes border thinking and local histories as coordinates of larger global designs. For this reason, he suggests that the unraveling of this historical design as an ongoing one, binding the processes of national formation and the construction of national subjects, from medieval central Europe to twentieth-century America.

To achieve an understanding of that global design, Paredes establishes three basic features of the *corrido* border ballad form in *"With His Pistol in His Hand."* As José David Saldívar points out, Paredes's analysis shows that in its form and content, "(1) the *corrido* is a multifaceted discourse, with reflexive, narrative, and rhetorical-propositional elements; (2) *corridos* as social texts tend to be historical and personal; and (3) *corridos* make assertions that derive from the collective outlook and experience of the Mexican ballad community on the border" ("Chicano Border Narratives" 172). Rather than serving simply as celebrations of an achieved identity, Paredes's writings from *"With His Pistol in His Hand"* forward continually urge an interrogation of what constitutes Mexican and American social space—as arenas of polity, of race, and of gendered identity in the twentieth century. "Every Mexican knows that there are two Mexicos," notes Paredes in one of his early essays. "One . . . is found within the boundaries of the Mexican republic. The second Mexico—the *México de Afuera* (Mexico abroad) as Mexicans call it—is composed of all the persons of Mexican origin in the United States" ("Folklore of Groups" 3). The composite hybrid of these two Mexicos is what Paredes refers to as Greater Mexico. Concerning these transcultural domains created by the Mexican labor diasporas of the nineteenth and twentieth centuries, Paredes adds, "What is often not known is that their limits are not defined by the Customs and Immigration offices at the border. . . . These regional folk cultures thus include regions of two nations" (7). In Texas, the well-defined geographical feature of the Rio Grande became the international line. But as Paredes pointed out, "The river, once a focus of regional life, became a symbol of separation" ("Problem of Identity" 25). His work attempted to explain how that focus became a symbol of separation and then to show that the Greater Mexican community in fact cut across imaginary borderlines and symbolic immigration checkpoints. In doing so, his project was also to document the undocumented styles and realities of the diasporic, transcultural Mexican American social imaginary expressed on the symbolic level (Paredes, "Folk Base").

Below the level of an explicit understanding of the doctrines and beliefs of the borderlands social world, Paredes identified two other levels of understanding at work: the level of embodied understanding, at work in the ways we are taught to behave and which become second nature to us, governing the experiences of everyday life; and the kind of understanding expressed in ritual, symbol, the spiritual spaces in works of folk art, and the imagination generally. The imagination of which I speak in this context constitutes a property of the collective social world, not merely a faculty of the spiritually gifted unique individual. This explains why I am referring to it as participating in the work of the social imaginary and to its artistic results as an aspect of the social aesthetic. Because of these layered understandings, constituting a network of leitmotifs within both Paredes's ethnographic and literary writings, the individual point of contact with the imaginary, as well as the "national" culture or political event, are always seen as one surface and a very local inflection of a much broader transindividual and transnational phenomenon that can be read according to a hemispheric dialectic of similarity and difference on the level of public agency and symbolic action. At base, Paredes's ethnographic work thus signals the emergence of new hemispheric studies of the Americas and the need for the development of new postcolonial optics attuned to the nuances of these multiple levels of understanding.

The Work of the Imagination

Yet Paredes's work seeks still more. It also attempts to display the power of culture to configure the borders of the modern American nation and to shape the identity of the subject within the civic traditions of the nation. His literary writings, like his ethnographic and folkloric studies, acknowledge the social dimension of difference, the complexity of identity, and the limitations of homogeneous community. Repeatedly, this acknowledgment occurs aesthetically, in the shapes and nuances of a variety of oral forms and gestures, symbolic expressions and articulations, that is, in the formulaic patterns that disguise and sometimes reveal the limits of community and identity in their relationship to the discourses and realities of power within the arena we have come to know since Habermas as the public sphere. In describing the public work of the private imagination, Paredes was well aware that it could serve a variety of purposes, not all of which were purely public, properly emancipatory, or easily governable. Still, in its public function, imagination could serve as a generative site in which individuals and groups responded to the global forces of modernity, adjusted them to their own practices of the modern, and set the groundwork for the mobilization of collective identities. Culture could thus become a way to talk about difference and its mediations.[24] As we shall see, this recognition on Paredes's part of the dialectic between the pull to sameness and the forces making for difference formed the basis for his growing recognition of the need to speak of modernity not as a singular phenomenon but as multiple and plural, as, in other words, "alternative modernities."[25] This would occur particularly after his experiences in Japan and other parts of Asia. Within these alternative modernities, modern institutions and practices might indeed converge as elements of a singular form of modernity, but distinct cultures would find ever new forms of differentiation resulting in astonishingly new (and alternative) modes of accommodation to the modern.

The patterns of this recognition of the need for differentiation are already unmistakably evident in Paredes's literary writings from the thirties, forties, and fifties. Paramount among the writings from that period is the novel *George Washington Gómez*, a novel written and completed, although not circulated for publication, during the time that Paredes worked as a newspaper reporter in Brownsville during the Depression era. In addition to the novel, Paredes also wrote two volumes of poetry and a variety of newspaper feature articles on the folk life of the people of south Texas during this time.[26] In a different creative mode, Paredes also composed original musical pieces for public performance, first as a solo entertainer and then with one of the first major Texas-Mexican recording artists, Consuelo "Chelo" Silva, whom he married in 1939.[27] In the years immediately before the American entry into the war that had already broken out in Europe and Asia, Depression-era relief had not made a difference in the lives of the people of southernmost Texas. Surviving *la Chilla* (the squeal), as the Depression was termed by Mexican Americans, required Paredes to piece together work as a journalist, writer, and musical performer with employment at the Pan American Airways plant at the Brownsville airport doing final assembly work on Lockheed fighter-bombers bound for England and the European front. In these anxiety-filled days before the American entry into the war, Paredes was looking for a way to lessen the shrillness of "the squeal," to put food on the table, and to consolidate his various talents. The way to accomplish all of this, he believed, might be the still wondrous new technology, scarcely two decades old and only just having been extended on the border to the periphery of capitalism: the radio.

Border Radio

By day, Paredes mounted .50-caliber machine guns on lend-lease warplanes bound for combat over England, France, and Germany.[28] By night, he hosted a live radio program and performed his own compositions on the public airwaves. In his Pulitzer Prize–winning study of the Depression era, the historian David Kennedy points out that "the political and social effects of radio were only beginning to be felt in the late 1920s, let alone understood" (228). A decade later, by the 1930s, the low-powered hundred-watt transmitters of the early years of radio broadcasting, reliably beaming their electronic messages only a few miles from their home transmitters, were rapidly being replaced by networks of multistation one thousand–watt transmitters. These networks, assembled under the names of the National Broadcasting Company in 1926 and the Columbia Broadcasting System shortly thereafter, quickly acquired a massive proportion of the radio market. To compete with the new networks and to evade US federal regulations concerning the suitable use of public airwaves, a few enterprising rogue media entrepreneurs began to experiment with giant 1 million–watt single-station transmitters capable of flooding an entire region and hemisphere with the voices of the newly expanding mass cultural market (Fowler and Crawford 9).

In nineteenth-century *corridos* of conflict, anyone running from the law typically made a quick break for the border. Beginning in the 1930s, radio created a whole new breed of so-called radio outlaws, those who ran for the border and built and operated the first of the megawatt-powered "border blaster" broadcasting stations capable of beaming programming across immense distances (Fowler and Crawford 1–14, 29).[29] Media writers Gene Fowler and Bill Crawford explain that "the men and women who created border radio were frontiersmen of the ether, imaginative experimenters who came to *la frontera* seeking freedom from the restrictions of the American media establishment" (1). Connoisseurs of the art of "shuck and jive" without equals, these first moguls of the airwaves and media trailblazers were escaping what by the late thirties had become an entertainment medium oppressively controlled by a few large corporations and strictly managed by federal regulators. Attempting "to maintain orderliness" and provide "tasteful advertising and potted-palm programming" that was uncontroversial and "decidedly unadventuresome," the joint forces of corporate and federal control threatened to advance the death of radio before its time. "Given this environment," note Fowler and Crawford, "border radio blasted like a blue norther across the American airwaves" (8), except that this "blue norther" emanated from the south, from *la frontera*.

3 Dr. John R. Brinkley, "the goat gland doctor," stand-
ing next to his private airplane, San Antonio, Texas, 1936.
Reproduced with the permission of the Institute of Texan
Cultures at the University of Texas at San Antonio,
L-0919-K, the San Antonio Light Collection.

The giant among giants of the border radio stations was without
question Dr. John Brinkley's XER (1931–35), later XERA (1935–40),
and later still reincarnated under the call letters of XERF (1947–60),
beaming from Villa Acuña, Coahuila, Mexico, "near the silvery Rio
Grande and romantic Old Mexico," across the border from Del Rio,
Texas (Fowler and Crawford 64). With its megawatt transmitter, re-
puted to fry birds on the fly that strayed too close to its towers, XERA,
"the Sunshine Station between the Nations" (16), could be heard in
every major metropolitan market in the country and was capable of
muscling the local stations off their assigned spots on the kilocycle
dials (44). Depending on weather conditions, XERA could even be

heard in Europe, Japan, New Zealand, and Australia. Dr. Brinkley's name had become notorious even before his voice blasted it across the airwaves in 1931. In pioneering a bizarre procedure of organ transplantation—the insertion of "goat glands" into the scrotums of Midwestern farmers, judges, businessmen, and average citizens looking for the masculine sexual fountain of youth—Brinkley had already become a multimillionaire and a person of considerable influence. Brinkley's pitch was a challenge to his listeners: "If you are a red-blooded 'he-man' with a real backbone, we will hear from you. . . . Dr. Brinkley is anxious to help you if you are man enough to help yourself" (36). Judging from Brinkley's accumulation of prodigious wealth, many perfectly healthy red-blooded he-men, figuring that no amount of masculinity was ever enough, rushed to his clinics for satyr-like potency. It is frightening to speculate what might have happened had Dr. Brinkley chosen to implant bull glands. Actually, bull glands might have made more sense, but goats were cheaper.

Probably the first of the modern masters of public relations and a genius in the use of media for self-promotion, Brinkley quickly understood the immense power of radio, using it with amazing adroitness to defend his medical practice and clinic against charges of quackery and malpractice from a variety of medical associations. Buying airtime on local stations at first, he soon decided that it was much more advantageous simply to buy the radio stations outright. When regulators, this time from the Federal Radio Commission (FRC), continued to hound him, he had the stroke of genius to move his clinic and to build a powerful new station (XERA) beyond the reach of the FRC in Mexico. In 1941, the recently elected Mexican president Manuel Avila Camacho, claiming that the radio station was controlled by "foreigners sympathetic to the Nazi cause," ordered the expropriation of Brinkley's station. So XERA—the home of "the goat gland doctor," mystics and astrologers, pitchmen of all sorts, religious fanatics, and hillbilly music—passed into history. Even today one is likely to hear on the border the familiar joke: "What's the fastest thing on four legs? A goat passing the Brinkley Hospital" (Fowler and Crawford 66). In a later phoenixlike resurrection, the station's original license was renewed under the call letters XERF, and the folksy "Sunshine Station between the Nations" became the home of one of the greatest rock and roll rebels and the popularizer par excellence of the 1950s, the late-night prowler Wolfman Jack. Powered by the frenzy of early rock and roll and Wolfman's all-night howls, XERF remained on the air until 1960.

What do the goat gland doctor, Wolfman Jack, and Américo Paredes have in common? Border radio. This is what Paredes had to say about radio station XERA:

> Of course, I was exaggerating when I said that my mother and I listened to Agustín Lara all the time. We also tuned in to a very powerful radio station, XERA in Villa Acuña, just across from Del Rio. A man who called himself Dr. Brinkley ran it. Ever hear of him? He was a quack. He claimed that he could implant goat testicles into men to make them potent again. Well, in those days, they would say "goat glands." It's amazing how rich he became! . . . We would tune it in because he would play the best of the new Mexican music: *tríos*, and *duetos*, and so on. He also played American music, jazz, and the Carter Family, too, in other words, hillbilly, country music. So I was getting quite an education in music during the nine months out of the year that I spent at home in Brownsville just listening to the radio.

On the border, a dazzling array of sonic rhythms were disseminated from these megawatt rogue stations—ranging in style from hillbilly and traditional country western, to parlor pop, jazz, blues, and folk balladry, including Spanish-language *rancheras* (country music), *conjuntos* (ensembles), *tríos* (trios), *duetos* (duets), and the newly emerging and astonishing catalogue of Afro-Caribbean beats. Digging at the earthy roots of American folk music, radio impresarios like Dr. Brinkley were striking gold by blending these gorgeous sounds, thereby inventing in the 1920s and 1930s the idioms of commercial American pop music. The music critic William Hogeland explains that "by turning themes that were already outmoded among music sophisticates into a porch version of ragtime and blues," groups like the Carter Family "invented commercial country music" from out of the mother lode of American vernacular music. "Tricky, full of backbeat and surprises," their "favored rhythms often involve the syncopation of piano ragtime and jazz, cutting-edge urban sounds in their day."

And all the while, from this clever, idiosyncratic, and ultimately irresistible mélange of repertoires, new stars were being born on the air. Aspiring to stardom as a singer and composer, Paredes jumped at an opportunity to become part of what was clearly becoming in the 1930s the radio fusion of the border when he was offered a chance to

host his own live radio show. Broadcasting from a small local Brownsville radio station, Paredes's variety show *El músico y poeta*, offered in
English- and Spanish-language formats, provided an evening of cosmopolitan pop romance and passionate *latino* flair. Styled after the
artistic genius of the incomparable Mexican singer-composer Agustín
Lara, popularly known as *el músico poeta*, the musical poet, Paredes's
radio review was both a tribute to and an emulation of the artistry
of the great originator of *la canción mexicana* (the romantic Mexican song).[30] Lara's extraordinarily popular shows, *La hora íntima de
Agustín Lara* and *La hora azul*, the *Intimate Hour* and the *Blue Hour*,
launched in 1930, featured Lara's strikingly original voice singing passionately heart-wrenching interpretations of familiar tunes, as well as
debuts of his own compositions in each broadcast (Aura 47–50). Paredes's version of Lara's format featured the intriguing pan-Latino
harmony of popular music, including *orquesta, conjunto, paso dobles*,
rumbas, boleros, *danzones*, tangos, merengues, and, *guaguancos*, the
music of Veracruz, Havana, San Juan, Bogotá, Caracas, Buenos Aires,
Mexico City, and the American Gulf Coast and southwestern borderlands.

This musical repertoire may serve as an index to a cultural historical
moment when it was still realistically possible to entertain the utopian
hope for what Diego Rivera had envisioned as "Pan-American Unity"
in a magnificent set of murals painted for the Golden Gate International Exposition in San Francisco in 1940.[31] Rivera's murals imagine
a panhistorical, panhemispheric unity of Indian, Latino, Hispanic,
and Anglo-American figures crafting a uniquely pan-American new
world. Rivera's modernist utopian dream was not unique. It lay at the
center of the vision of poets like William Carlos Williams, Nicolás
Guillén, and Américo Paredes. This was a moment when the shores of
the Gulf of Mexico and the Caribbean still served as sites of convergence for the Americas rather than as the zones of division that they
were to become after the 1959 Cuban Revolution and the ensuing US
embargo of the island. In the immediate prewar years, radio magi-
cally opened an electronic floodgate through which flowed a wave of
Latino popular and dance music and all of its accompanying cultural
gestures.[32] This free flow of ideas and forms seemed to offer the promise of a hemispheric cultural market without borders. Paredes's musical vocabulary added this massive flow of Latino values, manners, and
taste into the border region and beyond. In addition to presenting the

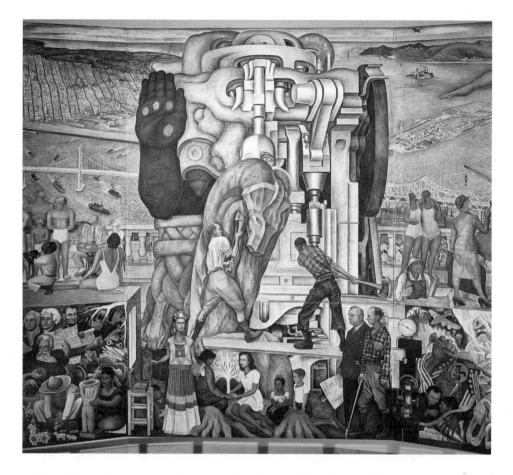

4 Diego Rivera, *Pan-American Unity*, 1940 (San Francisco City College). The organizing committee of the Golden Gate International Exposition in San Francisco commissioned the huge, multipanel mural. The mural is now housed on the campus of San Francisco City College. All rights reserved. Reprinted with the permission of the City College of San Francisco. www.riveramural.com.

hottest boleros, tangos, and rumbas, Paredes's radio review offered classical guitar, ensemble repertoires, and original guitar and piano compositions with a dash of the *conjunto* and *corrido* sound.[33]

Walter Benjamin and other media critics of early twentieth-century forms of mass culture had argued for the superlative uniqueness and magical power of the new entertainment technology of radio. In an essay of 1932, Benjamin, for instance, commented concerning radio that "the masses it grips are much larger [than that of theater]; above all, the material elements on which its apparatus is based and the intellectual foundations on which its programming is based are closely intertwined in the interests of its audience" ("Theater and Radio" 584). Siegfried Kracauer, his contemporary and an equally brilliant critic of the emerging mass media, had taken more skeptical note of the extravagant possibilities of mass culture, seeing its potential of becoming what he termed mere "mass ornament," especially when it separated itself out from the interests of its popular audience. With regard to the newly unfolding communication technologies, Kracauer cautioned against having those new media become the provinces of "unique individuals" rather than of whole communities: "Those who have withdrawn from the community and consider themselves to be unique personalities with their own individual souls also fail when it comes to forming these new patterns [of mass ornamentation]," he argued (*Mass Ornament* 76).[34]

Taking advantage of the technological opportunity to reach much larger audiences than those of previous entertainment forms while attempting to maintain a vital connection to their communities, radio shows such as Paredes's sought a middle ground, attempting to stake out new material and intellectual bases that were closely intertwined with the interests of the popular audience without becoming mere mass ornamentation. On the one hand, they constituted a throwback to the earliest days of radio when the new technology, by the very nature of its limited range, served areas only scarcely larger than local neighborhoods and catered to the discrete needs of the home community. On the other hand, radio shows on the United States–Mexico border such as Paredes's variety broadcast and those of radio station XERA differed in one vital respect from earlier radio programs and from programs in other regions of the country. They served a transnational audience and reflected a bilingual aesthetic, spilling their values and tastes across two national airwaves and helping make the Rio

Grande border, improbable as it may have seemed at the time, "the romance center in America" (Fowler and Crawford 9).

To be sure, the historian David Kennedy correctly argues that in the 1930s "radio assaulted the insularity of local communities. It also, not incidentally, catalyzed the homogenization of American popular culture" (229). And yet, shows such as Paredes's *El músico y poeta* also worked across the grain as direct counters to the homogenizing effects that mass-market radio and the newly consolidating culture industry were having in other regions of the United States and Mexico. Elsewhere, radio served to undermine the viability of local cultures by interjecting the homogenizing influences of the music, speech, and style of the metropolitan culture. On the border, something quite different was occurring. Here, radio was messily undoing the neat bifurcation that the divide of the geopolitical border had created in the mid-nineteenth century between the northern and southern Americas. The glitzy voices and down-home sounds carried by the electronic ether waves of border radio shows offered a way of reconnecting the transnational region through an alternative national language, in two registers, at the beginning of the era of electronic telecommunications and globalization.

Arráncame la Vida

Looking to expand his repertoire of musical registers and broaden his audience beyond the local scene, Paredes one day invited on his show a strikingly attractive and immensely talented young woman who was gaining a substantial following for her brilliant renditions of a sexy new sound, the Cuban-born, African-based rhythms of the bolero. Her name was Consuelo "Chelo" Silva. Graced with a "low sultry voice" by turns "gravelly and dulcet" and able to strike exact tones tempered with melancholy and defiance, Chelo Silva seemed born to sing on the radio, exactly the kind of musical enchantress made for the dynamics of wireless transmission in the days of AM broadcast—its ghostly static and low hisses of silence adding to the power of her voice (Del Toro, Strachwitz, and Nicolopulos). Like Greta Garbo, Edith Piaf, or Lola Beltran in other musical regions being shaped in the 1930s by the emerging culture industry, Silva could tease her radio audience into romantic rapture with the ener-

5 Consuelo "Chelo" Silva, *La reina tejana de los boleros*,
c. early 1950s. Cover art reprinted with the permission of
Chris Strachwitz, Arhoolie Records, Arhoolie.com. CD 423.

getic rhythms of her lyrical phrasings. Garbo-like in her radio musical
allure, she was also apparently Garbo-like in her willingness to test the
imaginary borders between male and female sensuality, and rumors
of her crossing them existed. Whatever may have been the truth behind the innuendos, Paredes was immediately taken by the young
singer, and she became a regular on his radio show. It is probably
no coincidence that shortly after Silva joined Paredes on the transnational airwaves he was invited to bring his act for live broadcasting to
none other than the neighboring superstation on the border, Brinkley's radio XERA. In this manner, Chelo Silva and Américo Paredes
became part of the outlaw stratospheric-broadcasting, goat gland–
pitching, hillbilly-yodeling, down-home mixing of music in English
and Spanish that made for the everyday magic of border radio. In the
course of their experience of performing and touring together over
the following months, while continuing to appear live on Brinkley's

megastation, Paredes and Silva embarked on a passionate and stormy love affair (Del Toro, Strachwitz, and Nicolopulos). They were married in 1939. The marriage, however, proved as tempestuous as their courtship, and as short-lived. Paredes wanted to develop and amass his own original repertoire; Silva desired to explore broader musical horizons, perform songs by other composers, and tour with other bands.[35] Consuelo Silva, it seemed, was not going to offer either the consolation or comfort promised by her name. Paredes, in turn, was not able to deal with a woman like Silva.

Although their divorce was not settled until 1947, they had already ceased to share their music and their lives by the early 1940s.[36] After her marriage with Paredes ended, Silva's career initially declined. As late as 1948, she worked as a window decorator at the local J. C. Penney department store in Brownsville, also raising their son, Américo Paredes Jr. Silva continued to sing in local venues and on the air when she could, hoping to revitalize her career as the recording industry re-emerged from the wartime decline caused by the severe restrictions of raw materials from which records were pressed. In the early 1950s, she received her big break by winning a recording contract with Ideal Records.[37] By the mid-1950s Chelo Silva had become a major recording star in Mexico, the United States, Latin America generally, and Spain, and had been dubbed *la reina tejana del bolero*, the Texas queen of the bolero, for her famously sultry interpretations and renditions from a woman's point of view of the universal theme of love in all its variations: "Love affairs gone awry, betrayals, and desires that could not be subdued," as the liner notes to one of her CDs puts it (Del Toro, Strachwitz, and Nicolopulos). After the breakup of their relationship, while Silva's musical career rose to star status, Paredes's musical aspirations declined to the point that he soon ceased to perform publicly altogether. It was almost as if Silva had been that most distressing kind of muse, one whose presence caused almost as much affliction as did her eventual absence. From that brief and passionate attachment, both later preserved only the jagged and bitter emotions that formed the quintessence of a tango or bolero by Agustín Lara: "Arráncame la vida [Rip out my life] / con el último beso de amor [With a final kiss of love], / arráncala, toma mi corazón [Rip it out, take my heart]"(Lara 24).

War and the Responsibilities and
Virtues of Citizenship

Through the early war years, as his marriage with Silva was collaps-
ing, Paredes continued hosting his radio show by night and supporting himself through his journalism and defense-industry job arming
bombers for the European front by day. By 1944, the end of the war
was still not yet in sight. Like many thousands of young men and
women of his generation, Paredes saw more and more of his friends
and family members volunteering and being drafted for service in
the armed forces. Exempt from the draft because of his work for
Pan American Airways and Lockheed, Paredes continued to face the
question of the responsibilities of American citizenship. His older
brothers, who had been born and raised on the Mexican side of the
border, urged him to renounce his American citizenship and return
to ancestral family lands near Matamoros, Mexico. His friends and
younger brother on the American side argued for the possibility of real
political power for a postwar cohort of Mexican American veterans.

The contradictions of serving in the American army were not lost on
Paredes. Like C. L. R. James, who challenged, "Why Negroes Should
Oppose the War," Paredes in Jim Crow, segregationist Texas debated
whether Mexican Americans should accept the obligations of citizenship when its rights continued to be deliberately and systematically
withheld. If citizenship involved both virtues and obligations, then
should not rights precede, or at least accompany, the responsibilities?
This remains the classic question for contemporary theories of citizenship.[38] Like many men and women of color of his generation engaged in the public discourse of the era, Paredes measured the possibility that service in the US Armed Forces might ultimately bolster
the validity of the claim to a Mexican American stake in national identity and American citizenship. In the end, Paredes and many others
like him concluded that it would only be appropriate to demand the
fulfillment of the virtues of citizenship if its obligations, particularly
to aid in the defense of the nation, were met by electing to fight for
them. The struggle to secure full citizenship was a conflict that by
1944 had been fought out but not resolved either by force of arms or
through acts of law on the US-Mexican border for nearly a century
since the signing of the Treaty of Guadalupe Hidalgo. In full histori-

cal irony, the horrors of modern war in Europe and the Pacific now seemed to offer the possibility for an active embracing of the virtues of citizenship.

The Asian Pacific War and the Postwar Moment

And so, in late 1944, Paredes decided to quit his defense-related job at Pan American Airways and the Lockheed bomber assembly plant and allow himself to be drafted into the armed forces. Paredes arrived in the Pacific in time to join the US Eighth Army in the occupation of Japan. In its practically minded wisdom, the US Army took note of his experience as a newspaperman and assigned him first as a staff writer and then as the political writer for *Pacific Stars and Stripes*, the official journal of the US Armed Forces in the Pacific. As a Mexican American correspondent for the US Army newspaper, Private, then Corporal, Paredes covered the aftermath of the war in the Pacific, the occupation of Japan, and its stormy transition from a militaristic feudal monarchy to a modern liberal-democratic society under the scrutiny of the Supreme Commander for the Allied Powers (SCAP), US Army General Douglas MacArthur. Paredes occupied a front-row seat at the war crimes military tribunal for the Far East (MTFE), interviewed wartime prime minister and chief "war criminal" Hideki Tojo in Sugamo prison, and witnessed the proceedings that marked the ending of one hot war and the beginning of the cold war.[39] Later still, based in Japan and China for the American Red Cross, Paredes traveled throughout China and Korea, observing the Chinese Revolution and the political crises that eventually culminated in the Korean War.

Writing in English for *Pacific Stars and Stripes* as a representative of American military power and in Spanish as a special correspondent for the Mexico City daily *El Universal*, Paredes offered in his articles from this period a spellbinding, compelling bilingual view of the shift from American continental expansion to overseas empire. He documents the dawn of globalization and the emergence of the transnational new world order.[40] During this epochal era, at the opening of the processes of globalization that we in another century are still struggling to understand, between Texas and Japan, Paredes first began to conceive of the clash of nations, cultures, and races in a startling new way. This vision would serve to complicate the rationales for the established orders that were already emerging during the early years of the cold war.

After having finished his tour of duty in the army, Paredes remained in Asia and worked for the Red Cross as the chief administrator for the distribution of relief aid and medical and humanitarian supplies in Japan, China, and Korea. He stayed until the months just before the beginning of the Korean War in 1950, the first of what would prove to be the continuing flare-ups of the cold war and a defining moment in the era of postcolonization. Through all of these events, Paredes observed and wrote about the power of national cultures, languages, and literatures as activities informing the apparatus of the cultural and political hegemony of the ruling classes.

In the midst of these world-historical events, Paredes met a Latina Japanese woman in a Tokyo Red Cross club for homesick American soldiers one day in 1947. Enchanted by her person and intrigued by her fluent Spanish, Paredes courted her, finalized a divorce from Chelo Silva, and married Amelia Sidzu Nagamine, the daughter of a Uruguayan national mother and a Japanese diplomat father. Expelled from Latin America with the rest of the Japanese diplomatic mission at the beginning of the war, the Nagamine family had returned to Tokyo and lived there throughout the years of the massive Allied air raids that devastated the city and killed thousands of civilians. Now, like the rest of their countrypeople, the Nagamines were attempting to relearn to be Japanese as a conquered people in an occupied land in a world turned upside down: Amelia's father by becoming the principal of a school, and she by working for the American Red Cross. By now marrying into it in 1948, Paredes became even more deeply attached to this world than he had already been.

With Amelia Nagamine de Paredes, he returned to Texas in 1950 to finish his BA, MA, and PhD degrees in English literature and folklore at the University of Texas at Austin. After a year teaching at Texas Western College in El Paso, Texas, Paredes returned to the faculty of the University of Texas at Austin as an assistant professor of English. During these tumultuous and hectic postwar years, settling into the life of an academic as an untenured assistant professor and as the father and husband of a young family, the manuscripts of his literary work—including the novels, the short stories, the poetry, and his other creative writings—remained actually intact but effectively lost. Over the course of the next thirty years as a scholar, Paredes was to produce, according to the anthropologist Richard Bauman, "the most important and influential scholarship of our generation on the folklore of Greater Mexico in general and of the Lower Border in particular" (ix–x).

The Archaeology of the Border

But the creative work had apparently vanished. Only when Paredes retired from the University of Texas as the Dickson, Allen, and Anderson Centennial Professor Emeritus of Anthropology and English in 1984, did he finally find respite enough from his many research, teaching, and professional duties to recover these early projects, including the manuscript of the novel *George Washington Gómez*. Other manuscripts, also presumably lost and mainly forgotten, were returned to him after Chelo Silva's death in 1988, and these too became the renewed focus of Paredes's work.[41]

From 1986 to 1990, in his retirement, Paredes began working on transcribing manuscripts literally falling apart at the touch of a hand. Over the next several years, Paredes would continue what he described as the "archeological" project of recovering this material from a half century before (*George Washington Gómez* 3). When the novel and other works were finally published, Paredes unequivocally stipulated that they appear in unedited form, precisely as he had left them when he had last worked on them in the 1930s and 1940s. The published works were to be an exact record of a moment in time, not an updated historical reconsideration of the past. At one point Paredes thus remarked about these works that it seemed to him now, as he neared the end of his life, as if the books had been written "by a man I no longer knew."[42]

During the years between the time of the original composition of the literary manuscripts and their final preparation for publication, Paredes's literary concerns with the folklore and history of south Texas, with the discourses and realities of power and their relation to official and unofficial narratives of history, and with the experiences of everyday life on the US-Mexican transcultural borderlands had become the substance of his scholarship and ethnographic work. The source of these concerns about the nature and substance of border knowledge, however, was manifestly present in his pre- and immediate postwar literary writings, elaborated not yet in the language of social science and empirical research but in the vernacular discourse of the social imaginary, in song, narrative, lyric, and journalistic prose.

Border Knowledge

Following a logic outlined by Enrique Dussel concerning discourses and realities of power in the American transcultural context, Walter Mignolo has argued that the long history of the emergence of Western global hegemony has built a frame and a conception of knowledge based on the distinction between epistemology and hermeneutics. In so doing, it has rendered subaltern other kinds of knowledge and discourses of knowledge. Mignolo employs the term *subaltern modernities* to describe this form of "border knowledge" (Mignolo 13). The world of the subaltern is excluded from rationality and validity, and hence, from history. According to Mignolo, border knowledge thus constitutes knowledge from a subaltern perspective; it is conceived from the exterior borders of the modern/colonial world system as a response to the encounter between them (11). Furthermore, the domains of that kind of knowledge are dynamic and expanding. "That long process of subalternization of knowledge is today being radically transformed by new forms of knowledge in which what has been in the past subalternized and considered interesting only as object of study becomes articulated as new loci of enunciation" (13).

Fifty years before the current focus on the issue of coloniality and its relationship to history, power, knowledge, and subaltern modernities, before our focus on processes of globalization and the transnational nature of economic and social forms, and before the related questions of imagined communities and the transnational imaginary, Américo Paredes addressed these same issues of the coloniality of knowledge in the context of border modernities. The United States–Mexico borderlands have long supported a web of relationships that transcend the US and Mexican nations.[43] In both his literary and scholarly work, Paredes attempted to specify what the local conditions of history, border knowledge, and transnational interactions in the borderlands region might be. In his prospective version of subaltern modernities, folklore and history serve as the repositories of border knowledge from a subaltern perspective. Thus, concerning that vernacular knowledge, Paredes would later write that "folklore is of particular importance to minority groups such as the Mexican Americans because their basic sense of identity is expressed in a language with an 'unofficial' status, different from the one used by the official culture . . . the Mexican American would do well to seek his identity in folklore. If the Mexican American will not do it, others will do it for him" ("Folklore" 1)

At moments such as this, and at many others in his writings, Paredes was fully aware that conceptions of identity and subjectivity imparted by the traditional social environment were linguistic in nature. They are contained, as Antonio Gramsci once remarked, in "language it-self," in "common sense," in "popular religion," and therefore also "in the entire system of beliefs, superstitions, opinions, ways of seeing things and of acting, which are collectively bundled under the name of 'folklore' " (*Selections* 323). At the time that Paredes began his folk-lore studies at the University of Texas, J. Frank Dobie served as the dean of Texas-Mexican folklore studies. An exponent of folklore as local color and the picturesque (precisely the way of conceiving folk-lore that Gramsci and later Paredes would refuse), Dobie appeared satisfied if his materials told a good story (Limón, *Dancing with the Devil* 50–51). His style contrasted starkly with the more social sci-entific method of scholars like Stith Thompson, whose historical-geographical work consisted of methodological studies on how to col-lect, select, and classify materials comparatively over space and time. Both techniques tended to slight the importance and historical sig-nificance of folklore as an expression of a community's conception of the world and life in determinate time and space and strata of so-ciety. A third strain of folklore studies, especially of the folklore of the West and Southwest, was exemplified by the work of scholars like Aurelio Espinosa. Espinosa argued that the origin of Mexican culture was Spain and that it was there that one would find the meanings of Mexican cultural forms.[44]

Paredes's scholarly work was unlike that of Dobie, Thompson, or Espinosa in its attention to the nature of folklore as a *critical* discourse. His work was based on empirical data gathering and ethnographic research scrupulously conducted in reference to its determinate his-torical context. Moreover, his use of empirical methods was highly in-formed by what he perceived as the need to qualify traditional ethno-graphic research by using better sampling methods and striving for objectivity as an ideal (Paredes, "On Ethnographic Work"). At the same time, there was more at issue than simply more careful collection methods. "Closer to the heart of the problem is the matter of language, a truly thorough knowledge of the language, both standard and dialectal," he claimed (75). The crux of the matter for a science of anthropology, as well as for an accurate historical record, according to Paredes, was that all too often it "ignores the nuances of human interaction" (83). It had aimed at compiling data without taking much into account "either the rhetorical and figurative uses of language or the structure of any given speech event, which may demand one response rather than another" (83).

The nature of folklore as the study of the social performance of verbal arts required that it attend to the nuances of performance in specific and variable settings and in relation to the processes alive in the linguistic interaction among individuals. Without an understanding of the contextual nature of any folk utterance, therefore, one could not "know what the expression really means to the people who use it. We can find its true meaning only if we know *how* and *when* it is used. Words in themselves have no meaning; their meaning is given to them by the particular context in which they are used. So to study *verbal context* without a thorough knowledge of *performance context* is a futile exercise indeed" (Paredes, "Folklore" 9). By their very nature, words have "true meaning" not ready made internally in the word or even less inside people's heads but in context. As Paredes conceives it in these studies, meaning emerges *between* people when words are performed collectively, expressing what in Spanish is called *sabidurias popular*, or dialogized collective wisdoms.[45]

In contrast to official conceptions of the world and narratives of historical process, folklore offered for Paredes a conception of the world that was not systematic, formalized, elaborated, or centralized. These discourses with unofficial status were by definition multiple, performative, sometimes contradictory, and they always afforded the possibility of multiple allegiances to truth. Mikhail Bakhtin describes a remarkably parallel situation when he argues that the cultural world consists of both "centripetal" and "centrifugal" forces. In contrast to the centrifugal "official" narratives that "seek to impose order on an essentially heterogeneous and messy world," the "unofficial" centrifugal ones "continually disrupt that order" (Morson and Emerson 30). Attitudes and feelings, undercurrents of emotion, and the messiness of the commonplace proceedings of everyday life not recorded in official documents may have profound consequences on events. Like Gramsci, Bakhtin sought in his theories of language to give individuals and social ensembles (the self *as* a social historical bloc, Gramsci would say), their due.[46] For both, meaning emerges as a product of a community's active work of intercourses and social discourses that come wrapped in contextual layers. Folklore thus designates the continuing problematics that constitute the popular wisdoms and traditions of the folk, ones that do not always line up in neat patterns of organized opposition to the authorized histories of the nation. For this reason, as Paredes once wrote, folklore remembers, but not as history remembers; folklore works by "building its own timeless world out of the wreck of history" ("Folklore and History" 58).[47]

As he sought to know whether folklore could put to order the "wreck of history" (58), Paredes also had to ask who constituted "the folk" to be studied. Who possessed folklore? What counted or passed as folklore? In addition, what could folklore do? Antonio Gramsci had already proposed that folklore should be studied "as a conception of the world and life."[48] Its features, he argued, were implicit in the "determinate (in time and space) strata of society and in opposition . . . to 'official' conceptions of the world . . . that have succeeded one another in a historical process" ("Observations on Folklore" 360). At the same time, Gramsci understood that there existed popular norms that in fossilized conservative and reactionary forms reflected the conditions of past life. Still, folk ideas and beliefs did sometimes align as "a series of innovations, often creative and progressive, determined spontaneously by forms and conditions of life which are in the process of developing and which are in contradiction to or simply different from" the norms of the governing strata (361).

In his own analyses, Paredes sought to identify the conservative aspects of traditional Mexican culture even as he attempted to describe those "creative and progressive" folk ideas and beliefs that did give agency to the Mexican American folk, which he termed *las clases subalternas*. He wished to elevate their mestizo art forms to the level of respect accorded the stately romance traditions deriving from Spanish Moorish culture.[49] Moreover, for Paredes, folklore constituted vernacular history in the making, sometimes offering the only surviving evidence of another history, adulterated, dismembered, and mutilated by the official narratives of the nation. This was also the sense in which he considered his own literary work to be a form of literary archaeology, committed to sifting through the highly unstable and dynamically shifting strata of sedimented layers of history, always with an eye for the exposed historical signs of the past, in the hope of re-membering the wreckage of the past.

Thus, concerning the methodology of a proper science of ethnography and folklore, Paredes would claim that "with legendary material and with the self-justificatory kind of performance, it is even harder to distinguish the interpretive from the literal. The ethnographer . . . must be very conscious of the informant as a potential performer. He must also keep in mind the existence of mutual stereotypes in himself and the people he is studying" ("On Ethnographic Work" 110). As lively as scholarship has proven on the immense contributions that Paredes's work has had in shaping our understanding of the folklore, ethnography, and social poetics of the cultures of the American Southwest, the significance of Paredes's own creative life as an imaginative artist and as a literary performer in his own right is just beginning to be understood. Viewed from the perspective of literary production, Paredes's ethnographic and anthropological work takes on a richer complexity and deeper nuance. And as definitive as Paredes's work from the 1950s forward has been in establishing a foundation for border knowledge, an understanding of Paredes's Depression-, World War II-, and cold war–era writings sharpens into clearer focus the profound nature of his transnational vision and its social aesthetic.

Beyond the North-South axis of the United States–Mexico border studies paradigm, Paredes brings an experiential understanding of the developing West-East axis of late twentieth-century American global politics. Unlike former paradigms of American literary and social history traversing an East-West axis "of frontier symbols and politics," or even of a North-South axis of "issues of slavery, Reconstruction, and Jim Crow segregation," as cultural critic Amy Kaplan has aptly identified them (Kaplan 18), Paredes requires us to map US hemispheric and global imperialism differently. "The conquest of Indian and Mexican lands in the antebellum period cannot be understood separately from the expansion of slavery and the struggle for freedom," argues Kaplan (18). Nor, she continues, can slavery, Reconstruction, and Jim Crow segregation be understood separately from the events of 1848 and 1898 in Mexico, the Caribbean, and the Pacific, or of 1945–50 in Japan and Asia (18–19).

Precisely so; however, to our understanding of the movements of peoples from East to West and South to North, Paredes's work adds the historically determinate and geopolitically concurrent movements of West to East and North to South. In seeking to document the unwritten history of the south Texas borderlands, Paredes brings his experience of cold war geopolitics, Asian cultural and racial conflict, the contradictions of American democracy, and the heterogeneously dialogical nature of border culture to the task.

Inventing the idea of Greater Mexico as an imaginary social space consisting in transnational communities of shared fates, Paredes allows us to make sense of the new geographies of citizenship in an era of the emerging globalization of capital with its intensified flow of ideas, goods, images, services, and persons. He allows for the possibility of a theoretical repositioning of modern citizenship in new multicultural versions. For this reason, it is a mistake to see Paredes's Greater Mexico simply in a cultural-nationalist context. It represents instead a far more complex imaginary site for the emergence of new citizen-subjects and the construction of new spaces for the enactment of their politics outside the realm of the purely national. It takes the special form of the social imaginary that I am here terming "the transnational imaginary." Current debates on the meaning of citizenship in its historical setting have focused on the ways in which processes of decolonization and migration, as well as social identities based on ethnicity, race, and gender, point to the existence of other than national identities as the basis for defining citizenship. As an imaginary space of real political and historical effect, Greater Mexico represents an early, direct challenge to the traditional language of citizenship and liberal democratic notions that tie it indissolubly to state membership.[50]

This revised sense of citizenship particularly comes into play concerning the relationship between Paredes's Greater Mexico and the transnational imaginary, on the one hand, and the idea of a national polity, on the other. What is perhaps confusing to conceive is that both social structures, a nationalist and a transnationalist one, can be vitally present in the same historical moment. Today, both trends exist. As almost every item in the news these days confirms, we are far from abandoning the idea of the nation as a viable category of political and personal identity. At the same time, however, something else has also become visible on the political horizon, namely, a loosening of national categories on various levels, including the economic, political, and personal experiential. This loosening has been with us at least since the post–World War II years. We have to live with the one (the nation) even as we see something else (the post-nation) emerging. It is not at all clear which one of these will prove the way of the future. However, what is clear is that both experiences are with us, almost as social imperatives, and that citizens must respond to both. How, then, do we make sense of the national in the midst of an emerging transnational, and vice versa? Paredes addressed these questions with his notion of Greater Mexico.

Furthermore, since we have to live within the nation, how can we compel it to be responsive to other forms of national identity, polity, and rights? These questions, too, converge on the multicultural issues that almost all modern nations must face today. That is where the concepts of "shared fates" and "cultural citizenship" have their most vital function; they allow for a way of dealing with multicultural politics in our everyday lives. There is really no inconsistency here at all, simply a messy attempt to deal with a confoundingly complex and evolving process in the current historical moment.

How Paredes's personal experiences as an American soldier, journalist, and humanitarian aid worker in postwar Japan and Asia affected his understanding of the social imaginary and transnational sites, as well as of the different relations between national and postnational forms of citizenship generally, and between Anglos and Mexicans in the United States–Mexico borderlands specifically, is one of the central questions I pose in this work. How may we define communities of belonging and the borders of belonging in the realm of the transnational? What stands between Texas and Japan?

Social Aesthetics and
the Transnational Imaginary

The answer to these questions has everything to do with the terms of my title, *The Borderlands of Culture: Américo Paredes and the Transnational Imaginary*. I have already indicated why border studies and borderland theory are pertinent to my argument. I will have more to say about the significance of the borderlands shortly, as well as about the role of culture and the cultural arts in social history. For the present, however, it is important to see that folklore is the general form in which cultural production takes on a manifestly social function in Paredes's remapping of the American borderlands. Fiction, representing the work of the imaginary, especially in its role of figuring an alternative symbolic mediation of the real, is the mode within which the critical work of folklore is enacted.[51] The manner of this relationship is what I will call Paredes's "social aesthetics." It partakes in what anthropologist Néstor García Canclini has described as one aspect of culture, namely, its assumption of an "indecisive position that attempts to imagine what can be done with quantities which are not overly certain, whose accumulated and expressive potentials are yet to be discovered" (*La globalización imaginada* 10).[52] The uncertain quantities whose unexpressed potentials remain undiscovered are the intrinsically ideological formations of the social world. To understand the special form of social communication realized in works of the imagination that attempt to express those formations constitutes for Paredes precisely the task of a social aesthetics. It helps us understand the extraverbal import of the imaginary as a way of reorganizing, regrouping, and revaluing values.[53]

I should also say a word about the relationship between the social imaginary and the transnational. I have used the term *social imaginary* in the preceding pages to refer to the intellectual schemes one may use in thinking about social reality. But I also mean by *social imaginary* something much broader and deeper, such as when Charles Taylor uses the term to describe "the ways people imagine their social existence, how they fit together with others, how things go on between them and their fellows, the expectations that are normally met, and the deeper normative notions and images that underlie these expectations" (*Modern Social Imaginaries* 23).[54] Recourse to the ways that people imagine their social existence will continue to emerge in this book as one of Paredes's most important analytical moves.

Elsewhere Paula Moya and I have argued that American fiction in general is transnational to the degree that it must be seen anew as a heterogeneous grouping of overlapping but distinct discourses that refer to the United States in relation to a variety of national entities. Even in the earliest periods of US national formation in the early nineteenth century, American literary discourses were already produced by a large variety of popular forms, genres, styles, and modes uneasily grafted together to form symbols of plurality and respresentativeness (1–2). We point out that "the frontier, the backwoods, the antebellum

South, and the Old Southwest provided indigenously heterogeneous idioms that vastly confounded efforts to describe a singular American national voice speaking with a New England accent" (11). Our call to see American literature as heterogeneous and multiple was intended as a challenge to traditional American literary historiography, asking for it to shift enough to allow it to respond to a transnational framework within which literary works produced by a diverse range of residents and citizens of the United States could be interpreted. As the US frontier moved west and southwest (especially after 1848), encountering other nations and native idioms, the transitive nature of American discourses was historically—but not historiographically—established. Indeed, the influences on American literature of nations other than England and of idioms that do not originate in the English language have been unevenly and inadequately incorporated into the larger narrative of American literary historiography. My work on Paredes hopes to provide a chapter in that larger project to see American studies in a transnational context.

That transnational context is imaginary because it focuses on the way ordinary people imagine their social surroundings. As Taylor observes, "This is often not expressed in theoretical terms, but is carried in images, stories, and legends" (*Modern Social Imaginaries* 23). The imaginary figures in a very real but fundamentally different syntax of codes, images, icons, tacit assumptions, convictions, and beliefs that seek to bind together the varieties of American national discourses. It "makes possible common practices and a widely shared sense of legitimacy" (23). Among other codes and symbols formed by the social imaginary, a foundational one is the language of citizenship in which claims of belonging, community, and right are formulated and expressed as a discourse of citizenship.[55] The transnational imaginary is thus to be understood not only ideologically but also as a chronotope, a spatial and temporal indicator of a real contact zone that is historical and geographical, cultural and political, theoretical and discursive. The borderlands are populated by transnational persons whose lives form an experiential field within which monologically delineated notions of political, social, and cultural identity simply do not suffice. The geographical particularity and historical specificity of the border region thus mark it as a category of an immediate reality.

Looking West to East and South to North, I begin this consideration of the literary writings of Américo Paredes with a discussion of his life in south Texas and in Japan and Asia, and of the roles that those regions and their histories played in his formation as one of the founding figures of twentieth-century Mexican American intellectual identity. History, folklore, and the particular features of border thinking broadly lie at the core of his concerns. I offer my discussion as a prehistory of the development of one version of late twentieth-century borderlands thinking.

A LIFE IN THE BORDERLANDS

> To the memory of my father
> who rode a raid or two with
> Catarino Garza;
> and to all those old men
> who sat around on summer-nights,
> in the days when there was a chaparral,
> smoking their
> cornhusk cigarettes and talking
> in low, gentle voices about
> violent things;
> while I listened.
> —Américo Paredes, dedication to
> *"With His Pistol in His Hand"*

In various places in his writings, Américo Paredes sometimes offered glimpses of his family's history, especially so when it seemed connected to the history of the United States–Mexico border region. During the final years of his life, he contemplated the possibility of writing a full-blown autobiography of his life in the borderlands. In the end, however, he decided against it, primarily because he felt that the autobiographical form was simply too majestic a genre for what he considered in complete sincerity a relatively unexceptional life. Instead, he decided to write a series of short vignettes—part memoir, part fiction—that he came to describe as the elements of a larger collective story, "a family autobiography."[1] He actually achieved only a few of these pieces, and only one was published in his lifetime.[2] In the meantime, Paredes had begun to organize his family autobiography in the form of reminiscence and oral history. Several interviews, letters, and autobiographical sketches from the final decade of his life document this project.[3] In what follows, I present the body of some of that autobiographical material as Paredes shared it with me in the form of an extended interview that I conducted with him and his wife in their home in Austin, Texas, on March 2–3, 1995. Numerous additional details emerged later in daylong conversations during an extended trip to south Texas in November 1998.[4] Some of the information that Paredes provided on those occasions was an elaboration of conversations and correspondence we had conducted since the mid-1980s when we were colleagues at the University of Texas at Austin, the same period during which he had first shown me the manuscripts of his prewar and postwar writings. In the course of these interviews and conversations, I asked Paredes about the history of his family in south Texas. What did he know about them? Who were they and how did they influence his own later attempts at understanding the structure of Mexican American political, social, and cultural life?

A Family Autobiography

AMÉRICO PAREDES: I was born in Brownsville, Texas, on September 3, 1915. But I really come from both sides of the border, from people with very strong family traditions that extend to the present from the time of the early colonial period. This was true both of my mother's side of the family and of my father's side. My mother's maiden name was Clotilde Manzano Vidal. She was raised by her grandfather, Don José María Vidal, her maternal grandfather, after both her parents had died when she was just a little girl. I don't know very much about Don José except that he had been born in Cataluña, Spain, and that he was an unusual man for his time. He was, for example, the only person on either side of our family to earn a college degree until my generation.

Not all the Vidals lived on the Texas side of the border. Oh no, Don José lived on the Mexican side. In fact he was *presidente municipal* (mayor) of Bagdad, Tamaulipas, during the French occupation of Mexico and when Bagdad was a thriving port, the customhouse port of first entry for all of northern Mexico. In those days, especially during the American Civil War, Clarksville, Brownsville's port city on the Texas side, and Bagdad, across the river on the Mexican side, were outlets of cotton for the Confederacy. Blockade-runners and smugglers thrived in both towns, especially during those final days of the war. But smuggling and the trading of contraband of all sorts as a way of life already had a deep tradition in the borderlands, long before the American Civil War. After 1835, when Texas won its independence from Mexico, and before 1848, when the boundary between the United States and Mexico was set at the Rio Grande, the region between the Rio Grande and the Nueces River to the north was disputed territory. Livestock and other goods were constantly being run across the border in both directions. So it was only natural that running the Union blockade became big business at the Texas-Mexican border. After the Civil War, both towns at the mouth of the Rio Grande were destroyed by a hurricane. Up to this point, Bagdad had been a bustling cosmopolitan port, a fabulous city, really, with merchants from all parts of the world, and cargoes of smuggled goods to and from the Confederacy. I remember people saying that you could hear all the languages of Europe and many from Africa, Asia, and the Near East in the busy streets of Bagdad. There was a lot of mixing—linguistic, social, and other kinds—in that port town.

As I said, Don José became its *presidente municipal* during the middle part of the nineteenth century. I don't know much more about him except that he was politically an Imperialist. That is, he was a supporter of the political faction that backed Maximiliano, archduke of Austria, during the French occupation until Maximiliano was captured and executed by republican Mexican armed forces in 1867.

Don José was of Catalonian descent, and he knew some English. Occasionally, he would take his family, including my mother, to San Antonio on his business trips. In those days, from the perspective of the border region, San Antonio was the farthest northern limit of the known universe. Even now when somebody tells me they're from Houston, I don't remember later whether they live in Fort Worth or Dallas. All those places vaguely blend together; they are simply part of *el Norte*.

Now Don José raised fine horses. Another peculiarity of his, other than that he was college educated, was that he also raised sheep. Of course, among cattle-raising people, that was a real oddity. And yet, apparently he couldn't stand even the smell of mutton! He would bring his horses to San Antonio to sell. Saddle horses. As I said, sometimes he would bring the family on what they called the *diligencia*, which, as far as I know, was something like a stagecoach. Once, on his way to San Antonio, he stopped among some *alemanes* (Germans).

Alemanes is what the border people called the Czechs, the Poles, as well as the Germans who settled in central Texas. All of these central European newcomers were simply *alemanes*, as opposed to the English-speaking Anglo-Texans who were called *americanos* or gringos. My mother once told me that on one of these trips Don José wanted to buy some *chickens*. So he stopped at a German farmhouse and asked whether they would sell him half a dozen *kitchens*. In his own way, he knew English. He would make mistakes like that sometimes. [laughter] No, the *alemanes* understood what he wanted all right. It helped that he also happened to be fair of color and light of skin, so he got along with them. He wasn't discriminated against. That was Don José Vidal, my maternal great-grandfather.

My mother's people, the Vidals, were an interesting family. My mother's father, my maternal grandfather, Mariano Manzano, was born in Asturias, Spain. He came to Bagdad as the navigator in a ship that was captained by his father, Ignacio Manzano. And it happened one day that he fell in love with one of Don José's daughters, my grandmother, Julia Vidal. Don José had been the captain of the port, and when he became *presidente municipal*, his new son-in-law, Mariano Manzano, became captain of the port. My grandmother Julia had four children, my mother and three sons, José María, Mariano, and Eduardo. But Julia died in childbirth when my mother, Clotilde, was just two years old. My uncle Eduardo later returned to settle in the Brownsville area, around 1928, when I was thirteen or fourteen. He had come to the United States as a member of a Mexican exile group, El Partido Liberal, men who were anarchists dedicated to overthrowing the government. He also belonged to the IWW (Industrial Workers of the World), the Wobblies, and was involved in trying to organize labor unions among the *mexicanos* in Colorado, where there were copper mines, and in the coal mines in Oklahoma. This was my mother's brother, Eduardo. His politics influenced me greatly during the time that he lived with us. My mother's two other brothers also later moved to Texas. José María went to San Antonio, where he worked for the railroad as a shipping clerk and became very much part of the Italian colony in that city. But Eduardo became, as I was saying, a labor organizer and a radical. In the course of his travels, he met a man who was *puro indio*, a Tlascalan Indian from around San Luis Potosí, and married his daughter.

Shortly after the death of my grandmother Julia, my grandfather

Mariano became the telegraph operator of Matamoros. And, one day, climbing a telegraph pole, so the story goes, he fell and was killed instantly. So that now left my mother and her brothers orphans, and it was Don José, their grandfather, who took over responsibility for them and raised them as his own. Other than these few things, we don't know too much about that side of the family.

Now in contrast to my mother's family, my father's people were very strong *juaristas* and Liberals, supporters of Benito Juarez's revolutionary party in the wars to free Mexico from French imperial control. They were on the opposite side of the political spectrum from Don José and the rest of my mother's family, in other words. But on the border in the mid- and late nineteenth century, the period that I'm now describing, everyone seemed to find a way to get along since life had to be lived as an everyday affair.

The Paredes and other families in the region came to New Spain in 1580 with Don Luis de Carvajal to colonize what is now the northern Mexico region of Nuevo León and Coahuila. These colonists, for the most part converted Jews, were called *cristianos nuevos* or *marranos*. Over the next two hundred years, their descendants moved north from that area to colonize what is now the Texas—Mexico border area, from the Pánuco to the Nueces Rivers. This now became the province of Nuevo Santander. I learned from my older brothers, who did the research in government and church records in the 1960s, that my great-great-great-great-grandfather (my *quinto abuelo*, as we say in Spanish), Don Pedro González de Paredes, was one of the leaders of the new settlements along the present Rio Grande.

In the early nineteenth century, my great-grandfather, Don Leandro Paredes Ybarra, had a ranch south of the Nueces in what was then the northern part of Nuevo Santander, but he was forced to give it up after 1848. After the war, his son, my grandfather Pedro Paredes Cabrera, developed a large ranch on the Mexican side of the Rio Grande with the help of other relatives, the Cisneros family.

Don Pedro's eldest son was my father, Justo Paredes Cisneros, born in 1868. I have to tell you about my father now. He was in some ways a strange man, too. You might look at my essay on "The Undying Love of 'El Indio' Córdova" and you'll have some idea of what his side of the family, the Cisneros clan, was like.[5] The Paredes, the Cisneros, and other families related to us had reputations as great composers of the traditional Spanish verse *décimas*, ten-line poems that were improvised and sung. According to stories I heard as a child during the summers I spent on the family ranches downriver from Matamoros, a man known in border folk tradition simply as "El Indio" Córdova apparently sometime in the mid-nineteenth century asks our kinsman Don Santiago María Cisneros for the hand in marriage of his daughter, Francisca Cisneros Gómez. But Córdova doesn't just propose, he composes his request in the elegant and complex folk verse form of the *décima*. Taking Córdova's *décima* as a challenge, Don Santiago composes his own verses to refuse the request in no uncertain terms. Their poetic duel of contra-*décimas* became legendary in no small part because of the romantic story that produced it. Here you had this urbane, cultured Indian in love with a beautiful young country girl who was denied to him in marriage because he was a *fuereño*, an outsider. It probably also had something to do with the fact that she was a member of one of the area's largest landowning families and he was not. These poetic duels in *décima* form also occur in other American contexts, particularly in Cuba, you know.[6]

I heard these stories and the *décimas* themselves recited countless times in gatherings of the extended family. For us, knowing the *décimas* became a way of establishing our identity as someone who belonged to a distinctive poetic and familial circle. Poetry and history served that same end, and even as a young boy, I was fascinated by the ways that stories and songs defined us as a community.

Patriarchy, Cultural Tradition, and Rebellion

AMÉRICO PAREDES: Now I'm going to mention something else that I haven't talked at all about before, but it is related to what I want to say about my father and his family. It concerns Renato Rosaldo, an anthropologist from Stanford. He wrote a book in which he contrasted three works: *"With His Pistol in His Hand,"* Ernesto Galarza's *Barrio Boy*, and *The House on Mango Street* by Sandra Cisneros.[7] Well, I thought he was way off the mark. To compare those three works is like comparing apples and oranges and pears. Sandra Cisneros was writing fiction. Galarza was supposed to be writing his autobiography. His book is called *Barrio Boy*, even though we never get to the boy, and the barrio is almost nonexistent. The book is really all about a little town at the edge of the sierra where Galarza grew up as a fatherless child. To my mind, Galarza gives a very idealistic view of that little town. For example, the book begins with the Mexican Revolution. When the revolutionaries come into the town, all the boys of military age go into the mountains to hide so that they won't be forced into service. Now we are supposed to believe that there wasn't a single person in that town who belonged to the *revolucionarios* and wouldn't tell the revolutionaries where those boys were hiding!

Anyway, Renato Rosaldo holds up Galarza's story as a model and thinks that my book comes up short by comparison because he feels that I have idealized the community from which my people came on the border. What bothers me about Renato Rosaldo's discussion is that in the first place, he forgets that I was not writing an autobiography like Galarza or fiction like Sandra Cisneros. To use legal terms, perhaps not correctly, I was writing a brief. I was being an advocate for my people. Enough had been said about them negatively that I wanted to point to the exceptions, the remarkable ways in which their communities held together under great external pressures from discrimination and other social injustices. "Weren't there," Renato asks, "people who did not follow the traditional views about doing what their parents told them and following the old communal ways of thinking?" that I describe in *"With His Pistol in His Hand"*? Yes, of course there were. Just as I could have mentioned in talking about Gregorio Cortez that some Mexicans really were outlaws. But that was not my purpose. Walter Prescott Webb and others had said enough about Mexicans as outlaws. I talk about what I saw myself — even in the late 1920s — namely, that people still shared a communal spirit. When they slaughtered a steer, for example, they would distribute it to the whole community, not just keep it for themselves. And then next time somebody else slaughtered, and that way everyone always had fresh meat. They didn't have to refrigerate it. In fact, it wasn't only the Mexicans who did it that way. After *"With His Pistol in His Hand"* was published, I remember a man of Czech descent visited me and said, "That's exactly what my people used to do."

The people of the south Texas border area lived in tight-knit patriarchal communities. Now, there certainly were people by the 1920s who were not following the old traditions and who were challenging the old way of life. Or others who were criticized when they slaughtered a steer because they kept all the good parts for themselves. [laughter] But those were the ones who were the exceptions because they were attuned to the wave of the future, not to the traditions of the past.

Or another example, in the days before the river was dammed, it would flood annually. Communities would join together when the river was flooding to shore up the levies. I remember—I was a little boy staying at my grandfather's ranch along the river when it happened during the summer—men coming back, my cousins coming back from the river, exhausted and muddy from fighting the river. They had finally stopped the flooding river, but they would say, "So-and-so's family never showed up. They went to Matamoros instead." [laughter] So, yes, there were exceptions to the old traditions, but the most important exception, the most important thing that Rosaldo attacked, was that the people couldn't have been that close-knit and that there must have been rebels among them who did not follow the traditional way. Of course, there were.

I offer this long disquisition in order to get to my father's story as a story of resentment and dissent. My father was the eldest in his family, and so he was supposed to inherit the whole place and uphold the old values. But because he did not, instead, the second son, Vicente, inherited. I have a son that I named Vicente for my uncle because it was to his house that we went in summers when I was a boy. Uncle Vicente was almost like a second father to me. But my father himself was just the kind of rebel to the cultural and social system that Renato Rosaldo asks about. It was a culture that required that the patriarch be taken as the representative of God on earth. His word was the absolute and final authority. The sons and daughters were expected strictly to keep the traditions and customs of the culture. In those days, for instance, even a grown son, a man with children of his own, would not dare smoke in front of his father, unless his father first gave him permission. It would be the height of disrespect to do so.

The Four Rebellions of Justo Paredes

AMÉRICO PAREDES: So it was in this context that I was saying that my father was a rebel and rebelled four times. The first rebellion took place when he was just a boy in the 1870s, when he ran off with a band of outlaws. He was able to get away with this first act of rebellion because his father, Don Pedro Paredes, had fought in the resistance against the French and was very well respected by many friends who had served in the *juarista* revolutionary army and were still serving in the army of Porfirio Díaz. Also, my grandfather still had land in Texas that he inherited through the Cisneros side of the family. And my father, as the eldest, was due to inherit his father's position and authority.

After the French were driven out of Mexico, Porfirio Díaz had attempted to seize power, and my grandfather had helped him by providing horses and cattle and other supplies for his troops. He and a man by the name of Rómolo Cuellar were probably two of the most important people who helped Díaz on the border. Cuellar later left the border region for Mexico City where he became quite a cultured cosmopolitan general, and his daughter became interested in the opera. My grandfather, however, went back to his ranch. He felt that the big city was a corrupting influence, and he wanted nothing to do with it. To my father, who was just a little boy at the time, my grandfather's military friends who visited resplendent in magnificent uniforms were heroic figures.

They would say to my grandfather, "Pedro, let us take this little boy to Mexico. We'll get him into the Colegio Militar." My grandfather, wary of the insidious influences of the cities, always said, [gruffly] "No; I don't want him to be corrupted." And of course my father as that little boy would look in awe at those men all dressed in gold lace and bright military splendor and wanted to be just like them. I think he came to resent his father in certain ways.

My father's first rebellion against his father was cloaked by the official story that he had been kidnapped by bandits. According to this version of the story, my father was riding from Quijano, which was a ranch at the time, to Matamoros, and that he was—it's a rather romantic story, really—that he was stopped and robbed by an outlaw gang who threatened to kill him. But it turned out that the outlaw chief had been *caporal*, a foreman, on my grandfather's ranch. And so when the *caporal* discovered who the boy was, he said, "We won't kill Justo Paredes. We'll take him with us."

What my uncle Vicente used to tell me was that nothing of the sort really happened. Justo just ran away with the outlaws. There was no kidnapping. In any case, when he was taken or ran away, he had been riding an old gelding that was in good enough shape to trot from their ranch to Matamoros and back. But later, when he and the outlaw band were chased by the *rurales*, fine horsemen on magnificent mounts, that poor animal showed what it really was, a swaybacked bag of bones whose belly almost scraped the ground. And so the rural police rescued, or captured, Justo and returned him to his father. I learned some of these things from my father, some things from my uncle. My uncle used to say that later people from all the neighboring ranches would gather around just to look at that ludicrous bag of bones Justo had been riding as an outlaw, and they would just laugh at the thought of it. That was the first of my father's rebellions, in the 1870s.

My father's second rebellion occurred when he ran away again, this time to Monterrey, sometime in the 1880s. Apparently he did fairly well in Monterrey. He used to say that he started selling fruit in baskets in the street. But then he and another person got enough money together to acquire a little hotel. I'm sure it wasn't the Ritz Carlton or anything like that. Just a place where people could have a room when they came to the city. But then he got sick with arthritis or something that threatened to cripple him completely. That was when he returned to his father's ranch—because he did come back—and he was so ill, they say, that he had to be helped off his horse. His father forgave him for running away from home a second time, and that apparently cured him.

His third rebellion occurred in the 1890s, when my father really did become a rebel, joining Catarino Garza's armed uprising on the border.[8] I mention that in the epigraph to *"With His Pistol in His Hand."* From his south Texas ranch near Brownsville in 1891, Garza led a rebellion against the Díaz regime under a manifesto, a plan, as they called it, which had all the *requisitos* (essential elements) of the revolution of 1910. Catarino Garza really was a precursor to the revolution of 1910. And my father joined him. I'm not certain how much of a revolutionary he really was or whether he was just doing it to spite his father, who was a strong Díaz man. In any case, this rebellion ended when my father was wounded in a skirmish with *porfirista* troops. They had him then, since Porfirio Díaz had a very strong relationship with the American authorities and Garza's rebels couldn't escape by crossing the river back into the United States. Those who did cross were arrested by the Americans and were turned over to Díaz, who immediately executed them. But since my father was wounded, he was hidden and not turned over to Díaz's police. He recovered from his wounds, and he was sent to New Mexico, he used to say, to hide

6 Justo Paredes and Clotilde Manzano de Paredes, c. 1890s.
Photograph courtesy of Alan and Vincent Paredes.

as a sheepherder. From there, he was smuggled back to Monterrey. Finally, a cover story was made up that claimed that he had been in Monterrey all along and could thus come home safely without fear of reprisals.

Justo and my mother were married at the end, at the very end, of the century, after he settled down from his Garza rebellion experience. My oldest brother was born in December of 1899. After his marriage to Clotilde, Justo seemed to have reformed and to have ended his rebellious ways. He built a house just across the road from my grandfather's house, and they had three children born there: the eldest, Eliseo; a daughter, Isaura; and a third, Lorenzo, my only surviving brother, who was born in 1904.[9]

But apparently my father had still one more rebellion left in him. So, in 1904, he decided to bite the bullet and just tell his father that he was leaving Mexico and moving across the river to Brownsville. For a while, I understand, my father and grandfather were estranged because of my father's decision to leave Mexico for the United States, his fourth rebellion.

Our family had owned land on the south side of the Nueces River, but had been forced to abandon it after 1848. My father always swore that he would never own a piece of land in Texas because, as he put it, "I am not going to pay money for land that had been taken away from our people!" So, even though my father did move to Brownsville, he refused to buy property. We finally did come to own a piece of land in Brownsville between Fourteenth and Van Buren Streets, but only much later. And really, my older brother bought it, not my father. So, you could say that my father kept his vow not to pay for stolen land. By the way, that house in Brownsville still stands.

So, that's how I came to be born in Brownsville. And my father did very well with that move. I am speaking about what I have been told, because all of this happened, of course, before I was born in 1915. The rest of the family who stayed in Mexico started on the way down, partly because after the revolution of 1910 the *agraristas* confiscated most of the good cattle land, and mainly because changes finally caught up with them. The old forms, the old folkways, no longer worked.

Texas Politics and Life on the Border
at the Turn of the Century

AMÉRICO PAREDES: By the time that my father moved our family permanently to Texas, he already had good connections with Judge Jim Wells and the Kenedys, the political bosses of south Texas with whom he had become friendly.[10] Through the influence of Wells and the Kenedys, he became a political boss himself,[11] even though he was a Mexican citizen until he died. But there was a strange arrangement, at least in Texas at the time. To vote, all you had to do was prove that you were a resident of the county. Apparently, they didn't ask them whether they were citizens [laughter] because my father remained a Mexican citizen until the day he died.[12] Yet he became a political boss. And he owned a saloon called Sobre las Olas (Over the Waves). You might notice certain things in his story that are similar to situations in *George Washington Gómez*. The back of the saloon was a gathering place for the local politicians.

In *George Washington Gómez*, I called the saloon El Danubio Azul (The Blue Danube). I changed the name but kept the idea of the waltz. My father loved that Mexican waltz "Sobre las olas" by Juventino Rosas. Everyone today thinks of it as a Russian composition because it was used as the musical theme in that movie *Doctor Zhivago*.[13] But it was really a Mexican waltz! Anyway, my father did very well as a saloonkeeper and politician. Things fell apart once Prohibition began, however. Even more new Anglos were now arriving in the valley, and it was no longer possible for a Mexican to have political power. But when I was born, he still had that saloon and was politicking, buying poll taxes for people, and things of that sort.

The politics of the ruling sectors of the time was characterized by the Democratic Party. Really there were two wings of the Democratic Party. They were known among the voters as the Blues and the Reds. Just as I represented it in *George Washington Gómez* and as the *corrido* "Los sediciosos" says it: "Ya la mecha esta encendida / con azul y colorado" (Now the match has been lit / burning blue and red). There was also a small Republican Party, which at that time was quite liberal in a sense because they were the opposition trying to undercut the Democratic machine. Really, whether the Reds or the Blues won the election, the machine remained the same. Judge Wells and the county and state party machine controlled it all. But after things fell apart, my father went back to Mexico. He still had some land. Really, he continued to move back and forth across the border. When he was a young man, my father didn't do very much with cattle because my grandfather raised cattle and horses and sold his horses to the Díaz people. They went south. My great-grandfather Vidal took his horses north—they were good saddle horses—to San Antonio. But my father said that he had two outfits, one to take care of the cattle and one to take care of the horses. My father said that he never liked to be a model nursemaid to cattle. He liked horses, and so he, too, raised horses; that's what he did. But he was never a farmer or anything of that sort.

The place that we bought in Brownsville I remember was on the edge of town so that he could raise his horses. He planted a banana grove. I remember that we used to get fresh bananas from that grove. When the weather was like it is today, warm and humid, I would go and cut the half-ripe bunches. The tree had a big, or rather two, two great big trunks. They would wrap up the bananas in old clothes and put them in the trunks, and put the ones that were half-ripe over the wood-burning stove, and we would eat roasted bananas. And I remember he used to plant okra—I've always loved okra—as well as a few other things. But then later the older boys convinced him to move back to what was the edge of the barrio. Fourteenth Street was the boundary for the Cuatro Veintiuno, another barrio, the four twenty one. On the other side of Fourteenth Street was La Perla. And the kids used to fight each other some times. They weren't gangs like the ones today, though.

So my father's fourth rebellion was to move to Texas in 1904. My older brothers and sister, Eliseo, Isaura, and Lorenzo, were born in Matamoros, Mexico. The rest of us, beginning with my sister Clotilde, were born in Brownsville, Texas. Lorenzo later became an American citizen. Eliseo was always very patriotic about Mexico. He finally went back to live in Matamoros and did very well over there, in fact served as the city historian of Matamoros for a number of years.

Gender Formations on the Border

AMÉRICO PAREDES: Of my brothers and sisters, Eliseo was the oldest, born in 1899 and lived until 1988. Then Isaura, in 1902, who died relatively young in 1936. Lorenzo, who is still living, was born in 1904. Then Clotilde, whose first husband was named Oscar del Castillo. In fact, I have nephews named del Castillo still living in Brownsville. The youngest of my sisters, Blanca, was born in 1910 and died in 1930. I have also outlived younger twin brothers, born in 1920. Eleazar died in 1975, and Amador died almost ten years later, in 1984.

Clotilde's first husband's mother was a Cuellar, related to the Rómolo Cuellar whom I mentioned earlier. But she divorced him and married a man named Ceballos. When they married, he was working for Pan American Airways. The airline transferred them to New York City, but my sister, who was a very strong, self-willed character, like my Tía Pilar about whom I've recently been writing, didn't like New York, so she made him apply for Florida. For Miami. She didn't like Miami either, so she had him move to California. And it was there, very close to Stanford, that they lived, in a little town called Millbrae. As a young man, I used to visit Clotilde and walk to Stanford from Millbrae.

The youngest of my sisters, Blanca, died on Easter Sunday of 1930. I still remember that date. Blanca was going to marry this young man who lived across Fourteenth Street from us. Cisneros was his name, Luis Cisneros. She was going to marry in June 1930, but she died before she could. From pneumonia. But she was very influential in my younger years. She read to me. She bought me books. For example, I read Lamb's *Tales from Shakespeare* when I was young because she [pause] . . . she bought it for me. And I know, sometimes I wasn't very happy that she'd give me books for Christmas. [laughter] I don't remember whether it was Lamb's complete book or whether it was selections from it, but I do remember that it had illustrations. The pictures were colored. The stories were *Macbeth, Hamlet,* and all of the famous plays. I also remember that she read to me from a number of books that dealt with Irish and Norse mythology. These were children's books. I remember Sigurd, especially, who was used as a figure of the warrior. It really was a big shock for me to lose her, and I have always felt guilty about it.

Why guilty? That Easter season we had gone to visit my uncle Eduardo at his farm. He had returned to south Texas, as I was telling you earlier, in 1928, when he gave up the life of radical politics. He leased some land on the American side and started farming it. We used to go there for picnics and family outings because it was on the river's edge and a very lovely place, really. It must have been in March because she died on Easter Sunday. We had gone on an outing to my uncle's ranch, and I don't know how it was, other than that when you're young, when you're a kid, you do crazy things. I remember that I jumped into the river and was swimming around with all my clothes on. When it was time to leave, they got me out of the river, with my clothes, dripping wet. It was already dusk. In those days the notion that it's always safe to be cautious just didn't exist. So when I decided to sit on the fenders of the farm truck for the ride home to dry off, nobody objected. At that time, the trucks and cars had big fenders and running boards that you could just stretch out on. We went from the ranch, which was halfway to Boca Chica beach, all the way home, some ten to fifteen miles, with me sitting on the outside of the car in the cool dusk of the evening in my soaked clothes. Of course, as my clothes dried, I was completely chilled, and by the next day, I was as sick as I could be. I had gotten pneumonia from riding on the outside of the car in the cold damp air in my wet clothes all the way home. It was Blanca who nursed me through my pneumonia, but she caught it from me. I survived and she died. It has always bothered me very much, thinking that I was the cause of her death. . . . But with her books, she influenced my life immensely.

7 Américo Paredes and his sister, Blanca Paredes, c. 1920s.
Photograph courtesy of the Américo Paredes Papers, 1886–
1999, Benson Latin American Collection, General Libraries,
University of Texas at Austin.

All of my sisters were formidable persons. They took guff from no one. At times they would even talk back to my father, something the sons would never dream of doing. They were feisty and would often exasperate my mother. She said they reminded her of Tía Pilar, my father's only sister.[14] Tía Pilar was an old woman by the time I knew her, but she was still tall, spare, and straight and was a dead shot with her Winchester .30–.30 rifle, the equal of any man on the border. Any predators that threatened her chickens didn't last very long within her range. The only time anyone knew her to have missed a target was because a mule got in the line of fire just as she squeezed off a shot. It was just as well that she killed the mule instead of her intended target, her son-in-law!

Her daughter, Della, had showed up at Tía Pilar's house one day with bruises on her face. My aunt cleaned her up, fed her, put her to bed, and went out with her rifle. When her son-in-law approached the riverbank to water the livestock, Tía Pilar was waiting for him. She drew a bead, pressed the trigger . . . and a mule got in the way. By the time she had worked another round into the chamber, the son-in-law had scurried away into the bushes to hide. She yelled at him to come out, but the son-in-law was not about to do that. Just then, Tío Alberto, Pilar's husband, and her boys rode up and took the rifle away from her. Tía Pilar paid for the mule, and Della went back to her husband. They say that he never hurt her again.

Coming back to my siblings, while Blanca had taught me to read English, my brother Eliseo taught me to read in Spanish. Even when I was real little, he used to buy me books in Spanish. "Esteve una viejecita que no tenia que comer, sino . . . ," I forget now how that rhyme goes, ". . . pan y miel," (there was an old woman who had nothing to eat but . . . bread and honey) I think. So I learned to read block letters. Long before I went to school, I had learned to read Spanish and English. Blanca would speak to me only in English, while Eliseo taught me to read in Spanish. So I was a bilingual reader before I entered school. Then, after me, following me by about five years, were my twin brothers, Amador and Eleazar. I don't know whether you knew them. You probably knew Amador who was principal of an old grammar school in Brownsville. Eleazar lived in Kingsville. Those were the last two. They're both dead now.

I might mention why I was named Américo, because things get printed, and you know what happens when something is printed,

printed, and reprinted. It becomes gospel. My sister Clotilde, not long before she died, gave an interview to someone by the name of Kimberly García. Clotilde told her that I had been named Américo because my mother, no, my father, greatly admired the great navigator Amerigo Vespucci, and so he had named me for him.

Now my father certainly did have an admiration for Vespucci, along with a number of other historical figures. But if he had named me for any historical figure, he might have named me for Benito Juarez or somebody like that. The fact of the matter was a little more interesting, really. My mother had an aunt, one of her mother's sisters, I forget her name, who married an Italian. Remember that Brownsville was a port city and that there were a lot of different people always around. Another of my mother's aunts married a Greek named Nicolás, who was known as Nicolás el Griego. But this aunt, I don't remember her name, married an Italian named Alessandro Tomasini. They changed the name to Alejandro. Tomasini had been a navigator in the old sailing vessels that visited the ports of Bagdad, Brownsville, and Matamoros. I don't know what he did later. I'm not certain whether they had no children at all or they didn't have any male children. In any case, Tomasini, my mother's uncle by marriage, made my mother promise that she would name her firstborn son after his countryman, Amerigo Vespucci. Well, her firstborn *was* a son, but at about that time, an uncle of my father named Eliseo Cisneros died. It was the custom in those days to replace the names of members of the family who passed away. So my older brother was named Eliseo. Then my brother Lorenzo was born. But in the meantime, my father had lost a brother named Lorenzo, so he named Lorenzo for him. Finally, when I was born, nobody died, I guess. So, I got the name of Amerigo Vespucci that had been promised to the uncle by marriage on my mother's side. It took three, tries but my mother finally fulfilled her promise!

Fictional Memories: Mr. White

AMÉRICO PAREDES: I've been trying to write down some of my memories from childhood recently, and one that I have shared with you concerns someone in that neighborhood whom I'll call "Mr. White." I guess the first thing I remember about him was that he owned the most elegant car I ever saw. It was a touring car, pearl gray, and just about as long as a funeral hearse. Besides the seats front and back, it had folding seats in the middle that could be raised to carry even more people. We never saw those folding seats unfolded, but Mr. White's two nephews would tell us about them.

Mr. White moved just across the street from us into what had been the Hagerty house soon after the Hagertys moved away. The Hagertys lived there for a long time. It was the only house in the neighborhood with a concrete sidewalk. The Hagertys had two daughters, who loved to roller-skate on the sidewalk. They were half Mexican. Or half Spanish, as they called themselves. But the mother looked like other Mexican ladies in the neighborhood. She talked to the girls in Spanish just as our mothers talked to us.

We were fascinated by that concrete sidewalk, but we stayed away from it. We didn't own roller skates anyway. And they were girls. So we would just watch them skate to the end of their sidewalk and stop when they hit the grassy slope to get from the graveled street to our doorsteps.

And then, there was their father. He was an Anglo, but when we talked about him, we never thought of him as Mr. Hagerty. Or as *el viejo gringo*, even. To us he was always *el rinche*. Because that was what he was, a retired Texas Ranger. Once a *rinche*, always a *rinche*, people used to say. He always wore his gun, so we were properly scared of him. When he was around, we stayed as far away as we could from the concrete sidewalk.

Once, when we thought there was nobody home, Daniel García tried to ride on the sidewalk with an old little kid's wagon of his. The old *rinche* came roaring out, and Daniel took off, leaving the wagon behind him. Daniel had done it just to see what would happen. He was like that. He died not long afterward, drowned in the *resaca* (lake). We had been told there were tree stumps in the *resaca* bottom. So Daniel found out by diving in.

One summer day, we woke up to find the Hagertys were gone. They left early in the morning. Movers came by later in the day and took away their things for them. We kids knew something had happened, but our elders wouldn't talk about it when we were around. And soon afterward, somebody else moved into the house and made us forget about the Hagertys. That was Mr. White, with his beautiful gray touring car.

Whenever we saw Mr. White, he was already dressed up, no matter what day of the week it was. In suits with matching ties and socks and hats. He was very friendly, always passing the time of day with the neighbors on his way to and from his beautiful car. We rarely saw Mrs. White; she was always busy in the house or backyard.

The Whites had no children, or they had grown up and moved away. We never found out, we never asked. But his nephews were staying with them that summer. They lived in Houston, which we knew was a very big place.

That was when we found out that the reason the Hagertys had moved away was because Mr. Hagerty had been arrested·for murdering a man. Now the details were told and retold. It had happened in the bar of a hotel, right downtown. Men used to gather at the bar there, on late afternoons for a few drinks and conversation. White men, that is, lawyers, doctors, bankers. People of that sort. Over in a corner there was a shoe-shine "boy," an old black man who had his stand there. Nobody else except the bartenders.

When on that particular afternoon old man Hagerty walks in. Already half drunk. He comes up to the bar and tells everybody how hot it is outside. Nobody pays any attention to him, not even the bartenders. He sees the black man in the corner and yells at him, "Boy! Come here!" The black man gets to his feet and says, "You calling me, suh?" "You know I'm calling you, you black bastard!" And he takes out his gun and goes toward the black man. "I'll teach you to talk back to a white man!" "What are you goin' to do, suh?" "I'm gonna kill you, you son of a bitch!" The man fell on his knees and begged for his life. And old man Hagerty put a bullet into his head as he was kneeling there. In front of a dozen white witnesses. That was too much, even for the Texas of the 1920s.

Right after he was arrested, the family moved to Harlingen. Where people didn't get excited over a white man killing a black man. So they said. He stayed over there all the time he was out on bail. It was soon after old man Hagerty was arrested that Mr. White moved into the house across the street where the Hagertys had lived. At times people would talk about Mr. White when they thought we weren't listening. But we couldn't make much of what they said. "Se las está vengando," they would say, "He's getting even." Or they would say that Mr. White had a lot of balls: "Tiene muchos huevos." After old man Hagerty went to prison, Mr. White moved away from our neighborhood. We woke up one morning, and he and his touring car were gone. And the house empty again.

It was then that I fully understood what people had been saying. For Mr. White was black. He was a conductor on the trains that came into Brownsville from the north. Living in old man Hagerty's house was a dangerous thing for him to do, but he did it and stayed until he was ready to leave. He was pretty sure we were on his side. There were some black families living in our area. They were Mexicans who happened to be black. Mr. White was a Negro who happened to be an American. More or less. But there were the cars that started cruising up and down our street, cars that had never driven around our neighborhood before. Full of white men, who would stare and stare at the house where Mr. White was living.

We were sorry to see him go. All of us kids missed the gray touring car. As for me, I also missed Mr. White's two nephews. They taught me a lot of English. English I had never heard in school or seen in the books I read. It was not until I was in college that I found people who were interested in that kind of language. They usually were professors of literature. I could understand that. The way Mr. White's nephews talked had a poetry all its own. Gamy. Not for polite ears. But poetry nevertheless. So Mr. White's nephews were part of my education, though I forgot their names and what they looked like long ago.

But I will never forget Mr. White. All dressed up, coming and going to and from his gray touring car, saying cheerful hellos to all his neighbors. And never letting on that he knew (what we also knew): that at any moment a white bullet might come crashing into his black skull.[15]

School Days on the Border:
Into the 1920s and 1930s

AMÉRICO PAREDES: The schools play such an important role of cultural formation in my various literary writings that I should say something now about my experience of the formal public school system. As I said earlier, by the time I came of school age, I already could read block letters in English and Spanish. School age at that time was seven. And I knew some English as well. The thing is that I had the misfortune of being born on the third of September, and the school year began on the thirty-first of August. On that day, I was still six years old, so they would not take me. I was sent instead to a little school that was really a kind of holding pen, you might call it. Some nuns who were refugees from Mexico where the revolution was still raging were running it. That would have been 1921. But the religious wars were still going on, the Cristero Wars. I remember the teacher was called Sor Xaviera. I never knew what her real name was. They spoke to us only in Spanish, and we learned how to pray. And that was about all I remember that we ever did. The only thing else I remember is that there was a boy, a refugee also, whose name was Zapata, and the nuns were horrified at the mere mention of that revolutionary name. [laughter] So I don't remember too much about that year except that we did a lot of praying.

And some of the kids came up with a version of the Lord's Prayer that I still remember: "Padre Nuestro que estás en los cerros / Tú cuidas las bacas, y yó los becerros" (Our Father who art in the hills / You take care of the cows, and I will tend to the calves). [laughter] The poor nuns, they were praying the Lord's Prayer while we were making fun of it. That is the one thing I remember about that school. I entered school really at the age of eight because of that year's delay, but I caught up. I know that by the time I was ten, I was in the third grade. And that was in the old grammar school. Later it was called Washington Park. It's now called Putegnat School, I think. I remember the first time I was ushered into its cool, quiet hall by my parents on enrollment day. Even today that subtle, spicy aroma peculiar to its floors and woodwork, perhaps from the oil used in its cleaning, still lingers there and reminds me of those days.

My first-grade teacher was Miss Josefina Castañeda. She was the older sister of Carlos Castañeda, the historian. She and María, her sister, taught first grade. And, of course, it was a very easy transition because she spoke to us in Spanish as much as in English. So I didn't have any problems in the first grade.

In the second grade, they would begin to look for high school students; tracking is what they call it now. Students with potential for high school were put in the "high" grades. Students without it were put in the "low" grades. Was it a coincidence that Anglos were in the high grades and Mexicans were in the low grades? They put me in the low second grade with Miss Annie Putegnat for whom that school is named now. Miss Putegnat was born in Brownsville and was one of the pioneers of the city's school system. She was a teacher during the term of the public school in the 1890s, and for over forty years she taught and was the principal in that same school. To many people Miss Putegnat and the old school were synonymous. But to use Newt Gingrich's language, she was a bitch. Usually to the boys. She was all right with the girls. Thanks to my brother and sister, however, I had such good background that I stayed with her just the first semester, and I was moved to high second, mostly with gringos, in the second semester. All of the cultural and social divisions of that world were fixed right there.

My third-grade teacher, I remember was named Mrs. McCallum. I pieced together some of my memories of her class for episodes in *George Washington Gómez*. You know, you take bits and pieces and put them together in creating fiction. It was in third grade that a friend named Luis Villalón fell in love with an Anglo girl. I even remember her name. Her name was May Carpenter. And she was square. She had a square face. Square figure. We used to call her Miss Square. I don't know what Luis saw in her. But he wrote her a letter, a love letter. And May went and gave it to the teacher. The principal took him from room to room, making him read the letter out loud in each classroom, and whipped him in each room. I created Miss Cornelia [in *George Washington Gómez*] from aspects of Miss Annie Putegnat and Mrs. McCallum.

After them, I had another very interesting teacher. Her name was Miss Bell. Later I found out that her first name was Ellie, Miss Ellie Bell. She was my fifth-grade teacher. At that time, the grammar school was a two-story building. That autumn of 1928 we had a hurricane, heavy rains and high wind, and the old schoolhouse, almost forty years old at the time, began to crack at the walls in the upper floor. I remember we used to march in and out of the building. We had a phonograph, a Victrola, and we'd line up outside and the Victrola would play a march, and we all would march in. Of course, we were in the high grades, fourth and fifth. And during that storm, they played the phonograph while we marched out of the building! Little did we realize as we quietly fled down from the upper floor to the lower during the height of the storm that the death knell of the old building was ringing. As we marched down the stairway at one end of the hall, we could see jagged cracks developing in the walls. Most of us thought it very funny, and we went tittering down the stairs despite the grave look on our teachers' faces. So the building was condemned. Grammar school pupils were transferred to the junior high school building.

Miss Bell went with us when we passed to the junior high school, which was at Palm Boulevard and Elizabeth Street. Something very simple now seems to me very strange about junior high. In junior high school, three Anglos—they were all three boys—and I were put in a special class. I still remember their names: Lavern Bohlen, Buford Beson, and Donald Abbot. For no reason that I can imagine, we were given a special class in ancient history. Later I wondered why we were given that special class. Of course, at that age, you don't ask. We just enjoyed it. The class was wonderful: one teacher just for the four of us, almost like a tutorial really. I've always loved prehistory and ancient history. That was all we studied. I became a very good friend of those three boys, but my relationship with them was very interesting. While we were the best of friends in class, we lived in separate worlds after school. When we returned to class on Mondays, they would speak about what they had done together over the weekend. The three of them had been together over the weekend. Of course, I wasn't included there. I had my own friends who were *mexicanos* in other classes.

Many years later I got a call from a man who said he was a traveling salesman and that he had been told by his wife to say hello to me when he was in Austin. I asked him who his wife was. Her name, her maiden name, was Bell, he said, Ellie Bell. It turned out that he was talking about my old teacher, Miss Bell. But at that time I was writing *"With His Pistol in His Hand"* and teaching two or three freshman classes, raising a family, and so on. I didn't have time to meet with him. So the next time he came to Austin, he called again, and I told him I would like very much to get in touch with Miss Bell. One of the things I wanted to ask her was why we four boys had been selected for that special class in ancient history. "Well, you can't," he told me. "She's dead." Ellie Bell had died. So I never knew why we were given that special class. It was a one-of-a-kind enrichment class in junior high, very odd.

Now, what I remember about high school at this late date is two teachers. I don't remember their names, but I know that one was our English teacher and the other was our history teacher. I used to give the history teacher an especially hard time. With another student, a girl from Laredo, I think, or Rio Grande City, whose name was

Elodia, I used to attack the textbook history lessons that the teacher gave us. Elodia was my ally when we tore into the teacher and the textbook. We were always arguing about what the textbook said about Texas and American history. But our teacher was very patient with us. I later used the name of Elodia for the character in *George Washington Gómez* who is a fiery, radical political leader.

The other teacher was my English teacher in my junior year, and she shouldn't have been teaching. I think that what happened in those days was that Anglo women who weren't able to get a job anywhere because they were, well, not qualified for anything else would come down to south Texas and would be hired as teachers. Now I had real arguments with this person, and the strongest argument we had was over Walt Whitman. I had learned and loved poetry since I was a child. I was even trying to write poetry myself by then. I loved poetry. But all the poetry I knew had the classical Spanish language meter and rhyme and an unmistakable verse form. Some blank verse that I enjoyed didn't have rhyme, but it had at least a very definite metric line. Poe, William Cullen Bryant, and of course all the poetry in Spanish. The *décima* and other kinds of poetry I had learned as a boy all had definite form. With Walt Whitman, I was confronted with a poet who used none of these. I'm told he's a poet; even that he is a great poet. And I'm supposed to like him. But why? Because the teacher tells me he is a great poet! [laughter]

She never read aloud to us. I think back now, and I think that if she had, I would have understood Walt Whitman. But she didn't, so we had these horrible arguments, and finally they got so carried away that she said I would have to apologize to her. I didn't apologize, so she failed me. We had been assigned a term paper that semester, and I had received permission to write a short story instead. It's nothing to brag about, but the story was published in the school annual. She had given me an A for that. I had As in everything else. But she failed me anyway. I had to apologize.

Meanwhile, I had also been writing poetry. One day I happened to see a notice on the bulletin board announcing a statewide poetry contest being sponsored by Trinity University at Waxahachie, Texas. So I decided to submit an entry on my own. All by myself. I was taking a typing class because, with the rest of the *mexicanos*, I was not considered college material and so had been put in the practical life classes. Instead of taking, let's say math — I was very good at and loved plane geometry and algebra in the lower grades—I was put in business arithmetic and typing. In other words, in classes where I might learn something that might serve me if I was going to be a shoe clerk on Elizabeth Street, or something of that sort. Anyway, in my typing class I typed a poem I had written entitled "Night." I entered it in the college poetry contest. And I won first prize. When the news came, I still had to go and apologize to her, and she relented and passed me in her course. Later, I found out that she had passed me but had given me a C. But by that time I was already taking senior English, so it didn't matter.

When the news came, our principal—I mentioned this in the talk I gave when I retired—whose name was J. W. Irvine, came to congratulate me. I don't remember what the "J. W." stood for because everyone called him "Red," Red Irvine. Here's an interesting thing. He was a coach. They called him Red because his face was always red. He was from east Texas. And he coached the football team quite well. I think they went to the semifinals of the championship playoffs, or something of that sort. But they had to come up north—somewhere, Fort Worth or Lubbock, or some place—to play. And it was very cold. The Brownsville players were not used to playing in that kind of weather, so they lost. The Brownsville Screaming Eagles. So they fired him as a coach and made him principal and dean of the college instead. Something less important than coach of the football team, I suppose.

But it turned out that it was a wise decision because he was an intelligent, a very intelligent, man. I took a course in what was called civics with him. He was impressed by my work. I first heard the term *New Deal* from him. Before Roosevelt used it, there was somebody named Stuart Chase, I think, who had written a book called *A New Deal*. So Red Irvine really was impressed, and especially not only that I had won this first prize but that I had done it all by myself. If I had tried to have the English teacher help me, I would never have gotten anything. So he recognized me during graduation for having won the prize. The recognition was nice because I was doing pretty badly by then because of the economic squeeze of the Depression.

Later, I ran into that English teacher who had given me such a hard time, and she asked me, "Did they give you anything for your poetry prize?" I told her that they had given me a tooled leather cover for a book. And she said, "Well, that's good. They might have given you a book of lousy poetry." [laughter] I looked at her, and she said, "All I mean is that it might not have been very good poetry." [laughter] That was her opinion of poetry.

In junior college, I had a very good teacher, Miss Heiman, who was a beautiful reader and really understood the importance of the oral performance of poetic language. She had heard about what had happened to me in high school concerning Whitman's poetry. So, one day, we were discussing a poem written by somebody on the death of Lincoln. Miss Heiman looked over at me and said, "Of course, it doesn't compare with Walt Whitman's 'When Lilacs Last in the Dooryard Bloom'd.' Don't you agree Mr. Paredes?" [laughter] I just looked down. After class, I went to the public library and took out a book of Whitman's poetry, and I sat there and read and read it until I got to "Out of the Cradle Endlessly Rocking." All of a sudden, it was as if doors opened for me, and I saw something there, something that might have opened for me in my junior year in high school if this excuse for a teacher had known how to read poetry. I think she told us Whitman was a great poet because someone had told her she was supposed to think that Whitman was a great poet. But because of Miss Heiman who really could read and perform poetry, I finally understood the greatness of Whitman.

Depression Years and the Immediate Prewar Era

AMÉRICO PAREDES: High school was a seesaw for me; up and down, up and down. Junior college was little better. Though I had to work most of the time, I did what I could of homework at school. I did two years of junior college, starting in 1934. The school was called Browns-ville Junior College at the time. I was saying earlier that these were the days of the Great Depression, and to make ends meet, I worked at several different jobs. But I still had time for poetry. For a good part of the period of the 1930s, I was part of a literary group that met in Matamoros. The group was made up of friends of my brother Eliseo, who was a successful merchant in the city by that time. These men were Freemasons, intellectuals, and literary men and included Garza Flores, the publisher of the newspaper *El Regional* in Matamoros. I published some of my earliest articles there, including a satirical piece I called "Diccionario moderno mundial" ("Modern Global Dictionary"), all under the pen name of Guálinto Gómez. The literary group also included Garza Griego and Sabas Klahn.[16] After 1940, I stopped seeing that group. But while it lasted, we would meet to read poetry and discuss the latest in Mexican politics. We would read Rubén Darío, Amado Nervo, Federico García Lorca, Gabriela Mistral, and many other poets of the day. We would especially pore over the section of *La Prensa de San Antonio* dedicated to literature. The section was published every Monday and was called "Lunes literarios." It also printed classical literature and translations from new and classic works.[17]

The 1930s was the period of César Augusto Sandino's revolution in Nicaragua, and we were very attuned to the political struggles in Latin America. Sandino, who was murdered by the Somozas in 1934, was one of my boyhood heroes. Another was Lázaro Cárdenas, the revolutionary general and president of Mexico who expropriated Mexican oil from foreign companies in 1938. The work of Emma Tenayuca, political and labor activist in San Antonio, especially moved me.[18] I managed later to work her into one of my stories, using her as my inspiration for the figure of Chonita in "The Hammon and the Beans." All through this period, I was an angry young man; angry at the way *mexicanos* were treated in Texas and the rest of the Southwest, and angry about social inequality and economic injustice. The other members of the reading group were constantly urging me to renounce my US citizenship and become a Mexican citizen. But I wasn't exactly taken by what I saw of Mexican nationalism either. A piece I began writing at that time, "Tres Faces del Pocho," (The Pocho's Three Faces/Phases) was an early attempt to satirize Mexican nationalism and its failings. In part because of the influence of my uncle Eduardo, about whom I spoke earlier, who had belonged to the anarchist Flores Magón group, my own politics were really quite radical.[19] I've often thought that if there had been a Communist Party cell in south Texas at the time, I would have joined it. By 1939, however, war had broken out in Europe, and gradually everything started to change, even in south Texas.

Radio Nights and Chelo Silva Days

AMÉRICO PAREDES: Throughout this period, I was a newspaper reporter and also tried my hand at singing and playing the guitar professionally. I had my own radio show for a short period when I was performing with Chelo Silva. I was also working as a reporter for the local newspaper, the *Brownsville Herald*. I did a variety of articles and features, especially dealing with the Mexican folklore of the lower Rio Grande. I believe I've mentioned before that the editor of the *Herald*, a man by the name of Hart Stilwell, wrote a novel that he titled *Border City*.[20] It's a romance, really, but also about the early labor movement in south Texas, the white labor struggle, that is. Stilwell was constantly trying to pick my mind for ideas for the book. One of the minor characters is a very angry and naive young Mexican reporter. Stilwell claimed that he based the character on me. I hope I wasn't as silly as he made that character out to be!

In the late thirties, south Texas was still in the depths of the Depression. I was trying to do a number of things just to make ends meet. I was probably trying to do too many things at once. Antonio Ortiz, musician and composer, and director of the Monterrey symphony, had taken me under his guidance and tutored me in all kinds of music. I learned flamenco and classical guitar, as well as piano. All the while, I was working as a reporter and attempting to write literature. After graduating from junior college in 1936, I began to write seriously. *George Washington Gómez* was the result.

About this time, in the late thirties, I was offered the opportunity to do a radio program. A man by the name of Raúl Cárdenas arranged with the local radio station in Brownsville for me to do a show that would be called *El músico y poeta*, styled after Agustín Lara, who was called *el músico poeta*. They wanted me to host a musical show where I would play my own original compositions and perform other things as well. And they were even going to pay me a few dollars per show, so I jumped at the chance! I composed about sixty songs for the program and arranged five or six others for piano. With Eva Garza and Mattias Serrata, who backed up with guitar, we performed on the air and toured in south Texas. Serrata was later killed in France during the war. And, of course, at this time, in 1939, I married Chelo Silva, with whom I had been performing. She had played with Mike Moran up to that point. With Chelo Silva in our group we would sometimes travel to Villa Acuña, Coahuila, to perform live on the powerful radio station XERA. I spent most of my time performing music on local radio stations and composing popular songs. I did write some short stories, including "The Hammon and the Beans," and others that have been lost. The marriage with Chelo Silva didn't work out. We just drifted in different directions. But we did have a child together, Américo Junior.

I was trying to write original compositions for us. She wanted to perform other things as well. A large part of my books and papers did not survive my divorce in the mid-forties. What was salvageable (or happened to be salvaged) was due to my mother's efforts.

By 1940, I was also working part time for Pan American Airways. I continued working at the Brownsville airport for Pan American after the war began. My job was quality control, checking the mounting of .50-caliber machine guns on fighter-bombers being ferried to the front in England.[21] These attack bombers, Lockheed Vegas, I believe, would be flown from Lockheed factories in California to Brownsville, where they received final preparation for the European theater of war. I remember vividly that as part of the preparation of the bombers for combat, each would receive a black box, installed by a special crew and protected by a squad of dangerous-looking military police. I later realized that these were the then top-secret Norton bombsights that were being installed in the bombers.

World War II and Postwar Japan, 1944–1950

AMÉRICO PAREDES: The work I was doing for Pan American Airways was classified as defense-related work, and so it gave me deferred status in the draft. I stayed on in that position until 1944, when I gave up my deferred status and allowed myself to be drafted into the army. Partly a guilt trip; I guess I felt that since my younger brothers and all of my friends were in action, I should be too. Partly because I wanted to get out of Brownsville. I was already twenty-nine, rather old to be drafted, but I decided to do it anyway. So I was drafted in 1944 and sent to Fort Sam Houston for basic training. I remember that I scored 140 on the Army IQ test and so was immediately accepted into the Criminal Investigations Division of Army Intelligence and sent to Camp Robinson in Little Rock, Arkansas, for special training. I was finishing training at Camp Robinson when word came that the war in Europe had ended. And then later, on a train first east to Camp Rucker in Alabama, then back west to Oregon and Washington, we heard that new secret weapons, atomic bombs, had been dropped on Japan.

I landed in Nagoya, Japan, in late 1945, as part of the US army of occupation with the first troops to arrive in that country. I was assigned to the 11th Replacement Depot outside of Okazaki as the *Stars*

8 Américo Paredes, Camp Robinson, Arkansas. US Army Intelligence training, 1945. Photograph courtesy of the Américo Paredes Papers, 1886–1999, Benson Latin American Collection, General Libraries, University of Texas at Austin.

9 Américo Paredes and Horst de la Croix, newly arrived in Japan, c. 1946. Photograph courtesy of Alan and Vincent Paredes.

10 "The Inquiring Reporter." Cartoon done by Américo Paredes and Horst de la Croix, *Pacific Stars and Stripes*, August 5, 1946. Reprinted with the permission of *Stars and Stripes*, a Defense Department publication. © 2003 *Stars and Stripes*.

and Stripes correspondent. The nearest big city was Nagoya, which was about 150 miles from Tokyo. Within walking distance, just over a hill, was Gamagori, a beautiful seaside town untouched by the bombings. Another *Stars and Stripes* staffer by the name of Horst de la Croix and I spent many of our evenings in Gamagori, often coming back after curfew. We published the camp newspaper and were attached to GHQ (general headquarters), so as headquarters staff and newspapermen, we didn't have to follow the rules of military life as strictly as other GIs did. We called the newsletter the *11th Depot G Eye Opener*. I was the editor, Horst did design, and with a couple of other staffers, we did articles of interest, bits on what entertainment was available for the bored GIs, and a variety of other humorous pieces, including a comic strip by Bruce McIntyre, who had been a Walt Disney cartoonist before the war.[22]

From there, probably because of my experience as a newspaperman in Brownsville and because of the newsletter that we had edited, Horst and I were transferred to *Stars and Stripes* in Tokyo in early 1946. Shortly after I joined the paper, a man by the name of Barnard Rubin, who had been the political editor and was a committed leftist, probably a member of the Communist Party, was sent home in something of a scandal for his political views. I took over his beat and became the political editor.[23]

Rubin wrote very good articles. I remember one on the experiences of Nisei American soldiers of the First Cavalry Division who had served as translators, interpreters, and in screening prisoners during the war. Now in Japan, they were traveling to their ancestral homes to find their surviving relatives. One article was about the experience of two Nisei who had gone to find their families in Hiroshima and Nagasaki. He had a column also where he wrote about things like the tearing down of the old feudalistic system and the emergence of new political parties, students, and miners on strike, mass meetings, and demonstrations, and the creation of real democracy in Japan. He showed how the "liberal" and "progressive" parties were made up of people who had either tacitly or actively supported the wartime military government and its policies. Gradually, Rubin's columns began to show that it was mainly the Communist Party that had resisted the imperial war government and that at base, a modern, democratic Japan would need a realignment of power along class lines. More importantly, he was showing how US companies and Japanese firms were in cahoots before the war and now again during the occupation to reshape postwar Japan. He was making a case for greater artistic freedom for Japanese writers, artists, and filmmakers, not so much from US occupation restrictions, but from those of the Japanese ruling classes.[24]

It was eerie and wonderful to be in Tokyo in those days. I lived in a one-room, six–tatami mat residence in Setagaya-ku. Probably every single person in the occupation forces wanted to have a look at the Japanese capital. When I arrived, it was still a half-ruined city. But what struck me the most was the poetry of politeness of the Japanese. In just these few months since the end of the war, we could walk the streets and byways of Tokyo at all hours, singly or in groups, as safely as if we were strolling down Main Street back home. By the end of 1945, there was a regulation forbidding the carrying of weapons of any sort. But we had stopped carrying weapons right away. Really, the peacefulness of the Japanese bewildered us when we remembered Pearl Harbor, the many atrocity stories that were circulating, and the recent bitter fighting in the Pacific.

In Tokyo, business was booming. Americans landed on enemy soil, stacked their weapons, and went shopping, souvenir hunting, for kimonos, obis, silk fans, fine lace, ceremonial dolls, and art prints; everything sold. The department stores in the Ginza were cleaned out very quickly, and you had to hit the side-street black market shops to find anything interesting, like samurai swords and Japanese field binoculars. There wasn't a thing you couldn't buy in the Ginza if you were American, had money, and knew where to look. In the side streets and the train stations, young women offered themselves for a box of field rations or a bar of chocolate.[25]

In the spring of 1946, I had the memorable experience of being allowed to interview Hideki Tojo. As political editor of *Stars and Stripes*, I covered the first few months of the trials, until I was discharged from the Army late in 1946. One day another of the defendants, sitting behind Hideki Tojo, lost his cool and slapped Tojo on his bald pate. It caused a sensation, and I wrote a page-one story for *Stars and Stripes* about it.[26]

During the arraignment of Tojo and the twenty-seven codefendants before the military tribunal for the Far East at the War Ministry building in Tokyo, Hideki Tojo was sitting there gravely listening to the proceedings when all of a sudden one of the other defendants seated behind him got up and slapped him on his bald pate, twice! The man who slapped him was someone by the name of Shumei Okawa, one of the other defendants. Okawa certainly added color to an otherwise routine proceeding by slapping Tojo. I was sitting in the front row of news correspondents, and I had seen that Okawa was acting very nervously after the noon recess. He twisted and squirmed in his chair like a schoolboy and wiped his eyes as if he were weeping. Finally, at one point, he took off his coat, revealing gray pajama tops. He unbuttoned the pajama top, and the US Army colonel in charge of military security for the war crimes trials reached around Okawa's neck and buttoned his pajamas from behind. Suddenly, Okawa half rose from his seat and slapped Tojo, who was seated in front of him, on the head. Tojo half turned and smiled embarrassedly as MPs (military police) restrained Okawa, who grinned delightedly at his little joke.

Later in the afternoon, a short recess was called and photographers were allowed to see the prisoners. When a newsreel cameraman started to film Okawa, he got up and slapped Tojo's shining dome again! The tribunal president Sir William F. Webb had to call the court to order. The prisoners were taken out for a recess, Okawa babbling as he was led out. When the court convened again later that afternoon, Okawa was seated out of reach of Tojo's head. Okawa wept through most of the last part of the proceedings. He was considered a brilliant man before the war. He had been an officer of the South Manchurian Railway and was alleged to have been the organizer of the Mukden Incident in 1931, which provoked Japanese attacks against China. Okawa was a propagandist for the expulsion of the white races from Asia by aggressive war.

In November 1948, all the defendants were found guilty except two who had died, and Okawa who was declared insane. In late December of 1948, just before Christmas, Tojo and six others were hanged in Sugamo prison. In my article for *Stars and Stripes*, I described Okawa's behavior as "neurotic." The lieutenant in charge of PR for the trials, a prissy man with a venomous desire for revenge on the Japanese, read "psychotic" for "neurotic" and decided that I and the whole press corps covering the trials were trying to get the defendants off for reasons of insanity. When I showed up next morning, he came up to me as I was talking to the foreign correspondents covering the trials. He called me to attention and then gave me the dressing-down of my life—right there, in full view of everyone—accusing me, and by implication the other newspapermen present, of being apologists for the Japanese criminals. I stood there and took it; after all, I was a soldier. But the correspondents were audibly calling the lieutenant a bastard and a son of a bitch. Watching from outside our group was the colonel in charge of the MPs guarding the prisoners. As soon as the lieutenant was through chewing me out, the colonel made his way to where I was and said, "If we want revenge on these Japs, we should take them out and shoot them. What their soldiers did, our GIs did the same thing. I know it." I never knew his name, but I can still remember him. He was a tall, athletic man, but well into middle age, with short-cropped white hair on a round head. He didn't say anything we didn't already know, but hearing it from him made a difference. Someone must have got to the lieutenant, because the next morning he came up to me, smiling, and said he had a surprise for me. He took me down a hall, opened a door, and there was Hideki Tojo himself. The lieutenant was giving me a chance to interview Tojo all by myself. The problem was that I was not prepared for any such interview, so Tojo and I just passed the time of day for a few minutes through an interpreter, and that was it.[27]

Really, it was a very uncomfortable experience. There was Tojo, the great statesman and warrior, a taciturn man, trying to retain as much dignity as he could under the circumstances, and me, an ordinary GI, with bad and limited Japanese and nothing to say. I really had nothing to ask him. In a way, I felt sorry for him because I knew that he was being accused of war crimes that had in fact been committed by both sides.

In late 1946, I was discharged from the army but decided to stay in the Far East. I ended up staying on for five years after the war ended, working with the American Red Cross. I did get one big scare during this time: I was diagnosed with TB [tuberculosis]. As it turned out, however, luckily for me, they had confused the patient files, and I was not the one with tuberculosis; some other poor GI had it instead. During that time, I continued to write, mainly short stories.

In the Far East, I did more writing than before. I had a good deal of time and opportunity. Most of my stuff was ineffective. I did a good deal of research, and preliminary writing, on a novel about Will Adams, an English pilot who was shipwrecked in Japan during the seventeenth century. He married a Japanese wife and became a technical adviser to the shogun. Gave up finally; I couldn't get the feel for life in seventeenth-century Japan. I understand that someone did write a novel, *Shogun*, about Will Adams ten or fifteen years ago.[28]

The Red Cross assigned me to China to help with the distribution of medical and humanitarian supplies after the war and at the beginning of the communist revolution. In October 1946 I was sent to Shanghai, a strange and great city, and was billeted with two other Red Cross men at the Swiss House on Bubbling Well Road. It was clear that civil war was breaking out. I slept and had breakfast there and was driven to the office, about a forty-five-minute drive from there. Dinner and lunch—it was called tiffin—were at the home of the head of the Red Cross in Shanghai, my boss, a man by the name of Jim Moody. Dinner was at 9 PM every day, with great formality and cooks, butlers, and houseboys cluttering up the place. I would be driven back to Bubbling Well Road, usually around midnight. It was a strange experience being waked up [*sic*] in the morning by a boy who called me, a south Texas Mexican, "Master." I could see what the communist armies in the north were fighting for. There were troops everywhere, rifles armed and long, shiny bayonets ready.

Everything was really expensive in Shanghai. I remember arriving and having the young man who was in charge of my finances exchange US $100 for me. He went out into the street and returned a few minutes later with a wad of bills. He counts them out: "One hundred thousand, two hundred thousand, three hundred thousand, four hundred thousand, and five hundred thousand Chinese dollars." "You're in luck," the young man tells me. "Yesterday the exchange rate was only at 4,120 to the US dollar." I felt rich with half a million Chinese dollars, until I entered a humble little beer joint and ordered a beer. The Russian waitress says to me in broken English, "Five thousand dollars, please." So now I felt really poor, until walking back to my hotel room I noticed that next to a shining sedan parked on the curb was a family, in tattered rags, shockingly dirty, and covered with open sores. Their faces were horribly disfigured by smallpox. The man was barely supporting himself on the shoulders of a boy who could have been no more than eight years old. The woman led the man by the arm. Of the three, only she was not blind.[29]

It was really romantic to go with a Chinese woman, following her down the streets with all those Chinese men staring at me with hate in their eyes and finally going into this place where she lived and not knowing whether the papers would say the next day that a Red Cross man had been found in an alley with his throat cut. The Chinese seemed to lose no sleep loving their brothers from across the sea. Their faces were hard even in repose, and they all seemed to hate the foreign barbarian. I read that in Hong Kong they did something about it too. It was really rough there; the place was crowded, and it took hours to get anyplace in town, the traffic was so heavy. There was a lot of color, though, and enough dives to see a lot of adventure if you had the money to spend.

Horst de la Croix, one of my army buddies who became my lifelong friend, worked in the art department section of *Stars and Stripes*.[30] He and I came up with an idea that when we finished our tours of duty, we would drive across China and Russia back to Western Europe and Germany where he had relatives. It was the kind of thing only a young man would think of doing. I found out that there was a trail of a sort that a Jeep could make from Shanghai to Chunking. But even though the Jeep might make it, there was no gasoline along the way. I joked with Horst that unless we could arrange to carry enough gas, the only way to make it would be to convert the Jeep into a wood burner for the trip. The trip up the Yangtze by boat to Chunking would take about three or four weeks. We could get a Jeep since there were quite a few of them in Shanghai. The filthy-rich class among the Chinese owned them even though they cost about $23,000, American dollars, that is, delivered in Shanghai. Customs and customs graft were terrific bringing things into China. All of this pointed out to me that the contrast between rich and poor was much greater in China than in Japan. The poor were poorer and dirtier, even in Shanghai, which certainly was not in the starvation belt. The rich were certainly rich. I hadn't seen such shiny cars as I saw in Shanghai in a hell of a long time.[31]

Over the next couple of years, I traveled to Tsintao, Tientsin, Chingwantao, Peiping, and other places besides Mukden, Changchun, and Tehhui in Manchuria. I also was in Seoul, Korea, in March of 1948. Seoul, the city of the Chosen people, whose face is the face of a baby that has lived ten thousand years. Part of their flag was red and part was blue. In 1948, the political situation in Korea was described as "tense." Police, which were a military organization, more like a militia, paraded, chanted, and counted cadence outside my window from dawn till dusk. Two of them stood perpetual guard outside our portals, to protect us from the outside world, perhaps. However, I wandered, sometimes at dusk, around the outside world, the lower world, since I'm such a low person at heart, and no harm came to my unarmed, trusting, wide-eyed self. But I really had little time for sightseeing. I wanted to finish that assignment in Korea in less than six weeks if possible. They were trying to talk me into staying three months.

Back in China, I remember traveling endlessly throughout the countryside on long railroad trains, sometimes by air, distributing what medical supplies we could. Everywhere I went all I could see was the suffering of the people. And that the communist army was winning. After 1947, I became the head public relations officer in China for the Red Cross. In that capacity I again traveled throughout northern China, checking to see that Red Cross materiel was being used properly, that is, not in support of combat operations. By 1948, the whole project began to be phased out, and so I returned to Japan where I started a magazine that was intended to help introduce newly arrived American GIs to Japan.

In China, I was homesick for Tokyo and everything that went with it. When I would go out into the streets in China such phrases as "Go-men nasai," (sorry) "Chotto matte kudasai," (please wait a second) etcetera, kept coming into my mouth in dealing with the Chinese. But I did not understand their language. I remember seeing a Chinese play in Shanghai one Sunday afternoon with the head of the Red Cross section. The play was an old traditional kind, with the high falsetto voices and the weird wailing songs. Japanese music was Western and modern compared to this. I knew I'd have to hear several more of those plays before I would be able to appreciate them. The costumes were gorgeous, though, as were the movements of the dancers.

Another thing I remember about Shanghai was their street vendors. They had such queer, musical cries. There was one in particular who sold crabs. His cries were almost identical with the opening notes of those heavily oriental songs of the gypsies of southern Spain. Every time I heard him, I always half expected him to finish the bar so the guitar would say thrum-tara-rum; THRUM-TARA-RUM-RUM; thrum-tara-rum-rum . . . rum. Other street vendors carried little sticks, which they would clack together to advertise their wares. Late at night, I would hear the clacking of the sticks and wonder what they were selling.[32]

Housing was awful in Shanghai. All Shanghai residences seemed to be in compounds. There were groups of houses surrounded by a communal wall with just one gate, which was usually guarded at night by a Chinese policeman or personally hired watchman. As winter set in, things got worse. More unrest, more stealing. I couldn't blame those people when I saw the condition they were in. The poor, of course. The rich were as rich as one might imagine.[33]

Amelia Sidzu Nagamine

AMÉRICO PAREDES: On October 13, 1947, my life changed radically. Visiting the American Red Cross Ginza office, a friend by the name of Jerry Davis introduced me to Amelia — and things quickly came to a head. By October 31, I was smitten; by November 11, I had told her I loved her; by November 13, we had decided to marry. Here was what I had dreamed about, and in spite of all my comments about never doing so again, I fell — for good. We understood each other. In the middle of all of this, I had to leave for Tokyo for assignments in Manchuria and Korea for the American Red Cross, but by May of 1948, I was back in Tokyo permanently, and we were married that month. But because Amelia was half Japanese, she fell under the ruling of a Japanese Exclusion Act, which did not allow Japanese nationals entry into the United States. It wasn't until 1950 that we were allowed to enter. Even then, all we were to be allowed was a six-month visa, with the possibility of one six-month renewal. So when we returned to the United States, it was with the understanding that we would be able to stay only for one year. I received my BA in one year because I understood that after that year, we would have to leave the United States for good.

What was ironic about all this was that Amelia was *not* a Japanese citizen. She was officially a citizen of Uruguay. Yes, Amelia's maiden name was Nagamine, but she was raised in Argentina, Chile, and Mexico. Her father, Naoya Nagamine, was from on old samurai family and was in the Japanese diplomatic service, working as a consulate officer in various Latin American countries in the 1920s and 1930s. At the time that Amelia was born, he was stationed in Buenos Aires. Her mother, Doña Julia, from Uruguay, had returned to Montevideo to be with her family when she was ready to give birth to Amelia, and that's how she came to have a Uruguayan passport. Amelia grew up speaking Spanish with her mother and learned Japanese from her father. Later in the 1930s, when her father was posted to Mexico City, Amelia also learned English, British English. She learned American English later, when her father was stationed

11 Américo Paredes and Amelia Sidzu Nagamine, c. 1947. Photograph courtesy of Alan and Vincent Paredes.

12 Américo Paredes and Amelia Sidzu Nagamine, c. 1948. Photograph courtesy of Alan and Vincent Paredes.

13 A birthday celebration in Tokyo, c. 1948. From left to right, Naoya Nagamine, Amelia Nagamine, Américo Paredes, Julia Nagamine, and Horst de la Croix. Photograph courtesy of Alan and Vincent Paredes.

on the Mexico-California border, in Mexicali, I believe. They also spent some time in Panama, I believe. When World War II broke out, Amelia's father was a consulate officer in Chile, but as noncombatant nationals of an enemy nation, they were expelled and forced to return to Japan with very little notice and next to nothing of their personal possessions. Amelia, her brother Hideo, and her mother, who had grown up as a *latino americanos*, now had to learn to be Japanese. And so they lived out the war in Tokyo, witnessing, enduring, and surviving the countless American air raids of that city. Amelia always reminds me that of the two of us, she was the one who had combat experience.

We met, as I mentioned earlier, in October 1947. By that time, I had finished my tour of duty with the army and had started working as the public relations officer for the American Red Cross. To keep up her Spanish and to help the family during this time of terrible hardship and confusion in the years after the war, she, too, was working for the Red Cross, translating for Puerto Rican GIs, who for the most part spoke only Spanish. Amelia was fluent in English, Spanish, and Japanese, so she was perfect for the job. The way we met was that one day I entered the commons room of the Red Cross office in the Ginza and all of a sudden, I realized that I was overhearing a charming young Japanese woman speaking fluent Spanish off in a corner with a group of Puerto Rican GIs. A Japanese woman speaking Spanish—now, that really intrigued me. I had been seeing another lady at the time, a woman named Madeleine. But when I heard Amelia say, with a wonderful little flirtatious lilt to one of the Puerto Ricans, "¡Hasta luegito!"—it was all over for me! I walked over to Jerry Davis and asked him to introduce me, and my life changed on the spot. She had totally captivated me. We left Japan on July 13, 1950, and because of the change in the date line, we arrived in California on July 13, 1950. That date remained a special one for us as our son, Alan, was born one year later, on July 13, 1951.[34]

Texas in the 1950s and the Origins of
"With His Pistol in His Hand"

AMÉRICO PAREDES: When I returned from Japan, even though I'd taken a few correspondence classes at the Tokyo Army College during my service in the army, I didn't have an undergraduate degree yet. I had two years of junior college from the Brownsville Junior College, but that was it. So we were undecided as to what we were going to do. Amelia had a Uruguayan, not a Japanese, passport. But American immigration law has a history of being racist, you know. In those days, no matter what their origin, if a person was 50 percent or more of Japanese descent, they were not eligible for permanent residence in the United States. We found out that because of the Japanese Exclusion Act, we would be allowed to stay in the United States only long enough for me to complete the BA, but not the PhD. Amelia could not stay in the United States longer than the maximum of a year—two six-month periods. So we had to scale down our plans. Or I had to scale down my ideas. Instead of thinking of preparing for the PhD, I decided to prepare myself for a quick BA and journalistic work. And for that reason the undergraduate courses I signed up for at the University of Texas emphasized literary criticism, creative writing, philosophy, and government, to give myself the best background, as good a background as I could, for a career in journalism. I expected that we would leave for Mexico or Canada after that.

It took me two semesters and two summer terms to finish the requirements for the bachelor's degree. I started in the fall of 1950 at the age of thirty-five, and I had completed all of the requirements by fall of 1951. Now, in the meanwhile, the immigration law had changed. So by using a legal loophole in the law, Amelia was able to cross the border at Matamoros, stay with my brother Eliseo for a short period of time, and then return as an "immigrant" to the United States from Mexico. For that reason, her immigration records show that she entered from Mexico, not that she came from Japan: because officially she entered the United States from Matamoros, sponsored by my brother Eliseo, who resided there.

At the University of Texas, I started taking courses in literary criticism and history. I was also taking courses in creative writing with Professor Gerald Langford. Literary criticism at that time was basically I. A. Richards's *Practical Criticism*. Professor Alex Sackton, who later became a very close friend, was my first advisor (he has passed away now). When I went to register at the university as a returning war veteran, I didn't know anybody. In my first advising session with Alex Sackton, I told him what I wanted: "The first thing I want is this course in practical criticism," I said. Of course, that pleased him immensely since he was the person teaching the course in criticism. Now the course was, well, all we read was Richards's *Practical Criti-*

cism, a way of reading which focuses exclusively on the text. We were not supposed to have anything to do with questions about the origins of the writer, who he was, she was, or anything of that sort. In other words, no social, historical, or biographical context at all.

He would give us a couple of literary texts, which he was pretty sure we didn't know, and using the methods of *Practical Criticism*, we were supposed to compare the two and say which of the two we thought was better and why. I had trouble with the assignments just once. Of the two texts we were given for one assignment, I immediately recognized that one was about as popular a text as you might want. It was the last few paragraphs of *Tarzan of the Apes*. Of course, I had read all of Burroughs, so I identified it immediately. I thought that the other text was also very ordinary writing, quite silly, really. Both texts dealt with trying to make up one's mind. In my essay, I said, "neither of the two has earned much to commend it. Both are rather ordinary writing, having to do with the psychological moment." I said that the first example was simply a nice piece of popular fiction. A cussing old lady must have written the second one. It turned out that the other was by Henry James! [laughter] About the only thing I ever liked of Henry James was *The Beast in the Jungle*. But his novels, I just couldn't tolerate them. So, Sackton was very disappointed with me. In fact, he gave me an A- for that essay anyway, but he told me to read more Henry James. [laughter]

One of the prizes I received for my creative writing that year was five hundred dollars worth of books. I used the prize money to purchase the complete works of Henry James. I plowed through them, but I must admit that I still didn't like them. I had a choice to get anything with that money, and I emphasize that I did choose Henry James. But it just never took.

But the reason for this long-winded aside is that the idea for *"With His Pistol in His Hand"* first came to me as one of Alex Sackton's essay assignments. I guess I could say that one particular assignment of his really changed my career. For that assignment, Sackton gave us two versions of the ballad "Sir Patrick Spence" to compare.

I wrote that of the two versions we were given, one certainly reads better than the other: "The king sits in Dumferling toune, / Drinking the blude-reid wine: / 'O whar will I get guid sailor, / To sail this schip of mine?'" But the other version, particularly when it is sung, is a much better one: "The king sits in Dumferling toune, /

Addrrinkinggg the blude-reid wwwiiine." I went into the matter of
the *performance* of the ballad because I was a musical performer myself, remember, and therefore, naturally, performance oriented. My
judgment was made on the basis of my experience as a singer and
a performer myself, not because I had read anything on the theory
of performance. There wasn't anything written about performance at
the time. But I knew it because it was something I had lived. So again,
Sackton was disappointed. In fact, I saw that he had originally given
me a B+, and then had erased it and given me an A-. He said, "If
you are interested in this sort of thing, Américo, you should go see
Professor Robert Stephenson."

Robert Stephenson was a very odd man; we might use the word
weird for him today. He was an associate professor of English *and*
Spanish. A very erudite man. But he never published anything. He
just read. He learned languages. He only taught two courses, one on
the ballad, and one on the folktale. So I went to see Stephenson in the
second semester of my first undergraduate year at Texas and took a
course that he taught on Russian literature in translation. And I began
to work with him. Later, Alex Sackton—we had become very good
friends by now—lamented the fact that he had sent me to Stephenson because, he said, "I thought you would have made a good literary
critic." But instead, I worked with Stephenson and turned to folklore and ballads. Then, when things were settled with Amelia's visa
and she was allowed to stay in the United States, I was encouraged
by a number of people in the faculty to do a PhD. I started working
with Stephenson because when I talked to him about the possibility
of staying on to do a PhD, he said, "Why don't you work on songs
from your own background?"

That was in 1951. It hadn't occurred to me to work on Mexican ballads because I didn't think that the English department would allow
me to do graduate work on Spanish-language *corridos*. But Stephenson encouraged me to do just that. So, with the aid of my veteran's
benefits and the GI Bill, which covered my tuition and fees, I entered
the master's program at the University of Texas at Austin in 1951. That
fall I made a trip to the Texas-Mexican border area to collect materials
for a master's thesis. At that time, I didn't have a tape recorder, just a
text of songs that I knew. The idea was not to use my own remembered
versions, but to get them from the people who still sang them. And
so I spent the Christmas holidays of that year collecting data. And

from those first samples, I selected some for my master's thesis. The master's thesis was a collection of ballad texts, really, and some background and critical information for each one. That first effort later became the basis for the book *A Texas-Mexican Cancionero*. Though much later, of course, in the 1970s.

On that first trip to collect ballads I wasn't concentrating on "The Ballad of Gregorio Cortez." No; not even on *corridos*. I collected a number of other kinds of songs that are not *corridos*. You can see that in *A Texas-Mexican Cancionero*. Of course, the *corridos* predominated. So that became my master's thesis. I received my master's in 1953. I had started teaching freshman English in the fall of 1951, as soon as I had received the bachelor's degree, which I finished that summer. That in itself was something of an experience since I had taken freshman English in the fall of 1934. But, of course, I'd been writing, editing, and things of that sort as a professional journalist, so I was quite prepared to teach composition.

After I completed the master's thesis, Stephenson suggested that I now do my dissertation on the same topic. He had been directing the work of another man who was also working on folklore, especially on the *corrido*. Norman Laird McNeil was his name, known as "Brownie" McNeil. I recall that he had a beautiful tenor voice. He was my age, also born in 1915. But for some reason, he had not been in the service at all. He didn't have that fourteen-year interruption that I had, during which I had been in the army and a journalist. But McNeil had taught. He was very well known in a number of Texas folklore societies. And for his master's thesis, he had written something called *Corridos de asuntos vulgares* (*Ballads of Everyday Matters*). Even though McNeil sang, the work was only concerned with texts. And I think it was because Stephenson was supervising McNeil's thesis that he suggested that I do something on that same kind of material. So that was when I chose to work on "Gregorio Cortez."

The Gregorio Cortez *Corridos*

AMÉRICO PAREDES: I wanted to write on a *corrido* about border conflict. Before the war, I had been writing protest verse, and other things, in Spanish. And then when I looked at what I had written over the years, I saw a pattern emerge from those border stories: of the peace-

ful Mexican who is goaded into violence by Anglo injustice. A similar pattern struck me when I studied the songs that I had collected,
and, of course, I had been hearing these songs since I was child. I had
been listening to these *corridos* and hearing the legends and the explanations of the *corridos*. I could have done a study of the Kansas Trail
corridos because that sequence is also very interesting. But it doesn't
have this element of protest. "Gregorio Cortez," of what I knew at
the time, seemed to fit the idea I had formed of the *corrido* hero. So
that's why I chose him.

When I started digging into it, the local newspaper helped me out
by printing a little notice that I was looking for material on Gregorio
Cortez. During one of the many trips we made to south Texas, one
evening Amelia and I were in Matamoros and had stopped at the
Texas Café, a nice place to go to for dinner and drinks. Anyway, we
were sitting there having dinner when a man from another table got
up, came over, and identified himself. He asked me if I were Américo
Paredes. I said, "Yes." And he said, "Well, in Austin there are people
you can talk to who knew Gregorio Cortez." And he gave me the name
and address of a family in Austin. When I returned to Austin, I went to
see them, and they told me that they knew Valeriano Cortez, Gregorio
Cortez's son. The next time he came to Austin—we were living in student apartments at the time—I interviewed Valeriano Cortez. He lent
me his copy of an early recording of "El corrido de Gregorio Cortez."

At that time, I hadn't even put my hand on a tape recorder, let alone
owned one! But I borrowed one, taped the recording, and gave it back
to Valeriano Cortez. Chris Strachwitz of Arhoolie Records now has
one of these tapes that has the earliest recording of "El corrido de
Gregorio Cortez," done during the 1920s. The song continued to be
recorded and played into the 1930s and 1940s. And then I really did
a job of research. I started digging, and the more I dug, the happier I
became, because everything I found fit the pattern and the situation
that I had hoped to find about border conflict and social justice.

I found an excellent source of factual materials in the records of
the Texas Court of Criminal Appeals. All of Cortez's convictions were
appealed except the last one, when an all-Anglo court found him not
guilty in Corpus Christi. But all of the others were appealed. All of
the records from the first trial were in the proceedings of the court
of criminal appeals, sometimes with all kinds of wonderful details.
For example, when the court of criminal appeals overturned his conviction for the murder of Schnabel—the constable who was killed

when Cortez did kill Sheriff Glover—there were even diagrams showing where Cortez was during the gunfight and where Glover was
and where Schnabel was—way, way in another place. The diagrams
showed clearly that there was no way that Cortez could have killed
Schnabel. A drunken member of his own mob killed Schnabel. So I
got a lot of good material from this source. Then I went to Judge Colquitt's papers because Colquitt was the one who pardoned Cortez.
And also, the papers of Ed Hudsell, where I found, for example, even
how tall Cortez was. He was 5' 9." And a physical description. He
was of medium complexion. He was neither dark nor fair. Things of
that sort. Also, what he did. I learned, for example, that in prison he
was a barber. I interviewed a number of other people who had known
him. So I had a very solid basis for the case I was making. Also, I used
the newspaper accounts. I used, remember, the Anglo newspapers,
which were mostly biased against Cortez. Yet, for example—I think I
mention that in the book—in the same issue of the newspaper there
was an article of how Cortez looked after he had been captured: "He
had beautiful wavy black hair, a man with a lot of presence," and the
article mentioned that though he was questioned in Spanish, whenever the interpreter would make a mistake, he would correct him. In
other words, he knew English to a good extent. They also praised him
for his coolness, you know, his woodcraft, in the ways he had avoided
capture, and so on. A beautiful picture of him emerged from those
Anglo newspapers.

In the same issue, one newspaper, probably the same page, there
was another article lamenting the fact that he had not been lynched
when he had been captured. For that reason I felt that the reports in
the Anglo, English-language press could be trusted. Then there were,
of course, a lot of legends already being told about Cortez. So the
work really is several works, of course, trying to take into account the
story as told in the *corridos*, in the courts and other historical records,
and in the popular imagination. The first part of my study was my attempt to show border Mexican communities from their own point of
view, not that of Walter Webb. And Renato Rosaldo later criticized
me for it. He said, "There must have been people that rebelled and
didn't fit the ideal pattern." I've never talked to him about that. I'd
tell him, well, I could tell you about my father [laughter], who didn't
fit the ideal pattern at all. But that's the way the idea for the dissertation, and then the book *"With His Pistol in His Hand,"* developed.

After 1953, I began serious work on Gregorio Cortez, on folklore, *co-rridos*, and on border conflict and social justice. In a very real sense, I had come full circle to *George Washington Gómez*, but the novel was very far from my mind during those years.

My doctoral committee included the most respected folklorists of the time. Mody Boatright, who was a very good friend of Dobie, was on the committee, as was Professor Stith Thompson, who was Mr. Folklore at that time, not only in the United States but also in Europe. He had retired from Indiana University, which has always had a very strong folklore faculty. Thompson had come to Texas as a visiting professor for a year, and they put him on my committee. He liked the manuscript, probably because he saw something of his historic geographic method there. Not something that I like. But he said that he was going to recommend the manuscript to the University of Texas Press, recommend it for publication. So the manuscript went to the editor, Frank Wardlaw, with Stith Thompson's imprimatur.[35]

Meanwhile, I left for my first teaching job in El Paso. Wardlaw was a very nice person, but again, very much of an admirer of Webb and Dobie, you know. I didn't think that I had been too harsh on Dobie, but Wardlaw called me at Texas Western College in El Paso and said they had read the manuscript and they liked it, but I would have to make some changes before UT Press could publish it. One was to remove all the derogatory comments about the Texas Rangers because he didn't want the press to be sued. He also wanted me to remove what he took to be derogatory comments about Professor Webb. So I told him, "Frank, why don't you just send me the manuscript back, and I think I'll try somewhere else." He must have had visions of this manuscript being printed at, say, Indiana, as "the manuscript that the University of Texas Press would not touch," or something like that. He backed down from those suggestions. A young woman at the press did a very good job editing the manuscript, cutting it down. For example, in the original manuscript, I had included a lot of discussion on the *décima* and other things that really did not belong. She tightened it up very well. And it appeared in 1958.

When it came out, it was reviewed favorably in the northern parts of Texas. I think it was a Dallas newspaper and a Houston newspaper that gave it very good reviews. Now, of course, newspapers in Karnes County, where the Cortez incidents took place, just plagued me for it. And one man, who was a librarian for the Texas Historical Association, wrote that I had done nothing but glean suspect data from the newspapers. That just wasn't true. A lot of good research went into the writing of the book.

But that is the way it came about. It didn't take, as I think I've already told you. UT Press was new, still relatively new at the time having been established only in 1950. When they published a book, they normally gave it a lot of propaganda. Usually they had a book-signing party at the University Co-op, and they would have a display outside in the vestibule with copies of the book for sale. In my case, nothing of the sort happened. The press met its obligations and published it. Rather, they printed it, but they did not publish it. After it was printed, I went looking for it, after it appeared, at the University Co-op. And I found one copy. Filed under "Western Americana," or something like that. Of course, it was in the *W*'s. Way down there at the bottom of the shelf where no one could see it. No book-signing ceremony or anything. In Brownsville, a bookstore by the name of Hargrove's did have a book-signing ceremony. So I told Wardlaw about it, and he finally relented. In Brownsville, you couldn't sell very many books at that time, but some were sold. In fact, Rolando Hinojosa tells me that he and his sister went and bought a couple of copies when they heard about it, and that was it.

So the book almost disappeared. It might have except for the fact that the Texas Folklore Society publishes an annual, and in those years that they don't have a particular volume of their own to offer, they use a book written by a member of the society. Boatright and Dobie were the society. And so that year, they decided to use my book for distribution to the members of the society. About four hundred copies were distributed to members. Oh, another thing that Wardlaw insisted on was that for the first thousand copies, I would receive no royalties. The first thousand copies were not sold in about five or six years. The only ones that sold were those that went out to the members. It wasn't until the Chicano movement in California discovered the book in the 1970s that it really took off. And it still is in print. Still being reprinted and sold everywhere.

I later found out through Wardlaw that a retired Texas Ranger had come to see him and wanted to know my address. He said that he was looking for me to shoot me. I don't think he ever really intended to waste a bullet on me. He just wanted to pistol-whip me. That's what he wanted. [laughter] But Wardlaw, to his credit, did not give the man my address. [laughter] Instead, he convinced him that if he thought that the book was unfair he should write his own book. And so he did. Of course, he cribbed my book for all the facts, but he used them in a way supporting his biased view. UT Press published it in 1959. I don't know if it ever sold or anything. So that's the way I got into the topic of the ballads concerning Gregorio Cortez.

I left the University of Texas in 1956 after receiving my PhD degree and returned in 1957. And again, I almost . . . I really felt like tearing up that PhD diploma after I received it because . . . I couldn't find a job! I received only two job offers. One was at Pan American College down in Edinburg, which was a junior college at the time, and another at Texas Western College, where there were only two PhDs in the whole English department—the chairman and one Chaucer scholar who was an alcoholic. All the rest, including the full professors, were MAS. So here I come in with a PhD. I wasn't very popular. I had become a very good friend of Gerry Langford, and I phoned him and told him, "I'm going to look for work outside of academia; I'm going to go back into government work." Go out for the CIA, maybe, I didn't know what. And Langford said, "Don't do it. We're going to get you back here." And they did. By that time, Professor Stephenson had retired and they needed someone to teach the courses he used to offer. So I returned to the University of Texas in 1957 after one year at Texas Western and started teaching those two courses that Stephenson used to teach. But I finally got them to change the courses into two different courses: one a graduate course, which became what is still labeled 394M, "Mexican Popular Culture" in anthropology, and the other, English 325, "Life and Literature of the Southwest." And out of that, the folklore program at the University of Texas developed. In 1966, I was invited to join the faculty of the Department of Anthropology, and so from that point on, I had half my appointment in English and half in anthropology.

The Literary Imagination

AMÉRICO PAREDES: I had started composing short stories in the 1940s and continued writing them into the 1950s when I returned to Austin from Japan. During that period, I also wrote the other novel that I'm working on now, *The Shadow*. I wrote it while I was still a graduate student and won a prize for it. Now, as for the short stories, I won a short story prize for those too, and received five hundred dollars worth of books. For the novel, I got five hundred dollars, which came in very handy. I recently noticed that I have two addresses written on the paper that I used to cover the manuscript when I was sending it to publishers, an Austin address, and after a certain point, an El Paso address. So I must have sent it out at that time, during the mid-1950s. Nobody was interested in it. They wanted me to make different changes to give it more local color.

But that was after *"With His Pistol in His Hand." George Washington Gómez*, that was another matter. My divorce from Chelo Silva didn't become effective until 1947. I had been in Japan two years by that time. As a result of the confusion of the breakup, a number of my papers got lost, including the manuscripts of the novel that my mother had and of some of the short stories I had written before the war. As I was working on *"With His Pistol in His Hand,"* way back in the back of my mind, I knew that I had the manuscript of a novel somewhere. But I never thought of it consciously. If I had ended up teaching literature and criticism, I probably would have gone back to work on *George Washington Gómez* after I returned from Japan. But as it was, I was too busy to focus on my own creative writing. First, getting my bachelor's; next, beginning to work on my dissertation; and then I went straight into the work on the Cortez materials. So the way I would explain it was that when I wrote *George Washington Gómez*, of course, I was a very angry young man. When I came back from the war, I was a very angry middle-aged man [laughter], but with the same desire to say these things. And I won't say that I didn't know the novel was there when I began working on *"With His Pistol in His Hand,"* but I never actually went directly to the manuscript.

In fact, I didn't have a chance to get back to it, from 1944 when I was drafted to the time that I retired in 1984. Before I left Brownsville, I decided that since this novel was not going to get published, I should try to make some short stories out of some of the chapters. The chapter that I call "The Night of the Baile," in which Guálinto gets into a knife fight, is one that I tried to make into a short story. And I also excerpted a piece from an early scene called "The Last Blow," where an Anglo drummer is killed. I might also point out, in my own defense, that I was not completely prejudiced against the Anglos, because the really unpleasant murder in the novel is one of

Mexicans killing an Anglo. I did try to make a few short stories from the novel way back then, without success. In fact, I found some of those attempts among the manuscripts of my short stories when I looked later. But the manuscript of the novel was there in Brownsville for forty years in the form in which it was eventually published.

And then, of course, when Amelia and I finally returned from Japan, I got the manuscript of *George Washington Gómez* back, just as I have just recently recovered the manuscript of *The Shadow*. I have yet another one that I never finished called *The River Man*. I might not ever finish that one at all because I also have the *décimas* book that I want to work on and something else that I am calling "Gringo, Greaser, and Other Neighborly Names." Roger Abrahams and Dick Bauman used *And Other Neighborly Names* as the title of a Festschrift that they edited in my honor. I was just too deeply involved in scholarly work and my teaching to pursue creative writing for all those years. So, the anger that I felt in the 1930s in the creative writings, I was now venting in the scholarly work on the Cortez book in the 1950s. Now I had a great deal more to write about because I had never heard of Walter Prescott Webb until I came to Austin. I was pretty harsh on Dobie in the novel because I didn't know him when I was writing the novel. Later, when I came to the University of Texas, I finally did meet him. I found him to be a very lovable old . . . fraud. I was invited to his house several times, and I think we even visited him at his Paisano Ranch. But as I said, he was a lovable old fraud [laughter] as far as Mexican materials were concerned.

The interesting point is that I had not read J. Frank Dobie's writings on Texas folklore when I was still living in Brownsville. Dobie did come to Brownsville once, to give a talk. I don't remember now whether I was a senior in high school or I was in junior college at the time, because we used the same auditorium. It may have been an assembly of both schools. In any case, it had nothing to do with the high school commencement ceremony as I depicted it in the novel. Dobie just spoke; and a very, *very* poor impression he made on most of us. Now I was sitting close to the front, and even though my hearing was very good when I was young, I could barely hear him because Dobie was not a very good public speaker. He was very good in small groups, but not at all in front of large audiences. That day he said a few things that really bothered me. I don't even remember now what it was he said that bothered me, but I know that it really did anger me. I remember that at one point he told the story about the coyote and the rabbit, even though he vulgarized it a little bit for theatrical effect. And that was that.

Dobie was constantly in the news at that time. His books were being highly touted for the truth of their representations of Texas folklife. I wanted to know more about him, so after his talk I went directly to the library to read the newspaper stories about him. And it was in the newspaper that I really found out about him. I read his pronouncements, because that's what they were, *pronouncements*. One in particular that I remember really irked me. He was quoted on this— I know it may not have even been Dobie who said it, or even exactly what he said. But nevertheless, he was identified in one article as a man who "knew Mexicans better than the Mexicans knew themselves." That really irked me. Everywhere everyone claimed that he was the best authority on Mexico and the Spanish language. But he didn't even know the Spanish language! For example, it was only recently, I think, that dictionaries have stopped giving the etymology of *chaps* as *chapparejos*. That word does not exist in Spanish.[36] But they got it from Dobie's books!

So I started reading about Dobie. My favorite story to hate about Dobie was the one in which apparently he had been asked to explain the etymology of the word *mojado*, wetback, meaning a Mexican who has crossed the US border illegally. Now, how do you translate *mojado*? You wouldn't call someone a "wet," or a "wet one," because those words meant something else in those days. Those were the days of Prohibition, and to call someone a wet or a dry meant something entirely different, having to do with the consumption of alcohol, not with illegal border crossings. So that's why *mojado* came to be translated as wet*back*. But Dobie's version was more colorful: this is the way Dobie was said—and I want to emphasize that I had not read his books yet at the time—this is what he was quoted as saying in feature articles: [Mimicking Dobie] "What happened was that Mexicans would swim across the river, and as soon as they swam across, they would lie down in the sun. And when they awoke, all their clothes were dry except their backs. So anytime you saw a Mexican with a *wet back*, you knew that he had just swum across the river." Now, notice that Dobie's explanation involves two stereotypes. First, the Mexican is too dumb to take his clothes off before he crosses the river, too stupid to put them on some kind of raft and float them across, which is what they did, of course. And second, as soon as he comes out of the river, what does the Mexican do? He's so lazy that he falls asleep in the sun! [laughter] So, that *really* got to me. Dumb *and* lazy! I read about Dobie and that story on the etymology of *wetback* at the time that I was writing *George Washington Gómez*, and so I decided to take advantage of the opportunity to satirize him. I gave the Dobie character the name of K. Hank Harvey and got my revenge by making him look ridiculous.

At the time I wrote those scenes in the novel I had never met Dobie. I had heard him speak once, but I had never even read any of his books. I've read them now, of course, and I guess they didn't change my mind about how little he really knew about Mexicans or the Spanish language. When I did get to know him, we would talk about a number of things, but never about Mexicans and never about Spanish. To the end of his life, he never knew a word of Spanish. But that is why that section of the novel is so vitriolic. [laughter] It was a representation of my feelings about this figure called J. Frank Dobie and what I had read about him.

When I began to think about publishing *George Washington Gómez* in the 1980s after I retired, several people suggested that I also publish some of my poetry. So I thought I would try to publish the poetry first. I sent the poetry collection to Nicolás Kanellos, the editor at Arte Público Press in Houston. He liked it, but we couldn't agree on a title. I had titled the collection simply *Versos varios* (Various Verses). Nick said, "Get a better title." For several weeks, we would exchange letters, trying out different titles. I would say, "How about this title?" He would respond, "No, I don't like it. How about this one instead?" which I wouldn't like. And we were doing that, going back and forth, when in one letter he asked me, in exasperation over the delay in the publication of the poetry, I think, "Do you have any fiction I could publish?" And I said to him, "Well, I have this novel that I wrote fifty years ago." This was already in 1990. Nick was interested, so I managed to rescue the manuscript, as I mentioned earlier, from among papers that my mother had been holding for me for half a century. I dug out the box containing the *George Washington Gómez* manuscript. It was typed on newsprint, the cheapest kind of paper available during the Depression. By 1989, it was yellowed and crumbling to pieces. I put the pieces together with Scotch tape, assisted by Francis Terry [of the University of Texas Folklore Center], and retyped a more or less clean copy so that Mrs. Terry could put the whole thing on computer diskettes. That is why I call the original manuscript an archeological piece in the acknowledgments.[37]

When I submitted the manuscript of *George Washington Gómez* to Nick Kanellos, I told him, "I'll submit the novel for publication if you will agree to one condition: to publish it exactly as it is—as a fifty-year-old work, without the usual editorial work you normally do on a contemporary manuscript. Don't make any changes at all, even in the spelling." The novel shows some of the quirks of the date of its composition. For instance, in the 1930s I had gotten into the habit of writing *cigaret*, with an "–ret" spelling instead of "-rette," which was a journalistic convention of the time. Nick agreed to that, so *George Washington Gómez* appears exactly as I left it in 1939.

Guálinto Gómez in *George Washington Gómez* is very different from Gregorio Cortez as he is represented in the ballads about him. The two are almost opposites of one another, a traditional hero in Cortez versus a modern antihero in *George Washington Gómez*. Why? I suppose that at that time I saw Gregorio Cortez, Jacinto Treviño, and other *corrido* heroes at more or less the same level of heroic intensity. They represented for me the old values in heroic resistance against a new political and social order. I guess I had made a separation in my mind between the *corrido*, as an artistic form that was part of a larger social life, and other art forms that are more a part of academic life. And I suppose I may have thought that I was writing a novel that was much more autobiographical than it turned out to be, since Guálinto in *George Washington Gómez* does not take the path in life that I finally chose.

I want to emphasize that: *George Washington Gómez* is *not* my autobiography. In fashioning my characters I used what I experienced, what I saw and heard, but they do not represent particular persons. Also, as the narrative developed, some characters changed in ways that I had not anticipated. Once I started writing, Feliciano, Guálinto's uncle, for example, became more and more important. Toward the end of the story, I think, he's a much more appealing character than Guálinto Gómez. I began Guálinto's story, I suppose, by basing it on my own experiences in school. But then I expanded his story and took it in a different direction than my own life had taken. When I was in my twenties, I was a fiery, loud radical. When I returned to the States in 1950, I was still a radical, but I had learned in my work as a journalist in Japan that understatement and irony—sarcasm, some people have called it—can hit harder than loud words. The work I did later between 1950 and 1980— *"With His Pistol in His Hand"* and *A Texas-Mexican Cancionero*, in particular—found initial disfavor with publishers because of their subject matter and because of their tendency toward irony and satire.

I did get a number of incidents and events in the story not from *corridos*, but from the legends and stories that developed alongside the *corridos*. Take what happened during the *sedicioso* (sedition) period, for example. People like my mother, who had no use for the *sediciosos*, influenced me quite a bit. She said all the seditionists did was get a lot of innocent people killed, and so she didn't like them at all. My father was rather neutral because he had belonged to the political party that ran Brownsville.

My mother's people, the Manzanos, who remained on the Mexican side of the border, weren't enthusiastic about the *sediciosos* either. The uncle I mentioned earlier, and who was a labor organizer, claimed that he had been sent by the Partido Liberal and the Flores Magón brothers to contact Aniceto Pizaña, with Luis de la Rosa, supposedly the leaders of what came to be known as the Sedicioso Revolt in 1915. He had been sent to contact Pizaña because Pizaña was a member of the Partido Liberal, and the Partido Liberal, of course, was interested in starting a revolution, an anarchist revolution in Mexico. In fact, they fielded an army and took to the field under a red flag. Of course, they got nowhere with that symbolic gesture. For the Mexican people, *la bandera mexicana* (the Mexican flag) is a strong symbolic force, and they won't easily turn to a movement that is not nationalistically based, certainly not to one that acts under the red flag of socialism.

My uncle Eduardo claimed that the Flores Magón people had sent money to Pizaña to buy weapons for the revolutionaries in Mexico. But because Pizaña had done nothing, my uncle was sent to the Brownsville area where Pizaña had a ranch, a place called Los Marranos, to contact Pizaña and find out what was wrong. My uncle was taking some tremendous risks to approach the rebels since the reprisals by the Texas Rangers were vicious, and they were indiscriminate with their violence. But he went anyway. When he arrived at Pizaña's ranch, he was told that Pizaña wasn't there. So, then, he crossed the river and tried to contact the *magonista* army, but was not able to contact them either. And I think it was just as well. So he returned to Brownsville, and by the time he was back, Pizaña's ranch had been raided by the Rangers, and an open revolt was on. What happened, he would later tell me, was that Pizaña used the money from the Flores Magón brothers to start the *sedicioso* revolt in Texas instead of buying weapons for the revolution in Mexico.

According to my uncle, the *magonistas* did not sanction the revolt of the *sediciosos*. They gave money to Pizaña so that he would buy weapons for the revolution in Mexico. My uncle claimed that he himself was never a *sedicioso*. Earlier, I told you about my father who was one of Catarino Garza's men when Garza tried to overthrow the Díaz government back in the 1890s. I was interested in all those things because there was a family connection. My uncle, in the matter of the *sedicioso* uprising, and my father's participation in the Garza rebellion were part of the history that I was raised with and wanted to represent in my fiction.

The *sediciosos* fought under the red flag of anarchism and supposedly even wrote a manifesto, "El plan de San Diego," in which they lay out a plan to establish an independent border republic in the border region. The origins, time period, and authorship of this manifesto are still very uncertain.[38] As far as I know, no bona fide Spanish-language copy of the "Plan de San Diego" has ever appeared, only what are purported to be English-language translations of Spanish originals. If these texts are translations of an original Spanish text, then whoever translated them was someone who didn't know Spanish very well. When Spanish-language texts thought to be original documents have surfaced, you could tell immediately that these were really translations from an English source. For example, I have seen documents in Spanish that refer to *los viejitos*, the old men of the area. Only someone who knew very little Spanish would say *los viejitos*, rather than the more proper *los ancianos*. I've always suspected that whoever did these English-language texts was trying to fabricate an uprising in order to justify the slaughter of hundreds of innocent Mexicans by the Rangers as they put down the rebellion. It's possible that a Spanish-language original is in somebody's possession, in his or her family *castaña*, the family strongbox. Border families used to put all of their important papers in these *castañas*, things like official documents, birth certificates, marriage documents, letters, journals, and genealogies. One of my pet projects that never got off the ground was to organize something I would have called "Operation *Castaña*," to sort through the holdings in the old family trunks of the border region. My guess is that if an original of the "Plan de San Diego" exists, somebody somewhere has it in the family *castaña*. Because it's strange that a Spanish version shouldn't exist.

But let me return to the difference between Guálinto Gómez and Gregorio Cortez as political actors. I know that many readers are very disappointed with the ending of the novel, finding the course of Guálinto's life not at all what they expected from him. Remember that I made no revisions on *George Washington Gómez* in 1990 when I finally went back to the manuscript. Had I done so, I might have dropped part 5 and ended the novel at the end of part 4, with Guálinto Gómez sallying forth to fulfill his destiny as the leader of his people and the founder of the *movimiento chicano*. Originally, I had planned a long novel, a two-volume work, perhaps. Parts 1 through 4 would deal with life on the border in the far and recent past, from the turn of the century to the 1930s. In part 5 we would move into the present, my present as a reporter for the local paper and an observer of the social and political problems of the town in the 1940s. First, it was necessary that my main character go away to college, so he could get a law degree. Then, he would return home to participate in local affairs, as I was witnessing them around 1938 or 1939. The problem was that though I could send Guálinto Gómez to the University of Texas, I could not go with him. I had never been to Austin or a university campus. The closest thing to a college campus I had ever experienced was the Brownsville Junior College. I knew that in order for the continuation of the story to work, there would have had to be a jump in time, with some cautious details of Gómez's years away from Jonesville worked in through flashbacks. Once I got Guálinto back to Jonesville, he could begin practicing law, and I would be writing again about things I knew well enough.

But I never got around to writing that version. Instead, I stayed with the first version of part 5, which had George G. Gómez, as Guálinto styled himself in his assimilated persona, returning to Jonesville to set up his law practice. He had left with a deep hatred toward all Anglos. He returns with an Anglo wife. He has rejected, at least on the surface, all he had stood for before he left for college. Remember that the 1930s and 1940s was the time of the emergence of the Latin middle class and the League of United Latin American Citizens

(LULAC). I tried to represent through Guálinto Gómez how members of this new middle class were trying hard to assimilate, to pass as "white," to bring up their children as monolingual English speakers. In Guálinto/George, however, a deeply seated conflict was supposed to be foreshadowed by his dreams as described in part 5. His conflict would have been exacerbated when he discovered that his father-in-law, Frank Dell, had been one of the Rangers who had murdered Gumersindo Gómez, Guálinto's father. In the extended version, I had intended that George Gómez would change his mind about assimilation. But finally, I decided that it would have been much too sentimental to give the novel a "come-to-realize" ending, with a reborn Guálinto leading his people in their struggle for social and economic rights. I realized that leaders would emerge unexpectedly. The unexpected leaders would be people like Elodia and Antonio Prieto, the minor characters in the novel. They would lead the way; and lawyer George would be what he was, a follower.

All of this, except for the first draft of part 5, was still in very rough outline form in the fall of 1939. Then Hitler invaded Poland, and World War II began on September 3, my birthday, no less. Things were no longer the same, either in the world at large or in Jonesville-on-the-Grande. During 1940, I revised part 5 into its present form and set the novel aside until some other day. That other day would be a long time coming.

Politics, Music, and Intellectual
Life on the Border

AMÉRICO PAREDES: Of my own politics during the period of the 1930s and 1940s, I have already mentioned that Emma Tenayuca, the labor organizer and Communist Party leader, was one of my heroes at the time. But I didn't know much about organizations outside of our own border area. We were very insular in south Texas, you know. I did know about LULAC. In fact, when I got older, I was asked to join. I didn't because I considered *Latin* a kind of "weasel" word. I told them that I would join them if their organization were called LUMAC, League of United *Mexican* American Citizens. It was my feeling that when Anglos called us "Latins," it was because they were avoiding the term *Mexican*, since they didn't want to insult us. In Texas, *Mexi-*

can was a dirty word, not to be used in polite company. It was never used except as an insult. So I never joined LULAC. My older brother Lorenzo, because he was older and he knew some of the people who were in LULAC, was also invited to join. He even attended some meetings, but in the end, he didn't join for another reason. Lorenzo was a militant atheist, has been all his life. So when they started talking about God, Lorenzo said, [gruffly] "I'm not going to join any organization that talks about God."

That's why he didn't join them. No, to a great extent I was a loner; I was not a joiner. I would not have joined LULAC. The concern about assimilation is what is involved in my poem "The Four Freedoms." Roosevelt came to office in 1934, I think, or 1933. In some ways, of course, he was liberal. At least he talked like a liberal, the Good Neighbor Policy, and so on. It seemed like a good idea, but it wasn't ever really applied. If it had been, I would have voted Democratic. I don't think I ever voted very much in those days until I returned to Austin in the 1950s. But I would have been a Democrat. Really, I had my doubts about the whole political process. My brother and his friends made me think of myself as a Mexican rather than as a Mexican American. At the time, I thought of myself as a *mexicano* who happened to be living in Texas. But in those days, one was rather cynical about the whole political thing. When World War II started, the Mexican government allowed the United States to draft Mexican citizens without their consent. So that rankled a bit.

I wasn't aware at the time of the work of other Mexican American writers. It was never mentioned in the press in south Texas. I didn't know about George Sánchez and his books until later in Austin, for example. That was my main objection to LULAC because at that time the LULACs were extremely assimilationist. They counseled their members not to speak Spanish at all to their children, to bring them up as American citizens and nothing else. I feel that multiculturalism—I never called it that at the time—and bilingualism are important. I was more in sympathy with publications like *La Prensa de San Antonio*, which attempted to create a bilingual culture for Mexican Americans. I did know Alonso Perales's book, *En defensa de mi raza* (*In Defense of My Race*, 1937). But again it was in Spanish, you see. By 1940, I was involved in a lot of things. I don't think I was reading as much, for one thing. That's when I was working for Pan American Airways. Also, I was in one of my musical periods. I was doing more music than reading or writing.

14 Américo Paredes, portrait published in *Cantos de adolescencia*, 1937. Courtesy of the Américo Paredes Papers, 1886–1999, Benson Latin American Collection, General Libraries, University of Texas at Austin.

As for other Mexican American writers of the times, people like Arthur Campa, for example, I came to know about them much later.[39] Campa, too, was very much of an assimilationist, though he did some very important work in the early days. Carlos Castañeda, however, I did know very well. Although he was born, in Camargo I think it was, he grew up in Brownsville. In fact, he was a classmate of my oldest brother at the Catholic school, San José Academy. Personally, I didn't meet him until I came to Austin. But I knew of him very well because two of his older sisters were teachers, elementary school teachers in Brownsville. In fact, I understand that they put him through college. Josefina and María. Miss Josephine, as she was called, was my first public school teacher. So I knew the Castañedas very well. I had corresponded with Castañeda, so when I published a horrible little collection of poetry in 1937, I sent him a copy.[40] And he wrote me a nice letter back, you know, very noncommittal. When I came to the University of Texas, of course, I looked him up because I knew of him very well by then. He was a historian. I had read one book of his, *The*

Mexican Side of the Texas Revolution.[41] I found it in the public library because that book was given some publicity in the local paper, which was my chief source of information. Frankly, I was disappointed because I thought what I would find would be "our" side. But, no, he mentions just different documents and things of that sort. It doesn't compare to *Verdadera idea de la primera campaña de Tejas* (True Account of the First Campaign in Texas) (1837) by Ramón Martínez Caro. So I was disappointed. Anyway, there were a lot of dry documents, you know, when I had expected he would be shouting, "We was robbed!" Of course, he would never say anything like that, as he was very much of a gentleman. His major work was on the history of the church in Texas and other parts of the United States. He was very, very religious. He was decorated by the Spanish government way back before the revolution in Spain. I always related to him even though, as I said, I didn't meet him until I returned to Austin.

The same thing goes for Ernesto Galarza. I never met him either. He was in his own little sphere in California, and I was here in Texas. I had hoped to meet him, but he died before I could. I finally ended up giving a memorial lecture in his honor at Stanford. But I never met him. But I knew of his work, and I admired his work.

As for music as an art form suitable for the expression of the anger that I felt in those days, well, I suppose I was aware of the power of music ever since I began to talk and listen to the stories about our communities. That's what the *corridos* were created to do. You know, there was an advantage to not having a radio before radios were common in homes. We had what were then, I suppose, top-of-the-line phonographs. Our own was a Victrola. We didn't use the word *fonógrapho*. It was *la victrola*. And almost everybody in the family, I mean my elders, bought records. My father would buy arias, historical vignettes, and comical skits on records. For example, my father bought something called *La batalla del segundo de abril.* I still remember that. Both sides were seventy-eight RPM. Then there was Mr. Bell, Ricardo Bell, an Englishman who became a very popular clown in Mexico. We had records of his. My father liked records of that sort. Now, my brother, Lorenzo, he liked more current records in Spanish, but he also bought records in English. And my sisters also bought records. So I was getting quite a varied musical education from records even at a very early age. When radio finally did come along, my mother and I would listen to nothing but Agustín Lara. She was very senti-

mental about Lara. In the early days of radio, we had fooled around
with a crystal radio set, but it wasn't until the early 1930s, or maybe
as late as 1935, that we got a real radio and gave the phonograph away.
Later in the 1950s, I happened to come across that same phonograph
in some ranch south of Matamoros. We had given it to my uncle Eduardo Manzano for his farm. In fact, I used to go there, and we would
dance to that phonograph. He finally got a radio, and in turn gave it
to an uncle on the Paredes side, Gregorio, on the Mexican side. And I
remember even hearing it there. Then they got rid of it, and it landed
next with some family south of Matamoros. One day, I was with a
cousin who was a rural policeman in Tamaulipas. He said to me, "Let's
go visit that house over there. I want to show you something." When
we walked in, he said, "Do you recognize this phonograph?" It was
that same old Victrola. So I was getting quite an education in music.
For example, my father liked Caruso. The phonograph gave me a very
broad music education because of the varied tastes of my elders. We
listened to whatever was popular. Up until the mid-1930s, I would say.
I think this morning I woke up with "My Blue Heaven" in my mind.

Oh, and jazz, yes. Of course. We bought lots of jazz records. My
brother and my sister especially listened to jazz. Now after radio became available, we would listen to music on the radio. Of course, I
was exaggerating when I said that my mother and I listened to Agustín
Lara all the time. We also tuned in to a very powerful radio station,
XERA in Villa Acuña, just across from Del Rio. A man who called himself Dr. Brinkley ran it. Ever hear of him? He was a quack. He claimed
that he could implant goat testicles into men to make them potent
again. Well, in those days, they wouldn't say "testicles"; they would
say "goat glands." It's amazing how rich he became! He had once had
a station in the Midwest, but the authorities had shut it down. So
he just moved it across the border. His station could be heard all the
way into the Middle West. We would tune it in because he would play
the best of the new Mexican music: *tríos*, and *duetos*, and so on. He
also played American music, jazz, and the Carter family too, in other
words, hillbilly country music. So I was getting quite an education in
music during the nine months out of the year that I spent at home in
Brownsville just listening to the radio.

The three months of the year that I spent in the country at my
uncle's, what had been my grandfather's ranch in Tamaulipas, I heard
live music. The *corrido* was especially strong there. And, of course, the

décima. And the discussions that accompanied the music. A *corrido* would be performed and then people would discuss it. So along with the music, I was also getting a lot of our history from the Mexican side of the border, at what had been my grandfather's ranch. I think I mentioned that my father rejected it and came over to the American side instead. My uncle, my father's brother, who followed him in age, his name was Vicente. The ranch had been passed down to him, and so it was his home then. But he kept us—me and my brothers, who were twins—for three months out of the year. For those three months out of every year, we were doing nothing but running around, swimming, horseback riding.

For me, the real interesting part began in the evening when the old men sat around and talked about how Mexican generals Mariano Arista or Pedro de Ampudia had lost the battle of Palo Alto in 1846, the first encounter between Mexican and American forces during the Mexican War, or about other stories dealing with the history of our region.[42] And the narrators were real performers. They didn't just tell the stories in a conversational manner. They acted them out in a dramatic way. They might say, "Íbamos andando cuando, allá oimos que disparaban. Pow. Pow. Pow." (We were walking along when, off in the distance, we heard some shots. Pow. Pow. Pow.) [laughter] And with sound effects, just like that, they would make the story come alive for us. I would be sitting away from them because I was just a kid, with the rest of the children. I was too young to be admitted to the inner circle closest to the speakers. But I would listen. Ghost stories, and legends, and history, all kinds of stories of that sort.

In the daytime, when the men weren't around, the women would take their turn and talk, to each other and to the children. I give some example of how women would perform as storytellers in the article "The Undying Love of 'El Indio' Córdova," where the women would also talk and be heard. And there were also books that were not available to me, only through the public library, in Spanish. Popular books. So I was getting that side also. But the music, the music that I got in the country was very closely related to our history, the kind of history that we did not get in books. And maybe more importantly, the music expressed the resentment of what has been done to us. So the whole thing came together.

Literary Influences and the Creative Process

AMÉRICO PAREDES: It was much later that I first read Mariano Azuela and Juan Rulfo. Azuela I didn't read until I came back from Japan. But I had read Altamirano and writers of his generation. Most of those I read on the Mexican side at the ranch. And, of course, we also read poetry of the group Amado Nervo, Gutiérrez Nájera, and poets from the Porfiriato.[43] The kinds of things that educated people were reading at the time. And I read isolated things out of books, and the literary section called "Lunes literarios" from *La Prensa de San Antonio*. Some of those books we read also in Brownsville. After 1940, I was working for Pan American Airways. A friend by the name of Sabas Klahn had gotten me the job. We would have lunch in his car, and we would read together sometimes. Read aloud from different authors, Gutiérrez Nájera, and others. And talk. The ranch people knew mostly the older literary figures from the Juarez period and, of course, also José Jaoquín Fernández Lizardi, *El periquillo sarniento* [*The Itching Parrot*], who went back to the very beginning of the republic also.

I like to tell people that Mexicans come in all colors, shapes, and sizes. [laughter] My stories in part were about that. One of my stories, "The Gringo," for example, was inspired by something that Mody Boatright once told me. He mentioned once that he had heard about a battle between some so-called cowboys, who were really cattle thieves, and some Texas Mexicans. The American cowboys would cross the Nueces River into the disputed south Texas grazing lands and steal cattle from their Mexican neighbors. He claimed that there had once been a battle in which a number of Texas Mexicans and some Anglo Texans had been killed or wounded. One of the casualties was apparently a young Texas Mexican who was fair-haired and light-skinned. In the confusion of the skirmish, the Americans mistake him for one of their own, doctor him, and take him back home with them. But when they get home and the young man regains consciousness, he speaks only Spanish. The Americans realize that despite the fact that he doesn't look Mexican, he is Mexican. And so I asked Boatright, "Well, what became of him?" I don't know whether he knew or whether he just didn't want to say, "Well, I don't know what happened to him," was his diplomatic reply. But of course he knew; they killed him. And that was the germ of this particular story.

Most of my stories were based on people I had known or incidents I had experienced. Take the story, "When It Snowed in Kitabamba," with the curious character named Meniscus. Well, that was a story I wrote after the war and that really was worked over quite a bit in the creative writing workshop that I took with Gerry Langford at the university. In "When It Snowed in Kitabamba," a story I had begun while I was in Japan, I was trying to dabble in symbolism. The story is set in occupation Japan after the end of the war in the Pacific and is about an American army captain named Meniscus who has an exaggerated view of his country and his commanding general, General Douglas MacArthur.

A meniscus is a kind of crescent from the inside, a concave surface. And it fits the story because he is flawed in that way: Meniscus always believes that the shortest distance between two points is a straight line. I thought his name said something about his flawed character. And his exaggerated idolization of MacArthur, of course, also fits. There were officers who idolized MacArthur, you know. After Meniscus shoots himself, the Japanese couple who are washing his body and changing him notice that his legs are bent in, crescent shaped. But that detail did not seem to carry the story in the original version. So I changed it a lot, including adding the scene where I have him stumble and fall and make him ridiculous. But I had chosen the name Meniscus because at the beginning he was going to be bowlegged and unable to walk the straight line that he always was talking about.

Talking about MacArthur, did you ever hear the one about the psychiatrist? Well, right after the war, a young psychiatrist who was just incredibly good had come to great prominence in Vienna. I mean, by his late twenties, he already had surpassed the work of all the great analysts of the past, Freud, Adler, Jung, and everybody else. It was obvious that he was going to be an incredible scholar and analyst. And then all of a sudden his health declines and, almost immediately, he dies. So there he goes, up to heaven, sad as can be. He has to approach the Pearly Gates, of course. And as he approaches the gates, he's feeling pretty low, going along quite slowly, dawdling along, really, and grumbling, because he has been cut down in the bloom of his youth, with fame and success all before him. When he gets to the Pearly Gates, he sees that Saint Peter is looking down toward him very anxiously, eager for his arrival, waving for him to hurry. "Doctor! Please! Please hurry! Hurry!" says Saint Peter. "Why, what's going on?" asks the young psychiatrist. "Well, we've got a terrible psycho case here that none of these other guys who are already here, Freud, Adler, Jung, none of them, have been able to do anything about. You were called because we thought you might be able to help us." "Who is it?" asks the young analyst. "It's God," says Saint Peter. "He thinks he's Mac-Arthur." [laughter] [44] That shows you what most people thought of MacArthur at the time. He put himself above the emperor of Japan, who was the son of heaven, after all! Anyway, that was part of what I had in mind in creating this captain who had a picture of MacArthur in his office. Some of those later stories—and the comic ones also, of course—meant a great deal to the few people who saw them, the Johnny Picadero stories, for example.

I wrote those stories when I was still in Tokyo. There was a small group of ex-soldiers who had stayed on in Japan after the war working in different capacities. They were all very good friends of mine. I've mentioned Horst de la Croix, I believe. It was for people like him that I wrote those stories. Just for laughs, you might say. The stories developed out of little bits and pieces of things that had really happened. Because Horst and I were in special services, we didn't have to make reveille or anything. So we would go over the hill, and on the other side was the Inland Sea, and there was a resort hotel there for soldiers who were on leave. We were on leave everyday after five o'clock. We would go and have a good time, and we'd return very late. There was no bed check for us or anything. Once we stopped at the kitchen, and we met this *puertorriqueño*. The *puertorriqueños* that were in the army, some of them could barely speak English. That's how I met Amelia who had a job interpreting for them. This particular man was overjoyed because we spoke Spanish, and he gave us all sorts of things.

Horst de la Croix spoke Spanish. He had a very good education. In fact, he also spoke French and German. He was born in Germany. And English, of course. And he learned Japanese very quickly. So the Puerto Rican cook would give us things, and we'd go home. We lived in a little barracks, but all by ourselves. In the morning, we would have cheese, butter, and bread that the *puertoriqueño* cook had given us. So we'd have our own nice little breakfast. We'd have beer instead of coffee for breakfast. [laughter] We would show up at the very last moment at the office because we were with a camp newspaper, and I also was a local correspondent for *Stars and Stripes*. And the major was always talking about making colonel. So these are some of the little things I put together and used in the various stories.

That was true about the Johnny Picadero stories as well. I had thought of writing a whole cycle of those Picadero stories. I had written them originally for the group of men I was associated with at *Stars and Stripes*. But once I was away from that group, I lost interest. They were men who had very good educations. In fact, I was the least educated of the bunch with just two years of college. Horst, for example, already had his master's degree from Berkeley. And there were others like him. So they stimulated this sort of intellectual and critical thing in me. But when I returned to the States, that kind of story just didn't ring true anymore. I did write one more story with Picadero going to visit his friend Pablo in Coahuila. I enjoyed writing those stories, and the little group that read them enjoyed them. But when I decided to look around to see what might be publishable, well, I thought those might work.

The critical power of joking and jesting was another part of my training, if you want to call it that, on the border and in town. Training in the joke! Analyzing some of those stories myself, I do find that I use humor often, even in "The Hammon and the Beans," with that tragic little girl, Chonita. I'm still amused when I imagine Chonita going around and around in heaven with butterfly wings on her back. I've always felt that humor and tragedy somehow coincide. In fact, the reason that "Over the Waves Is Out" got published in the first place was because the editor of the *New Mexico Review* found it very funny. Now, I had not intended it to be funny, even though there were some comic passages in it, for example, when the father and the mother start arguing. I parody Hemingway since I had read Hemingway then. But I didn't know Hemingway at the time that I was finishing *George Washington Gomez*.

In my early years, Mark Twain and Charles Dickens were the authors that most influenced me. I read many others, of course, in high school and junior college, mostly writers in English and Spanish before 1920. It was after I finished *George Washington Gómez* that Hart Stilwell, the editor of the *Brownsville Herald*, loaned me a few books. It was only then that I first learned about Faulkner, Hemingway, Dos Passos, Wolfe, and Russian writers in the late 1930s and early 1940s. And I read a lot later in the Tokyo Army College after the war. They had a very good library.[45] I parodied Hemingway in "Over the Waves Is Out," and the father looks ridiculous when he takes his gun out and wants to join the chase and says that Davila couldn't catch scabies much less a criminal. "No pesca ni la roña," we say in Spanish. [laughter] Those stories tend to be basically about serious topics, the conflict between fathers and sons, for example. But I also wanted to include humor; there was always an element of comedy. Even in "When It Snowed in Kitabamba" there is an element of comedy.

From Pocho to Proto-Chicano

AMÉRICO PAREDES: A number of critics have gotten interested in my verse lately because they think it reflected an early interest in community identity that Chicanos would later develop more fully, using for the most part different literary techniques. I used mostly the very well-known traditional techniques. But I saw, of course, the relationship there. That's why I have called myself a proto-Chicano. Except that the word *Chicano* was not used in that way at the time that I first started writing. I knew the word *Chicano* as an affectionate way of saying *mexicano*.

My sister, Clotilde, had a daughter named Esperanza, who was nicknamed "la Patti" by her maternal grandmother, who was a Cuellar. Patti was a red-faced, precious little thing. My brother, my eldest brother Eliseo, the one who was *muy mexicano* (very Mexican), lived next door to us. One time, my sister and her daughter came to visit us, but we weren't in. We were next door at my brother's house. So Clotilde and her daughter went across to Eliseo's house. Patti was dressed as a little cowgirl. You know, little boots, vest, frilled skirt, and so on. Very cute. My brother looked at her and said in jest, but with a harsh tone of disapproval to our sister, "¿Y quién es esa gringa que traes tú aquí?" (And who is this little *gringa* that you have here?) [laughter] The poor little girl didn't understand the words, but definitely felt the tone of disapproval, and she burst out in tears, sobbing, weeping, and crying inconsolably. So my brother goes and pats her on the head and said, "No; no. No es gringa. Es pura Chicanita" (No; no. She is not a gringa. She's a pure Chicanita).

That was the first time I heard the word *Chicana* or *Chicano* used, in the late 1920s. Afterwards, I always heard it used in that way, just as a clipped form of *mexicano*. All this nonsense that it comes from the Aztec just isn't so. Sixteenth-century Spanish had a [sh] sound. But it was written with the letter *x*. And it had the [ch] sound too. And now it still has that [sh] and the [ch] sounds. So the Indians were not going to confuse those two sounds. *Mexica* [meshíca] became *mejíca* [mehíca]. The *x* [sh] took over the [h] sound. Later, the grammarians decided to write it with the letter *j* and took the *x* to represent the Latin sound [ecks], as in *extra*. When I got to Japan in 1945, the Japanese still called cake soap, that is, Western soap, *shabón*. And *shabón* it had been in Spanish in the sixteenth century when they introduced the product and the term to Japan.

So the word for Mexico was *Méshico*. Thus a Mexican was a *Meshíca*. And that is the way the Spaniards pronounced it. When it changed, the Mexicans decided to keep that *x* to represent the [h] sound. But *jabón*, and a number of other words like that, were still pronounced with a [sh] sound. Spanish has a tendency to make the [ch] sound to denote *cariño*, tenderness. Look at the number of names that express tenderness that way: Encarnación becomes "Chon." Nepumuceno, "Cheno." Rosario, "Chayo." And you could go through a whole list of words in which the word is clipped in certain ways, and it begins with a [ch] sound. In fact, in baby talk it's used pretty often just that way. Yes, as in Chonita. That's a feminine diminutive of the name Encarnación. And for Jorge, you would say "Choche." There is any number of names like that. So as far as I can tell, *Chicano* began as a way of saying *mexicano*, especially if you were away from Mexico and thinking about it tenderly.

In those days, the vernacular expression we used for Mexican American was not *Chicano* but *pocho*. This is an example of turning an end around and pointing it in a different direction. José Vasconcelos is the one that named us *pochos*, meaning half-baked, or stupid.[46] So I decided that I was going to call myself a *pocho* and be proud of it. [laughter] And I mention it again, in this poem that I dedicate to Sabas Klahn, at the end: "Eres méxico-tejano, / ¡eres pocho, como yo!" (You are Texas Mexican / you are a *pocho*, just like me). So later, it was just a matter of using *Chicano* instead of *pocho*. I was tuning into that wavelength, even in the 1930s and 1940s.

Looking back, I definitely see the concerns that I had in the 1930s and 1940s reflected in the writings of the 1960s and the 1970s. Yes, very definitely so. It's reflected in a desire to identify, to go from one extreme to another. First, *mexico-americanos* were ashamed of their Indian origins, and so they all wanted to be Spaniards. Now, they all wanted to be Aztecs and identify with Cuauhtémoc, roasted feet and all. [laughter]

I've always used the term *Chicano* itself in the political sense. I call myself a Chicano when it's a political matter. Otherwise, I prefer to think of myself as a *mexicano*. Of course, I applauded the Chicano

movement, and I encouraged it. I got to know many of the first generation of Chicano activists pretty well, people like the historian Juan
Gomez-Quiñones and the poet Alurista. I was arrogant enough to
think of them as my intellectual children. Of course, they had started
on their own, but I think I did influence them to a certain extent.

The Checkerboard of Consciousness

AMÉRICO PAREDES: All of this emerges in a scene in *George Washington Gómez* where Guálinto realizes he isn't one single identity, but
rather a composite of identities. I referred to it as a "checkerboard of
consciousness." The idea came really from my own experiences on the
border. Now if I had been born on the Mexican side, never having
much to do with Anglos and Anglo-American culture, I might indeed
have been able to experience myself as only one personality, even if
it was a personality hostile to Anglo America. But even as a young
boy, I had daily contact with that other world, especially through my
schoolteachers. Some of them, whom I loved, showed me a great deal
of respect, and affection even.

Other Anglos, besides my teachers, were also very decent, especially those who were part Mexican, anyway. So I always got to see
both sides. To put it another way, I always saw Anglos as human
beings. And some of them I had a great deal of affection for. When
I was young, I even fell in love with an Anglo girl when we were in
school. I called her Carolina, which was not her real name. It was
a very innocent sort of thing. So I did not see all Anglos as monsters. Yes, all *rinches* were monsters to me, I won't deny that. Mexicans included under the rubric *rinche* almost all law enforcement officers, since they were all apparently out to kill Mexicans or beat them
up whenever they could. The immigration officers were also always
known as *rinches*. In fact, some of them were retired Rangers. So I
think that the idea of the checkerboard of identities emerged from
the experiences of my daily life, learning to live with both sides of the
divide.

I don't know whether that's a peculiarity, a personal peculiarity
of mine, but I have tended in the past to compartmentalize certain
things. For example, when I started working on *"With His Pistol in His
Hand,"* I never thought of *George Washington Gómez*. It was in a dif-

ferent compartment of my consciousness, covered up. When I was on the Mexican side during those years, which ended about 1930, there were certain things that my relatives down there felt and knew that I did not completely share with them. I could stand back and see some of the things that they couldn't see. That was always especially true concerning the Anglos.

But I think that what I'm calling the checkerboard of consciousness also gave me more of a sense of humor. I see in today's newspaper, for example, that the popularity of *I Love Lucy* is now considered nostalgia. Well, I've always loved that show. [laughter] But I forget which one of my colleagues criticized it as being sexist. And now it's racist because the Cuban is always made into the comic butt of the jokes. Well, I never saw it that way. In fact, the comedian is a woman, an Anglo woman. What about Burns and Allen, where Gracie Allen was the comedian? The comedian has to get him or herself in certain situations, and the straight man has to stand outside of the comic situation. I never have thought of *I Love Lucy* as either sexist or racist. Sometimes, I'll be doing something else in another part of the house and an episode *of I Love Lucy* will come on the television, which is always on. I'll always drop what I'm doing and come running to watch it. Well, running is an exaggeration; more like a fast shuffle! Anyway, I think I've seen almost every episode. Lucille Ball was a wonderful comedian. I think after Chaplin, there hasn't been anybody like her at all. And Desi Arnaz was a pretty darn good musician. You know, come to think of it, now that I'm somewhat deaf and slow, I understand Ricky's English better than his Spanish! [laughter] When Ricky starts into his rapid-fire Spanish, sometimes I just can't keep up!

Another part of the checkerboard for me concerns the nature of the disciplines and which way I go in disciplines. Though I never studied anthropology, I've always been interested in anthropology. And in history. So when I started teaching graduate courses in anthropology, I created a course called "Materials and Methods in Folklore" because we emphasized folklore. This is now the course on the introduction to graduate folklore at the University of Texas. In the course I would take students back to the beginnings of British anthropology in the nineteenth century, and it was quite obvious that anthropology was sanctioned and supported by the British Empire because of what it could show about controlling the natives.

This reminds me of a story I once heard. Now I can't cite you chapter and verse, but there was a celebrated instance of a native group in southern Africa that could not be controlled. And the anthropologists found that the center of power was located in the stool that the chief sat on, the actual material object! So the British officials arranged to steal that stool, and they then controlled the native group very easily. Another story, which I heard from some Argentine ethnographers, was that in the backwoods of Argentina there were still people—partly indigenous, partly mestizos—who believed that every seventh-born child was a witch. So when a seventh child was born, he or she would be strangled. The authorities tried to stop the practice, but they couldn't because they were dealing with a tightly closed traditional society. Finally, a very enlightened ladino governor arrived in the region who resolved to do something about the killing of these children. What he did was he publicized the news that he, the governor, would be the *padrino* (godfather) to every seventh-born child. That governor was a good anthropologist, whether he had studied anthropology or not. He had wisely and consciously created for the native group a conflict between their beliefs. Were people going to let the seventh-born live and risk that the child might really become a witch? Or were they going to kill the child and lose the opportunity to be able to say, "Mi compadre, el governador" (My child's godfather, the governor")? [laughter] So that stamped out the killing of the seventh child immediately. After many seventh children were born and it turned out they were not witches, it completely allayed that sort of thing. The British were especially good at using customs and beliefs to control people, particularly in Africa.

Now this does not mean that a lot of anthropologists were not interested in the people. But they had to fund their research, and this was the way that they were supported, by working with the colonial officials. The matter of prejudice was of course especially what interested me when I started working in anthropology. I was working with groups of people who were very, very tolerant, who thought of themselves as being completely devoid of prejudice. And yet even among them, there were those unconscious prejudices. I remember talking to a man once who was not an anthropologist, but was a graduate student as I was. He was fair-haired, and we were talking about not having to shave very often. I told him, "Well, you don't have to worry about it so much because your beard is blond." And he started lecturing me about thinking that blond hair was superior to black hair.

I thought, "Wait a minute. I never said anything of the sort." So I said, "You ask your wife whether at times she doesn't use peroxide on her arms." I knew her, and she had rather black hair. And she was there and said, "yes," that she used peroxide to bleach that hair so that it wasn't as noticeable. "The reason I'm complaining that I have to shave more than you do is that my dark hair shows more readily than yours. I'm not saying that your color of hair is superior to mine. You're expressing latent prejudice, and you're not aware of it."

I also noticed that the anthropological attitude was to use informants as though they were information machines—you pressed the right button and out came some data—and failed to see them as human beings. So I think that British anthropology was definitely an imperialist tool, and to a certain extent American anthropology as well. John Gregory Bourke is a good example of that. He used his knowledge of Indians to help the US Army control them in the late nineteenth century. Later, when he was posted on the border in south Texas, he did the same thing studying Mexicans.[47] But most modern anthropologists, I think, are really trying to understand. Unfortunately, they are betrayed by the fact that they sometimes have a lot of latent prejudices.

A Shadow on the Border

AMÉRICO PAREDES: As for my more recent work, I have come back to a novel, *The Shadow*, that I wrote while I was a graduate student. I was doing a number of things at the time that I first wrote it, but I had been playing with the idea of a story about postrevolutionary Mexico for a long time. The idea for this one also came from stories that I had heard. One of my uncles on my mother's side, a Manzano who lived on the Mexican side, would come to visit my mother, and he always had stories to tell. He was, as they say, *muy burlista* (a jokester). One of his stories concerned an *agrarista*, a supporter of land reform, from southern Mexico who had come to the Tamaulipas region and appropriated a good deal of land after the revolution. One of the local landowners whose land had been appropriated by the *agraristas* felt particularly aggrieved by these appropriations, and so he had hired a professional assassin to kill one of the *agrarista* leaders. The assassin did kill the man, but bungled his escape and so was caught by the *agraristas*. They were wise enough not to shoot the assassin out of hand. Instead, they took him to Matamoros, where he was interrogated and made to tell who had hired him to assassinate their leader. Of course, by that time, having heard how things had been botched, the landowner who had hired him had already escaped across the river to Brownsville.

And that was the basis of the story. My uncle's friend, the *presidente* of the *ejido* (collective farm), claimed that as he had been riding his horse at a walk down a little road in their *ejido*, the horse had been frightened by some kind of shadow. He learned later that on that day at almost precisely the same moment, the *agrarista* leader had been assassinated. The shadow he had seen, he believed, was the dead man's spirit fleeing this life.

So he told my uncle, "I know what's wrong with me. Estoy asustado" (I am suffering from fright sickness). But at the same time, my uncle's friend did not believe in those old folk superstitions. He was a rational and modern man. He no longer believed in those irrational folkways. So he was caught in an irresolvable internal conflict: between his emotions, which told him that he had seen the shadow of the dead man's spirit, and his rationality, which told him that dead men's spirits don't walk the earth. And he died of that impasse between the two. We all thought he died of some disease, from any one of a number of ailments prevalent along the border at the time. But more importantly, he thought he was dying of *susto*, or "fright sickness."[48] And that was the point that I used for the story.

I don't know what to think about the border now. Today, the border has become notorious because of all the drug trafficking and illegal border crossings, of course, and the fact that Mexico is in such a bad economic condition. Waves of poor people think that their future is in the United States. And so they come. Most of them stay along the border on the Mexican side. They don't do their economy any good. Yet many of them have lost their lands to ladinos, as in Chiapas. I feel a strong sympathy for people in Chiapas, Oaxaca, and places like that. NAFTA, of course, has brought the question of Mexican immigration to the forefront again, but the maquiladoras have as well. They have done a great deal in destroying the lower Rio Grande Valley on both sides because they built factories—they're American factories, of course—that pollute the river with a kind of pollution that didn't exist before, pollution that you can't get rid of with chlorine. Today you have cases of children being born without brains, anencephalic children. I have not been to the border for several years. In fact, it saddens me to go to the border now, especially across the river to Matamoros. Matamoros was once a nice little town, but with hoards of people coming up from the interior of Mexico with the intention of going across the border, the situation is now very bad, very bad.

During the revolution, the refugees coming over were a different kind of refugee. They were the upper classes, which of course could be executed if they stayed in Mexico. And they brought all they could with them. Gold, silver, jewels, and so on. And they tended to think, "Well, we're going to live in this country. Let's adapt." In the *Can-cionero*, I have a little piece of this zarzuela at the end of the book, which was sung by refugees that lived in Brownsville. "Como estamos en tejas el inglés hay que aprender para que con nuestros primos nos podamos entender" (Now that we're in Texas, we're going to have to learn English so that we can understand our cousins). [laughter]

The people that were descended from the original settlers, who felt a strong sense of indignation because they had been the *dueños* (pro-prietors) and now they were the servants, tried to avoid the Anglos as much as they could. And of course, in this way they were hurt-ing themselves. I disagreed with the LULACs in that they wanted us to forget our culture, our language. But I think it was very important for us to learn English to be able to defend ourselves. For example, the protest writer that I knew best when I was a boy was Perales, who wrote *En defensa de mi raza* in Spanish. Who read it? Spanish-speaking Mexicans. It didn't affect the Anglos. I thought that was the reason that I had to write in English. I was trying to reach a wider audience. So I think that was the division at the time. Later, in *Uncle Remus con Chile*, I do bring up a different kind of opposition. When I started working on that joke book, I thought in terms of Anglos versus *mexicanos* everywhere in Greater Mexico. But then I saw that cultural conflict has many layers. There was also the Mexican on both sides of the border against the *agringado*; *los de este lado contra los del otro lado*; *los de ambos lados en contra de los chilangos* (against the as-similated Mexican; those from this side of the border against those from the other side; and both of those against the central Mexican people).[49] Significant changes have taken place both in Mexico and the United States since I first started working.

But the complexity of this new border situation basically doesn't af-fect my original notion of Greater Mexico. Greater Mexico begins at the border of Guatemala and extends all the way to the Great Lakes, to New York, or wherever there are *mexicanos*. They vary from one place to another, but to my mind, they're basically the same. The differences are in degree of acculturation. Some of them don't speak Spanish anymore, or don't speak it very much. It's a problem. But it's still a Greater Mexican problem. Of course, I look at Greater Mexico from a cultural viewpoint, not from a political viewpoint. But now, perhaps the Mexican ruling party, the PRI [Partido Revolucionario Institucional], is finally going to break apart and changes will occur in Mexico. I hope that NAFTA does work for all the people. NAFTA looked very good for the ladino, but not for people in Chiapas who had been dispossessed of the land and who now have less and less to hope for. Unless Mexico is going to do what the United States did one time in their history: exterminate the native peoples. Or tried to, I should say.

I remember that once in the 1970s, that I was working with a group, a consortium, of universities to take a group of Chicanos to Mexico, to give them some idea of what Mexican culture was really like. We had tried to show them that we were connected to Mexico, to try to combat the idea that we Chicanos sprang out of nothing, that we had nothing to do with those Mexicans over there because we're Aztlán. One young man from Santa Barbara, I think, couldn't speak Spanish at all. He was very embarrassed about it. In Oaxaca, we visited some of the *pueblos indígenos* (indigenous villages), and of course, the Mexican official in charge of the visit showed us in a very paternalistic way that they were trying to get the Indians to learn Spanish and forget their ways. Those Chicanos were scandalized. "What you're doing to these people are what the gringos are doing to us," they howled. So there you have another complication to the story: how will Mexico deal with its own racism? That's a different kind of shadow on the border. It's a very complicated situation. I hope you may live to see the solution to it. I don't think I'll live long enough to see that day myself.

I think that's enough reminiscing. I'm starting to sound like one of my former colleagues in the English department who used to say when he went on too long, as he often did, "It's not that I'm verbose; it's just that I don't know when to stop talking!" But I do want to thank you for your patience in listening to me, and for allowing me to remember.

II

FICTIONS OF THE TRANSNATIONAL

IMAGINARY

3

THE CHECKERBOARD OF CONSCIOUSNESS

IN *George Washington Gómez*

> The true picture of the past flits by.
> The past can be seized only as an image
> which flashes up at the instant when it
> can be recognized and never seen again.
> . . . For every image of the past that is
> not recognized by the present as one of
> its own concerns threatens to disappear
> irretrievably. — Walter Benjamin, "Theses
> on the Philosophy of History"

In an essay entitled "Dialectical Materialism and the Fate of Humanity," the Caribbean revolutionary and thinker C. L. R. James observed that "Over a hundred years ago, Hegel said that the simplest reflection will show the necessity of holding fast the positive in the negative, the presupposition in the result, the affirmation that is contained in every negation, the future that is in the present. It is one of the signs of the advanced stage of human development that this is no longer a mere philosophical but a concrete question"(161). James's analyses of culture, writing, and politics are particularly instructive in the ways they consider issues of cultural production in relation to personal consciousness and across national boundaries and historical eras.[1] Here, as in other of his writings, James is concerned with situating the past in relation to the present in order to extract from it a politics for a possible future.[2] For James, this constitutes the crucial project of historical narrative. A different future appeared unimaginable if the past of the black subject could not be rewritten, since the past had never been captured from the standpoint of the black subject.³ Yet even while James was certainly correct to emphasize the epistemological and political implications of the relationship between the present and the future, the last few decades of the twentieth century proved to have been marked less by speculation on the future than by what Fredric Jameson has called "an inverted millenarianism." Jameson employs the phrase to describe the contemporary situation "in which premonitions of the future, catastrophic or redemptive, have been replaced by senses of the end of this or that (the end of ideology, art, or social class; the 'crisis' of Leninism, social democracy, or the welfare state, etc., etc.)" (*Postmodernism* 1).⁴ Given the astonishing rapidity with which near the twentieth century's end communism collapsed in the Soviet Union and its Eastern European former client states, one might understandably be tempted to add to Jameson's list of inverted millenarianisms the end of Marxism, communism, revolution, and even of history itself.⁵ In a very different vein, Jameson maintains that "taken together, all of these perhaps constitute what is increasingly called postmodernism" (*Postmodernism* 1). In 1984, when Jameson first wrote these words, he could hardly have anticipated the astounding rapidity with which these various finalities actually occurred by the end of the twentieth century.

If in the wake of these inverted millenarianisms we are indeed on the threshold of what the first George Bush enounced as "a new world order," then, with continuing crises worldwide, we still remain distinctly in the depths of an old *dis*order. This may hold even more true after the regime of the second George Bush. As it is, we are left to ponder what a truly new world order might look like in a post–cold war, post-Marxian, postcolonial, poststructuralist, postmodern, indeed, postcontemporary era. What affirmations might sublate each of these "posts" and their present negations? With the denunciation of all metanarratives by postmodernists, how are we to read today the possibility of liberatory solutions to crisis and to conceive of James's future in the present?

Border Writing and the Future in the Present

Cultural critics, ethnographers, and sociologists on both sides of the border seem to agree that if an answer to these questions exists, one of the places where it might be found is in the borderlands. To paraphrase the Mexican sociologist Roger Bartra, the special forms of hybridity emerging from the postnational terrain located between disenchantment and utopia that is the United States–Mexico border seems particularly rich in possibilities (13–14). As we shall see, the names for these possibilities presently are none other than *modernism, modernity*, and *modernization* in their shifting interplays of cultural, political, and economic structures. If modernization is something that happens to the economic base of a society, and modernism the ideological form that the superstructure takes in reaction to that development, then perhaps modernity, as Jameson suggests, "characterizes the attempt to make something coherent" out of the relationship among them (*Postmodernism* 310). Chicano and Chicana discourse, situated on the time-space border between North American and Latin American world experiences, constitutes a prime instance of the articulation of this interplay, in the form of discourse that has come to be known as border writing. Its modernity consists, as Jameson suggests, in the manner of its description of the ways persons experience producing and living with (or without) the products of the new industrial and cultural technologies.

According to the cultural critic Emily Hicks, border writing is that kind of postcontemporary discourse that exhibits a "multidimensional perception and nonsynchronous memory" (xxiii). Similarly, the critic Alfred Arteaga claims that in Chicano and Chicana poetry, "two nations are imagined in English and in Spanish and differentiate themselves at a common border, yet Chicano border space is a heteroglot interzone, a hybrid overlapping of the two" (277–78). The Chicano scholar Rafael Pérez-Torres claims that Chicano literature "signals a movement toward mestizaje, toward hybridization and crossbreeding on a cultural level that reflects the racial mestizaje which has produced the Chicano people" (8). *Nonsynchronicity, heteroglossia*, and *mestizaje* are the terms that seem to characterize the postmodern border at century's end with the disarming consistency of a near truism.

Yet in this bordered world space between Mexico and the United States, "the abrupt opposition between the traditional and the modern does not work," claims the Mexican ethnographer Néstor García Canclini (*Hybrid Cultures* 2). García Canclini contends that hybridization supersedes notions of mestizaje since the former term "almost always refers to religious fusions or traditional symbolic movements," while the latter tends to be limited to "racial" mixtures alone (11). In another essay, García Canclini refines his version of hybridity by explaining that it encompasses *"all the processes that combine discrete social structures or practices, which already existed in distinctly separate forms, to create new structures, objects, and practices in which the antecedents merge"* ("Rewriting" 279; emphasis original). Renato Rosaldo has pointed out, however, that "hybridity can imply a space betwixt and between two zones of purity," or it "can be understood as the ongoing condition of all human cultures, which contain no zones of purity because they undergo continuous processes of transculturation (two-way borrowing and lending between cultures)" (Foreword xv). The resolution between these two versions of hybridity and the mestizaje of the border remains a central problematic in the cultural studies of the borderlands. Bartra attempts to resolve the tension when he speaks about a "post-Mexican condition" emerging from the "constant transgression of all borders" in a hermeneutical escape from the cage of nationalism (14).

Despite divergences of emphasis about the nature of cultural difference at the border, then, these and other critics do agree that the multidimensionality and nonsynchronicity of border writing emerge from its capacity to see from both sides of the border simultaneously and describes a two-way process of borrowing and lending. Its characteristic heterogeneity issues from its ability to configure concepts from within two cultural contexts intertwining in the *"multitemporal heterogeneity* of each nation" (García Canclini, *Hybrid Cultures* 3, emphasis original). *Multidimensionality, hybridity,* and *heterogeneity* should be added as the watchwords for describing life in the modern borderlands and the border writing that it has occasioned. These differential qualities of the borderlands as a "heteroglot interzone" are nothing less than the dialogical equivalents of C. L. R. James's dialectical "future in the present."

In James's formulation we find a hint of how the unresolved tensions of these borderland concepts were first apprehended and interrogated in the moment of their emergence as the normative condition in the new era of globalization experienced on the border. Paraphrasing James, we might well ask, then, what affirmations were available to sublate present negations in these initial stagings of the future of the past? With the loss of synchronic, organic, uniform metanarratives, how are we to read today the possibility of liberatory solutions to crisis? Returning to James's notion of the future in the present might well offer a fruitful way of reading Paredes's literary productions for what they can teach us about the modernist origins of the processes of cultural and subjective formation that characterize life in our own postcontemporary age.

Américo Paredes is widely recognized as one of the chief architects of the domain of Mexican American cultural studies and is celebrated for having established the very ground for border writing. His best-known contribution to American cultural history remains *"With His Pistol in His Hand"* (1958), a study of ballads of US-Mexican border conflict. Renowned as an ethnographer, literary critic, and social historian for well over fifty years, Paredes also gained in the last years of his life a reputation for his accomplishments in the creative arts. In late 1990, Paredes furthered his study of the border by publishing a novel titled *George Washington Gómez*. Written between 1935 and 1940, the novel lay deferred by the pressures of everyday life for fifty years before its appearance. Set at the beginning of the twentieth century, written near mid-century, and published near the end of the century, Paredes's novel as a curiously polytemporal text addresses the central social issues of the modern era: the fate of the individual in relation to the collective experience of a community in the process of modernization. As a product of the Great Depression, the novel thus speaks from the past to the present. It also expresses from that past the status of today's ethnic subject and the formation of what Norma Alarcón has termed "ethno-nationalism" (57), issues that James characterized as elaborations of the future in the present.

In *George Washington Gomez*, we thus have a prefigurative instance of a new form of subjectivity captured in the process of construction from the discontinuous network of strands made up by the discourses and practices of politics, ideology, economics, history, sexuality, and language across national borders. Paredes's novel offers the future in the present in ways that both prepare for his own future ethnographic and literary historical work and anticipate the nexus between the sociopolitical and ethical-subjective in contemporary borderland representations of identity. The novel pulls from the residual elements of traditional culture the patterns that conceive the subject and then interrogates those patterns in the light of its dominant, modern formation to suggest other, untried designs for imagining a new ethnic consciousness in the form of "subject-effects."[6] As Paredes's novel shows, these subject-effects were already visible in the early moments of twentieth-century modernity.

Identity and Social Conflict

In an essay titled "The Problem of Identity in a Changing Culture," Paredes maintains that "conflict—cultural, economic, and physical—has been a way of life along the border between Mexico and the United States" (68). He adds that the patterns of conflict originated in the early nineteenth century in the present area of south Texas demarcated by the Nueces River to the north and the Rio Grande to the south (see figure 2, page 30). By the early twentieth century, these patterns of conflict had become constitutive of the entire discourse that has come to be known as the culture of the border.

Following Paredes, the anthropologist Renato Rosaldo reminds us that borders are hardly innocent spaces but rather "sites where identities and cultures intersect" (*Culture and Truth* 149). Gloria Anzaldúa, in sharp addition to both Paredes and Rosaldo, notes that "The U.S.-Mexican border *es una herida abierta* (is an open wound) where the Third World grates against the first and bleeds. And before a scab forms it hemorrhages again, the lifeblood of two worlds merging to form a third country—a border culture" (3). Rosaldo and Anzaldúa thus agree with Paredes that in those borderland contact zones between conflicting cultures, identity becomes a central problematic, linked explicitly to racial and economic, as well as to psychological and ethical, categories.

Because of their historical and geopolitical positioning as one of the easternmost outposts, first of colonial New Spain, and then of the newly independent Republic of Mexico, the people of the present-day south Texas region—people of Mexican culture—argues Paredes, experienced first the conflict with Anglo-American culture that would soon affect all of the Mexican borderland settlements of the Southwest. The narrative of this conflict in Texas can stand as a version of the history of New Mexico, Arizona, and California as well. That border history shows that in Texas by 1835, the Anglo-Texan fight for independence from Mexico had left the Mexican Texan a dispossessed foreigner on his own native land, culturally Mexican, politically American, but in reality not quite either. Like their ancestors who had been sent to settle the northern regions of the nation in order to fill the gap between the central Mexican seat of government to the south and the far-off Anglo-Texan colonies to the north, the inhabitants of the borderlands lived "an in-between existence" 73).

After 1835, this hallmark of Mexican American identity as an in-between existence became even more intensified. Paredes's *"With His Pistol in His Hand"* was a study of the border ballad tradition—the *corrido*—that arose chronicling this history of border conflict and its effects on Mexican American culture. Paredes there remarked that "borders and ballads seem to go together, and their heroes are all cast in the same mold . . . During the Middle Ages there lived in some parts of Europe, especially in border areas, a certain type of men whose fame has come down to us in legend and in song. . . . People composed ballads about men like these; legends grew about them, and they became folk heroes to be studied and argued about by generations of scholars" (xii). As the oral folk history of nineteenth-century Mexican American resistance to Anglo-American political and cultural power, affecting both subjective and collective identity construction, the Mexican American *corrido* functioned as an ideological expression of what Raymond Williams, in another idiom, calls the "residual" cultural order. "The residual, by definition," says Williams,

> has been effectively formed in the past, but it is still active in the cultural process, not only and often not at all as an element of the past, but as an effective element of the present. Thus certain experiences, meanings, and values which cannot be expressed or substantially verified in terms of the dominant culture, are nevertheless lived and practiced on the basis of the residue—cultural as well as social—of some previous social and cultural institution or formation. (*Marxism and Literature* 122)

These lived "experiences, meanings and values" of traditional Mexican American communities (effectively formed in the past, but still active in the present cultural process) expressed in nineteenth-century and early twentieth-century *corridos* centered on folk heroes who represented the community's collective resistance to the newly dominant Anglo-American power. Typically in the *corrido* of intercultural conflict, a hardworking, peace-loving *mexicano* is goaded by Anglo outrages into violence, causing him to defend his rights and those of others in his community against the *rinches*, the border Spanish rendering of Texas Ranger.[7]

Reluctantly, but with deadly conviction, the protagonist of the "heroic Border *corrido*" arises "with his pistol in hand" (Paredes, *"With His Pistol in His Hand"* 232) to defend his community and to represent iconically in the idiom of heroic male discourse the communal fight against injustice. The *corridos* memorializing the deeds of these heroes tend to be multifaceted "*narratives, reflexive,* and propositional in semantic intent and *poetic* in technique" (McDowell 45, emphasis original). By the end of the nineteenth century, the *corrido* had emerged as the dominant socially symbolic act of the Mexican American community, inventing in its ritualized performance the very possibility of a narrative community and instantiating the idea of a unified and legitimate transnational subject whose life of struggle was worthy of being told.

George Washington Gómez is set against this history of cultural-political conflict chronicled in the United States–Mexico border ballad. It takes especially as its moment the 1915 uprising in south Texas by Mexican Americans attempting to create a Spanish-speaking Republic of the Southwest. Dismissed in official histories by Anglo-American historians as "Mexican bandits," the *sediciosos* (seditionists) were in fact acting under a carefully considered revolutionary manifesto, the "Plan de San Diego." That manifesto called for a union of Texas Mexicans with American Indians, African Americans, and Asian Americans to fight social and political injustice. Answering deep-seated feelings of anger and frustration over Anglo oppression and injustice, the seditionist movement of 1915 was an early expression of many of the same grievances that later motivated the Chicano movement and other social movements of the 1960s. Its manifesto constituted an early enunciation of the viability of coalition politics among internal Third World groups in the United States.[8]

Los Sediciosos

In 1915, bands of armed men under the leadership of Aniceto Pizaña and Luis de la Rosa raided Anglo military posts, ranches, rail lines, and depots along the border. In the end, the seditionists were crushed by the power and numbers of the American military forces brought in to quell the uprising. Of the major seditionist movement leaders, de la Rosa withdrew from the fray early on, while Pizaña was arrested on the Mexican side of the border by Carranza officials and detained in Mexico City. Bloody terror swiftly followed revolutionary resistance as the Texas state police, the infamous Texas Rangers, set out to enact reprisals against the entire Mexican American population of south Texas.[9] *Corridos* immediately appeared to articulate the seditionist position, to memorialize it, and to offer a critique of it. One version of these *corridos* recounts the events in this manner:

En mil novecientos quince,
que dias tan calurosos!
voy a cantar estos versos,
versos de los sediciosos.

En ese punto de Norias
ya merito les ardia
a esos rinches desgraciados
muchas balas les llovia.

Ya la mecha esta encendida
por los puros mexicanos,
y los que van a pagarla
son los mexicotejanos.

Ya la mecha esta encendida
con azul y colorado,
y los que van a pagarla
van a ser los de este lado.

Ya la mecha esta encendida,
muy bonita y colorada,
y la vamos a pagar
los que no debemos nada.

[In nineteen hundred fifteen
How hot were those days of perdition!
I am going to sing you these verses,
Verses of those in sedition.

In that place known as Norias
How warmly they burned
Those disgraceful Rangers
Met with bullets that stormed.

And now the match is lit
By the true-born Mexicans
And those who will pay for it
Are the Mexicotexans.

Now the match is lit
glowing bluer and redder
and those who will extinguish it
Are on this side of the border.

Now the match is lit
so beautiful and red,
and we're going to pay
Who owe nothing instead.][10]

Before 1915, the *corrido* genre had served as a folk vehicle for the expression of the racial and cultural tension that had existed along the United States–Mexico border since at least the mid-nineteenth century. It also functioned symbolically as a representation of the integrated character of the organic Mexican community from which it arose.[11] "Los sediciosos," the *corrido* printed above, is a classic instance of how these ballads appear spontaneously and anonymously in the wake of social crises to analyze and commemorate the events of which they speak.[12] At the same time, "Los sediciosos" stands as a turning point away from the unitary form of the *corrido* toward a more complex vision of the community, one faced with the ambiguities of modernization and the emerging transnational character of the region. With the regional economies of northern Mexico and the American Southwest in the process of "full-scale industrialization and commercialization," the borderlands were emerging as "both a barrier and a bridge between nations" (E. Young 20). This twentieth-century song strikingly alters the organic quality of the nineteenth-century *corrido* as a genre and a form, expressing a cohesive sense of community. Now we hear instead the voiced expression of growing divisions within the twentieth-century Mexican border community, a bifurcation between the *puros mexicanos* (true-born Mexican nationals), on one side, who have ignited the rebellion, and the *mexicotejanos* (American-born Texas Mexicans), on the other side, who will have to pay for the lighting of the fuse.[13]

And there was hell to pay. In the aftermath of the seditionist uprising, hundreds of innocent Mexican American farmers and ranchers were slaughtered by Texas Rangers, summarily executed without trial at even the slightest suspicion of possible alliance with or even sympathy for the seditionists. Many were murdered simply because they happened to be working near sites of seditionist action, making for terrifying instances of guilt by contingency. This reign of terror virtually cleared south Texas of landholding Mexican Americans, making feasible the Anglo development of the region into its capitalist agribusiness formation in the 1920s. Montejano points out that "the agrarian development of this period can be seen as the last in a series of crises that eroded the centuries-old class structure of the Mexican ranch settlement. By the 1920s, the Texas Mexican people had generally been reduced, except in a few border counties, to the status of landless and dependent wage laborers" (*Anglos and Mexicans* 114). Before 1848, the vast majority of *mexicano* laborers had been employed as skilled or semiskilled workers on the farms and ranches of the landholding Mexican elite. When the more diversified market economy introduced by Americans entering the region after the mid-nineteenth century supplanted the traditional ranching economy of the Southwest, it also transformed the region's social structure and cultural life. The historian David Guitiérrez thus argues that "on the broadest level, Mexican Americans experienced vast structural displacement as the local economy shifted rapidly from a pastoral one, based primarily on ranching and subsistence farming, to a capitalist one, increasingly based on commercial agriculture, trade, and later, the large-scale infrastructural development of the region" (*Walls and Mirrors* 24).

At virtually the same time that C. L. R. James was exploring how the past is conceived in relation to the present and the future by subjects whose status as subjects has been open to question, Américo Paredes was completing a novel attempting to reconceptualize the past in order to imagine a different set of symbols of the future. *George Washington Gómez* situates us in the midst of the deliquescent historical transformations occasioned by the modernization of the border, changes that had been underway since the middle of the nineteenth century but were now coming to a head in the early twentieth century with the full-blown industrialization of agriculture. In the heroic *corrido* of border conflict, the warrior hero is doomed to honorable but certain defeat in his fight against the limitless power of Americanization and modernization. Paredes's novel takes its tonal key, however, not from narrative as *romance corrido*, as an allegory of vindication and redemption in defeat. Instead, he turns to the pathos expressed in a song like "Los sediciosos" concerning the tragic fates of those innocents from whom was exacted the cost of that bitter transitional defeat. Paredes's subjects for the substance of his narrative are not warrior heroes but the nonheroic innocents who dwell darkly in the shadows of history and live its internal contradictions and hierarchical complexities in the mode of irony.

Interpellating the Subject

The social critic Richard Johnson has claimed that one may arrive at a functional definition of that slippery term *culture* indirectly by focusing on related key words such as *consciousness* and *subjectivity* (45). *Identity*, as the signifier of differentiation within consciousness and subjectivity, implies these terms as well. Identification is central to naming. "When we name things," says Paredes, "we give them a life of their own; we isolate them from the rest of our experience. By naming ourselves, we affirm our own identity; we define by separating ourselves from others, to whom we give names different from our own" ("Problem of Identity" 31). What we cannot name, we cannot talk about. When we give a name to something, as when we assign an identity, we may empower ourselves because now we can think and talk about what constitutes that identity. In *George Washington Gómez*, the issue of identity is raised from the first pages of the novel as we meet the main characters—Gumersindo and María Gómez, María's mother, and her brother Feliciano García—discussing the naming of the child born in the midst of the seditionist uprising and its bloody aftermath:

> The baby, meanwhile, was feeding greedily at his mother's breast. Born a foreigner in his native land, he was fated to a life controlled by others. At that very moment his life was being shaped, people were already running his affairs, but he did not know it. Nobody considered whether he might like being baptized or not. Nobody had asked him whether he, a Mexican, had wanted to be born in Texas, or whether he had wanted to be born at all. The baby left the breast and María, his mother, propped him up in a sitting position. She looked at him tenderly. "And what shall we name him?" she wondered aloud. (15)[14]

The answer to her question exemplifies one version of US-Mexican subject formation in the American West and Southwest, an American postcolonial variant of the "processes of subjectification" that Homi Bhabha has identified with colonial discourse and the formation of the colonial subject in general (*Nation and Narration* 5–9). We already know the literal answer to her question: the baby is the title character. Positioned as a subject by the material actions and symbolic rituals of the community into which he has been born, the child also has a figural presence and a prefigural future in the present already underwritten by the class, race, and gender relations in which he will live his life. Indeed, the naming ritual that we witness at the beginning of his story invokes the power of baptism and makes concrete the abstract process of subjectification that has already configured the child even before his birth.

In response to María's question as to a proper name for the child, the other characters, her husband, mother, and brother, offer each in turn a variety of symbolically loaded names for the child. Each option indicates an alternative narrative within which the child's destiny might unfold. So, in series, we get first, Crisósforo, a name of grandiose and idiosyncratic proportions, considered as a sign of the baby's presumed singularity and in relation to the legend of Saint Christopher, *Christoferens*, the Christ-bearer and bringer of light. Next, we get the name of José Angel, a name also serving as a mark of traditional religious value, but focusing on patriarchal descent ("Joseph") and on the child as a presumed harbinger of spirituality ("angel"). The names of Venustiano and Cleto, alluding to Mexican revolutionary leader Venustiano Carranza and to one of the leaders of the ongoing sedition, Anacleto (literally, "the elect"), are suggested as signs of revolutionary commitment. And then we even get the father's own name, Gumersindo, a name of Germanic origin indicating strength and offered as a cipher of ancestral continuity. It is considered and, curiously, rejected like the rest. Finally, the child's mother speaks: " 'I would like my son . . .' she began. She faltered and reddened. 'I would like him to have a great man's name. Because he's going to grow up to be a great man who will help his people.' " Gumersindo responds jocularly, saying, "My son . . . is going to be a great man among the Gringos," and then adds in sudden inspiration, "A Gringo name he shall have!" asking, "Is he not as fair as any of them?" (16). Gumersindo thus introduces into this symbolic moment of subject formation the reality of the issues of caste, race, and color. We might see this moment as an exemplary instance of Althusserian interpellation, the process whereby an "individual" is "appointed as a subject in and by the specific familial ideological configuration in which it is 'expected' once it has been conceived" (Althusser 176). Once appointed as a subject, the configured individual may then respond to the pressures of ideology through the functioning of the category of the subject. At issue immediately in the novel, then, as the baby is called to a determinative racial and national identity, are questions of subjectivity and consciousness, especially as these concepts relate to culture and citizenship.

Trying to recall what "great men" the gringos have had, Gumersindo considers before exclaiming: "I remember . . . Wachinton. Jorge Wachinton" (16). The grandmother's attempt to say the strange name "Washington" is processed in an even more pronouncedly Mexican form, emerging phonetically as "Guálinto . . . Guálinto Gómez" (17). " 'It's a good name,' said Gumersindo. 'How do you like it, *viejita*?' María smiled at the term of endearment. 'It is a very good name,' she said" (17). And so both names stick: the official and formally antithetical name of George Washington Gómez, and the familiarly transcodified name of Guálinto Gómez. The present clash of identities that is the substance of Guálinto Gómez's future life is instantiated at this originary moment when the various discourses that might have ordered and will order his life are signaled to us. A "foreigner in his native land," the child in his story will follow out the commands implicit in the ideologies unconsciously projected in his "very good name," ideologies that will position him as a subjected representation of the imaginary relations to the real conditions of existence in the early twentieth-century borderlands of south Texas.[15]

Each of the names—those considered and rejected, as well as the one chosen and immediately transformed into its dialectal equivalent—signals a different set of speech genres and promises to inscribe the child into a particular discursive history. As M. M. Bakhtin points out, speech genres, certain combinations of forms of utterances, underwrite permissible locutions in daily life and, more important, serve as normative restraints on our most intimate intentions; they form the legitimate borders of what we can say and not say ("The Problem of Speech Genres" 60–62). The textual instance at hand represents two sets of such speech genres at work. On the one hand, we have the utopian hopes and dreams of the father and mother, who optimistically project a future of reconciled differences with their crossed references to the child's promised Mexican and American destinies. Counter to the evidence of their own historical experience, they innocently believe that the two destinies can cross. On the other hand, we have the historically validated misgivings of the child's uncle Feliciano concerning the impact of those crossed destinies on Guálinto's actual lived experience. As he departs the scene of ritual naming, Feliciano, soon to be the child's surrogate father, sings some verses from one of the most prominent of the *corridos* of border conflict, "El corrido de Jacinto Treviño": "En la cantina de Bekar, se agarraron a balazos" (In Baker's saloon, they shot it out).[16] Prefiguring the violent murder of the gentle Gumersindo by Texas Rangers in the following chapter, the song activates an entirely different speech genre to guide the unpredictable interaction between the child's Mexican nurturing and American enculturing.[17]

The interplay between these binary oppositions moves the novel's ideological plot, but in decidedly more complicated patterns than the dialectics of difference structuring the border *corrido* normally allow. In neither context is *difference* simply a code word for liberal tolerance and homogenizing complacencies. Nor is *dialectics* here simply synonymous with synthesis. In both instances, we have moved considerably beyond the politics of consensus.[18] While dialectic in the Hegelian sense can be contained within a single consciousness overcoming contradiction in a monologic view, the dialectic we encounter in the borderlands depends on the centrality of an ongoing dialogue between contending discourses, opposed in contra-diction, that cannot be resolved into one voice and thus has no equivalent in other conceptual systems.[19] For this reason, one special way in which the dialectic may be defined under these conditions is "as a conceptual coordination of incommensurabilities" (Jameson, *A Singular Modernity* 64). How and why this is so forms the substance of the narrative of the life of Guálinto Gómez.

The Problem of the School

The continuing instability of the title character's name signals the precariousness of this ideological plot throughout the remainder of the novel. In crucial early scenes, before he enters the American schools,

the child is known as Guálito Gómez, a name he and his uncle like
to explain is "Indian" in order to forestall the complications of having
always to legitimate Guálinto's right as a Texas Mexican to the name
of George Washington. These idyllic preschool years will later serve
as the edenic counterpoint, the largely untroubled duration of no-
time before the fall into history, that might ironically reemerge to
save him for history. In the narrated present, however, once the child
enters school, his heart and mind become the battleground of cultural
hegemony:

> So, . . . [Guálinto] began to acquire an Angloamerican self, and as the years
> passed, . . . he developed simultaneously in two widely divergent paths.
> In the schoolroom he was an American; at home and on the playground
> he was a Mexican. Throughout his early childhood these two selves grew
> within him without much conflict, each an exponent of a different tongue
> and a different way of living. The boy nurtured these two selves within
> him, each radically different and antagonistic to the other, without realiz-
> ing their separate existences.
>
> It would be several years before he fully realized that there was not one
> single Guálinto Gómez. That in fact there were many Guálinto Gómezes,
> each of them double like images reflected on two glass surfaces of a show
> window. The eternal conflict between two clashing forces within him pro-
> duced a divided personality, made up of tight little cells independent and
> almost entirely ignorant of each other, spread out over his consciousness,
> mixed with one another like squares on a checkerboard. (147)

To raise the question of identity as this passage does is not to celebrate
it or fix it as something that is knowable and known as an a priori. We
are nowhere near an era of political correctness and identity politics.
What follows instead in the course of the narrative of Guálinto's history is a systematic exploration of the creation of a normalized notion
of identity in the early twentieth-century modern borderlands from
out of the dual fragments of Mexican and American social forms. This
normalization is to be accomplished as much by the American school
system, which attempts to pass off ideology in the guise of truth, as
by the economic system, which commodifies the complex differences
of identity by reflecting the multiplicity of Guálinto's selves as one
single specular image in the "glass surfaces of a show window" in the
marketplace.

Equally at work, even if repressed from the conscious levels of the narrative, is the fixation of Mexican gender ideology that identifies Guálinto as a belated heir to the tradition of armed resistance represented most vividly by his uncle Feliciano, the true inheritor of the warrior tradition. Given this perplexing interplay of determining racial and gender discourses, from this point on, identity will not be available except in the form of a fantastical mediation. That mediation, figured in this passage by the cubistic image of the checkerboard of modernist consciousness, becomes like a space of specular performance, providing a scene from what Wallace Stevens, writing contemporaneously with Paredes, would call in his "Notes toward a Supreme Fiction" a "Theater of Trope" (397).[20] The mise-en-scène of Guálinto's performance in his theater of trope includes the existential materials of daily life along with those psychological ones from the deep, raw material of social life in which the identity form is imprinted in the early versions of an emergent twentieth-century mass culture.

This catoptrical theater of reflecting showcase windows, as Walter Benjamin has argued in another but related context, is not accidental but symbolic, a representational stratagem associated with the devaluation of the world of subjects by the very nature of the commodity form ("Theory of Remembrance" 162). The magic mirrors of the marketplace exist precisely to confound identity and blur the relation of the subject to commodities in the object world mingled with its reflected selves in the reflecting glass. They allow the passerby to see him- or herself reflected on the "glass surfaces of a show window" in equivocal illumination, with pleasing amplitude, and illusory integrity in relation to commodities.[21]

In a subsequent passage, the connection between consciousness and the mirror motif veers away from tropes of reflection, inner consciousness, and subjective integrity toward the related and even larger matters of national identity and social physiology:

> Consciously [Guálinto] considered himself a Mexican. He was ashamed of the name his dead father had given him, George Washington Gómez. He was grateful to his Uncle Feliciano for having registered him in school as "Guálinto" and having said that it was an Indian name. He spoke Spanish, literally as his mother tongue; it was the only language his mother would allow him to use when he spoke to her. The Mexican flag made him feel sentimental, and a rousing Mexican song would make him feel like yelling. The Mexican national hymn brought tears to his eyes, and when he

said "we" he meant the Mexican people. . . . Of such matter were made the basic cells in the honeycomb that made up his personality. (147–48)

But even here, the initial characterization turns out to be romantically, not to say, sentimentally, incomplete. It implies that we might be able at some point to read the identity of the subject correctly in relation to its experience of the Mexican object world that fills the private, affective world, "literally as his mother tongue." From this view, determining the position of the subject in the real would be enough to recognize the content of ideology and its source. A particular experience of reality could thus be said to set the content of ideology. Paredes denies, however, that the identity of the subject may be understood solely by virtue of its conscious positioning for, as we learn, in addition to the "cells that made up his personality" as a Mexican, there are others that make Guálinto Gómez something else again:

> There was also George Washington Gómez, the American. He was secretly proud of the name his more conscious twin, Guálinto, was ashamed to avow publicly. George Washington Gómez secretly desired to be a full-fledged, complete American without the shameful encumberment of his Mexican race. He was the product of his Anglo teachers and the books he read in school, which were all in English. He felt a pleasant warmth when he heard the "Star-Spangled Banner." It was he who fought the British with George Washington and Francis Marion the Swamp Fox, discovered pirate treasure with Long John Silver, and got lost in a cave with Tom Sawyer and Becky Thatcher. Books had made him so. (147–48)

The narrator of the novel, then, would have us see Guálinto's identity and formation as a subject as an effect of an immense network of causal strands that includes the state public school and its lists of required readings. But that network also includes more broadly "politics, ideology, economics, history, sexuality, language," as Gayatri Spivak has argued in relation to other colonial situations ("Subaltern Studies" 13). Here, the official histories of American colonial contexts and revolutions crowd in against those instilled by the oral traditions of the formal and informal schooling Guálinto receives as a Mexican American. This other schooling, attained in the legends, beliefs, and folk customs of his family, including most prominently through the border *corrido*, dispels the possibility of there existing a single, homogeneous, and authentically determining cause for this particular subject.

Still, Guálinto's American self is not to be read simply as a latent repression of the Other, ready to break through from unconscious levels of the psyche to overwhelm the manifest Mexican identity of his conscious self. The mediation between the terms is infinitely more complex than the classical scenario of true and false consciousnesses might imagine:

> In school Guálinto/George Washington was gently prodded toward complete Americanization. But the Mexican side of his being rebelled. Immigrants from Europe can become Americanized in one generation. Guálinto, as a Mexicotexan, could not. Because, in the first place, he was not an immigrant come to a foreign land. Like other Mexicotexans, he considered himself part of the land on which his ancestors had lived before the Anglotexans had come. And because, almost a hundred years before, there had been a war between the United States and Mexico, and in Texas the peace had not yet been signed.
>
> In all this he was no different from other Mexicotexan school children in Jonesville. (148)

Realizing for the first time that he is neither a Mexican nor an American, Guálinto, like "other Mexicotexan children in Jonesville," lacks even the advantage of his parents who, as combatants in a racial and class war against an implacable enemy, did know who they were precisely because "in Texas the peace had not yet been signed."

Ratios of the Self

For the parents, conceptions of identity and subjectivity imparted by the traditional social environment are available and validated in many ways, not the least of which is folklore.[22] The narrative of their identities, troubled and painful as it might be, is nonetheless ascertainable, reinforced by the icons of Mexican material culture, and especially by the expressions of the popular imagination: the jokes, riddles, popular sayings, legends, and songs—in sum, the entire repertoire of speech genres of their collective vernacular life experiences that name a way of life. These forms of typical utterances express the specific themes associated with communal identity in highly standardized ways. The limits of the meanings of such expressions are rigidly determined.[23] In the traditional *corrido*, for example, the most formal articulation of

the folkloric speech genres that name the embattled form of this identity, the fate of the individual and of the community are not separate.
Rather, self and community are imagined as if integrated in a synthetic symbolic structure, offering a semblance of aesthetic coherence,
as among the various stanzas of a *corrido*. Folklore is the symbolic
logic through which their differential, Spanish-language, Mexican,
racialized, gendered, and economic being can be integrated with only
the most tenuous of links to the official English-language, American worldview and its different "conception of the world and life"
(Gramsci, *Osservazioni* 215).[24]

For the children, however, an altogether different ratio of speech
genres and symbolic logic applies. The schools, the church, conventional party politics, the emerging mass media, and most enticingly,
consumer commodity culture all play them into the domains of locutions beyond their understanding. For them, "gently prodded *toward
complete Americanization*" rather than violently repressed for being
Mexican, subjected to the interpellative work of both traditional
Mexican folklore and the ideological system of assimilation to American modernity, identity both is and is not what it seems to be. Learning to speak across these two sets of speech genres means learning
to negotiate the restrictive possibilities of what can be spoken within
each set. Within this doubled system of generic control—American
on the one hand, and Mexican on the other—historical forces and
social trends that do not sort out into clean antitheses shape the children. Reality is far more complex and differentiated. In this borderlands version of Du Boisian double consciousness, priority cannot be
easily assigned to one or the other because of the constant give-and-
take between the normative impulses of the one versus the even more
normative qualities of the other's everyday speech.

Consequently, what is at stake for the children is not simply a life-
style choice of mere preference between neatly opposed alternatives
but a more fundamental epistemological crisis of subject formation.
Should Guálinto remain a Mexican, or should he become an assimilated American? Does he have a choice? If he does not, then who or
what chooses? As Paredes shows, the ratios and proportions between
those alternative formations are not static, but always in the process
of being made and unmade. Moreover, the sorting out of the shifting relations among those ratios of the self involve, inescapably, the
narrative *telling* of their evolving configuration.[25] The epistemological
crisis of the borderlands subject can be most meaningfully resolved

only allegorically, in narrative, as a problem of social aesthetics. Let us see how and why this is so.

Agency and Subject-Effects

In *George Washington Gómez*, American and Mexican systems of enculturation each acquire causal status by seeming separately to produce the effect of an organic, primary, active subject. Guálinto the American would thus be seen as the product of a pluralist American melting-pot ideology, while, simultaneously, Guálinto the Mexican would be the shaped product of a sustaining traditional world. But as Paredes brilliantly shows, in the early modernist era of the twentieth century, the apparently homogeneous, deliberative subject of borderland cultures emerges less as either a sovereign and causal, or a dependent and affected consciousness than as the doubly crossed subject-effect of both American ideological and Mexican folkloric systems.[26] Rather than full subjective agency, we are given the simulation of fullness and agency experienced acutely as the in-betweenness of the borderlands of culture.

These double Mexican and American culture systems each acquire within their own spheres a presumed priority by virtue of their apparent production of a formed subject. However, this subject is then also taken to be an active causal agent, itself willfully capable of producing and reproducing the effects of both the American ideological and Mexican folkloric configurations within which its own singular fate is said to evolve. Hence what might initially have been conceived of as a double cultural systemic cause must now be regarded as the dual effects of a (bifurcated) sovereign subject. Concurrently, the presumed sovereign subject remains the affected product of ideology and tradition. Within these doubly crossed negations, the sovereign Mexican American subject, initially conceived as a formed effect and then as a forming agent, now takes the form of what Gayatri Spivak has described as the prototypical subaltern subject. The subaltern subject appears as "the effect of an effect, and its positing a metalepsis, or the substitution of an effect for a cause" ("Subaltern Studies" 13). This metaleptic ground demarcates the social space of the bordered subject as well, encompassing both the figural construction of willed behaviors and the elaboration of ideological processes of subjectification. Now, if in the wake of this double deconstruction the category of the subject is to remain a viable one, it must henceforth be seen as the marshalling of a category that is at once essential and provisional, sovereign and bifurcated. It is a compelling form of what Spivak terms the "strategic use of positivist essentialism in a scrupulously visible political interest" ("Subaltern Studies" 13). This doubly crossed figure constitutes Paredes's proleptic rendering of the future in the present, an elegant prefiguration of the bordered subject of postmodern Chicano and Chicana narrative.

Other types of national narratives constructed to provide the etiologies of identity, such as narratives of the so-called immigrant experience, for instance, simply will not apply to the situation of such bordered, *trans*cultured subjects. Positioned in the borderlands of culture, metaleptic figures such as the one Paredes depicts in Guálinto Gómez exist on a much more problematic and unstable ground of heterogeneous determinations and crisscrossed negations: "Hating the Gringo one moment with an unreasoning hatred, admiring his literature, his music, his material goods the next. Loving the Mexican with a blind fierceness, then almost despising him for his slow progress in the world" (Paredes, *George Washington Gómez* 150). In the foreword to "Black Roses," writing in his own voice, Paredes describes Guálinto's predicament by noting that "the Mexico-Texan is alone," confused in social, racial, and even linguistic terms: "Small wonder then that such an individual is confused even in ordinary conversation by his bilingualism. When he tries to express himself beyond the realm of everyday thoughts, he finds his mind divided as his heart has been. Especially true is this since thought, customs, ideals, and his literary forms are as different as they are in English and Spanish. The result is a struggle between the two languages for mastery in the individual."[27]

The remainder of Guálinto's story is concerned with what it would take, materially and psychologically, to imagine a dialogue between the two languages vying for mastery within his consciousness, to envision how one could conceptualize what one can by definition not yet conceive since it has no equivalent in current experience.[28] Formed ideationally as a mirror image of the Anglo-American subject and against the traditional Mexican subject, Guálinto becomes the precursor of a new middle class, partially assimilated and wholly alone, the quintessential buffer between Anglo-American and Mexican American modernity. Paredes's novel attempts meticulously to imagine the affirmation that is contained in the crossing of these negations and in what they signal about the future in the present. The conceptualization of identity offered at the novel's end can thus in no way be taken as a precritically ideal one, a teleological arc of completed development. Instead, in the end, Guálinto's identity remains sociologically and dialogically problematic to a disturbing degree.

The term *identity* has had as complicated a history, as has the other term, *culture*, to which I have related it throughout this discussion. Identity, too, might be best approached functionally and indirectly, rather than essentially and substantially. Theodor Adorno has argued that

> in the history of modern philosophy, the word "identity" has had several meanings. It designated, for example the unity of personal consciousness: that an "I" remains the same throughout all its experiences. This is what was meant by the Kantian "I think, which should be able to accompany all my representation [*Vorstellungen*]." Then again identity meant what was supposed to be regularly or nomethetically [*gesetzlich*] present in all rational beings, or in other words thought as logical universality; including the equivalence with itself of every object of thought, the simple A = A. Finally, the epistemological meaning: that subject and object, however mediated, coincide. The first two levels of meaning are by no means strictly differentiated, even in Kant. Nor is this the result of a careless use of language. Identity rather shows up as the zone of indifference between psychology and logic within idealism itself. (*Negative Dialectics* 142 n.)[29]

These several versions of identity with which we have been concerned —psychological coherence, rational congruence, epistemological mediation—hint at two others also at play in the complexity of identity of Paredes's novel. The identity of the legal subject, sanctioned in its individuality by the state apparatus and represented before the law as a citizen, and the identity of the economic subject, reified into a singularly commodifiable object, are versions still to be considered briefly. Of the first three notions of identity that Adorno contemplates, we have already said enough to establish the case that Paredes's novel acknowledges their force in the critical construction of a subject within a given social position.

However, as I have suggested, it is not the psychological, the logical, or the epistemological that determine the identity of the subject alone. Historically, the languages of US-Mexican self-formation have also spoken the discourses of the citizen-subject and the economic subject. The former speaks to the subjectivity of citizenship as legal status, that is, as full membership in a particular political community. The latter is concerned with subjectivity as economic activity, where the extent and quality of one's subjectivity is a function of one's participation in the economic bounty of a community.[30] For the sake of brevity, I will treat these forms of identity together, as different yet similarly articulated with the psychological, rational, and epistemological forms prescribed by the public educational and private familial roles within which an identity is created for the legal and economic subject.

On the Periphery of Capitalism

Paredes's novel uses the genre of the realistic historical narrative to express this intersection of discursive formations and real control of the means of production and coercion, working in consonance to produce an economic and cultural hegemony in south Texas:

> For more than half a century Jonesville remained a Mexican town, though officially a part of the United States. A few English-speaking adventurers moved in, married into Mexican landowning families, and became a ruling élite allied with their Mexican in-laws. But Spanish remained the language of culture and politics, and Mexican money was legal tender in local commerce. Then came the railroad early in the 20th century, and with it arrived the first real-estate men and the land-and-title companies, and a Chamber of Commerce, of course, which renamed the little town "Jonesville-on-the-Grande" and advertised it to suckers from up north as a paradise on earth: California and Florida rolled up into one. Mexicans labored with axe and spade to clear away the brush where the cattle of their ancestors once had roamed. To make room for truck farming and citrus groves. And the settlers poured in from the U. S. heartland, while Mexicans were pushed out of cattle raising into hard manual labor. It was then also that Jonesville-on-the-Grande came to have a Mexican section of town. (36)

This passage from *George Washington Gómez* gives the history of the American Southwest in brief. It describes one version of how US-

Mexican identity was constructed and mediated through the struggle over language, culture, politics, capital, and real property. It relates the process by which Mexican American enclaves of precapitalist organization, formerly tolerated and exploited, were transformed by the "prodigious expansion of capital into hitherto noncommodified arenas" (Jameson, *Postmodernism* 36).[31] This is the penetration into the local scene of the Southwest by what Ernest Mandel has identified as the third stage of late capitalism, namely, multinational capital.[32] Largely self-sufficient Mexican farms and ranches in existence before the advent of market capitalism had been destroyed by force of arms and the penetration of a market economy into the American Southwest following imperialist expansion after 1848 and throughout the remainder of the nineteenth century. The social transformations were completed by the alliances through marriage of "a few English-speaking adventurers" with "Mexican landowning families" to become a new "ruling élite." These new class alliances, plus the shift from one mode of production to another, now made what used to be a Mexican town into an American city with a Mexican barrio.

In this last episode of what might be called the narrative underwriting of American Manifest Destiny, the imaginative topography of the contemporary borderlands of culture comes starkly into view. And what we see is the cultural resistance to American "capitalization of the margin" (Flores and Yúdice 59), the transformation of the Mexican Southwest into an American winter garden of agricorporate dimensions. Paredes's novel represents the loss of one mode of production and the entry into another as the moment of entry into modernity.

While in the previous era of subsistence ranching and small farming awesomely static feudal hierarchies of class and gender reigned, severely limiting the experience of freedom by the poor and by women, the logic of that society nonetheless produced relations of identity that provided a vision of totality. Experience coincided with the recognition of the social form that governed the experience. Now, with the passage from feudal patriarchal forms to classical market and monopoly capital forms during the mid- to late nineteenth and early twentieth centuries, fissures and contradictions emerged between the lived experience of individuals and the structure of the conditions of existence of that experience.[33]

The transformation of the political geography occasioned by these structural shifts at the level of the base also occasioned a cultural re-mapping at the level of the superstructure as the newly imposed borders between nations and peoples emerged as the loci of subjective redefinition and resignification. In the wake of these material and symbolic transformations, identity thus becomes in Paredes's novel what the social critics Juan Flores and George Yúdice have described as the nature of Latino identity in general. It is an identity that finds itself perpetually attempting "a fending off of schizophrenia, of that pathological duality born of contending cultural worlds and, perhaps, more significantly, of the conflicting pressures toward both exclusion and forced incorporation" (60). Or, as Paredes's narrator at one point remarks concerning the conflicting pressures resulting from the dislocations of the mode of production and the representation of the individual within the new social structure:

> The Mexicotexan has a conveniently dual personality. When he is called upon to do his duty for his country he is an American. When benefits are passed around he is a Mexican and always last in line. And he has nobody to help him because he cannot help himself. In the United States he is not the only racial group that often finds the going hard. But while there are rich Negroes and poor Negroes, rich Jews and poor Jews, rich Italians and Poles and poor Italians and Poles, there are in Texas only poor Mexicans. Spanish-speaking people in the Southwest are divided into two categories: poor Mexicans and rich Spaniards. (195–96)

The cultural-political duality of Mexican American identity is complicated here by adding to the external pressures of class, race, and color the internal mechanism by which racially mixed mestizo Mexicans become white European Spaniards. All it takes is capital. The narrator elsewhere claims that "The word Mexican had for so long been a symbol of hatred and loathing that . . . it had become a hateful and loathsome word" (118).

Understanding this relationship between the word *Mexican* and poverty, middle-class persons, anxious to dissociate themselves from the American denigration of the word and the culture, now sought to become "Spanish," another name for white.[34] This figural transformation obliquely suggests the continuing ideological dissimulation of Anglo-American racial categories. By "conveniently" dividing "Spanish-speaking people" into two categories, "poor Mexicans and rich Spaniards," dominant historical narratives enforce a particular social hierarchy. Paredes is attempting to make clear that history and knowledge are not in this instance the disinterested production and representation of essential facts; they are instead the decidedly interested elements of "a subject-constituting project" (R. Young 159).

In the face of such practices, a concrete manifestation of what Spivak describes as the "epistemic violence" exacted on the colonized subject ("In a Word" 130), the formation of the dual identity—Mexican and American, and yet not either essentially—is clearly neither tied simply to coercive power structures nor to essential features of race, class, or ethnicity alone. It is linked as well to vested constructions of specifically represented objects, with no existence or reality outside of their discursive representations. One is either "a rich Spaniard" or "a poor Mexican" (or greaser, spic, *sebo*, and "other neighborly names" commonly used for Mexicans in the United States, as Paredes points out elsewhere), independent of racial or historical factors. For as decidedly social constructions, the identities denoted by the terms *Spaniard* and *Mexican* do not cross. The viciousness of this dynamic is all the more destructive for its very pliability in an era when, as the narrator tells us, the Mexican "is called upon to do his duty for his country" and becomes only then conveniently "an American." Once the crisis has passed, and the benefits are distributed, he reverts to his former role: "He is a Mexican and always last in line."

Earlier in the novel, Paredes had represented in the character of El Negro, a seditionist rebel, the mixture of black and Mexican, "a nigger-greaser," according to one of the Texas Rangers (11). In the ensuing years, wealth has transformed El Negro into the well-respected Don Agustín de la Vega, the "Chief of Customs at Morelos," the Mexican city across the border from Jonesville (75). Moments such as this highlight the complexity of racial politics in the prewar borderlands throughout the novel. However, perhaps nowhere is the complexity more sharply drawn than in a scene involving characters from another racial group, Japanese Americans. Invited by their teacher to a high school senior-year party at a place called La Casa Mexicana, Guálinto and his friends arrive at the gathering only to be denied admission because they are Mexican. Given the chance to enter if he identifies himself as white and a Spaniard when challenged by the doorman, Guálinto refuses to abandon his friends and stalwartly claims that he is "a Mexican" (173). Guálinto's white friends and his girlfriend, María Elena Osuna, from one of the wealthiest families in the region, enter easily. So do "Jimmy and Bob Shigemara," who were "the sons of a prosperous Japanese truck farmer" (170). The

Shigemaras were "fat, well-fed boys who talked a glib, smooth English" and claimed that they were "not the same as the Chinese. 'We're much more civilized'" (170). The irony of Mexicans denied entry into La Casa Mexicana is emphasized by the ease with which the Shigemaras claim and are accorded social precedence because of their father's wealth.

The complexity of factors determining subjective identity is ultimately most forcefully represented to Guálinto when a former Texas Ranger, his future father-in-law, says to him: "George Washington Go-maize. . . . They sure screwed you up, didn't they, boy? . . . You look white but you're a goddam Meskin. And what does your mother do but give you a nigger name. George Washington Go-maize. . . . It don't sound right" (284). Straddling the multicultural ground proves too much for Guálinto Gómez, and he attempts to resolve his ambivalences by changing his name. He now forswears the bewildering unreality of his former composite names: the American George Washington, with all of its own now mixed racial signals, alluding, as the old Texas Ranger understands, not to a founding father, but to other Washingtons of color, like George Washington Carver or George Washington Cable. And he rejects as well the Indian-sounding name Guálinto and all of its associations with familial, cultural, and local history. Instead, he takes the simpler, if not quite neutral, name George G. Gómez (284).

Fantasy and Critique in the Public Sphere

In the wake of these scenes of identity negotiation within the heterogeneous mix of American racial identities, Paredes offers one other dramatization of borderland responses to the steering mechanisms of early twentieth-century American modernity. Guálinto's efforts first to resist the homogenizing pressures of the American school system and then to embrace his parents' original dream to become a "leader of his people" are both subverted when he instead becomes, in the days just before World War II, an officer in army counterintelligence. His job is, ironically, "border security" (299), spying on the newly emerging political organizations formed by his former childhood friends who represent the next stage of resistance to assimilation. This disowning of his family's and his community's history is achieved within a specific horizon of blurred personal and social experience that leaves

Guálinto at novel's end deeply unsettled. He finds himself strangely troubled by a recurring dream, itself a return of repressed boyhood daydreams.

In the dream, he imagines himself leading a victorious counterattack against Sam Houston's army at the decisive battle of San Jacinto in 1836, the very battle that had led to the creation of an independent Anglo Republic of Texas. In his dream, Guálinto rewrites history: the Mexican dictator Santa Anna is hanged before he can bring ruin upon Mexico, and all traitors aligned with him are dispatched. Victorious Mexicotexans take command of their own fate, history is undone, and "Texas and the Southwest . . . remain forever Mexican" (281):

> He would imagine he was living in his great-grandfather's time, when the Americans first began to encroach on the northern provinces of the new Republic of Mexico. Reacting against the central government's inefficiency and corruption, he would organize *rancheros* into a fighting militia and train them by using them to exterminate the Comanches. . . . In his daydreams he built a modern arms factory at Laredo, doing it all in great detail, until he had an enormous, well-trained army that included Irishmen and escaped American Negro slaves. (282)

On the verge of quite self-consciously losing himself as a twentieth-century premovement *mexicano* into the American melting pot, Guálinto's political unconscious returns in the form of a collective memory from the nineteenth century—instantiated by the sense of self offered by his father's, his uncle's, and his mother's lives—to offer an alternative ideology and different self-formation. In this return of the repressed, not of the classical unconscious but of historicity itself, Guálinto's buried memories and childhood daydreams erase the apparently resolved identity crisis by reinscribing over that presumed resolution the provisional quality of its instrumental form. If history can be erased and overwritten, repressed and forgotten, then perhaps another kind of history, an anamnestic history, can be layered over prior ones, making them lose their forgetting.

As we have seen, the discursive speech genres of birth certificates, educational degrees, career dossiers, service records, marriage licenses, and legal court records bind George Washington Gómez institutionally to a formidable identity discourse. Now the simpler structures of a precritical utopian dream emerge from the repressed to trouble the stability of his newfound bourgeois self. In this process, Guálinto's self-formation is powerfully shaped by the Anglo-American public sphere he has chosen to embrace as an assimilated middle-class American. He continues to be authored as well, however, by experiences and discourses of experience that by now have retreated into the unconscious fantasy structures of his life. It is for this reason that at the point of complete denial of his Mexican past, Guálinto can in the residue of his daydreams and fantasies "end up with a feeling of emptiness, of futility":

> Somehow, he was not comfortable with the way things ended. There was something missing that made any kind of ending fail to satisfy. And he would stop there, to begin from the beginning a few days later. But he had outgrown those childish daydreams long ago. Lately, however, now that he was a grown man, married and with a successful career before him, scenes from the silly imaginings of his youth kept popping up when he was asleep. He always woke with a feeling of irritation. Why? he would ask himself. Why do I keep doing this? Why do I keep on fighting battles that were won and lost a long time ago? Lost by me and won by me too? They have no meaning now. (282)

Flores and Yúdice maintain that Latino "self-formation is simultaneously personal and social (or private and public) because the utterances and acts through which we *experience* or gain our self-images are reaccentuated in relation to how genres have institutionally been made sensitive or responsive to identity factors such as race, gender, class, religion, and so on" (65). In times of crisis, such as in the crisis of stability indicated by the name *postmodernity*, "private identity factors or subject positions may become unmoored from institutionally bound generic structures" (65).

In the case that Paredes presents in this novel, perhaps the issue has less to do with the stylistics and formalisms implied by the term *postmodernity* than with the configurations of identity put at stake by the shifting relations of material and cultural production on the US-Mexican border in the first decades of the twentieth century. This "unmooring" of the subject position from the bonds of institutional ideology (that might be more advantageously associated with modernity, modernism, and projects of modernization than with postmodernity) could explain why Guálinto's "childish daydreams" and "silly imaginings" leave him "with a feeling of emptiness, of futility." It is for good reason that Adorno has claimed that "identity is the primal form of ideology" (*Negative Dialectics* 148).

Situated in the realm of the imaginary, Guálinto's daydreams fuel a discomfiting primal and utopian self-formation that stands against the one that our hero has supposedly consciously chosen under the various signs of his interpellation. That is to say, the fantasy structures of the unconscious always return, bringing with them a historical memory that has the practical function of designating an alternative, even if deeply latent and tenuous, content to the formed subject of history. "Fantasy," in this sense, as Jameson has written, "is no longer felt to be a private and compensatory reaction against public situations, but rather a way of reading those situations, of thinking and mapping them, of intervening in them, albeit in a very different form from the abstract reflections of traditional philosophy or politics" ("On Negt and Kluge" 171).

If birth certificates, diplomas, career dossiers, service records, marriage licenses, and legal court records are the speech genres that mark the social arenas where meanings are articulated, negotiated, and distributed by the collective body of the public, then dream and fantasy in response to public matters may register an alternative "social horizon of experience" (Negt and Kluge 2). Negt and Kluge maintain that the public sphere is where public and private experience intersect and "everything that is actually or ostensibly relevant for all members of society is integrated" (2).[35] As a response to unbearable real situations, fantasy may merely serve as an expression of alienation. But precisely because fantasy cannot be easily circumscribed or repressed, it can also be the site for an "unconscious practical critique of alienation" (32–33). For Guálinto in this instance, these alternative public spheres remain only latent and repressed, situated as they are within knowledges formed by the anxiety of the clash between the everyday real and the utopian imaginary. However, the fact of their continued existence, even if only in the attenuated forms of daydream and fantasy, signals the possibility of their emergence as critique in other, more opportune historical eras.

Engendering Border Discourses

At least as significant as the precritical utopian impulse emerging at the novel's end to disrupt any reading that attempts to forge a simple, undialectical relationship between true and false consciousness, between resistance or assimilation to Anglo-American culture, is one other latent emplotment, namely, the story of gender formation. In Paredes's novel, as in all of his other writings from this period, gender and sexuality are articulated through and through with matters of identity formation and the creation of stable subject positions. A fully gendered reading would be concerned not only with the separate fates of Guálinto's mother, María, and his two sisters, Carmen and Maruca, as they fulfill their familial roles as mother, daughters, sisters, nieces, and wives. It would also be concerned with how that fate is legislated by Mexican patriarchal ideology, expressed most starkly in the guiding speech genre of the text, the *corrido*.

Numerous Chicano cultural critics, including Renato Rosaldo, Gloria Anzaldúa, Norma Alarcón, María Herrera-Sobek, Sonia Saldívar-Hull, and others have rightly pointed out that the Mexican *corrido* expresses a specific construction of male mastery, articulating ideologies of resistance and historical agency with ideologies of masculinity. This articulation privileges and enforces male dominance. The symbolic politics of the *corrido* thus represent a special instance of the infiltration of the late nineteenth-century US-Mexican public and private spheres. With regard to the Texas-Mexican *corrido*, and its warrior hero in particular, Joanna Pavletich and Margot Backus argue that the gender-coded icons and images that predominate in these songs —lone heroes with pistols in hand, violent confrontations in cantinas, scenes of mortal combat, and mythic horsemanship—all help produce a male-gendered aesthetic space. This space creates only secondarily and by supplementarity "a grieving female, domestic space" occupied by women and children (132). The authority of male icons and images within the *corrido* is such that "the moments of greatest cultural, political, and aesthetic weight [are] simultaneously its most powerfully gendered moments" (132). These gender-coded moments of confrontation within the *corrido* valorize, narratologically and thematically, the patriarchal *corrido* hero, who, though vanquished in the end, is constructed as a figure of monumental historical consequence and moral substance whom his Anglo persecutors cannot rival. Drawing its energies from a sexual and gender system in which the sexually male is articulated to the socially male in terms of presence, action, eloquence, and meaningfulness, the *corrido* celebrates in the mode of romance autonomy, patriarchy, and resistance—even while it laments the patriarch's certain defeat.[36] As a socially symbolic act, the *corrido* both draws from and adds to the patriarchal constitution of US-Mexican culture. As gender-coded discourse, it identifies that community and represents it in monologically male terms.

Paradoxically, that same symbolic importance also enables an interrogation of the patriarchal structure of the traditional culture. This is so because while the *corrido* links patriarchy and resistance, it also unconsciously joins patriarchal authority and defeat, since in the songs of border conflict the hero is invariably killed, captured, or exiled from his home. Reading Paredes's novel as gendered discourse points to the ways in which a new dialectical articulation, not now between patriarchy and resistance, but between patriarchy and defeat, emerges as historical inevitability in the emplotted form of disillusion and loss. If we can conceive of the *corrido* as analogous to the classical epic, representing an archaic world of heroes who, as Bernard Knox maintains, "belonged to the time when men were stronger, braver, and greater than men are now" (21), then the novel represents a more ironic era, when the world and the men who inhabit it are neither quite so translucently heroic nor so transcendently monumental.

One might well argue, therefore, that given the single-minded, implacably male-dominated articulation of resistance in the *corrido* of border conflict as filtered through the related but diminished form of *corrido*-inspired narratives, the characters represented in these narratives could not but be prescribed by ethical and political limitations. We come up against the borders of this male-gendered discourse throughout the novel, but perhaps nowhere more poignantly than in the failed utopian vision at the end of the narrative. The link between the Mexican patriarchal discourse of the *corrido* and a certain political vision is surely one reason for the decline of the *corrido* as a viable resistance form in the 1930s and the rise of other genres that do not constrain themselves so readily by failing to interrogate patriarchal ideology.[37] Perhaps more important, however, this understanding of the restrictions of patriarchal social forms accentuates the crucial centrality of the *non*heroic (not to be confused with *un*heroic) agents of history for subsequent political courses of action.

With the end of the historical moment of armed struggle after the sedition of 1915, the interventions of resistance permitted within the personal and socially symbolic cultural spheres became all the more crucial. But to the extent that these emergent acts of symbolic social resistance continue to be articulated with uncritical, male-dominant, gendered discursive systems, and hence with the limits of such systems, their own viability as enunciations of liberation will remain, inevitably, equally in doubt. It is evident that the new historical situation arising at the end of the nineteenth-century that Paredes at mid-twentieth century was working to relate required new formal strategies. It required a new poetic language and a new bilingual aesthetic, in short, a wholly different subaltern modernity for overcoming the impasses and contradictions that the values and social structures of a former era could no longer pretend to resolve. The invention of these new languages and forms was Chicana and Chicano modernism itself.

The vibrant flowering of writings by Chicana writers after the mid-twentieth century seeking to raise those articulations of race, class, and gender to the level of critique corroborates the point about the bankruptcy of patriarchally invested, male-gendered social texts that fail to interrogate the procedures by which an authentically determinative subject-effect is produced. Even today, after two decades of Chicana feminist critique, it is still worth repeating that in the texts of the borderlands, gender factors, no less than those of class and race, have functioned to create a heterogeneous field that problematizes the general notion of an undifferentiated Chicano (male) subject.[38]

Earlier I mentioned that the represented social fates of Guálinto's mother, María, and his sisters, Carmen and Maruca, as they fulfill their familial roles as mother, daughters, sisters, nieces, and wives would have to be read as part of any general resolution of the novel's narrative trajectory. Certainly when read in the context of the guiding generic emplotment of the *corrido* and its warrior hero ethos, Guálinto's story excludes his mother and sisters from the roles of agents of history. However, as we have just seen, the *corrido* narrative leads to implacable contradictions concerning warrior heroes and historical agency. What happens, then, to the non-*corrido* figures that do not aspire in real or imaginary terms to the status of warrior hero? What is the effect of their literal elision from the text on the symbolic resolution of its story? What mode can their story assume?

María, who initiates the events of the novel with her dreams that her son is "going to grow up to be a great man who will help his people" (16), remains so static in her role as *madre de familia* that even Feliciano, the only true heir to the warrior code in the novel, becomes like her "eldest child" (264). In the novel's emplotment, María cannot exist outside of her role as mother, even in relation to her brother.

Likewise, Guálinto's eldest sister Carmen, as smart and self-conscious as Guálinto in every respect, is nevertheless represented as agreeing to withdraw from the role of agency. She assents to leave school to care for her ailing mother and to help her younger sister Maruca through an unwanted pregnancy. Although each sister eventually moves into the world on her own, neither can be described as having available to her even as a future aspiration the fully achieved agency of subjectivity as their community defines that role.

And while the hostile, opposing Mexican and American cultural forces continue to collide around them, situated in the borderlands between the warring sides, neither sister sides passionately with either. Carmen settles into the anonymity of Mexican American married life in Jonesville even as the assimilated Guálinto, now known as "George," dismisses her for having kids that "looked like Indians" (285). Maruca retreats to a utopian California with "a middle-aged Anglo widower" (290) and completely disappears from family history.

Thus while Guálinto and his sisters equally suffer under an enforced Americanization, they do so in gender-specific ways. Rita Felski has pointed out that women have experienced the logic of modernity not only through "the hierarchies of class, race, and sexuality but by their various and overlapping identities and practices as consumers, mothers, workers, artists, lovers, activists, readers, and so on" (21–22). These distinctively feminine encounters with the forces of modernity and the shaping of modernization of the kind that Felski identifies as being at the core of modernism remain absent from Guálinto's story. We do not learn how Carmen and Maruca position themselves in relation to the logic of modernity. For the sisters, sentimentality and romance fail as alternative plots of their stories. While their brother chooses to leave behind his Mexican enculturation and to cross over into complete Americanization, he does so under the sign of the privilege of deciding what borders to cross and which communities to double cross.

The sisters' respective choices and lack of alternatives leave open the question of the very meaning of community. As Chandra Mohanty puts it in a different but related context, "Who are the insiders and outsiders in this community? What notions of legitimacy and gendered and racialized citizenship are being actively constructed within this community?" (188–89). How porous are the borders of this community? Who may traverse the lines defining them? In what direction may the crossings proceed? Are there no mediators, then, moving across the symbolic and real borders of community described within the novel, capable of creating a new hybrid, an assimilated nation of modern citizens in the transnational contact zone of the United States–Mexico borderlands? If one could exist, what might be the nature of a fully emancipated imagination unshackled from its binding limitations and capable of resolving these formidable questions?

George Washington Gómez repeatedly rejects the agency of the heroic figure within the historical present, but it also offers no alternative future plot to replace heroic action either. The novel continually represents the idea of the warrior hero and its gender politics in ways internally contradictory, dynamically complex, and, finally, reflective of the heterogeneity of border life. Where are we, then, at the end of the novel when left with a hero whose heroic status has been undermined through and through and with no one to take his place?

The Ethnic Bildungsroman and the
Emergence into History

In *The Historical Novel*, Georg Lukács argues that even in the most passionate and divisive of civil wars, "large sections of people have always stood between the camps with fluctuating sympathies, now for this side, now for the other" (37). This does not mean that these "non- or not passionately participant popular masses can remain untouched by the historical crisis," he maintains (37). On the contrary, it is often precisely these nonheroic characters, the inconsequential figures, who in their psychology and destiny represent social trends and historical forces too weak to be measured and too deep to be perceived but make a difference. They are the ones deeply moved by the world-historical forces swirling around them and whose feelings underlie world-historical shifts (37). These figures are for the most part women, peasants, working-class subjects, and sexual outsiders, the subalterns of hegemonic society relegated to the margins of historical narratives by virtue of their conditions as social outsiders. The fates of these characters at the margins of historical narratives figure the necessary stratagems by which a community reimagines the older, patriarchal family model of resistance in the process of attempting to create a new, emancipated imagination in order to survive the transformations of modernity as a community, as a nation, even though partitioned by class, race, and gender divisions.

Guálinto Gómez represents the contradictions and limitations of that nonheroic historical position in his attempted construction of an authentic identity beyond ethnicity. In the plot of his story, we get less the achievement of authenticity than a representation of the aspect of its historical becoming. *George Washington Gómez* is, therefore, quintessentially an instance of what we might term the ethnic bildungsroman. As Bakhtin, writing at the same time as Paredes, employs the term, a bildungsroman is the type of novel that "can be designated in the most general sense as the novel of human emergence. A human being can, however, emerge in quite diverse ways" (*"Bildungsroman"* 21). One way in which a human being may emerge is in the complete integration of the social process with the development of the person.[39] In their historical novels, authors like Walter Scott, Honoré de Balzac, and William Faulkner inherit what Jameson has called "a social and historical raw material, a popular memory" (*Postmodernism* 405). This historical memory then becomes the raw material for social narrative. Moreover, the fiercest loyalties and furious divisions that bind or problematize the social processes of a community are inscribed synchronically in that raw material of popular mnemonics. Jameson further contends that "the conditions of thinking a new reality and articulating a new paradigm for it therefore seems to demand a peculiar conjuncture and a certain strategic distance from that new reality, which tends to overwhelm those immersed in it" (405).

In *George Washington Gómez*, Paredes, too, gathers the historical raw material of popular memory, especially as it is articulated in the form of the story of human emergence. Like the hero of classical nineteenth-century bourgeois narrative, Guálinto's narrative is one of emergence as he undergoes an education in moral choice. The narrative of his life shows him evolving from within as he negotiates those choices that simultaneously shape his destiny and control the narrative plot of his biography. Differently from the bourgeois narrative of education, however, Guálinto's story of ethnic education is shaped not only by his premeditated acts of individual will but also by the transpersonal and transinstitutional structures of race and geopolitical power. Clothed in the intellectual protocols of the American middle class, he engages in "a set of social practices that includes language, dress, speech, eating habits, religious and cultural practices," but in the context of racism (Bogues 11).[40] Taken together, these extradiscursive practices constitute a set of powerful but highly unstable conditions that give the possibility of "moral choice" meanings different from what they would be in times and places not shaped by the destabilizing conditions of race and ethnicity.

With insidious results, Guálinto embraces the values of the American middle class at the cost of the cultural, political, and historical narrative that has named him as a future leader of his people. How to imagine a new reality and articulate a new paradigm for conceiving of the multicultural politics that Guálinto intends to experience is the substance of the questions that Paredes conceptualizes in the story of education featured in *George Washington Gómez*. In what political language might he speak? What do the terms of political language mean in the context of subalternity and racial oppression? Recourse to answering these questions and understanding the complexities of the synchronic conditions in Guálinto's story of emergence is available in Stuart Hall's discussion of Antonio Gramsci's relevance for the study of race and ethnicity, to which I now turn.

Race, Ethnicity, and Societies
Structured in Dominance

In his reading of Gramsci, Hall offers a useful model for a preliminary understanding of the contradictions and limitations that Paredes is representing in the life of his ambiguous hero on the border and the diverse ways in which his life emerges from the social processes of the borderlands. First, as Hall explains, Gramsci emphasizes the necessity of "the emphasis on historical specificity" for any understanding of the morphology of racism (Hall, "Gramsci's Relevance" 435). Gramsci means to underscore the ways in which the general features of racism are "modified and transformed" by specific historical contexts in which racism is active. This means that one is always dealing with specific racism*s*, not racism in the abstract. From Gramsci's general point about racisms, it follows that Guálinto's experience with the Anglo world will thus of necessity not be that of his father, his mother, or even of his uncle Feliciano. The changing nature of historical conditions also explains why Gramsci gives considerable weight to differences among national characteristics and to the regional unevenness of historical development. In the novel, we see Guálinto struggling to define an alternative response from within a shifting historical and economic social structure, and the nature of that response cannot be predicated in advance.

Gramsci also shows that one may not reduce questions of class to those of race or vice versa (Hall, "Gramsci's Relevance" 435–36), and that the "class subject" that attempts to act within structures shaped by patterns of class and race is "non-homogeneous" in its makeup (436). This means in the case of Paredes's ambiguous hero that the modes of exploitation of different sectors of the labor force are not the same and will exert no one form of hegemonic pressure to produce one form of unity. As Hall explains, "We would get much further along the road to understanding how the regime of capital can function *through* differentiation and difference, rather than through similarity and identity, if we took more seriously this question of the cultural, social, national, ethnic and gendered composition of historically different and specific forms of labour" ("Gramsci's Relevance" 435, emphasis original).

Given these factors of nonhomogeneity, Gramsci thus can show that there is a political consequence to the noncorrespondence between economic, political, and ideological dimensions of the social structure. The consequence is to abandon any idea of how classes "*should . . .* behave" and focus on "how they actually do behave, in real historical conditions" (Hall, "Gramsci's Relevance" 438). This argument for historical reality over ideal normativity gives a rationally compelling, if ultimately not an emotively satisfying, rationale for the puzzlement of Guálinto's turn to assimilationist politics at the novel's end. When the force of realpolitik in the 1940s among middle-class Mexican Americans was assimilation, Paredes's hero could not act differently if he wanted to remain true to his newly chosen class allegiance. In the most ironic of turns, by choosing assimilation, Guálinto might in fact be best positioning himself to become what his parents originally desired for him, "the leader of his people."

Hall makes a similarly compelling argument with respect to Gramsci's treatment of the state. Gramsci breaks with the notion of the state "in an exclusively coercive, dominative and conspiratorial manner" (Hall, "Gramsci's Relevance" 438) and allows us to look more carefully at the "institutions and processes in so-called 'civil society' in racially structured social formations" (438) than we have in the past. Doing so allows us to see how institutions forged the complex unities of competing identities available to the racialized subject of Guálinto Gómez. As Hall argues, "schooling, cultural organizations, family and sexual life, the patterns and modes of civil association, churches and religions, communal or organizational forms, ethnically specific institutions, and many other such sites play an absolutely vital role in giving, sustaining and reproducing different societies in a racially structured form" (438–39). Reading the role of these institutions through Gramsci thus allows us to see more clearly the point of Paredes's story, namely, the centrality of the "*cultural* factor in social development" (439), that is, the "actual, grounded terrain of practices, representations, languages and customs of any specific historical society" (439, emphasis original). These practices, as we have seen throughout our reading of *George Washington Gómez*, underscore the ways in which the common sense of a specific historical moment takes root in and helps shape popular life, its "national-popular" character, and forms "a crucial site for the construction of popular hegemony" (439).

Finally, Gramsci's work in "the ideological field" allows us to see more clearly how in the case of Paredes's Depression-era novel " 'racism,' if not exclusively an ideological phenomenon, has critical ideological dimensions" (439). Ideologies are "necessarily and inevitably contradictory," and the "self" that underpins them "is not a unified but a contradictory subject and a social construction" (440). Understanding this complexity allows us to understand particularly in Guálinto's case the reasons for "the 'subjection' of the victims of racism to the mystifications of the very racist ideologies which imprison and define them" and "how different, often contradictory elements can be woven into and integrated within different ideological discourses" (440).

For the character Guálinto, the relevance of these aspects of structures of race and ethnicity point out why the narrative pathways of his life yield no singular, unitary way, or still less, a traditional story of emergence, vindication, salvation, and redemption. Between his desires and their fulfillment, between his beliefs and his actions, between his words and the checkerboard of his consciousness that underpins them, there exist sedimented, elastic environments of other words, belated desires, inchoate beliefs, and contradictory knowledges in conflict with one another that do not vindicate, resolve, or redeem.

Their articulation is difficult to penetrate, but their complex inter-relationships—merging in moments, recoiling violently at others—form the social and historical environment within which the narrative of his life is individualized, given stylistic shape, and made to embody the social atmosphere of this moment in history. In this way, the historical dialectics of difference shaping Guálinto Gómez's life are interwoven with the social dialogues surrounding it and with the future, which it anticipates, provokes, and orients itself toward. In the end, Guálinto's individual fate is of less concern to the narrative than is the social significance of its articulation with the future.

Articulating the Future

Taken together, the heterogeneous features formulated by Gramsci's notions of hegemony and of the subject shaped within social formations structured by race and class offer one way of understanding the contradictory motives and ambitions of the unfolding story of Paredes's nonheroic hero in becoming, Guálinto Gómez. They constitute the ethnicity of this bildungsroman as a tale of emergence and transition. This does not mean, however, that we will easily reach the end of the process of his becoming. In fact, because his story ends before his final emergence into maturity, Guálinto never fully gets out of his past, but continues to live within it. In his classic study of the form of the bildungsroman, Franco Moretti argues that youth is the necessary and sufficient condition of the hero of the modern era (4–5). "Youth," claims Moretti, "is, so to speak, modernity's 'essence,' the sign of a world that seeks its meaning in the *future* rather than in the past" (5, emphasis original). In the plunge into what Marx had called the "permanent revolution" of modernity for which a cultural ground had not yet been conceived, the youthful attributes of inner restlessness, wanderlust, and mobility are invested with symbolic centrality. We invest them with symbolic import because of their role in allowing youth to imagine the possibility of a future world that does not yet exist. The transitoriness of youth figured by mobility, travel, and interiority becomes the very token of the dynamism and unpredictability of modernity. Built on such sharp and unstable contrasts as an untenable past and a volatile future, it is inevitable, according to Moretti, that "the structure of the *Bil-*

dungsroman will of necessity be *intrinsically contradictory*" (6, emphasis original).

In *George Washington Gómez*, we see the formlessness of this mobility figured in the instability of the hero's historical position, between social classes and racial communities, and between a past not yet done with and a future not yet differentiated from the past. In the trajectory of his life, the present does not appear as the end point of a seamless forward movement. Instead, the present flows riverlike in a slow and sometimes reversible course of swirls, eddies, cross- and countercurrents. The future cannot be simply an end point, a neutral space of desire and anticipation. Inevitably, the future comes freighted with the melancholy anxiety of an unknown moment of reckoning and judgment of the present. Guálinto's life is thus linked by metonymy in the most fundamental of ways to the bordering river whose waters, described by Paredes in "The Rio Grande," meander to "die so very gently / By the margin of the sea" (*Between Two Worlds* 15–16). Formulated as a potential for a future reconstruction in more self-consciously gendered narratives, the undoing of the apparently stable subject position denoted by the name George G. Gómez serves brilliantly as the marker of the boundaries of the borderlands of culture that postmodern Chicano and Chicana literature would traverse problematically at the end of the twentieth century. The articulations of the complex unities structured in dominance of the borderlands required no less than this anticipatory full return to the possibilities of the future, with all of its unpredictable instabilities.

Throughout Paredes's narrative, this anticipatory potential of the future remains precariously fragile. Fantasy might as easily serve to dissipate practice and undermine its intent; the critique of privilege associated with male gender remains latent and repressed, the traces of its course deferred and displaced. The unsettled quality of our hero's identity remains a mark of the unavailability of unified solutions. At the margins of history, fluctuating between his uncle Feliciano's values and the temptations of a homogenizing American melting-pot identity, Guálinto opts for the nonheroic path of Americanization and assimilation by choosing to blend into middle-class life and the very same white supremacist society that has murdered his father and erased his history. Still, the sublimation of the possibility of historical agency into the political unconscious does not represent the end of praxis, but only its transference into an unspecifiable future.

In his "Far East Notebook no. 3," Paredes writes in an entry dated November 7, 1949, concerning the ending of the novel:

> Today I also decided that the first volume of GWG, which is already written, has been since before Army times, will stand as it is. It does not need any better ending, the way it ends, with Guálinto in despair, is good enough. But I have definitely decided it will be a Trilogy, of which what is written will be the first volume. The main theme will be what I had originally thought it should be, the efforts of Guálinto to be the helper and leader of his people; the world is in a mess and he tries to right some of its wrongs. The ways he goes about trying to help, the obstacles he meets in his way, and the final results, will be my story. (Américo Paredes Papers, box 8, folder 14)[41]

Thus in the final scene of the novel, to the great dismay of readers who would have much preferred the integrative, heroic ending of the border *corrido* to the problematically despairing and decidedly non-heroic ending we actually get, Guálinto dismisses the core Mexican values that he has grappled with over the course of his life. He denies the dualities implicit in the image of the checkerboard of consciousness, his divided personality as a US-born Mexican. In the end, he rationalizes with an awesomely serene lack of self-consciousness that the circumstances of modernity and modernization on the border are such that the only pragmatic pathway available to someone like him is full assimilation and the complete negation of the past, an attempted forgetting of history with a vengeance.

In his daily interaction with Anglos, in blending into the world of American business, defense, and national security, and in his intermarriage with an Anglo woman, Guálinto makes of assimilation a choice that one could reasonably make. Certainly, assimilation was a historical choice that many middle-class Mexican Americans of the generation that came to personal and political maturity in the years of the Great Depression did make. He is thus an exemplary instance of how American society operates, allowing individuals to imagine broadly a spectrum of possibilities for subjective self-verification. In this manner, Paredes displays the malleable quality of both universal and ethnocentric consciousnesses and shows, moreover, how personal identity can serve as a bolster to repressive and limiting ideologies. Social categories are not static; they are conditions that people may traverse. But traverse to what end? *George Washington Gómez* concludes with that open question and its horizon of unresolved possibilities. All of which makes the work profoundly, prototypically, a historical novel. In this unique moment, a radical historicism is achieved with Guálinto's violent disjunction of his past from himself.

Not surprisingly, in the end we are not able to specify in satisfyingly concrete and definitive terms the nature of a completed Chicana and Chicano subject position through the figure of George Washington Gómez since the historical valences of the terms *Chicano/Chicana* were at mid-century decades away from being sounded with energetic ideological force. However, we may at least articulate some features of its subject-effects: it fluctuates between essential and provisional forms of identity, desiring the wholeness of sovereignty while experiencing its own relentless bifurcation, living its territorial ambitions in a transterritorial public sphere, and expressing its univocal dreams in a bilingual tongue. These are not contradictions of logic but dialogizations of consciousness. Situated in the borderlands of culture, the Mexican American subject Paredes imagines in *George Washington Gómez* exists on an unstable ground of double negations. Yet through these self-negating subject-effects we can glimpse the future of the past through which Chicana and Chicano subjectivities would one day emerge into real history. Paredes saw the task of the now thoroughly deconstructed warrior-hero narrative not in the conservation of the past but in the redemption of the hopes of the past.

The ending represented in Paredes's novel is thus hardly apocalyptic, or even prefigurative of an "inverted millenarianism." It is, rather, an initial and tentative expression of the now widely explored complexities of Chicana and Chicano subject identity as a "heteroglot interzone, a hybrid overlapping" of two messy domains in reciprocal fluxion, only partly identifiable as an Americanized Mexican world, on one hand, and a Mexicanized American realm, on the other. Hovering between his view of himself and others' view of him—each affecting the other continually in the checkerboard of his consciousness—Guálinto Gómez could make nothing absolute of his Mexican or American identities.

In its systematic breakdown of the binary Manichaeanisms implicit in the term *Mexican American*, *George Washington Gómez* is an expression that can be described only as post-modern par excellence.[42] It serves powerfully as a sign before its time of the state of Chicana and Chicano literature at the end of the twentieth century. Moreover, in

its archeological work of collecting, sifting, categorizing, and analyzing the present signs of the incompletion of the past, Paredes's novel
recounts the possibility of wresting from within the realm of the past
the hope of freedom in the future. It turns out that this is but another way of articulating what C. L. R. James, Paredes's contemporary
in the exploration of subaltern modernity, was rendering as the affirmation contained in every negation, the future that is implicit in the
present.

TRANSNATIONAL MODERNISMS

Paredes, Roosevelt, Rockwell, Bulosan,

and the Four Freedoms

> Nations, like narratives, lose their origins in the myths of time
> and only fully realize their horizons in the mind's eye.
> —Homi K. Bhabha, *Nation and Narration*

The Mexico-Texan he's one fonny man
Who leeves in the region that's north of the Gran',
Of Mexican father he born in these part,
And sometimes he rues it dip down in he's heart.

For the Mexico-Texan he no gotta lan',
He stomped on the neck on both sides of the Gran',
The dam gringo lingo he no cannot spik,
It twisters the tong and it make you fill sick.
A cit'zen of Texas they say that he ees,
But then, why they call him the Mexican Grease?
Soft talk and hard action, he can't understan',
The Mexico-Texan he no gotta lan'.

If he cross the reever, eet ees just as bad,
On high poleeshed Spanish he break his had,
American customs those people no like,
They hate that Miguel they should call him El Mike,
And Mexican-born, why they jeer and they hoot,
"Go back to the gringo! Go lick at hees boot!"
In Texas he's Johnny, in Mexico Juan,
But the Mexico-Texan he no gotta lan'.

. . . .

Except for a few with their cunning and craft
He count just as much as a nought to the laft,
And they say everywhere, "He's a burden and a drag,
He no gotta country, he no gotta flag."
He no gotta voice, all he got is the han'
To work like the burro; he no gotta lan'.
—Américo Paredes, "The Mexico-Texan"

In the foregoing discussion, we have seen how Paredes's ethnographic fame rests on his foundational work in the 1950s and 1960s on the ballads and everyday folklife of Mexican Americans and on his subsequent elaboration of that work during the 1970s and 1980s. His initial scholarly contribution from this early period, *"With His Pistol in His Hand,"* was a masterful work of cultural criticism decades ahead of its time. In an epoch when the intellectual modes dictated either an old historicism or a restrictive new critical formalism, *"With His Pistol in His Hand"* went insistently against the grain of the usual analytical methods. Combining literary, sociological, ethnographic, and historical analysis of traditional border ballads, it offered a new way of doing folklore. It documented the unofficial historical records of the borderlands and bore witness to their traditions of vernacular critique, all the while providing a stinging rebuttal and a devastating deconstruction of the established white supremacist hierarchies that operated as the common wisdom and official history of the region.[1] "To dramatize his sense of culture as a site of social contestation," José D. Saldívar notes, Paredes "located the sources of meaning not in individual subjectivities, but in social relations, communication, and cultural politics" ("Américo Paredes and Decolonization" 295).

Before Paredes, the cultural politics of Texas and the Southwest were the singular product of the Anglo-American imagination, responding exclusively to the hegemony of Anglo-American material interests. But as Michel Foucault reminds us, "Where there is power, there is resistance" (95). After Paredes, with the publication of his critical work, the cultural politics of the region began to be cast in the decidedly different mold of biculturalism, reflecting the multicultural realities of the American social world. To this immensely influential body of scholarship were added during the 1990s a collection of essays,

Folklore and Culture on the Texas-Mexican Border (1993), and a study of jokes, jests, and oral narrative, *Uncle Remus con Chile* (1993).

During the last decade of the twentieth century, Paredes's literary works added another dimension to his imposing array of work in the historical and ethnographic realms. These literary works also address the predicaments of contemporary borderlands cultural politics, identity formation, and social transformation, but they do so in a different way. Given the contemporaneity of their concerns, it is curious to learn that the literary works published during the final period of Paredes's life were not pieces of the contemporary moment, nor even products of the 1950s and 1960s. They were instead products of the thirties and forties, decades before that of his mature scholarly work. As products of an era other than those of the twentieth-century fin de siècle, they belie their postmodern, post–Chicano movement thematics and publication dates.

George Washington Gómez, which I have just discussed, and the collection of poetry *Between Two Worlds*, to which I now turn, both written during the years of the Great Depression in the Texas-Mexican borderlands of deep south Texas, advance with imaginative force the sophisticated insight of Paredes's later exemplary transdisciplinary work of social criticism and cultural intervention. They prefigure crucial aspects of postmodern Chicano and Chicana writing from a high modernist, premovement historical moment. Together with the later scholarly work, the novel and the poetry can now be seen in retrospect as part of a larger imaginative project to offer what Héctor Calderón correctly identifies as "a redefinition of the borderlands [as] . . . a historically determinate geopolitical zone of military, cultural, and linguistic conflict" (22). This project seeks as well to invent a figural discourse of national epic proportions appropriate to the reconstruction of a new narrative of a truly hemispheric American social and cultural history at the borders of modernity. In doing so, Paredes intends in his poetry to outline the contours of subjectivity absent from other discourses of the modern.

Modernism on the Border

Paredes's literary productions are richly marked by the flavor of their origins in the era of high literary modernism in both its Anglo-

European and Latin American varieties. They are also self-consciously steeped in an unwavering resistance to the residual effects of nineteenth-century American imperialism and its racist aftermath, as well as to the continuing effects of twentieth-century capitalist transformations of production in the Southwest. Paredes's literary writings, but especially *Between Two Worlds*, composed during the very moment of what could arguably be called the historical divide between the modern and the postmodern, represents the bifurcated, interstitial, differential quality of the kind of writing that in its post-contemporary form has come to be called border writing.[2] Looking as it does from its liminal present both to the past and to the future, speaking an oddly dual idiom that simultaneously celebrates a lyrical history and forebodes a prosaic future, *Between Two Worlds* might well emblematize the features of that postmodern border writing, were it not for the fact that it predates the notion by more than half a century. At the same time, it should be noted that deconstructing unities of history and even of subjectivity does not imply for Paredes that only chaotic and idiosyncratic histories can be written. There are definite episodes of historical transition to be identified; there are definite consequences to modernity to be described.

Despite what could be shown as his work's allegiance to a certain aesthetics of canonic modernism, I wish to show in this next section of my study that the crux of Paredes's work in lyric and narrative poetry is the *form* that his modernism takes in the interstices between the northern and southern American hemispheres. Another way of conceiving this formal modernism on the border is to see it as an element of what I am here calling "transnational modernism," or, the experience of modernism—the ideology of the modern—in its transitive mode. I wish to organize my approach to Paredes's poetry along three broad themes: (1) attitudes toward the space of modernism as representation and construction, including the social, national, geographic, historical, and imaginary spaces of representation; (2) theories of the production of subjectivity, including the subjectivity of the artist, of the reader, and of their represented subject positions, especially as citizens; and, (3) assumptions about the ontology of the object, from aesthetic formalism to deconstructively based interpretations of a belief in the a priori existence of the object.[3] By focusing on these three themes—space as representation, the production of subject positions, the ontology of the object—modernism in its

most standard, canonical form can be read as a rhetoric of representation, rather than through the usual critical legacy of formalism and
the avant-garde.

The concept of a unified modernism has been under considerable reformulation for over the past twenty-five years, with increasing intensity in the last decade. The mid-twentieth-century analysis
of modernism, which literally mapped a succession of stylistic devel-
opments in a genealogical pattern, has long been abandoned. Today,
the lineage of modernism as formal innovation, the legacy of the
avant-garde, and the place of high art within European and American
twentieth-century cultural history have all been held up for question
through the methodological tools of feminist theory, queer studies,
deconstructive approaches to history and textual analysis, varieties of
historicisms old and new, postcolonial and postmodern theory, and
the rigors of cultural studies. The undoing of the hegemonic unity of
modernism has proven a complex process, the result of work in diverse
fields. The work of Theodor Adorno and Max Horkheimer, Walter
Benjamin, Georg Lukács, and Raymond Williams has proven crucial
in this regard. More recently, Paul de Man, Jacques Derrida, Stuart
Hall, Edward Said, Terry Eagleton, and Fredric Jameson have developed the insights of the early theorists of modernism.[4] Because of
this rewriting and reconfiguring of twentieth-century culture under
the aegis of critical theory, high-art modernism, canonic modernism,
is no longer unquestionably granted a privileged place by virtue of
its aesthetic concerns. This questioning of the privilege of the modern and of modernism has been made especially crucial by scholars
such as Johanna Drucker, Linda Hutcheon, Rita Felski, Judith Butler,
Eve Kosofsky Sedgwick, and Gayatri Chakravorty Spivak.[5] Yet even
these rewritings contain critical assumptions that are the legacy of
modern art and theory. Even so, the emphasis on formal innovation
and the oppositional role of the avant-garde remains central to critical and theoretical texts. The ghosts of received tradition have largely
been driven away from the cutting edge of thinking about modernity, but concepts of form, formalism, subjectivity, and history remain tenacious in their hold on assumptions about what constitutes
"the" modern.

Modernity, Transculturation, and Metalogues

This is why, even though I understand modernism in the traditional sense, I also offer the term *subaltern modernity* for reading Paredes's work through the idea of transculturation, a word borrowed from the Cuban sociologist Fernando Ortiz. The concept of *transculturation* articulates the assimilation of one cultural group to another under the pressure of differential political and economic power. Ortiz employs the term in this way:

> With the reader's permission, especially if he happens to be interested in ethnographic and sociological questions, I am going to take the liberty of employing for the first time the term *transculturation*, fully aware of the fact that it is a neologism. And I venture to suggest that it might be adopted in sociological terminology . . . as a substitute for the term *acculturation*, whose use is now spreading.

> *Acculturation* is used to describe the process of transition from one culture to another, and its manifold social repercussions. But *transculturation* is a more fitting term.

> I have chosen the word *transculturation* to express the highly varied phenomena that have come about in Cuba as a result of the extremely complex transmutations of culture that have taken place here, and without a knowledge of which it is impossible to understand the evolution of the Cuban folk, either in the economic or in the institutional, legal, ethical, religious, artistic, linguistic, psychological, sexual, or other aspects of its life. (97–98)

From Ortiz's notion of transculturation, I wish to retain especially his idea that at the point where one encounters the syncretism of cultures, one finds that the formerly independent structures are reshaped in formidable ways. Each element participating in the syncretic experience of transculturation undergoes a process of mutually caustic interaction and violent change. This process is "always exerting an influence and being influenced in turn" by everyone else in the mix of cultures, such that in the end, each transcultured individual ends up being "torn from his native moorings, faced with the problem of disadjustment and readjustment, of deculturation and acculturation—in a word, of transculturation" (98). Mary Louise Pratt has noted that the term *transculturation* describes "how subordinated or marginal groups select and invent from materials transmitted to them by a dominant or metropolitan culture" (6).[6] *Transculturation* is the term Paredes himself would later use to describe the interactive process by which different cultural groups within Greater Mexico and Mexico proper experienced the pressures and complexities of life in the borderlands and how they negotiated what they absorbed from the dominant culture and why ("Folklore of Groups" 8). Transculturation is not a matter of evading the dominant culture, but of choosing how one must confront it. Beyond the possibilities of agency, however, it is nevertheless the case, as the critic John Beverley reminds us, that "transculturation does not overcome subaltern positionality; rather, subaltern positionality operates and reproduces itself in and through transculturation" (61).

In addition to the notion of transculturation, I use here the many deconstructions of the hegemony of a fictive modernist autonomy and unity to consider why certain positions within modernism have been kept from consideration. Chief among these is formalism itself, which is primarily concerned with the aesthetic issues appropriate to understanding the textual characteristics of modernist works. At the same time, I will also consider social and cultural history, with their powerful emphasis on the dynamic relations between ideology and representation, and between the economic basis of power and the activity of production and reproduction. I wish to consider both the diachronic lineage of formalism and the synchronic analysis of poetry as ideological formations by attempting to describe the rhetoric of representation in Paredes's works, examining their codes of representation. I pose in this section of the study the possibility of identifying aesthetic visions of a modernist imaginary in terms not defined by nationalist ideologies but remaining open to the consequences of transnationalism, that is, moving from a vertical and bipolar conceptualization of culture (high and low) to one that is decentered and overdetermined (a counterculture of modernity).[7] My concern will be to see how the idea of modernism as a social construct is developed and debated in European and American contexts and how issues of class, race, and gender identity modify it. Subject, object, and the space of representation stand as the organizing concepts of my investigation into Paredes's transnational modernisms.

Paredes's *Between Two Worlds*, as a product and a symptom of the end of modernism at the peripheries of modernization, suggests how commonly held characterizations of modernist ideologies as ahistorical and apolitical are not adequate for explaining the cultural productions of writers actively engaged in decolonization struggles on the margins of sanctioned history and in the borderlands of high culture. The figural languages of Paredes's verse exert force politically as unofficial discourses at the margins of official versions of history; they also function aesthetically as metalogues whose discursive shapes recapitulate their themes of revision.[8] In his poetry, Paredes would construe the relationship between modernity and the nation as the defining condition for the borderlands subject-citizen.

To gain a sense of the formative effect of the historical and political categories on modern literature as a whole, it is first necessary to recognize the peculiar constructions of modern nationalism in the context of competing nationalisms (the existence and stubborn persistence of regional voices, popular styles, or minority-group identifications) *within* the borders of the nation and that these competing nationalisms are articulated in different imaginative registers attempting to define a native idiom and a distinctive cultural identity. I am seeking to account for what some today are denoting as the postnational subject—but which I am calling the transnational subject— in the very midst of that subject's formation. Paredes's works demonstrate that this subject in process, displaced and dispossessed in the official narratives of literary history, offers a substantial critique of the traditional justifications of modernity. Far from celebrating identity as an accomplished end, this view of the subject in process, never complete, problematizes, as Stuart Hall has said, "the very authority and authenticity to which the term, 'cultural identity,' lays claim" ("Cultural Identity and Diaspora" 222).

The works I examine seek to remap the cultural space of modern literary history and to contribute to the ongoing critical revision of the entire narrative of cultural nationalism and its place in mid-twentieth-century global politics. In the process, they participate in what Fredric Jameson, in a related idiom, has called the "cognitive mappings" of the new type of collective social space and cultural practice where resistance to forces of domination might be effectively marshaled and enacted (*Postmodernism* 409). Indeed, these writings urge us to interrogate what constitutes social space—as an arena of polity, race, and gender—even as they display the power of culture to help shape (and not merely reflect or express) the nation and the subject of that nation at the symbolic level. These works thus participate in the production and documentation of a transnational modernity.

Finally, my readings mark the development of a transnational modernist aesthetic that limits both a traditional modernism and an uncritical or celebratory multiculturalism. For Paredes, writing at the height of the modern, the allure of a modernist aesthetic persisted even as he recognized its limitations for capturing the heterogeneity of culture. The transnational imaginary offered an alternative way of accounting for the differential world he inhabited and described.

Nationalism and Literature

At the beginning of the twenty-first century, with many nations once thought fully consolidated now finding themselves challenged and, indeed, sundered by " 'sub'-nationalisms within their borders— nationalisms which, naturally, dream of shedding this sub-ness one happy day," as Benedict Anderson puts it—it is increasingly clear that the end of the era of nationalism is "not remotely in sight" (*Imagined Communities* 3). Even as the epoch of multi-, trans-, and even postnational isms bears down on us, the idea of "nation-ness" remains "the most universally legitimate value in the political life of our time" (3). A work such as Paredes's *Between Two Worlds* proves crucial to an understanding of modernity in relation to nationalism precisely because it demonstrates with astonishing clarity the fundamental link between basic political economy and ideas of culture, on one hand, and the joint constructs of modernism and the nation, on the other. Neither apolitical nor ahistorical, Paredes's modernity is formed by the historical and political legacy of the Mexican American communities of the borderlands.

To gain a sense of the formative effect of the historical and the political on Paredes as a modernist poet, we need first to recognize the peculiar constructions of American nationalism and the construction of its national literature. The sociologist of culture Sarah M. Corse claims that "national literatures have traditionally been understood as reflections of the unique character and experiences of the nation" (*Nationalism and Literature* 1). As an alternative to the traditional argument for a reflective relation between national literature and national character, Corse proposes a sociological conception of literature that attempts to take into account the relationship between textual content and the context of its mode of production, and the "identity formation processes of the nation-state" (4). Focusing on the "social, cultural, and political processes of literary *use* and national identity *construction*," Corse proposes that "both national literatures and nations themselves are socially constructed under identifiable political and historical circumstances—and that the two processes are deeply interwoven" (4, emphasis original). This model is congenially applicable to Paredes's literary, journalistic, and scholarly writings both by nature of their intellectual disposition and of their disciplinary formation. As Paredes explores the question of modern cultural nationalism in the borderlands and identifies the contradictions that beset it, he anticipates and heralds topics in the sociology of literature, the new American studies, the new literary history, and the new social history of art.[9]

Under these new conceptions of the nature of national literatures, works of literary production, like nationalism generally, are to be seen as "cultural artifacts of a particular kind" (B. Anderson 4). In the United States, the search for a uniquely native national literature has emerged as one of the defining features of that literature—so long as it was written in English and came from New England. The need for distinction from and parity with British and continental literatures in the late eighteenth and nineteenth centuries meant that this native national literature would symbolize national identity. This also meant that the artifacts constituting the national literature would be formed as much by defining pressures from outside the nation at its peripheral borders as by those emanating from the inner central heartland. The particular constellation of ideologies that demarcate the boundaries of that bipolar construct make up, as Homi Bhabha suggests, its imaginative horizon (*Nation and Narration* 1).

In his poetry of the 1930s and 1940s, Paredes represents the limits of the Anglo-American cultural and political horizon, limits precisely instantiated at its borders by the emergence of a modern new Mexican subject, neither Anglo-American nor Mexican national, but rather the product of the newly self-imagined difference between these two separate nationalisms. A lyric poet at the end of the era of high modernism, Paredes sought to create poetic figures to account for what we are today denoting as the postnational Latino subject in the very midst of that subject's formation.

The Imaginary "Cit'zen of Texas"

The subject in process that Paredes describes in his poetry existed in an empty discursive realm, outside of formal American histories and absent from Mexican intellectual concerns. Attempting to redress those dual exclusions, Paredes imagines a history and a future for borderland citizenry from within the lived situation of their double exclusions. That imaginative project constitutes what I am calling his vernacular poetics in order to account for Paredes's bardic role in the symbolization of these new borderland identities.[10] In "The Mexico-Texan," cited at the beginning of this chapter and one of his earliest creative efforts in this vein, Paredes explicitly reveals the inadequacies of the American promise of full participation in citizenship and a share in national identity for those caught between Mexico and Texas: "A cit'zen of Texas they say that he ees, / But then, why they call him the Mexican Grease?" (*Between Two Worlds* 58). "The Mexico-Texan" figures the migrant workers, the day laborers, and the families in transit of the mid-Depression-era borderlands, to be seen everywhere, standing around street corners, hands in pockets, waiting for a day's work, a restless population that moved through south Texas, Arizona, California, all over the Midwest, and across the Rio Grande into Mexico, available to whoever had work and a few dollars to pay them. Of the Mexico Texan's national identity, Paredes thus writes: "He no gotta country, he no gotta flag / He no gotta voice, all he got is the han' / To work like the burro; he no gotta lan.' " People like the Mexico Texan were *ciudadanos imaginarios*, imaginary "cit'zens" of a mythical country, figured ironically against both Mexico and Texas, but in reality neither here nor there. Theirs was a country where national borders expanded or contracted and could be respected or ignored but where nothing changed as they could be "stomped on the neck on both sides of the Gran.' " This was a world between worlds where everyone seemed dispossessed in one form or another, creating, at best, regional affiliations and passionate alliances with yet unrealized national cultures. The Mexico Texan was thus Paredes's metaphor of a figure in process, a person to be invented, whose allegiances were yet to be determined, in transit toward an unspecified locale that he was to call in one of his poems from this period "ahí nomás," an indeterminate elsewhere, "just over there." To understand better the transitory dynamics of modernity within the history of the borderlands subject and the manner of its expression in cultural production within this political landscape, however, we must first turn to the narrative of history itself and situate our subjects in their social context on the border of modernity.

Franklin Delano Roosevelt's Four Freedoms

On the afternoon of January 3, 1940, Franklin Delano Roosevelt entered the Senate chamber to deliver his annual message to the Congress. With the impact of the European war fully in everyone's mind, Roosevelt thought it natural to approach the State of the Union address "through a discussion of foreign affairs" (Roosevelt 1).[11] At the same time, he warned, "The social and economic forces which have been mismanaged abroad until they have resulted in revolution, dictatorship and war are the same as those which we here are struggling to adjust peacefully at home" (1). Recently elected to a third full term, Roosevelt and his New Deal legislation, dealing with "food, homes, railroads, money, trees, and jobs" (8), had come to be identified rightly with the features of *homo oeconomicus* rather than with the qualities of *homo spiritualis*. In a subtle shift from quantity to quality, Roosevelt now argued that the three great constitutional phrases— *common defense, general welfare,* and *domestic tranquility*—calling for the promotion and assurance of a good and just life within the country—required listeners to see the internal welfare of the American citizenry and its peaceful adjustment to "social and economic forces" in the context of the international framework of intertwined political and economic interests (1). Roosevelt thus reminded his audience that "you are well aware that dictatorships—and the philosophy of force that justifies and accompanies dictatorships—have originated in almost every case in the necessity for drastic action to improve internal conditions in places where democratic action for one reason or another has failed to respond to modern needs and modern demands" (1). Responding to these "modern needs and modern demands" moreover required, according to Roosevelt, a renewed commitment to the traditional ethical and moral propositions best expressed politically under the banner of "basic human rights" (Greer 10–11). "The permanent security of America in the present crisis does not lie in armed force alone," Roosevelt continued. "What we face is a set of worldwide forces of disintegration—vicious, ruthless, destructive of all the moral, religious and political standards which mankind, after centuries of struggle, has come to cherish" (8). In his great call for a renewal of "moral values" in political terms to combat these "forces of disintegration," Roosevelt now claimed that

> in 1933 we met a problem of real fear and real defeatism. We faced the facts—with action and not with words alone.
>
> The American people will reject the doctrine of fear, confident that in the 'thirties we have been building soundly *a new order of things*, different from the order of the 'twenties. In this dawn of the decade of the 'forties, with our program of social improvement started, we will continue to carry on the processes of recovery, so as to preserve our gains and provide jobs at living wages. (8; emphasis added)

Through Roosevelt's multistep "process of recovery," represented by the policies of the New Deal, the "American people" (as distinct from the American *nation*) were gradually being cured of their psychic fear and economic depression. Addressing the real needs of the people as citizens would cure the ills of the nation as an imagined institution. He thus felt that "jobs at living wages" might well still the citizenry's understandable fears and provide an authentic kind of national security that armed force alone could not. Implicitly, however, Roosevelt's goal in 1940 was not simply to rehabilitate the nation by offering its people economic security; he was as keen to salvage the nation's collective psyche from the corrosive effects of "real fear and real defeatism" and to redirect the narrative of its history away from the trajectory of a world-historical narrative that seemed frighteningly impelled by very real "forces of disintegration."

One year later, on January 6, 1941, with American entry into the war now less than a year away, Roosevelt returned again to Congress to elaborate further on the ethico-political "new order of things" for which his policies had already laid the ground and to expand on his narrative of national renewal. In the days before his annual State of the Union address to Congress and the nation, Roosevelt had fretted over how best to address in one unified line the lingering effects of spiritual and economic crisis, the need for a revaluation of political standards in moral terms, and the real urgency of preparing for the coming war. At the very brink of war, its shadow practically touching the shores of the American continent, Roosevelt now again urged Congress to prepare the ground for this new order by understanding that national security certainly involved vigilance and action on the international stage and in foreign policy, with the United States continuing to serve as the "arsenal of democracy" with the establishment of the Lend-Lease Act (Roosevelt 668). Nevertheless, he was also still profoundly aware of how national security depended on the internal stage of domestic affairs. So now, in 1941, Roosevelt again argued, "As men do not live by bread alone, they do not fight by armaments alone. Those who man our defenses, and those behind them who build our defenses, must have the stamina and the courage which come from unshakable belief in the manner of life they are defending" (670). Consequently this was no time, he pleaded, to stop thinking about "the social and economic problems which are the root cause of the social revolution which is today a supreme factor in the world" (670). Having linked national security and domestic tranquility in the alleviation of the national depression, private individual interests thus having assumed public collective significance (Arendt 33), Roosevelt looked ahead, even beyond the war that the United States had not yet officially entered, to "the ultimate objectives of American policy" (Greer 12) to sketch a vision of what the nation might one day be. What emerged from that vision was an extraordinarily felicitous formulation: The Four Freedoms. "In the future days, which we seek to make secure," Roosevelt proclaimed in his now celebrated phrasing, "we look forward to a world founded upon four essential freedoms":

The first is freedom of speech and expression—everywhere in the world.

The second is freedom of every person to worship God in his own way—everywhere in the world.

The third is freedom from want—which, translated into world terms, means economic understandings which will secure to every nation a healthy peacetime life for its inhabitants—everywhere in the world.

The fourth is freedom from fear—which, translated into world terms, means a world-wide reduction of armaments to such a point and in such a thorough fashion that no nation will be in a position to commit an act of physical aggression against any neighbor—anywhere in the world. (672)

Cynics mocked that Roosevelt here offered no more than a utopian vision of a distant millennium (Greer 12). Roosevelt himself, however, had insisted in his message to the nation that his grand idea of the Four Freedoms was "a definite basis for a kind of world attainable in our own time and generation" (672). Even more grandly, for him the Four Freedoms constituted both a renewal of the American commitment to basic human rights and an extension of those personal rights into the transpersonal arena of world politics.

The Four Freedoms, of speech and worship, and from want and fear, had, as the historian Eric Foner points out, "an unmistakably liberal cast" (223). At various times over the next few years, Roosevelt would compare the Four Freedoms with "the Ten Commandments, the Magna Carta, and the Emancipation Proclamation" (Foner 223). They represented the culmination of Roosevelt's lifelong commitment to liberal democratic notions of justice and fundamental human rights.[12] The New Deal agenda for American renewal, to be understood as an ethical revaluation for the elimination of spiritual and economic maladies, was now turned outward on the world in general. Modern social conditions in 1941, on the eve of the American entry into the latest of the great imperial European world wars, precluded that on the international as on the national scale "the social and economic problems which are the root cause of the social revolution" affecting the world could be ignored.[13] "The world order which we seek is the cooperation of free countries, working together in a friendly, civilized society" (672). To this end, then, Roosevelt asked "all Americans to respond to that call" (671), concluding that "our strength is our unity of purpose" (Roosevelt 672).

Now what is at stake in Roosevelt's momentous pronouncement of a world order built on the groundwork of the Four Freedoms is nothing less than a renewed commitment to an ideal vision of a unified American nation working to effect that brave new world order under the pressure of "modern [American] social conditions." In a hegemonic move worthy of the most enlightened of liberals, Roosevelt urged the personal liberties guaranteed in the Bill of Rights as the constitutional ground for the construction of both a modern new American nation and a modern new world order formed in an American image. Emerging from an older Republican disorder built on neurotic fears and shaken by real depression, the nation's, and the world's, unity is here called into existence as a Democratic system of cultural signification, "as the representation of social *life* rather than the discipline of social *polity*" (Bhabha, *Nation and Narration* 1–22, emphasis original). The narrative of global and national unity that Roosevelt elegantly unravels displays exactly this conceptual divide between lived experience of social life, on the one hand, and the institutionalized structuration of that experience in the social polity, on the other. It also exemplifies perfectly Benedict Anderson's thesis that "nationalism has to be understood, by aligning it, not with self-consciously held political ideologies, but with the large cultural systems that preceded it, out of which—as well as against which—it came into being" (12). The ideology distinctly at work here is that of freedom in its exceptionally American forms.

Norman Rockwell's Four Freedoms

"Talk of freedom," as Eric Foner notes, "permeated wartime America." The outbreak of war with the Japanese attack on Pearl Harbor occasioned an outpouring of "books, pamphlets, and advertisements intended to arouse patriotic sentiment, market war bonds, . . . and give concrete meaning to wartime ideals" (225). Illustrators, artists, and composers from cartoonist Walt Disney to muralist Hugo Ballin and composer Robert Russell Bennett dedicated artworks representing Roosevelt's Four Freedoms in patriotic fervor. Without a doubt, however, Norman Rockwell created the most celebrated of these representations. This was so much the case that, as Laurie Norton Moffatt, director of the Norman Rockwell Museum, observes, "in the minds of many, Rockwell's images became interchangeable with Roosevelt's concepts" (Murray and McCabe ix).[14]

In his autobiography written almost two decades later, Rockwell reminisced that at the outset of the war he had been looking without success for an idea for a poster that would contribute to the war effort and "make some statement about why the country was fighting the war" (Rockwell and Rockwell 338). No single work of art had yet managed to portray the "four essential freedoms" as powerfully as Roosevelt had. In Vermont, Rockwell struggled to find a way of picturing America's soul. Then, one night, while tossing and turning in

15 Norman Rockwell, *The Four Freedoms: Freedom of Speech*, 1943. Reprinted with the permission of the Norman Rockwell Family Agency LLC, John Rockwell and the Norman Rockwell Art Collection Trust, and the Norman Rockwell Museum at Stockbridge, Massachusetts.

16 Norman Rockwell, *The Four Freedoms: Freedom of Worship*, 1943. Reprinted with the permission of the Norman Rockwell Family Agency LLC, John Rockwell and the Norman Rockwell Art Collection Trust, and the Norman Rockwell Museum at Stockbridge, Massachusetts.

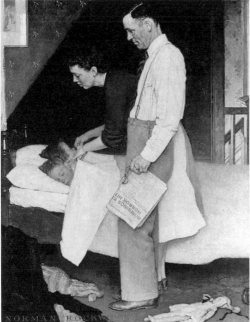

17 Norman Rockwell, *The Four Freedoms: Freedom from Want*, 1943. Reprinted with the permission of the Norman Rockwell Family Agency LLC, John Rockwell and the Norman Rockwell Art Collection Trust, and the Norman Rockwell Museum at Stockbridge, Massachusetts.

18 Norman Rockwell, *The Four Freedoms: Freedom from Fear*, 1943. Reprinted with the permission of the Norman Rockwell Family Agency LLC, John Rockwell and the Norman Rockwell Art Collection Trust, and the Norman Rockwell Museum at Stockbridge, Massachusetts.

bed, he found the feeling behind Roosevelt's expression of the "four essential human freedoms":

> I suddenly remembered how Jim Edgerton had stood up in a town meeting and said something that everybody else disagreed with. But they had let him have his say. No one shouted him down. My gosh, I thought, that's it. There it is. Freedom of Speech. I'll illustrate the Four Freedoms using my Vermont neighbors as models. I'll express the ideas in simple, everyday scenes. Freedom of Speech—a New England town meeting. Freedom from Want—a Thanksgiving dinner. Take them out of the noble language of the proclamation and put them in terms everybody can understand. (338–39)

In four consecutive weekly numbers beginning with the February 20, 1943, issue, the *Saturday Evening Post* published Rockwell's representations of the American soul in four achingly sentimental scenes. Rockwell's posters conveyed a simple, if not altogether unambiguous, message. They portrayed carefully selected images of an American way of life based on fundamental civic, social, and political institutions: the democratic process, the church, and the family. Lester C. Olson proposes that "the posters promoted identifications which constitute the tenets of a conjoined religious and political perspective" (16). *Freedom of Speech* was the first of Rockwell's illustrations published in the *Saturday Evening Post* on February 20, 1943. The scene depicts a town meeting in Vermont, viewed from the perspective of a participant, perhaps turning around from a position within the audience to hear the words of a plain American workingman. Despite differences of age, gender, and social class among the represented figures, the unifying purpose of the gathering is made manifest in the gazes of the citizens focused on the central figure, an embodiment of the spirit of the commonwealth of American democracy in the town hall meeting.

Freedom of Worship, which appeared the following week, focused on the centrality of religion in American civic life and depicts individuals of divergent backgrounds worshipping, in the words of the slogan superimposed on the illustration, "each according to the dictates of his own conscience." *Freedom from Want* and *Freedom from Fear*, appearing on the next two consecutive Saturdays, converge on the central role of the family in the creation of that American civic religion. In *Freedom from Want*, Rockwell invites the viewer's participation in the scene by archly inserting himself turning toward us from the lower right-hand corner of the frame, as if to greet us, just having entered the scene. A grandmother serves an enormous turkey to the gathered extended family, joyously anticipating the bountiful fruits of American freedom. In this scene of classic Thanksgiving overabundance, Rockwell "fuses family, country, and God into a celebration" (Olson 17) in a manner very much akin to what Rousseau in *The Social Contract* describes as "civil religion." Existing alongside of and clearly differentiated from formal religion, this "profession de foi purement civile" (profession of faith which is purely civil) is essential for the creation of a cohesive commonwealth, contends Rousseau.[15] In contrast to spiritual religion based on individual belief, the civil religion of the citizen is based on "sentimens de sociabilité" (expressions of social conscience) elicited precisely to join the citizen with the virtues of the state and ensure the social conscience of the good citizen ("Du contract social" 468). Of all of the civic rituals that create an intimate relation between religious notions, the self-conception of the state, and the private life of its citizens, the uniquely American version of this performance of social conscience is surely the celebration of Thanksgiving Day. This profoundly national holiday probably stands as the best example of the profession of civil faith at work in American life in the way that it "serves to integrate the family into civil religion" (Bellah, "Civil Religion" 179). Rockwell's paintings proved so powerful in their effect because he there articulates the profoundest commitments of American democracy and the most fundamental beliefs of ordinary Americans.

The final painting in the series, *Freedom from Fear*, takes viewers even more deeply into the emotive needs of the citizenry. Rockwell now leads his audience into the children's bedroom as a mother tenderly tucks them into bed and a pensive father looks on. As Olson points out, "The scene is peaceful, except for the unsettling headline on the newspaper the father carries: 'Bombing Ki—Horror Hit—,' and in smaller print: 'Women and Children Slaughtered by Raids'" (18). In a world at war where women and children are being slaughtered daily, the bedroom scene becomes an almost too smug representation of American peace, tranquility, and security.[16]

The illustrations elicited an enormously positive response, and the *Post* was deluged with requests for reprints of Rockwell's illustrations. As the historian Robert B. Westbrook points out, Rockwell's *Four*

Freedoms illustrations quickly became the best-known paintings of the era, enduring national symbols reprinted in the millions and distributed all over the world (203). "They appeared," wrote Ben Hibbs, the editor of the *Saturday Evening Post*, "right at a time when the war was going against us on the battle fronts, and the American people needed the inspirational message which they conveyed so forcefully and so beautifully" (qtd. in Rockwell and Rockwell 343).[17] What was the message that these illustrations conveyed "so forcefully and so beautifully"? "It was," writes Westbrook, "that Americans were fighting World War II to protect essentially private interests and discharge essentially private obligations. And, in two of the four paintings, the message was that the people of the United States were fighting for the family" (qtd. in Rockwell and Rockwell 203).

Carlos Bulosan: "Freedom Is Not
an Intangible Thing"

Each of Rockwell's illustrations published in the *Saturday Evening Post* was accompanied by complementary essays reflecting on the meaning of each of the Four Freedoms. Some of the most celebrated writers of the age, including Booth Tarkington, Will Durant, and Stephen Vincent Bénet, wrote the essays.[18] For the essay dedicated to the most problematic of the private and familial representations of the Four Freedoms, *Freedom from Want*, the editors of the *Saturday Evening Post* selected a young, virtually unknown Filipino writer by the name of Carlos Bulosan.[19] Unlike the nostalgic representations of an American past that really never quite existed as portrayed in Rockwell's epideictic paintings, Bulosan's essay looked forward to a possible American future where those outside the American social mainstream—migrant farmworkers, union organizers, cannery laborers, black victims of segregation, Asian and Latino immigrants—might be allowed to experience real freedom. For these Americans, "freedom meant having enough to eat, sending their children to school," and the desire to share in the unfulfilled promise of American democracy (Foner 227).

Bulosan himself was so outside the social mainstream at the time that he was selected to contribute an essay almost by accident. As the series was in preparation, the *Saturday Evening Post* associate editor

Stuart Rose had chanced one day to be in the offices of Bulosan's literary agent and read there an outline of Bulosan's projected autobiography. In the words of the *Saturday Evening Post*, Rose "found in it a rare quality, a quality which he felt should go into the text of Freedom from Want" (Hibbs 4).[20] In his late twenties, Bulosan—like so many other Filipino, Mexican, black, and white workers—was living on the periphery of the American dream, experiencing more the America of *The Grapes of Wrath* than the one imagined in Rockwell's *Four Freedoms* paintings. Bulosan was a journeyman laborer, working odd jobs, picking berries and fruit in the Northwest, making a living as best he could bumming from small town to small town during the Depression and, as he admits, had never experienced the freedom from want. In fact, Bulosan was so far on the edge at the time of the commission that when the nightmare of all writers occurred—the *Post* inexplicably lost his manuscript—he was barely able to recover from the near disaster. The editors of the *Post* tracked him down in Tacoma and requested the carbon copy of the essay. There was none; Bulosan had abandoned the only working draft of the article in the tavern where he had written it. Bulosan tells his side of the story in a letter to his agent, quoted in the *Saturday Evening Post*: "Today your telegram came telling me the article was lost. I was worried because I didn't make a carbon copy. In fact, the draft, the only draft, was left on a table in a beer tavern in Tacoma. I rushed to Tacoma. I almost cried when the manager produced it. It was spilled with beer and one end was burned. Some drunk must have used it to light his cigar" (qtd. in Hibbs 4).

From experience, Bulosan understood that for Americans like him freedom from want was something that lay as a possibility in the future, not something experienced at the Thanksgiving Day dinner table. In the *Saturday Evening Post* essay, Bulosan would thus say about Americans like himself:

> If you want to know what we are, look upon the farms or upon the hard pavements of the city. You usually see us working or waiting for work, you think you know us, but our outward guise is more deceptive than our history. . . . We celebrate labor, wisdom, peace of the soul. . . .

> But we are not really free unless we use what we produce. So long as the fruit of our labor is denied us, so long will want manifest itself in a world of slaves. It is only when we have plenty to eat—plenty of everything—

that we begin to understand what freedom means. To us, freedom is not an intangible thing. When we have enough to eat, then we are healthy enough to enjoy what we eat. Then we have the time and ability to read and think and discuss things. Then we are not merely living but also becoming a creative part of life. It is only then that we become a growing part of democracy. . . .

What do we want? We want complete security and peace. We want to share the promises and fruits of American life. We want to be free from fear and hunger. ("Freedom from Want" 12)[21]

Against Norman Rockwell's painting of a family Thanksgiving gathering celebrated to overindulgence at a time when people worldwide were dying of starvation because of global warfare, Bulosan's words appeared haunting and sharp. Unwittingly, by juxtaposing Rockwell's bountiful surfeit, a typical scene of American overabundance, with Bulosan's lean language, the editors of the *Saturday Evening Post* were illustrating the necessity of the reciprocal relationship between the liberal democratic state and its citizens. The state was obliged to provide a minimal level of subsistence for all of its citizens if all of its citizens were to owe the state the duties and obligations of loyalty, allegiance, identification, and, ultimately, self-sacrifice. Moffatt justly observes that "President Roosevelt and Norman Rockwell addressed, each in his own way, a profound question of citizenship: what are the national goals which justify asking citizens to make ultimate sacrifices?" (Foreword to Murray and McCabe x). Bulosan responded by calling for "a democracy worth defending" ("Freedom from Want" 12) on behalf of those American citizens who were "not really free" because they were without "Freedom from Want." He spoke for all those who could legitimately wonder "if we are really a part of America" (Westbrook 204).

Bulosan's essay in the *Saturday Evening Post* sequence on the Four Freedoms gets squarely at the issues of national and individual identity and the rights of citizens in relation to the pledges of American democracy. It was chosen by the editors of the *Saturday Evening Post* precisely because it offered, as Foner explains, an extension of the American promise into the postwar future, rather than a retreat to Rockwell's imagined past of white American small-town life (227–28). For working men and women of color, the failure of the nation's institutions to live up to the declarations of the Four Freedoms amounted to a critique in practice of the rights and obligations of citizenship (Westbrook 195). If the traditional foundations of the democratic state, such as freedom from fear and want, did not form part of the experience of their lives, on what possible basis could political duty and obligation to the state be justified?

As the political theorist Michael Walzer has argued, in the context of war, the general problem of the citizens' obligation to the state becomes even more acute because the state requires that citizens risk their lives for the sake of the state. In the liberal democratic tradition of Thomas Hobbes and John Locke, the purpose of the state is primarily to secure and protect individual life. Locke, for instance, explains in *The Second Treatise of Government* (1690) why people found it advantageous to move from the freedom of the state of nature into the restrictions of civil society. Locke maintains that the only reason why anyone "divests himself of his natural liberty and puts on the bonds of civil society" is by agreeing to unite with others in order to create "a community for their comfortable, safe, and peaceable living amongst one another" (95). In creating forms and structures of governance, he continues, people "make one body politic" and begin to feel "safe and secure." Furthermore, in doing so, they "are united and combined together into one coherent, living body," and from this congregation of security and purpose the very life of the commonwealth arises, declares Locke: "This is the soul that gives form, life, and unity to the commonwealth" (212). Locke is specifically referring here to the system of laws embodied in legislative forms that make up civil society. However, his words evoke the psychological and emotive factors related to the very human desire to belong, to form part of the field of care of a larger community of shared self-interest. The commonwealth of the state provides comfort, coherence, safety, and security, and in the process it creates the very unity and soul of a nation's living body, its affective sensorium. Citizens should protect the state because it protects them. Walzer turns the Hobbesian and Lockean view against itself with the argument that when citizens "protect their protection they are doing nothing more than defending themselves, and so they cannot protect their protection after their protection ceases to protect them. At that point, it ceases to be their protection. The state has no value over and above the value of the lives of the concrete individuals whose safety it provides" (82).[22] This is exactly the point that intellectuals like C. L. R. James, Emma Tenayuca, Carlos Bulosan, and Américo Paredes, writing from the margins of the state's protection, were making in the years leading up to Pearl Harbor.

That there existed profound ambiguities, as well as fissures and cracks, within the ideologies of enlightened liberal democratic self-interest and the culturally determined narrative of American history underwriting Roosevelt's Four Freedoms address to the nation is all too well known. The historian Tom Nairn has argued, and economic conditions of late twentieth-century America have exemplified, that the uneven development of capitalism inscribes within the modern nation social progression in an alternate cycle with economic regression, imbricating both "progress and regress in the very genetic code of the nation" (345–46). Consequently, the course of national history can never run smoothly. History offers ample instances of how, in moderate doses, nationalism can provide a positive, collective identity; however, it shows concurrently that in immoderate or irrational doses, nationalism creates negative, even lethal, chauvinisms. In either case, what is apparent from a glance at the rhetoric of national discourse, for example here in Roosevelt's usage in reference to the crisis of the Great Depression, is the psychologistic cast of its tropes and metaphors. As Locke suggests, there is nothing accidental in this link between the structures of the nation and the makeup of human subjectivity: nationalism explicitly provides one way of joining the subjective conditions with the material modes of production. Bulosan expressed this relation by asking, "What do we want?" His response that "we want complete security and peace. We want to share the promises and fruits of American life. We want to be free from fear and hunger," challenged the liberal bourgeois rhetoric of the Lockean commonwealth to live up to its promise. The emotive needs of the citizen-subject underwrite the legitimacy of Roosevelt's "essential four freedoms" and Norman Rockwell's interpretation of freedom in the context of an American civil religion founded on private, familial-social, and cultural structures. This critique of the shortfall in that relationship between the citizen-subject and the democratic nation is pertinent to the discussion of Paredes's analysis of the centrality of the Four Freedoms in prewar American thought. Like Bulosan, he worries about the tangible reality of freedom and is concerned with the reasons for the Mexican American's commitment to American political and national institutions in the years immediately before and after the second Great War.

Américo Paredes's Four Freedoms

What is surely less well known than the ambivalences of American nationalist ideology is how the traditional narrative of national destiny that Roosevelt and Rockwell tried to reimagine in liberal democratic terminology at the end of one historical era and on the verge of another was received and revised at the margins of the nation. As Bulosan and Paredes show, that revision proved particularly crucial for those other Americans—African Americans, Asian Americans, and Native Americans. Viewing this response not only allows us to fill in historical gaps in our cultural history but also allows us to understand through dialectical counterreflection the very production of that cultural knowledge itself. In *Between Two Worlds*, Paredes offers a striking series of poetic responses to Roosevelt's millennial vision, and Rockwell's sentimental one, of American freedom. His responses become evident in numerous ways and in various idioms in a number of Paredes's literary works, but in none more directly than in his own recension of the Four Freedoms in a poem of that title:

Lengua, Cultura, Sangre:—
es vuestro mi cantar,
sois piedra de los mares
y muro del hogar;
este país de "Cuatro Libertades"
nada nos puede dar.
Justicia . . . ¿acaso existe?
La fuerza es la justicia,
palabras humorísticas: Justicia y Libertad.
Nos queda sólo la Raza,
nos queda sólo la Lengua;
hay que guardarlas siempre
y mantenerlas vivas
por una eternidad. (*Between Two Worlds* 58)

[Language, Culture, Blood:—
my song is yours,
you are rock of the seas
the hearth wall of the home;
this "Four Freedoms" nation

can offer us nothing.
Justice . . . does it even exist?
Might is justice,
amusing words: Justice and Liberty.
We have but our Race,
we have but our Tongue;
may we always preserve them
and maintain them alive
for an eternity.] [23]

Paredes's poem "The Four Freedoms," dated 1941, was written in direct response to Roosevelt's State of the Union address of January 6 and before Rockwell's illustrations and Bulosan's ironic critique in the *Saturday Evening Post*, which appeared in 1943. The sentiment of the poem is exactly consonant with that of Bulosan's essay. In fact, so central to Paredes's thinking are questions about the meanings of Roosevelt's Four Freedoms that at one point he considered entitling the collection of his poetry from that era *The Four Freedoms*.[24] If freedom meant the right to speak, worship, work, and live pretty much as one pleased as long as one did not interfere with others, Americans had found freedom, and the ruling segments had been singularly liberal with immigrants and other outsiders. But if freedom meant democratic cooperation in determining the ideals and purposes of the social and economic institutions of the country and the creation of a community of shared fate, then indigenous natives, Mexicans, Filipinos, African Americans, and every other immigrant and racial group had not known freedom. Anglo-American culture was guilty of what every dominant race is guilty of, the imposition of its own culture on minority peoples. That this imposition and the process of Americanization had been at times relatively mild in comparison to the horrors of cultural purity that came to light in 1940s Europe did not alter its quality.[25]

   In marked contrast to Roosevelt's universalizing discourse of national unity that sought to extend that local unity globally, Paredes cites the communal aspects of local culture, language, and "race" as the real mainstays of freedom. In this context, "la Raza," which I have translated as "our Race," plays an ambivalent role, for what Paredes implies with the deployment of the term is less a genetic consanguinity than a culturally fashioned collectivity ("la Raza" may also be translated colloquially as "the People," "the Folk," or "the Community"). Rockwell's version of the Four Freedoms conveys the message that "Americans are fighting to protect the opportunities they had, as Americans, to provide for the material needs of themselves and their families" (Westbrook 204). Paredes renders the notion of the Four Freedoms altogether differently. Freedom is not an expression of private value or even of a common civil religion, but an active communitarian process involving collective identity and shared articulations of mutual security based on ethnic and linguistic solidarity. The special status of race and ethnicity in relation to American freedom thus proved central to Paredes at this point in his life. Especially as the United States braced itself for the war, Paredes felt aware that the usual distinctions between "aliens" and "citizens" in American life were soon to become even more crucial than they had already been in determining who received justice and liberty and who did not. In perilous times, as the legal scholar Geoffrey R. Stone has written, "it is reasonable to suppose that [citizens of an enemy nation] have divided loyalties and pose greater risks of subversion than either American citizens or other noncitizen residents. . . . Even resident aliens who are not citizens of an enemy nation may pose special risks because they do not have the same allegiance to the United States as American citizens" (283). In his poetry from this period, Paredes was expressing the risks and suspicions that Mexican American citizens, treated as aliens in their native land—"En tu proprio terruño serás extranjero"—faced in the conduct of their everyday lives. Even though his people were neither citizens of an enemy nation nor resident aliens but bona fide American citizens, Paredes understood that their loyalty and allegiance to the United States would inevitably be open to question.

Like C. L. R. James, who had characterized Roosevelt's Four Freedoms as "ridiculous" examples of the bankruptcy of bourgeois thought ("Dialectical Materialism" 151), and Carlos Bulosan, who wondered to whom these Four Freedoms were truly available, Paredes here speaks as if overwhelmed by the liberal vision's immense inadequacy. Roosevelt's speech implied that the New Deal had secured for Americans the benefits of the Four Freedoms and now sought only to extend them to the rest of the world. Rockwell's paintings urged an interpretation of Roosevelt's Four Freedoms as statements about the obligations of Americans to their nation in crisis. This obligation was a duty owed principally to the American family as the very mainstay of democratic institutions, indeed, of the American way of life itself. Bulosan, James, and Paredes stand for the reaction of intellectuals of color to Roosevelt's Four Freedoms. They represent the decolonizing project of rethinking the very concept of freedom, not from the perspective of Euro-American humanism, but from the perspective of the African, Asian, and American imperial and colonial subject as they enquire under what conditions the Four Freedoms might actually come to be for all Americans, and even, as Roosevelt claimed, for people "everywhere in the world." Short of that utopian possibility, what indeed might justify the participation of subaltern Americans as citizens in the defense of the nation? In others of his poems, Paredes offered additional visions of obligation, duty, and citizenship as alternatives to Roosevelt's and Rockwell's versions.

For example, in a poem of 1937 entitled "Mi pueblo," ("My People" or "My Town"), Paredes made the localization of culture articulated in his poem "The Four Freedoms" even more explicit by dedicating the poem "A mi barrio, El Cuatro Veintiuno" (To my barrio, the Four Twenty-first):

> Eres cierta incertidumbre entre cielo y podredumbre,
> del abismo y de la cumbre el destino te formó
> citadino y campirano, eres yanqui-mexicano,
> eres méxico-tejano,
> eres pocho, como yo! (*Between Two Worlds* 48–49)

> [You are certain incertitude between the heavens and corruption,
> destiny shaped you from the abyss and the summit
> urbanite and country dweller, you're a Yankee-Mexican,
> you're a Mexico-Texan,
> you are a *pocho*, just like me!]

Like language and culture, and even "race" itself, identity here is conceived distinctly. It is a conceptual invention of the community, created to guarantee justice and liberty as aspects of experience rather than as abstract platitudes of political economy or ideology. What provides the subjective repertoire of the Mexican American social mechanism is assuredly not a sentimental vision of small-town American family life, nor even less so a romantically constructed ideal *Geist* (spirit) of the *Volk* (folk). By 1937, evidence of the nightmares that uncritical cultural nationalism and celebrations of racial purity could lead to was plentiful with the ascendancy of fascism and Nazism in Europe. Race and nationalism, blood and soil, were the very principles of National Socialism thought, and they were echoed in eerily frightening ways by American Jim Crow racism. Thus Paredes offered another vision of liberty, the subject of another poem, "La libertad" (1942). It, too, speaks to the Rooseveltian Four Freedoms and Rockwell's interpretations:

> Raza morena y mestiza
> ¡oh, semilla de grandeza!
> llevas en ti la entereza
> que te da la juventud. . . .
> Indio descalzo, trigueño,
> que llorando vas tu suerte,
> indio, ¡qué diera por verte
> soberano de verdad!
> Con el estómago lleno,
> bien vestido y bien calzado
> y en tu destino confiado—
> ésa es la libertad. (*Between Two Worlds* 62)

> [Swarthy, mixed race
> seed of nobility!
> you bear with you the integrity
> that youth gives to you. . . .
> Barefoot, dusky Indian,
> who weeping bear your fortune,
> Indian, what would I give to see you
> Sovereign in truth!
> With a full stomach,
> well dressed and well shod
> and confident in your destiny—
> that is liberty.]

"Libertad" here is a material, concrete property of collective interactions, not an abstract thing reified from an assemblage of personal freedoms. Its features are solid, perceptible, and attainable. Its blazon here, too, as in Bulosan's essay, is not an "intangible thing," but a well-fed, well-dressed, well-shod *indio* standing in the sovereignty of truth and the confidence of destiny, ready to build a future of peace and security. "Youth" marks Paredes's "dusky Indian" as the agent of the future.

Paredes takes Roosevelt's New Deal discourse of freedom and its notions of justice and liberty as metaphors, mere stand-ins, "amusing words," ("The Four Freedoms" 58) for something not amusing at all, namely, a state of democratic sociability not yet fully realized for all Americans. Standing outside of the regime of liberal democracy, Paredes's Mexico Texan seems, as his poem of the same title puts it, "one fonny man": "A cit'zen of Texas they say that he ees, / But then, why they call him the Mexican Grease? . . . The Mexico-Texan he no gotta lan'" (*Between Two Worlds* 26). If as in Locke, property and the ownership of land equate the citizen and the bourgeois and constitute the basis for active subjectivity, what role is there in civil society and the public sphere for that "fonny" figure who finding himself under two contradictory obligations winds up without a homeland, as someone who "no gotta lan'"? To what extent could he really use the institutions, practices, and experiences denoted by the sphere of the Four Freedoms? Under the repressive social and political conditions of the Depression-era borderlands, was democracy even possible? The answer to these questions was not so "fonny." To answer them would require moving this figure divided between two worlds out of the realm of subjection and inequality. It would mean defining new social spaces outside the repertory of possible actions, beyond the frontiers of nations and the limits of previously existing social imaginaries, and envisioning a transition into a sphere of democratic self-authorization as a fully integrated citizen-subject.[26]

In rethinking the relation between the private subject of liberalism and the loyal political "cit'zen" of social democracy, Paredes requires us in these poems to move beyond the distinction between personal freedoms and public rights. Extending far beyond the suspect myths of blood and tongue, the cultural identity of *la Raza*, the Folk, as Paredes construes it, exists in the uneven development of history and global economies. It is situated on the margins of *cierta incertidumbre*, a certain incertitude, embodied in the subjective figure of the *pocho*, the hybrid mestizo, the "cit'zen" who "no gotta lan,'" crosscutting the seemingly impermeable lines of cultural sovereignty. In this state of affairs, labor and creative work make for the real sources of cultural and political affiliation, which are but other ways of describing a cultural form of citizenship.

The sovereignty of the *pocho*'s identity is by no means certified, however. Marked by the certain incertitude of local conditions, the *pocho* is undeniably liable to the barbarisms of history. Hence the next poem, "Alma pocha," of 1936, written in ironic response to the great and gaudy centennial celebrations of Texas independence:

> En tu propio terruño serás extranjero
> por la ley del fusil y la ley del acero;
> y verás a tu padre morir balaceado
> por haber defendido el sudor derramado;
> verás a tu hermano colgado de un leño
> por el crimen mortal de haber sido trigueño.
> Y si vives, acaso, será sin orgullo,
> con recuerdos amargos de todo lo tuyo;
> tus campos, tus cielos, tus aves, tus flores
> serán el deleite de los invasores;
> para ellos su fruto dará la simiente,
> donde fueras el amo serás el sirviente,
> Y en tu propio terruño serás extranjero
> por la ley del fusil y la ley del acero. (*Between Two Worlds* 35–36)

> [In your native homeland a stranger you will be
> by the law of the rifle and the law of cold steel;
> and you will see your father shot to death
> for having shed his sweat;
> you will see your brother strung up from a limb
> for the mortal crime of having been born olive-skinned.
> And if perhaps you do survive, it will be without pride,
> with bitter remembrances of what once was yours;
> your lands, your skies, your birds, your flowers
> will be the delight of the invaders;
> for them the fruit will sprout,
> where once long ago you were the master a servant you will be.
> And in your homeland a stranger you will be
> by the law of the rifle and the law of cold steel.]

The poem counterpoises the grim reality of present conditions, "la jornada tejana," the arid Texan wastelands, with the utopian memory of long-lost days. Nature's former beauty, its panoramic vistas, the land's living richness are now another's and mock the former master, now a servant, with their fecundity. Calling the "Alma pocha" (the feminine soul of the *pocho*) a stranger in her own homeland, Paredes's speaker, "destiny," *el destino*, echoes other poems of the collection.[27] In "Rose Petals," from the same year, another voice describes, now in English, "A sad, sad longing / That is almost pain / For something that I one day was / And wish to be again." Assaulted by "the law of the rifle and cold steel," the *alma pocha* remains, nonetheless, "la que sufre, / la que espera" (she who suffers / she who hopes).

Again, in another poem from this same mid-1930s period, titled "Ahí nomás" ("Just Over There"), Paredes reminds us that the Mexican American's conditions of existence are not by any means unique, but constitute a fundamental aspect of a broader American history:

> "Indian, dark brother from whose ancestors
> Half of my father's fathers sprang,
> You who know all these ragged mountains,
> Up to the nests that the eagles hang,
> 'Where do your weary footsteps take you?' "
> . . . .
> Long was the road that he had to travel,
> Difficult, rocky his journey was,
> But with a shrug and a smile he answered,
> "Just over there. *Sí ahí nomás.*"
> . . . .
> Should I encounter along my journey
> A sister soul that is drawn to me,
> Who rhymes with me in a perfect couplet,
> Whose voice is pitched on my selfsame key,
> Touching my arm, she will stop me, ask me,
> "Where are you going? *¿A dónde vas?*"
> And with a shrug and a smile I'll answer,
> I too shall answer, "*Ahí nomás.*" (*Between Two Worlds* 22)

The poet's *alma pocha* here finds kindred souls among native first peoples, and among women, all of whom have trod with "weary footsteps" the ages of "bitterness and despair." The "sister soul" is the mediator of the alliance among the "dark brother," the poet, she "Who rhymes with me," and the landscape. Cida S. Chase points out that this poem has "clear correspondences with '*Ahí, no más . . .*' from *Notas del alma indígena* (Notes on the Indian Soul), by the Peruvian nativist poet José Santos Chocano" (191)[28] Chocano's major works *Alma América* (1906) and *Fiat lux* (1908), to which Paredes is also directly alluding, express the ideals of the beauty of the natural landscape of America and the wonder of its native cultures.[29] But Paredes is also after much more than correspondences with the American landscape.

At issue for Paredes is a profound realignment of mestizo and Indian fates. The Mexican anthropologist Guillermo Bonfil Batalla has claimed that in Mexico "mestizos are the contingent of 'de-Indianized' Indians" (42), that is, Indians assimilated to the social structures created by Spanish colonialism. Mestizaje as racial mixing and cultural assimiliation, argues Bonfil Batalla, is different from the much more radical process of "de-Indianization" by which Mexico has disavowed its "Indian face" (39). "De-Indianization" is a caustic "historical process through which communities with particular and distinctive features are forced to renounce that identity, with all the consequent changes in their social organization and culture" (42). Thus, the social differences between mestizos and Indians cannot be explained simply by different histories of racial mixture. De-Indianization results from the much more destructive forces of ethnocide that ultimately block the historical continuity of a people as social unity and as a culturally differentiated group (Bonfil Batalla 42). While celebrating his pocho identity, Paredes here chooses not to deny his Indian heritage behind the claims of mestizaje. Instead, aligning himself as a U.S.-Mexican pocho and mestizo with the aspirations of native Indian peoples whose "goals" and "distant dreams" remain "just over there," he imagines something else: that the "journey" "up to the heights, where the eagles scream" is the path leading outside of solipsistic confinement, even of mestizaje, toward the larger symbolic realm of freedom for his entire, multi-racial, "pueblo multiforme" (*Between Two Worlds* 48).

This movement toward inclusive freedom is signaled formally in the poem another way. The interlingual rhymes between *"Ahí nomás"* and "was" of the first part of the poem give way to the monolingual rhyme of *"¿A dónde vas?"* and *"Ahí nomás"* at the end of the poem. In all of these details, the poet is taking advantage of his ability to write in and work across two poetic traditions. Here, the grammatical construction *alma pocha* allows for a great deal of figural free play concerning the fecundity, fruitfulness, and erotic destinies of Mexican

American life, as these various poems make plain. Taken together, the metaphoric patterns, bilingual constructions, and thematic arrangements of these poems offer the possibility of a new form of modern art writing as a borderlands alternative to the domain of bourgeois modernism.

These then are the conditions under which Mexican Americans received Roosevelt's Four Freedoms message to the nation and the popular translations of its declarations as represented by Rockwell's paintings and posters. Unevenly distributed and selectively applied, the Four Freedoms of justice and liberty seemed to some "palabras humorísticas," "amusing words" ("The Four Freedoms" 58).[30] Less amusing was the fact that even into the new decade of the 1940s, the Great Depression of the 1930s (colloquially termed *La Chilla*—the squeal, in south Texas Spanish) still held Mexican America tightly in its grip. To make ends barely meet, the young Paredes enterprisingly worked several jobs in Brownsville, Texas—as a newspaper reporter covering the Mexican neighborhoods at half the wage rate of Anglo reporters, as a weekly radio variety show host and entertainer, and as an installer of .50-caliber machine guns on US Army fighter-bombers bound for embattled Britain. Of that period and the Depression Paredes writes in his novel *George Washington Gómez*:

> La Chilla, Mexicans called it. The Squeal. Or perhaps a euphemism for that most useful of Mexican expressions: *La Chingada. Estamos en la gran chi-i-illa, compadre*. La Chilla. Sugar is two cents a pound and men are two cents a dozen, Mexicans half-price. Flour costs a quarter a sack, and a quarter costs all of a man's efforts and the little pride he has left. La Chilla. Long lines of men sitting in employment offices with a gloomy hope in their eyes. Long lines of women standing in the street before relief agencies, hunger and humility on their faces. . . . Relief rations are limited, and the Mexican gets more dirty looks than groceries at the RFC, the *ora sí*, as he calls it, the "Now's the Time." For one decent meal at last. (195–96)

Coming of age in the midst of the cultural and social havoc wrought by the transformations of the borderlands by economic crisis and the plunge of the world into global conflict, Paredes responded by inventing in the imaginary realm the possibility of a new kind of decolonized consciousness on the border. He listened to the poetry of the folk as it punned and joked in two languages about the struggles of daily life in the Depression-era borderlands and tried to enunciate the possibility of a sustaining cultural identity. Through his poetry, he forced the questions of the obligations and duties of citizenship owed to American liberal democracy and looked for answers in the cultural terms of an alternative modernity. For these reasons, Paredes's poetry from the 1930s and early 1940s represents a crucial shift of consciousness in the symbolic history of progressive American ethnic thought as it struggled to imagine the possibility of justice and liberty within the context of America's Four Freedoms.

5

PAREDES AND THE MODERNIST

VERNACULAR INTELLECTUALS

George I. Sánchez and Emma Tenayuca

> Every social community reproduced
> by the functioning of institutions is
> imaginary. — Etienne Balibar,
> "The Nation Form"

To gain a fuller sense of the range of Paredes's modernist project and the depth of its originality, we must turn eventually to other poems of the collection. First, however, it will be well for establishing a sense of the moment of uneven historical development from which Paredes speaks and to understand the prefigurative importance of what he says to look at some other contemporaneous records of the people who continued to be, in the title words of the historian and educator George I. Sánchez's 1940 seminal study, a *Forgotten People*. It is crucial to remember that the range of possible responses to the hegemonic narrative of American destiny was severely circumscribed for the Depression-era generation. Attempting to refigure the disfigured narrative of their history, Mexican American intellectuals of the period found themselves relying to a surprising degree on the same liberal rhetoric of American national unity that we find in New Deal reformist statements such as discussed. Whether they spoke from a culturally conservative position that advocated the possibility of the kind of cultural pluralism that William James and other American pragmatists had championed since the turn of the century or whether they spoke from a leftist position committed to class struggle, these writers tended to deploy the very same discourse of modernity and modernization that we find in Roosevelt's Four Freedoms and Rockwell's illustrations.

Paredes's contemporaries in vernacular thought looked to justify the reformation and modernization of Mexican American identity by positing a unity in plurality—e pluribus unum. In stark contrast, Paredes attempted to imagine a radically new ground for identity within a new *mexicano* consciousness under the sign of a vernacular aesthetic.[1] George I. Sánchez offers a good place to begin to understand Paredes's difference. An excellent advocate of the notion of cultural pluralism, like other Mexican American intellectuals, activists, and academicians of the 1930s and 1940s seeking to describe a new Mexican identity within the bounds of the modern American nation, Sánchez attempted to construct reformist narratives that would counter the enforced constructions of Anglo-American history and would realize instead the visions represented by their own community's myths of blood and tongue.

George I. Sánchez and the Forgotten People

Looking retrospectively at New Deal politics and rhetoric after a lifetime's struggle fighting racism, exploitation, and cultural devastation, Sánchez—a distinguished scholar, educator, and political activist—in 1967 was to reflect mournfully that the New Deal of Franklin Delano Roosevelt had raised hopes for a better life. "The National Youth Administration, the Civilian Conservation Corp, the Works Progress administration, and related federal agencies constituted an honest-to-goodness war on poverty, and we Spanish-Americans were among the poorest of the poor." "But," he adds, "the New Deal did not last long enough. Washington turned its eyes to foreign parts" (vii). Indeed, "In those distant younger days" of the 1930s and 1940s, says Sánchez,

> though I did not ignore reality, I did harbor a modicum of optimism. Maybe, somehow, the forgotten people of my homeland would be remembered and redeemed. Maybe as the nation grew more affluent, and wiser perhaps, it would roll back the pages of history and pay the long overdue debt it incurred when it forced itself on my people. I had hopes, though very slim ones, that, at the very least, a repentant nation would help us lift ourselves by our bootstraps. Instead, it took away our boots! (vii)[2]

To outline that bootstrap history of Mexican Americans, Sánchez first had to counter the official histories of the Southwest still largely promulgating the romantic versions of the Spanish conquest offered both by Anglo writers like Charles F. Lummis and by Mexican American folklorists like Aurelio M. Espinosa.[3] In contrast to these mythographers, Sánchez introduces an unromantic history. He argues that, first as Spanish colonials, then later as Mexican republicans, the Mexicans of the Southwest became a culturally dispossessed people after 1848 with the Treaty of Guadalupe Hidalgo. They "were thrust suddenly out of their traditional social and economic setting into a radically different one" he claims (12). Orphaned from one national culture and made the "stepchildren" (15) of another, after 1848 the newly made Mexican American was placed by the treaty "at the mercy of forces about which he was totally ignorant and which he was woefully unprepared to meet" (15). Still as unprepared to act in their new political and cultural environment in 1940 as their ancestors had been after 1848, today's Mexican Americans continue to "battle their own cultural inadequacy" (13), adds Sánchez. Without the proper ideological tools to build a new cultural life as assimilated Americans, the Mexican Americans "are unprepared to act in their new environment—unprepared because of centuries of isolation. They have no tradition beyond the sixteenth century. [The Mexican American] is not yet an American culturally, the Treaty of Guadalupe notwithstanding" (13). Using the experience of his native New Mexico to characterize that of Mexicans in general, Sánchez carries his analysis beyond that of mere cultural inadequacy and notes pointedly, "In the march of imperialism a people were forgotten, cast aside as the by-product of territorial aggrandizement" (12): "The Spanish-American of New Mexico was left to the mercy of waves of exploiters: merchants, cattle barons, land grabbers, venal politicians—merciless all. We were not given schools, so we remained ignorant of the new way of life that had been so ruthlessly thrust upon us" (vii). Because of this failure of the dominant culture to provide the proper implements of acculturation into this "new way of life," "today we find these humble people still struggling unsuccessfully to make their age-old patterns work in an unresponsive setting" (12–13). They are a populace "ignorant of modern ways" nonetheless "thrown into a situation which would task the most enlightened societies" (18).

To combat this ignorance of modern ways and the resulting effects of underdevelopment and exploitation, and to "stem the tide of political and economic regression," Sánchez assumed that in 1940 as in 1848 one must first "envision a plan for the incorporation of the New Mexi-

can into the American fold" (19). The degree to which "this fundamental aspect of cultural incorporation was neglected" (21) throughout the nineteenth century can be deduced, he notes, by the woefully
inadequate state of education of the contemporary New Mexican.
No "effective program of cultural rehabilitation" being enacted, the
New Mexican today persists in carrying "inferior and obsolete practices and beliefs" and maintaining "a traditional way of life that is
below current standards" (28): "Midst the wreckage of his economy
and his culture, and unprepared for the new order of things, he is
pathetic in his helplessness—a stranger in his own home" (28). Because of the nature of this complex of cultural and economic problems, the New Mexican remains outside Roosevelt's "new order of
things," "a stranger in his own home," and "in a position comparable
to that of . . . other subject people" (29). And as a subject people,
Mexican Americans in their inferior status were in large measure the
result of the failure of the United States to recognize the social responsibility it assumed when it brought these people forcibly into
American society (40). Appropriating the political rhetoric of American democracy against itself, Sánchez anticipated Bulosan's later cry
for freedom from fear and hunger when he proclaimed caustically,
"The legal right to 'life, liberty, and the pursuit of happiness' is an
empty privilege when the bare essentials of Americanism and of social
welfare are wanting" (40).

In the rehabilitation of the *mexicano* to "the new order of things,"
Sánchez believed that Mexican Americans could be "modernized at
no loss to cultural values" (54). Rather, the traditional values of the
community could be accommodated to the new order. Between tradition and modernity, no compromise was necessary; tradition could be
accommodated within the new order of things. Chief in the reforms
that Sánchez thus advocated was a major improvement in the quality
of education. To this effect, he argued that the "responsibility of education . . . is not only that of educating for a changing society but that
of changing . . . society" (85). Sánchez clearly saw that as an agent of
the state apparatus, "the curriculum of the educational agencies becomes, then, the magna carta of social and economic rehabilitation;
the teacher, the advance agent of a new social order" (86). The elaboration of this new social order entailed for Sánchez an expansion of
current practices to those at the periphery of this order, but not yet
a reconceptualization of the notion of pedagogy, one that might re-

define existing notions of community, language, societal space, and possibility to create a new pedagogy of the vernacular.

Short of this new pedagogy and while having undergone this cultural rehabilitation, a type of cultural modernization to which other subject peoples in similarly colonized situations have been condemned, this modern "New" Mexican, the prototype of a new breed of multicultural American, might yet well be finally "fitted to make his contributions to American civilization." According to Sánchez, "That contribution might well embody worthy elements of his culture—language, music, folklore, architecture, foods, crafts, and customs" (91). Equipped with the symbolic and material tools to compete with other Americans, the Mexican American might turn his rehabilitation to the benefit of the dominant culture, like a modern-day Greek bringing the refinements of culture to a latter-day Rome. At the dawn of a new modern age,

> girded with good health, economic security, social self-sufficiency, education, and the ability to compete for a living wherever he may be, the New Mexican can set forth from the limited prospects of his present environment and embark towards new horizons. Released from the handicaps of his present situation, he need no longer be a problem child, a culturally unassimilated subject, but a respected and self-respecting American. Thus, armed with the culture of his country, incorporated into the American fold, he is no longer the stepchild of a nation. Freed from cultural bondage and from the despair of dire poverty, the New Mexicans will have harvested the true fruits of their conquest and will cease to exist as a forgotten people. (98)

If there ever existed a people that could be termed by virtue of their geopolitical situation "new" Mexican, that people under the pressures of harmful neglect virtually no longer exists but has vanished into the cultural amnesia of the American grand narrative of assimilation and incorporation. In its place there stands to stride into modernity a differently "new" Mexican who will have been fashioned from the process of modernization as a legitimate "self-respecting American." Only then might these new Mexicans be said to have gained authentic existence and ceased "to exist as a forgotten people."

Thirty years later in a tribute to the memory of the late George I. Sánchez, Paredes, by this point himself a respected member of the American academy, would return to these words to underscore the constitutive "unity of education and culture" for the man ("Jorge Isidoro Sánchez" 121). Attempting to summon a terminology proper to the description of an activist before the era of activism, for someone he describes as "a forerunner of the Chicano movement" (126), Paredes would turn to the contours of social justice in everyday life for his answer. It was the nature of Sánchez's courage that he wished to praise. He derided as "a strange commentary on the subtle ways of brainwashing," the fact that "many of our young Chicano writers have accepted machismo as an ineluctable part of their ethnic make-up and, even more, have attempted to elevate the cult of the *macho* into a kind of Chicano mystique." He scorned as he had in his fiction and poetry from the 1930s and 1940s the contemporary vogue of "the cult of the bully—the *matón* [the killer] and the *castigador de mujeres* [the abuser of women]" as undeserving of "a place in our scale of values" (125). In place of the cult of machismo and its false versions of masculine virtue Paredes offered instead as a value of a higher order the "willingness to face death for a cause." Paredes proposed the figure of George I. Sánchez as the model of a better form of *mexicano* masculine worth. In sharp contrast to the posturing bullies, the hollow macho killers, and the cowardly abusers of women, Sánchez represented for Paredes something of infinitely greater value and worth, a kind of civic virtue, which Paredes termed in Spanish *valor civil*: "*Valor civil* is courage that requires no weapon but the will itself; it is the courage of the unarmed and peaceful citizen who will not flinch before threats of violence. *Valor civil* is the ability to stand steadfast for what you think is right, come what may. George Sánchez had *valor civil*. He was a fighter for the things he believed in—way back, many years ago, when very few fought alongside him" (125). Paredes's remarks were intended "not as captious observations on the recent past but as a hard look at the future" (126). Still, he was fully aware that the paths leading to that future of achieved citizenship and attained national affiliation within the United States would require a different orientation and a different sense of the public sphere, activated here as *valor civil*. Attaining full status as a citizen subject would require an interlingual rendering of the old values and traditions of the warrior hero into the new virtues of the modern citizen hero agitating within the arenas of social and political institutions for the right to live in peace. The result would be not simply an acultural material account of what happens in the transition to modernity but would require an understanding of what happens to our relations to one another, society, time, national space, and the values of good citizenship with the coming of the modern era. *Valor civil* would be one way of bridging the legal principles of society (civic virtues) with the moral domains (courage and ethical values) of individuals who stand outside the public sphere because they are not allowed a place within it.[4] Writing in the 1970s, when the momentary euphoria after the initial successes of the civil rights movement had begun to recede and was being replaced by the sobering realization that "reaction has set in" (126), Paredes made of Sánchez an exemplary instance of the new citizen of the republic of the future, one regulated by the reign of value and civic virtue. Paredes understood that figures like Sánchez would be required as bolsters against the frustrations of the even darker times that still lay ahead. In 1940, however, when Sánchez was completing *Forgotten People* and Paredes was still arming bombers for a terrifying world war by day and hosting a radio show by night, these insights were still only wildly utopian impulses that both men found difficult to entertain realistically.

Emma Tenayuca: The Popular Front and the Mexican Question

Almost an exact contemporary of Américo Paredes, Emma Tenayuca was born in San Antonio, Texas. A child of working-class parents in that harshly segregated south Texas city, Tenayuca learned revolutionary politics listening to radical voices protesting the extreme versions of the Jim Crow laws that governed Texas society in the first half of the twentieth century.[5] In 1937, as a young woman of twenty-one years, Tenayuca joined the Communist Party and by 1939, already a veteran of numerous strikes and workers' actions in San Antonio, she had been elected state chair of the Communist Party of Texas. Her fiery speeches at workers' rallies, meetings, and picket lines across the city quickly earned her the nickname of "La Pasionaria," after the impassioned Basque orator Dolores Ibárruri during the Spanish civil war.

Writing with her husband Homer Brooks in a major article of 1939, Tenayuca observed that Mexican Americans and Mexican nationals in the American Southwest share "a common historical background and are bound by a common culture, language, and communal life" (261). In daily life, both were segregated from Anglo-American communi-

19 Emma Tenayuca, national committee-woman of the Workers Alliance of America, in Bexar County Jail, San Antonio, Texas, following filing of unlawful assembly with disturbing peace charges in connection with attempt of ousted WPA workers to stage a sit-in at WPA headquarters, protesting cut in rolls. 1932.

20 Emma Tenayuca, organizer for the Workers Alliance of America, with others, protesting alleged beatings by Border Patrol. Federal Building, San Antonio, Texas. February 23, 1937. Published February 24, 1937.

Both reproduced with the permission of the Institute of Texan Cultures at the University of Texas at San Antonio, L-1575-C and L-1540-A, the San Antonio Light Collection.

ties throughout the Southwest. Did this common cultural and political experience, however, constitute the grounds for national unity? Where did Mexican Americans, descendants of the original inhabitants of the region after 1848, and Mexicans who had emigrated into the region in the nineteenth and early twentieth centuries, plus the masses of newly arrived Mexican nationals, belong? What national affiliation and cultural stake to the rights and obligations of citizenship could any of these three groups, representatives of three different stages in the Mexican labor history of the Southwest, claim within the United States?

In autobiographical comments, Tenayuca points out that by 1937 she had read Marx's *Wage Labor and Capital* (1847) and, along with other readings she encountered during "this revolutionary time in American history," it had catalyzed her thinking ("Living History" 14). One result of this reading was her essay with Brooks; "The Mexican Question in the Southwest" offers an elaboration of her readings in Marx. It speculates on what a redeemed American nation might look like that might be able to truly incorporate the Mexicans of the Southwest into the national polity. Writing in the party journal the *Communist*, Tenayuca and Brooks questioned whether the Mexican people of the Southwest constituted their own separate nation or formed a segment of the Mexican nation within the United States (262).

Reading Stalin's classic definition of a nation as "a historically evolved, stable community of language, territory, economic life and psychological make-up manifested in a community of culture" (8), Tenayuca and Brooks conclude that since the Mexican people of the Southwest lacked two important aspects of nationhood, namely, territorial and economic community, they could be conceived neither as a separate nation nor as a segment of Mexico proper: "Historically the Mexican people in the Southwest have evolved in a series of bordering, though separated, communities, their economic life inextricably connecting them, not only with one another, but with the Anglo-American population in each of these separated Mexican communities. Therefore, their economic (and hence, their political) interests are welded to those of the Anglo-American people of the Southwest" (262). Connected to Mexico culturally and linguistically yet separated from its sovereignty, and inextricably tied to the economic and political interests of the Anglo-American world while "not regarded as part of the American nation," Mexicans in the South-west were situated at a historical crossroads, experiencing a differential loss. Neither one nor the other, they saw their situation in fact more akin to that of dispossessed former slaves, "the Negro people in the south today." The "super-exploitation of the Negroes" perpetrated by southern racism had been carried over into the Southwest and "ap-plied to the Mexican population." Exploitation had taken the forms of extremes of "wage differentials" between whites and people of color, "disenfranchisement" with the elimination of voting rights, "suppres-sion of the Spanish language, of the native culture of the Mexicans" in the schools, and "social forms of discrimination" of the most basic kind at all levels of society (261). Anticipating contemporary analyses of the Latino in terms of an internal Third World, this treatment of Mexicans in the Southwest, claim Tenayuca and Brooks, is "a carry-over to the United States of Wall Street's imperialistic exploitation of Latin America" (262).

Focusing on the categories of territorial and economic community in the consideration of a Mexican American national culture, the fac-tors of a coherent historical evolution, a homogeneous community of language, and a shared psychological makeup manifesting a com-munity of culture, Tenayuca and Brooks thus offer an extraordinarily important early critique of nationalist paradigms as a solution to the question of *mexicano* subjectivity. These factors are precisely the ones that Paredes would also draw on to answer the same question, but with a differential turn, as he contemplated the nature of a Mexican American cultural citizenship. With the making of Greater Mexico as an analytical concept, Paredes would bypass the apparent necessity of the binary situation, of being either Mexican or American exclu-sively, in an attempt to imagine a social formation between nation-states where cultural citizen-subjects could claim and exercise rights in the civic, public sphere of open debate and exchange, and in the ideational domain of the subject.

Writing in the era of the Popular Front, Tenayuca and Brooks understandably attempted to follow the Stalinist version of dialecti-cal materialism. They claimed that "from the historical point of view the forcible incorporation of these areas [the formerly Mexican terri-tories of the Southwest] in the United States was progressive, in that it opened up for development these territories which until then had stagnated under the inefficient, tyrannical, and semi-feudal control

of Mexico" (257). While this line of thought may edge perilously close
to the perverse logic of American Manifest Destiny with its justification of imperial conquest because American imperialism supposedly
came to lighten the natives' darkness, Tenayuca and Brooks are actually arguing something else. They believe that in having opened up
the possibility of progressive development, the American bourgeoisie
itself was now liable for the continued underdevelopment of the region and its people. By not having regarded the Mexican people of the
Southwest as part of the American nation, the American bourgeoisie
itself was called into account for the present crisis, for it "continued to
hinder the process of national unification of the American people by
treating the Mexican and Spanish-American people as a conquered
people" (262).

The intensification of social and political action on the part of Mexican and "Spanish-American" activists during the 1920s and 1930s
"signalize the awakening of the Mexicans and Spanish-Americans in
the Southwest." Tenayuca and Brooks can thus proclaim that these renewed struggles represent the beginning of a new stage in the struggle
for social justice: "*The task is now to build the democratic front among
the Mexican masses through unifying them on the basis of specific needs
and in support of the social and economic measures of the New Deal*"
(263; emphasis original).

Pointing with approval to the formation of Josefina Fierro's Congress of Spanish-Speaking People as evidence of the new Mexican
desire for unification, Tenayuca and Brooks identify the main objectives of this movement for Mexican unification as "a people's
movement, uniting the interests of large and important sections of
the population, . . . who, in alliance with the country's democratic
forces, . . . , can free themselves from the special oppression and discrimination in all its phases that have existed for almost a century"
(264). In this struggle, action against "economic discrimination,"
for "educational and cultural equality," against "social oppression,"
and against "political oppression" constituted the foremost objectives.
While not purely a labor movement alone, the proletariat aspect of
the Mexican population as a whole nevertheless required that in order
for it to be most effective, it needed to bring about "the closest relationship with the labor and democratic forces in the Anglo-American
population of the Southwest" (265). This broad coalition should include the possibility of working even with such groups as the League

of United Latin American Citizens, which until recently had served as an exclusionary "petty-bourgeois native-born" (265) instrument for achieving Americanization by complete assimilation, argued Tenayuca and Brooks.

The solution to the problem of the Mexican in the Southwest lay, then, in removing economic and political barriers to employment and in facilitating the cultural development of the Mexican people, which would also help eliminate the conditions responsible for their status as unskilled workers. Resolving these conditions could lead to a crucial progressive revitalization of American democracy in general, added Tenayuca and Brooks, for, as Engels wrote, "No people oppressing other people can be free" (qtd. in Tenayuca and Brooks 267). Likewise, since the exploitation of the Mexican people in the Southwest was, Tenayuca and Brooks claimed, "in many respects a continuation of the special exploitation and oppression to which the Negro people in the South have been subjected . . . [a] blow against the oppression of one will be a blow for the freedom of both" (267).

Internationally, the Mexican and Spanish American people's movement in the United States could have a profound bearing on the relationship between the United States and Latin America, for unless "the 'Good Neighbor' policy begins at home, with respect to the treatment of the Mexican people, it will be difficult to convince Latin America of the sincerity of this policy" (267). With the growth of fascist influence in Latin America, the winning of the people in the Southwest for "an anti-fascist peace policy and for continental solidarity of the Western Hemisphere" (267), and as a barrier to Nazi-financed Mexican fascists, meant the necessary recognition of "the historical rights of the Mexican people in the Southwest" (268). The achievement of such a movement, Tenayuca and Brooks conclude, will be "a decisive step forward toward the national unification of the American people" (268).

Frantz Fanon has shown how in the struggle for national liberation the affirmation of the existence of precolonial culture represents "a special battle-field" (*Wretched of the Earth* 209). In that struggle, cultural workers take their stand "in the field of history" to establish the legitimacy of the claim to the status of nation by renewing contact with "the oldest and most pre-colonial springs of life of their people." This work on the part of native intellectuals proves vital because "colonialism is not simply content to impose its rule upon the present and the future of a dominated country. Colonialism is not satisfied merely with holding a people in its grip and emptying the native's brain of all form and content. By a kind of perverse logic, it turns to the past of the oppressed people, and distorts, disfigures and destroys it" (210). It is not surprising, therefore, that the efforts of the native to rehabilitate him- or herself and to escape from the claws of colonialism are often "logically inscribed from the same point of view as that of colonialism" (212). In making his point about the contemporaneous colonized world in 1963, Fanon cites the condition of the Mexican communities as typical of colonized space in the present time. In their analysis, Tenayuca and Brooks will point out that the Mexican communities of the United States resemble those of Mexico in so far as they are all defined in a subaltern relation to white America.

Situated between social democracy and Stalinism, Tenayuca and Brooks contemplate the political condition of their epoch as Fanon describes it. Their conception of Popular Front antifascist struggle, characterized by modernist notions of progress and uneasy alliances with traditional culture, entirely typical of the historical moment, is one that other historical eras will find easy to scorn (particularly after the astonishing announcement of the Nazi-Soviet pact of 1939), but which in its vital moment seemed the only viable political option in the face of shockingly massive oppression. As the historian Emma Pérez has noted, in order to effect truly radical decolonizations of mind and space, intellectuals of the time would be required to imagine still unimagined constructions and practices. They would need a "decolonial imaginary" that was yet to be articulated (4).

As a young labor organizer in the early 1930s and a veteran of the vicious suppression of labor, Emma Tenayuca knew the brutality of the power that dissent and demands for justice were up against in the realms of the imaginary and the real. In labor action against the Finck Cigar factory and the pecan-shellers' cooperatives in San Antonio, which were shamelessly exploiting a largely Mexican and female workforce, Tenayuca had learned the power of the state to enforce its will viciously, and of collective identity to stand against oppression (Ruiz 79). Of these experiences of physical threat, incarceration, and possible deportation, Tenayuca was later to write, "I think it was the combination of being a Texan, being a Mexican, and being more Indian than Spanish that propelled me to take action" ("I Saw" 8). Her experiences had taught her that the way of Americanization was "a sterile path" (Tenayuca and Brooks 255–56), leading "nowhere except a possible split between the native and the foreign-born [*mexicano*]" (Tenayuca and Brooks 266). For this reason, the integrationist strategy for fighting racial discrimination and social injustice on the part of moderate liberal middle-class groups such as the League of United Latin American Citizens offered no solution to the question of *mexicano* national subjectivity.

Orthodox socialism also appeared incapable of offering a direction as it proposed solutions only to traditional, orthodox national entities. Both alternatives failed to understand that in the United States, *mexicanos* had been changed into something else that no longer corresponded to the notions of nationality and the national identity denoted by the names *American* and *Mexican*. Tenayuca saw herself as "a Texan, a Mexican, and more Indian than Spanish." Thinking from these multiple subject positions, she understood that an answer to the question of *mexicano* national identity in the context of the capitalist modernization of the Southwest would have to come in the context of something beyond the constraints of liberalism and socialism. It would also have to come from a position beyond assimilation to American modernity or repatriation to a Mexican homeland that, even if it ever had been, was no longer home. Alicia Schmidt Camacho is correct to argue that "neither socialism nor liberalism could conceive of the self-determination of oppressed peoples apart from their subjection to development" (87).

The answer would almost certainly have to come from beyond the borders of traditional nationalism and the modern nation-state. What would be the nature of such a space beyond nationalism? Tenayuca and Brooks understood that the solution to the question of the Mexican in the Southwest could only lie in "the cultural development of the Mexican people" (266). What that cultural development would look like and how to attain it remained questions not yet fully determined. In the case of the national formation of *mexicanos* in the Southwest, that new nationalism could only be produced as the projection of individuals into the fabric of a collective narrative, the recognition of a common history, a mutual tradition, and a sense of shared fates. That is, its real existence could only come about in terms of an imaginary shift in the national community toward liberatory aspirations for reform and social revolution. In the years of the Great Depression and of the beginning of the Second World War, the possibility of such a shift seemed nothing less than a utopian fantasy. The movement into that metacultural utopian realm would require the transcendence of the former structures of the nation-state and of the constraints of ethnicity. Its articulation would call for an alternative, counterdiscursive tongue available in the lyric content, the forms of musical expression, and the narratives of deep desires for fulfillment available in the vernacular consciousness of the folk.

THE BORDERS OF MODERNITY

> Tradition remembers but not as history
> remembers . . . building its own timeless
> world out of the wreck of history.
> —Américo Paredes, "Folklore and
> History"

The reason for this excursus into the historical documents of Mexican American modernity should now be apparent. Despite the profound discontinuities among the varieties of ideologies represented by Roosevelt's and Rockwell's liberal New Deal Four Freedoms, George I. Sánchez's *Forgotten People*, and Emma Tenayuca and Homer Brook's socialist "The Mexican Question in the Southwest," each shares with the others a deliberate construction of consciousness, reflecting a particular cast of modernity and modernization that seems to speak for the age. Liberal and Popular Front politics alike participated in similar ideological justifications of modernity and modernization with their promise of "progress, homogeneity, cultural organicism, the deep nation, the long past" (Bhabha, *Nation and Narration* 4). Seeking to refigure their disfigured history, Mexican American intellectuals deployed the liberal rhetoric of American national unity to justify its reformation—but not to imagine the framework of a new modern *mexicano* consciousness. In stark historical contrast, Paredes, as a young native intellectual seeking to invent a site of decolonized consciousness, offered a difference. With his poetic reprise of Roosevelt's Four Freedoms, his artistic work represents an important shift in consciousness and prefigures an era of renewed cultural integrity in the imaginary ground between two worlds in the borderlands of culture.

States of Permanent Crisis

For Paredes, if justice and liberty are to be attained by *mexicanos*, they will have to be through the work of an alternative, residual imaginary available in vernacular material culture, race, and language. In the poem, "Mi pueblo," Paredes had signaled as much:

> Ah, mi pueblo, no lo ignoro; yo soy pardo, incoloro,
> mas cual pájaro canoro llevo un canto dentro mí;
> ese canto que me llena con su aroma de azucena,
> aunque seas "tierra ajena,"
> ese canto es para ti. (*Between Two Worlds* 49)

> [Oh, my people, I will not forget it; I am colorless, mixed race,
> But like a songbird I bear a song within me;
> that song that fills me with the aroma of a lily,
> even though you might be "another's land,"
> that song is for you.]

Against the ingrained racism of official culture and its sanctioned historical narratives in the Southwest, and even against the reformed cultural pluralism advocated by other Mexican American intellectuals of the period, Paredes employs the metaphorical bonds of blood and kinship ("La Raza," "sangre," "Mi pueblo") expressed through language ("la lengua") and song ("mi canto"). He uses them as tropes for cultural continuity and the historical basis of community. "What the eye is to the lover—that particular, ordinary eye he or she is born with—language—whatever language history has made his or her mother-tongue—is to the patriot," writes Benedict Anderson. "Through that language, encountered at mother's knee and parted with only at the grave, pasts are restored, fellowships are imagined, and futures dreamed" (154). As a young man, Paredes may not have been a political nationalist, but he certainly was toying with the ideas of cultural nationalism. Understandably, then, language and language history figure prominently in his poetry.

In the instance of the bilingual poem "The Four Freedoms" that I discussed earlier, the language Paredes uses is Spanish. However, it is a Spanish that is in constant dialogue with English, the language of the title of the poem. Between the English title and the Spanish body of the poem, Paredes describes an interlingual space between two worlds that is richly situated to examine relations of social objectification, test out patterns of resistance, and imagine the liberating reconstitution of empowered subjects. Even in a monolingual poem like "Mi pueblo," the *pocho* who speaks is the product of this double linguistic consciousness, a *yanqui-mexicano*. Cumbrously shaped cognitively and emotively at the intersection of the American and Mexican linguistic communities, *pocho* consciousness is anything but secure.[1] In fact, decades later, in an essay of 1978, Paredes would assert in reference to this era that "the *pocho*, living between two cultures, existed in a state of permanent crisis" ("Problem of Identity" 47). Its very doubleness creates the state of permanent crisis.

At this earlier point in time, however, Paredes can still imagine that through the discourse of a new border consciousness—expressed as a heteroglossic, vernacular tongue—pasts could be restored, fellowships imagined, and futures dreamed. Paredes's rebellion as a poet comes precisely from this linguistic history, from within the deepest recesses of his bilingual soul, speaking through a polyphonic, double tongue. Like the great Cuban poet of social protest and revolutionary struggle Nicolás Guillén (1902–89), whose sensuous Caribbean rhythms in his poetry from the 1920s he echoes in many of his finest lyrical works, Paredes here marshals the deep structures of English and Spanish linguistic strata and metrical rhythms to transform what could be instruments of oppression and censorship into vehicles for liberation.[2] Another way of measuring the distance between Paredes and his Mexican American contemporaries in their divergent understandings of race, culture, and language and the construction of the modern new Mexican subject is to read his poetry with an ear to its distinctive intertextual affinities. Doing so allows us to see Paredes's accord with an amazing array of alternative modernities voiced in African American, European, and American modernist poetry and an emerging new world empire of rhythm.

Sons, Sones, y Sonetos

Even in his earliest poetic efforts collected as *Cantos de adolescencia*, Paredes had already sensed the hermeneutic possibilities of music as a pathway to that new consciousness. For this reason, he devotes a section of that work specifically to the topic of *la música*. The poems gathered there, including "Guadalupe la Chinaca," "Canciones," "Paso Doble," and "Rumba"—all written in 1934—celebrate the ambiguously compensatory power of the rhythmic muse to communicate beyond the power of mere language. "Guadalupe la Chinaca," for example, refers to the popular Mexican resistance to the French imperial intervention of the mid-nineteenth century. The Mexican folklorist Rubén M. Campos identifies "La Chinaca" as a riposte on the part of liberal Mexican women in favor of Mexican independence to conservative women who supported the French imperial regime.[3] Paredes's poem is more like a jazz ostinato, providing the background to the solo improvisation of the traditional Mexican political song "Canto de Chinaca." His rendition of the classic nineteenth-century protest song reinterprets the original with its superpatriotic, nationalist, xenophobic intent. He takes the liberal response to the conservative's intentions to transform Mexico into a Franco-European state and resituates it in the context of twentieth-century imperial threats. In rejecting French cultural influence, he underscores the repudiation by Mexican intellectuals, artists, and nationalists of any different culture in the service of a literary and national revolution against the colonial tradition.

Likewise, "Rumba" reaches beyond Mexican social and political identity to establish links to the mystic sensual rhythms of Afro-Caribbean and Latin Mediterranean song. "Paso Doble" runs this same energy through the "ritmo arrobador" (entrancing rhythms) and "fiera y palpitante melodía" (wild and palpitating melody) embodied in the fiery dance of a sensuous "gitana" (gypsy woman), evoking the most consequential Spanish-language "gypsies" of Paredes's poetic moment, García Lorca's *Romancero gitano* (*Gypsy Ballads*) (1928) and *Poema del cante jondo* (*Poem of the Deep Song*) (1931), compositions alive with the vibrant images and hypnotic rhythms of Andalusia and the European south. *Poema del cante jondo* in particular includes two beautiful songs, "Baladilla de los tres ríos" and "La guitarra," that resonate with Paredes's themes of the doubled river that flows remorselessly to the sea and of the strummed guitar that weeps for distant things (García Lorca, *Collected Poems* 96–97, 98–100).

With their own irresistible southern setting, Paredes's early lyrics teem with García Lorca's eerie sensuality and the beguiling physicality of the world, as if taking García Lorca's words as their motto: "A poet must be a professor of the five bodily senses" (García Lorca, *Gypsy Ballads* 1). The concrete luxuriousness of these early poems based on traditions of the Spanish peninsular deep song and gypsy *seguidilla* (dance) couple Paredes's insistent themes of love and death, sensuality and memory, evoking the living presence of the past. It is consequently not in the least surprising to find in García Lorca's first published collection of poetry, *Libro de poemas* (1924), a poem entitled "In Memoriam," expressing the torment of loss in the poet's tender heart, which might have served as a companion model for Paredes's version of Tennyson's memorial (García Lorca, *Collected Poems* 74–75).

Even while they situate us within the cultural hybridity of the Caribbean New World and its social and racial ambiguities, interestingly enough both "Rumba" and "Paso Doble" are in fact based on European models in another sense as well. Both are courtly Petrarchan sonnets. Gustavo Pérez Firmat has made an elegant argument concerning the apparent contradiction that arises when Nicolás Guillén in his poetic writings similarly mixes uniquely New World American vernacular social modalities with the quintessentially Old World high-culture artistic form of the Italian sonnet. Pérez Firmat resolves the seeming contradiction of this startling hybridization by noting, "As its name indicates, the sonnet was initially a musical form; a *sonnetto*, literally, is a brief song, or—to express it in terms closer to Guillén—a brief *son*. As the paronomasia suggests, the Cuban *son* and the Italian sonnet, are distant relatives, for both are musical forms. The *son* is Cuba's native sonnet, and the sonnet is Italy's native *son*" ("Nicolás Guillén 323).[4]

Predictably, given Paredes's lifelong enchantment with poetry and song, *sonetos* and *sones*, music and musical forms are distinctly the subjects of his sonnets "Paso Doble" and "Rumba" as well. Both insist on the power and the preference of the "fiera y palpitante melodía" (wild and palpitating melody) ("Paso Doble") and the African-born "bailes bacanales" (Bacchanal dances) ("Rumba") over what the poet disdainfully calls the "suaves madrigales" (soft madrigals) of Old World forms. Even while the poet dismisses the madrigal as a form and the Spanish origin of the paso doble by claiming that Spain vindicated itself by knowing how to "despachar a tierra extraña / lo mejor de su sangre brava y noble" (dispatching to foreign lands / the best of its courageous and noble blood), he also understands the fact of the poetic and musical genealogies that tie Old World to New

World forms and does not disdain them. In this instance, the implied analogy the poet would have us perceive is that just as European music is transformed in contact with American realities, the sonnet form, too, becomes something else in this musical exchange, as do its composers.[5]

The mystic transformation works both ways, affecting both the American cantos and the European *sonnetos*. As Pérez Firmat suggests, the writing of sonnets in the context of American hybridity involves transformations at surprisingly subtle levels: "To write a mulatto madrigal or a *mestizo* sonnet is to transform, to transculturate, two of the 'whitest' literary forms, two genres whose whiteness extends even to their conventional content" ("Nicolás Guillén" 319). Filled with youthful ardor, idealistic melancholy, and unbounded poetic ambition, the *Cantos de adolescencia* and an unpublished manuscript from the same period entitled "Black Roses" are virtual catalogues of conventional peninsular and New World genres and prosodies put to unconventional use, expressing the raw spontaneity and mysterious joy of life on the border between North and South. In addition to the sonnets previously mentioned, we find there hymns, romances, heroic verse, *rimas* (rhymes), epitaphs, madrigals, elegies, cantos, and *décimas*, some of which are original creations, others of which are renditions or translations of Ben Jonson, John Keats, Tennyson, Algernon Charles Swinburne, and the nineteenth-century Spanish poet Gustavo Adolfo Bécquer and the French poet Francis Jammes.

All of these forms and citations serve as the testing ground for the young poet's apprenticeship in heterometric verse. Even though Paredes's writings do not specifically cite the works of García Lorca or Guillén, his poetry, as we have seen, shares much with both. He does mention a thorough schooling in the *modernismo* of Rubén Darío, Manuel Gutiérrez Nájera, and Amado Nervo, with a smattering of José Martí and Leopoldo Lugones. Nevertheless, his poetic work of the 1930s was much closer in temperament, style, theme, substance, and rhythm to the twentieth-century mulatto *sones* of the Cuban poet and the Andalusian *baladilla* (ballad) and *cante jondo* (deep song) of García Lorca than to the works of Spanish American fin de siècle poets. The spiritual preciosity of Nervo or the rhetorical extravagances of Darío and other *modernistas* remain elements to be transformed in his work. More like his other main poetic muse in *pos-*

modernismo, Gabriela Mistral, Paredes learned the power of passion as a defining element of the idioms of American verse. Only in one feature is Paredes unambiguously aligned with the *modernistas*—in his adoption of their transculturation of the Parnassianism and symbolism of continental verse by juxtaposing and assimilating it to the singular, unique, and aesthetically definitive phenomenon of New World letters: the historical reality of American mestizaje. Like his contemporary in hybrid verse Guillén, Paredes seeks to "add color, and even local color" (Gustavo Pérez Firmat "Nicolás Guillén" 319) to the whitewashed figures of the sonnet. Through heteroglossic mestizo verses such as the sonnets of *Cantos de adolescencia*, "Black Roses," and later *Between Two Worlds*, Paredes's poems voice the vernacular aspirations of subjects removed from history by imperial conquest and capitalist expansion.

The new Mexican consciousness that Paredes conceives in his bilingual poems now streams into other discourses seeking curricula for new meanings. It moves in the cognitive, social, and political-economic space between two worlds and speaks a multilingual tongue. And it pursues courses different from those taken by both the progressive modernity of Roosevelt's New Deal rhetoric and the pluralistic ideologies of other Mexican American reformers of the day. In this as in other matters, Paredes anticipated analytical formations and discursive strategies that lay decades in the future.

Bordering on the Avant-Garde

Since the appearance of Peter Bürger's *Theory of the Avant-Garde*, critics have understood the function of the modernist revolutionary avant-garde as a turn against the institutional apparatus on which the work of art depends, a turn against the status of art in bourgeois society as an autonomous entity, and a protest against art's lack of social impact even as art was reintegrated into the praxis of everyday life (Bürger 23–24). For this reason, it makes sense, as Robert Kaufman emphasizes, to differentiate between "*avant-gardist* attempts to enact a collapse of art into life" and "*modernist* attempts to preserve aesthetic autonomy and a rigorous separation of art from life" ("Negatively Capable" 368). Paredes's poetry offers a graceful crystallization of the revolutionary avant-garde impulse to make art politically useful

—yet with a modernist difference. His modernism revolts against the normalizing function of tradition; it lives on the experience of rebelling against all that is normative.[6] Art in this sense, far from being an institutionalized object with disinterested autonomy, constitutes a particular cultural practice, a strategy, and a production whose particular features are tied to a particular locale. That modernist art often proved easy prey to just the institutionalization and reification that it most feared is perhaps the best indicator that the modernity of modernism itself was not an ontological quality ascribable to an ideal work of art. Instead, it constituted an aspect of a cluster of historical practices situated and then configured in a particular locale that could be defeated and superseded. But it could also be refashioned. Read in this manner, the alignment between modernity and history, with modernity serving as the defining term against which history is to be assessed, must be sorted anew. For instead of privileging the temporally new, we must now reconfigure the new in relation to the locally and spatially situated manners, features, and flavors of a given locale.

In this reformulated situational sense, modernism becomes a conjunctural social movement mobilized to face what the social geographer Edward W. Soja has called "a continuous process of societal restructuring that is periodically accelerated to produce a significant recomposition of space-time-being in their concrete forms" (27). Modernism is, at base, "the cultural, ideological, reflective . . . theory-forming response to modernization" (29). And it can be directly linked, then, as Soja goes on to suggest, "to the objective processes of structural change that have been associated with the ability of capitalism to develop and survive, to reproduce successfully its fundamental social relations of production and distinctive divisions of labour" (26–27). Modernity also powerfully involves the manipulation of human geographies as instrumentalities of social control, productivity, and consumption. Part of the story of the invention of a modern America therefore involves the solidification of spatial consciousness figured in the territorial boundaries of the continental nation at the borders of modernity. Many of Paredes's poems emphasize just this situational quality of subjective space and human geographies by focusing on the subjective workings of metaphors of marginality, peripheries, transitions, diasporas, and, of course, the geopolitical border itself.

Moreover, because the modern cannot be conceived apart from its temporality, any attempted revision of the experience of the modern in relation to concepts of modernity must also take into account its relationship to its historical prefigurations in the traditions that it seeks to modernize. In the earliest of his lyrics, Paredes seeks to accomplish just such a revision and to capture an avant-gardist stylistic mood reminiscent of Walter Benjamin's tone of "revolutionary nostalgia" (Eagleton "Capitalism" 136). Terry Eagleton has defined this revolutionary nostalgia as "the power of active remembrance as a ritual summoning and invocation of the traditions of the oppressed in violent constellation with the political present" ("Capitalism" 136). Paredes's modernity is thus paradoxically most starkly visible wherever in his writings he turns in a Benjaminian mode to "the power of active remembrance" in opposition to the allure of "the political present" ("Capitalism" 136).

Human Geographies: The River That Flows Nowhere like the Sea

The lead poem in Paredes's *Between Two Worlds*, entitled "The Rio Grande," written in 1934 when Paredes was only eighteen years old, offers a good example of this process of active remembrance as an index of the modern. The poem dates from the period of the *Cantos de adolescencia*. It exemplifies the focus on the geographic specificity of the south Texas border region as a critical social space for the political artist. It also displays Paredes's nostalgic imaginative attempt to reconfigure the nature of the modern dividing line between real historicities and concrete spatial knowledges. The centrality of this poem to his poetic project is exemplified by the fact that it is one of the handful of his published poems that Paredes wrote completely and separately in both English-and Spanish-language versions, as if conducting a trial of the poetic modalities available in each idiom. The Spanish version, "El Río Bravo," dates from July 21, 1936, and was first published in the December 14, 1936, issue of *La Prensa de San Antonio*.[7] Although the two versions are the same poem about the same border river, the one in Spanish uses the Mexican appellation Río Bravo for the river that Americans call the Rio Grande to designate the US-Mexican boundary. In both poems, the border-marking river assumes political and allegorical status as it exhibits an almost Benjaminian revolutionary nostalgia and, with its own circuitous meandering, performs an allegory of active remembrance of tradition in violent antagonism to the political present:

> Muddy river, muddy river,
> Moving slowly down your track,
> With your swirls and counter-currents
> As though wanting to turn back.
>
> As though wanting to turn back
> Towards the place where you were born,
> While your currents swirl and eddy,
> While you whisper, whimper, mourn;
> . . .
> Till you die so very gently
> By the margin of the sea. . . .
> We shall wander through the country
> Where your banks in green are clad,
> Past the shanties of rancheros,
> By the ruins of old Bagdad.
>
> Till at last your dying waters,
> Will release their hold on me,
> And my soul will sleep forever
> By the margin of the sea. (*Between Two Worlds* 15–16)

> Río Bravo, Río Bravo
> que en tu cauce lento vas
> con frecuentes remolinos
> cual si quieren ir atrás,
>
> cual si quieren tus corrientes
> sobre el cauce devolver
> a buscar ignotas fuentes
> que les dieron vida y ser
> . . .
> así vas . . . a morirte lentamente
> a las márgenes del mar.
>
> Pasaremos por los campos
> que se mirarán verdear,
> por jacales de rancheros,
> a las ruinas de Bagdad.

Y tus aguas moribundas
en lo azul se perderán,
mientras duermo dulcemente
a las márgenes del mar. (*Cantos* 26–27)

Earlier, I commented that in this poem Paredes seizes a historical
memory that is in grave danger of being lost and that embodies the
memory in the reality of local space. Paredes's images of the doubled
river represent the inseparability of history and locale, of time and
space. The river metaphor thus stands as a classic instance of Bakhtin's
idea of the chronotope as a constitutive category of the project that
Bakhtin calls "historical poetics." In his essay on the chronotope, written almost exactly contemporaneously with Paredes's poetry, Bakhtin
proposes that "in the literary artistic chronotope, spatial and temporal
indicators are fused into one carefully thought-out, concrete whole.
Time, as it were, thickens, takes on flesh, becomes artistically visible;
likewise, space becomes charged and responsive to the movements of
time, plot, and history" ("Forms of Time" 84). Bakhtin also points
out that "novelistic chronotopes" are frequently "deeply infused with
folklore motifs," such as the motif of the road. "At [the] heart" of the
chronotope of the road, he urges, "is folklore" (120). Bakhtin's link
of the chronotope to folklore is crucial here for an understanding of
Paredes's use of the related figure of the deep-swirling river and the
mnemonics of art. In both instances of novelistic and folkloric discourse, what is at issue is the narrativized trajectory of everyday life.
The English-language title of the poem even emphasizes the grandeur
of the river's flux, while the Spanish-language version evokes the wild,
ferocious, even angry, aspects of the river's course.[8] In both versions,
the river's trajectory is heterogeneously and multiply voiced. Paredes
utilizes precisely this narrativized characteristic of the image of the
river—as a spatio-temporal relationship and as concrete and discursive experience—in both lyrical and novelistic forms to realize life and
illuminate the relics of lost history along the banks of the river.

As a chronotopic intersection of time and space, the Rio Grande/
Río Bravo has been the literal site of much history and conflict since
its establishment after 1848 as the geopolitical borderline between
Mexico and the United States. In Paredes's figural evocations, the
great rush of the river's tide in its headlong flood toward "the margin
of the sea" figures the seeming inevitability of the stream of history

and the arcing oblivion of historical forgetfulness. At the same time, with its "aguas moribundas," dying waters, it puts before us mythically, like the great River Styx, the margins between the quick and the dead. The river forms at once the frontier between the known and the imagined worlds and the barrier between the past and the future, the margins between what we remember and forget.

The "swirls and counter-currents" that make it seem to turn on itself, causing it to return to its origin, simultaneously undercut the eastward flow of the Rio Grande in its journey toward the Gulf of Mexico and disrupt its smooth, teleological run from known to imagined, from past to future. They allude to a complex relationship between the living and the dead. The Spanish-language poem even more powerfully than the English-language text emphasizes this doubled motion toward and away from "ignotas fuentes," unknown sources. From the narrative present, the binational, bilingual speaker reflects on historical origins, even while projecting toward a future perfect temporality of culmination, "a las márgenes del mar" (by the margin of the sea). Until the moment that it enters that engulfing sea, the river drifts toward the sea in the same way that the flow of history holds us, or as a body engulfs the soul. The abandoned "shanties of *rancheros*" and the "ruins of old Bagdad," archaic relics from the colonial past of south Texas and of earlier stages in the development of the present mode of production, evoke in different registers the economic base of a declining world and the Oriental mystery of crumbled empires. Both images represent in reality, however, the shattered *mexicano* culture that once persisted but is now gone.

The river poem is thus in part a death song: it elegizes two distinct historical moments. First, it recalls the remnants of a precapitalist, eighteenth-century Mexico-Texan ranchero economy. Then, it memorializes the ghost-town ruins of an early nineteenth-century petite bourgeoisie entrepreneurial class that founded the trading center of Bagdad, Tamaulipas, in the decades before the establishment of the Anglo-Texan colonies, before Texan independence, and before the coming of the latter-day imperious Anglo capitalist agribusiness formations in the late nineteenth and early twentieth centuries.[9] The historical consciousness Paredes elicits here in a nostalgic mode is a revolutionary recollection of both of these social moments. The poem's elegiac tone offers a lyrical evocation of the quelled surges of history that those distinct moments represent.

Paredes's point in his poems of the doubled river is that the counter-currents of history are contradictory, refractory, and liable to turn back on themselves, endlessly diverting from linear trajectories and achieved entelechies. The duplicitous "hidden" currents that "swirl and eddy" beneath a placid surface dissemble a "troubled, dark" depth. The river can thus metamorphose fascinatingly from moment to moment, indolent and passive in one course, vibrant and dashing in another, as in this evocation of 1935, "Moonlight on the Rio Grande":

> The moon is so bright it dazzles me
> To look upon her in the eye,
> She lies like a round, bright pebble
> On the dark-blue velvet sky,
> She hangs like a giant pebble
> In the star-incrusted sky.
>
> The Rio Grande is bent and brown
> And slow, like an aged peon,
> But silver the lazy wavelets
> Which the bright moon shines upon,
> As bright as the little silver bells
> On the round hat of a peon. (*Between Two Worlds* 28)

An "aged peon" one moment, an insolent blade sporting "little silver bells" the next, the river flows its figurative course, defying the limitations of two separate worlds. But in each manifestation, the river man, the peon of the poem, is the historically real personage of the foot soldier, the pedestrian farmhand, the moveable pawn who has shaped the history of the border region.[10] In each of these river poems, Paredes is working out the specificity and vitality of subjective experience on the border and exploring the multiple configurations of social life that have characterized life at the periphery of capitalism. He gives special place to the ways Mexican Americans have experienced modernity and to what social geographer Edward Soja has termed the "time and space, history and geography, sequence and simultaneity, event and locality, the immediate period and region in which we live" (25). Soja goes on to suggest that "just as space, time, and matter delineate and encompass the essential qualities of the physical world, spatiality, temporality, and social being can be seen as the abstract dimensions which together comprise all facets of human existence. . . .

each of these abstract existential dimensions comes to life as a social construct which shapes empirical reality and is simultaneously shaped by it" (25). This active and dialectical construction of the social by the spatial and the temporal and spatial by the social gives rise to the construction of human geographies and is one of the defining features of modernity (27). Its representation as a relationship of reciprocity forms part of Paredes's poetic project as well.

In another river poem, a beautiful sonnet entitled "A orillas del Bravo" ("By the Banks of the Bravo"), Paredes again returns to the quintessential qualities of the physical world along the river that also marks the political instance of a limiting border to describe the abstract dimensions of social being as such: "La brisa que se queja entre la rama / acaba con el día calcinante / y esparce sobre el agua murmurante / aromas de amapola y de retama" (The breeze that laments among the branches / ends with the calcined day / and scatters across the murmuring waters / aromas of poppies and *retama*) (*Between Two Worlds* 47). In the poetic moment, the lamenting breeze bred of the "calcined" day's heat forsakes the heated shore to caress instead the soothing river's waters with the embalming aromas of wildflowers and medicinal herbs. All the while, the melancholy character of the scene is reinforced by the mournful movements of the long, pendulous leaves of the *retama*, a native tree resembling the weeping willow. In this way, the material world is imbued with the disembodied presence of the registering poetic eye that takes the scene and shapes it, as much as the scene shapes it. We should note, moreover, one additional border feature of the poem, namely, the fact that this river sonnet, too, is a Spanish-language poem and like "El Río Bravo" refers to the Rio Grande by its Mexican name. As was the case for the sonnets "Paso Doble" and "Rumba" from *Cantos de adolescencia*, here, the melodious, classical lines of the lyric disguise the fact that the poem instantiates a basic borderlands political outlook. Standing on the Mexican right bank looking across to the American left bank, the poet seems to slip out of his American self and acquires another subjective identity in a Mexican imaginary mode. As in the earlier river poems, then, the Rio Grande is a political line that divides but does not separate, defines but does not differentiate.

As Paredes would have it, rivers are spaces and temporalities; they are topographies and teleologies; they are histories and concretized social spaces. As figures to be understood, they stand as signs of knowledge as well as of power. Like another great American modernist, Langston Hughes, Paredes thus might well have written: "I've known rivers . . . / I've known rivers ancient as the world and older than / the flow of human blood in human veins. / My soul has grown deep like the rivers" (Hughes 23). As courses of history and trajectories of cultural space, Paredes's rivers constitute tropes of a liminal state between origin and end, abstraction and concretion. They must be gazed across, followed in time, and traversed in space. In the African American modernist tradition, concert music, the blues, and jazz became symbolic expressions of social memory and anticipation in the era of the Harlem Renaissance. Langston Hughes claimed that he composed "The Negro Speaks of Rivers," his first published poem, in 1920 while traveling on the train from Saint Louis through Texas on his way to visit his father in Mexico City. Crossing the Mississippi in the gathering dusk, the sight of the Mississippi evoked for Hughes the historically determining effect of life along other rivers for black and working peoples of America. Like the great poets of the Harlem Renaissance examining the role of African American folk music in the liberation aesthetics and political debates about racial performance, social memory, and national identity spirituals, Paredes here too looks at rivers, and for the same reasons. He focuses on the ways that rivers as metaphors of deep tradition and symbols of music can express an understanding of the course of history.[11]

In this, too, Paredes's poems participate in the modernist mode of another American poet, Wallace Stevens, who evokes in "The River of Rivers in Connecticut" another river scene:

> There is a great river this side of Stygia,
>
> . . .
>
> In that river, far this side of Stygia,
> The mere flowing of the water is gayety,
> Flashing and flashing in the sun. On its banks,
> No shadow walks. The river is fateful,
> Like the last one. But there is no ferryman.
> He could not bend against its propelling force.
> A curriculum, a vigor, a local abstraction
>
> . . .
>
> Call it, once more, a river, an unnamed flowing,
> Space-filled, reflecting the seasons, the folk-lore

Of each of the senses; call it, again and again,
The river that flows nowhere, like a sea. (533)

Stevens's magnificent poem signals the tropological features of river poems: their course is "fateful," no mythological "shadow" haunts their shore. They instantiate "curriculum" and "vigor" in the form of "a local abstraction," and, most tellingly, they are emblematic of the social ecology of place, "reflecting the seasons, the folk-lore / Of each of the senses" of a region's cognitive geography, making it like a Kantian phenomenon perceivable as an object and knowable as an idea.[12] And all of this strikes us not cognitively but sensorially as the river "flows nowhere, like a sea." Reveling in the fluid, poetic rhythms of the American vernacular, Stevens offers here, as Jameson observes, "indigenous credentials of a high-cultural 'vernacular' order" (*A Singular Modernity* 168).

This curriculum of history realized as social space in the recurring trope of centers and peripheries in the poems of Langston Hughes and Wallace Stevens, paradigms of American modernism, is never far from Paredes's poetic designs either. However, his rhythms derive from a decidedly different cultural vernacular order. It is hardly fortuitous, therefore, that the musical genre of the *corrido*, the kind of narrative folk song to which Paredes would repeatedly turn in order to draw the "seasons, the folk-lore / Of each of the senses" of the border region, takes its name from *correr*, the Spanish word for "to run" or "to flow." *Corridos* flow swiftly and without embellishment, as Paredes later explained in the introduction to *"With His Pistol in His Hand"*, rendering local abstractions in the folklore of the senses. In his concern with the curriculum of the borderlands, Paredes was ever conscious of its persistent links to the real and the imaginary fluid boundaries of the bordering river. The chronotope of the river in effect defines the artistic unity of his literary work in relation to the geography and history of the border, materializing and condensing time and space in dynamic and contrapuntal interrelationship in the medium of the poetic word. This explains why the literal "Río Bravo" and "Rio Grande" figure so prominently in Paredes's social aesthetics. They represent one aspect of the confluence of ideas represented by the great modernist rivers whose symbolic flows James Joyce was contemporaneously reciting as "the waters of babalong," (103) describing their course as the "rivering waters of, hitherandthithering waters of. Night!" (216) in *Finnegans Wake* (1939).

The Dirge of the Heliotrope

This concern with the curriculum of the real and the imaginary fluid boundaries figured in the river poems is so overwhelmingly present to Paredes's symbolic forms that even when, as in a poem entitled "Flute Song" (1935), their forms seem of secondary consideration, they in fact become the dominant theme:

> Why was I ever born
> Heir to a people's sorrow,
> Wishing this day were done
> And yet fearful for the morrow.
>
> Why was I ever born
> Proud of my southern race,
> If I must seek my sun
> In an Anglo-Saxon face.
>
> Wail, wail, oh flutes, your dismal tune,
> The agony of our birth;
> Better perhaps had I never known
> That you lived upon the earth. (*Between Two Worlds* 24)

The initial four-line stanza of this poem sets a tone of sorrow, appropriate to the social conditions of which the poet speaks. However, as we have seen throughout our discussion of Paredes's poetry, elegy is far from the final mode of his work. The "wail[ing] flutes" accompanying "the agony of our birth" certainly denote the classical funereal dirge and heroic lament, but they also connote something altogether different: the music of the poetic song itself.

The numerous references to, and outright imitations of, the rhythms of popular Mexican and Afro-Caribbean music, including *corridos*, tangos, boleros, and rumbas, emphasize the importance of poetic song and popular music to the evocation of the social world that Paredes represents. So while sorrow certainly characterizes the lived reality of the subjected Mexican American people of the borderlands, destined to seek their "sun / In an Anglo-Saxon face," the dominant key of "Flute Song" is registered by the poet who is "proud of my southern race." In this poem sung from the perspective of the south, lyrical sorrows and dismal tunes are in fact dialogical counters and reaction formations. They have been mobilized to face the challenging question of what is to be done, given the grim reality that his "southern race" has indeed been born, that the northern Anglo-Saxon does undeniably live on the earth, and that the Mexican American, situated between the two, must perforce seek his sun in an Anglo-Saxon face. Thus, while "Flute Song" appropriates the rhetoric and prosody of elegy, it nevertheless refuses the ideological consequences of its imaginary social geography. It opts instead to overplay the melodious line, the cultural boundary, and threshold of meaning, that must be bridged in the process of cultural production by choosing forcefully and continually to reject self-marginalization and to counter the hegemonic national narratives of Anglo-Saxon America by imagining other, perhaps more enlightening, heliotropes.

Mnemonic Drums

This confluence of cultural, historical, and poetic ideas is readily visible as well in a poem such as "Africa" (1935):

Africa! Africa!
Black soul with a song
And a chain.
Africa! Africa!
Black soul with a long
Cry of pain.
Carved piece of jade,
Soft beauty made
In the depths of the jungle's fierce breast
To the music of the drums,
Of the tremulous drums,
Of the live, sobbing drums . . .
Of the drums!
Of the drums!!
Of the drums!!!
That incite such a curious unrest.
Africa! Africa!
Bare back burden-bent,
Choked cry in the night.

Africa! Africa!
Bare back that has felt
The whip of the white.
The song remains,
I can hear it echoing yet
To the rolling of drums,
Of the ominous drums,
Of the live, throbbing drums . . .
Of the drums!
Of the drums!!
Of the drums!!!
May you never forget. (*Between Two Worlds* 18–19)

The percussive rhythms of these verses are strikingly reminiscent of their exact contemporaries from the Harlem Renaissance, the paronomasia of Jean Toomer's "Song of the Son" ("In time, although the sun is setting on / A song-lit race of slaves; it has not set") or Lewis Alexander's "Enchantment" ("A black body—dancing with beauty / Clothed in African moonlight") (qtd. in A. Locke 137, 149–50). Paredes's poem resonates with the certainty of how art, song, and dance function as historical knowledge. Like the African American modernists, Paredes, too, here makes lyrical poetry act like "the music of the drums" as a medium in which history is brought to bear on the kinds of ontological questions and issues raised in philosophical discourse and brought into a position of prominence in situations of social, cultural, and political conflict (Kutzinski, *Against the American Grain* 144). The most important of these questions for African Americans and Mexican Americans alike is that of cultural identity and historical foundation emerging from a shared experience of racial oppression and social injustice. The drums, then, serve as metaphors for history and memory, and for figurative poetry itself, the very form of the social vernacular aesthetics to which Paredes always attends. They reverberate with the hypnotic intensity of life ("the music of the drums / . . . the tremulous drums / . . . the live, sobbing drums"), and the insistence of change: "Of the drums!!! / That incite such a curious unrest." The insistence of their beat—"May you never forget"— underscores the ways that memory and history work upon the mind, to stimulate *anamnesis*, the loss of forgetting.

As in Baudelaire, memory for Paredes becomes an instrument of historical description, a way of showing how, in modern society, because of the increasing number of shocks produced by the changes of modernization, the defense mechanisms by which people normally protect themselves in everyday life against the shock of modernity are no longer merely personal ones. Instead, a whole series of mechanical substitutes intervene between consciousness and its objects on the transpersonal level, shielding us yet also depriving us of any way of assimilating what happens to us, or of transforming our sensations into any genuinely personal experience. For Baudelaire, this is the function of truly modern "Mnemonic Art," to render the glory of the aesthetic from the tension between the past and the present in memory, not from the immediate study of life ("Painter" 15). In Paredes's version, the progressively intensive repetition of the song "of the drums!!!" serves the mnemonic function, expressed in the mode of self-knowledge, forged in oppression, fired in the struggles against racism, and tempered by the bath of kinship created among those viscerally responsive to the call of the African drums.

Here, too, Paredes's poetic lines sound with the beat of an Afro-Caribbean rhythm, as if straight from a poet like Nicolás Guillén in his "Canción del bongo": "Esta es la canción del bongo: /—Aquí el que más fino sea, / responde, si yo llamo" (This is the song of the bongo drums: When I call, everybody, even the most refined, respond) (qtd. in Pérez Firmat, "Nicolás Guillén" 324). Paredes's version of the call of the African drums also speaks of call and response and adds to the rhythms of self-knowledge the historical dimensions of a mnemonic beat: "The song remains / . . . May you never forget."

Baudelaire proclaims the beginning of modernity in Constantin Guy's illustrations by declaring them as prime instances of what he calls "l'art mnémonique" ("Painter" 15).[13] Mnemonic art is that activity in which "exaggeration" aids memory (16) and where the external "attitude and gesture" (18) of the artistic exaggeration discharges a "luminous explosion in space." Its radiant effect is what Baudelaire now calls "La modernité," adding "c'est le transitoire, le fugitif, le contingent, la moitié de l'art dont l'autre moitié est l'éternel et l'immuable" (it is the transitory, the fugitive, the contingent, the half of art whose other half is the eternal and the immutable).[14] This compromise in the domain of art between the transitory and the immutable is not unlike the compromise of Hegel in the realm of history itself, where for Hegel a general meaning was immanent within the particular moment of history. For Baudelaire, the transitory, fugitive element of everyday life contains within it "le fantastique réel de la vie" (the fantastic reality of life) (15; 1166). Paredes's drums here similarly beat the rhythm of remembrance and commemoration in their attempt to hold off forgetting and keep the past alive from an instance of transitory history. However, his mnemonic art attempts to sound the fantastic reality of life by representing its transitoriness not as a function of the luminosity of art but rather of the historical chains of oppression and injustice. The drums resound with memory, but they do not speak to the past or of seduction by the past. Instead, their mnemonic rhythm is the source of the "luminous explosion in space," producing proleptic memories of future freedoms still to be achieved. Like Langston Hughes who vows that while "America never was America to me / . . . America will be!" Paredes hears in the music of the drums the melody of a modern American idiom in which the achieved promise of America will someday exist.

Mestizo Modern

At the very moment of the development of a distinctively Mexican American modernism through these self-consciously polyphonic forms, Paredes is simultaneously aware of its borders and limitations. Chafing against those boundaries, he was still casting about for more effective means of capturing the power of vernacular culture to express its differentiation from both Mexican and American modernity, the specific symbolic cartography of what Wallace Stevens terms a region's "folk-lore." As an apprentice in modernity, Paredes already had begun to understand the contradictory overlap and coexistence of two incommensurable realities that constituted his experience of the modern. In the prologue to his *Cantos de adolescencia*, for instance, he expressed his sense of what can only be termed a nascent double consciousness in the context of his *méxico-texano* identity: "¡México-texano! Fenómeno sociológico, planta de tiesto, hombre sin terruño propio y verdadero, que no es ni mexicano ni yanqui. . . . [El autor] se sintió un momento netamente mexicano y al otro puro yanqui" (Mexico-Texan! A sociological phenomenon; a flowerpot plant; a man without his own proper, authentic native land, neither Mexican nor Yankee. . . . In one moment [the author] felt himself strictly Mexican;

in the next, purely Yankee) (3). With dreadful objectivity, he recognizes himself as "a sociological phenomenon," a preposterous oddity existing both inside and outside of two discrete national realities. He goes on to say, moreover, that while his initial poetic experiments had been entirely in English, a tongue in which he admits "I feel more sure of myself . . . than in my own" (4), he has opted now to speak in his Spanish mother tongue. He confesses that where grammatical errors have crept into his Spanish verse, he has eliminated them, but not entirely. He has deliberately allowed a few to remain "because to my mind, they could not be removed": "Así—en aquellas palabras— 'sentí' lo que quería decir. Decirlo de otra manera fuera no decirlo" (Thus—in those very words—I "felt" what I desired to say. To say it otherwise would have been not to say it) (4).

Paredes here distinctly avoids the lure of romantic conceptions of race, the folk, and the nation in situating himself neither in one nor the other hermetic space of essential purity but in the incommensurable sensorium—what he "felt"—produced in his very heart by the riverlike, free-flowing dialogics of borderland social and discursive relations. The articulation of this reality would require a disruption of the rules of grammar, a rejection of the traditions of classical form, a translation from one tongue to another, even if, perhaps, ultimately only fitfully achieved. In these exploratory texts, Paredes is contributing to the emergence of a New World counterdiscourse of modernity emerging throughout the Americas and the Caribbean. The modernity of poetry would attain fullness not by abandoning the sensible reality of the past, but by surpassing it via subsumption from the perspective of a kind of hybrid mestizo alterity that Enrique Dussel was later to call transmodernity.[15] The utopian dream was, of course, that from the dross of the everyday, this new counterdiscourse of transmodernity might answer to the alchemy of nationalisms produced in the borderlands of the Americas by the wizards of modern capital.

Whatever shape the form of the modern might eventually take, however partial its present realization, the features of a better way of articulating it as a counterdiscourse were beginning to take recognizable contours in the poems Paredes composed in the 1930s and early 1940s between two worlds. Already it was becoming clear to Paredes that the modern poem would have at least three distinct modalities, giving it a distinguishably mestizo modern flavor.[16] The modern poem would need to be (1) *racially indeterminate* in its reflection of border identities, requiring a heteroglossic blend of mestizo hybridity that was Anglo and Mexican, Euro-Hispanic, African, and Indian simultaneously, all in dialogical intercourse. It would need to be (2) *transnational* in order to express its derivations from the nationalistic discourses of one nation to which it was affiliated culturally but not politically, and of another nation to which its cultural and political affiliations were perpetually up for grabs. And it would need to be (3) *diasporic*, *migratory*, and *transitory* in its hemispheric, perhaps even global, reach. Taken together, these characteristics comprised the features of a subaltern *trans*modernity as a uniquely transnational crossing of symbolically articulated, deeply differentiated, cultural signifying systems, the implications of which for political praxis were yet far from fully evident. They would compose the features of a New World poetics and help configure an alternative modernity expressed aesthetically in the form of the mestizo modern.

When taken in relation with the eternal and the immutable, the transitory and the fugitive are significant, claims Baudelaire, because together they constitute "the age, its fashion, its morals, its passions" ("Painter" 3). Between modernization as an economic transformation and modernism as a cultural vision, modernity served as the mediating element, neither purely economic nor entirely cultural in nature, which translated the historical experience of the one into the aesthetic modality of the other, as fashion, morals, and passion. In his poems, Paredes, too, realized that to utter modern poetry in any other way than with regard to the fantastic reality of life in all its circumstantial, racially indeterminate, transnational, and transitory nature would be as if not to give it voice at all. The transmodern poems of this hemisphere would require nothing less than a dialogical tongue, a bilingual aesthetic, in order to incite critical reflection and articulate the laws of the heart.

7

BILINGUAL AESTHETICS AND

THE LAW OF THE HEART

> There are no shadows. Poetry
> Exceeding music must take the place
> Of empty heaven and its hymns,
> Ourselves in poetry must take their place,
> Even in the chattering of your guitar.
> —Wallace Stevens, "The Man With the Blue Guitar"

> Empieza el llanto
> de la guitarra. . . .
> Es inútil callarla.
> Es imposible
> callarla.
> Llora monótona
> como llora el agua,
> como llora el viento . . .
> Llora por cosas
> lejanas.
> —Federico García Lorca, "La guitarra"

> In folk poetry, not only does the performer have the task of
> bringing the "part" assigned him to temporary life, but he
> can re-create the text at will. In the end, it is the performer
> who is the poet—for the brief moment that he performs.
> —Américo Paredes, "Some Aspects of Folk Poetry"

Américo Paredes's reputation as a scholar rests in no small part on his lifelong project of overturning the historical strategies of containment that have limited the modes through which everyday Mexican American life has been described historically. His critical project was decades ahead of its time in its resolve to overturn the narrative clichés and historical commonplaces through which Anglo writers and historians had formerly represented Mexican American life. What was true of the scholarship of the late 1950s, 1960s, and 1970s is also true of his last published works, including the novel *George Washington Gómez,* the volumes of poetry *Cantos de adolescencia,* and *Between Two Worlds,* the collection of short stories *The Hammon and the Beans and Other Stories,* and a final novel, *The Shadow*—all of which were written in the 1930s, 1940s, and early 1950s. These works offer a striking confirmation of Adorno's notion that "modernity is a qualitative, not a chronological, category" (*Minima Moralia* 218).

In a variety of fascinating ways, these imaginative works address the predicaments of contemporary ethnic cultural politics, identity formation, and social transformation in the context of what I am here calling a bilingual modernity and transnational modernization. Paredes's lyrical forms already function as snippets of cultural critique and social analysis to show how culture, knowledge, and power are interlinked as social constructions that might be challenged and reconfigured. And they do so in a curiously modern and bilingual way. To exemplify this bilingual modernity, I turn now to the beautifully evocative lyrics of a poem written in 1935 and collected in *Between Two Worlds* entitled "Guitarreros" (Guitarists).

> *Bajaron el toro prieto,*
> *que nunca lo habían bajado . . .*
> [They brought the black bull down never before brought down]
>> Black against twisted black
>> The old mesquite
>> Rears up against the stars
>> Branch bridle hanging,
>> While the bull comes down from the mountain
>> Driven along by your fingers,
>> Twenty nimble stallions prancing up and down
>>> the *redil* of the guitars.

One leaning on the trunk, one facing—
Now the song:
Not cleanly flanked, not pacing,
But in a stubborn yielding that unshapes
And shapes itself again,
Hard-mouthed, zigzagged, thrusting,
Thrown not sung,
One to the other.

The old man listens in his cloud
Of white tobacco smoke.
"It was so," he says,
"In the old days it was so." (29)[1]

Paralleling the allegorical course of his river songs and the human geographies and social spaces that they represent, Paredes's many poems about music, singing, and poetry also involve ideas concerning social space, temporality, and Mexican American modernity in a multilingual mode. As we have seen in the preceding discussion, some of the poems from *Between Two Worlds* are entirely in Spanish, some entirely in English. Others, such as "Guitarreros," are subtly bilingual. In the instance of this poem, the title and the epigraph are in one language, while the rest of the poem—except for one crucial word—is in another. The point of Paredes's bilingual aesthetic is precisely to direct our attention to this play between languages and cultures as sites where modes of consciousness are made and unmade in the dialogical space between cultures and traditions. Its goal is to incite critical inquiry by reflecting on the ways that one may use poetry—and its central sensorium, the heart—as a tool of cognition.

Quite apart from the starkly modernist imagery of the first few lines, reminiscent of Pound's or Stevens's most sublime moments, "Guitarreros" is of great interest for its elegantly self-conscious representation of the complex interplay among history, geography, poetry, language, and what I want to call the transnational modern in two cultural and linguistic registers. It speaks of male relationships and the sensuous experience of shared song and poetry. It is also about the havoc wrought by changing modes and relations of production with the advent of twentieth-century capitalist economies (modernization, corporate agribusiness, and capital markets) within the ranching communities of the Southwest at the end of the nineteenth century. Cormac McCarthy's trilogy consisting of *All the Pretty Horses*, *The Crossing*, and *Cities of the Plain* has chronicled these themes and values as features of the postmodern borderlands.[2] Paredes's fiction and poetry address them as a project of social aesthetics five decades earlier.

In "Guitarreros," the human geography and the social structure related in Paredes's river poems—figuring a divided social space that both encompasses and includes—is reduced to the ritualized performance site of the song itself. The poem locates us beneath the "branch bridle hanging" canopy of an "old mesquite." Two *corridistas*—traditional ballad singers—perform in this rich sociopoetic pastoral space a traditional ballad, "El corrido del hijo desobediente" (The Ballad of the Disobedient Son), some verses from which are cited as the epigraph to the poem: "Bajaron el toro prieto, / que nunca lo habían bajado." Simple as the poem may seem, closer examination quickly reveals that the symbolic implications of the song and its unitary scene far exceed its locally circumscribed sociotextual space, even while the bilingual aesthetics of the moment remain the paramount concern of the poet.[3] In Spanish, the word *guitarrero* implies much more than its literal English equivalent, *guitarist*. For the term *guitarist*, Spanish offers us two alternatives. In the first option, a guitarist could be a *guitarista*, someone who aspires to the artistry of the instrument. In the second option, a guitarist might also be a *guitarrero*, that is, someone who has attained the full mastery of artistic performance with the guitar. To get a sense of the subtleties of the bilingual aesthetics exploited by the poem, however, we must first turn briefly to the traditional nineteenth century *corrido* to which Paredes's poem refers. The most instructive form of this exercise would be to listen to a musical performance of the classical ballad, since performance is what is at issue in both the song and the poem. Failing that, I cite the lyrics of the *corrido* in full here.[4]

El hijo desobediente
Un domingo, estando herrando,
se encontraron dos mancebos,
echando mano a sus fierros
como queriendo pelear.

Cuando se estaban peleando,
pues llegó su padre de uno:

—Hijo de mi corazón,
ya no pelees con ninguno.—

—Quítese de aquí, mi padre,
que estoy más bravo que un león
no vaya a sacar la espada
y le parte el corazón.—

—Hijo de mi corazón,
por lo que acabas de hablar
antes de que raye el sol
la vida te han de quitar.—

—Lo que le pido a mi padre,
que no me entierre en sagrado,
que me entierre en tierra bruta,
donde me trille el ganado.

Con una mano de fuera
y un papel sobre-dorado,
con un letrero que diga,
"Felipe fue desdichado."

—La vaquilla colorada,
que hace un año que nació,
ahí se la dejo a mi padre
por la crianza que me dió.

De tres caballos que tengo,
ahí se los dejo a los pobres,
para que siquiera digan en vida,
"¡Felipe, Diós te perdone!"—

Bajaron el toro prieto,
que nunca lo habían bajado,
pero 'ora si ya bajó
revuelto con el ganado.

Y a ese mentado Felipe
la maldición le alcanzó
y en las trances del corral
el toro se lo llevó.

Ya con ésta me despido,
con la estrella del oriente,
esto le puede pasar
a un hijo desobediente.

[*The Disobedient Son*

On a Sunday afternoon branding
Two young cowboys did meet,
Each going for their blades
Each looking to fight.

As they were fighting,
The father of one arrived:
—My dearly beloved son
Do not fight with anyone.—

—Get away from here my father
I feel more fierce than a lion,
I do not want to draw my sword
And split your heart in two.—

—My dearly beloved son,
Because of what you have said
Before the next sunrise
Your life will be taken from you.—

—I only ask of my father
That you not bury me in sacred ground,
That you bury me in common earth,
Where the stock may break and tame me.

With one hand out of the grave
And in my hand a gilded sheet of paper,
With an epitaph that reads
"Felipe was accursed."

The red yearling,
Born but a year ago,
I leave there to my father
For the upbringing that to him I owe.

My three stallions
I leave there to the poor

So that at least they may pray,
"May God forgive you, Felipe."

They brought the black bull down
Never before brought down,
But now indeed the bull is down
Thrown in among the herd.

And as for this cursed Felipe
The sacrilege caught up with him
And within the confines of the corral
The bull took him away.

With this I say farewell,
By the light of the eastern star;
This can happen to
A disobedient son.]

In the Chattering of Your Guitar

In the "corrido del hijo desobediente," a prodigal son disobeys his
father's plea that he not fight another young cowboy. The son then
compounds his misfortune when, in the heat of the moment, he not
only disregards his father but even threatens him with the same phallic
violence that the disobedient son wishes to inflict on his antagonist:
"Quítese de aquí mi padre / que estoy más bravo que un león / no vaya
a sacar la espada / y le parte el corazón." The son's words threaten-
ing his father represent a supreme violation of patriarchal authority,
of the phallocentric system, and of communal protocols. They manifest a complete failure of respect for the uncompromisable quality of
paternal authority and the ritual law of the elders. Moreover, they express an unguarded flaunting of the symbolic oedipal order. Given
the primal nature of the son's insolence, the words, not surprisingly,
bring down on the young man's head the father's heavy curse and
doom the fractious son to death before the next sunrise. So fierce is
the certainty of this doom, and the power of the symbolic word of the
father that calls it forth, that the song's diachronic narrative of male-
on-male violence abruptly halts with the father's curse in the fourth
quatrain. Nothing remains for the disobedient son but to lie down
and be buried. So the narrative jumps ahead elliptically in the fifth

quatrain to the disobedient son's synchronic acceptance of his fore-told death, and to his despairing attempts to salvage what honor he can from his disgrace. As he lies dying, he makes his final requests—to be buried among his livestock in unsanctified ground ("Lo que le pido a mi padre . . . que me entierre en tierra bruta / donde me trille el ganado") with one hand out of the grave ("con una mano de fuera"), holding as his epitaph a gilded sheet on which is to be written, "Felipe fue desdichado."[5]

With his dying breaths, the disobedient son then wills away his most prized possessions, a red yearling to his father and three stal-lions to the poor of the community, so that they might pray for his forgiveness ("¡Felipe, Diós te perdone!"). In most versions, the *co-rrido* ends with the two lines that Paredes cites as the epigraph to his poem: "Bajaron el toro prieto, / que nunca lo habían bajado." These last verses tell of the breaking of a black bull, one never before brought down, to graze with the rest of the livestock ("revuelto con el ganado"), presumably in fulfillment of the disobedient son's last testament, donating his cattle to the poor, but also suggestive of the breaking of symbolic masculine sexual force.

José E. Limón points out in an excellent reading of the structure of the "anxiety of influence" in Paredes's poem that in identifying the epigraph as a verse from "El corrido del hijo desobediente," we realize that the *guitarreros* of Paredes's poem are singing this spe-cific song. The poem is "about the imagined singing of this particu-lar corrido" (*Mexican Ballads, Chicano Poems* 49). However, the focus of Paredes's English-language poem is not, as we might expect, the Spanish-language *corrido* itself, but rather the ritualized performance of the *corrido*, the artistry of its composition, the enacted commu-nal ties that the performance ritual instantiates, and the nostalgic re-membrance of a time when, as the poem in its concluding verse says, "It was so . . . / In the old days it was so." The bilingual modernity of "Guitarreros" emerges less from its overt linguistic features such as code switching, interlingual references or puns, or the use of ver-nacular Chicano argot, than from the deeply embedded bicultural elements of the discursive moment it represents. How and why this is so forms the crux of Paredes's bilingual aesthetic and a key to the modernity of its keynote themes.

In one of his later works, a scholarly monograph titled *A Texas-Mexican Cancionero*, Paredes would argue that the nineteenth-century ballad form popularly termed *corrido* is based on the medieval *romance corrido*. With its sources in medieval ballads, the *corrido* is chiefly a male performance genre whose pragmatic vernacular aesthetics sought to instruct and delight its audience with stories that celebrated, interpreted, and dignified the symbolic values of the community. Its special quality in the United States–Mexico borderlands is as the chronicle of that community's attempt to resist the encroachment of dominant Anglo culture in the last half of the nineteenth and the early part of the twentieth century.[6]

Of major significance in both *corrido* performance in general and in Paredes's poem in particular is the gendered nature of this bilingual scene. While women might occasionally perform *corridos*, especially in the "organized audience" situation of the intimate family setting, more often than not, and especially in extended family gatherings or in formal ceremonial settings, "men were the performers, while the women and children participated only as audience" (Paredes, *Texas-Mexican Cancionero* xxi). In these special ceremonial occasions, only the "oldest and wisest men had the privilege" (xxii) of narrating the histories that situated the song and of singing the *corrido* tales drawn from the heroic worldview of masculine virtue and value. In "Guitarreros," Paredes takes this point of the performance aesthetic as the central feature of his poem. The specific ritual of performance—male elders only in a rural, pastoral setting sharing the pleasure of song and recollection—more so than the song itself draws our attention and mediates the achievement of a collective, masculine-gendered, subtly homoerotic *mexicano* identity.

Citing "El corrido del hijo desobediente" as the epigraph to his poem, Paredes thus activates as an element of the present the entire expressive tradition of the Spanish-language *corrido* genre, as well as of its gendered oral performance ritual. These traditions then become the latent narrative of a manifest narrative of celebration in English-language poetic verse. Why this is significant becomes apparent when we recall the social function of the *corrido* genre in the Mexican American community. As the oral folk history memorializing the late nineteenth-century conflict between Mexican American tradition and Anglo-American hegemony, a socially symbolic intervention into subjective and collective identity construction, the *corrido* constitutes a crucial illustration of the residual cultural order continuing as an effective element of the present.[7]

Through the citation of "El corrido del hijo desobediente," Paredes wishes to show how certain experiences, meanings, and values of a lapsed agrarian, precapitalist, patriarchal order now no longer entirely verifiable in terms of the dominant culture are nonetheless still imaginatively lived and practiced through the residue of the cultural institution of the *corrido*. They are also active in the social formations still marginally figured by the *guitarreros* of the song and by the old man in the poem who affirms that "It was so . . . / In the old days it was so." The apparent simplicity of "Guitarreros" masks the complexity of its multiply layered scores that resonate deeply with the fullness of stories, songs, and local histories. Like the allegorical course of the bordering river in others of Paredes's poems, here the flow of the song's poetic speech is polytemporal, multiply accentuated, and surges along—bound not by the unidirectional, single axis of grammatical forms, but by the polychromatic, multidimensional axes of musical form and notation.

In a high modernist mode, it evokes cultural institutions and social formations abstractly, with the forceful clarity of one of Picasso's paintings of guitars and guitarists, with the most economical of lines, the starkest of images: "the bull comes down from the mountain / Driven along by your fingers, / Twenty nimble stallions prancing up and down the *redil* of the guitars." Uniting history and lyrical song in one complex figure—"Hard-mouthed, zigzagged, thrusting, / Thrown not sung"—the river poems and this and others of Paredes's ritual performance songs serve as figural markers of the power of poetic language to evoke residual elements within the contemporary human geography. All in all, the depicted scene certainly seems to represent a comfortingly nostalgic image of organic male consciousness celebrating its rich historical patrimony, *macho a macho*, in premodern time and space. At once a song, a manifesto, and a memory, the poem offers a strong opening for a unitary celebration of that macho ethos.

Macho Chiasmus

But before we get too comfortable with this manly reading, we would do well to note that at first glance, because the citational structure and memorializing tone of the poem predominate so powerfully, it is easy to underestimate the profound discomfort with which Paredes's poem regards this nostalgic scene of male bonding and tradition sharing. Two features of the cited *corrido* and Paredes's poem should give us pause: first, we should not overlook the strangely enigmatic quality of the epigraphic citation itself, *"Bajaron el toro prieto, / que nunca lo habían bajado."* Nor should we ignore, second, the bizarre image in the cited *corrido* of the disobedient son's hand protruding from the grave and gripping in stony rigor mortis the script of his own epitaph, "Felipe fue desdichado." The strikingly graphic qualities of epigraph and epitaph work here hand in hand to effect a powerful deconstruction of certain aspects of the traditional, male, Spanish-language residual culture that both song and poem seem to celebrate without qualification. Let us see how this is so.

We will recall that in "El corrido del hijo desobediente" the disobedient son dies making an oddly catachrestic final request. He wishes to be buried among his livestock in unsanctified ground so that, in a complete reversal of his former relation to them, in death he might now be broken and tamed by his wild stallions and cattle, as he once broke and tamed them. This is the figure of chiasmus, "a grammatical figure by which the order of words in one of two parallel clauses is inverted in the other," as the OED states, and a special instance of the trope of catachresis, "the application of a term to a thing or concept to which it does not properly denote." In this instance we have a special case of a borderlands crossing, a chiasmus, in which the disobedient son exchanges places with his wild animals and as the former tamer of the herd, now becomes the tamed. Ultimately, these new pairings challenge the validity of defining relations of mastery in any binaries: father/son, old/young, obedience/disobedience, inheritance/disinheritance, and more obliquely perhaps, but still operative in this instance, the binaries of masculine/feminine, heterosocial/homosocial.

As if that catachresis were not weird enough, the disobedient son also gruesomely requests to be buried with one hand protruding from the grave, holding his own epitaph. The epitaph gilds the grim reality of the fact that the disobedient son's supplication is surely, at best, only an ambiguous acknowledgment, if not in fact a partial denial, of his own responsibility for his unpardonable sin. In Spanish, to be *desdichado* means, as I have noted, "to be ill-fated, or wretchedly sorrowing." As it happens, *desdichar*, the root verb form of the participle, also means, "to contradict oneself, to gainsay by word or deed." The Spanish-language *corrido* indirectly acknowledges, then, that Felipe is certainly ill-fated, but he is so not through the power of some trans-personal destiny, but because in the agency of his own historical being the disobedient son contradicts and denies the very values of manhood, patriarchy, patrimony, and respect defending which, presumably, he died in the first place.

Traditionally, why do machos fight one another to the death if not to defend their challenged or insulted masculinity? In doing so, they reveal a repressed anxiety and desire for recognition in the fullness of (sexual) being. To paraphrase Saint Luke, then, Felipe in death is, as he was in life, a sign which shall be spoken against, a sign of contra-diction (*desdicho*), in fact, the very sign of his own contra-diction (*desdichado*).[8] In the undoing of his life and the body of his contradictions, represented by the synecdoche of his hand equivocally signing from the grave, the disobedient son literally loses his integrity.

The final, enigmatic verse of the *corrido*, the first two lines of which Paredes cites as the epigraph to his poem, is likewise charged with suggestive ambiguity. In the *corrido* proper, these concluding verses telling of the breaking of an unbroken black bull seem almost irrelevant to the story of the disobedient son. Indeed, this quatrain seems so distantly connected to the archetypal narrative of filial disobedience within the pastoral patriarchal order that some variants of the song simply excise it, cutting out the bull, so to speak. One early anthology of Chicano literature reprints the ballad precisely in this manner (Castañeda Shular, Frausto, and Sommers 179). That is to say, in the uncut versions of the song, the lines about the black bull supersede the primary narrative of the son's disobedience. They introduce by metonymy a larger theme, that of the closing of a mythical epoch.

Because of these variations, excisions, and perplexing ambiguities, it is very tempting to read the relationship between the disobedient son and the black bull as simply a contrivance of emplotment. In fact, however, the relationship between the symbolic "toro prieto" and the paradigmatic "hijo desobediente," as Paredes would have us see, is anything but contrived. A quick reference to the *Diccionario de mejicanismos* reveals what Paredes, who grew up in the transnational borderlands of south Texas and *norteño* Mexican ranches, obviously knew, namely, that the verb *bajar* used in the song in reference to the bull, has the vernacular, northern Mexican, south Texas usage of "breaking and taming livestock." In short, it is exactly synonymous with *trillar*, the verb naming Felipe's reversed relation to his animals (111; 1087). Moreover, the verbs *trillar* and *bajar* that the song uses to indicate the taming of wild stallions, bulls, and disobedient sons also share another meaning, expressly, "to subdue," as in the exercise of power implied in the subjection of a beaten warrior to the victor, or a people to a ruler, or a bride to a man. All of these meanings share a place in the now sharply compromised phallocentric system of the song; its vanity and pride subdued.

In both the *corrido* and the poem, then, what at first sight seems like an unremarkable and uncritical celebration of a utopian masculine absolute past of unitary sociocultural value is instead something else. Both the *corrido* and the poem exhibit the taming and breaking of a social formation under the weight of its own "contradictory" (*desdichado*) value structure. In displaying that economic and social collapse, rather than celebrating masculine power, the poem contrives to unravel an entire system of values. In complete dialogic reversal, the young buried macho, former breaker of stallions and bulls, now lies broken and subdued by them. The rising intensity of the song leads directly to this virtuoso turnabout of those meanings, especially as the chiasmus reverses the direction of the subjection. What is more, the gilded script naming the self-contradiction of his values by his own actions, which in death he embodies, openly marks his grave. This unraveling critique is performed in the mode of bilingual metonymy, through the science of the beautiful (aesthetics), in the provenance of the modern. With dialogic intensity, *corridos* such as that of the disobedient son contradict and negate the very truths and authenticities that they desire to uphold. Surely, this is the point of the mediated image of macho chiasmus here.

In point of fact, many years after having written this poem, as a scholar of the *corrido* form, Paredes would argue precisely that by the 1930s "when Mexico's Tin Pan Alley took over the *corrido* . . . its decay was inevitable" and the genre no longer clearly served its former critical function. The demands of the modern, newly consolidated global American culture industry and its dependent Mexican counterpart, claimed Paredes, "wore the folk material thin" to produce what he came to call "a pseudo-*corrido*" ("Mexican Corrido" 138–39). Laboring to meet the needs of the modern consumer, mass entertainment, the culture industry under the growing demands of the developing commercial radio, film, and audio recording industries for more and more products, the anonymous folk balladeers of the *corrido* were overwhelmed by commercial songwriters. Mexican Tin Pan Alley commercial songwriters creating products for consumption in the newly commercialized form of the *corrido* in the 1920s and 1930s produced music that mimicked a tradition, simulated the gestures of a tradition, or simply invented one if it did not exist.

Down a Dark Tin Pan Alley

This "invention of tradition" was especially true, Paredes would argue decades later as an ethnographer of Greater Mexican culture, for the fabrication of a Mexican national identity and its link to Mexican masculinity.[9] In an essay originally published in Spanish as "Estados Unidos, México y el machismo" (1967), Paredes offers a devastatingly critical genealogy for the absurdly exaggerated version of Mexican masculinity notoriously identified as machismo. Far from representing a traditional type of masculinity in opposition to a debased modern version, Paredes argues, machismo as an expression of the gun-toting, braggart and bully, facing death with false bravado was an invented tradition, a product of cultural romanticism, reflecting the ideological needs of a newly emergent state groping for a distinctive national subject identity. As the anthropologist Kate Crehan concludes, "the context for this particular 'invention of tradition' was the very specific one of Mexican nationalism and its struggle to define, always in the shadow of its powerful northern neighbor, an autonomous Mexican identity" (198). It reflected, moreover, the class structures of that emerging society, especially in the *corridos* promulgated by commercialized Mexican popular song and film:

> Then appear the *corridos* for which Mexico is known abroad, the same ones cited repeatedly by those who deplore *machismo*. . . . Such *corridos* were disseminated in Mexico and abroad by the voice of popular singers like Pedro Infante and Jorge Negrete. That is to say, these were moving-picture *corridos*. And when one says moving-pictures, one says middle-class. These have been the songs of the man from the emergent middle class, a man who goes to the movies, has enough money to buy a car, and enough political influence to go around carrying a gun. During World War II, it was the middle class that became emotional hearing Pedro Infante sing:

¡Viva México! ¡Viva América!   Long live Mexico! Long live America!
¡Oh pueblos benditos de Dios!   Oh, nations blessed by God!
("The United States, Mexico" 221)

Paredes points out the class basis of this notion of masculinity and the influence of the United States in its construction. Not the least of the contentious arguments that Paredes makes in this essay is for the close genealogical relationship between Mexican machismo and the figures of the North American frontiersman and cowboy whose supposed manliness was venerated by myth, legend, history, and Hollywood, as well as celebrated by American presidents from Theodore Roosevelt at the beginning of the twentieth century to George W. Bush at the beginning of the twenty-first century. In both instances, the Mexican and the American one, Paredes claims, "machismo betrays a certain element of nostalgia; it is cultivated by those who feel they have been born too late" ("The United States, Mexico" 234).

In "El corrido del hijo desobediente," this nostalgia disguises a mystified desire for an archetype that the economic and social history of the Southwest will simply not entertain. This is the point of Paredes's bilingual aesthetics. Having become so powerfully identified with the failed ideologies of a defeated ranchero, patriarchal, and precapitalist world, unable to resist the encroaching hegemony of modern cultural commoditization, the *corrido* in both its newly commodified and traditionally residual forms from this time forward would either have to evolve or give way to new symbolic constructions that could layer different, richer, and more viable alternatives to the lyrics of former songs.

Likewise, the failed virtues celebrated in countless *corridos*, graphically monumentalized in this instance by the disobedient son's epitaphic hand holding not the archetypal pistol in hand but the gilded pronouncement of his contradiction, are replaced now by a modernist poetic aesthetic and script that memorialize even as they supersede. Unbending patriarchal authority and uncompromising male violence such as that celebrated, or at least memorialized, in a *corrido* like the one discussed could not prevent the destruction of that former way of life that had now receded into the legendary past ("In the old days it was so"). Nor could it contest the modern historical erasures that Paredes in the 1930s was witnessing and documenting in his poetry. This may well explain in part why neither the patriarchal social formations nor the heroic border *corrido* survive to oppose the processes of twentieth-century modernization. Other versions and newer forms authored by different persons would have to arise to fulfill that function in another age.[10]

Moreover, his recognition of this historical process explains why Paredes sings a song about the ritual of singing rather than simply singing the song of patriarchal authority itself. He is, finally, less concerned with representing the decline of a particular community and the nostalgia for a premodern world than with rendering the very processes of change and creative adaptation. The cultural critic Robert E. Livingston thus correctly points out that "whatever might be said about its ultimate political allegiances, the movement of literary modernism derives much of its energy from its resistance to an institutionalized cultural order and its ever-keener awareness of the transnational dimension of aesthetic production" (152). The case of Américo Paredes's modernism illustrates Livingston's point precisely about the links between modernism and the critique of an officially sanctioned institutional order and an emerging insight to the transnational character of aesthetic production.

Llora por Cosas Lejanas

The transnational character of aesthetic production in Paredes's poetry emerges constantly, but not always in the use of a bilingual idiom. When the poems are bilingual, however, we are on special notice that something distinctive is about to occur. This is particularly the case in "Guitarreros." *Redil*, as the only Spanish-language word in Paredes's poem apart from the epigraph, requires our special attention because of the web of transnational allusions it justifies. First, the "*redil* of the guitars" as a figure in the poem for the livestock pens and enclosures of ranches that once existed (in the "old days it was so") makes the guitars synecdoches of an economic and social formation that also no longer exists. Second, since *redil* comes from *red*, meaning "net," it may also be a metaphor for the ten strings and fretted necks of the two guitars. This metaphor in turn creates a visual corral for the guitarists' eerily disembodied fingers, represented as "twenty nimble stallions prancing up and down the *redil* of the guitars." Third, in addition to being a synecdoche for the guitars themselves, the "*redil* of the guitars" is also the small circle of men whose song brings the bull down from the mountain, "driven along by your fingers." A fourth strand of allusions created by *redil* refers to the character constellation of the poem. If there are three characters in the poem, two guitarists singing, "One to the other," and an old man who listens to their song and comments about the "old days," then the poem reproduces exactly the reduced character constellation as well as the confining topoi of "El corrido del hijo desobediente," with only its two fighting cowboys and an intransigent patriarch making up its entire cast. As in the ballad, the poem hints at another perspective beyond the nostalgic old man and the *guitarreros* with their guitars yearning for faraway things, namely, that of a poet who stands aside to witness and record the alignments of their mutually defining circumstances. Together, these multiple strands of allusions emanating from the *rediles* of the guitars form the fold of its intertextual *red*, or poetic net of the poem and the song.[11]

Bad Guitars and Lying Women

A poem written almost a decade later and half a world away adds yet a fifth component to the figures of the guitar and the guitarist that Paredes explores here in "Guitarreros." In "Guitarras y mujeres" ("Guitars and Women"), the poet mocks his own macho blindness by recalling some painfully sententious lines that in full naïveté he had once composed about women and guitars: "Las mujeres mentían / como las guitarras malas" (women lied / like bad guitars). Another male voice immediately challenges the disingenuous poet by asking with archirony whether it is perhaps not the other way around, that "mienten las guitarras / como las malas mujeres" (guitars lie / like evil women) (*Between Two Worlds* 69).[12] With this coy reversal, we find ourselves back in the problematic trope of "El corrido del hijo desobediente" and its macho chiasmus. In this instance, with the chiasmus of a crisscrossed exchange between lying guitars and evil women, how are we to know which way the irony cuts? In that of the lying women or of the bad guitars? Lying guitars or evil women? Or, is this instead a conundrum to be resolved only uniquely, concerning the particular individual, woman, or guitar? The poem concludes with precisely that question: "¿Es cuestión del individuo? / ¿la mujer? /¿o la guitarra?" (is it a question about the individual? the woman? or the guitar?). As in the earlier instances of macho chiasmus, the figure reproduces the stereotype while simultaneously undercutting its implications. We are once again in a situation that explicitly challenges the validity of defining relations of mastery in terms of the hierarchical binaries of masculine/feminine, truth/falsehood, or good/evil. In retrospect, from the vantage point of this later image of the *guitarras malas*, the good guitars of "Guitarreros" can hardly be regarded as unambiguous instruments of truth telling. Instead, Paredes's personified guitars should be understood as near avatars, embodied representations of the principle that expressions of what is good or bad, or truth or lie, are corralled in the *rediles* of the very cultural gestures that they presume to signify.

While the *guitarreros* of the poem and the singers of ballads celebrate nineteenth-century economies and mourn the passing of their enmeshed social-gender relations and negotiations, the modernist poet cannot commemorate the world within which they lived without being aware of the constraining nature of its cultural idioms and forms of sociability. Perhaps nowhere else in his poetry of the 1930s and early 1940s than here with his guitars is Paredes most consummately a modern.

The Kings of Modern Thought

We should recall at this point that the source of the title and epigraph to Paredes's *Between Two Worlds* is Matthew Arnold's great poem of 1852, "Stanzas from the Grande Chartreuse."[13] In this poem, Arnold retraces the near elegiac contours of Wordsworth's alpine journey limned in the "Prelude," "the convent of Chartreuse / Received us two days afterwards, and there / We rested in an awful solitude—" (Prelude [1805], Bk vi, lines 422–24). Like Arnold following Wordsworth poetically, Paredes returns to his own undiscovered country between two worlds, the borderlands of south Texas and northern Mexico. In this poetic reprise, he reiterates the symbolic phrases of his community's master narrative of the *corrido*, but without the historical amnesia of the sexual politics of the original score and in full acknowledgment of its rhetorical and tropological self-negations. *Anamnesis*, not amnesia, drives Paredes's revisionary song.

The literary critic David DeLaura has pointed out that Arnold's

"Stanzas from the Grande Chartreuse" is not so much a lament for former times and beliefs as it is an expression of Arnold's hopelessness over the impotence to which melancholy stoicism reduces us (20). Here are Arnold's lines:

> Wandering between two worlds, one dead,
> The other powerless to be born,
> With nowhere yet to rest my head,
> Like these, on earth I wait forlorn.
> Their faith, my tears, the world deride—
> I come to shed them at their side. (lines 85–90)

In the "Stanzas from the Grande Chartreuse," Arnold imaginatively considers and rejects various historical attitudes that in former times he feels have served effectively to stave off the dread of the unknown future. He enumerates them in order to refuse them in sequence. First, he rejects Christian faith, now simply "gone" (line 84). Then, he sees the flaws in his own codes of conduct and ethics, which he had absorbed from his former "rigorous teachers . . . masters of the mind" (lines 66, 73) and sees them as now "outworn" and "out-dated" (lines 100, 106). Finally, Arnold turns away even from the mentalities of "the kings of modern thought" because they are merely silent, dumb, and passive as they "wait to see the future come" (lines 115, 118). Bound as he is between two worlds, Arnold still does allow of another historical possibility. It is one, however, that he wistfully acknowledges is ineluctably unavailable to him: the poetic vision of a future realm, "powerless to be born" (285).

This vision of what we might call, paraphrasing Arnold, the realm of the kings of *post*modern thought is unmistakably what animates Paredes's antinostalgic, counterdiscursive modernist work. Arnold, "between two worlds," dispiritedly resigns himself to his former ethical codes, judging himself totally unfit for the life of "action and pleasure" (line 194) offered by the fearsomely burgeoning modern world of the mid-nineteenth century (DeLaura 21).

As cultural historian Regenia Gagnier notes, by the time that Arnold published *Culture and Anarchy* (1869), he had resolved his fears by turning to aesthetics, or "Culture," as a solution to faithlessness, anomie, and the machinery of modernity. In *Culture and Anarchy*, "Culture" for Arnold means "trying to perfect oneself and one's mind as part of oneself." But human perfection as culture conceives it, writes Arnold, "is not possible while the individual remains isolated" (qtd. in Gagnier, *Insatiability* 107–8). Paredes, too, turns to culture as a solution. But unlike Arnold, Paredes embraces the idea of the undiscovered country, figured in the differential condition of life between two worlds. That liminal space marks a zone of critical deconstruction and constitutes the site where Arnoldian "action and pleasure," unattained even by the cultured individual, might be finally realized. As a master performance artist at the peripheries of modernism, Paredes sees the shared activity of culture, figured here in the performance of the *corrido* and the poem about the performance, as a profoundly social activity.

With the breaking and taming of the disobedient son in the Spanish-language *corrido*, and the singing of his story in an English-language poem, Paredes tells a heteroglossic lyrical narrative: of the collapse of a feudal, patriarchal, and sexual social order under the weight of its own contradictory values, hastened by the corrosive power of the modern. History is one name for the dialectical play between these mutually complicit values and ideologies, dystopias constructed from within utopias. And the site of this utopia is the human geography of critical social space, played out here in poem and song as the fatally resolved oedipal conflict between father and son and the fracturing of the pastoral patriarchal order under the mark of modernity.

Where does the critique of this social order leave us, however? If the eroticized warrior hero of a former era lies dead and buried with his contradictions exposed, who then is to take his place? With the ironic debunking of patriarchal macho values, are we left only with the irony of modern poetic vision? The English-speaking poet who serves up the contradictions and their unresolved tensions does not quite seem up to the role of cultural hero, warrior or otherwise. In contrast to the two patrimonies, one based on male violence and power, the other on male performance genres in rigidly stratified gender and sexual patterns, the bilingual discursive space of the poem offers an alternative figurative domain.[14] As in the archeological work of folklore itself, we are left here to deal with the exposed historical signs of the past and the curriculum of its contradictory flows.

A new vision of self and society, a dialogic world not based on static notions of male privilege and desire, nor of unitary concepts of self or community, emerges from the bilingual space of the poem. It is not present *in* either Spanish or English, but situated in the critical mediation *between* the two languages, interlingually as it were, an early version of what Arjun Appadurai has termed "transnational public culture" emerging in the new global "diasporic public spheres" (21). It is what Heidegger in the book on Nietzsche, talking about Descartes, means when he claims that modernity is not in the subject or the object but in the relational *situatedness* and *positionality* of the two.[15] In "Guitarreros" that situational modernity rises from the realm of the transnational public culture and the social aesthetic between two languages and cultural discourses.

The Law of the Heart

A word about this social aesthetic seems necessary, then. Heidegger argues that as logic comports itself toward the true, and ethics toward the good, so aesthetics comports itself toward the beautiful (78). Aesthetics is consideration of the beautiful in relation to peoples' state of feelings and is thus at home in the realm of the human visceral sensorium. In an essay on ethics, *Theory of Moral Sentiments* (1759), the eighteenth-century philosopher Adam Smith held that virtuous actions were also by definition beautiful. Virtue is beauty, and beauty virtue. Now, recalling etymologies with the help of the OED one more time, we should recollect that *virtue* is derived from the Latin *virtus*, meaning "manliness, valour, worth, etc." "Human society," writes Smith,

> when we contemplate it in a certain abstract and philosophical light, appears like a great, an immense machine, whose regular and harmonious movements produce a thousand agreeable effects. As in any other beautiful and noble machine that was the production of human art, whatever tended to render its movements more smooth and easy, would derive a beauty from this effect, and on the contrary, whatever tended to obstruct them would displease on that account: so virtue, which is, as it were, the fine polish to the wheels of society, necessarily pleases; while vice, like the vile rust, which makes them jar and grate upon one another, is as necessarily offensive. (qtd. in Eagleton, *Ideology of the Aesthetic* 37)

In this way of thinking about the beautiful, the whole of social life, including ethics and politics, is aestheticized into a harmoniously encompassing social aesthetic. Terry Eagleton thus points out that virtue is the easy habit of goodness. A good society is one in which people conduct themselves gracefully, where the law is not external to individuals but lived out in the heart, as the very principle of one's free identity. "Such an internal appropriation of the law is at once central to the work of art and to the process of political hegemony. The aesthetic is in this sense no more than a name for the political unconscious; it is simply the way that social harmony registers itself on our senses, imprints itself on our sensibilities" (Eagleton, *Ideology of the Aesthetic* 37). Critique and sensibility thus unite in judgment and help create the law of the heart.

While one way to read this aestheticization of the social totality in the unity of critique and sensibility is to see it as justification for the way things are, it may also, alternatively, "be read as a discourse of utopian critique," contends Eagleton (38). If this is so, then, we would expect that from the margins of the social whole a very different reading would emerge, respecting the function of aesthetics as something other than a tool of hegemony. Regenia Gagnier points out that "from Kant on, modern aesthetics was seldom about the beautiful object alone (formalism) but rather about the relation between the receptive subject and the object" (Gagnier, "A Critique of Practical Aesthetics" 264). Elsewhere, Gagnier notes that for this reason, the "Kantian judgment of taste is neither simply subjective, relating to the consumer, nor objective, relating to the object" ("Critique" 264).[16] Aesthetic judgment resides precisely in the conceptual space of the relation between subject and object. But what exactly is at stake in this alternative reading of the relation between the receptive subject and the perceivable object?

In aesthetic judgment, says Kant, we put our own prejudices aside, and we put ourselves in everyone else's place.[17] A portrait of *enchiladas de mole* is not beautiful because I happen to enjoy eating *enchiladas de mole*. If we judge it beautiful, it is because it meets other, community, standards for judging it beautiful. My saying it is beautiful, does not make it so. As opposed to mere egoism and selfish judgment, the aesthetic is communal. It points to a utopian alignment of subjects united in the deep structure of their shared field of being. In the political realm, individuals are bound together for external, instrumental ends. Social life would collapse if it were not held together by force. The cultural aesthetic domain, by contrast, is one of noncoercive consensus. Culture and the aesthetic thus promote unity based

on their effectuating human responses of mutuality in their most intimate subjectivity in relation to the object world. They allow us to
internalize the social consensus in an uncoercive way.

With this way of reading the Kantian aesthetic and its role in the
construction of meaning and critique, the beautiful turns out to be
just the political order lived out on the body—in the way it strikes the
eye, pleases the ear, soothes our skin, and stirs the heart. However,
Paredes is not trying to aestheticize morality and society in quite this
way. Instead, he wishes to elicit that state of feeling—as a practice,
and as a way of life.

Kant's notion of the aesthetic as the *relation* between a receptive
subject and a perceived object warrants in Paredes's poetry a relation
always to be understood in the context of a specific historical moment and profoundly situated societal locale, what I am calling a social aesthetic.[18] As a lived experience, its political motivation unfolds
from its attempts to present historically and dialectically contextu-
alized views of these states of feeling as phenomena of consciousness. As a practice, its formal and rhetorical impetus appears, not surprisingly, as understatement, contradiction, parody, satire, burlesque,
and most frequently, irony. Paredes accesses and enacts the social aesthetic through all of these modes.

Writing about contemporary Mexican folk art, the anthropologist
Néstor García Canclini notes that if we could free the concept of the
aesthetic from its elitist and Eurocentric connotation to include the
more "rustic" arts and crafts, then we would be able to "include under
the name of art expressions that handle in a different manner the tangible and imaginary relations of individuals with other individuals
and their environment" (*Transforming Modernity* 107). In providing
social experience in this differently mediated way, Paredes offers a
strikingly distinctive form of aesthetics, a bilingual vernacular aesthetics that asks us to be able to reside comfortably between two worlds.
His bilingual aesthetics is in the fields of sensuousness and feeling
what dialectics is in the area of thinking, which is why we may regard it as a kind of dialectics of sensuousness. The articulation of this
dialectics of sensuousness in idioms of refractory male violence and
power allows us to envision an alternative, if surely utopian, model of
identity to ones based on the monological word of the father. Guiding
us through complex structures of feeling, this dialectic of sensuousness offers an alternate mode of analysis, one linked not to the logic of

the intellect but to the logic of the heart. Art, community, and critical moral culture are at least in part the substantial products of that
modernist bilingual aesthetic.

In a poem entitled "Esquinita de mi pueblo" ("The Corner of My
Community"), composed in 1950 in the weeks after his return from
Japan, Paredes reflects exactly on this process of living the carto-
graphic imaginary between two worlds:

> At the corner of absolute elsewhere
> And absolute future I stood
> Waiting for a green light
> To leave the neighborhood.
> But the light was red. . . .
> That is the destiny of people in between
> To stand on the corner
> Waiting for the green. (*Between Two Worlds* 114)

Unable to sanction fully (nor live uncritically) the ideological structures that the "old man" of "Guitarreros" and the other inhabitants of
the poet's "neighborhood" occupy, Paredes sings instead of twentieth-
century constructions of narratives about narratives and the revisions
of history that such metanarratives might allow: "Not cleanly flanked,
not pacing, / But in a stubborn yielding that unshapes / And shapes
itself again."

This process of shaping and unshaping is precisely the marker and
the substitute of the limits of a monolingual aesthetics. It charts what
in "Esquinita de mi pueblo" Paredes alternately maps as "the corner of
absolute elsewhere / And absolute future." That is, between the emergence of a properly modernist style and the representational dilemmas
of the new capitalist world system, Paredes's verses exploit their contingency to history, "the destiny of people in between," and the utopian glimpses of achieved community, "Waiting for the green" that
this contingency allows. Indeed, as I have tried to show, in exploring
its styles and testing its ethics, Paredes offers us something very like
what Jameson calls a "cognitive mapping" of the imaginary borders
of modernity within the real conditions of existence.[19] At moments
such as this, tracing out in aesthetic figures relationships that turn
out to be all too real social affinities, Paredes's poetry accomplishes
Wallace Stevens's requirement that poetry must "exceed music" and

"take the place of empty heaven and its hymns" ("The Man With the Blue Guitar" 167).

The concluding lines of Paredes's prologue to the collection *Between Two Worlds* say: "I am aware that if this volume finds any favor with the reader it will be mostly as a historical document. It is thus that I offer it, as the scribblings of a 'proto-Chicano' of a half-century ago" (11). These "scribblings" annotate one way that the desire for social harmony registers itself on our senses, imprints itself on our sensibilities, and becomes the law of the heart at the borders of language in the transnational spaces between two worlds.

8

BORDER SUBJECTS

AND TRANSNATIONAL SITES

The Hammon and the Beans and Other Stories

> The war of manoeuvre must be considered
> as reduced to more of a tactical than a
> strategic function. . . . The defenders are
> not demoralized, nor do they abandon
> their positions, even among the ruins, nor
> do they lose faith in their own strength or
> their own future. Of course, things do
> not remain exactly as they were.
> —Antonio Gramsci, "War of Position
> and War of Manoeuvre"

Like his contemporary in the philosophy of working-class culture Antonio Gramsci, Américo Paredes in the 1930s and 1940s had already grasped the notion that power relations occupy a continuum in societies structured by class dominance, which is to say, in modern capitalist societies.[1] For Gramsci, power can be exercised as brute force at one extreme of the continuum, or as willing consent at the other. In one of his notes from the *Prison Notebooks*, Gramsci writes that "the State is the entire complex of practical and theoretical activities with which the ruling class not only justifies and maintains its dominance, but manages to win the active consent of those over whom it rules" (*Selections* 244). As an instrument of social control, the state may exercise power in multiple forms of "practical and theoretical activities" for the enforcement of its sovereignty. It may also accomplish it by winning "active consent." Hegemony extends over the whole field of power available to the state. Edward Said expands on Gramsci's position by explaining that culture serves state power in a particular way: "Culture serves authority, and ultimately the national State, not because it represses and coerces but because it is affirmative, positive, and persuasive" ("Reflections" 171).

Modifying Gramsci's notion of hegemony, Anthony Bogues argues that although Gramsci's position recognizes "the partial agency of social groups who are dominated," it is not sufficient to describe the situation of the colonized subaltern subject in Africa or the Caribbean. In those contexts, "dominance . . . did not necessarily express itself in hegemony," but in outright coercion. Under conditions of dominance, counterhegemonic practices developed that only "sometimes derive from some of the ideas of the colonial West, . . . while simultaneously drawing from other belief systems" (174–75). The strong parallel between slavery and colonialism in the Afro-Caribbean world and the racialized social structures of the American western frontiers and borderlands is one that Paredes continually sought to explore.

Unlike the official state intellectuals of the day who in their mythopoeiac renderings of the American West and Southwest sought to legitimize the power of one particular vision of American culture, and unlike even oppositional Mexican American writers who sought to pluralize that legitimacy, Paredes sought instead precisely to *de*legitimize. His critiques of the existing paradigms and stereotypes did not intend simply to respond to the cultural politics of the day. Instead, the sources of Paredes's critical folklore are drawn from outside the conceptual schematics of hegemonic culture, intending to describe a cultural system functioning as a counterpoint to both hegemony and counterhegemony on a regional and global scale.

Reflecting on the relationships among the ideas of the so-called minority, the nation, and narration, the postcolonial critic Homi Bhabha has written that "The marginal or 'minority' is not the space of a celebratory, or utopian, self-marginalization. It is a much more substantial intervention into those justifications of modernity—progress, homogeneity, cultural organicism, the deep nation, the long past—that rationalize the authoritarian, 'normalizing' tendencies within cultures in the name of the national interest or ethnic prerogative" (*Nation and Narration* 4). As we shall now see, it is precisely these justifications of modernity that Paredes interrogates in many of the finest of the short stories collected in *The Hammon and the Beans and Other Stories* (1994) as he sought to articulate the discursive systems of Greater Mexico. These stories offer multiple versions of the contradictory ways in which Mexican Americans sought to become new national subjects in the decades following 1848 and after the full incorporation of the Southwest into American modernity in the first half of the twentieth century. His critiques of American modernity provide powerful additions to the ongoing revision of the unquestioned prerogatives of the entire narrative of American nationalism.

Paredes's initial short stories are set, not surprisingly, in his home region, the south Texas border country. In that region, by the mid-1930s, when Paredes began to write his fictions, many of what had been for generations small family-owned or family-tenanted farms and ranches, held and worked in common, were now being taken over by large, corporate agribusiness interests, organizing production for a newly developing competitive global market.[2] In the process of this shift from family to corporate relations of production, Mexican Americans became increasingly displaced onto smaller and smaller parcels of land that they worked primarily through contract sharecropping, thus "ensuring the availability of cheap resident labor throughout the year" (Montejano, "Frustrated Apartheid" 138). Already in the late 1910s, however, with the coming of new irrigation and large-scale farming technologies, ranch land bought cheaply from *tejanos* was being "resold dearly as farmland—all on the basis of water" (Sandos 70). As Anglo investors, speculators, and settlers arrived in large numbers into the region in a land speculation boom that changed the cultural and ethnic character of the region from Mexican to Anglo-American, even sharecropping became increasingly economically unfeasible for white landowners. Increasingly, they found that they could make more money by hiring Mexicans as wage laborers than by leasing parcels of land to them. Especially at harvest times, agricultural work now came to be handled by a migratory workforce itself controlled, as Montejano points out, by various economic and legal means (i.e., wage fixing, mobility restrictions, vagrancy laws, etc.) allowed by the unchecked control of state power. These labor controls amounted to a program of labor repression and legalized discrimination that was efficient, thorough, and ruthless.

In the face of this growing oppression and deterritorialization, many

Texas Mexicans sought ways of expressing their frustration and out-
rage. The historian James A. Sandos has demonstrated how the anarchist politics influencing sectors of the contemporary revolutionary movement in Mexico was also being heard in the United States
through radical media outlets. The revolutionary newspaper *Regeneración* published by Ricardo Flores Magón offered for some natives
of the south Texas region a strategy of resistance to the unjust displacements and outright oppression to which they were subjected and
which had become a way of life.[3] *Magonista* anarchist ideas were disseminated throughout the region and "became progressively more
militant about the need for direct action to redress the wrongs done
to Mexicans and Tejanos on both sides of the river" (Sandos 74). The
anarchist program of "direct action" (a code phrase for revolutionary
praxis) came to mean for some Texas Mexican sympathizers of Mexican anarchist revolutionary thought the reclaiming of the land that
had been taken from Mexico and Mexicans after 1848 by staging an
armed uprising against the United States.

By late 1914, conditions seemed ready for this sort of direct action.
And so, in January 1915, a tiny group of *magonista* revolutionaries
based in San Diego, a small ranching community on the border in
Duval County in south Texas, acted. Following the dictates of the
revolutionary "Plan of San Diego," a manifesto for a full-blown rebellion against American imperial domination of former Mexican territories, was set in motion. According to the broadsides announcing the manifesto, plan supporters, marching under a red banner,
would reclaim all of the former Mexican territories now comprising
the American West and Southwest and proclaim a multiethnic social revolutionary Republic of the Southwest. Its political and social
revolutionary principles clear, the plan offered membership only to
"the Latin, the Negro, or the Japanese race" (Sandos 81). Moreover,
American Indians were promised that "their ancestral territory would
be restored to them in return for their support" (81). A later revision
of the plan pronounced an even more revolutionary program. It now
called for complete social revolution, "decried the exploitation of land
and labor by whites and denounced their racist discrimination against
people of color" (83). It pronounced, finally, the establishment of "the
Social Republic of Texas."[4]

Following the principles outlined in the anarchist-inspired, ideally
conceived blueprint for revolution, armed Mexican guerilla fighters

crossed the Rio Grande on July 4, 1915, and attacked Anglo ranches, burned railroad bridges, cut telegraph wires, and killed several white Americans. Reprisals followed quickly, and over the next two years, the notorious Texas Rangers and other law enforcement agencies set out with vigor to effect "the long-standing Ranger practice of ridding [the] area of Mexican 'undesirables'" (Sandos 91). As one contemporary Anglo-Texan observer described the volatile scene in 1916: "A Ranger can shoot a poor peon with impunity, and he is scarcely even asked to put in the usual plea of self-defense, which is as a general rule an untrue one anyway. No race, however ignorant or downtrodden, is going to submit to this for long without feeling an overwhelming sentiment, not only against the rangers themselves, but against the race from which they come" (Lewis 178). Residents of the lower border coined a new word—*rangering*—to describe the summary execution of Mexican Americans suspected of participating in or even sympathizing with the rebellion (Sandos 92). Instead of inspiring fear, the bloody Texas Ranger reprisals provoked condemnation, anger, and retaliation on the part of *magonista* sympathizers like Luis de la Rosa, a former deputy sheriff of Cameron County, and Aniceto Pizaña, a respected rancher from the Brownsville, Texas, vicinity.[5] Over the next year, de la Rosa and Pizaña, subscribers to the anarchist newspaper *Regeneración* and adherents to the "Plan of San Diego," attacked the implements of the Anglo-Texan modern system of commercial agricultural production: the ranches, irrigation pumping stations, railroad trains and depots, and automobiles. Using guerrilla tactics, they burned bridges and railroad trestles, cut telegraph and telephone wires, and ambushed Texas Ranger and US Army patrols, and even struck "the major symbol of Anglo domination, the enormous King Ranch" (Harris and Sadler 387). The "seditionists," as they came to be called in the contemporary *corrido* about the rebellion discussed earlier, performed what they conceived as acts of war. They intended nothing less than to reclaim land stolen from Mexico by the United States, reject the changes wrought by the Anglo capitalist mode of production in the border region, and establish a new border republic.[6] The upshot of revolutionary action was that "by the fall of 1915, south Texas was on the verge of a race war" as an Anglo "backlash of massive proportions" created a reign of terror aimed at virtually eliminating the Mexican American population in general from south Texas (Harris and Sadler 108).[7]

Of Mimicry and Romance

The titular story of Paredes's collection, "The Hammon and the Beans," and a number of the following stories are concerned precisely with the "Plan of San Diego," its revolutionary creed, and the racial hatred and political tension that has persisted to the present day in south Texas in the aftermath of the bitter fighting, the so-called border troubles, of 1915–17. In Paredes, we are not immediately concerned with that revolutionary struggle. Instead, the focus lies on the effects of that struggle and the end of the heroic past of Mexican American armed resistance to Anglo-American hegemony. This marks it as an era of transition from a moment of direct action to one of symbolic and cultural resistance. It is the transition that Gramsci describes as the shift from the "war of manoeuvre" (the consolidation of forces marshaled in direct opposition to hegemony) to the "war of position" (a shift from direct opposition to hegemony to a confrontation with it from within its formations and on its own terms) ("War of Position and War of Manoeuvre" 229–30).[8]

Similar to Gramsci's political analysis, Paredes's imaginative one looks forward to the beginning of a new stage of Mexican American resistance to Anglo-American control of the Southwest. Conflict between the Mexican and the American social worlds will occur henceforth in the realm of culture and ideology. Paredes writes in full awareness that, as Gramsci puts it, in this new stage of cultural conflict "among the ruins" of a former era, "things do not remain exactly as they were" ("War of Position and War of Manoeuvre" 227). The stories of *The Hammon and the Beans* represent brilliantly the difficult dialectic between a Mexican past and an American future for Mexican Americans living on the border at the margin of modernity and modernization. At special issue in this dialectic is the manner in which an evolving sense of a uniquely Mexican American masculinity will be displayed with all its anxieties highlighted in the margins between the American and Mexican national cultures.

The immediate past is represented unambiguously by the "Plan of San Diego" rebellion of 1915–17. With its links to the Mexican Revolution, international anarchism, socialism, and the heroic resistance struggle of the Flores Magón anarcho-syndicalist movement, the sedition represents the phase of direct action, now quickly receding into the legendary past. The future is represented much more opaquely by the stories of the troubled children who must cross the ever-present border between their parents' Mexican past and a yet unspecifiable American future. Squeezed between what has been and what might be, between tradition and modernity, this represented present often seems retrospectively to the narrators of the stories like moments of mere pathos and diminished possibility.

Like most of the stories, "The Hammon and the Beans" is set in the lower Rio Grande Valley of south Texas, the region of the most intense border conflict.⁹ Paredes's first-person narrator recreates the mood of life on the border in the first two decades of the twentieth century, a historical moment when the heroic resistance of men like the *corrido* hero Gregorio Cortez, and even of the "Plan of San Diego" revolutionaries Luis de la Rosa and Aniceto Pizaña, is already fading into the hazy, and unhistoricized, past. Brownsville, Texas, Paredes's hometown, is sketched here as it will be in all of his later fiction and poetry as "Jonesville-on-the-Grande," a place of shockingly diminished heroic quality, and with all the feel of a town suffering under the heel of occupation by a victorious foreign army. The narrator reminds us, "It was because of the border troubles, ten years or so before, that the soldiers had come back to old Fort Jones" (*Hammon* 4).

In the wake of the border troubles, Fort Jones serves in the story as a metaphor for the paternal presence of the US Army of occupation, and as a literal reminder of the force behind that presence. The "high wire fence that divided the post from the town" (4) is an objective correlative of the political and cultural distance that separates the occupying army from the Mexican American citizens of Jonesville. "We stuck out our tongues and jeered at the soldiers," continues the narrator. "Perhaps the night before we had hung at the edges of a group of old men and listened to tales about Aniceto Pizaña and the 'border troubles' " (4). However, the oral histories told by the old men must compete for the children's allegiance with other official histories of revolutionary resistance that the children are learning from their books in their American schools. The stories are not about the seditionist "Plan of San Diego" but of an alternative national formation, "about George Washington . . . and Marion the Fox and the British cavalry that chased him up and down the broad Santee" (4).

In ideological terms, what the scene of everyday life offers the child-narrator is an ongoing dramatization of the conflicts between the

residual elements of the child's traditional community and revolutionary ideals and the forces of the new dominant American culture, a conflict being fought for the hearts and minds of the Mexican
American children. The opening scene of the story makes concrete
the power of American ideology in the physical presence of the army
fort and the spiritual influence of the American school. That ideological power struggle, as seen through the eyes of the child narrator
and the outcome of which is already painfully obvious, is precisely
what the story is about: "And so we lived, we and the post, side by
side with the wire fence in between" (5). As it turns out, however, the
separation between the two is not as inviolable as the initial scenes
of the story lead us to believe. While "none of us ever went to Fort
Jones," there is one child who did, "a scrawny girl of about nine"
(6) named Chonita. Every evening Chonita would enter the forbidden grounds of the fort "to the mess halls and [press] her nose against
the screens and [watch] the soldiers eat" (5). The daughter of impoverished working-class parents who live in a one-room shack charitably
provided to them at no cost by the narrator's parents, Chonita is not
only more daring than her playmates, she "was a poet too" (6). She
would return from her forays into the fort with the refuse from the soldiers' meals for her hungry family. To the amusement of her friends,
she also emerged from the army post with comic emulations of the
soldiers "calling to each other through food-stuffed mouths": " 'Give
me the hammon and the beans!' she yelled. 'Give me the hammon
and the beans!' " (6).

Her mimicry and her daring are the instruments of her poetry.
Mimicry here hardly emerges as a passive act; instead, it is a tactic of
discursive responsiveness. By appropriating the foreign tongue that
the soldiers speak, Chonita is able to both amuse her friends and assert
a kind of mastery through her unexpected linguistic ability that her
subaltern position does not otherwise allow. Still, discourse, whether
heteroglossic or monologic in tonality, is not in itself the equivalent
of material, economic, historical, or military power. Almost, but not
quite.[10] The dialogizing of discourse is not an inevitability nor is freedom a certainty. Chonita learns her mimicry and performs it outside
the purview of the walls of power. Under the cover of camouflage,
mimicry articulates that which it disavows. The child mimes what she
does not have, namely, the ability to satisfy her literal hungers. Her
mimicry is thus at best two-edged. It undermines the arrogance of

the American soldiers' extravagance. Nevertheless, it underscores the fact of her subservience. The other Mexican American children, like the narrator, children of the middle class, in egging her on and pretending that Chonita "could talk English better than the teachers at the grammar school" (6), reinforce that they do not have to mime the fulfillment of their desires, while Chonita to her fatal peril undeniably does.[11] The narrator thus finds it "a pretty poor joke" (6) when the other children tease the poor little girl, but he loses track of her and her mimic escapades when he unexpectedly takes gravely ill.

One evening shortly thereafter, the local Mexican American doctor, a friend of the family, appears at the narrator's home seeming very distraught with the distressing news that Chonita has died. What has killed her, the narrator's father asks rhetorically. The effects of neglect, abuse, and all the ills of oppression and chronic poverty, the doctor responds. While he mourns the little girl, he denigrates her "brute of a father" (7) for his disreputable behavior the night of her death. He is not aware that this man is Chonita's stepfather, not Chonita's biological father. Her real father had been "shot and hanged from a mesquite limb" for the offense of "working too close to the tracks the day the Olmito train was derailed" (8). The reference to events related to the sedition of 1915 identifies Chonita's father as one of the countless innocent victims of the Texas Ranger terror following the failed rebellion of 1915. In the midst of an ensuing heated political discussion among the adults about "radicals," "bandits," "outlaws," and "leaders of the people," the narrator is ignominiously sent to bed by his mother. In bed, away from the adult conversations that he has been overhearing, the boy drowsily muses over what he has heard and only half understood concerning the heroic acts of men who lived and died before he was born. He begins to confuse and transpose the heroes of the American Revolution (Marion the Fox) and those of the Mexican Revolution (Villa, Zapata) by conflating what he has learned at school with the stories and legends he hears at home: "Emiliano Zapata's cavalry charged down the broad Santee, where there were men with hoary hairs" (9). The cold loneliness of this vision reminds him of poor Chonita, who according to his mother, is "in Heaven now. . . . She is happy" (7): "I thought of Chonita in Heaven, and I saw her in her torn and dirty dress, with a pair of bright wings attached, flying round and round like a butterfly shouting, 'Give me the hammon and the beans!'" (9). His mother's poignant words and the pitiable vision of the little girl as a forlorn angel with "torn and dirty dress" and "bright wings" really hold no comfort. As he has already admitted, "In later years I thought of [Chonita] a lot, especially during the thirties when I was growing up. Those years would have been just made for her. Many's the time I have seen her in my mind's eye, in the picket lines demanding not bread, not cake, but the hammon and the beans" (7). In another age the fragile, malnourished "butterfly" might have found life not in the narrator's mother's deferred vision of a plentiful afterlife, nor in begging scraps from the army kitchens, but in radical politics or collective action, demanding social justice on the picket lines with her oppressed sisters and brothers. Her poetry might have been real rather than mere mimicry, its effects social and not simply discursive. "But it didn't work out that way" (7), the narrator admits.

In these last few paragraphs of the story, Paredes consciously echoes Mark Twain, one of the authors whom he was reading most closely during the period that he began writing prose fiction.[12] At the beginning of the *Adventures of Huckleberry Finn*, naively embarking on the course of actions that will fundamentally alter his life and its relationship to the basic ideals and beliefs of his home community, Huck Finn feels the mournful loneliness of subjectivity. As he lies awake in the dark night, Huck says: "I felt so lonesome. I most wished I was dead":

> The stars was shining, and the leaves rustled in the woods ever so mournful; and I heard an owl, away off who-whooing about somebody that was dead, and a whippowill and a dog crying about somebody that was going to die; and the wind was trying to whisper something to me and I couldn't make out what it was, and so it made the cold shivers run over me. Then away out in the woods I heard that kind of a sound that a ghost makes when it want to tell about something that's on its mind and can't make itself understood, and so can't rest easy in its grave and has to go about that way every night grieving. (6)

In the dark night of his soul, Paredes's narrator does not hear the classical harbingers of death, as does Huck Finn. Instead, he senses something that proves to be just as ominous: the military and political markers of social death. He is haunted by the ghosts of Emiliano Zapata, the brilliant military leader of the Mexican Revolution, and Francis Marion, known as the "Swamp Fox" by the British for his disruption of their forces with his outstanding guerilla tactics during the American Revolution. Each vision contends for his heart. As his mind drifts among heterodox thoughts about these figures of heroic romance at play with his mind, all of a sudden from the stark cold loneliness of night he hears the homeless notes of the bugle emerge from the nearby army base: "The cold voice of the bugle went gliding in and out of the dark like something that couldn't find its way back to wherever it had been" (9). The heroic age of direct action "with pistols in hand" seems now irretrievably, forlornly distant from the present historical moment.

As in *Huckleberry Finn*, whatever heroism might yet arise will come only from the naïveté of children. Envisioned in the narrator's imagination as a forerunner of Paredes's own childhood heroine, the great Depression-era labor organizer and secretary of the Communist Party of Texas, Emma Tenayuca, Chonita represents the noble possibility of revolutionary action, mimed and deferred. However, since it is mimed and deferred, there can be no falsely victorious ending to the story of border romance. In later life, the narrator fully understands this. His night of mourning for Chonita is the source of his memorial to her: the story of her brief life of poverty on the periphery of power. That written monument is one that might initiate the conditions for a reawakening of the spirit of direct action, one that might eliminate the possibility of other little girls having to suffer Chonita's mournful fate. The child's name, a diminutive form of the name Encarnación, Incarnation, in reference to Christ as the "incarnate word" of Catholic salvation, can thus only be read ironically, for the incarnation of the dialogic word of liberation in this instance remains profoundly unfulfilled. The text of her story thus becomes, like the *corridos* and "tales about Aniceto Pizaña and the 'border trouble'" that the narrator overhears, an occasion for the expression of a symbolically deferred solution to the determinate contradictions of history in the present.

Dionysos on the Border

The second story of the collection, "Over the Waves Is Out," also deals with the intersection of generational conflict, the value of the aesthetic, and the formation of the modern American nation in the borderlands after the uprising of 1915.[13] In this tale, another young boy hears the mysterious call of music in the night and imagines it to be a signal from the muses that he has been elected as one of the precious few in his rude surroundings on the border called to their seductive melody. We quickly learn that the child has been hearing instead the noise from one of the newfangled contraptions that have recently begun to invade the borderlands, a wireless radio playing in a nearby bakery. When a disgruntled accordion player willfully destroys the radio by blasting it with his shotgun, destroying it no doubt in the spirit of the original Luddites and saboteurs threatened by the allure of the modern, the young boy is left to reconcile his illusory status as one of the aesthetic elect with his pathetic insight that the arts of musical production and reproduction are as liable to the vagaries of mechanization as the relationships between fathers and sons are liable to misunderstanding. Here as in other places, the signs and markers of modernization are both economic and cultural, including Victrola phonographs, radios, motorcars, and movies.

As in "The Hammon and the Beans," the decline of the heroic age of direct action and revolutionary resistance and the implications of that decline for expressions of masculinity again emerge as the subject here. But while in "The Hammon and the Beans" the narrator's understanding of the passing of that era is linked to a child's tragic death, in "Over the Waves Is Out," the recognition of the end of the historical moment of direct action with pistols in hand is not tragic but comic, and indeed almost bathetic. As in the first story, the insight to the reduced nature of present reality comes indirectly, from the discrepancies between what the narrator describes, what he hears, and what he later comes to understand. In addition, as in the first story, the understanding that comes with that view of the past does not preclude the possibility of future victories in the conflict between oppressors and oppressed. It does, however, admit to the necessity of its deferral to other times and other methods.

"Over the Waves Is Out" is again focused on the experiences of a young boy. The major conflict this time is not cultural, between Anglos and Mexicans, but generational, between fathers and sons. The father claims to have once ridden with Pancho Villa's revolutionary armies and, as a deputy sheriff of Cameron County, has possibly served alongside the "Plan of San Diego" leader Luis de la Rosa. The son, who in his fantasies would "dream he was a minstrel in the court of El Cid Campeador," is no warrior hero; instead, he "had always wanted to be a musician" (10). The father will not allow his son to become a musician "because he had once known the man who composed 'Over the Waves' " and he was known to have "succumbed to drink and women, which led him to a tragic end" (10).[14]

One evening, miraculously, the boy begins to hear music as if welling sensually from inside of him: "He was lifted up in a sea of piano music which continued to pour out of him, churning and eddying about him in glowing spirals, slowly burying him in a glittering shower until he fell asleep" (12). On another evening, the music begins anew, as we find the boy again floating about on the beautiful sounds. This time, however, the music is abruptly interrupted by the sound of a gunshot down the street at the neighborhood bakery. The boy follows his father who is hurrying along, buckling on his pistol belt as he runs. The boy notices that his father's voice as he runs toward the sound of gunfire is brisk and eager, strangely unlike his father's usual voice. At the bakery, someone has shot at a radio, scared the baker, run for the border, and escaped across the river into Mexico, leaving the boy's father no opportunity for the glory of former days. On hearing the story of the boy's musical hallucinations and after considering the possibility that the boy has experienced no Apollonian or Dionysian mystery but has only been hearing the radio in the bakery (which has apparently offended at least one listener), the sheriff gives the boy, over his father's objections, a player piano.

Returning home, the father "took out his gun as he walked, cocked it, and uncocked it, sighted along the barrel, twirled it around and put it back in its holster" (21). When he begins to tell his son again of other midnight chases and is corrected by the boy concerning details of a story he has apparently heard numerous times before, the father admits that "it's hard to remember [the details] at times, it's been so long ago. So long, long ago" (22). The boy himself, back in his musical dream floating harmonically over the waves, is blissfully unaware that the player piano he has just been promised is not the piano of his dreams. In their separate reveries, neither father nor son is present to the other as each lives and dreams of a past and future world. But suddenly the boy is jarred back to the present. The shock that follows his realization that "you don't have to practice with that kind of piano. You just pump the pedals" (22), is followed by another: the son's realization of the father's anticipated pleasure in pumping the pedals himself as he listens to the sentimental love song, "Over the Waves." Stopped in his tracks by the dual revelations, the boy watches his father "disappear into the night. He felt very sad and very old and very much alone" (22).

The degeneration of the heroic revolutionary past is here subtly allayed by Deputy Sheriff de la Garza's declining age and by his son's intoxication with the sensuality of music. In both cases one senses a certain diminishing of the potential for heroic behavior; and yet, the narrator's compassionate irony serves not so much to undercut the protagonists as to express their ambiguous position between two worlds, between two ages and two cultures, with no certainty as to which way their destinies will be played out. Their partial illusions, as well as their partial insights about each other, serve as critiques of their self-assured visions of themselves and of each other. For the father, his rediscovery of his past musical consciousness opens the possibility of a genealogical reconciliation with the self that his own father had denied him and with the son whom he has perhaps misapprehended. For the boy, the seductive power of music survives only while the force of his illusions is strongest, hence his feelings of sadness, age, and solitude at the story's end. But these sensations of sadness, age, and solitude might also allow him to participate in his father's history, comprehending the story of his life now not as the irrelevant songs and tiresome tales of nostalgic old men, but as the substance of his own historical fate.

While this alternative melody serves to harmonize the discord between father and son, it also carries with it a contrapuntal line: the countervailing absence of women's song. The boy's allegiance to music and the arts initially separates him from his father's masculine values. As it turns out, however, even Deputy Sheriff de la Garza is capable of sensing what the child feels as he remembers his own father's denial of his sentiment and affect. Significantly absent from this male interchange are all of the women in the family. Yet, in reciting the contradictory truths of patriarchal consciousness and male genealogies, Paredes's story offers unconsciously an image, albeit as a negative truth, of women's consciousness. This position of negative truth concerning women's consciousness was one in which Paredes would continue to remain most comfortable and safe. It would take other voices in other historical moments to speak that consciousness directly. Here, however, the consolidation of male solidarity, with the acceptance of the heterogeneity of male affective response, seems necessarily to drive to the margins of narrative any women's presence.

Paredes's story unwittingly shows how oppositional border narratives often attained hegemonic patriarchal force by repressing women's consciousness. The hegemonies at stake, as it turns out, are not simply those exerted by state power and cultural ideologies from outside the Mexican American community but those created from within Mexican patriarchal structures of power as well.

Violent Death: "¡Unos Cuantos Piquetitos!"

"Macaria's Daughter," composed circa 1943, is perhaps the most gripping of Paredes's stories that deal with the power of sexuality and violence. It attempts to imagine a social revolution tied neither to anarchist uprisings nor to cultural or symbolic action, but to the feminine consciousness not represented in the other fictions. The story narrates a tale mournfully prosaic enough of the murder of a young Mexican American woman (who "looked like Hedy Lamarr") by her husband, Tony, a man who "was short and squat with long powerful arms and a very dark, pushed-in face that was almost noble in its ugliness" (25). But what separates Paredes's treatment of this plot is the austere irony that allows readers to view through a dense, multiply temporal, complex narrative frame, simultaneously the young wife's naively ambiguous desires and her husband's mounting murderous jealousy and desperation over her presumed unfaithfulness. Marcela, the young wife referred to simply as "Macaria's daughter" throughout the narrative, has been constructed by her mother's identity (Macaria's identity as a woman of the night), by her mixed Anglo-Mexican blood (her father is an Anglo door-to-door drummer), and by her resemblance to figures of the Hollywood silver screen (her resemblance to Hedy Lamarr). The limitations enforced on Mexican and American women by harsh and merciless patriarchal cultures define her even more completely. In the tableaulike ending of the story, a plaster image of the Virgin of Guadalupe with "its brown Indian face" stares down on Marcela's murdered body from the altar in a corner of the couple's shabby shack. The young wife's torn and mutilated form, stabbed multiple times by Tony's knife, thus becomes an extension of the symbology of women's victimization and an abject mark of the dreadful power of abstract male ideologies of control through real violence. Even though the young husband *would* rather

21 José Guadalupe Posada, *"Horrible suceso: Fraguado por el demonio y destruido por el admirable y portentoso milagro de Nuestra Señora de Guadalupe"* [A Dreadful Incident: Hardened by the devil and undone by the admirable and marvelous miracle of Our Lady of Guadalupe]. Typical of the numerous images of disasters, calamities, and violence represented in the popular broadside press of late-nineteenth and early-twentieth century Mexico, this Posada engraving depicts the horror of male abuse of women as a war between the devil and the Virgin of Guadalupe. Reproduced courtesy of the Department of Special Collections, Stanford University.

have not murdered her, he nevertheless feels the community's un-voiced ethical imperative that he *must* kill her in order "to keep being a man" (25).

Frida Kahlo's approximately contemporaneous painting, *Unos cuantos piquetitos!* (*A Few Small Nips*), picturing not the symbology but the reality of male reign of terror and woman's blood, might serve as emblem to "Macaria's Daughter." Kahlo's painting was in-spired by woodcuts and prints of Mexican illustrator José Guada-lupe Posada (1852–1913) who rendered gruesome murders and ghastly accidents, and by a contemporary newspaper account of an actual crime, the horrendously brutal murder of a woman by her husband.[15] Posada's lurid broadside sheets and woodcut prints, as Kahlo well understood, offered a salient glimpse into one part of the popular Mexican imaginary concerning violence toward women. The art his-

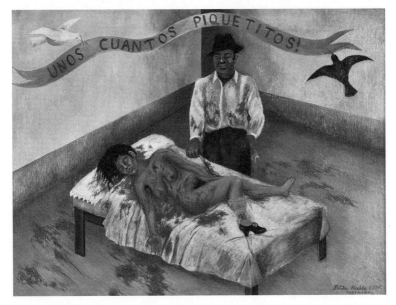

22 Frida Kahlo, *¡Unos cuantos piquetitos!* 1935. Reproduced with the permission of the Museo Dolores Olmedo Patiño © 2005 Banco de México Diego Rivera and Frida Kahlo Museums Trust. Av. Cinco de Mayo No. 2, Col. Centro, Del. Cuauhtémoc 06059, México, D.F.

torian Sarah Lowe points out that "In keeping with Kahlo's sardonic sense of humor, the title of Kahlo's painting derives from the killer's answer upon being charged with murder: 'But I only gave her a few small nips'" (85).[16] In Kahlo's painting, the idea that the representation of a woman's bloody murder may be aesthetic is shockingly undercut by the realistic representation of the splatter of her blood onto the edges of the painting and even onto the frame itself. In Paredes's narrative, the polytemporal vividness of the story's descriptions serves the same problematizing function by pointing out the distancing quality that artistic representation of violence produces.

In form and content, Paredes's story thus uncannily echoes Kahlo's shocking indictment of male pornographic fantasies, linking violence and female sexuality in appalling imagery drawn from the Mexican popular imagination and its stereotyped images of what it means "to be a man." The difference, however, is that in Paredes the horrific indifference of the killer in Kahlo's painting is displaced partially from the husband onto the Anglo policemen who gaze on Marcela's exposed and torn body and reflect on its still, sensual beauty. This scene from the beginning of the story when the policemen first discover the murder before the flashback of the middle portions tells the events leading up to it, turns our attention to male violence and the female body:

> "Hello, Tony," said Mac.
>
> "Hello," the man said.
>
> Mac walked into the room. "Where's the knife?"
>
> "There." Tony pointed toward the bed. Another policeman came in and looked at the woman. A car drove up outside, and the driver yelled to the patrolman standing in the doorway, "What is it, Pete?"
>
> "Mexican killed his wife," shouted Pete.
>
> "Oh," said the man in the car. He drove away.
>
> The others were looking at the woman. "He tried to cut her head off," one of them said.
>
> "Naw," said the other, "look at them breasts. He worked on them more."
>
> "Geeze! There's more'n thirty, forty cuts on that body."
>
> Mac went over to Tony and patted his shoulder. "Too bad, Tony," he said. "Was she in love with another guy?"
>
> Tony's ugly face came alive. "No!" he said savagely. "No!"
>
> "Now, now," Mac said, "we all know why a man kills his wife."
>
> The youngest of the policemen was looking at the woman's thighs, which her tattered skirt did not wholly cover. They were white and incongruously whole. "Gosh," he said, "she must have been pretty" (24–25).

The syncopated cadences of the Hemingway-esque prose render it morally equivocal, bifurcated, and polyrhythmic as the policemen's noir dialogue serves as the counterpoint to Tony's abject "No!" denying his wife's betrayal. Mac and Pete express one half of the bifurcation, the perspective of the manly male view that "we all know why a man kills his wife"; and Tony, the second, an excruciatingly plaintive inability to stem the runaway imperative of male possession of female sexuality. The professional, hard-bitten callousness of the policemen's words does not obscure the fact that their gazes focus on Marcela's breasts and thighs and the fact that "she must have been pretty." In the bifurcation, Marcela herself has been erased from the scene; her identity replaced by the anonymity of the phrase "the woman," repeated three times in the short passage.

The jazzy rhythms of the story notwithstanding, reminiscent of

Hemingway's best stories such as "The Killers" (1927), the issue for both Kahlo and Paredes is the shocking brutality of coercive male power, if not compelled then at least heedlessly condoned by the destructive masculinist values of an entire community:

> He wondered why it was necessary for him to do it. To keep on being a man, they said. The withered old men would sit around in the shade, smoking their cigarettes and talking about him. . . . they were waiting out there, especially the women. When he came home that morning there was nobody out on the street, nobody in the yards. He knew they were all inside, waiting for him to do it. . . . The women especially. Until they heard her screams, telling them that justice had been served, that their own virtue had been affirmed. (25–26)

Adding to his critiques of state-condoned material and epistemic violence in other places, Paredes here now includes the use of male compulsion on women as another form of coercive subjection. The "withered old men [who] would sit around in the shade, smoking their cigarettes and talking about" Tony's violence are akin to the "old man [who] listens in his cloud / Of white tobacco smoke" and affirms that "it was so. . . . In the old days it was so" of the poem "Guitarerros." And both prefigure the "old men who sat on summer-nights . . . smoking their cornhusk cigarettes and talking in low, gentle voices about violent things" of the dedication to *With His Pistol in His Hand.* The *corrido* subjects of both "Guitarerros" and *With His Pistol in His Hand* simultaneously commemorate and undercut violence. For as "Macaria's Daughter" now reveals, violence used as a means to the end of enforcing power has numerous valences. As Walter Benjamin notes in an essay titled "Critique of Violence," it has at least a double social function: the "first function of violence is . . . the lawmaking function," while the second one is "the law-preserving function" (241). Law-preserving violence is proleptic violence, the fury of which is as undeniable as violence that enforces law. In both instances, the subordination of women to men consists in the use of violence as a means of socially sanctioned terror, preserving community under duress. The outcome is the subjugation of women and their interests to male-defined notions of fidelity, desire, and community, with catastrophic consequences for both women and men. Paredes's indictment here of the ethos of male violence against women in both its lawmaking and law-preserving modes could not be more profound.

"A Cold Night," another story from the early 1940s, also deals with the sanctioning of violent death. This story was originally one of a group included in a collection entitled *Border Country* that Paredes submitted to and won first prize in a literary contest sponsored by the Dallas *Times Herald* in 1952. In personal correspondence to me on December 13, 1992, Paredes explained that "the judges declared it the best story submitted though the same collection included 'The Hammon and the Beans' and 'Over the Waves Is Out.'"[17] "A Cold Night" focuses on another child and another scene of death. Neither his father, a day laborer working to remove stumps from the cleared chaparral to prepare for the development of new commercial farmland, nor his mother, whose face "reminded him of the face of the Virgin of Guadalupe" (36), understand why suddenly one day the child is afraid to pray the "Avemaría": "Now and at the hour of our death. Amen." Having inadvertently been witness to the brutal beating death of a man in an alley behind the church, the boy is so disturbed by the merciless violence he has witnessed that he is now also completely repulsed by, and can only express his hatred of, a God who carelessly allows such violence to exist in the world. "Terrified by the thought that at any moment he could become a corpse like the man in the alley" (38–39), he is not comforted by his mother's advise that he "just love God" (39). However, he continues to carry an amulet of the dark-skinned Virgin of Guadalupe, whom he prefers to the image of the white-skinned Virgin Mary in the church because of her "nice familiar Indian face . . . beautiful . . . all-embracing, all-forgiving" (38). Also in contrast to the serenity the child associates with the Indian Virgin stands the figure of "Christ [who] writhed bloodily on his cross" with a "bloody head and wounded side" (40), and who was now too much like the man murdered in the alley to sustain faith and provide comfort for the little boy. In a scene reminiscent of a short story of Tomás Rivera titled "Y no se lo tragó la tierra," ("And the earth did not part")[18] but in fact anticipating it by twenty years, the boy systematically curses God and all the saints and is struck not by divine retribution but by "the supreme meanness of it all" (40). Left now without transcendental stays to authenticate his being, the child hears only the wind eerily whispering his name ("Ramón. Ramón. Ramón") and imagines it to be "the lonesomest sound" he has ever heard. But as in Rivera, the celestial solitude and universal loss the child feels at the story's end is surmounted by a sense of cold determination that might well serve as the ground for a more substantial base for a materially performative authentication of identity at some future point.

The Color of Mexicans

With the story titled "The Gringo," a vignette of historical romance, Paredes seems to shift away from the analysis of gender ideologies and the formation of male subjectivity to return to the primal scene of defeat and deterritorialization, the opening days of the US-Mexican war. In 1846, after Texas had sought and won annexation into the United States, US Army General Zachary Taylor led part of his forces into the disputed trans-Nueces area of south Texas, north of the Rio Grande. Claimed by both the Republics of Texas and Mexico after the Texas War of Independence in 1836, the south Texas region had remained during that ten-year period culturally Mexican, even if it was politically indeterminate. The annexation of Texas by the United States together with General Taylor's move southward to the Rio Grande was tantamount to an act of war. It was matched by a Mexican resolve to defend the disputed territory and the northward movement of a Mexican armed force led by General Pedro de Ampudia to Matamoros, Mexico, across the river from Brownsville, Texas.[19] The titular gringo of the story is not a gringo at all, but a fair-skinned, blue-eyed Texas Mexican boy caught in the midst of these geopolitical events associated with the creation of a continental American nation. His story offers another take on the narratives of nineteenth-century American national formation from the perspective of the inhabitants of the former Mexican territories occupied by the United States after 1848. Having been wounded by real gringos in an earlier ambush north of the Nueces, his father and brothers killed while he is spared when mistaken for one of the Americans because of the light color of his skin, "the gringo" (whose name is Ygnacio) is nursed back to health by the daughter of one of the Americans. When he awakens and attempts to speak to her, she warns him not to utter a word as she has already guessed the truth of his racial identity and understands that a certain lynching will follow the revelation to her father and brothers of the fact that he is Mexican. The young woman, appropriately named Prudence, tends Ygnacio's wounds, attempts to teach him some basic survival English, and after her father discovers the truth of Ygnacio's identity even tries to convince her father that since Ygnacio is after all "white" he can perhaps be taught to be "a real Christian" (53). Plainly, Ygnacio's cultural and linguistic contaminations as a Spanish-speaking Mexican, not his skin color, are the reasons for the hatred of the Americans. At a hint that a romantic attachment between the daughter and Ygnacio might be forming, in the father's eyes "the Gringo" is quickly transformed into just another "greaser," fair skin or not. With the daughter's help, however, young Ygnacio manages to escape back into the disputed territories and then cross safely into Mexico proper. As in the story of Chonita, linguistic traits override other concerns, but only temporarily, as we shall see.

In Matamoros, wearing identifiably American clothes and boots and carrying a brace of "horse pistols with powder and shot" (54) given to him by the American woman, "the Gringo" is suspected as an American spy, especially when he warns about the might of Taylor's approaching army. His physical appearance, which has just saved him among the enemy, now conversely puts him profoundly at risk among his own people. His actions compromise him as well. Thinking to re-cruit guerrilla forces to aid Ampudia and his poorly equipped troops in their coming fight with Taylor's invading army of real gringos, Ygnacio warns: "Our only hope is if our rancheros fight them the way we know how. In guerrillas" (47). Ygnacio surmises that by stealthily maneuvering around the American army, hitting quickly, and run-ning to hit again later, guerilla warfare–style, the poorly equipped Mexican forces might just be able to check the firepower of the Ameri-can guns. But just as his cultural and linguistic traits set him at odds against the Americans, his fair features and physical appearance mark him for suspicion among the Mexicans. Once more, the power of the social life of discourse becomes the marker of difference with which Paredes is concerned.

Preparing to set an ambush for a patrolling US cavalry unit, Ygnacio is finally goaded by his doubting countrymen to prove his allegiance as a true Mexican. When the American patrol stops short of an ambush the guerillas have set for the patrol, Ygnacio decides temerariously to ride toward their position, hailing the Americans troopers as if he were one of them, attempting to lure them into the trap. His trust in his appearance as a fair-skinned, blue-eyed Mexican who looks like a gringo proves to be fatally misplaced. Ygnacio is given away again by the material reality of his own linguistic habits and vernacular speech patterns when he calls out to the Americans in his Spanish inflected English: "Thees way, boyss!" (56).

It is May 8, 1846, at Palo Alto, Texas, the date and site of the first major encounter between American and Mexican armed forces during the US-Mexican war.[20] As his ruse fails and when his old-fashioned horse pistol misfires, "the Gringo" unsheathes his machete and attempts to ride down an American cavalry officer who calmly awaits him astride his mount, armed not with a cavalry saber but with one of Samuel Colt's new six-shot revolvers in hand.[21] The technology and symbology of weaponry is significant. Before the arrival of the Anglo-American in the Great West, the Mexican had contested American Indians for control of the region armed primarily with lance and knife. After 1838, however, when Colt produced his first revolvers, the balance of power shifted remarkably on the Great Plains away from mounted Mexican lancers toward rapid-firing Anglo gunmen (Paredes, "The United States, Mexico" 228–29). The man with the pistol, a symbolic and real instrument of power, hereafter comes to dominate in the popular Mexican and American imagination as the active subject of history. Facing the weaponry of the new American technology and commerce of war, a rapid-firing revolver, armed with only the broad and heavy machete, a weapon and tool indicative of decidedly precapitalist modes of social organization, "the Gringo" rides headlong into history as "the guns of Palo Alto went off inside his head" (54). In the last instant of his life, Ygnacio stands against what must surely seem like the massively unstoppable force of American historical destiny, the taking of the trans-Nueces region of south Texas serving as mere prelude to the seizure of the entirety of the northern Mexican territories that were to form after 1848 the American West and Southwest. Moreover, Paredes represents with Ygnacio's doomed charge yet another epochal shift: the advent of modern warfare and the replacement of chivalrous individual heroism with modern technological ingenuity. In the various thematic strands combined at the story's end, Paredes thus articulates the disjuncture between the socio-spatial levels and social practices of race, nationalism, gender roles, and the developing implications of US continental expansionism.

Machos Undone

Some of the stories turn away from the specificity of south Texas history and return instead to one of the ongoing motifs of *The Hammon and the Beans and Other Stories*, namely, the pathos of enforcing and enacting the macho role of manhood. This motif is especially the subject of "Revenge," but on an entirely different register. Here, the protagonist, named Anastasio, is a country boy affecting the city style, who seeks revenge for the killing of his brother. However, word arrives with the figure of his hard-edged country cousin, Apolinar, that Anastasio has already dawdled too long, for the killer has himself been done in by one of the banal tragedies of everyday modern life: crossing a street he has been hit and killed by an automobile. Just when Anastasio begins to feel released from the obligation he is dreading, to uphold his macho identity, the adjudicating cousin intervenes. Apolinar, a "tiny young man" wearing "tiny blue trousers, wide at the hips, narrow at the cuffs in the country style" (71) is the opposite of Anastasio, who wears his trousers in the city style, "narrow at the hips, belled at the bottom" (69). As cousins, they do share one physical feature, "a red, feminine mouth" (71).

Apolinar subtly spurs the increasingly reluctant Anastasio into maintaining his suddenly questionable reputation as "a *macho* with *huevos*" (73), as someone "bigger and stronger and meaner than anybody else" (73). Apolinar reminds Anastasio that the man's death does not complete Anastasio's vow of revenge since he has sworn to laugh over the dead man's grave. "You didn't get a chance to kill him," he observes, "but you can still laugh over his body. If you really want to, that is" (73). As in "Macaria's Daughter," where the husband feels compelled to kill in order "to keep being a man," Anastasio's fate has been cast for him too. Norman Mailer has claimed that there is no injunction more mysterious than the one "to be a man" (interview with Terry Gross). What does it mean to be a man? The typical answers involving expressions of male violence and sexuality seem now irrelevant. Even the "plump breasts" and "haunches rippling under their thin covering" of a young girl walking ahead of the cousins fail to rouse Anastasio's "enthusiasm" (75). With the heightened sensibility of all-consuming fear, Anastasio feels the mystery of the injunction as he walks laggardly through the hot, dusty streets of Jonesville to the dead man's house, as if toward his own funeral.

Cowed more by his cousin Apolinar's merciless glance and taunting gestures than by the presence of his enemy's family, Anastasio does indeed eventually bring himself to perform his revenge. He enters the home of his enemy intending to laugh over his corpse. In a startling progression of irony, however, the dead man's father overhears Anastasio's muffled sound, takes the laugh for a heartfelt sob of loving grief, and compels Anastasio to join in the funeral cortege and attend the burial ceremony of his son. All the other toughs in the town lining the route of the cortege, present to mediate the enactment of revenge and decide the privilege of masculinity, now are treated to the grotesque sight of Anastasio in the ludicrous position of being surrounded by the pitiable throng of the dead man's grieving family and thus of having to feign mourning for his deceased enemy.

His laugh taken for a sob and hence linked to the grief-stricken, wailing and moans of the women, Anastasio is positioned by his own ambiguous actions in the feminine social space of grieving, the very space that he had most sought to avoid. In this extraordinarily exposed and vulnerable position, even the traditional symbol of his manhood works against him, as he is "extremely conscious of the weight of the pistol concealed under his coat." The "bulge of the pistol" (79) tucked into his pants notwithstanding, from the perspective of the hierarchized patriarchy, Anastasio is completely undone as a macho. He knows that "the whole *barrio* is laughing at me by now!" (82). Apolinar, subtle ironist and wily master of coercion, having surely anticipated the limits of Anastasio's masculinist pose all along and insidiously connived in its collapse, is the interesting figure here. He bears witness to the scene from aside, critically projecting the limits of masculinity and adjudicating its perversely performative pathos. When the story ends with his ambiguous figure "laughing softly" (82) — and thus participating in the general scorn of his cousin's macho pose — the basic ground of Mexican masculinity is put at stake with a vengeance.

With "Macaria's Daughter," the story "Revenge" offers yet another version of Paredes's sharp-edged, unsentimental deconstruction of the code of the traditional masculine warrior hero. And while this debunking of the ethos of the macho does not mark the complete undoing of its phallocentric value system that Chicana writers will later extend, it nevertheless offers a preliminary, unsentimentalized prefiguration of the critique to come. Together with other of his writings from this period, it suggests that Paredes was beginning to understand how gender ideologies that may have helped shape a community had also undoubtedly compromised and betrayed it. Perhaps no surer proof of an emergence to modernity exists in Paredes's creative works than this protocritique of the performance of sexual politics.

Modernity remains the backdrop to the story "Brothers" as well. In this instance, the unlikely "brothers" are a German immigrant boy, Fred, and Arturo, a Mexican American native of Jonesville. According to the boys' teacher, Fred's grandfather left Germany after "the Great War" "to stand up for freedom and justice for all. For the brotherhood of man" (84). At the beach one day, playing cowboys and Indians in the "language of the movies," Arturo's Spanish-inflected English marks him as not quite a standard American. But so does Fred's German-accented speech. Linguistic quirks aside, the two are consummately linked in child's play as they imitate with refined skill the cowboys-and-robbers romance scenarios provided by Hollywood. The silver screen provides access to a mimetic brotherhood that seems capable of transcending real historical and ethnic differences. However, that utopian illusion is sorely tested by the hypocrisy of Fred's father when "the little white boy and his dark-brown playmate" (84) ask him whether, since the apparent homonyms Spanish *ya* and German *ja* both denote "yes," it is possible in German to say *sí* and mean *ja*. For if such linguistic relations are possible, and since as Fred's father says, "all men are brothers" and "at bottom speak the same language," then, as the boys reason, they might turn out "to be related," and brothers in truth (87). The German father looks at the Mexican American boy and dismisses the preposterous thought, acidly ordering his son to return to his side of the wire fence separating the Mexican and Anglo sections of the Jim Crow beach. It is the late 1930s, and even though Fred's father has apparently emigrated from Germany in reaction to Nazi racism, his toleration for interracial friendships goes only so far.

A Border Romance

The short story "Rebeca" describes two distinct time periods in the life of the eponymous character: an early one, rehearsing an almost idyllic epoch of rural, premodern life on the banks of the Rio Grande, and a later one, representing the rhythms of the modern urban space in the city of Jonesville. In the rural scenes, we learn that Rebeca, the youngest daughter of Don José María Chapa and Doña Cenobia Chapa, is a model daughter and an excellent cook to boot. Anticipating the sentimental plot of Laura Esquivel's *Like Water for Chocolate* by forty-plus years, Paredes tells us "the kitchen was her joy, her work of art" (95). As it does for the characters in Esquivel's domestic idyll, Rebeca's serenity comes from a near total identification with her gendered role of culinary labor: "Everyone praised her *asado de puerco*. Her *frijoles rancheros* had just the right amount of cilantro. Her *tortillas de harina* were a marvel; her *buñuelos* melted in your mouth. And her way with north Mexican tamales, slender and delicate, was incredible" (94). Her joy as a food producer is blunted by the conditions of her work. While her sisters labor five days a week, from breakfast through before supper doing the general housekeeping, Rebeca works seven days a week, from five in the morning when she makes her father's coffee, until bedtime. Only then, after she washes the dishes and prepares the next day's meals in order to keep everyone happily fed, is she free. "She quickly realized that her beloved kitchen was also her prison" (94). To escape this prison, she dreams of a little house "where she would be the mistress" (95).

That romance dream of love with a guitar-playing, dark, Rudolph Valentino–like countryman from Mexico named Chano Quintana and the compromised pastoral that it represents ends when the lure of city life and modern ways pressure her into marrying instead "a pink-faced young man" from the city, Alberto Medrano. In marriage "Beto" proves cruel, hard to please, and even brutal to their children, so that over the years Rebeca "yearned for the old days at her father's ranch" (102). Now, in the story's present, with her children grown and her culinary magic no longer producing the delight it once did, Rebeca has taken up another means of oral pleasure to fill her emptiness, smoking up to two packs of cigarettes daily. Illusions of romance and serenity completely dispelled, Rebeca is diagnosed with terminal lung cancer. The new serenity she finds while contemplating her own death eludes her when she learns that she is not sick at all. The clinic has mistakenly switched her X-rays with those of another truly unfortunate patient. Crushed by the prospect of what everyone takes to be her miraculous good fortune, in the end Rebeca takes up her cigarettes again—to tempt fate, to provoke an untimely rupture of the imprisoning routine of wife and mother, or perhaps simply to annoy her husband.

In the story "Rebeca," too, Paredes is thus concerned with the de-

fining parameters of Mexican American masculine and feminine subjectivity and with displaying the ways that traditional family home
life provides at one and the same time a sustaining ideology of identity construction and a limit to an entire community's potential for
human validation. The familial social space itself thus becomes as contested a site of equal historical and subjective weight as the geopolitical space of the border region itself. Within these social and political
spaces, terrains of cultural geography, Paredes represents once more
the complex intersections, overlappings, and collisions of discourses
that structure this historical period.

Of particular significance in this regard is his representation of an
evolving notion of gender identity and sexuality in the newly Americanized borderlands. Especially in the stories discussed here, gender
identities and relations are inconsistent, malleable, and liable to idealism, sentimentality, romanticism, and abject violence. Male identities
in particular are characterized by arrogance, illusion, bluster, cruelty,
and the bad faith of unresolved contradictory impulses. The origin
of this fractured domain of practices that comes with "being a man"
in these stories is only partly ascribable to the influences of Mexican
traditions of masculinity and its failure to keep up with the demands
of a modern age. There is no signal here that there once existed a premodern moment of traditional masculinity free of the problematics
outlined in these tales of confusion.

Paredes is working out here the possibility that the particular brand
of male ideology associated with the heroes of these stories is not
simply a residual element of the feudal world of the eighteenth and
nineteenth century borderlands. It is also associated with the particular features of the class structures and gender ideologies related to
the creation of a capitalist world structured by class dominance. Paredes would return to this issue in numerous ways at other times in
his life. But in these stories from the 1940s and early 1950s he is expressing imaginatively what he would in later life as an ethnographer
and historian of the cultural history of Greater Mexico and in relation to the concept of machismo conclude, namely, that "to feel poor
and to be poor are not exactly the same thing . . . often the first is
a necessary condition in doing away with the second" ("The United
States, Mexico" 234). The articulation of what it means to be a Mexican American male in the context of modernization and from a subaltern position turns out to be available only, as Gramsci surmised

about the nature of subaltern knowledge, "via a series of negations" (*Selections* 273), imagining oneself one way in order to find a way not to be so.[22] Perhaps in this way, searching among the ruins of former traditions, we might be able to locate alternative possibilities of future communities freed from the corrosive constraints of both hegemonic and traditional gender ideologies.

9

NARRATIVE AND THE IDIOMS

OF RACE, NATION, AND

IDENTITY

In the mud huts of China,
The tile-roofed paper houses of Japan,
In the straw-thatched *jacales* of old Mexico,
The rain-blackened shacks of Arkansas,

Here is my fatherland, these are my people,
My beloved,
Black, yellow, brown–
And even if their eyes are blue–

These are my people,
The bleeding wounds upon the feet and hands
Of humankind
—Américo Paredes, "Pro Patria"

Le Sage ne rit qu'en tremblant.
—Charles Baudelaire, "De l'essence du rire"

I continue my assessment of Paredes's post–World War II–era writings by returning to the question of national belonging and the transnational imaginary. I wish to relate this notion to Paredes's argument that ethnic, racial, and national identity are formed in the crucible of border violence and cultural conflict. In 1966, reflecting on the course of nineteenth-century border history, Paredes wrote:

Being Mexican meant remaining inviolable in the face of overwhelming attacks on one's personality. Under those circumstances, for a Mexican to accept North American values was to desert under fire. Such a situation—creative of folk groups defined as minorities—is not historically unique. It has been repeated many times with other peoples whose identity has been menaced. Among people within their own borders—the Poles, let us say, the Finns, the Irish, or the Greeks—such a situation has created an intensified nationalism. In contrast, other peoples who have existed as minorities within a dominant group—the Jews in Europe, for example—have maintained their identity through very close cultural bonds. The border Mexican American, because of his special relationship to the United States, made use of both these solutions. ("Folklore of Groups" 10)[1]

Paredes is here pointing to the ways that Mexican Americans share survival strategies with other peoples residing in border countries worldwide.[2] One strategy is "intensified nationalism"; another is the construction of internally cohesive "close cultural bonds." *Nationalism*, and, in particular, *ethnic cultural nationalism* of the kind that was to become the watchword of Mexican American political activism during the years of the Chicano movement, are terms loaded with problematic possibilities. As the mainstays against the assaults "on one's personality" that for Mexican Americans have constituted their attempted participation in the American polity, the terms offer the promise of survival. At the same time, history has shown ethnic and cultural nationalisms, as strategies for resisting domination within that polity, to be problematic in the extreme. They are certainly potentially limiting to the individual who experiences intensified nationalism under conditions not of one's own making. Experiencing Japanese, Chinese, Korean, British, French, and American nationalisms at their worst in Asia, Paredes was shaken from the comfortable sense that being rooted in a community was a wholly positive thing in the face of assaults on one's personality. It was shocking to realize that ideas based on separatism, race hatred, racial supremacy, nationalisms, and prejudice of all kinds, in both their more and less virulent forms, sprouted from those very same kinds of roots that had nourished his own sense of *tejano-mexicanidad*. To experience ethnic or racial identity under these conditions was thus in part to understand the contradictions of ethnic and racial identity. How might one conceive of national identity under these highly charged and difficult conditions? How might one do so in a world of evolving traditional ethnicities and emerging new ones? Within the limits of reason, what might serve as the desirable path to an acceptable future with a sense of accomplished community? How might changing ethnicities add, or detract, from the sense of a larger national unity and national coherence? In the context of the differentiated and heterogeneous social conditions of newly modernized societies, what was the integrative function of citizenship? With minor variations, these questions remain the vital issues of our times in numerous countries across the globe. Demonstrably, they are the substance of the racial and nationalist matters Paredes was observing in Japan and in his travels in Asia during the immediate postwar years.

In reference to the concept of identity, the literary critic Satya Mohanty has urged the need to explore the possibility of "a theoretical understanding of social and cultural identity in terms of social location" (216). Mohanty's exhortation is one with which I agree. I take the case of Paredes's works from the 1930s, 1940s, and 1950s as instances of an imaginary of such an understanding. They constitute especially significant illustrations of how identity and social location may be conveniently collapsed into the vexed questions of American citizenship and national identity in the context of the newly emergent issues of globalization, the transnational, and their effect on national identity and national belonging.[3]

For Paredes, the abstract issue of citizenship was primarily an incontrovertibly concrete matter. The status of the Mexican American people of the Southwest after 1848 as citizens stood at the forefront of his thinking as a journalist, creative writer, and scholar. The historical circumstances of 1848 altered dramatically and in material terms the experience of former Mexican nationals, immigrant Mexican nationals, and US-born Mexicans as settlers, resident aliens, and citizens of the United States. While their relationship to Mexican culture is irrefutable, so is the impact of the new relationship to US citizenship and national identity. Paredes is concerned in all of his literary writings with understanding precisely the nature of the aesthetics and politics of bilingualism, multiculturalism, and the transnational reality of life in the borderlands.[4] As I have noted, in employing the term *Greater Mexico* later in his career, Paredes was getting at the nature of American cultural diversity and its implications for the modern nation-state. The United States–Mexico borderlands comprised for Paredes something very much like what later scholars would describe as a "multination state" of polyethnic makeup creating dynamic, and perplexing, pluralities of cultural and political identity, rather than two autonomous nation-states interacting in strictly binary terms.[5]

Race and Power in the Pacific

In their exploration of the transnational imaginary, not all of the stories in *The Hammon and the Beans and Other Stories* are set in the borderlands. Seven of the stories take us from the geographical, if not the social, space of early twentieth-century south Texas and into the World War II Asia Pacific theater of operations, the postwar occupation of Japan, and the opening days of the Korean War. In these narratives, the issues remain, as in the south Texas stories, the intersections of race, power, and conquest. Now Paredes attempts to account as well for the extraordinarily fierce Manichaean nature of the war in Asia by linking domestic American racism with the conduct of its armed forces during the war and the postwar occupation.

To understand how racism influenced the conduct of the war in the Pacific, Paredes takes us first, in the story entitled "Little Joe," to infantry basic training at Camp Robinson, Little Rock, Arkansas. An Anglo narrator named Watson reflects on the curious experiences of a fellow trainee, Little Joe, who comes from the Texas-Mexico border. Watson and the other white American recruits cast Little Joe in the role of a knife-wielding killer, like all of his kind essentially endowed with the bloodthirsty impulses of a savage cutthroat, that is, as a being possessed of special powers of nonhuman evil. "One must remember," notes Paredes, "that in the 1930s supposedly scholarly studies still were being published in Texas depicting Mexicans as treacherous and cowardly, a degenerate product of miscegenation between Spaniard and Indian" (*Uncle Remus con Chile* 11).[6] Here, the stereotyped and blatantly racist construction of Little Joe has created such an exaggerated image of him that even the biggest man in the squad, a Minnesotan named Great Big Johnson, is petrified with fear whenever Little Joe cleans his bayonet: "That little guy, he don't look like much, but don't cross him. I'd hate to do that" (*Hammon* 112). The reality is that Little Joe is a neat, quiet, polite, south Texas boy, perhaps even a scholar-musician at heart, and hardly a cold-blooded killer at all. In contrast to the image of the Mexican in American popular culture, notoriously portrayed as a knife-wielding killer in the media coverage of the Zoot Suit Riots of 1942–43 and symbolically presented as a primal brutal force in World War II novels like Norman Mailer's *The Naked and the Dead*, Paredes's Little Joe is not primordially linked to the harsh power of uncivilized savagery. He is simply a decent human being attempting to live under the constraints of the prevailing Jim Crow, segregationist, white supremacist American ideology that keeps Mexicans and blacks in their subordinate place.

C. L. R. James, writing in *The Socialist Appeal*, the Socialist Workers Party newspaper in September 1939, had posed the question people of color faced at the onset of the war, implicit in Paredes's "Little Joe": "Why should I shed my blood for Roosevelt's America, for Cotton Ed Smith and Senator Bilbo, for the whole Jim Crow, Negro-hating South, for the low-paid, dirty jobs for which Negroes have to fight, for the few dollars of relief and the insults, discrimination, police brutality, and perpetual poverty to which Negroes are condemned even in the more liberal North?" ("Why Negroes" 28). Denied the core principles of democracy as formulated in the Fourteenth and Fifteenth Amendments that guarantee the political rights of American citizens, or as expressed in Roosevelt's famed Four Freedoms, the experiences of Mexican Americans, African Americans, Native Americans, Asian Americans, and other American people of color during World War II exposed the hypocrisy of American critiques of Nazi and Axis racism. Mailer's caricature of a Texas Mexican in *The Naked and the Dead*, Sergeant Julio Martinez, is typical of the prevailing mood of the times. Of the various soldiers in Mailer's archetypal platoon experiencing fearsome combat in the South Pacific, only Julio Martinez is consistently represented in exaggerated metaphors of animal terror. In fact, at one point he is compared as reacting to the sounds of combat in conditioned panic, like Pavlov's dog, and is described at another as having the *"poise and grace of a deer"* but always *"nervous and alert as if he were thinking of flight"* (18, 63, emphasis original). Called "Mex" and "Japbait" by the other characters, Mailer's Mexican American speaks an infantile English, acts "instinctively," understands "intuitively," and cringes with "inferiority" when required to speak with superiors, personified as "White Protestant" (591, 92, 691). Paredes's Mexican American soldiers are nothing like Mailer's. Instead, they are reflective, doubting, amusing figures, active agents of their own fate, illustrating far more complex versions of the experience of racialized combat in the Pacific than Mailer portrays.

Paredes extends this critique in "The Gift," a captivity narrative of a different flavor than that of the classic one set in the American wilderness. Here, we find ourselves in a Japanese prisoner of war camp "out in the jungle, in the middle of nowhere" (*Hammon* 118). In this instance, we focus on the ranking captured American officer, Navy Lieutenant Commander Young, who is gripped by an abject fear of the Japanese. His captors have completely broken his spirit. While readily admitting, "we were all afraid," the narrator observes that Young "was afraid in a different way" (119). The look in his eye "was like a crack in a thick wall through which you could see the scared soul of Lt. Commander Young. Now the Japs had broken the wall, and fear poured out of him, drenching him from head to foot" (119). Because of this abjection, Young regularly informs on the other American prisoners to spare himself the wrath of his jailers. After several of the men are brutally beaten and executed by the Japanese because of Young's treachery, his fellow prisoners "started making plans to kill Young" (122). His fellow prisoners also know the narrator, as in the earlier story, only as "Mex," an expression of the conflicted racial politics among the Americans. In the ritual drawing of straws to determine who among them will "sacrifice himself to save the rest" (122) and execute their commander, Mex draws the short straw. "I knew it would happen," he says; "all my life I've got the short end of the stick" (122). Waiting in the latrine to ambush Young, the narrator loses his easy despise for Young as he contemplates his own beheading for the assassination he is about to commit: "I thought about how the edge of the sword would feel when it hit the back of my neck. . . . Then I was really afraid, and I knew how Young felt and why he ratted on us all the time" (123). Before the narrator can act, however, Young is finally pushed too far by his captors. He strikes back at one of them, killing the more sadistic of the Japanese guards, a man called Monkeyface by the Americans.[7] Facing the Japanese executioner's sword, to the surprise and newfound respect of his men, Young accepts his death sentence calmly, maybe even heroically. The narrator, having made himself ready to play the fall guy in killing Young and then at least partially identifying with him, in the end takes on Young's role completely.

Spared execution because he is not in the hut when Young kills the guard, in complete ironic reversal, the narrator is suspected by his comrades of having revealed the plot to save himself. When he is granted the "gift" of life by both circumstance and the good grace of a young Japanese lieutenant's mercy, the narrator feels "lucky" at his deliverance. However, the uncertainty of the guilt of his survival diminishes any sense of joy he might otherwise have felt about his luck. Freed from his captivity, the narrator now wonders about the propriety of having felt lucky: "I should have, shouldn't I? . . . I couldn't have done anything else, could I?" (124). These questions mask the unanswerable ones: Why had he survived when the others had not? What had he done to survive?

Le Comique Absolu

The US Japanese occupation force is the subject of the story "When It Snowed in Kitabamba." At war's end, the US Army General Douglas MacArthur became supreme commander for the Allied powers (SCAP) of occupied Japan. As SCAP—"an acronym applied both to the Occupation headquarters and the general himself"— MacArthur "radiated authority and self-assurance" (Schaller 22–23). Although the public had grown accustomed to press releases portraying him as a "heroic" figure, many in Roosevelt's administration had by the end of the war grown weary of his grandstanding and self-promotion.[8] Two years later, Truman's administration, too, was dealing with MacArthur's "messianic certainty" about the course of his policies as supreme commander. Shortly before the Japanese surrender, in a memorandum of June 17, 1945, Truman had written about MacArthur:

> Mr. Prima Donna, Brass Hat, Five Star MacArthur. He's worse than the Cabots and the Lodges—they at least talked with one another before they told God what to do. Mac tells God right off. It's a great pity we have stuffed shirts like that in key positions. I don't see why in hell Roosevelt didn't order Wainwright home [in the disastrous Philippines campaign] and let MacArthur be a martyr. . . . We'd have had a real General and a fighting man if we had Wainwright and not a play actor and a bunco man such as we have now. (qtd. in Schaller 21)

In his most acerbic manner, Truman then contrasts real leaders and generals such as Robert E. Lee, Dwight D. Eisenhower, and Omar Bradley to the "Custers, Pattons and MacArthurs" (Schaller 21). It was nevertheless true that even though there were those who called

MacArthur "Dugout Doug," many Americans revered him and saw him as having orchestrated the defeat of Japan in the Pacific. Cutting an "Olympian image of a 'lone figure' guiding through inspiration," MacArthur cultivated this image and encouraged "the idea that he alone determined the course of events within Japan" (Schaller 23).

Captain Meniscus in Paredes's story is one of the many who were taken in by the image and venerated MacArthur. An unabashed idolizer of MacArthur, obsessed with neatness and order and the idea of his heroic figure, Meniscus understands that his duty as occupation forces chief of Kitabamba is to transform the Japanese into straightforward Americans. He is methodical, direct, and, like his hero, "loved to issue his little orders" (*Hammon* 129). He hates "circumlocution" and the "circumnavigation of things" (129). His annoyance at one of his men, the company clerk Corporal Hogg, is compounded by his suspicion that Hogg's barely disguised insolence expresses a deeper mockery of everything that Meniscus values. For instance, Hogg is rumored to have composed a ditty that Meniscus finds particularly offensive: "Chewing gummo, chocoretto, / Yamamoto was her name; / All she had was gonorrhea, / But I loved her just the same" (132). Meniscus protests against the implications of "Chewing gummo, chocoreto" in the song, allusions to the price of sexual favors in postwar Japan, the ubiquitous American chewing gum and chocolate bars.[9] The song disturbs Meniscus' prim self-righteousness with the taunt that the American occupiers really are no better than "lecherous carpetbaggers," "blackmarketeers," and "degenerates" (132) concerned only with the "back-alley rot" of debauchery. Instead, Meniscus "knew there was no truth in the song. His men were good, clean American boys" (132). A few pages later, Corporal Hogg and another soldier, Master Sergeant Fatt, discussing the other coin of the occupation realm, American cigarettes, reveal the extent of Meniscus's naivety. Scheming to convert American occupation luxury into personal gain, they do the numbers for conversion of currency in the black market with the precision of accountants: "Cigarettes brought thirty yen a pack. Thirty yen was two dollars in cash and about fifteen dollars in goods and services" (138).

Furthermore, as the motto of his undeviating obsessions, Meniscus keeps in his office some words that MacArthur once uttered in his near presence framed underneath a portrait of MacArthur: "The shortest distance between two points is a straight line" (130). In his irrational compulsion and excessive zeal to represent the superiority of American ways and impress the Japanese with the precision of American methods, the captain has turned the delivery of the daily mail from Tokyo on the 3:19 train into an intricate, arcane, and darkly ceremonial ritual. The daily scene is a bizarre enactment of the straight and narrow path, replete with martial music, crisp files of army MPs lining his route to the mail train, and his own march of eccentric solemnity to retrieve the mailbags:

> Every day, with the arrival of the train, a little ritual was enacted at Kitabamba in which Meniscus was the chief actor and the crowd of townspeople both audience and supporting cast. Across the square was the railroad station, and from the doorstep of Meniscus' headquarters (straight as a piece of string stretched between the two points had been able to make it) a low narrow boardwalk ran unerringly to a post on the station platform. The post was marked with a sign which said, "Kitabamba, 27th Military Government Headquarters, Captain Meniscus commanding." (140)

Like MacArthur himself, who followed an almost invariable routine in his daily schedule in his attempt to radiate authority and certainty in his methods, Captain Meniscus attempts to cultivate a heroic persona for himself and amaze the conquered Japanese. All of this would be mildly comical were it not for the fact that Meniscus in his lust for the "straight" way believes in MacArthur's motto so entirely that he is fully capable of sadistic cruelty in enforcing the superiority of the straight American way. Meniscus torments his Japanese servant who barely understands a few words of English by exhorting him to "Straighten up!" (133), tracing for him with pencil and straight-edge ruler the shortest distance between two points (135), and making him "straighten the same thing again and again" (136). Daily, Meniscus puts him through a torturous explanation of the solemnity of the unbending motto and of what he understands to be its implications of "devotion to the unswerving path of duty," American style (140).

From such elevated solemnity, only a fall can ensue. And so indeed, when one day the unforeseen occurs and it snows in Kitabamba, "a vague uneasiness seized him" (137). The captain's dogged short march between two points is sidetracked when, distracted by thoughts of one of Corporal Hogg's capers, he slips and falls awkwardly, and repeatedly, in the snow, turning his pretentious show into a ridiculous slapstick farce. Earlier, when warned by his company clerk that it might snow, Meniscus had dismissed the reports of previous snow days as mere "folktales," protesting with ludicrous self-assurance, "There has never been any snow in Kitabamba. The records show that" (130). His sergeant and his company clerk laugh with derision behind his back at his false certainties and his outrageous pretensions. Now, after the fall, the gathered Japanese are much gentler with their conqueror than are Meniscus's own men. At first, the Japanese are mildly "amused" (147) by the man's comic comedown and "watched delightedly, with open curious faces, this strange New Year's ceremony of the conqueror" as each time that he attempts to rise he falls again in the freshly fallen snow (147).

Their bemusement quickly turns into mournful wisdom as with "an ancient sadness in their eyes" (147) they witness something much deeper than the suffering pathos of an arrogant, petty tyrant's tumble. They are moved by the spectacle of their shared fellowship of fallenness. Meniscus, however, "seeing their faces and the pity and the fellowship in them, became enraged at the sight" (147). He finds it unbearable that the Japanese have witnessed the deflation of his pretensions and, worse, that even while seeing the hypocrisy and falsity of his pathetic ceremony, they continue to feel pity and sympathy for him. The various comic registers of the scene, from laughter and humor to irony and satire, strip Meniscus's pretensions of the false casing that surrounds them, leaving them painfully visible for all to see. In a shocking final twist, the story ends with Meniscus putting his sidearm into his mouth, killing himself because of the humiliation.

In an essay titled "On the Essence of Laughter," Charles Baudelaire observes that "the power of laughter resides with the one who laughs, never with the object of laughter. It is not he who falls who laughs at himself, unless he is a philosopher, someone who has acquired, by habit, the ability to reflect upon himself [se dédoubler] and attend like a disinterested spectator upon the phenomena of his *I*" ("De l'essence du rire" 982). Such a self-reflective capacity within consciousness between two moments of the self, argues Paul de Man, is not an intersubjective relation at all, but is in fact essential to the nature of irony itself. However, the laughter of the witness to the fall is surely a mark of intersubjective difference to the one who has fallen. It denotes the superiority of one subject over another, "with all the implications of will to power, of violence, and possession which come into play when a person is laughing at someone else—including the will to educate and to improve" (212). In relation to Captain Meniscus's tumble, the superiority implicit in the laughter of his sergeant and company clerk is clear: they disdain his posturing and mark their distance from him with their laughter. Meniscus himself is hardly philosophical enough to "reflect upon himself and attend like a disinterested spectator upon the phenomena of his *I*."[10]

In this oddly comic narrative, however, the laughter of the Japanese comes closer to the moment of Baudelarian comic *dédouble-ment* than does that of the sergeant and the clerk. Meniscus's pratfall moment represents for the assembled Japanese who view his level-ing stumble less the registers of vaudevillian hierarchies of superiority and inferiority than an implicit recognition of their *own* separation from themselves, especially in relation to their American conquerors. In laughing gently with Meniscus's fall, and killing him softly with their pity, implicitly they lament their own fallen state as a vanquished people. They thus attain the condition of the philosophical comic, or what Baudelaire calls *le comique absolu* (the absolute comic). Ironi-cally, their sense of humor also grants them an encompassing vision of a shared sense of historical fate with their bumbling conquerors that can only be termed democratic.[11] From their shared sense of fal-lenness, in effect a position of philosophical wisdom, they can pity Meniscus's fall and express fellowship with his humiliating defeat. Doing so, they also force him fatally to contemplate the shallowness of his own understanding of them over whom he has lorded as an ironical stand-in for the master of false superiority himself, supreme commander and conqueror Douglas MacArthur.

The power of laughter that ultimately kills Meniscus takes one final, darker aspect. In the moments before he dies with a pistol in his mouth, Meniscus overhears the corporal and sergeant who "choked back a laugh" talk about his tumble: "But he looked so goddam funny for a minute there . . ." (149). More ominously, however, Meniscus now understands that the "moil inside him" caused by his fall is noth-ing to the tangled confusion of his "straight" obsessions that the reve-lation of other deeper secrets is about to create. What he overhears the corporal mercilessly spin tells him that he has been discovered: " 'Anyway, it serves him right, putting on those silly airs. I guess he doesn't know I'm on to him.' 'You sure?' 'Sure I'm sure. He must have changed his name when he left town. I was just a kid, but I re-member him' " (149). In having changed his name mysteriously to

Meniscus, meaning "free from curvature, bending or angularity," according to the *OED*, the captain has unconsciously disguised his angularity by naming it and thus bringing it directly into the open. In his obsessions with the undeviating pathway of the straight, however, Meniscus ironically reveals the symbolic negation of his unspoken desires. The *OED* notes the American slang usage of *straight* as "heterosexual" and "not homosexual." *To go straight* means "to cease homosexual practices." Since these usages date from 1941, it turns out that "When It Snowed in Kitabamba" is an extended investigation of what it means and costs to be "straight" in 1945.

Japanese Mexicans

"Ichiro Kikuchi" is predicated on a different and yet equally peculiar turn of irony and on the patterns of global immigration. This story is based on an actual experience of a young friend of Paredes's wife, Amelia Nagamine.[12] In the story, the titular Ichiro Kikuchi, born and raised on a farm near Cuernavaca in the state of Morelos, is the son of a Japanese father, Keigo Kikuchi, and a Mexican mother, María de los Angeles Bermúdez de Kikuchi. As in other of Paredes's fictional accounts, real historical processes involved in the creation of hybrid cultural spaces stand at the fore of "Ichiro Kikuchi."

Beginning in 1897, thousands of Japanese immigrated to Mexico, concentrating their communities on the Mexican West Coast and the central regions, including the environs of Cuernavaca.[13] By the 1940s, three generations of Japanese Mexicans had dispersed throughout Mexico, in some cases marrying Mexican nationals, and had installed themselves peacefully in the community. They and their children had begun experiencing the blurring of Asian and American identities in Mexico (Ota Mishima 56, 58, 83). On December 8, 1941, Mexico broke diplomatic relations with Japan, drastically altering the peaceful relations between Mexicans and Japanese. In the context of this debacle, what were now the links between Mexico and Japan? What was the identity of Mexicans of Japanese origin?

Addressing these questions, Paredes turns once again to names and the process of naming to indicate the hybrid cultural space that his characters inhabit. Narrated from the point of view of one of these Japanese Mexicans, the story informs us that in Japanese, the "given name" Ichiro "means 'first born'" (151). In Spanish, Ichiro Kikuchi has been baptized with the name "Juan Guadalupe": "Juan for San Juan, the town where [his mother] was born, and Guadalupe for Our Lady, the Mother of all Mexicans" (151). Already at the moment of naming, Ichiro's doubled identity is problematic. His Buddhist father resents the fact that his Catholic mother has baptized him at all. Despite this initial unhappiness, Ichiro Kikuchi grows to young adulthood on his Japanese father's and Mexican uncle's farm, contentedly growing flowers in Mexico. With his father's catastrophically ill-timed insistence that he travel to Japan to maintain his Japanese identity in late 1941, however, Ichiro Kikuchi finds himself unable to return to Mexico after the attack on Pearl Harbor and the breaking of diplomatic relations between Mexico and Japan.

In Japan, Ichiro Kikuchi experiences the other side of cultural difference, "being only half Japanese and not knowing the language," and especially so after "Mexico declared war against Japan a few months later" (154). The young Japanese Mexican is put "to work on the government radio broadcasting to Spanish America" (154) and three years later is drafted into the Japanese Imperial Army. He is ordered into action and immediately captured by Americans in the battle for the liberation of the Philippines. It is now 1945, and the Japanese army is very different from the proud, disciplined, able force it once was. Ordered to fight to the death, Kikuchi's unit of "old men, schoolboys and people like me" instead surrenders, tragically misjudging the good faith of the American GIs to whom they have entrusted their lives. Contrary to the belief that it was only the Japanese who wantonly killed their prisoners, the fact was that the war in the Pacific was for both sides "a war without mercy": "No quarter, no surrender. Take no prisoners. Fight to the bitter end. These were everyday words in the combat areas, and in the final year of the war such attitudes contributed to an orgy of bloodletting that neither side could conceive of avoiding" (Dower, *War without Mercy* 10–11). Many Japanese fighting men did die instead of surrendering, but they did so in part because of "the disinterest of the Allies in taking prisoners" (11). By 1945, US troops in the field were routinely killing Japanese who attempted to surrender (Dower, *Embracing Defeat* 285). About to be executed with his entire unit, Kikuchi is digging his own grave when an American soldier assigned to execute the prisoners notices a chain and pendant hanging from Kikuchi's neck. Bending more closely to identify the object, the American soldier demands to know what it is that Kikuchi is wearing. Kikuchi recognizes that the American "was Mexican. . . . An American Mexican. So I answered in Spanish, 'A medallion. *La Virgen de Guadalupe*'" (156).

For the Mexican American soldier, later identified as a sergeant named Melguizo, the medallion of the Virgin of Guadalupe is more than an apotropaic trinket. It represents the reality of life itself in the midst of the horrors of Asian Pacific combat and raises the Japanese infantryman who wears it from the anonymity of war's cruelty and violence into the brotherhood of shared fate. The soldier can see that Kikuchi is not only a fellow Catholic, but apparently also a fellow Mexican. So when Kikuchi speaks in Spanish to the Mexican American GI, he confirms what the GI has already surmised. The Mexican American faces a Japanese Mexican. With this confirmation, Sergeant Melguizo lifts Ichiro Kikuchi from the grave he has just dug, and leads him to the rear where a few prisoners are being held. With the echoes of the volleys that kill his comrades in arms reverberating around him, Kikuchi does not feel "any regret, any shame" (156) that he has been spared while the rest die.

Later in Tokyo after the war, the shock of having recognized himself partially in the demonized Japanese Other proves too much for the Mexican American GI, as he turns away from Kikuchi who is attempting to thank him for the gift of his life. Race hatred bred at home, displaced in combat onto a vicious and odious enemy, returns at this moment too uncomfortably close to home and so Sergeant Melguizo refuses to acknowledge that he has ever had anything to do with Ichiro Kikuchi or his life. Here again Paredes represents the situation that C. L. R. James suggested Americans of color would face in World War II and anticipates the contradictions posed for Americans of color by other imperial postcolonial struggles in Korea and Vietnam. In the Manichaean struggle between irreconcilable antagonists, with merciless extermination the goal of each side's efforts, the defining line between war crimes and justifiable action becomes as blurred and ambiguous as the line between luck and fate, between national and cultural commitment. In the struggles fought within these intersecting vectors of loyalty, patriotism, and citizenship, as Ichiro Kikuchi concludes, "there are no heroes now" (159).

War Crimes

In "Sugamo" Paredes takes the issue of war crimes one step further as he represents the fate of a black American soldier accused of murdering a Japanese civilian during the Korean War. Sugamo was the prison where the victorious allies kept the prime minister of Japan, Hideki Tojo, and other Japanese military leaders until they were tried and executed for war crimes after World War II. The scene is set against the background of American determinations of international justice.[14] As he awaits trial for the murder, Private Jewel C. Jones mulls over what he conceives to be the polite, good-natured, childlike qualities of the "gooks" and contrasts their "difference" as "funny little people" and "a race of kids that never grew up" (160). From his cell in Sugamo prison, he observes a group of Japanese playing baseball and experiences "a cozy, secure feeling, standing up so high above them, looking down at them" (161). All this is juxtaposed with the oppressively racist attitudes of the American MPs who guard him and with the norms of the white supremacist society in which he has learned to respond to names like "coon" and "kinky-head" (161).

In complex time sequencing, Jones flashes back first to action in Korea, when enemy forces overrun the frontline troops, forcing rear-area service troopers such as he into combat. After a day's heavy fighting for survival, the lone surviving commander of their unit orders Jones to escort a prisoner to headquarters, located "far to the south [beyond] the faint rumble of battle" and to "be back in fifteen minutes" (167). Private Jones understands the major's impossible order as it is clearly intended — code words implicitly condemning the prisoner to death. It is physically impossible for him to take the man to the rear area and return in fifteen minutes. Jones's pride in having been selected as "a man with brains" who "understood" (167) the intent behind the order is short-lived. The young Korean prisoner quickly perceives what is about to happen and pleads for his life, uttering the only words he knows in English, "Thank-you-thank-you-thank-you" (167) — before Jones blasts him with his automatic weapon.

In a second-level temporal sequence, we learn that after this harrowing moment, Jones's commanding officer has rewarded him with the precious gift of leave time from the battlefront and a return trip to Tokyo. In Tokyo, Jones is refused the services of one of the bar girls, apparently because he is black. When the bar manager attempts to deflect Jones's anger in his limited English, madly flipping through a pocket dictionary to find words to explain to the enraged black man, and finding only the words "Thank you, s' . . . Thank you, s' . . ." rolling from his mouth, the distinct temporal realities of then and now collide for Private Jones. He lashes out brutally at the bar manager as he had at the prisoner pleading for his life. This time, however, instead of blasting the man begging for his life with an automatic weapon, he beats him to death with a liquor bottle.

Back in present time, the black soldier Jones is sentenced to death for the murder of the Japanese bar manager, while being jeered by redneck MPs. What pressures lead this black American soldier to need to prove his worth as a "smart" soldier to his white commanding officer by executing an unarmed prisoner of war? What anger explodes at the sight of the young Korean prisoner's desperate pleas for mercy? What confusions do a Japanese bar manager's frightened attempts to explain why a Japanese prostitute is not available to Jones activate in Jones? Finally, how does Jones's murder of the Japanese man relate to the racial taunts of the policemen who guard him? The double jeopardy of racism, its destructive force whether one expresses it or receives it, remains the unresolved issue of the story.

Devaluing Hiroshige

"The Terribly High Cost," set in postwar Tokyo, continues this exploration of American racism during the occupation of Japan. Consisting really of two stories in one, in the frame narrative a particularly vapid university professor, Travis Williamson, and a visiting Indianan friend, Peter Richards, discuss the origin of a rare Hiroshige print that Richards has presented to Williamson.[15] Williamson, whose office is full of "books and colorful pictures" of "the life and literature of the Southwest" and "reproductions of paintings by Tom Lea" (169) misjudges the value of the Hiroshige print because it is not an "original." Richards explains how he received the print (a rare collector's piece from the original nineteenth-century block and not simply, as Williamson has supposed, the copy of a print) in Tokyo after the war as a gift from one Kunio Yoshida, a janitor with the Civilian Property Custodian's office for which Richards worked during the occupation of Japan.

Yoshida's tale forms the inner narrative of the story. According to

Richards, Yoshida is like all the conquered Japanese: "Shabby and sad-looking, always bowing at every American in sight" (172). The "shabby and sad-looking" figure of Yoshida transposes the fate of Japan after the defeat, a reminder of the power imbalance between the victors and the vanquished. When Richards gets to know him better, he learns that Yoshida has a degree in American literature from "an Ivy League school" (173). Labor market conditions in occupation Tokyo being not especially favorable for professors of American literature, Yoshida is obliged to support his war-ravaged family as a janitor. Yoshida's father, an old-style samurai, broken by the war, subsequently commits suicide by jumping from the cliffs at a popular suicide spot, the beautiful nearby town of Otani.[16] The expenses surrounding the death put Yoshida in worse financial straits until Richards gets him a position at a two-year college in the Tokyo Army College for American occupation personnel, working as a teaching assistant in a course on American literature offered by an incompetent American professor: "Kunio would do everything but stand before the class and lecture" (182). The ironic twist of having a Japanese national teaching American literature to Americans "through a dummy" (182) American professor is superseded at the ending only when Yoshida's daughter commits suicide after having been jilted by a Hawaiian Nisei corporal. Paredes is again concerned with the double crossings of enforced postwar transculturations—defeated Japanese instructing their conquerors and Japanese Americans victimizing Japanese nationals—anticipating the reversals of fortunes that postwar power realignments would produce. Not the least of those reversals is the fact that the Americans see the Japanese characters in defeat as having been saved from their own worst qualities, but only to the extent that they embrace American values. Here, as in other stories, that embrace is always partially sexualized.

Asides on the Oboe

The final two selections of *The Hammon and the Beans*, "Getting an Oboe for Joe" and "The American Dish," are broad farces narrated in a parodically picaresque mode by a roguish, salacious character, a self-styled "crazy Mexican" named Johnny Picadero and his Mexican national sidekick, Pablo López.[17] If the *burla*, or mockery and ridicule, of these stories is not quite burlesque, then neither are they quite picaresque either; perhaps *mock* picaresque is closer to the style and intent of the Picadero stories. In either case, "Getting an Oboe for Joe" and the subsequent "The American Dish" are survivors of a projected cycle involving the *pocho* character Johnny Picadero, the son of Mexican Juan Brito y Duero.

> My father is from beautiful San Fernando, not the place in Califa but that town deep in Tamaulipas, where all the people are supposed to be one-eyed. The main reason is that all they eat is dried beef, which is tough and rubbery. They grab a hunk of it with their teeth and pull and pull, and finally a piece comes off and hits them in the eye. Over and over, all the time. My father has both his eyes, but he squints a lot. (186)

We are now far from the historical time and place of Japan. This is apparent when we realize that the San Fernando that Johnny declares to be his ancestral ground is not the real historical town in central Tamaulipas, Mexico, but a place of the cultural imaginary, the fabled town of traditional Mexican lore, notorious for being a village of fools. In the Mexican tradition of the *burla*, as Paredes in the later years of his life as a folklorist would report, San Fernando is a sleepy provincial town and a symbol of the backwoods, "from which eager hicks come to the city to make good" (*Folktales of Mexico* 42). To emphasize the "hick" nature of San Fernando, Johnny contrasts it to the hip urbanity of "Califa," urban youth patois for California. As Johnny narrates his family history, we learn that when his father immigrated into the United States, the *rinche* who processed him wrote down Juan "Picadero" for "Brito y Duero": "Perhaps the character [the immigration officer] had just been to a bullfight. . . . Who can tell. At least he could have made it Picaduro [or, stings hard], my father likes to say, and he grins and looks at me sideways. He thinks I don't catch on" (186–87). Unlike the fools from which he springs or the dolts among whom he lives, Johnny is an urbane *bato al alba* (a cool dude) in metropolitan San Antonio, Texas, and a soldier in the US Army. The Johnny Picadero stories were to be a set of caricatures of various "types" of Mexican and American characters as represented by the popular imagination on both sides of the border.[18]

The point of "Getting an Oboe for Joe" is simple enough. It deals with an attempt to locate an oboe in postwar, late-night, party-time, occupation Tokyo for a forlorn Mexican American baker who is not capable of producing his magic in the mess tent kitchens without music to soothe his soul. A whimsical *fabula* and nutty burlesque, it quickly escalates into a wildly implausible series of misunderstandings that end with Johnny Picadero nearly thrown into the stockade. In the midst of a slapstick ride from Kamakura to Tokyo in a stolen army Jeep—a raucous run involving Keystone Kop US Army MPs, seedy characters from the Tokyo dark market and the demimonde underground—and Johnny Picadero's dodging of the military police by donning a kimono and passing as a Japanese, we are asked to recall the realpolitik of south Texas. The bizarre incorporation of social critique of American racism into a screwball scenario marks these stories with Paredes's signature tropes of irony and parody.

Arriving in postwar Japan, the Chicano *pícaros* are immediately on the make. They quickly realize that they can avoid having "to spend the rest of [their] time in the Army at some post out in the boondocks." All they need to do is to get jobs with "I&E," the Information and Education (that is, propaganda) section of the occupation offices. They apply for and are assigned to an army newspaper "within walking distance of Kamakura and a short drive to Tokyo" (188). In Tokyo, hunting a source for the oboe, Johnny meets a sleazy Korean small-time gangster "on the Ginza" who promises to get him "some oboe" (191). Naively acquiescing, Johnny finds himself in an area of Tokyo beyond the Ginza in "a street full of people, men and women and more women and men" (191). "Lots of oboe here," smirks the Korean. Furious about the deceit and his own naïveté, Johnny dumps the Korean who, not quite ready to be discarded, tries to con him once again, this time by playing on their racial solidarity as mutual double outsiders, "blood brothers" (192), in a forbidden world now inundated with white men.

Once again on his own, still wandering the streets of Tokyo, Johnny meets yet another character, this time an ambiguously identified "young Japanese man dressed like a student" who in perfect English asks whether he isn't "the American inquiring after an oboe" (196). Recognizing that Johnny is now confined to the liminal shadows and unable to walk the streets openly because by this time the US Army MPs are closely on his heels, the young man named "Hiroshi" facilitates a transformation in reverse. Just when many Japanese are Americanizing, Johnny now crosses in the other direction, taking off his army uniform "cap and combat boots" and pulls on a kimono. "You look very Japanese," says Hiroshi, and adds with exquisitely sardonic irony, "you look like the Emperor" (197). Not sure how exactly to take this last drollery, Johnny admits that "not even my friend Pablo would know me in that kimono" (197). Wearing the kimono, Johnny becomes, as Hiroshi says, "invisible. . . . For all practical purposes." That is, invisible to the Americans.

Hiroshi now guides the transcultured and differently racialized Johnny to the underworld at the margins of legitimate, lawful society, the burgeoning Tokyo black market. With his chocolate and cigarettes as barter in hand, not uncoincidentally both products of the indigenous Native American world that *mestizo* Johnny has criss-crossed with Japan this evening and also the coin of the occupation black market realm for the pleasures of the night, Johnny finally encounters the most elegant antique oboe in the world. But as in the master plot of the episodic picaresque that Paredes has used to structure his tale, just at the point of an all-too-easy happy conclusion, contentment is apparently avoided as the US Army MPs catch up with our hero. With the ensuing chase, we shift generic modes as the story now repeats the events narrated in the most famous of border *corridos* of cultural conflict, but this time as farce, not tragedy: "Just like Gregorio Cortez," says Johnny; "so many of them just to catch one Mexican!" with "their forty-fives in hand."[19] In true slapstick form, the army cops have raided the wrong house, and it is unintentionally up to Johnny to lead them down the path to the next circle of this surreal, seductive hell, the real black market den. And there they find the makings of the new world emerging from the still smoldering ruins of napalmed Japan. However, the infernal smoke rises from different fires than we might have imagined: "There's a big party going on in there, with all sorts of people besides the native element. A Chinese or two, or maybe they're Koreans. Two civilian whites and a couple of our guys in uniform, a lieutenant and a sergeant. . . . The lieutenant and all the rest just sit there on the floor, around some little tables where they have been drinking sake and smoking something that is not tobacco, for sure" (199). The cultural forms that worked in one age to narrate the story of heroic resistance still provide the raw materials in the present age, but in the vastly different idiom of comedy. Johnny Picadero's labors to find an oboe for his friend prove fruitless, but all's well that ends well since it is not plot resolution that Paredes is after in this story but slapstick intrigue and the heterogeneous power of alternative discursive forms. Like the jokes, riddles, puns, and other whimsical verbal play that Paredes would collect as a folklorist years later, the Picadero stories represent an entirely different kind of discursive strategy for cultural survival and personal identification. As in others of his fictions, names and naming are still the issue here, but the trajectory of the plot is one designed to deal with a different set of social conditions after the world war and the emergence of a new stage of global history.

From the despair and desolation of devastated Tokyo, new subcultures were emerging at the periphery of the old feudal order and the new democratic one. Dower notes that the end of the war and the destruction of the austere prewar authoritarian military government created a sense of desolation in Japan. But it also produced extravagantly flamboyant new expressions of iconoclasm and self-reliance in the mixing of American, British, Australian, Russian, Japanese, Chinese, Korean, Formosan, and Okinawan peoples among the ruins of the old colonial world. Their intermixing at the margin "came to exemplify not merely the confusion and despair" of the transformation of the old regimes "but also the vital, visceral, even carnal transcending of it" (*Embracing Defeat* 122). Paredes's little slapstick comedies represent his own understanding of the ambiguous nature of Japan's repudiation of its stultifying prewar severity and its postwar embrace of the self-indulgent commercialization of pleasure, desire, and the promise of fulfillment that also came with democracy and modernization during the era of the American occupation.

The Last of the Culomula

"The American Dish," the second of the Johnny Picadero tales, continues in the mock picaresque mode. This story, too, follows the madcap capers of our rambunctious antihero in the borderlands of culture. The rhythm of the story is not the somber 4/4 beat of the *corrido*, but, as in the previous story, the full-speed, nonstop pacing of a Marx Brothers movie, or better still, of a Cantinflas escapade or a Tin Tan *burla*. In this story, too, the comic mode is probably closer to burlesque than to the picaresque. Johnny is not quite the *peladito* (urban tramp) that Mario Moreno made famous in his Cantinflas films. Nevertheless, the distance between the Mexican *peladito* and the Chicano *bato al alba* is not vast. Moreno's character of Cantinflas has been described as "the Aztec equivalent of Chaplin's [tramp], challenging middle-class decency, hypocrisy and smugness with his incomprehensible speech and anarchic spirit" (Medina de la Serna 167).

Another prototype for the Johnny Picadero character much closer in cultural style is undoubtedly the role of Tin Tan, made legendary by the inimitable comic borderlands actor Germán Valdés. Born in Mexico City in 1915 but growing to maturity in Ciudad Juarez on the Texas Mexican border, Valdés emerged from the *teatro frívolo*, or frivolous theater, the popular theater of the 1930s. In the character of Tin Tan, Valdés created an elaborately comical, zoot-suited Mexican American *pachuco* (mid-twentieth century Chicano hipster), always wearing an enormous smile. With Tin Tan, Valdés succeeded in lampooning the stodgy world of the middle classes on both sides of the border. As the cultural historian Rosa Linda Fregoso notes, "Tin-Tan blended working-class forms of expression and dress and came up with a Mexican version of the U.S.-Mexico border type: the pachuco. Tin-Tan's parodic characterization of the pachuco provided a critique both of U.S. treatment of Chicanos and Mexico's neglect of its emigrants to the United States" (54). With the character Tin Tan, Valdés created the type of the overly Americanized Mexican urban youth, replete with complex bilingual, bicultural idioms that would serve as the paradigm of the border urban clown for decades to come. The type of this character reached its apogee in the late twentieth-century comic films of Cheech Marín and his version of the Chicano "vernacular aesthetic" (Fregoso 55).[20]

The association of these early twentieth-century Mexican films and latter-day Chicano movies is an apt one. The golden age of Mexican filmmaking coincided with that of the Hollywood studios before the rise of television and constitutes a rich matrix of images that predict the iconographic evolution of postwar Mexican aesthetic sensibility.[21] Paredes adapts the idioms of this cinematographic era as the dominant generic form to organize his Picadero tale. Its plot structure is not that of oral or written narrative, but of the stylized pictorial mode of Hollywood and Mexican comic burlesque film. In this segment of what were intended to be a series of episodes concerning Johnny Picadero, our hero is back home in "San Cuilmas" (Mexican American slang for San Antonio, Texas) in early 1950s cold war America after horrifying combat in the Philippines and Okinawa followed by four transformative years in the occupation army. Now Johnny travels to Mexico to visit his Mexican former comrade in arms and best friend Pablo López, who like fifteen thousand of his Mexican national countrymen saw action in the Pacific serving in American armed forces.[22]

In this installment of the Johnny Picadero cycle, the satire targets Americans who think they can pass as Mexicans because they know a few clichéd things about Mexico, such as how to order chile con carne in a Mexican restaurant. Johnny sardonically points out that "chile con carne" is really "an American dish," that is, ersatz Mexican food, unless one means the phrase literally, intending to order a dish of meat and *chile picante*, something quite different from what Americans call chile con carne. In their Americanized usage, the words literally do not match up to the intent of their original Mexican meaning. The story, therefore, links this false and literal understanding of Mexico with the unalloyed greed of American venture cultural capitalists looking for sleazy opportunities in postwar Latin America.

"The American Dish" is set in the Mexican countryside. The prankster encounters cold war "spies," a delectable Miss Ross, an altogether different kind of American dish, and the shady operatives of a fly-by-night American film company stealing Mexican cultural capital by illegally filming "the tribal dances of the Culomula Indians" before they pass into history with the last of the Mohicans (229). Picadero is a classic trickster, a harlequin figure out of the Cantinflas and Tin Tan universe of Mexican movies, willing to lie, cheat, and bamboozle anyone blocking his path out of the confining demesne of social injustice and racism. His comic style, out of the commedia dell'arte, traveling theater, and music hall tradition, is based on the stratification of meaning between everyday discourses in both English and Spanish and on the possibilities available for isolating from these strata multiple levels of intentionality. Here, as elsewhere, then, parody and irony prove central to Paredes's intent. In these last two stories, comedy, burlesque, and caricature in the form of the parodic names of the fictional Indian tribe and of the zany main character do not diminish the sting of his earlier satires, but extend the critique into the realm of style as they unmask and reveal the false, hypocritical—or simply banal—adequation to historical reality.

As in "When It Snowed in Kitabamba," in the Johnny Picadero stories laughter becomes the ironic medium through which the Baudelarian philosophic detachment of the absolute comic necessary for the recognition of mistaken, mystified assumptions about superiority and inferiority, and even the acknowledgment of difference, can take place. Related to the comedic spirit that in later life as an ethnographer and folklorist Paredes would celebrate in his collection of jests, oral histories, legends, and anecdotes, *Uncle Remus con Chile*, the Johnny Picadero stories explore the rhetorical modes available to revisionary and alternative history. Alive to the magic, absurdity, and ludic anima of daily life, Paredes's burlesques take the long way around to social realism.

Dialogic Prosaics

Paredes's stories taken as a whole, whether set in Texas or Japan, are multiform in style, speech, and voice. As in the poetry that in most cases preceded the fiction, Paredes's strength lies in displaying and exploiting the possibilities for satire and irony. He is testing the possibilities for writing the kind of political critique that comes from the experience of living at the periphery of heterogeneous linguistic levels, in English and Spanish, in high formal discourse as well as in everyday vernacular idioms. These discourses and idioms emerge in different stylistic modes as romance, tragedy, or comedy. The direct literary-artistic narration in numerous diverse variants from first- to third-person, in realistic or experimental temporal form, in ironic or utopian mode, as well as in the stylization of everyday popular forms and its individualization of characters' speech offers a highly structured unity to the various works. Bakhtin has argued that "the language of a novel is the system of its 'languages' " ("Discourse in the Novel" 262). Paredes is not here writing novels, but he is concerned with displaying the system of "languages" that are always at play in dialogized form within a language and across linguistic systems. In marshaling a variety of diverse social speech genres and a diversity of individual voice types, all functioning within the crossed signs of Mexican and American speech characteristics and tinged in these instances with both formal Japanese and the informal argot of the postwar occupation era, Paredes displays the complex stratifications of meaning always at play within a national language. When multiplied by the interactions of his bilingual and multicultural subjects,

Paredes's characters serve the sociopolitical purpose of emphasizing internal stratification as an unavoidable feature of border consciousness as such. When he expands the idea of the border to include not only the imaginary geopolitical boundary line between two nations but also the more functional one of symbolic overlap between cultural groups, Paredes makes the idioms of race, identity, and nation the distinguishing features of his art. Representing the differing individual voices that flourish under such conditions of heterogeneity, Paredes makes the movements of social multiplicity the identifying marker of modernity. Reading them more than a half century after they were written, one cannot help but think that this is where American ethnic literature is going. It turns out that it is also where it has already been.

In all of Paredes's stories, whether in the modes of tragedy, comedy, or realistic narrative, the guiding rhetorical force is ironic wisdom, the self-knowledge that glimpses the discontinuity and plurality of levels within a subject caught between two worlds and comes to know itself by what it is not. Together with the poems written during this period, we can see Paredes's nascent ideas concerning the links among American postwar empire building, the emergence of what would later be termed globalization, and the construction of a system of world capital. A poem from this period, "Pro Patria," written in the days immediately after his arrival in Japan with the occupation army, expresses Paredes's sense of these global linkages directly:

> In the mud huts of China,
> The tile-roofed paper houses of Japan,
> In the straw-thatched *jacales* of old Mexico,
> The rain-blackened shacks of Arkansas,
>
> Here is my fatherland, these are my people,
> My beloved,
> Black, yellow, brown–
> And even if their eyes are blue–
>
> These are my people,
> The bleeding wounds upon the feet and hands
> Of humankind.
>
> And the sleek bastards in the swallowtails,
> They who can say which course the earth shall take,

How it should swing on its axis,
The sons-of-bitches in the stripèd pants,

They have the awesome task
Of making this fatherland of mine
Flourish in filth, thrive in a grave of garbage,
So that some other day we all may perish
In one grand shout of glory.

It is for this we breed
More numerous
Than a triumphant soldier's dream. (*Between Two Worlds* 84)

The "fatherland" is not a site of cultural romance or of romantic nationalism. It does not denote an ethnic folk. Nor is it locatable in any one particular cartographical space. It denotes instead the kinship of affiliation with other races and ethnic groups that already existed in Paredes's experience of the transnational borderlands of Greater Mexico but which accelerates to fruition in Japan under the consciousness created by a sense of shared oppression and injustice, as mutual recipients of race prejudice, and of having experienced the catastrophe of imperial conquest. In these stories, Paredes's virtuosity as a master storyteller and clear-sighted critic of contemporary ethnic culture is powerfully present. Creating a new historiographical space while critiquing the process of history making itself, the concluding stories of *The Hammon and the Beans and Other Stories* along with other contemporaneous writings represent further evidence of Américo Paredes's historical centrality as an artist and scholar of the American ethnic vernacular imagination experiencing itself in an inordinately textured transnational context.

THE POSTWAR BORDERLANDS

AND THE ORIGINS OF THE

TRANSNATIONAL IMAGINARY

The Occupation-Era Writings in *Pacific Stars*

and Stripes and *El Universal*

> What know you of sorrow, who wear not
> the traveler's cloak, nor on an unaccustomed
> pillow rest, groping for dreams till dawn?
> —traditional Japanese poem

As we have seen in the discussion of his prewar poetry and in the short stories from Texas and Japan, Paredes explored in a variety of discursive forms how the activity of being citizens affects the way we view ourselves. He was interested, that is, in understanding how culture constructs and interprets citizenship. In particular, he was concerned with democratic citizenship and its meaning in an emerging transnational world. In the context of the social and demographic transformations of the American Southwest that he was witnessing at midcentury, what role, if any, he wondered, did culture play in defining citizenship? How was culture political? How did different groups participate in building a national community? Was it possible to claim membership in a society, claim political and social rights, and become recognized as an active agent in American society while at the same time retaining real difference? Was it possible, in other words, for "foreign" or "alien" groups to become part of the coherent living body of American society while at the same time retaining or even developing cultural forms that kept other identities and heritages alive?

These questions are evident in all of his writings from the 1930s, 1940s, and 1950s. Throughout his life on the border and in Japan and Asia in general, Paredes was observing, thinking, and writing about the power of national cultures, languages, and literatures. He saw them as activities that informed the apparatus of the cultural and political hegemony of the ruling classes in the process of nation (re)building and of their affiliation with the idea of citizenship.

In these writings, Paredes asked: What would it take, materially and psychologically, to imagine a new identity and sense of belonging, and how could one conceptualize something that by definition could not yet be imagined since it had no equivalent in current experience? What would the harbingers of such an identity look like objectively? In both the literary texts and his other writings from the Far East as a reporter and member of the US Army of occupation in Japan, Paredes attempted meticulously to imagine, what it means for a member of a minority or marginalized community to belong to the greater cultural and national polity. At the dawning of the cold war, occupation Japan was to offer him an enormously fertile testing ground for his developing ideas on the relationships between culture, language, ethnicity, race, and national affiliation.

The End of an Era

On August 15, 1945, Emperor Hirohito of Japan took to the airwaves to exhort his countrypeople to "endure the unendurable and bear the unbearable." He admitted that the war had "not turn[ed] in Japan's favor." Two weeks later, on September 2, 1945, an awesome armada of American military forces arrived in Japan to accept the formal surrender aboard the American battleship USS *Missouri* in Tokyo Bay.[1] Almost as startling to the Japanese as the substance of Hirohito's speech, admitting defeat without actually naming it, and the appearance of the conquering Americans at their doorstep was the very fact itself that the emperor had spoken to them. John Dower remarks that "in the two decades since he had ascended to the Chrysanthemum Throne, Emperor Hirohito had never once spoken directly to his subjects" (*Embracing Defeat* 33). Dower's point concerning the emperor's speech and the issue of national belonging is crucial. In this prototypically modern media moment, Hirohito was not speaking to the

Japanese as fellow *citizens* of the nation; they were still the *subjects* of an imperial realm. But the relationship between subject and citizen was about to be severely redefined in postwar Japan. The moment of Hirohito's unprecedented emergence into the public sphere through the medium of radio marked an extraordinary, world-historical moment for Japan and the rest of Asia. It represented a complete realignment with the past, a break with tradition that would shortly be symptomatic of the need for the construction of a completely new social imaginary for Japan. With Hirohito's momentous radio address, the *subject* Japanese learned that the war that had permanently shattered their former lives had finally ended. They did not yet understand that a transition from wartime to peacetime, from feudal militarism to populist democracy, from monopolized industry to global market capitalism, from *subjection* to *citizenship*, in short from *Bushido*, the way of the gods, to *depato*, the way of the American-style department stores, was about to begin.

Having experienced the brutal twin blows of, as Hirohito said, the "cruel bombs [used] to kill and maim large numbers of the innocent" (qtd. in Dower, *Embracing Defeat* 36), the atomic weapons detonated over Hiroshima and Nagasaki, and months of massive firebomb raids "that had reduced fifty percent of urban Japan to cinders" (Schaller 3), the Japanese people steeled themselves now for what was to come.[2] On the brink of starvation, their society and economy at the point of near-total collapse, their cities were so utterly devastated that a new word was coined to describe them — *yaknohara*, or "burnt plains." With the "ferocious demonization of the enemy that was the staple of official propaganda" still working on their minds (Dower, "Contested Ground" 66), the Japanese were certain that they were entering a period of vicious recrimination under American military occupation, the first foreign invasion of their country in recorded history.[3]

For their part, Americans were still recoiling from the attack on Pearl Harbor, from the ferocious battles to the death in the South Pacific, and from the increasing verification of widely reported wartime rumors about the brutal treatment of captured Allied soldiers, sailors, airmen, and other civilians by their Japanese captors. The historian Michael Schaller has written that "even discounting for the hyperbole and passion of wartime rhetoric, the actual violence of battle made most verbal attacks appear understated" (4). Still, the verbal attacks were astringent enough. For example, a Gallup poll taken in 1944 revealed that 13 percent of the American public favored the complete extermination of all the Japanese after the war. When joined with generations of American anti-Asian prejudice, the mood of the time augured that the occupation would be a time of bitter retribution. Americans were apparently in no mood for reconciliation. Given this atmosphere of desire for reprisal and punishment, nobody could have predicted what actually ensued.

Determined to prevent an internal revolutionary upheaval that might tilt a defeated Japan in the direction of a Soviet-style regime, the new Truman administration opted for a more benign policy for the occupation of Japan than anyone had imagined. First would come a dismantling of the Japanese wartime structure of military governance. Simultaneously, an Allied powers military occupation would be set in place. But the aim of the dismantling and occupation would be to use existing Japanese structures and organizations "to speed thorough but nonvindictive demilitarization, democratization, and economic reform" (Schaller 8) rather than to impose punitive measures. In this manner, the victorious Allied powers hoped to make of Japan a formidable Asian anticommunist bulwark against what was already beginning to appear as the real threat to global peacetime security, the mounting power of the Russian Soviet Union.

In the seven years of the occupation from 1945 to 1952, the actual course of reform followed a delicate interplay between SCAP US Army General Douglas MacArthur and "the Japanese elites who maintained control of political and economic life throughout the Occupation" (Schaller 29). Although the occupation was nominally an Allied undertaking, in reality, the United States alone "determined basic policy and exercised decisive command over all aspects of the occupation" (Dower, *Embracing Defeat* 73).[4] These Japanese elites, traditional conservatives often described as "moderates" or even "liberals" by American policy makers, in reality sometimes proved to have had very questionable wartime records of accommodation with and downright support for the militaristic government policies of aggression. Nevertheless, working in concert with MacArthur's occupation policies, the traditional ruling classes emerged from the ruins of the devastated social and economic Japanese landscape to shape the course for the postwar reconstruction of a shattered Japan. As the cultural historian Linda C. Ehrlich tells it, "What followed was a time when Douglas MacArthur, the 'shadow shogun,' attempted to destroy the Japanese war machine, dismantle the *zaibatsu* (the domination of Japanese finance, commerce, and industry by a few families), and carry out land reform" (44).[5] In this period that the Japanese came to call "the confusion era" (Yamanashi and Rimer 23), Americans and Japanese interacted to a degree that neither could have predicted during the height of the war.[6] "The meeting of cultures went far beyond chewing gum, nylons, 'kissing scenes' in movies, and songs like 'You Are My Sunshine,' whistled by GIS" (Ehrlich 44).

At no time since the Taika Reform of 645 and the Meiji Restoration of 1868 had Japan been faced with as massive an adaptation of foreign social, political, and cultural institutional forms. The historian Harry Harootunian has argued that "between the two world wars, Japanese society underwent a massive industrial transformation" (x). This experience that established "modern life" marked the moment Japan was "overcome by modernity," engineered as a preemptive strategy intended to hold off the worst excesses of international modernization. Before the war, many Japanese felt that modernity had authorized a wholly negative "counterfeit civilization" that was shallow, derivative, and spiritually impoverished when contrasted to traditional Japan (Harootunian x). Now after the war, the aims, methods, and styles of the occupation would hasten and intensify this encounter with modernity in ways that could not have been imagined in the prewar period. A successful transition would require the Japanese finding resources in their traditional culture that, appropriately modified and transformed, would enable them to take on this new wave of modernity. Invariably, in dealing with modernity, Japanese writers and thinkers had "turned toward an indefinite past to envisage a cultural and communitarian endowment that anchored Japanese identity to constitute the sign of genuine authenticity and fixity in an environment of ceaseless temporal change" (Harootunian xxxii). Now the postwar occupation intended something altogether different for Japan. It intended no less than the transformation of Japan into a new society that would be, as the art historian Donald Richie notes, "humane, peace-loving, and democratic: in a word, American" (11).

Between Texas and Japan

In November of 1945, a few weeks into the beginning of this massive social transformation of a shattered Japan, Private Américo Paredes landed in Nagoya. Once the prosperous home of the Japanese aircraft industry, in the *après guerre*, Nagoya stood reduced to an ashen, barren landscape by the rain of incendiary bombs during the final months of the war. Almost immediately, Paredes began writing for *Pacific Stars and Stripes* and *El Universal*, reporting on the course of the new cultural, economic, and political forms forcibly superimposed on the ruins of the old.[7] In my research I have been able to identify seventy-four major articles and feature columns in *Pacific Stars and Stripes* and *El Universal* written by Private, then Private First Class, then finally Corporal Américo Paredes.[8]

Composed between December 1945 and August 1950, Paredes's writings from Asia broach a formidable array of topics. They include reports on the US supervision of the creation of a demilitarized, social democratic, anticommunist government for postwar Japan; news articles on the Japanese protests against the occupation apparatus; others on the frequent food riots due to the dreadful shortage of adequate supplies of basic foods and household staples; and special features on the emergence of a postwar arts and entertainment scene. Most dramatically, these writings document the changing status of women in postwar Japan and chronicle their roles in the sex and entertainment industries. They also include intriguing eyewitness accounts of the war crimes trial of Hideki Tojo, the general of the army and wartime prime minister of Japan, and of his twenty-seven co-indicted Japanese military and civilian leaders brought before an international war crimes tribunal.

In his writings from postwar Japan, Paredes attempts to capture the despair of the exhausted and impoverished Japanese, their anguish and regret mixed with the birth of hope in strange new forms and the simple joy at what Dower has called "the unexpected surcease of misery and death" that came with the end of the war (*Embracing Defeat* 38). What would this new postwar Asian world under American occupation look like? What shape would its political forms and social traditions take? How would its language, media, and arts evolve? Who were these new Japanese emerging from defeat? What would it be like for them to live in a homeland suddenly inundated with the affable and good-natured white men now quietly but unmistakably in control? Paredes's dispatches from the occupation frontline would address all of these questions.

Shortly before Paredes's articles began appearing in *Stars and Stripes*, a soldier by the name of Barnard Rubin, a political columnist for the newspaper, "a committed leftist, probably a member of the Communist Party," according to Paredes, and the managing editor, Ken Pettus, who had edited a CIO Woodworkers Union newspaper in Seattle before the war, had been summarily dismissed from the paper.[9] The army ordered Rubin and Pettus home under the same clouds of suspicion concerning loyalty, national allegiance, and national security that in 1945 were already darkening the American mainland. A series of articles in *Stars and Stripes* documenting the firing of the two men accused of "disloyalty" make for immensely fascinating reading as an early case study of cold war red-baiting and the evisceration of the American Left.[10] The firing of Rubin, in particular, a combat veteran with an honorable combat record in the bloody battles of the South Pacific, was so egregiously unjust that it received wide coverage back in the United States. Moreover, eighteen members of the newspaper's editorial staff signed a letter to the commanding officer of the Civil Information and Education (CIE) section, a euphemism for the propaganda wing of SCAP, protesting the firing of Rubin and Pettus and the "censorship" of their coverage of the emergent Japanese political and cultural world. The irony of the situation, that the Americans were there to teach the Japanese about "freedom of the press," escaped no one.

Although I have not been able to locate a copy of the letter to ascertain exactly who signed it, by this point in time Paredes had just joined the Tokyo staff of the newspaper and had been posted to Rubin's former beat as the political correspondent for *Stars and Stripes*. Paredes soon also took over Rubin's assignment as political editor, as well as the opportunities, obligations, and possible pitfalls that came with it. In an interview I conducted with Paredes in 1995, he described to me the temper of the times and his own political affiliations just before the war in this way:

> The 1930s were the period of Sandino's revolution in Nicaragua, and we in south Texas were very attuned to the political struggles of Latin America. The work of Emma Tenayuca, political and labor activist in San Antonio especially moved me. . . . All through this period, I was an angry young man, angry at the way *mexicanos* were treated in Texas and the rest of the Southwest, and angry about social inequality and economic injustice. The other members of a reading group I belonged to were constantly urging me to renounce my US citizenship and become a Mexican citizen. But I wasn't exactly taken by what I saw of Mexican nationalism either. . . . In

23 Américo Paredes
in the Tokyo offices of
*Pacific Stars and
Stripes*, c. 1946.
Courtesy of Alan and
Vincent Paredes.

part because of the influence of my uncle Eduardo . . . who had belonged
to the anarchist Flores Magón group, my own politics were really quite
radical. I've often thought that if there had been a Communist Party cell
in south Texas at the time, I would have joined it. By 1939, however, war
had broken out in Europe, and gradually everything started to change,
even in south Texas.

Paredes was not an avowed communist. However, his idols included
Lázaro Cárdenas, the hero of the revolution and the populist president
of Mexico who nationalized the foreign oil companies; César Augusto
Sandino, the Nicaraguan radical leader in the anti-imperialist struggles in Central America; the Flores Magón brothers of Mexican syn-
dicalist and anarchist fame; and most centrally, Emma Tenayuca, the
great socialist daughter of San Antonio, Texas, and the general secretary of the Communist Party of Texas during the 1930s. Paredes's
articles for *Stars and Stripes* are not about Texas but about the economic, political, social, and cultural turmoil in postwar Japan and
about the convoluted links between SCAP and the Japanese elites who
maintained control of political and economic life throughout the

occupation. So what happened in Japan? How did his experiences as an American soldier, journalist, and humanitarian aid worker affect his understanding of the United States–Mexico borderlands? What stands between Texas and Japan?

The winter of 1945, Paredes's first in Japan, was one of horrendous suffering for the Japanese: the harvest turned out to be one of the worst in decades, and its failure led to massive food shortages and unimaginable misery. The efforts of the American-installed government was so "woefully incompetent in rationing and distributing basic commodities" that, according to Dower, "for several years, newspapers routinely reported tallies of corpses that had been found in public places like railroad stations, where the famished homeless sought refuge" ("Contested Ground" 61).[11] Paredes's articles for *Stars and Stripes* talk about the hunger of the Japanese and the struggles of "leftwing Social Democrats and Communists" battling the police for equitable food rationing. Others of his articles report on massive rallies of "half a million laborers, agrarians, and white collar workers . . . singing the International, the Song of May Day, and the Red Flag song," "organized by labor [and] communists" agitating for labor reform. He writes about other "huge rallies organized by labor, communists and other elements to increase food allowances and denounce the formation of a conservative cabinet." And he marks "the first speech by a communist before the Japanese Diet."[12]

In addition, he reports on the changing political and social status of women with their first participation in the Japanese Diet, the parliament. In particular, he documents the increasing calls for the "protection of working women."[13] In the devastation of their society, women were all too often forced by desperation, sheer starvation, and destitution to the margins of respectable society. Paredes writes also on the emerging sex and entertainment industries around the Ginza commercial district of Tokyo. With the opening of their homeland to the occupation, the Japanese feared American rapacity in a quite literal way, writes Dower. "The sexual implications of having to accommodate hundreds of thousands of Allied servicemen had been terrifying, especially to those who were aware of the rapacity their own forces had exhibited elsewhere as well as of the huge numbers of non-Japanese women who had been forced to serve the imperial troops as *ianfu* or 'comfort women'" (*Embracing Defeat* 124). This matter of servicing the conquerors was also a subject that Paredes would address in his columns "Desde Tokio" ("From Japan") and "Desde China" ("From China") for *El Universal* during this period.

The Rebirth of the Ginza

In what can only be called an image from the emerging transnational, postcontemporary age, Paredes represents in one magnificent *Stars and Stripes* Sunday feature spread the sex industry as it "blossomed forth from the ruins" of bombed-out Tokyo to provide nightlife and "comfort" to the occupying quarter-million-man American army. The Ginza, reports Paredes, has become a "Japanese cross between Broadway and a Mexican marketplace."

You can buy almost anything on the Ginza.

Cucumbers and shoes, strawberries and pearls, fish of all kinds, shapes and odors, postcards and supposedly eatable concoctions with the consistency of axle grease—all can be had on the Ginza.

For a price, of course. In this Japanese cross between Broadway and a Mexican marketplace, one can buy a nice handful of cherries for 35 yen, just $2.30. . . .

Already people are going back to walking the Ginza on evenings. An estimated 400,000 parade up and down its sidewalks on a Sunday. Theaters and dance-halls are beginning to spring up again. . . .

Cabarets, dance halls and night clubs, which once populated "Tokyo's Broadway" were banned during the war, but soon after the surrender, little spots like the "Oasis of the Ginza," "Eden," "Manhattan," "Marigold" and others well-known to the American soldier blossomed forth from the ruins.

Japanese will tell you that these dance-halls were opened with no specific intent to cater to the soldier trade, since Japanese were also starved for a little dancing and funmaking as in the good prewar times.

At first, most of the cabarets were for soldiers, but now Japanese have their own places where they can cut a rice mat on their own. The food and employment situation has produced a plentiful supply of dance partners.

Surveys indicate that there are 3,000 dance hostesses in the Ginza establishments alone. Each of them gets a nightly cut of 50 to 100 yen. Most of them are former office workers, factory hands, waitresses, geishas and chorus girls.

Increasing numbers of girls from formerly well-to-do families, girls that had never worked before, are said to be taking up taxi-dancing to help out at home.

Today the Ginza is a shadow of its former self, but its old lovers and backers have great plans for it. By 1956 they hope to have "a veritable international shopping and amusement center" where the tired little shops and rundown dance halls now stand. . . .

All in all, it seems that the Ginza is reviving fast and that, if the planners dreams are realized, it may again be the beauty spot of Tokyo.[14]

The captions to the full page of photographs accompanying the article read in sequence, "—THE GINZA—CROSS-SECTION OF TOKYO;—THE GINZA IS HIGH-PRICED;—THE GINZA IS GAY," all of which descriptions with only the most modest of changes accounting for contemporary usages would ring true today. What is even more true than the photorealist pictorial sketch of the Ginza Paredes offers, however, is the reality of the social transformation that the rebirth of the "dance halls and night clubs" along this "Japanese Broadway" and "Mexican market" occasioned. In the shadow of "the food and employment situation"—no doubt Paredes's cynical use of SCAP speak for the conditions of near starvation and economic desperation that many Tokyoites confronted—the Ginza has become an urban mixing ground, a site of "con-fusion" where quite literally East and West met, touched, and erotically swayed to the rhythms of American swing and jazz, transcending their differences with body language, even if only for the moment of the taxi dance.

Moreover, it was not only Americans and Japanese who were mingling and mixing. As Paredes points out, "All the different Japanese types meet and mingle on the Ginza" as well: "Brightly colored kimonos and smart western dresses are seen side by side with beggar's rags and the blue, oddly designed coats that mark the carpenter's and artisan's trades." Class divisions enforced by hierarchies of tradition that before the war might have more strictly divided the Japanese had been loosened in the democracy of disaster, bringing together in the taxi-dancing shared embrace with Americanization "former office workers, factory hands, waitresses, geishas and chorus girls," and increasingly even "girls from formerly well-to-do families, girls that had never worked before." The caption to one of the photographs of several young Japanese women arriving for work at a cabaret alliteratively reads: "Slinky-looking Oriental sirens gather at a Ginza dance-hall doorway in early afternoon in preparation for a night's work as dance partners to gaiety seekers thronging dance emporiums nightly" ("Rebirth of the Ginza," July 21, 1946). The chic and fashionable Western attire of the young women in these photos makes it quite certain that they are not factory workers, waitresses, geishas, or chorus girls, but daughters of the "formerly well-to-do" caught up in the democratic leveling of hunger and necessity.

Writing in *El Universal* on the same topic, Paredes notes that "la Ginza" in Japanese means "la Silla de Plata" (the Silver Chair) and that Tokyoites call it "el Broadway del Oriente" (the Broadway of the East) ("Desde Tokio," August 11, 1946).[15] With the tremendous postwar resurgence of the Ginza business and entertainment district, supporting over a thousand separate businesses, many working primarily the black market, Japanese faith that la Silla de Plata would soon become "un asiento de oro" (a golden seat) was not misplaced. That golden future would be created in part by the labor of the "más de tres mil muchachas trabajando de bailadoras en los establecimientos de la Ginza solamente. . . . Todos los días se llenan sus filas con muchachas de buenas familias, quienes nunca habían trabajado en nada y ahora tienen que hacerse la vida bailando para no morírse de hambre" (more than three thousand young women working as dancers in the Ginza establishments alone. . . . Its ranks are filled each day with young women from good families, who have never had to work at anything and now have to make their livelihood dancing in order not to starve to death) ("Desde Tokio," August 11, 1946). From these scenes of "funmaking" in the "Broadway *de Japón*," Japanese businessmen, Paredes wrote, were already planning "un centro commercial y de recreo de estatura internacional" (a commercial and entertainment center of international stature).

The appeal of this glittering scene of commercial and entertainment nightlife in the context of the torched desolation of metropolitan Tokyo can hardly be overestimated. Quite apart from the extraordinarily vexing matters of the commercialization of sexual desire and of the necessity of women to sell their bodies under conditions of domination, these articles tell us something else. They articulate the emergence of postwar global structures of recreational commerce. Liberated from the wartime regulatory regimes that had stifled the traditional Japanese sensuality of the body, Tokyoites began to take their first steps into the postwar structures of recreational commerce in these American-style dance halls, indulging their senses as best they could (Igarashi 52–53). And in some instances, the future of their experience with the new American extravagance seemed only all too good to be true, as plans for a veritable international shopping and amusement center were already in the works.

Citizens of the Night

But the rise of these international shopping and amusement centers from the ashes of Tokyo is troubling, to say the least. Paredes thus notes how even as "the Ginza is busily rebuilding itself . . . a thriving 'dark market' trade" goes on along its sidewalks and side streets. Clearly, the "dark market" of the side streets of the Ginza led directly to the night lives of the "women of the dark," as the taxi dancers, bar girls, and prostitutes were termed by the Japanese. Dower explains that "the word for 'black market' was *yami-ichi*, for 'woman of the dark' it was *yami no onna*—written with the same ideograph for *yami* (darkness) in each case" (*Embracing Defeat* 139). With just enough Japanese to catch the pun, Paredes, too, makes the connection in his reference to the women of the Ginza soft-porn and hard-sex nightlife and links both to the men of the hard-core "dark market." Japanese women and men of the dark were the "harbingers of a hedonistic, materialistic, American-style consumer culture" (Dower, *Embracing Defeat* 138) that the inhabitants of the light were on the verge of embracing too. For in this dark embrace of Americans and their culture, the shift from the erotic soft sway of the taxi dance to the hard-core release of unbridled desire was in postwar Tokyo a relatively quick and easy move.

"The prostitute, together with the war orphan and black market merchant, was an icon of early postwar life," notes the literary critic Michael S. Molasky (103).[16] Concerning the "women of the dark," he adds that:

> The public seemed especially intrigued by the brash, iconoclastic street-walkers known as *panpan*, many of whom catered to the occupation soldiers. These women embraced not only the occupiers themselves but American mannerisms and fashion. Decked out in brightly colored dresses, strutting around in high heels and puffing on Lucky Strikes, the *panpan* elicited ambivalent responses: admiration and disdain, pity and envy, fear and desire. . . . Yet the *panpan* was above all a survivor of the

24 Women of the night, Tokyo 1948. "Prostitutes in the lower
level of the profession—the cheaper, less elaborate houses.
Some of them might have started out as amateur pan pan girls."
Courtesy of the Ohio State University Japanese Collections.
Reprinted and quoted with the permission of the special col-
lection, John W. Bennett, *Doing Photography and Social Research
in the Allied Occupation of Japan, 1948–1951: A Personal and
Professional Memoir.* John W. Bennett 2002.

25 *Panpan*, Tokyo, 1948. *Panpan* "solicited American
soldiers in particular, because these men had more money
than the military personnel of other Allied forces. These
photos were taken by an Army photographer with [John
W. Bennett] as guide and director, one long night in 1948.
Some forms of prostitution—in particular the pan pan
teenage amateurs—were the direct result of the presence
of GIs as sources of income and images of liberation."
Courtesy of the Ohio State University Japanese Collections. Reprinted and quoted with the permission of the
special collection, John W. Bennett, *Doing Photography
and Social Research in the Allied Occupation of Japan,
1948–1951: A Personal and Professional Memoir*. John W.
Bennett 2002.

postwar chaos, and in this regard nearly every Japanese who lived through the war could identify with her. (103)

Paredes had already remarked on the "brightly colored kimonos and smart western dresses" of the women of the Ginza in his July 21, 1946, piece for *Stars and Stripes*. Writing in Spanish for *El Universal* a few days later, Paredes directly associates the figure of the *panpan* and matters of love for sale with the desperation of the postwar chaos, observing, "the specter of hunger haunts the streets of Tokyo." From the beggar to the emperor, what occupies the minds of all the Japanese, he cries, is how to evade hunger, the hold of which on the bodies and souls of the populace seems to grow by the day. "Hunger is an offshoot of the insane war that bled Japan for fifteen years," writes Paredes, "changing the land from an orderly and tidy nation into a demoralized country, that is indescribably filthy, completely finished off by unrelenting bombardment . . . a land pulverized by the [American B-29] Superfortresses." Only the "antlike industriousness" of the Japanese people, he continues, and the benevolence of the occupation powers has staved off massive starvation ("Desde Tokio," August 11, 1946). Desperation also explained why in these years of acute deprivation and conditions of extreme poverty sex became an effective form of barter for men and women, but especially so for young women. In both English- and Spanish-language versions of his descriptions of the Ginza, Paredes underscores that the links between hunger, desperation, sex, and the commercialization of desire are acutely problematic, requiring acquiescence to their contradictions only under duress.

As the caption to a contemporary illustration from the Asahi Historical Photograph Library puts it, "The harshness of postwar life produced a sad but steady trade in 'women of the night,' who were called *panpan*. There were many such women who sold their bodies to feed their families" (*Asahi* 164).[17] And so, observes Paredes with sharp poignancy, "in the streets, in the train stations, especially around Tokyo and Yurakucho Stations, young Japanese women offer themselves for a box of field rations or a bar of chocolate. The people call them *'chocoreto no mumume'* — the chocolate girls" ("Desde Tokio," July 11, 1946).[18] Tokyo's Yurakucho district was in fact the classic site for the *panpan* and the sexual assignations joining conqueror and conquered in the early stages of the postwar commodification of desire.[19] An article in the *Japan Review* for 1949 picks up on Paredes's notion of the Ginza as "a Japanese cross between Broadway and a Mexican marketplace" by describing a stretch of Tokyo near Ueno Station as "the Broadway of the Flesh" (Kanzaki 5–6). As Paredes points out, even the argot of Japanese and American commercial intercourse mimicked these crossings and created new words, hybrid forms of speech, new discursive turns such as *chocoreto no mumume*, to designate their evolving intercultural relations, in lingo mixing GI English and underworld Japanese that came cheekily to be called "*pan*glish" or "SCAPanese" by the polyglot wits of the day.[20]

Women were in everyone's mind during the occupation, in Paredes's no less so than in anyone else's. He writes in that same column for *El Universal*: "Japan is enduring a second invasion—a feminine invasion. After MacArthur's edict giving Japanese women equal rights, the fair Nipponese sex has shown great verve and determination in assuming a new position in relation to the past." What was this new position? One of political equality. In that same article, Paredes goes on to point out that in the elections of April 10, 1946, thirty-nine women, with representation across the political spectrum of the contending parties, were elected to all levels of offices. Now, as Japanese men feared, even the holiest of sites were fair game for women as they sought to enter temples and religious shrines segregated by sex for hundreds of years. Paredes clearly delights in recounting the expressed shock of the Tokyo metropolitan press at this untoward turn of events. Emerging from marginal status to assuming a rightful place in the holy of holies, Japanese women were everywhere scandalizing traditional Japanese male society by assuming a position of equality within the body politic.

Paredes's articles focus on the persons marginalized in respectable society—unruly and aggressive leftists and communists, the prostitutes and procuring pimps, the maverick and entrepreneurial black marketeers, the denizens of the demimonde of self-indulgence and citizens of the night—"distinctive subcultures of defeat emerged, shocking yet mesmerizing symbols of the collapse of an old order and the emergence of a new spirit of iconoclasm and self-reliance" (Dower, *Embracing Defeat* 122). They represented Emersonian ideals with a strikingly Japanese twist. Paredes's actual and discursive forays to the borders of this emerging new social space—between the old and new orders within Japanese society, between Asian and Western cultural and racial formations, between the victorious American occupiers and the defeated occupied peoples of Japan—individually and as a group all constituted his initiation to the complexities of the new transnational modernity. The social space of this new transnational world would afford Paredes a site, a habitus, from which to revise, refashion, and energize his consolidating understanding of the nature of cultural difference and of life in the borderlands of the postwar intercultural contact zones. These are the features that characterize his articles from China and Japan, first to last.

Occupation Arts and Culture

Quite apart from cultural difference, however, Paredes was intrigued from his first days in Japan by the parallels between his native United States–Mexico borderlands world and this new Asian land. His first published article from Tokyo for *El Universal* establishes this parallel as it details an event that occurred in the provincial town of Gamagori, "on my first night in a Japanese city" ("Desde Tokio" May 28, 1946). On this evening, the similarities between Mexican and Japanese women were also on Paredes's mind. He describes how the geishas at an establishment to which he has been taken for a delicious seafood dinner served the guests dressed in "colorful kimonos reminiscent of the costumes of our Tehuanas," an indigenous people of Oaxaca and southern Mexico. More than the geisha's sensuous apparel, he writes, their "dark complexions and oblique eyes with long lashes" could have allowed them to pass for Mexican women. Beyond the nostalgia-inducing features of the geishas and the problematics of Japanese-Mexican racial passing that their skin color and facial features bring to mind, the universal language of music also plays on Paredes. As the evening progressed, his hosts offered him another intoxicating taste of Japan, that of music in the modern Japanese style. An elegantly attired geisha entered the room and tuned her samisen; Paredes waited impatiently for what he imagined would be the mysterious strains of an unknown Asian melody.

Instead, "por fin sonó el samisen con sus notas huecas y comenzo la voz de la geisha alta, dulce e inefablemente extraña" (at last, the hollow notes of the samisen sounded and the geisha's high, sweet, ineffably strange voice began its song). Inexplicably, astonishingly, the "exotic daughter of the sun" begins to sing, in Japanese, of all things, "Lamento gitano" ("Gypsy Lament"), a bolero by one of the greatest

Mexican popular composers of the mid-century, María Grever.[21] "I listened to the geisha as she finished her song with great satisfaction, like that of one who encounters a veiled woman, lifts her veil and discovers a former lover." With the geisha metaphorically unveiled, the transnational question remains: how did a romantic Mexican song come to be transcribed into Japanese, and perhaps even more bizarrely, why do the Japanese think of it as one of their own?

A comedy of Asian Pacific errors ensues as Paredes tries to convince his hosts that the Japanese song "es de mi tierra, es canción mexicana" (is from my native land, is a Mexican song). "But I thought you were an *American*," one of his confused hosts reasonably replies. "No—le respondí—. Soy soldado norteamericano, pero también soy 'mekishiko-jin" (persona mexicana)" (No, I replied. I am an American soldier, but I am also *"mekishiko-jin,"* a Mexican person). Unable to dispel the multicultural confusion or persuade his hosts, Mr. Nakano and Mr. Hirano, Paredes sings the Spanish lyrics of "Lamento gitano." "How beautiful," says Mr. Nakano. "And how odd that a Japanese song has been translated into Spanish." His nationalistic ardor enflamed, Paredes insists forcibly that it is the other way around, "Insisto en que es canción mexicana. Oiga usted. . . . A una canción mexicana le han puesto letra en japonés" (Pardon me, but I insist that this is a Mexican song. . . . A Mexican song that has been translated into Japanese). Taken aback by Paredes's impolitic ire and mindful of the fact that however he identifies himself, he is after all an American soldier, his more diplomatic hosts concede and let Paredes have it his way. Suddenly aware that he is acting like a boorish American and that he has not convinced anyone about his or the song's Mexican identity, Paredes departs the restaurant and Gamagori, understanding for the first time the confused nature of the transcultured world he has entered in occupation Japan. Back in Tokyo a few days later, he writes, strolling the Ginza and browsing the black market stalls in search of a guitar, as if stalked by the embarrassing scene in the Gamagori restaurant, he comes across the sheet music for "Lamento gitano," in Japanese, translated into English, advertised as an American tune.

In one of his very first articles for *Stars and Stripes* on March 24, 1946, headlined "A Sure Sign of Spring," on the opening of the first art exhibition in Tokyo after the war, Paredes describes the effects of what he now calls the "occupational overtones" produced by this interlayering of cultural expressions in the works on display at the Ueno Museum in Ueno Park.[22] Paredes here observes that along with the usual subjects of traditional Japanese paintings, engravings, and assorted print styles representing "Japan's pine trees and mountains," new forms using the colors of the traditional kimono but experimental in style and method were represented. The nude as a subject, off limits during the austerity of wartime Japan, according to Paredes's unnamed informant, was now amply represented, with "Goya-like abandon." Even more telling in terms of Paredes's recognition of an emerging Japanese cultural self-consciousness that not surprisingly included a pronounced American presence were the paintings of "American soldiers, including a sergeant playing cards," "a green-uniformed Marine, pipe in mouth," and "a Tokyo street scene cluttered with jeeps and American Army signposts."

But perhaps the most arresting images in Paredes's description of the art show are two paintings, one "a vividly-colored picture of a battered artillery piece overgrown with flowers," the other "a painting of bombed-out Tokyo Central Station with the subtly melancholy title of 'Winter Day.'" Countering the shock of defeat represented in these mournful paintings are images of work and peace as well, depicting "workers with hammers in their hands, . . . farmers tilling the soil," with titles such as *Back to the Soil* and *War, Peace, and Reconstruction.* Through the Civil Information and Education (CIE) section, MacArthur exercised supraconstitutional powers over all matters political and social. In the case of the visual and pictorial arts, "SCAP frowned on paintings of bombers, warships, or imperial shrine archways," writes Paredes. In his reading of these paintings, clearly appearing just below the radar screen of the occupation censor, Paredes is sensitive to the fact that Japanese artists were finding ways to express in the new modes available to them thoughts and emotions that had not been allowed by the Japanese wartime governments and that were now, in turn, forbidden by the new Allied occupation overseers.

Even while the basics of food, clothing, and shelter were in direfully short supply, "Japanese cultural consumers devoured American movies, jazz, and dancing" (Molasky 9). Writers, musicians, artists, filmmakers, and other cultural intellectuals like popular songwriters, thrived in the postwar atmosphere of unbridled energy and creativity, developing ingenious methods of circumventing censorship restrictions. With the collapse of Japanese wartime censorious mores, and despite SCAP's censorship policies, eroticism and the risqué blossomed in the same spirit of irrepressible energy and iconoclasm as had the black market. Documenting the ubiquity of this newfound erotic vitality in another story published a few days later, Paredes returns to the subject of cultural production in an article about the number one pop song on the Japanese radio airwaves. As in the case of the art show at Ueno Park, Paredes allows the material to speak for itself.

In this case, too, as in the restaurant in Gamagori, what catches Paredes's attention is the sensuality of music. The astonishingly upbeat tune titled "Ringo no uta" ("Apple Song") seems at first hearing to be an innocuous little ditty about delicious red apples. In reality, the song is a suggestive play on words, alluding to the novel and frowned on "forbidden fruit," the new fashion of full lip kissing. Paradoxically, while American film censors were wary of the newly liberated eroticism, they were nevertheless endorsing kissing scenes in the new Japanese cinema as an element of the new democratic norms that they were promoting.[23] For their part, the Japanese wondered at kissing: "Was it aesthetic? Was it hygienic? Was it Japanese?" (Richie 19). In his discussion of the "Apple Song," Dower points out, "There had been no tolerance of satire in Emperor Hirohito's war-mobilized nation, and precious little place for frivolity. This may help explain why the first great popular expression of relief and hope after the defeat involved an utterly frivolous paean to an apple" (*Embracing Defeat* 172).

From an otherwise remarkably unmemorable musical titled *Soyokaze* (*Song of the Breeze*) released in October 1945 (Sado Hachiro and Majime Tadashi), the "Apple Song," as Paredes notes, stands in sharp contrast to some of the darker, more somber scenes rendered in the paintings at the Ueno Museum art show. "A two-quarter time melody not quite Japanese" focusing on a lightness and airiness bordering on inanity, the "Apple Song" offers an escape from hard times and lightly points toward a new Japan (" 'Apple Song' in Number One Place," March 30, 1946). Paredes writes: "From the words it seems that the lyricist kissed a red, red apple. Then there was silence and gazing at the sky. The apple did not say anything at all to this show of affection, but the writer says he knew what the apple was thinking about all the time." That is the literal translation. Yet "the words mean much more than that to the people of Japan," continues Paredes. "The real meaning in unabashed English . . . would be as follows:

'I kissed her apple-lips; / She looked silently at the sky. / I could understand her mind. / Apple-lips, I love you—/ Beautiful apple lips.' "

The erotic power of full lip kissing unleashes inexpressible desires that can be understood from the glance of an eye or the turn of a phrase. Brightly colored dresses, high heels, and red lipstick were the fashion codes that identified a woman as one of the taxi dancers or a *pan-pan*, one of the army of women of the night who "fraternized" with American GIs. The multiply metonymic "apple-lips," figuring both a woman, her identifying red lipstick, and her eroticism, mark "Apple Song" as a gloss on the code language for the newly liberated Japanese sexuality. Paredes observes that "university students and other purists" say, "It's a corny song. . . . It stinks!" Yet he adds, "the great majority of the Japanese people don't seem to think so. Laborers, office girls and geishas, they all sing 'Ringo no uta.' " Drawing on his own rich experience with the power of popular music from his border radio days on megawatt-blasting superstation XERA, Paredes knows that mass culture appeals on a fundamental level to our deepest hopes, inexpressible wishes, and forbidden desires. As in the case of the new social dynamics facilitated by the newly flourishing Ginza dance halls and sexy cabarets, popular music here creates a space that allows for laborers, office girls, and geishas to share new pleasures by transgressing traditional social lines in the great postwar mixing ground of mass popular entertainment.

Dower points out that when famed pop singer Michiko Namiki performed the song in concert, "she threw apples to her audience while singing and they, it was suggested, tried to catch them as if reaching for happiness" (*Embracing Defeat* 173). A photograph published in the *Asahi Shinbunsha* for 1945 illustrates the symbolic associations between Michiko Namiki, her apples, and the return of desire for fulfillment on the part of the Japanese public in a time of scarcity (*Asahi* 164). At a time when real apples cost an exorbitant amount and food in general was frighteningly scarce, the "Apple Song," as Paredes suggested, offered a popular, if hardly sophisticated, but nevertheless deeply symbolic response to the privations and horrors of the recent past and the still terrifying future. Sensing, however, the underlying utopian impulses of the song and the amazing rapidity of the "confusion" of Japanese and American imaginary styles that it foretells, Paredes concludes his piece by noting, "One of these days someone is going to swing it. And then they'll really have something."

26 Michiko Namiki and the "Apple Song." "With its opening line 'Kissing a red apple . . .' and its slightly plaintive melody, the song struck a chord with people at the time and became a tremendous hit." October 1945. Courtesy of the Asahi Shinbunsha and the *Asahi rekishi shashin raiburari*.

As Paredes notes in another *Stars and Stripes* article, a review of the first postwar production of Shakespeare in Tokyo ("Tokyoites Enjoying Shakespeare Comedy," June 16, 1946), the results of the symbolic unfolding of the processes of globalization are startling, to say the least. It was more than appropriate, then, that this first production was *A Midsummer Night's Dream*, "Shakespeare's comedy about the foolishness of man and the unreality of things" ("Tokyoites Enjoying Shakespeare Comedy," June 16, 1946). The feeling of unreality of Shakespeare's play is heightened, notes Paredes, "by hearing Shakespeare in Japanese." The effect "drops the listening westerner from the heights of fancy to occupation soil with a queer thud" ("Tokyoites Enjoying Shakespeare Comedy," June 16, 1946).

Quite apart from Shakespearean productions, however, jazz and swing became the forms for expressing "the foolishness of man and the unreality of things." Within a few months of the beginning of the occupation, Paredes's earlier pop culture prediction would prove tellingly true as Tokyo would begin swinging with fancy footwork and jazzy rhythms to popular hits such as "Tokyo Boogie-Woogie," "Jungle Boogie," "Homerun Boogie," and even "Shopping Boogie," performed by the Japanese "queen of boogie," Shizuko Kasagi.[24] In a wry aside to his Mexican readers in *El Universal*, Paredes observed concerning popular dance that while American swing was certainly

27 Shizuko Kasagi dispelled the clouds of gloom hanging over postwar Japan with a spirited cry of "Hey!" in her song, "Tokyo Boogie-Woogie." 1947. Courtesy of the Asahi Shinbunsha and the *Asahi rekishi shashin raiburarî.*

in vogue, "los gustos musicales del japonés tienden más a la música dulce, al tango y al fox romantico" (the musical tastes of the Japanese tend more toward sweet music, the tango and the fox trot). He added archly on the success of postwar Latin flair: "El mexicano en al Japón ha creado gran fama como experto en el baile" (the Mexican has achieved great fame in Japan as an expert dancer) ("Desde Tokio," August 11, 1946).

Quickening the tempo and raising the volume, the war-winning transmutations in swing of traditional Japan were the audible indicators of exhilarating changes already in the wind. The final line of Paredes's "Apple Song" article mentions that the popularity of the tune was due in no small part to the fact that it was first conveyed to the public by another form of mass entertainment, cinema. Like jazz and swing, popular ditties, coupled with the power of cinema became symbolic expressions of one possible kind of change, moral as well as political liberation. Not to overdo the optimism, however, Paredes concludes the piece in typical casual understatement, observing that at present movies were not being made in Tokyo because the actors union was out on strike—fighting for a living wage.

Later that spring, Paredes continued documenting the extent to which Japanese society was experiencing confusing, wholesale change by reporting on a proposal by the Japan Romaji and the Kanamoji societies to promote the use of both romaji (roman letter style) and katakana ("stiff" style of syllable use) over the kanji (Chinese character) script. The main object of both societies, writes Paredes, will be "to effect the wholesale abolishment of Chinese ideographs without impeding the progress of current culture by means of the propagation of katakana and romaji" (May 30, 1946).

In each of these instances in his reports from the arts of the occupation contact zone, Paredes attempts to capture the uneasiness on the part of Japanese intellectuals and artists about their country's recent wars of aggression, their fear of the American occupiers, and apprehension about the rapid movements toward democratization and Americanization. Perhaps most forcefully, the feelings that Paredes wishes to represent with the historical fidelity of journalistic reporting are those evoked in images by Japanese artists focusing on their hatred of the crushing defeat and incomprehensible destruction caused by the war.

The Aztec Entertainment Mogul

In the midst of this nightmare of destruction, Americans in Tokyo were attempting to create a sense of normalcy, American style. United Service Organizations (USO) groups began touring immediately with the arrival of the occupation forces, theatrical performances were organized for the troops, philharmonic concerts booked, and even the first American beauty contest, the so-called Miss Stateside pageant, was produced. As if this idea for a beauty pageant were not bizarre enough, Paredes makes it even more delectably outrageous in his front-page spread for the special features section, complete with large double column photos, for the July 21, 1946, issue of *El Universal*. There he announces that the Tin Pan Alley impresario for all occupation cultural events in the Japan isles was, amazingly, none other than "un mexicano": "In this capital city, whenever a theatrical spectacular is produced, whenever a philharmonic concert is planned, or whenever a popular U.S.O. tour arrives to entertain Uncle Sam's soldiers, the first thing that has to happen is a meeting with a Mexican, . . . Johnny del Puerto, a native of the Aztec capital." Paredes's story documents the rise of this "chief of public entertainment for all Tokyo" whose offices were located, in total historical irony, at the grand Hibiya Theater, close to Hibiya Park, the very site where, as Paredes notes, "five years earlier the militarists rendered homage to the attacking heroes who died at Pearl Harbor."

The rise of a lowly Mexican infantryman to the high position of American entertainment czar in Japan, Paredes writes wryly, is a story "of which all Mexicans should be proud." A member of prominent Mexican military families and an announcer for popular radio stations in Mexico City before the war, del Puerto had completed and successfully pitched a project at the White House aimed at strengthening the Latin American flank of the defense effort and "uplifting the morale and culture of Latin American armed forces" in support of the allied effort. On the completion of this bravura public relations scheme, del Puerto had enlisted "in the ranks" of the US Army in Washington, DC. While biding time waiting for his genius as a radio announcer and crackerjack promoter-producer of entertainment spectacles to be recognized, del Puerto completed infantry basic training at Camp Wheeler, Georgia.

In July of 1945, del Puerto was shipped overseas. Arriving in the Philippines, he met up with the famed Mexican air force Squadron 201 (Escuadron Aero de Pelea 201), "The Aztec Eagles," a detachment of crack Mexican fighter pilots assigned to the Fifty-eighth Fighter Group of the US Army Air Force Fifth Air Corp. Flying Republic P-47 Thunderbolts out of Clark Field in the Philippines and also over Formosa, these Mexican combat pilots engaged in fierce close air support for US frontline forces. They were the first Mexican armed force to wage war on foreign soil since the nineteenth century.[25] The ranks of the Aztec Eagle Fighters numbered some of Mexico's best flyers, such as Lieutenant Reynaldo Pérez Gallardo, the son of a distinguished general of the revolution, later the commander of the unit. Del Puerto connected with Mexican buddies from the Aztec Eagles squadron, including the Mexican popular idol, "El Charro Cárdenas," and then later made his way back to the airwaves. Eventually, Johnny del Puerto arrived in Japan with the army of occupation in October 1945.

The rest, as we should say, was history. Del Puerto quickly rose to the top of the occupation entertainment industry apparatus and ascended to the role of impresario par excellence. An independent article in the feature section of the Sunday, May 12, 1946, issue of *Stars and Stripes* also reports on the American beauty pageant with full photo spread and names "Sgt Johnny del Puerto" as the originator of the idea.[26] In *El Universal*, Paredes describes how the entertainment mogul, taking pity on the troops "so recently engaged in mortal combat," set about to remedy the fact that, except for the cabarets and taxi dance halls in the Ginza, organized nightlife in Tokyo was, so to speak, dead. He presented his latest scheme to GHQ of SCAP, and with his usual golden touch became "chief of shows and entertainment."

At the time of his interview with Paredes, conducted in Spanish, of course, del Puerto was chafing with discontent, not satisfied with bringing routine spectaculars to the occupation troops. He now dreamed on grander scales. Hoping to comfort all sorts of sad and lonely soldiers so far from home, del Puerto had just come up with the plan for the first of these spectaculars, the idea for a "Miss Stateside" beauty pageant. At a time when the world has literally exploded around your head, what do you do to begin to piece it back together? Apparently, Paredes smirks, you find someone like Johnny del Puerto to help you dream upon a star, bizarrely, if necessary. The hugely successful beauty pageant was one such product of this Mexican's transnational imagination, working overtime from within Uncle Sam's army. And an inexhaustible imagination it was too, for as he coyly admitted to Paredes, del Puerto's "golden dream" was "to build a giant entertainment center in the very heart of Tokyo, situated in the Nippon Theater which would include swimming pools, cabarets, restaurants, soda fountains, movie houses, theaters, and other forms of entertainment for the Occupation forces." In short, envisioning the one-stop shopping hotspots of a future world, places like Las Vegas and Hollywood years before their time, Johnny del Puerto fantasized "the golden dream" of the multiplex entertainment Americanization of Japan, live and in the flesh, as a truly globalized fait accompli. To see the origin of Paredes's fictional Johnny Picadero in the historical antics of the real Johnny del Puerto is probably not very much of a stretch.

Modeling Democracy

By far the most numerous of Paredes's articles in *Stars and Stripes* and *El Universal* are those concerned with the political situation of postwar occupation Japan. What Paredes offers in many of his articles are objective pieces of no-nonsense reporting, often interspersed with the personal firsthand experiences of one or another Japanese informant. These first-person vignettes really turn out to be experiences of the group masquerading as personal anecdotes through which Paredes presents his American readers with a composite subject of the Japanese people. For example, in reporting on the confusion that many Japanese, especially those in the countryside, felt about the new democratic elections process, Paredes creates in *Stars and Stripes* a representative type of the "peasant" who "does not seem to think that the caliber of the native Japanese politician will improve" after the election (April 7, 1946).

From this vantage point, he can then opine, "Defeat and bad government before the war have made even the most intelligent among the rural population cynical about their officials." In response to the reporter's question about the quality of the candidates up for election, "an average Japanese farmer" complains about the indiscriminate plastering of election posters, a waste of hard-to-find paper: " 'See,' said one farmer, 'all those posters advertising one man. And I can't repaper the walls of my house because there is a paper shortage. Are politicians in the United States as foolish as that?' " With this question, left hanging unanswered, Paredes is able to cut adroitly in two different directions. One, in the direction of the newly foolish Japanese politician, and, two, toward the character of traditionally foolish American politicians who are serving as models for Japanese democracy.

The next day's issue of *Stars and Stripes* presents Paredes's front-page story with the photo of a massive protest march on premier Kijuro Shidehara's official residence by left-wing social democrats and communists in opposition to the premier's food distribution policies. Three hundred Japanese security police confront the demonstrators on entering the grounds of the premier's residence, and the affair, according to Paredes's report, "soon became a series of small melees." Only when a detachment of American MPs showed up firing several shots in the air did things settle down. "During the rioting with the police, a *Stars and Stripes* reporter moved among the fighting groups unmolested," Paredes writes. As a "representative of the American Army," he thus finds himself to have become an inadvertent arbiter of the Japanese civil strife when "several of the demonstrators came to the reporter . . . and complained that the police were shooting at them with pistols." He concludes his piece by voicing the complaints by the demonstrators, including those of one Setsuko Hani, a "woman Communist," that "there could be no democracy in Japan while men like [Shidehara] were in power" (April 8, 1946). The substance of Paredes's reporting often turns precisely on this point, attempting to show how the men coming to power under the occupation distressingly often do not represent authentic democratic interests. The collapse of the authoritarian state has simply led to a new stage of conflict in the modern public sphere over the very feasibility of self-determination itself.

Democracy and the Parable of the Melons

The question of what democracy meant stood at the forefront of the minds of the Japanese from the first days of the occupation. Understanding what it meant involved the refashioning of the very meaning of "Japan" itself. Paredes dramatizes the startling salience of the question in one disquieting vignette in one of his columns in *El Universal.* There he reports that in the autumn of 1945, having just landed in Japan with the first of the Allied occupation forces, he happened to be assigned to visit "un villorrio," a little one-horse dump of a village high up in the mountains:

> In order to reach the village I had to travel hours by train and then still more hours on foot. My mission was to interview the peasants concerning their economic situation to ascertain the shortages of provisions in the region. I was the first allied soldier to visit this place and I found the peasants as cooperative as they were hospitable. A few weeks earlier, they had been cutting bamboo poles and sharpening their points in order to defend themselves to the last man against the expected allied invasion, which had been avoided only because of the surrender. I found it difficult to question these villagers not because of any lack of cooperation on their parts but because they had so many questions for me. Almost all of them were variations on the same theme.

"What is democracy? How does it work? Exactly what is it? Please explain to us what democracy is." (July 26, 1947)

The plaintive nature and artless simplicity of the questions posed to Paredes by the peasants in this small village were not questions restricted to the backwater districts. They echoed throughout Japan, not just in metropolitan Tokyo. In the same column, Paredes narrates, again in Spanish, what he calls "La parábola de los melones" ("The Parable of the Melons"), which he heard from a Japanese political commentator:

> When the American "honeydew" melon . . . is planted in Japan it doesn't produce a fruit which has the same taste as that of the fruit planted in the United States. Differences in the climate and the Japanese soil are bound to be replicated in the end product. A honeydew melon planted in Japan ceases to be American and becomes instead a product of Japan. The same thing must happen with our enthusiasm for democracy. Even though America may be our mentor in the sowing, the result will have to be not American but Japanese with all of the inevitable variations caused by our differences of temperament and economic circumstances. When it matures our own native fruit of necessity will have to be something different from the fruit that furnished the seed.

Cultural interaction is not simply a one-way street. Paredes makes the point that as much as Japan was beginning a process of Americanization, an equally necessary Japanization of American forms and ideas was underway. With the collapse of Japanese feudal militarism, and the ascendancy of democracy worldwide, the very system that their leaders had "mocked, ridiculed, and dismissed as weak and incompetent," the Japanese people, with their "antlike tenacity" were "convinced now of the power and efficacy of democracy" and devoted all their energy to make themselves, first and foremost, "democratic." His column ends with the cautionary thought that democratization will need to be syncretic in style and hybrid in form. These were not new matters for Paredes. On this very different stage in Japan, the lessons that Guálinto Gómez had not learned in *George Washington Gómez* were rehearsed for Paredes with the momentous recalibration of the meaning of national culture and how one adapted, or not, the seed of foreign fruits. Many in power before the war, as well as those who now sought to fill the vacuum caused by the collapse of the prewar institutions, regarded the gift of democracy less charitably and with much graver reservations than had Paredes's source for the "Parable of the Melons." Many Americans agreed, believing that "the Japanese were utterly incapable of comprehending American-style democracy" (Dower, *Embracing Defeat* 284). In moments such as this one in *El Universal*, Paredes articulated for his Mexican readership that the Japanese were not taking to Americanization and democratization easily. He was coming to see how their embrace of American values, ideals, and fashions were likely to be as problematic and as fraught with ambiguities as were the seemingly innocent yet powerfully charged embraces in the taxi dance halls of the Ginza. Blurring the boundaries between "home" and "alien lands," Paredes's journalism offered his Mexican, Spanish-language readers a dramatically new, transnational perspective on the meanings of conquest, occupation, and cultural migration.

In Pharaoh's Army

Describing in *El Universal* the same demonstration in front of the premier's official residence that he covers in the *Stars and Stripes* article mentioned above, Paredes points out that in the midst of the bloody confrontation between the communists and the Japanese police, after shots rang out, members of the throng crowded around him as the literal representative and palpable embodiment of democracy. In demanding to voice their opinions to the prime minister, "Evidently, the demonstrators thought that they were practicing democracy pure and simple and that therefore it was my responsibility to defend them" (July 26, 1947). Yet, Paredes reported in *El Universal*, "The ordinary citizen continues to fly in pursuit of democracy. He doesn't ponder, 'Is something good? Is it bad?' He asks instead, 'Is it democratic?' Little by little the Japanese is beginning to forsake the idea that one must always obey 'the patriarch of the family,' whether it be the industrial family, the political family, or the national family."

An article in *Stars and Stripes* also deals with politics and democratic forms, but turns in particular to the lot of the Japanese peasant, who, history shows, has always taken it on the chin: "The Japanese peasant has supplied canon fodder to the Army and sold his daughters into prostitution to keep out of debt" ("Another Food Problem," April 14, 1946). In the midst of food shortages of such magnitude that it had been reported that "17 geishas in a fashionable hot springs resort had to take side jobs to keep alive," Paredes writes that "a *Stars and Stripes* reporter" visited a prosperous village to see for himself why the country was not able to feed itself. Starvation was a chief cause of death, especially among the outcasts of Japanese society—war widows, orphaned and homeless children, even mentally or physically disabled war veterans. He discovers that within these catastrophic conditions, the peasants are learning capitalist economics all too well. Instead of selling their rice on the controlled legal market at a prescribed low price, they are quietly siphoning as much of their crop as they can to the black market, even though the farmers of this village claim they are not doing so. Government bungling in the distribution of fertilizer required that farmers must turn to the black market to buy their share. Owners of fertilizer plants were waiting for prices of fertilizer to be deregulated before they increased production. "The capitalists won't get [their plants] in operation again until they get their price," claims one farmer. "If we have to buy fertilizer in the black market, how can you blame us for selling our rice in the black market too?" another villager asks. Even at the rural fringes of occupation Japan, Paredes finds the economic trafficking of the dark market transforming traditional culture and society. In response to Paredes's question, "Is the average farmer growing rich as some newspaper articles say?" the peasants respond: "Newspapermen are city people." Paredes's conclusion: "Maybe some farmers in the suburbs are making money from the city people, . . . but most peasants are as poor as ever." The article concludes with Paredes's observation: "Farmers also want to see in cultivation the land that was taken for war factories and airfields. Airfields were constructed on the best rice land, since runways have to be level" (April 14, 1946). In these articles from the agricultural prefectures, Paredes is delineating the despair, cynicism, and opportunism, as well as marvelous expressions of resiliency, creativity, and idealism "of a sort possible only among people who have seen an old world destroyed and are being forced to imagine a new one" (Dower, *Embracing Defeat* 44). With discomfort and uneasiness, he registers in these articles in *Stars and Stripes* and *El Universal* the appalling realization that as a soldier in Pharaoh's army, he represents to the Japanese the power and interests of American might and the traditions of its ambiguous democracy.

Hideki Tojo and the Spectacle of Justice

Over the following six weeks of April and May 1946, Paredes was to write twelve additional articles on the ultimately successful attempt by conservative and reactionary political elements, aided by American interests in the person of SCAP, to win control of the postwar government of Japan. The matters of electoral reform, land reform, agrarian improvements, food distribution, black market control, sexual and gender politics, and the accomplishment of the conservative agenda for the "reconstruction of Japan—mentally and physically, to rebuild the morale of the Japanese people and to give them international faith" (*Stars and Stripes*, April 16, 1946), continued to form the core of Paredes's reports. In this period of his reporting for *Stars and Stripes*, the dominant mode is that of irony. Paredes seems always ready with a turn of phrase, an unattributed quotation, a constructed composite character, or more subtle rhetorical ruses such as understatement, juxtaposition, or sardonic phrasing to signal the fact that American "democratization" during the occupation was clearly cast in an anti-communist, developing cold war mentality. In the cases of the arts, the press, and labor, "MacArthur advocated both a free press and labor unions, but would not tolerate either criticism of the Occupation or crippling strikes" (Ehrlich 45) such as the strikes in the movie studios. In the person of the new imperious figure of authority, MacArthur, SCAP was no less than "a supra-constitutional authority using unavoidably dictatorial methods to establish democratic rights in Japan" (Spaulding 13). In October of 1945, one Japanese observer had commented that SCAP policies of "reform from on high" smacked of "rationed-out freedom" and democracy by fiat (qtd. in Dower, *Embracing Defeat* 70). Given these contradictions of power, nothing less than familiar to someone who hailed from the periphery of the reach of American democratic ideals, Paredes's oppositional politics in *Stars and Stripes* proceeded under the signs of irony and paradox.

Nowhere were irony and paradox more necessary in Paredes's reporting for *Stars and Stripes* than over the subject of the international military tribunal for the Far East, the war crimes trials in Tokyo. Beginning in early April 1946, Paredes became the lead reporter for *Stars and Stripes* on the matter of the military tribunal and its spectacular show of international justice. In the April 30, 1946, issue, Paredes's front-page story details the indictment of Hideki Tojo and twenty-seven other defendants for "crimes against peace, conventional war crimes, and crimes against humanity." Charged with "planning, preparing, initiating and waging wars of aggression in violation of international law and treaties," the defendants were also to be tried for murder in having instigated by their leadership numerous "crimes against humanity." Paredes points out that the defendants are also accused of "surprise attacks," "using poison gas," "promoting the use of opium to weaken the will of the Chinese people," and "poisoning the minds of the Japanese people" by teaching them "harmful ideas of alleged racial superiority of Japan, her peoples of Asia, and even of the whole world."

In a follow-up article published the next day, May 1, 1946, Paredes gives the defendants their rejoinder, quoting Dr. Tadashi Hani, one of the Japanese defense lawyers, as saying "Tojo and other war crime suspects may be found guilty of breaking the peace, but they are not guilty of the charge of murder." Paredes also reports the defense contention that while in Nuremberg Nazis were being tried for genocide on the basis of masses of incontrovertible evidence, no evidence of the sort had been brought forth to indicate that Japanese leaders ever gave genocidal orders in the Asia Pacific theater of war. Furthermore, Paredes observes, the defense contended that the trials were "not proper" because of the "lack of good interpreters and competent Japanese lawyers." From his own experiences in south Texas, Paredes well knew the power of language as a tool of justice and injustice, and he returns frequently in his reports to the matters of translation and linguistic competency. Here, he is also careful to mention that the Tokyo metropolitan newspapers applaud the indictments to the extent that they might constitute a "supreme warning to all remaining reactionary forces in Japan." The warning goes out especially, he notes, to those now self-styled "liberals" and "pacifists" who despite having cooperated with the militarists before and during the war, are currently endorsed and legitimated as "democrats" by SCAP.

Paredes reports in the May 7, 1946, edition of *Stars and Stripes* that Hideki Tojo in response to the accusations registered his plea: "He said loudly, 'On all counts I plead not guilty.'" Paredes goes on to say that the defense argued that by tradition from time immemorial, war constituted a legal means of political action in international affairs. War as such, then, "is not a crime and . . . the very existence of inter-

28 Américo Paredes and Japanese friends, Tokyo, c. 1946. Courtesy of the Américo Paredes Papers, 1886–1999, Benson Latin American Collection, General Libraries, University of Texas at Austin.

29 Américo Paredes on Avenue Z, Tokyo, c. 1946. As soon as the US occupation army entered Japan, it redrew cities according to the American system of avenues and streets. In the Ginza and other places, English street signs often confused the local populace. Photograph courtesy of Alan and Vincent Paredes.

30 Américo Paredes's lead article on the indictment of Japanese war leaders for crimes against humanity, April 30, 1946. Reproduced with permission of *Stars and Stripes*, a Defense Department publication. © 2003 *Stars and Stripes*.

national law on warfare showed the legality of war as an instrument
to settle disputes between states in absence of an international legislature" (May 15, 1946). Defense attorney Captain George A. Furness
argued that since the very same nations sitting in judgment of the
Japanese defendants on the tribunal charged them with their crimes,
"it is obvious these nations believe the accused are guilty and should
be punished." Furness continued that the trial "can neither be fair,
legal or impartial under the circumstances of its appointment and
therefore has no jurisdiction." In Paredes's account, it is clear that the
main defense argument is that "nations fresh from the heat and hatred
of war" should not sit in judgment on the defendants (May 15, 1946).
The American chief of prosecution Joseph B. Keenan had successfully pursued judgment against high-profile American gangsters like
"Machine Gun" Kelly in the 1930s, but in his present attempt to cast
the Japanese leaders as hoodlums and gangsters, it was obvious that
he was well past his prime.[27] Paredes describes Keenan as maintaining
that "it would be necessary to bring men from Mars to get a neutral
court in this case. . . . But the test of impartiality, [Keenan] added,
was the conducting of proceedings in open court under the scrutiny
of the Japanese people and the whole world" (May 15, 1946).

What was indeed embarrassingly obvious under scrutiny was that
the European powers and the United States alone were seated in judgment of Japan. The tribunal neglected "Japanese aggression against
other Asian countries" (Igarashi 26). This was so even while the European nations continued to be colonial powers with records of imperialism longer than and at least as harsh as Japan. None of the colonized
nations they intended to hold onto now after the war was allowed representation on the tribunal. For many Japanese, as Paredes, too, had
come to believe, "the Allies had their own charges to answer . . . as regards the Pacific War" (Harries and Harries 175). In particular, many
believed that "the prosecution had failed . . . to prove Japan's sole responsibility for starting the war; and in what followed, America in
particular bore its share of guilt—Hiroshima, Nagasaki, and the in-
cessant incendiary and napalm raids on the residential areas of Japan's
cities, towns, and villages" (Harries and Harries 175).

Paredes's newspaper accounts of the proceedings of the tribunal
establish what historians have documented, "the trial's many un-
fairnesses, its weaknesses in procedure and, from an international
perspective, weaknesses at law" (Harries and Harries 175). In his
articles, while maintaining strict journalistic objectivity, Paredes at-

31 The military tribunal for the Far East, *Pacific Stars and Stripes*. The so-called Tokyo tribunal opened on May 3, 1946. Photograph from *Pacific Stars and Stripes*, May 4, 1946. Hideki Tojo with his "gleaming bald pate" stands in the middle of the first row of the dais for the accused, behind the two rows of desks for the prosecuting and defense attorneys. Shumei Okawa, in white, stands directly behind Tojo. Reproduced with permission of *Stars and Stripes*, a Defense Department publication. © 2003 *Stars and Stripes*.

tempts constantly to represent the Japanese defendants, especially Hideki Tojo, in a manner that grants them their due measure of humanity in the face of their demonization by the prosecution, other media, and American public opinion in general during the war crimes trials. He describes, for example, the chief justice Sir William Webb's terse labeling of normal defense motions for "specific findings of fact" as "almost contemptuous" and notes Webb's subsequent refusal to remove from indictment two defendants who had not been able to hear the accusations being made against them because of their prolonged hospitalizations. Yosuke Matsuoka, suffering from tuberculosis, had been "confined to an isolation ward of the Tokyo Imperial University Hospital" since early in the trial, while Shumei Okawa, "removed after his strange actions when the court opened" was now diagnosed as "suffering from a severe mental disease or disorder" (June 4, 1946). In each of these instances, understatement, indirection, and adept rhetorical placement of direct quotation allow Paredes to be journalistically neutral while conveying a composed dismay at what he had increasingly come to believe to be, at best, a hypocritical charade and, at worst, a prolongation of racist warfare. The rush to judgment had robbed events of their historical character and projected them onto the stage of spectacle.

Perhaps the most spectacularly compelling moment depicted in all of Paredes's *Stars and Stripes* articles occurred on May 3, 1946, the day of the opening of the military tribunal for the Far East. With a theatricality that bordered on voyeurism, the trial was conducted in full operatic irony in the former Japanese War Ministry building in Tokyo. The historians Meirion and Susie Harries point out that it is probably "unkind to stigmatise the packaging of the IMTFE as a melodrama" (Harries and Harries 135). At the time, the symbolism of using the former imperial War Ministry building as the site for the meting out of justice may have seemed appropriate rather than callow, as the Harrieses point out. In its report on the opening of the trial, entitled "War Crimes: Road Show," *Time* magazine also emphasized the spectacular quality of the event by likening it to the opening of "a third-string road company" and describing the setting as being more suited to "a Hollywood premiere" than to the deliberation of justice (24). Moreover, the *Time* article points out that "much care had gone into fitting the courtroom with dark, walnut-toned paneling, imposing daises, convenient perches for the press and motion picture cameramen" (24).

The twenty-eight prisoners were ushered into the "larger than life courtroom" wearing shabby prison garb. According to the Harrieses, they looked less like the genocidal demons of the roles they had been cast into than like "a gathering of ordinary old men" (135), or worse, "like schoolboys carrying their primers to class," according to *Time* magazine (24). In the midst of the atmosphere of reckoning and doom that the American prosecutors wished to create, the defendants "giggled and gossiped," while the chief prosecutor Keenan, "who look[ed] like W. C. Fields" ("War Crimes" 24), struggled to push solemnity. In all of its aspects, the courtroom scene took on the exaggerated trappings of cinematic justice and the spectacle of righteous deliberation, as if it were a theatrical road show produced for the benefit of history, broadcast to the world by an assembled mass of print and electronic media representatives.

From a spectacle of justice, however, the proceedings quickly degenerated first to melodrama and Hollywood kitsch, and finally, to pathetic vaudeville. The *Time* article again sets the tone of the day: "Nurnberg's impresarios had used simpler furnishings, relied on the majesty of the concept to set the tone. The German production had a touch of Wagner—elaborate vaunting of guilt, protestations of heroic innocence. Tokyo's had the flavor of Gilbert & Sullivan" (24). If not *The Mikado*, Paredes certainly has the tragicomic elements of opéra bouffe in mind as he delineates the scene in his page-one story on the opening of the military tribunal for the Far East, to which I now turn in full.

May 4, 1946. By Cpl Américo Paredes.

Tokyo—War crimes defendant Hideki Tojo was slapped smartly on his bald pate twice during his arraignment and that of 27 co-defendants before the Military Tribunal for the Far East at the War Ministry building in Tokyo Friday.

The slapper was neurotic Shumei Okawa, one of the defendants and self-appointed star performer of the proceedings. . . .

Tribunal President Sir William F. Webb, representing Australia, opened the proceedings with a statement in which he said that the coming trial was as important as any criminal trial in history.

"To our great task we bring open minds both on the acts and on the law," Sir William's statement said. "The onus will be on the prosecution to establish guilt beyond a reasonable doubt."

The day was taken up with the reading of the indictments, 47 counts of which were gone through Friday. . . .

The defense interrupted the reading of the indictment counts on two occasions. Prof. Kenzo Takayanagi of the Tokyo Imperial college, special defense counsel, interrupted the reading in the early afternoon to object that "there were substantial errors" in the Japanese translation.

Prosecution chief Joseph B. Keenan defended the indictment and the court ruled that the reading should proceed.

Okawa Entertains

After a 3:30 PM recess, during which Shumei Okawa caused a mild disturbance with his antics, one of Okawa's lawyers tried to introduce a speech into the record in which he made an appeal for his client. The court ruled that the speech was out of order. . . .

Five hundred spectators and 100 Allied and Japanese newspaper, movie and radio men were present at court Friday.

Chief of the Allied-appointed defense counsel is Capt. Beverly M. Coleman, USNR with Maj. Franklin E. N. Warren as his assistant.

Shumei Okawa, who added color to an otherwise routine proceeding, showed considerable signs of nervousness after the noon recess. He twisted and squirmed in his chair like a schoolboy and wiped his eyes as if he were weeping.

Finally, he took off his coat, revealing gray pajama tops. He unbuttoned these, and Lt. Col. Aubrey S. Kenworthy, chief of military security for the war crimes trials, reached around Okawa's neck and buttoned his pajamas from behind.

Okawa then asked for paper and pen. Lt. Col. Kenworthy gave him a pen and he wrote down messages which were later said to be unintelligible. He kept bothering Iwane Matsui and Kichiro Hiranuma who were seated on either side of him.

Suddenly he half rose from his seat and slapped Tojo, who was seated in front of him, on the head. Tojo half turned and smiled embarrassedly as two MPs restrained Okawa, who grinned delightedly at his little joke.

At 3:30 PM a short recess was called and photographers were given a chance at the prisoners. When a newsreel camera started to photograph Okawa, he rose, slapped Tojo's shining dome again. Tribunal President Sir William F. Webb had to call the court to order. The prisoners were taken out for a recess, Okawa babbling gibberish as he was led out. When the court convened again at 4 PM, Okawa was seated out of reach of Tojo's gleaming cranium. He wept through most of the last part of the proceedings.

Shumei Okawa was considered a brilliant man and a creative writer before the war. He was an officer of the South Manchurian railway and is alleged to have been the organizer of the Mukden Incident in 1931, which provoked Japanese attacks against China. Okawa was a fervid propagandist for the expulsion of the white races from Asia by aggressive war. Court officials said he had been acting eccentrically the morning before the indictments.[28]

Westward the Course of Empire

In November 1948, all the defendants were found guilty, excluding two who had died during their detention in Sugamo prison, and Shumei Okawa, who had been declared insane and whose judgment was deferred. Hoping for one more bit of symbolic "tragic expiation," after the guilty verdict, SCAP intended the executions to take place on December 8, 1948, the seventh anniversary (Japanese time) of Pearl Harbor (Harries and Harries 172–73). Due to last-minute judicial maneuvering on the part of the defense, however, it did not turn out that way. Instead, Hideki Tojo and six others were hanged in Sugamo prison on December 23, 1948.

The following day, Christmas Eve of 1948, Paredes penned a poem titled "Westward the Course of Empire":

Favored by Rome's solicitude
Hannibal drank his potion
while Cuauhtémoc swung from a *ceiba*
without benefit of trial.
You, Hideki, had your day in court
people believe in being civilized
where we are from.

Through the quickening twilight the bayonets gleam
the warheads are at ready
Carthage, city of triremes
Tenochtitlán, city of lakes
your time will come.
      Tokyo, December 24, 1948 (*Between Two Worlds* 111)

In correspondence from 1992 and in an interview I conducted in 1995, Paredes reminisced about the incident described in the newspaper article on the slapping of Tojo's "gleaming cranium" on the first day of the war crimes trial. Paredes recalled that in the article he had described Okawa's behavior as "neurotic." A lieutenant in charge of what in late twentieth-century parlance could only be termed "spin management" for the trials, apparently understood Paredes to be diagnosing Okawa as psychotic and severely reprimanded him in public. Later, attempting to atone for having dressed down Paredes so inappropriately, the lieutenant arranged for Paredes to have a personal interview with Tojo. The interview (through an interpreter) did not go well.[29] "There was Tojo, the great statesman and warrior, a taciturn man, trying to retain as much dignity as he could under the circumstances, and me, an ordinary GI, with bad and limited Japanese and nothing to say. I really had nothing to ask him. In a way, I felt sorry for him because I knew that he was being accused of 'war crimes' that had in fact been committed by both sides."

"America Is Demo*crazy*"

Paredes did mark Okawa's eccentric antics as "neurotic," but as he well knew, *neurotic* differs significantly from *psychotic*. The neurotic nature of Okawa's behavior can certainly be construed in Paredes's description of Okawa's antics, the account of the unbuttoned pajama tops, the mention of Okawa's "babbling gibberish as he was led out" of the courtroom, and the description of the double slapping of Tojo's "gleaming cranium." The *Time* magazine article on these events corroborates these details. The article, which appeared two weeks after Paredes's *Stars and Stripes* story, in fact uses Paredes's very words to report that Okawa "carried comic indifference into broad buffoonery" when he "twice darted from his chair to smack startled Tojo's gleaming pate." *Time* further noted that as Okawa was being led from the courtroom, "he babbled in high-pitched English: 'I don't like the U.S.; America is demo*crazy*'" ("War Crimes" 24).

The words that Paredes used to describe the opening day of the war crimes trials in Tokyo stand among the very few instances at which he departed from his typically restrained, understated style to articulate the absurdity of the moment, its histrionic quality, and the nature of its melodramatic mise-en-scène. In any case, Shumei Okawa, the principal surviving ideologue of the military dictatorship, an intellectual and early proponent of a kind of fascist Asianism, and apparently an accomplished racist, really was deranged. He was undergoing the psychotic erosion of his brain—by syphilis.[30] His defense counsel later rationalized Okawa's bizarre behavior by offering that Okawa had simply mistaken Tojo's bald pate for a table. The man who mistook a head for a table was later treated with one of the byproducts of modern warfare in an American hospital, the new medical technology of penicillin. He was cured and released unconditionally as a free man from the asylum in which SCAP had imprisoned him a week after Tojo and the others were executed (Harries and Harries 136).

In a column for the Mexico City daily *El Universal*, Paredes recounts the conduct of the tribunal as an alternating sequence of "dramatic and comic" moments. He speculates that perhaps because of its poor organization, or the want of professional stature on the part of the court participants in relation to the magnitude of their task, or perhaps because of the very real difficulties of meting out justice in languages as fundamentally dissimilar as Japanese and English, the proceedings were becoming a "tragedia de errores" (tragedy of errors). At center stage of the drama, seated in front of tribunal president Sir William F. Webb, was the demonized Hideki Tojo, according to Paredes, the very "symbol and personification of Japanese aggression, in whose person were concentrated all the crimes of the Japanese armed forces" ("Desde Tokio," July 11, 1946). And while the other defendants displayed a bewildering range of emotions, Tojo, the unwaveringly "dignified representative of a bloody era," writes Paredes, spent his days before the tribunal "hushed and impassive, like an idol cast in bronze, his bald cranium luminous beneath the sharp lights of the court" ("Desde Tokio," July 11, 1946).[31] Paredes offers the insight, rare for his moment in history, that as a "symbol and personification of Japanese aggression" and as the "representative of a bloody era," Tojo is the scapegoat and whipping boy for the Emperor Hirohito himself. The rhetoric of Paredes's description in the Spanish-language account of the same scene, more incisive here than in the English version, leaves no doubt where, between tribunal president Webb and stand-in war criminal Tojo, his own affinities lay. Justice enacted on the public stage was not justice, but a show that the enlightened Western powers staged for themselves.

When placed alongside the two newspaper articles about the war crimes trial of Hideki Tojo and the scene of madness that erupted during the opening day of the tribunal, the poem titled "Westward the Course of Empire" takes on special significance. Written the day after the execution of Tojo by the Allied powers, the poem adds another layer to Paredes's developing conception of how social transformation may be effected in a situation of complexly intertwined cultural strata. Different forums and different media require different strategies. The *Stars and Stripes* articles, governed by the reality of CIE censorship as represented by the lieutenant who publicly dressed him down for describing Shumei Okawa's actions as "neurotic," required one rhetorical strategy, that of subtle irony and quiet understatement. More than mere stylistic categories, however, the ironic, the parodic, and even the implied polemic are sharply marked poetic features that release Paredes's journalism from its confines to a monologic view enforced by the implied US Army censor. The Spanish-language column "Desde Tokio" in *El Universal*, free of the censor's touch and addressing a conservative, middle-class, Mexican readership, allows Paredes another cultured, lettered style, that of a more elaborately dramatic irony, a sarcasm with bite, articulated in the governing mode of the tragedy of errors. However, even in the case of the Mexico City newspaper, indirection and careful rhetorical strategy were necessary for his articles as well, Paredes soon realized. *El Universal*, too, had its own editorial restrictions that he had to observe carefully. Writing in his "Far East Notebook no. 1," covering the years 1947–48, Paredes noted about *El Universal*: "Just finished writing an article for them — and am just realizing what a reactionary paper it is. The Church is coming back fast in Mexico, and the Red witch hunt going on in the States is helping the trend" (Américo Paredes Papers, box 8, folder 12). Writing for *Stars and Stripes* and *El Universal* offered Paredes a vital education in rhetoric and language consciousness that would serve him to great effect when he returned to the American borderlands in the era of cold war and uncompromising segregation.

Together, the articles in *Stars and Stripes* and *El Universal* represent something akin to what Antonio Gramsci had termed "integral journalism," that is, one that "seeks not only to satisfy all the needs of (a given category) of its public, but also to create and develop these needs, to arouse its public and progressively enlarge it" ("Integral Journalism" 383). The ideas Paredes was gleaning here about how to create a critical audience and arouse it toward progressive action were ones that he would put to immediate use as a scholar-activist on his return to Texas in the early 1950s. *"With His Pistol in His Hand,"* his magisterial scholarly work from that period, would bear all of the marks of these lessons learned in Japan. At this point, however, Paredes was still an apprentice in integral journalism and critical praxis.

Here in these newspaper articles, as in a handful of poems written between 1945 and 1949, we find Paredes's first full expression of the necessity of linking the anti-imperial struggles of the peoples of the United States–Mexico borderlands with those of the people of Asia, and historically with the fates of conquered nations globally. Referring ironically to the rhetoric of progress activated in works such as George Berkeley's 1726 poem "Verses on the Prospect of Planting Arts and Learning in America" and Emanuel Leutze's nineteenth-century American expansionist-era mural in the US Capitol building titled

32 Américo Paredes in the US Armed Forces Institute offices, c. 1947. USAFI, a branch of the Civil Information and Education (CIE) Office of SCAP, offered over 450 courses for GIs. Courtesy of Alan and Vincent Paredes.

Westward the Course of Empire, Paredes's poem of the same title reflected on the newly globalized achievement of nineteenth-century American expansionist ideology.[32] Connecting his personal experience with Tojo to the grander course of global history by apostrophizing him, "You, Hideki," Paredes articulated his passionate sense of injustice by writing a poem of pathos, grief, and regret. Less an expression of the poet's lyrical self than of transhistorical relations of power, the poem invoked the long traditions of the elegy and apostrophe to focus on the courses of history and temporality beyond individual memory. Taken as a whole, then, the illocutionary force of these lyrical and journalistic writings was to articulate new understandings, mixing styles, forms, texts, people, acts, and memories in a process of critical expression. More than expressions of nostalgia or regret, Paredes's writings in English and in Spanish from Japan echo across linguistic worlds and cultural spaces, reverberating with pathos in their accentuation of Hideki Tojo's iconic gravitas and dignity being played out under the bright lights of history's judgment that reflected off his "gleaming cranium."

Subaltern Modernities

The articles that I have been describing are not the usual sorts of pieces that one finds in the pages of post–World War II *Stars and Stripes* or *El Universal*. It is true that many of the writers for the army newspaper were not typical newsmen; several of them were working-class men (there were no women on the staff of *Pacific Stars and Stripes* during the period) whose sympathies for labor and democratic ideals became evident in the kinds of stories they wrote. All were subject to the censorship imposed by CIE and their own political and ethical predilections. Paredes's articles walk a remarkably fine line between objectivity and well-tempered ironic criticism in their reporting on the Americanization of Japan. When one recalls that his predecessor as the staff political writer had been shipped home in disgrace as a "communist" for taking his job too seriously in the emerging red-baiting era of early cold war America, it is nothing short of astonishing to see how biting Paredes's reports frequently turned out. In fact, they serve as verbal masquerades, preludes to and essays (in an almost Montaigneian sense of *essai*) in the critique of social injustice that Paredes would undertake with his scholarly writings on his return to Texas in 1950. Like his literary works, his *Stars and Stripes* and *El Universal* articles constituted versions of the kind of resistance writing that Gramsci described as "skirmishes" in the "war of position" ("War of Position and War of Manoeuvre" 225–26).

In Asia, Paredes had experienced forms of imperialism, colonialism, nationalism, racism, class oppression, and sexual domination different from the ones he already knew. He had witnessed how Japanese, Chinese, and Korean writers, filmmakers, artists, songwriters, and everyday citizens struggled to render American modernity into their own equivalents through neologisms and other newly constructed meanings, resulting in uniquely Asian understandings and practices of modernity. That experience of difference proved crucial in the development of his ideas concerning the links between national culture, citizenship, vernacular identity, and the discursive understanding of their interrelationships under the twin terms of *history* and *folklore*.

Fifty years before the late twentieth-century focus on issues of globalization, transnationality, coloniality, and their relationship to history, power, knowledge, and subaltern modernities, Paredes explored the conditions of border knowledge. In these prospective versions of subaltern modernities, folklore and history serve as the repositories of border knowledge from a *trans*cultural perspective across a hemispheric horizon, North to South but also, as we have seen, East to West. Although our conception of Paredes's later work in folklore and ethnography has been correctly informed by an appreciation of its insistence on the racial politics of Texas and the borderlands during the first half of the twentieth century, it is clear that we must now add to this conception another axis.

During Paredes's time in Japan, a uniquely Japanese hybridity emerged from the contact with the American occupation. From the debris of disastrous defeat, a new national identity was being produced "that could encompass the memories of loss and devastation through the realm of everyday culture rather than through abstract political discourse" (Igarashi 12–13). In Japan, Paredes witnessed and documented how postwar Japanese society constructed narrative strategies to create continuities that masked the historical disjunction of defeat and transcended the loss it had endured.[33] How the experiences of these years and his understanding of those narratives of defeat contributed to the production of Paredes's writings of the 1950s, and particularly so to his seminal work *"With His Pistol in His Hand,"* is a matter that has not yet been fully comprehended by scholars of the American borderlands. These experiences and understandings help explain why in *"With His Pistol in His Hand"* Paredes would offer an ironic parallel between the executions of Anglo-Texan prisoners by the Mexican army under Santa Anna in Texas in 1836 and those of American prisoners by the Japanese army in the Pacific at the end of World War II. "Had Santa Anna lived in the twentieth century," writes Paredes in 1958,

> he would have called the atrocities with which he is charged [by contemporary American historians] "war crimes trials." There is a fundamental difference, though, between his execution of Texan prisoners and the hangings of Japanese army officers like General Yamashita at the end of the Pacific War. Santa Anna usually was in a rage when he ordered his victims shot. The Japanese were never hanged without the ceremony of a trial— a refinement, one must conclude, belonging to a more civilized age and a more enlightened people. (*"With His Pistol in His Hand"* 18–19)

When Paredes finally returned to the United States, he did so with the experience of having witnessed the emergence of America as a global power. Even at this early point in his scholarly career in the 1950s, Paredes was already aware that conceptions of identity and subjectivity imparted by the traditional social environment prove integral in the system of incoherent and often contradictory beliefs, superstitions, and the ways of seeing things and of acting that are common sense and folklore. In Japan, he had witnessed how everyday life was cultural through and through, steeped in traditions from the distant past of the folk in both content and form. Modernity for the Japanese certainly meant the starting point of the new. However, it also required the pulsating persistence of a past that was never fully past, requiring a concept of culture as the site of the transformation of life.[34] In his writings from Japan, we can see Paredes working out the implications of his initial observations of the deeply imbricated patterns of the interactions between history, folklore, and the particular features of national culture. All of these implications would carry over to and become the focus of his later, mature scholarly writings. His observations of the Japanese experiences of accommodation to postwar modernization provided him with a crucial model for understanding how alternative modernities functioned. The creative adaptations of the Japanese to the American occupation offered one way of understanding how new forms of sociability could emerge even from the barren landscapes of an utterly defeated culture. The transvaluations of modernity that he saw occurring in Japan demonstrated how dissent and opposition could grip one's spirit even in the midst of wholesale social yieldings to global modernization.

The questions he poses in his short stories, his poetry, and his journalism from occupied Japan and revolutionary China lie at the core of the matter of conceiving national belonging and the identity of the polity, especially as we are now engaged in what many are calling the era of transnationality and globalization. These experiences in the faraway places of East Asia changed the way that Paredes was to regard all fixed notions of national, ethnic, racial, cultural, and folk identity. With reference to China, Korea, and Japan, he came to understand the possibility of a shared Asian culture, bonded by differences and similarities. At the same time, however, he glimpsed the fundamentally unsettling dangers that traditional culture and folkism had unleashed when yoked to uncritically *völkisch* ideologies.[35] Moreover, as he notes in his personal notebooks from the period, as a racialized American he was acutely aware of the effects of racism in Japan itself, particularly about the outcast status of the "impure" Ettah class and the "primitive" aboriginal Ainu peoples of Japan.[36] When joined with the notion of a broader kind of cultural citizenship that Paredes suggests in his conception of Greater Mexico, it should be abundantly clear that the notion of national belonging he was forming in East Asia was one not based on an unproblematically folkic identity politics. It would be based instead on the inescapable conclusion that identity always involves a deep understanding of the raw politics of culture. Living in the complexities of the modern division of labor and an emerging global market would require individuals to forge affiliations beyond ethnicity and to share their fate as communities of like-minded persons. Conscious unities would have to supersede folkic bonds.

Paredes's wartime writings from Asia offer extraordinary insight to the postwar origins of what we can now call the transnational imaginary. They offer a fundamental view of the Asian world and the instrumental nature of the American war machine in the production of literal and imaginary contact zones, especially in relation to the connection between world war and subaltern identity, between world war and the emergence of the subaltern subject into the imaginaries of democratic citizenship. From Tokyo and from China, moreover, we get disconcerting insight to the place of the Asian woman's body as a site on which new subjective identities and social imaginaries were being negotiated, possessed, and occupied. Finally, the wartime writings bear testimony to Paredes's own personal transformation from a border subject with regional intuitions into a transnational citizen of an emerging global system figured by the intersecting lines of power relations, North to South and East to West.

In the aftermath of his momentous Asian experiences, it was becoming clearer to Paredes that the developing transnational American reality, where American identity was more a fluid process and less of a static fact, was to be understood as a cultural geography, or as a chronotope. In that place, experiences of the particular environment and temporality interacted with specific kinds of knowledge and ideology to create a unique sense of belonging. National identity was thus now to be understood as both discursive and real, populated by transnational persons whose shared lives intersected in complex ways with the heterogeneous meanings of symbols across two nations. The idea of a transnational imaginary is one way of describing and accounting for the differential world that Paredes saw developing globally and to which he would return to live and study after he left Japan in 1950.

In the borderlands at the mid-twentieth century, specific political and cultural features were generating a transnational Greater Mexico, spanning the real and imaginary geographies of North America and staging new cultural designs, the meanings of which could not yet even be imagined. It was a site rich with possibilities for the repositioning of citizenship, the emergence of subjectivities, and the invention of novel spaces for vernacular politics in the mode of subaltern modernity. Its structural features resembled those of the Black Atlantic as Paul Gilroy has described it, that is, as a concept capable of transcending "both the structures of the nation and the constraints of ethnicity and national particularity"(19) by allowing one to focus on the exchanges and transitions of persons *across* nation-states. Paredes's renderings of these crossings and transitions amounted to alternative descriptions of the process of modernity and rested on the idea that after the mid-twentieth century, modernity had become increasingly "global and multiple" and must be seen "from a transnational and transcultural perspective," as Dilip Parameshwar Gaonkar has noted (1). Paredes's chronicle of these alternative modernities observed a crucially important moment in the history of New World modernism and in the rise of transnational thinking among intellectuals of color throughout the Americas.

11

The Shadow AND THE IMAGINARY

FUNCTIONING OF INSTITUTIONS

> Sombras que sólo yo veo,
> me escolatan mis dos abuelos.
> —Nicolás Guillén, "Balada de los dos
> abuelos"

As if the questions of national and cultural identity and citizenship were not momentous enough in their own right, they became so in an acutely personal manner for Paredes during the summer of 1950 when, after having spent five profoundly transformative years in Asia, he desired to return to Texas with his new Japanese-Latina war bride, Amelia Sidzu Nagamine. In the years immediately after the war, Japanese nationals and their dependents were forbidden entry into the United States, even though no such restrictions had been imposed on German or Italian nationals. Because of this racist restriction, Paredes and his new wife had contemplated immigrating to Canada or Mexico where they might settle and Paredes could pursue his journalism or other public relations–type work. With the passage of Public Law 717 by the Eighty-first Congress, signed by President Harry Truman on August 19, 1950, however, their future suddenly cleared. It permitted entry into the United States to all "alien spouses and minor children of citizen members of the U.S. Armed Forces." The bill was immediately dubbed the "Soldier's Bride" law, or more colloquially among GIs, the "Oriental War Brides" bill. As reported in the *Nippon Times* of September 14, 1950, the legislation eliminated the need for special private laws enacted by Congress permitting an individual American serviceman to bring "his Asiatic bride" to the United States ("President Signs"). Restrictions did exist, however. A marriage had to have occurred at least six months before the enactment of the bill, and the prospective couple had to document a courtship of at least three months before the law applied. Moreover, the serviceman had to present proof of US citizenship, while the Japanese bride was required to provide "a copy of the bride's family register (*koseki tohon*)," the Japanese official document of ancestral affiliation. An additional requirement for the marriage between an American serviceman and a Japanese national to qualify under the legislation was "the claiming by the American citizen that he has legal residence in a state whose statutes contain no barrier to marriage between persons of different races" ("Japan-U.S Marriage").[1] These restrictions did not affect the Paredeses situation, and so on September 13, 1950, the two arrived in California as a newly minted war couple, with the questions of American citizenship, permanent residency, and national affiliation very much on their minds.

Inventing Greater Mexico

Paredes had begun composing his short stories in the 1940s and continued writing them in the early 1950s after he returned to the United States from his momentous years in Asia. Writing now at a moment of national crisis after the beginning of the cold war, Paredes drew directly from his experiences of the racial politics of border life for his postwar ethnographic writings and literary works in order to consider citizenship and national belonging in the context of twentieth-century labor markets and the cycles of modernization put into high gear by the great postwar global realignments of power. What constituted real and imaginary national difference? How was that difference symbolically activated? What role did national, ethnic, racial, or cultural identity play in the construction of real and imaginary borders? His heightened awareness of what comprises these differences after his years in Asia is what I am calling Paredes's comprehension of the transnational imaginary. In both his ethnographic work and in his literary writings of the postwar period, the *national* culture or political event emerges as a local inflection of a *transnational* phenomenon that can be read according to a hemispheric dialectic of similarity and difference.

During this period, besides beginning a family with Amelia Nagamine, completing requirements for an undergraduate degree, and beginning work on a doctoral dissertation, Paredes was also engaged in another literary project, a novel entitled *The Shadow*. As he explains in the preface to the novel, he wrote it while still a graduate student, "taking graduate courses in English and Spanish, teaching a couple of freshman English courses, and doing research for my dissertation," and he won a five-hundred-dollar prize for it. Despite this unpretentious early success, the novel did not find favor with editors and publishers, perhaps because, as Paredes conjectured in the interviews rendered in chapter 2, publishers wanted him "to give it more local color." Over the next several years, Paredes continued to rework the manuscript, incorporating the numerous "additions and revisions" suggested by well-meaning friends and editors, "patching and mending" (*Shadow* xi) to make the work more acceptable to publishers. In the end, still with no takers, Paredes claimed that "finally I gave up and turned to projects that held more promise, such as finishing my dissertation" (*Shadow* xi).

Like so many of his other literary works, *The Shadow* was a product of the vernacular imagination and the transnational border world with which Paredes's life was imbued. As Paredes notes in chapter 2 concerning the genesis of *The Shadow*, he wanted now to write a novel about post-revolutionary Mexico, land reform, the labor struggles in the borderlands, and the "irresolvable internal conflict" between emotions and rationality.[2] After his return to Texas from Asia and for the next forty years, Paredes was busy doing other things than writing novels. In the years approaching the end of his life, attempting to complete as many unfinished and deferred projects as his strength would allow, he returned to *The Shadow*. In personal correspondence of August 19, 1994, Paredes wrote that "I don't think I'm through trying to write—or to re-write old stuff."[3] The "re-writing of old stuff" in this case produced the final version of *The Shadow*.

As we have seen in the discussion of Paredes's poetry and short fiction from the 1930s and early 1940s, his prewar writings are almost entirely concerned with the Americanization of the Southwest and its native and Mexican peoples after the imperial conquest of 1847–48, as well as with the resultant human transformations that military, political, and cultural occupation required. The discourses that emerged from these nation-shaping events became what Paredes later called "the unofficial heritage of a people" ("Folklore, *lo Mexicano*" 1). While in his writings Paredes remained concerned with the fate of Mexico proper after 1848, his major interest clearly lay with the destinies of

33 Américo Paredes being interviewed on Mexican radio station XEO after the publication of *"With His Pistol in His Hand,"* 1958. Courtesy of Alan and Vincent Paredes.

34 Américo Paredes, back cover portrait to the first edition of *"With His Pistol in His Hand,"* 1958. Courtesy of Alan and Vincent Paredes.

those who remained in the occupied Mexican territories of the Southwest and the fates of those who subsequently came there from Mexico
to work and settle in the region during the massive labor diasporas of
the late nineteenth and early twentieth centuries. This almost complete focus on life on the American side of the border is as true of his
prewar literary writings as of his postwar scholarly work.

Furthermore, in addition to this concern with the changes in the social institutions of the region, in his literary work from this period Paredes also reflected on the effects on the traditional forms of Mexican
culture produced by the encroaching forces of American modernity
and transnational capitalist modernization. Traditional forms such as
the *corrido*, the *décima*, and other folk and high literary arts had once
served as the repositories of cultural wisdom and national identity,
formulating a kind of idealized cultural nationalism. Now the extreme twin pressures of Americanization and modernization severely
eroded the formerly cohesive qualities of traditional social forms. Paredes's works from this period, the novel *George Washington Gómez*,
the poetry of *Cantos de adolescencia* and *Between Two Worlds*, and the
short stories included in *The Hammon and the Beans and Other Stories*,
especially, document the reasons for this erosion and the decline of
certain of these traditional forms as expressions of cultural cohesion.

The reasons for the decline were multiple and complex, stemming
both from *external* attacks by Anglo-American social institutions on
the legitimacy of Mexican cultural forms in a modern American context and from the *internal* stresses, contradictions, and limitations of
those traditional forms in themselves. The warrior hero of the *corrido*
of border conflict, for example, a product of the patriarchal structure
of traditional communities with their intense suppression of women
and severe delimitation of gender roles, not to mention the internally
debilitating nature of their class divisions, could no longer stand up
to a fully critical gaze.

Under the pressure of this critical gaze, something else was required.
Only as an ideologically committed act of Sartrean intellectual en-
gagement, in the form of a legal brief responding as an advocate to
unjust accusations in the wholly partial courtroom of historical judgment and scholarly appeal, could the story of those formerly effective socially symbolic acts be narrated with a sense of loss. Paredes
attempted to do justice to that sense of loss and to refashion the distorted historical narratives of the day in his doctoral dissertation and

first published scholarly book, *"With His Pistol in His Hand": A Border Ballad and Its Hero* (1958). "To use legal terms, perhaps not correctly, I was writing a brief," Paredes maintained in interviews. "I was being an advocate for my people. Enough had been said about them negatively that I wanted to point to the exceptions, the remarkable ways in which their communities held together under great external pressures from discrimination and other social injustices."[4] *"With His Pistol in His Hand"* was the result of Paredes's grand fusion of aesthetics and politics into one voice of cultural advocacy.

As Paredes well knew, whatever the case for a fruitful appeal to the historical record might be, in the border regions of the Southwest, the socially transformative effects of the industrialization of agriculture had already occurred. This was especially true of south Texas, the zone that had traditionally constituted the heart of resistance for Paredes, both of overt armed rebellion and of direct political and indirect symbolic action against the worst injustices caused by the forced Americanization of the borderlands. As the old man in his poem "Guitarreros" averred concerning an idealized unitary past, "It was so / In the old days it was so." Perhaps it once had been; but after the modernization of the region, it was no longer so. By 1910, capitalist development had tended toward the virtual elimination of small farm and ranch holdings in Texas and the rest of the borderlands with a resulting destruction of all traditional peasantries. This process had not begun in nor was it limited to Texas or the American Southwest. In Mexico proper, an armed revolution was underway, induced by similar pressures from the vestiges of the colonial hacienda landowning systems and the new capitalist formations on the old patterns of communal agricultural life.[5]

After his experiences in Japan and Asia, the very paradigms of nationalist culture seemed now to Paredes to require revisionary formulations under the radical changes stimulated by the socioeconomic and cultural conditions and market forces border communities were subjected to during the Great Depression and the immediate post–World War II eras. So while his focus remained on the events north of the border, he understood now more completely the implications of the bordered nature of life in the region as a product of the Greater Mexican vernacular imaginary operating across state formations and transborder national economies. He sought to explain the complex and multiple relations among the various communities north and south of the new border that constituted his conceptual invention of Greater Mexico. Fragmentation and dissolution had not begun in and had never been limited to south Texas. The labor diasporas of the early part of the twentieth century had already displayed the developing nature of transnational forces to disrupt communities on a hemispheric scale. It was true that in south Texas "the river, once a focus of regional life, became a symbol of separation" (Paredes, "Problem of Identity" 25) after 1848. But the separation proved symbolic rather than real as people behaved as if the border did not exist. On the border "the general flouting of customs and immigration laws" occurred not so much as a form of social or ethnic protest but as "part of the way of life" (26). Now the border represented not so much a separating line as an associative field of transactions in human capital across enormous domains of social, economic, and semantic value. Thus it was that on his return from Japan Paredes devised *Greater Mexico* as a relational term to indicate the gathering of symbolic cultural forms at divisive imaginary national boundaries.

Imaginary Borders

The border created by these world-historical forces of social and economic realignment was, as Paredes would later claim, "imaginary and ill-defined" ("Problem of Identity" 25). Forming part of the imaginary, its limits for any one individual were "not defined by the Customs and Immigration offices at the border" (Paredes "Folklore of Groups" 7). Moreover, he would add, the social character of life under these new symbolic conditions, experienced as part of the everyday real, paradoxically now made "borders less meaningful than they once were" (Paredes, "Problem of Identity" 7).

In Japan and Asia in general Paredes had comprehended the limitations of cultural nationalism, the restrictions stimulated by a community's own internally divisive racial and class structures, and the effects of global realignment at the beginning of the cold war era. These were in addition to his familiarity with the homegrown factors of American racism and modernization. For these reasons, we can see the emergence in Paredes's writings from this whole period of a critical, nonunitary vision of the development of modern Mexican American subjectivity. That vision was dialogized across at least two languages and numerous idioms and discourses. It became Paredes's lifework to study and preserve this heterotopic, multilingual "unofficial heritage of a people" ("Folklore, *lo Mexicano*" 1) expressed in the varieties of the simple and complex forms of the verbal arts. His project became to create an ethnography of civic culture and sociability in order to understand the use of cultural idioms as "forms of social protest" that often meant much more than they said (Paredes, "Folklore, *lo Mexicano*" 10).

Discussing the nature of the "nation form" and its processes of "producing the people," Etienne Balibar writes:

> A social formation only reproduces itself as a nation to the extent that, through a network of apparatuses and daily practices, the individual is instituted as *homo nationalis* from cradle to grave, at the same time as he or she is instituted as *homo œconomicus, politicus, religiosus . . .* That is why the question of the nation form, if it is henceforth an open one, is at bottom, the question of knowing under what historical conditions it is possible to institute such a thing: by virtue of what internal and external relations of force and also by virtue of what symbolic forms invested in elementary material practices? Asking this question is another way of asking oneself to what transition in civilization the nationalization of societies corresponds, and what are the figures of individuality between which nationality moves.
>
> The crucial point is this: What makes a nation a "community"? Or rather in what way is the form of community instituted by the nation distinguished specifically from other historical communities? ("Nation Form" 93)[6]

The major difference between *The Shadow* and Paredes's other literary works is that this final novel addresses from the vantage point of the southern borderlands in Mexico all of the issues that the earlier works had represented from the American northern side of the border. *The Shadow* expressed Paredes's understanding that the fates of the Greater Mexican communities dispersed across the imaginary fields of the Americas were shared in historically real and incontrovertible ways. It represented his last great poetic attempt to show that the relationship between these real and imaginary communities was decidedly not antithetical on either side of the border. As Balibar explains, "*Every social community reproduced by the functioning of institutions is imaginary,* that is to say, it is based on the projection of individual existence into the weft of a collective narrative" ("Nation

Form" 93, emphasis original). Emerging from his transformational experiences of the transnational crucible that postwar occupation Japan represented, *The Shadow* expressed Paredes's hard-won recognition that the shared narratives of individual and collective Greater Mexican histories formed part of the processes of transculturation, economic transformations, and cultural displacements shaping and redefining nations and communities on a global scale, frequently with devastating local effects. This new social and political ground required an understanding of the imaginary functioning of the new institutions from which might emerge a "new citizenship" (Balibar, "Propositions" 723), formulated against prevailing notions of national belonging and figured in an imaginary citizenry of the Greater Mexican world.

Imaginary Citizens

The Shadow is set in postrevolutionary northern Mexico during the period of national consolidation when the fervor and idealism of revolutionary struggle begin to settle into their institutionalized forms. Here is the beginning of the novel:

> The noon was glaring quietness. There was no breeze, no movement. People were indoors, waiting for the fury of the sun to pass; outside, dogs and chickens panted in the shade-speckled dust. In the chaparral, life was also still. It had sought the cool, dark places and lay hidden from sight. There was a heavy loneliness in the hour, as if the whole world were dead.
>
> Only at the communal farm of *Los Claveles* was anyone astir. There, men in sandals and white cotton drawers worked in the fields, plowing the rapidly drying earth. They worked against time—time lost earlier in the year while their leaders made trips to nearby Morelos to talk to the authorities, while they sent petitions to Mexico City, while they marched through the old settlements where lived the original owners of the land they had "affected" and turned into an agrarian colony. Now they had the land, and they were working it, though they would have preferred to be in the shade like all men with some sense in their heads. But they stayed in the fields because Antonio Cuitla, president of the *ejido*, kept them there. (1)[7]

In these first paragraphs, we encounter the "glaring quietness" of the northern Mexican noonday sun. As in the opening scenes of *Pedro*

Páramo (1955), Juan Rulfo's contemporary magisterial novel of insurgent Mexico, we have entered a realm suspended in time and devoid of human activity, "as if the whole world were dead."[8] Under the devouring noonday sun, only men compelled to work are astir. The novel's protagonist, Antonio Cuitla, president of the *ejido*, the cooperative association at the collective farm of Los Claveles (The Carnations) keeps them there. Under his "calm, thoughtful eyes," the men work against the imperatives of time, the power of the elements, the rhythms of the harvest, and the dictates of human reason. Life itself is elsewhere and "lay hidden from sight." From this beginning, we are left to wonder what could have such power over "life" to structure its forms, rhythms, and shapes so thoroughly. Struggling to recover "time lost" in futile attempts to shape a civic life by "talk[ing] to the authorities" and sending "petitions to Mexico City," the peasants of Los Claveles must now set aside the political forms of public life and of historical nation building in order to return to the everyday rhythms of the world of commonplace agrarian labor.

In the noontime of these transitions, however, their labor is their own only in part, as they work not for mere subsistence, as before the revolution, but for the surpluses of capitalist development and modern nation building. Before the transition to the new processes of modernized industrial agriculture, their work would have been structured around the cycles of the day. This new form of work for profit rather than for sustainability requires that campesinos must work even when "they would have preferred to be in the shade," waiting for the fury of the sun to abate. To be sure, before the revolution, their labor and the land had not been their own either; it had belonged to the *hacendados*, the rich landowning families. Now, after the revolution, their labor and the land is still not their own entirely, since they work as a collective for the sake of the prosperity of the *ejido* in general. For centuries, the *ejido* system of landholding in the Indian villages had worked by combining communal ownership with individual use. The traditional Indian system of land tenure in the village *ejido* had not allowed for individual ownership of the land. Land was held in common tenancy. During the last decades of the nineteenth century, however, land reform measures had abolished common landownership rights, thus dispossessing Indians even of their communal village lands. Under the banner of land reform, the revolutionary constitution of 1917 had restored the communally held lands taken from village *ejidos* in the nineteenth century (Lomnitz 318–19). But in the meantime, everything had changed. "Ultimately an ambiguous concept of property involving state ownership of the land and communal usufruct by the villages," *ejidos* were the problematic cornerstone of revolutionary land reform (Joseph and Henderson 344). The *ejido* collective no longer worked according to the laws of traditional peasantries, but under the rule of a developing globalized modernity. As the novel opens, modernization has altered the peasants' relationship to the land, making them liable not to the rhythms of nature but to those of production.

Thus the *ejidatarios* (land grantees) have regained access to their traditional lands appropriated by agrarian reform and won back through a decade of hard revolutionary combat. However, the land is still not formally their own. Their collective labor is intended to create bounty for all and serve as the base for urban industrial development in a multifold Mexico consisting in small, educated, modern communities, balancing power with the central metropole and the forces of nature while retaining self-governance of their own affairs.[9] Their communal tenancy in the land is thus profoundly transitory, based as it is on utopian hopes that a newly collectivized agricultural economy will secure for them their own individual succession to prosperity and the status of democratic citizen—and will underwrite the belated entry of Mexico itself into capitalist modernity and liberal nationhood.[10]

The revolutionary constitution of 1917 had created a public system of education extending into remote agrarian communities. It had made land, the subsoil, and water properties of the nation and, correspondingly, had given citizens rights to portions of that national wealth. And it had specified a series of workers' rights and instituted certain legal protections from the worst predatory practices of capitalism (Lomnitz 319). But what of a private sphere from which the construction of a public sphere might be attempted? How might those persons excluded from the rights and privileges of citizenship as a civic reality participate in the enactment of new civic and cultural forms of sociability? What had changed for individual citizens in the years of the tempestuous irruption of the Mexican masses between 1910 and 1920? What explained now the resurgence of the practices of the old regime, the worsening of the lives of peasants and workers, and the growth of foreign, above all American, capital in the decades following the revolution?[11] In short, under conditions where one did not exist, how could one imagine a *citizen* who could participate in the shaping of the new nation and its new social imaginaries? Such are the questions that Paredes considers in *The Shadow*.

As he sits astride his sorrel, gazing at "his men working in the fields" (*Shadow* 1) Cuitla, a former revolutionary leader, now unwittingly replicates the role of caballero surveying his *peones*, unintentionally putting the lie to the fact of revolutionary change that he and his fellow *ejidatarios* have suffered to enact. Cuitla is a man "in his forties, with that hewn appearance of limb and features sometimes found in mestizos who have much Indian ancestry" (2). Cuitla's age and references in the text to the newly enacted Agrarian Code of 1934 (7) and flashbacks to events of the Cristero Wars of 1926–29 (66) place the time period of the novel as sometime during the mid-1930s, precisely the time when after a decade of civil war, there emerged in Mexico a new capitalist state.[12] In the aftermath of revolution, innovation was more economic than political, more corporate than individual, as the focus of reconstruction became the formation of a powerful modern state. The historian Alan Knight points out that "agrarian reform" was the central concern of the Cardenas presidency in 1936–37. "It served both as a political weapon to cut down opponents and as an instrument to promote national integration and economic development" (256–57). At issue was whether the land distribution reforms of the revolution and the turn to *ejido* collective farms "conceived of the *eijido* not as a temporary way station on the road to agrarian capitalism . . . but as the key institution which would regenerate the countryside, liberate the campesino from exploitation and . . . promote the development of the nation" (257).

In this period of postrevolutionary reconstruction, the agrarians at the Los Claveles *ejido* are engaged in the work of nation building, fashioning a new, modern, corporate Mexico from the ruins of the old country destroyed by revolution. This nationalist project and its attendant modality of patriotism had acquired in the 1920s what the Mexican historian Manuel Gamio has described as "an almost religious quality" (*Mexican Immigration* 128). But had it truly created the conditions for democratization and the flourishing of the citizen-subject?

Antonio Cuitla figures the uneasy blending of old and new in the construction of the modern Mexico. His "clothes were in the American style," but the way in which he wore his hat "at the back of his head" and gathered his shirttails "outside his belt and tied in a knot over his navel" were "concessions to the customs of his native village" (*Shadow* 2). The most obvious anomaly in his appearance on this day is a brilliant "red-silk kerchief Cuitla had about his throat." We learn subsequently that the red kerchief is his wife's, a gift he once offered her as a memento of their shared days of revolutionary combat when she was his *soldadera*, his "soldier's woman," and had followed him "all the way up to the battle line to bring him his tortillas and to pass cartridges while he fought" (53). Today, he has decided on "sudden impulse" and with "abrupt bravado," to wear it as a "brave bit of color burning bright against his sober clothes," perhaps as the only remaining emblem of those heroic days. Or was it instead a mark of "gaudiness, effeminacy, ease—those things he had put away from himself long ago" (18)?

As Cuitla gazes at his men in the field, the reality of the moment fades into a vision of the utopian future their collective labor might bring into existence:

> He saw them and he did not, for as he looked he did not see skinny little men in cotton drawers, sun-shriveled men sweating their lives into the sun-baked land. He saw green, waving fields, networks of canals, whitewashed houses, trim fences, and flower-bordered lanes. And moving about them a brown and happy race: harvesting, feasting, playing. And in the foreground, looking straight at him with confidence in his eyes, stood a brawny farmer, his child on his shoulder, his young wife by the hand, smiles of contentment and cleanliness and health. And it was all in several colors, as he had seen it many years ago on the cover of an educational magazine. (2)

Cuitla's vision here of "a brown happy race" is reminiscent of Paredes's poem "La libertad," written in 1942, where liberty is personified as a well-fed, well-dressed, well-shod Indian, standing in the confidence of destiny and sovereign over his own fate. In the poem, liberty marks a material, concrete property of collective interactions, not an abstract reification created from personal freedoms. Its features are solid, perceptible, and attainable. In the uneven development of history and world economy, situated on the margins of modernity, the mestizos of Cuitla's *ejido* stand outside the impermeable lines of cultural sovereignty. Cuitla's fantasy "in several colors" is a manufactured one, concocted "as he had seen it many years ago on the picture of an educational magazine," describing a life that might yet come to be but that is certainly not the one that the agrarians of Los Claveles lead. When the vision fades, Cuitla sees "his men in the distance, like little white dolls against the grey-green of the chaparral" (2–3), not in a pastoral garden, but against the arid land, behaving not like active agents in the construction of a collective modern mestizo nation, but like the manipulated "dolls" and "puppets" Cuitla "had seen on a streetcorner in Mexico City once" (3). Cuitla's millenary vision of an agrarian golden age looks not forward to socialism or even backward to its roots in precapitalist conditions, but to a glossy, modern, imaginary one, perhaps a product of the state's propaganda apparatus. The novel proceeds to question whether, under certain conditions, *only* imaginary communities are real.[13]

Antonio Cuitla's reverie takes an uneasy turn as he ponders the historical necessity of doing unpleasant things that "must be done" in order to fulfill that millenary vision, whether or not his men understand how those actions or that golden age will benefit them. Of his men, the narrator tells us, "He knew them well and he loved them. He had led them for a long time during the years of war, the years of killing other men who looked like you and talked like you" (3). It was for good reason that he and the men of the village had fought in Pancho Villa's legendary peasant army, the Division of the North (83). In those years of revolutionary conflict, victory had meant land, pure and simple, for the peasant revolutionary armies led by Villa in the north and by Emiliano Zapata, commander of the Southern Liberation Army. After the revolution, there would be no more rich and no more poor. All would be equal and live in peace. All would own land, and there would be no more exploiters. As Cuitla says at one point, "The great reality was the land" (67). Even one of the representatives of the prerevolutionary landed oligarchy, Don José María Jiménez, who figures large in the novel shortly, utters that sentiment in his attempted temptation of Cuitla's soul. In response to Cuitla's declaration that for the agrarians "corn is more important" than a "poetic" sensibility, the *hacendado* replies:

> "You are right. . . . And you well know how much I agree with you, how much I would like to see all these people, who are our people, yours and mine—he included Cuitla in the same category as himself with a broad wave of his hand—well fed, well shod." . . .
>
> "Yes," Don José María said, "the man in huaraches [sandals] has a place

close to my heart. And his welfare for me too is the first of all things. But in hailing the dawn of a new and better day, one may also regret the charm of the sun that is setting. (7–8)

Seeming to share in Cuitla's vision of a well-fed, well-shod peasantry as the bedrock for the new modern mestizo nation, Don José María in fact distorts it. Who "our people" are and what constitutes their well-being are precisely the issues that the revolution has not settled. Cuitla can express his desire more simply: "We have land, you have land. Why should we not be neighbors and live in peace?" (8). The revolution has not removed the question of land, which remains insoluble within the framework of agrarian commercial capitalism.

Still, the years of fraternal warfare have sharpened Cuitla's sense of loyalty to and responsibility for "the man in huaraches" whom he knew and loved, and who was "[his] burden and [his] pride." The fiery violence of the revolution had unleashed the concentrated charge of centuries of oppression, making Cuitla "an emancipated man, free in body and mind, no slave to either master or priest" (45). So even if his men cannot see where their recently won nationhood must take them, he is confident that he will know and have the conviction to take them, for after all, "They were Indians without shoes, how can they know?" (3). In the unease of these oppositions, the legacy of feudal peonage and racialized labor make the distinctions of class and race synonymous with and indicative of Cuitla's own internal divisions and of the contradictions of modern nationhood. These abstract issues resolve concretely on the matter of who wears shoes and who does not.

The reason for Cuitla's unease is his growing accommodation with the landowner-bourgeois classes who have lost property to land reform and are eager to retain the best portions that remain of their still rich and vast haciendas. Chief among the landowners of the region along the banks of the Río Bravo is the previously mentioned Don José María Jiménez, descendant of the original colonizers of the region of the northern border of Mexico, a cultured *hacendado* typical of the landed criollo class and the ancien régime, and a self-styled "modern, forward-thinking man" (24). From his "modern, neat little frame house" (24), Don José María had been "among the first to plant cotton in a large new way" and was now also "a cotton broker, who lent money on future crops to the less fortunate" (25). The revolution has transformed Don José María from a member of the landowning class into a member of the capitalist bourgeoisie through a process of gradual imbrication. Masses of people were involved in the struggle of revolution, but as John Womack argues, often "under middle class direction, less in economic and social causes than in a bourgeois civil war" (128). For this reason, Don José María's hold on Cuitla is not simply that of a reactionary feudal landowner in the process of reshaping himself into an agribusiness man; his hold is deeper than that:

> He talked eloquently of water supplies and water tables to them, for he could not talk to them of those other things which made the *estero* [estuary] dear to him, could not explain to them the link it was . . . to things that had gone before, to things these newcomer tatterdemalions knew nothing of because they were not made of the same stuff as he. How could one explain to bandits the vision of graceful wharves, of steamers coming upriver in the moonlight? Of romantic girls planning elopements, of colorful Austrian and French uniforms, of battles and horse races and the many bright and splendid things those banks had seen? (29)

In his conversations with Don José María, Cuitla comes away "feeling that in these talks there was something literary, something cultured and elevated" (6). The urbanity, learning, and wit wrapped in nostalgic romance for the era of French imperialism in Mexico, rather than the *hacendado*'s wealth alone, make for the seductions that tempt Cuitla into embracing Don José María's view of the world. That, plus Cuitla's own desire to be one of those propertied "riverbank men," rather than one of the newly shod Indians, impels the seduction.

Cuitla knows that his patron saint Anthony had resisted the lubricious temptations of the devil in the shape of a sensuous woman.[14] As a young man, Cuitla had enjoyed shocking his native villagers with his own obscene version of the legend of the saint: "If the devil ever appeared to him in the shape of a beautiful woman, the devil would get screwed" (80). In this modern temptation, however, Cuitla stands to "get screwed." His temptation will not occur through the seductions of devilishly alluring women, but through the daemonic illusions, in the form of Don José María Jiménez, of Old World urbanity and New World greed. Don José María stands as the figure of the class that benefits the most from an economic system based on native Indian rural agricultural labor, that is, on everything that is not urbane or European in Mexico. Cuitla's seduction proves dramatic because it points out the extent to which his desire for authenticity as a modern "reasoning man" (13), and which has to express itself in an alien language, forms the very basis for his undoing. The narrative now proceeds to show how the mythic structure of temptation in a spiritual sense is refashioned in the historical pattern of modern political economies.

Don José María contrives to manipulate Cuitla's own desires for acceptance as a progressive modern man as points of advantage for the benefit of the remaining landowners and himself. He amuses himself by spending "hours in Cuitla's *jacal* [hut], wearing his straightest face and talking about the most ridiculous things in the world . . . dropping at intervals a few carefully veiled ironies that were too subtle for Cuitla to understand and which he often took for compliments" (27–28). Don José María hopes to ensure that "no more of his land was affected under the agrarian law" (28) by establishing himself as a friend of the president of the communal association. To do so successfully, however, he must first arrange for the elimination of the greatest force of disruption and chaos in the region, Cuitla's "best friend" and comrade in arms, Jacinto Del Toro. Del Toro now enters the narrative as a symbol of the catastrophically destructive and unquenchably idealistic strands of the "uncontainable insurrection" (Schmidt Camacho 54) that results when the masses enter into the realm of sovereignty over their own destiny.

Hyacinthos on the Border

If revolution is, as Trotsky claimed, "a history of the forcible entrance of the masses into the realm of rulership over their own destiny," then Jacinto Del Toro is Paredes's symbol of the malevolence and violence that must accompany the overturning and complete transformation of the social relations of a society through violence (qtd. in Gilly, *Mexican Revolution* 337).[15] The contradictions of that overturning are contained everywhere in the novel, but perhaps nowhere more so than in the character's name, Jacinto (Hyacinth) Del Toro (of the Bull). A figure of centrifugal chaos and primal fragmentation, Jacinto Del Toro is "a wrecker" and "a destroyer" (4). Unlike the urbane, cultured riverbank landowners who compose Golden Age *décimas* and read eighteenth-century Italian romances, Del Toro is an "unlettered and rude" (28) man. What is more, Don José María knows cynically well that "now that the Revolution is over," Del Toro's ferociously devastating powers must be constrained (69). Only in that way can a new society be created from the ruins of the former world that is in fact not at all different from the world it replaces.

First among the contradictions figured in Del Toro is the name Jacinto itself: "*Hyacinth*, of all things" (28), as the snobbishly lettered Don José María snidely points out. Jacinto Del Toro, "the big black savage" who "was at the same time too cunning and too ignorant to be flattered," stands as a threat to the landowners in a way that Cuitla does not because Del Toro cannot be blandished by irony, co-opted by flattery, or seduced by urbanity. He stands in striking contrast to Cuitla, susceptible on all of these counts. As Cuitla himself understands, Del Toro's "thirst for more and more land. More and more trouble. More and more blood" (43) is constitutive of his being and therefore not about to be satisfied simply. He "loves trouble," says Cuitla. "He does not love the land" (4). Consequently, Del Toro stands in the way both of the landowners' desire for the status quo ante and of Antonio Cuitla's hopes for future gain from his carefully nurtured relationship with the *hacendado* class.

Among the rural folk of south Texas and northern Mexico, the name Jacinto is not an uncommon one. In fact, the name resonates with both historical and legendary significance. Historical significance derives from its allusion to the decisive battle in the Texas war of secession in 1836 at a site called San Jacinto, near present-day Houston. With the defeat of the Mexican general Antonio López de Santa Anna by an army of Anglo Texans and Texas Mexicans, an opening for the seizure of the rest of the Mexican borderlands was created for the United States. Moreover, two separate *corridos* of border conflict are directly concerned with heroes named Jacinto. One, "El corrido de Jacinto Barrera," concerns the exploits of a Mexican warrior hero during the revolution who represents the *sang froid*, devil-may-care attitude of the combative macho in the Mexican popular imagination. The other, "El corrido de Jacinto Treviño," concerns the actions of a Texas Mexican fighting for social justice in the Texas borderlands. Both songs activate the thematics of the place of heroic action in pursuit of ethnic and national identity, thematics of major concern in Paredes's *The Shadow*.[16]

The name Jacinto has another, classical, register as well. In Greek legend and as narrated in Ovid's *Metamorphoses* (10. 174–219), Hyacinthos was a young man of great beauty who fatally attracted the love of Apollo, who killed him accidentally while teaching him to throw the discus. Other versions of the legend relate that Zephyrus out of jealousy deflected the discus so that it hit Hyacinthos full in the face and killed him. In the various versions, however, the stories of Hyacinthos agree on the detail that from the bloodstained ground marking the young man's death, "there bloomed forth the wondrous [brilliant purple] flower" (Hamilton 115–16). After the death of Hyacinthos, Apollo "himself inscribed his laments upon the petals and the flower bears the markings of the mournful letters, *AI, AI* [Alas, Alas]" (Morford and Lenardon 240). The rites having to do with the death of Hyacinthos are thus clearly connected with vegetation, bloodletting, and flowery resurrection. In death, Hyancinthos nourishes the earth with his blood, and later, when the barren ground blooms with splendid hyacinths, the flowers are "his very self, changed and living again" (Hamilton 117). In Ovid, the links to commemoration and rebirth are even more striking, as Apollo cries in his grief, "You will be my theme as I pluck my lyre and sing my songs and you, a new flower, will bear markings in imitation of my grief" (qtd. in Morford and Lenardon 240). The various legends and rites associated with Hyacinthos marked the passage from the youthful verdure of spring to the dry heat of summer and the ripening of the grain and the memory of that transformation. As an underworld vegetation deity, Hyacinthos is thus specifically connected with the cycles and rhythms of death and regeneration through violence associated with the transformations of the agrarian world. The figure of Hyacinthos thus represents a close parallel to the Mesoamerican type of the *hombre de maíz*— "man of crops," the "spirit of corn"—typically a child or a vigorous young man. In Aztec, Tepecano, and Tarascan versions of this type, for instance, the man of crops dies and is buried, his corpse giving forth corn or other crops that emerge from his grave (Bierhorst 68). In both European and Mesoamerican mythic patterns, death and life are linked elements in a cycle of transformative fecundity.

Similarly, the patronymic Del Toro expresses Jacinto's primal qualities as a massively fecund character. As is true for Antonio Cuitla, whose name links him both to the temptations of Saint Anthony and to the vegetable world (*cuitlacoche*) as well,[17] the name of Jacinto Del Toro is thus doubly significant. Both his proper and patronymic names link him as a symbol and type of mourning, transition, and the rites of agriculture to the rites of death, fertility, and regeneration.

To be sure, in *The Shadow* Del Toro is primarily a symbol of destruction with little regeneration in evidence. His death marks the transition in the novel from a pre- to a postrevolutionary world, but without any assurances that the death sacrifice will fertilize the land. The mythic structure evident as a base for the novel in the use of names forces the question of why Paredes invites these associations to the deep structures of mythic thought. Neither Antonio Cuitla nor Jacinto Del Toro is, after all, a paradigm of sainthood or a fertility god. I believe the answer to the question emerges from the sedimented layers of desire represented in *The Shadow*. These levels of overlapping meaning insistently direct us toward the collective assembly of the desires deeply embedded in the political unconscious of this represented world. Figured in both images are the basic structures of the struggle between freedom and necessity—in the form of events that will not allow us to forget the ultimate fantasy of human liberation.

For Cuitla that fantasy emerges as a destructive force that overrides the fact of the deep friendship between himself and Del Toro. When Cuitla recalls their days as comrades in arms during the revolution, he remembers Del Toro "young, slim and quick, his pistol in his hand . . . killing his way to freedom" (67). Del Toro is so entirely linked in Cuitla's imagination with the elemental forces of devastation that "in all the memories he could call back . . . he saw Del Toro killing someone. A jovial man, really, but there were times when he grew restless and ugly, when he had to have his drink of blood, after which his whole being seemed replenished" (66–67). Desiring the fullness of the promises of land offered by the revolution, Del Toro is not satisfied with the arid parcels of the "grey green chaparral" that the agrarian code has allotted the former revolutionaries. He demands instead the rich dark riverbed land and the verdant fields that the landowners have kept for themselves.

> It was then that Del Toro began to talk about taking all the land up to the river's edge and driving the landowners out. And the men of the colony, discontent with their high, dry soil, tired of grubbing trunks out of the ground and living in the *jacales* they had made with their own hands, looked greedily at the cleared farms, the neat houses and the planted fields of the people along the river, and they listened to Del Toro. (29)

Now that the revolution is over, the danger that Del Toro personifies has not diminished in the least; it has only been awaiting its redirection. Since he is certainly on the verge of finding that redirection, "Don José María Jiménez had decided that Del Toro must die" (29).

At that very moment, an "agent of destiny" in the form of a man "dressed in city clothes with worn city shoes on his feet" and surrounded by "a sense of pursuit" (30) shows up and is hired by Don José María to ensure that Del Toro does not act before Cuitla can stop him. Led by the *hacendado* to the lonely place where Del Toro plows his allotted plot of land, Gerardo Salinas, the city-bred assassin, ambushes Del Toro as he bends over his work. But Del Toro does not die easily. Instead, he springs toward Salinas with "an expression of fierce hatred on his face that was almost delight" (37). Five furious shots from Salinas's automatic are necessary to bring him down before Del Toro finally falls "forward into the furrow he had begun to plow . . . [and] lay still, his face in the furrow, blackening the plowed earth with his blood" (38).

As Del Toro lies dying, Cuitla rides along a dusty rural road on his way to murder his "comrade and old friend" (5). Independently of Don José María's plot but certainly led by the landowner's suggestions, Cuitla has also concluded that in order to guarantee the gains of the revolution, Del Toro must die. He is already composing the justification of self-defense for the killing of his old friend by recalling the lines from "El corrido de Gregorio Cortez" to the effect that "la defensa es permitida":

> A man must defend himself. He would wound himself with Del Toro's revolver, just slightly, before the others came.
>
> His eyes, focused inwardly, came slowly and reluctantly to the actual world, to Antonio Cuitla riding along the dusty trail. And it was then he saw it.
>
> He saw it for an instant out of the corner of his eye. He jerked his head toward it, as the horse stopped short. The sorrel shrank back, back and down, as though gathering itself for one tremendous leap.
>
> The shadow was just beyond the animal's head. It was a dense, shapeless mass of black rising out of the middle of the road, where no shadow should be. It made no movement or sound. It was just there in the bright silence of noon.
>
> The horse shied, shaking its head. Then the shadow was gone. There was nothing on the dust of the road but the reflected brilliance of the sun. . . .
>
> The chaparral was still with the lonely stillness of noon.
>
> There was nothing there. (10)

At the liminal moment of transition in the "bright silence of noon" on a secluded country road, the destinies of Jacinto Del Toro, Gerardo Salinas, and Antonio Cuitla intersect as each begins to cross over from life to death. Moments later, still shaking off the terror of the eerie vision and "peering at the spot where he had seen — or thought he had seen — the thing" (11), Cuitla fires wildly into the thick brush at the sound and feel of movement within it and kills Del Toro's assassin. From this point on, Cuitla's own fate is set as he endeavors unsuccessfully to understand the nature of the vision he has encountered on this lonely noontime trail. What was the shadow? What enigmatic haunting has Cuitla experienced? Was it the ghost of an enemy understanding the nature of his betrayal? Was it the form of a friend compelled to warn him before fleeing this life that an assassin seeks him as well? Who or what was the shadow that crossed his path at the very moment that Del Toro lay blackening the earth with his blood?

Unlike Hyacinthos's death that anticipates regeneration, Jacinto Del Toro's transition from life is problematic in the extreme. Antonio Cuitla, whose names as we have seen are linked to temptation and to the corn, is left to decipher the meaning of that transition and of its possible connection to what he has experienced. He realizes that if solutions to his questions are possible, those solutions will have to come from the deepest and strongest roots of the ineradicable gains of the revolution, that is, from the mass consciousness that made revolutionary struggle possible in the first place. After a decade of massive suffering, death, and destruction, what has the revolution accomplished? Without that certainty, even the dead will not be safe from an enemy who can reshape "the very substance of history and memory" (Schmidt Camacho 58). This eerie event is the point of departure for Paredes's realistic novel as he examines how the opaque local effects of a ghostly global cause constitute the obvious and natural material for literature.

Susto

After presenting the killing of Del Toro early in the narrative and following Cuitla's uncanny vision of "a dense, shapeless mass of black rising out of the middle of the road, where no shadow should be," the novel then turns to Cuitla's struggle to understand the nature of his experience of the unfamiliar within the familiar. He is haunted by the memory of the shadow. As "a reasoning man" (13) with a "logical reasoning mind" (92), he does not wish to see himself as someone "frightened by nothing, like a superstitious Indian" (11). Cuitla grapples with the irresolvable tension between traditional beliefs that unseen elements from a supernatural realm can affect things in the natural world and his modern certainty as "a thinking, reasonable man" (13), that "the great reality was the land" (67). Anything beyond the material familiarity of a collective farm was mere evanescence, "a breath that the wind takes away" (67). "He had killed God long ago. Now Del Toro was gone, and he was sure that neither of them existed any more" (62). No ghosts or spirits to perturb the world.

But the questions and the obsession persist for Cuitla and along with them come memories, dreams, and finally the feverish hallucinations of mortal affliction, all of which imaginings center on the meaning of the shadow. The tales, sayings, legends, proverbs, and beliefs of his communal folk village, the entire repertoire of speech genres that make up the wisdom of the popular imaginary of the folk, which express and symbolize their shared provenance as a community, point to complexities and ambiguities that rationality cannot resolve. From that shared vision of the overdetermined nature of the real comes his conviction that the cause of his crisis is *susto*, or "fright sickness."[18] As Cuitla rightly understands, "Men actually died of fright sickness. If they believed they were going to die" (74).

What kind of fear is it that can cause a sickness unto death? What collective beliefs and fears are gathered in the thought that serves as an expression of their shared fates? A possible answer to these questions emerges as on his mortal sickbed, Cuitla drifts in and out of hallucinations and memories of the past:

> He lay there a long time, thoughts coming and going through his head, memories long forgotten, which with their bustling prevented the emergence of others that lurked in the dark corners of his mind. The Revolution came back to him in one loud dusty mass. Then the sweat and the shouting were gone, and he was back home in his village, sitting in the shade, laughing with some other boys his age while the girls went by to the spring, their earthen jars on their heads, their young hips swinging rhythmically beneath, their bare feet stirring the dust as they went. While the boys watched and laughed. Life had been good. (74)

Against the chaos of revolution, the vision of prerevolutionary village life arises with full nostalgic force. The communal agreements of that former era had created a sense of community and patterns of shared social life that in the aftermath of the revolution now seem desirable, and their passing something to grieve, as the death of Hyacinthos had produced the flower with the signs of sorrow marked on its petals. But those very same social patterns of life, governed by other indigenous "communal agreements" (*Shadow* 42), produced conditions that forced men like Cuitla, Del Toro, and innumerable others of their countrymen to seek work elsewhere. They had created conditions intolerable enough to compel peasant armies to force the *hacendados* to "turn over their land to men working under a different kind of communal arrangement, one backed by a political philosophy the old one had lacked" (*Shadow* 42). Antonio Cuitla's understanding of the differences between the two kinds of communal arrangements, the prerevolutionary one now romantically, nostalgically recalled, and the present postrevolutionary one, of ceaseless work in the noonday sun bitterly endured, is forged in the blazing heat of the cotton fields of Texas: "And now the village was gone and where he was it was hot, but with a different kind of heat, dry and fierce among the white rows. And he felt the tug of the cotton sack behind him and smelled the rancid smell of his own sweat, like old grease in which eggs had been fried. And again he was in the cotton fields of Texas, picking side by side with Jacinto Del Toro, his best friend" (74–75). Earlier, while casting through the wallet of Del Toro's assassin looking for clues as to the man's identity, Cuitla had found "a few Mexican bills," "the photo of a girl," "a small medallion," and "a clipping from a Mexican newspaper" (61). "The clipping was about the coming season in Texas and the need for pickers, the high wages being offered." All of which reminded him that before the revolution, "he, too, had gone to Texas when he was young" (61): "He had not carried a medallion to Texas, but he had taken many ignorant ideas that he had gotten rid of since. It was in Texas he first heard men talk of revolution, men of his own sort, talk about striking off their chains, and of the imprisonment of starvation. Yes, he had got most of his education in Texas. In the cotton fields and the coal mines" (62). The two moments, of pre- and postrevolutionary times, are linked for Cuitla by the common experience of the participation in the transnational labor markets of the late nineteenth and early twentieth centuries. The man who killed Del Toro is the man Antonio Cuitla was. The intervening years of crisis have altered precious little on that score, since in Cuitla's present,

Mexicans are still compelled to seek work in Texas. For Cuitla and Del Toro, Texas had held more than labor. "And Del Toro too. He also received his education there, especially at the Huntsville prison farm. Texas had a lot to teach the Mexican peon turned migrant laborer, who looked across the border for a new kind of life" (62). Texas held an "education," allowing both Cuitla and Del Toro to see their shared fates as braceros, as workers and comrades who live by the toil of their arms in the transnational labor markets of the developing commercial agricultural economy between two worlds. He had taken many ignorant ideas to Texas that he had gotten rid of since, and in doing so, he had learned about striking off the chains of their oppression and the imprisonment of starvation. Moreover, that transformation had occurred as a change in consciousness arising out of their shared activity as fellow workers within the very specific conditions of commercial agricultural labor. Through the reification of their subjectivities into racialized objects of labor, the "Mexican peon turned migrant laborer" attained class consciousness and became an agent of history. The laborers' understanding of the relations of production figured in that shared experience "in the cotton fields and the coal mines" of the transnational borderlands is the source of their potential liberation as a class. However, it is simultaneously their undoing as individuals in the crucible of the revolution.[19]

At the end of the novel and in the last paroxysms of his presumed fright sickness, Cuitla begins to see "*it* . . . the shapeless black lump" (92, emphasis original) that he identifies with the shadow first glimpsed on the day of Del Toro's death. The syndrome known as *susto* in popular belief is, according to one writer, "the loss of the spirit or soul due to a sudden shock. *Susto* may occur after a sudden fright, such as witnessing an accident or a sudden fall. This shock loosens the *alma*, or soul, from the body. Though nearby, the *alma* needs to be lured back into its person by means of herbs and rituals. The longer this illness goes untreated, the more serious the condition becomes. The symptoms include anorexia, lethargy, and depression" (Sandoval 78–79). Numerous remedies exist for *susto* in the folk pharmacopoeia. The most common one is the use of medicinal herbs in conjunction with the performance of a ritual *barrida*, or sweeping, where the afflicted person is placed between clean white sheets, with arms extended as if on a cross, and then swept by a folk healer, a *curandera*, with rosemary branches while reciting the Apostle's Creed.[20]

The aim of these healing rituals is to call back to the forlorn body the wayward soul of the frightened sufferer. Without a soul to fill it, the body remains a mere empty vesicle and the individual, no longer one with itself, is not the self. As Cuitla sinks more deeply into his illness, exactly who he is becomes the central question. What has the revolution made of him? Who is this man who shuns his wife, frightens his son, betrays his best friend, and disobeys the laws of tradition? The village healer, Anastacia Rendón, in her blindness sees as much, as her son Serapio informs Cuitla: "She is old and blind, she is not well. She has got it into her head that you are not you but someone else" (94). Her blindness links her to the shadow that Antonio now imagines constantly: "Sitting, watching. It watched him day and night, though it had no eyes" (92).

Increasingly the shadow becomes confused with and displaced by other hallucinations in Cuitla's delirious imagination. They appear in the forms of the *curandera*, rushing at him like a sacrificing Aztec priestess "in a robe of feathers, a knife in her hand" (95), of Don José María uttering his most reactionary jibes about the peasants as "apes" (96), and especially of Jacinto Del Toro, appearing "huge and black against the sky . . . with a quiet smile on his face, as if he knew something he did not want to tell" (98). All of these figures together now blend with the idea of "the shadow" to create a multivalent symbol not reducible to one neat value. As his *susto* reaches a point of crisis and Cuitla falls to the ground in choleric rage and feverish despair, he hears from among the men gathered around a fire outside his hut the beginning of a new haunting, this time from the melody of a song: "Someone was passing his fingers over the strings of a guitar, caressing them, pressing a thumb over them as one does with a ripe ear of corn, so that the notes pattered down like grain" (99).

In his final, dying moments, Cuitla hears the familiar opening chords of "El corrido del hijo desobediente," the story of a disobedient son who defies the codes of the patriarchal order through violence and lack of respect. As we observed in the earlier discussion of this *corrido*, the song tells of the interrupted transfer of patriarchal authority as the disobedient son dies disinherited by a traditional power structure that is in the end too rigid to accommodate his rebellion. In an arresting reiteration of the elegantly interlingual poem "Guitarreros" and of the symbolic system of *corrido* performance that Paredes was describing in his doctoral dissertation on "El corrido de Gregorio Cortez" (in progress at the time he was writing the novel),

Paredes returns to issues that had moved him since before his years in Japan:

> The guitar spoke its invitation to the voices, and the voices answered. They sang of the disobedient son. . . .
>
> Sword in hand, the son threatened his father, and the father cursed the son. Humbly he lay, waiting for death. . . .
>
> Let the son be buried in the wild and lonely earth. His arm will stick out of his grave, and in his hand there shall be a paper with gilded edges, on which shall be written that his was a life accursed. . . .
>
> The bull came down from the mountain. They had never brought him down, but now he came, with the herd all about him. The black bull that had never left the hills. (99)

In the song, the son is "disobedient" and "accursed" because he does not acknowledge that *his own actions* have contradicted and denied the very values of manhood, patriarchy, patrimony, and respect that define him. His curse is to have lived and died the contradictions of those values.

Watching the performance of the song from the doorway of his house, Antonio Cuitla notices that the singers performed "with their eyes shut and their heads thrown back, with an intense application to their task, as though they sang not from enjoyment but from a compelling need" (100). As the song ends, the same "compelling need" drives him to mount a horse with his last remaining strength in defiance of the conviction of his comrades that "he was already dead." And with the final lines of the song "about the bull, the black bull of the mountain in the light of the eastern star" still ringing, Cuitla rises in emblematic fury and rides "straight into the flames" at the center of the gathering, firing his pistol, insolently declaring his identity with the challenge and insult to his men, "I am Antonio Cuitla, father of all you bad boys!" (101) until, in the end, "he was left alone in the village, riding round and round the dying fire, still challenging the dark" (101).

A Social Aesthetics of the Borderlands

Paredes concludes *The Shadow* with the *corrido* of the disobedient son to underscore in the genre of musical expression and lyrical content the unresolved and possibly irresolvable dilemmas of the novel concerning the end of revolutionary struggle and the entry into modernity in the borderlands between northern Mexico and the American Southwest. Located between two nationalisms and the regulatory force of two nation-states, the inhabitants of Greater Mexico in the first half of the twentieth century were developing new relationships to work, ethnicity, identity, authenticity, nationality, citizenship and cultural integrity, that is, to the characteristic phenomena of modernity itself.

As an artist and a scholar of the vernacular imagination, Paredes was committed to an imaginative inquiry of the evolving form of the modern nation-state and of its relations to the fluctuating nature of its subject citizens in his writings. The Mexican ethnographer Néstor García Canclini has written that in the development of a modern Mexican citizenry, the "rapprochement of citizenship, mass communications, and consumption," had, among other aims, the necessity of giving "recognition to the scenarios in which the public is constituted" (*Consumers and Citizens* 28). The relations among those scenarios, Paredes came to see, were unrelentingly differential, interactive, heterogeneous, and painfully dissonant. Emerging from those modern transnational spaces was a notion of identity as a process of movement and mediation, a performance "not from enjoyment but from a compelling need" (*Shadow* 100), and, most pointedly, not constrained by ethnicity or national particularity, since those were the very conditions most caustically distorted by the processes of modernization. Acknowledging the diversity and heterogeneity of social position and, therefore, of social appreciation, claims García Canclini, "leads to finding in the diversification of tastes one of the aesthetic foundations for the democratic conception of citizenship" (*Consumers and Citizens* 28). Paredes was involved in working out in detail that notion of identity in relation to the aesthetics of the social over the next forty years of his life.

Perhaps this focus on modernity will also help to explain why at this point in the final scene of *The Shadow*, Paredes requires us to veer so sharply away from the realm of uncanny shadows to the realistic world of modernization. Writing in *"With His Pistol in His Hand,"* Paredes would later claim that "the somber, weird strain and the introduction of revenants and of supernatural signs of fatality (absent in the *romance*) are characteristic of such Mexican ballads as *El Hijo Desobediente*. . . . They give the balladry of the Lower Border a close resemblance to Scottish balladry" (143). Linked to the structural frame-works of other marginalized peasant cultures, the folk songs, popular festivals, and occult belief systems of witchcraft and *susto* that Paredes calls up in *The Shadow* appropriate the uncanny, the supernatural, and the weird to empty it of its spectral content and subvert it to express a differently coded message in the mode of romance.[21] This stress on the dialogical quality of the supernatural allows us to read its import otherwise, as an attempted tropological neutralization of the encroaching hegemony of bourgeois modernizations.

The climax of the supernatural occurs as Antonio Cuitla on his deathbed undergoes one final vernacular rite, the ritual healing of the folk *barrida*, or sweeping with a broom of medicinal herbs, in-tended to exorcise the evil spirit that has presumably possessed and altered him. Just then, at the very height of the uncanny, one last un-earthly apparition seems about to intrude, announced by the sound of a low "humming noise [that] had been hanging in the air . . . [and] grew until it became a roar" (*Shadow* 108). Once again, however, no ghost appears. Instead, materially and mechanically, "a broom of light moved across the dark and swept away the blackness" (108). This mechanized broom of light sweeping away the darkness comes from the headlights of automobiles, concretized forms of the new indus-trial technologies, signs and symbols of Fordism and their accom-panying human routinizations of Taylorism, carrying men sent from metropolitan Mexico City to check on the progress of the revolution at the peripheries of the nation. The concluding passage of the novel shows it to be surely wrong to imagine that Paredes's narrative posits a "ghost" or any other supernatural phenomenon to recuperate "an elided history and placing it in the present" (Alonzo 49). By giving reality to a ghost in a way that the novel never does, such a reading lit-eralizes and hypostatizes what in the novel remains profoundly reified. Paredes is writing realistic fiction, not gothic romance. The conse-quences of this formal and generic distinction are that the real and the imaginary cannot be separate and opposite categories but must remain relational terms, imbricated synchronically in both directions. Postulating either an imaginary or a real ghost as the resolution to the issues of the novel requires us to mix categories wrongly.

For this reason, then, the ending of the novel takes us in another direction than the supernatural. The narrator points out that in the days before his death "Cuitla had dreamed of a tractor, had seen himself enthroned upon it, driving it up and down the fields. But the dream, like everything else had been a dream" (91). The encompassing quality of the statement, "the dream, like everything else had been a dream," aligns Cuitla uncomfortably closely with Don José María, whose words that "life is a dream. . . . And dreams are also dreams" (81) refer to one of his Spanish Golden Age preferred sources of wisdom, Calderón de la Barca. It is easy to see why Don José María aligns himself with the great peninsular dramatist and the words of his imprisoned prince, Segismundo. As a genius who enjoyed both high spiritual and worldly honors, Calderón knew how to have his hero reconcile elements of conflict between the spiritual and material with consummate flair. His masterpiece, *La vida es sueño* (*Life Is a Dream*) (1636), begins in a world "not far removed from chivalresque romance," and its plot proceeds with romance variations of descents into enchanted underworlds or encounters with strange beings in enchanted abodes (Lewis-Smith 7).[22] Its action is pure invention yet "contains the shadows of history" (8). As Roberto González Echevarría has pointed out, it is in this kind of contained dualities that baroque poetry will forever be stalled (Echevarría 190–91).

Antonio Cuitla proves incapable of fabricating such brilliant reconciliations. While his story certainly includes romance plot elements, types, and inventions, it contains more than the shadows of history. The shadow of Cuitla's dream is hardly a distant, elided source to be recuperated for the present. Together with resources from the realms of art and imagination, this shade is both a psychological and historical bridge between the old and the new and an external symptom of symbolic reality within material history. For this reason, Cuitla's socialist realist tractor dream turns out not to be stalled in the fields of Don José María's spectacular indirections. Cuitla's dream represents a false alignment, only of oneiric form, with Don José María's notion that "life is a dream." His version is deeply rooted in proverbial formulas signifying the "transience of life and the consequent vanity of purely temporal values" (Lewis-Smith 12–13), unavoidably leading to the mutability of fortune. Cuitla's dream cannot be Don José María's baroque "life as dream," especially not in terms of its symbolic or ethical content. Accordingly, even in the midst of his most furiously deluded hallucinations, Cuitla remains fully capable of the blindingly lucid and intensely humanistic rejoinder, "Man makes himself. . . . Everything is possible" (*Shadow* 96). In the fatal grip of this final dream, Cuitla is not imprisoned by the shady life-is-a-dream idea of the *hacendado*, but continues to believe in sensorial, earthbound, historical action. On his deathbed, on the verge of escaping from all dreams and shadows, he understands that the crises of national reconstruction that he helped instigate failed the campesinos only because they did not go nearly deep enough to break capitalist domination of production and the exploitation of campesinos.[23]

Nevertheless, Don José María does have the last word when, whispering to the dying man, he viciously claims the victory of the modern: " 'Maybe you've heard the news, Antonio,' he said. 'About the highway to the sea. A paved road fourteen feet off the ground all the way from Morelos to the gulf. We will take our cotton to the gin in trucks. That will be progress. The *estero* will be drained. Then there will be bottom land for everybody. Much land, Antonio' " (113). The landowner's earlier nostalgia for "the glories that were lost" before the "rank foreigners from the north and the south" came to the border and "slowly pushed their betters from the land" (21), his desire for a "life of vigor and romance" conveyed by his resistance to the draining of the *estero*, now diabolically disappear. In the face of the profit to be made by the modernization of the region and its linkage to global mercantilism in cotton and other commercial crops symbolized by the construction of the newly "paved road," Don José María's sentimentality about the land melts away. In a story so richly integrated by patterns of crisscrossed dusty country lanes, the passage into full modernity and its problematical transitions is dramatically signaled by the stark technology of the modern road, opening the border region to the pragmatic pathways of transnational commerce.

In the end, Don José María willingly discards romance, sentiment, and nostalgia in favor of the profit gained from the draining of his precious *estero* and the trade in cotton promised by the opening of the roadway to the world. Between penurious tradition and luxurious modernity, there is no contest for the *hacendado*. For Antonio Cuitla, tradition and modernity are the horns of a dilemma on which he dies. As the black bull never before brought down finally is brought down, he too, like Jacinto Del Toro, goes down. His own acquiescence to the lure of urbanity, the taste of culture, and the force of reason cause the downfall. His fall is guaranteed when he places all of these desires above the well-being of the people he is supposed to lead toward the better life of the accomplished modern state and ignores the complicity between rationality and oppression so obviously revealed in the actions of the *hacendado*, Don José María Jiménez. Plunged into modernity by the destructive processes of revolution, the crisis of the political system, the deconstructions of national identity, and the temptations offered by social transformation, both characters experience *susto*. Both feel the shock of what Roger Bartra has described as the huge internal breakdown of a "complex system of integration and consensus," namely, "the end to specifically 'Mexican' forms of legitimation and identity" (47). The difference between the two is their distinct ways of negotiating a new integration in the face of the end of specifically Mexican forms of identity, and their different ways of relating to the shadowy traces of the past.

Cuitla's story is filtered through the strains of the song of the disobedient son and other *corridos* in *The Shadow*. It also develops from the novel *George Washington Gómez*, poems like "Guitarreros," and the short stories in *The Hammon and the Beans and Other Stories*. We see versions of it in Paredes's political and cultural reporting from Japan, which redefine ethics, politics, and aesthetics as belonging to related domains of knowledge. The cultural historian Paul Gilroy has argued, concerning the notion of the Black Atlantic as "a counterculture of modernity," that the work of "subcultures" of dissent, separate from the hegemonic cultural or linguistic mainstream, such as the ones emerging from the zones of the transnational imaginary on the borderlands of culture, frequently "appears intuitive." That is, rather than seeming critical in the Kantian sense of critique, the cultural idioms of ethnic and racial minorities, agrarians, the urban poor, women, and other subaltern groups, the marginalia of hegemonic society, seem *un*critical, merely subjective, and based on feeling. By extension, whenever these idioms are seen as *critical*, they are also often held to be socially disruptive and, consequently, both morally repugnant and aesthetically foul. Rational analysis of the social totality is unnecessary when intuitive logic creates a consensus grounded on the self-evidence of taste (38–39).

In Paredes's view, the work of vernacular cultures is something else again. As products of the popular imagination, folklore, popular culture, folk beliefs, and other verbal arts do their critical work at the level of "gut feeling," as a lived experience of the racialized, class-stratified, and gendered structures of everyday life. That same kind of aesthetic critique lies at the core of Paredes's work. In his writings, the verbal

arts do not only consider the world; they also explore the utopian possibilities of transforming it. In that utopian future of a transformed
world, these countercultures just might be capable of satisfying real
human needs. When the day of that liberatory experience arrives, "reason is . . . reunited with the happiness and freedom of individuals in
the reign of justice within the collectivity" (Gilroy 39). In this anticipatory manner, argues Gilroy, artistic expression becomes a crucial
way of resolving the demands of tradition and modernity within the
tension created by the difference between revolutionary collectivity
and individual self-fulfillment.

Communities of Fate

Yet if at every turn in the attempt to define an indigenously fulfilled
and uniquely bordered subjectivity we find only the difference between collectivity and subjectivity, how are we to create the congress
of shared provenance and common cause resulting in communities
of belonging within well-defined borders of belonging?[24] The great
waves of Mexican immigration caused by the labor diasporas of the
twentieth century and the massive increase in communication and
information technology introduced by modernization have brought
into crisis former beliefs in a single civic nation with a homogeneous
national identity which could be used as a model for national development.[25] As a result, the old models of national cohesion have
become problematical in the extreme. The foundational subject of
nationhood, the figure of the citizen, is undergoing such profound
transformations during the modern era that even the seemingly necessary connection between citizenship and the nation-state is today
being questioned. The sociologist Saskia Sassen thus proposes that
"the transformations afoot today raise questions about this [connec-
tion] insofar as they significantly alter those conditions which in the
past fed that articulation between citizenship and the national state"
(4). Moving beyond the older paradigms of national belonging, new
ideas, modes, and approaches have called into question the very idea
of the unitary nation, revealing its fictive bases in the narratives of its
purveyors. Nations and nationalisms of the kind that used to be may
no longer be intrinsic to the nature of the modern world. Faith in the
nation thus now seems touchingly naive.

The social theorist David Held has argued that each nation-state forms a "political community of fate" (*Democracy and the Global Order* 102). With increases in globalization and transculturation, however, some of the "most fundamental forces and processes that determine the nature of life chances" now increasingly cut across national boundaries and, consequently, diminish the sense of a shared political and social fate (103).[26] Countering Held's pessimistic view, the political theorist Will Kymlicka has suggested that what forms a "community of fate" is not the forces and processes people are subjected to, "but rather how they respond to those forces, and in particular, what sorts of collectivities they identify with when responding to those forces." Kymlicka thus goes on to say that "people belong to the same community of fate if they care about each other's fate, and want to share each other's fate—that is, want to meet certain challenges together, so as to share each other's blessings and burdens. Put another way, people belong to the same community of fate if they feel some sense of responsibility to one another's fate, and so want to deliberate together about how to respond collectively to the challenges facing the community" (*Politics in the Vernacular* 320–21). Kymlicka suggests that not simply issues of national identity, language, culture, or legality constitute communities of fate, although legal status is certainly of crucial importance in the determination of a sense of national belonging. Of equal if not greater importance are matters of mutual understanding and of articulating in cultural practices one's place within the national community. The payoff to the construction of a cultural geography of the kind denoted by the transnational imaginary is no less than the possibility of a state of affairs where multiple national political cultures and plural national collectivities might suggestively interact as communities of shared fates.

What new kinds of patriotism and sense of national belonging might follow from this revised version of citizenship? "How can we construct a common identity in a country where people not only belong to separate political communities but also belong in different ways?" (Kymlicka and Norman 377). What forms and elements might arise from these new relationships between citizenship and the national state that might produce what Saskia Sassen has termed "operational and rhetorical openings for the emergence of new types of political subjects and new spatialities for politics" (5)? For one thing, such a process might allow for truly meaningful democratic participation in the determination of the political and cultural life of the nation and mutual deliberation about how to respond collectively to the challenges facing the community of the Americas.

This question of belonging within diversity was already at the center of political and aesthetic concern throughout the hemisphere in the 1930s. The great Cuban poet Nicolás Guillén had voiced his sense of the shadowy nature of national belonging and personal identity in his "Balada de los dos abuelos" in this particular manner:

Sombras que sólo you veo,
me escoltan mis dos abuelos. . . .
África de selvas húmedas
y de gordos gongos sordos . . .
—¡Me muero!
(Dice mi abuelo negro.)
Aguaprieta de caimanes,
verdes mañanas de cocos . . .
—¡Me canso!
(Dice mi abuelo blanco.). . . .
los dos del mismo tamaño,
ansia negra y ansia blanca,
los dos del mismo tamaño,
gritan, sueñan, lloran, cantan.
Sueñan, lloran, cantan.
Lloran. Cantan.
¡Cantan!

[Shadows I alone can see,
my two grandfathers go with me. . . .
Africa of the humid forests
and the great, stilled gongs . . .
"I'm dying!"
(says my black grandfather.)
Waters dark with alligators,
mornings green with coco-palms . . .
"I'm tiring!"
(says my white grandfather.). . . .
both the same size,
black anguish, white anguish,
both the same size,

they shout, dream, cry, sing.
They dream, cry, sing.
Cry. Sing.
They sing!]

In Guillén, the shadows from the past are specters that simultaneously escort us into the future and vividly instantiate the synchronic co-existence of distinct modes of production, discrete political exigencies, and uniquely contrary cultural affiliations. His song thus undertakes the necessity of articulating those peculiar conjunctions that the entry into modernity has created, and the exquisite torment of its demands. Paredes begins here. Like Guillén, he surmises that in place of old local and national self-sufficiencies, we might have intercourse in multiple transnational directions. The struggles to find those alternative directions involve undeniable suffering and anguish. Nevertheless, both poets can imagine a way to sing about those cries of pain.

However, unlike Guillén, whose poem begins from the binarisms of Africa and Europe but ends in the monologic synthesis of the poet's voice, issuing a singular *balada*, Paredes turns elsewhere. Helping us envision oppositional practices and struggles that do not depend on binary thinking, on a notion of a unitary subject, or on a monologic of representation, the alternative notions of national identity, citizenship, and even of patriotism suggested in Paredes's works of the vernacular transnational imaginary ask us instead to consider differently. These writings urge us to inquire whether it is possible to conceive of other models of identity and cultural struggle that are inclusive and expansive. They allow for the accomplishment of a transnational and pan-American culture that does not privilege the one over the many but that can help hold us together as we share one another's fate, as we "dream, cry, sing," imagining a world beyond the specter of injustice.

Paredes's formulations of the transnational citizenry of Greater Mexico might allow us to understand the ways that the nineteenth-century borderlands connect to the realities of the twenty-first-century world, where in some regions of Mexico more than half of its citizens now live north of the border in Texas and California.[27] A century of transnational labor migration has inextricably linked Mexico and the United States. Today, entry into the era of globalization requires us to consider anew the concept of citizenship, acknowledging perhaps as Kymlicka proposes that "citizenship is not just a certain status, defined by a set of rights and responsibilities. It is also an identity, an expression of one's membership in a political community" (Kymlicka and Norman 369). However, because not all share, or have been allowed to share, equally in the political community of that public thing, the res publica, identification with a common culture may be possible only if we adopt a conception of "differentiated citizenship." 28

In his works from the 1940s and 1950s, Paredes was prospecting to what extent everyday vernacular practices create this sense of "differentiated" polity from out of the cultural gestures and social idioms of a language with unofficial status. The questions he was posing elsewhere hit a gold vein in *The Shadow*. Was it possible to claim membership in a society, claim political and social rights, and become recognized as an active citizen-agent in the labor market and the public sphere while at the same time retaining the multiple differences of one's identity? Could one imagine a *trans*national state of mind? Under what conditions might a differentiated form of citizenship serve as the guarantor of community? What difference did difference make enacted in other theaters of modernity? At mid-century, in the midst of the crisis of national identity occasioned by the rise of the cold war and its ruthless choices proposed in the name of national security, by the shattering conditions that have come to be known as postmodernity, and by the emergence of the late stages of postindustrial capital, these were the salient matters that Paredes was deliberating as features of the real and the imaginary.

CONCLUSION

A Transsentimental Journey

> Let us conclude by saying that even
> when dealing with the most modest
> matters of everyday life, the subject
> matter of our novelists has always been
> world-historical. — Roberto Schwarz,
> *Misplaced Ideas*

In the summer of 2003 I traveled to Japan to conduct research on
Américo Paredes's occupation-era experiences in Asia and to lecture
on the implications of that work in relation to the emerging topic of
the transnational as a category in American studies. I spoke at the annual meeting of the Japanese Association for American Studies and at
four additional colleges and universities in Kobe, Kyoto, Nagoya, and
Tokyo proper. The responses of my Japanese audiences and interlocu-
tors were remarkable for their intellectual acuity and their emotional
identification with the issues that Paredes's work raised. At one point
in a public question-and-answer session at Kobe University, for instance, one assistant professor, pressing me on a point I had made
about the relationships between citizenship and patriotism, suddenly
choked up and wept when he attempted to speak about his grandfather's participation in the attack on Pearl Harbor and his grandmother's experiences in Hiroshima. For everyone in the auditorium,
memory and remembrance in that moment ceased to be abstract and
academic.

Later in Tokyo, at Tsuda College, invited to participate in a graduate seminar offered by the history professor Masako Iino, I was impressed by the easy familiarity with which she scanned her book-
shelves and pulled down from one of them her working copy of *Pacific*

Stars and Stripes: The First 40 Years, 1945–1985, to show me Paredes's page-one article on the Tokyo war crimes tribunal. Contemporary studies of the Asia Pacific war did not end for professor Iino's American history students with the Japanese surrender, but extended into the "confusion era" of the occupation years and beyond. In the quiet setting of a sublimely sumptuous traditional teahouse garden near her home in Kamakura, she asked me about the legacy of Paredes, his sense of American and Japanese racism, and about the relation of scholars of my own affirmative-action generation to the work of someone from his era.

On still another occasion, one of my Japanese hosts, Professor Masako Notoji, a distinguished faculty member at the Center for Pacific and American Studies at the University of Tokyo, took me aside to share with me a personal family anecdote. Professor Notoji told me about a confrontation that had occurred sometime in the late 1920s between her father, a newly appointed assistant professor of agronomy, and the volatile young samurai, Hideki Tojo, an up-and-coming army officer and newly appointed commander of the First Infantry Regiment. In response to the professor's insistent demands that Tojo keep his men out of university research lands and that his men honor the sanctity of the research fields that the troops had been trampling in their maneuvers, Tojo had bristled at her father's words. Then Tojo had bowed respectfully, acknowledging the dignity of the agronomy professor's request, and agreed to curb his men from the research fields of the Tokyo Imperial University. Professor Notoji urged me to speak about this clash between military strength and intellectual integrity in prewar Japan.

Clearly, she desired me to see a different Tojo emerge from this family vignette of an incident more than eighty years in the past, not the demonic war criminal portrayed in the war crimes trials. Professors Iino and Notoji, as well as the young man in the audience at Kobe University, each helped me see processes of cultural memory instigated by the occupation still at work in contemporary Japan. They pointed out the lingering power of the memories of loss that haunted postwar Japanese society and that Paredes had witnessed firsthand as they took shape in the immediate postwar years.

In numerous instances, my Japanese hosts desired to learn more about Paredes and his work. They wished to understand what a Mexican American soldier from the United States–Mexico borderlands could understand about their plight as a defeated and occupied nation in Asia. How had that sympathy developed? How did it emerge under conditions of occupation-era censorship and the hypernationalistic vigilance of the early cold war years? Where had that understanding of the Asian transnational world led him? Why had he stayed in Japan so long, and why had he left it, ultimately, so thoroughly behind? These were more questions than I could answer at the time.

Perhaps the most trenchant question that I remained unable to answer then was one posed by another young professor at a seminar in American cultural history at the University of Tokyo, who asked me whether I considered Américo Paredes an extraordinary man. Or, was he rather an ordinary man working out from under exceptional circumstances? Was I concerned with the man or with the history? I saw his point. Was I offering a "cultural study" of Paredes's work, or was I engaging in a continuation of the project that Paredes initiated? Was I positioning myself within Paredes's critical epistemic geneal-ogy in order "to study" Paredes, or was I positioning myself in the genealogy that Paredes's work continues to open up? The moment of those questions proved to be one of profound crystallization for my thinking as I contemplated their implications.

The answer I gave at the time was the one that I have been attempt-ing to advance in this work. I have tried to resolve the issue of the disparity between personal and social history in terms of the relation-ship between Paredes's life story and the historical moment within which he lived and wrote. The point that I try to make is that for Pa-redes, that disparity is more apparent than real. As his family autobi-ography related, private lives can only be apprehended in their social terms. And the opposite also holds true. The ultimate efficacy and import of social movements can only be reckoned in personal his-tories. Beginning from this premise, Paredes's work made possible a whole range of inquiries concerning borderlands theory and transna-tional articulations of identity, personal liberties, the status of women within society, and the rights of citizens, even while it was at times constrained by the epistemic possibilities of his age and times as well as by his own limitations as a man of that epoch. The constraints on his vision of these possibilities were all too real. So, for example, the crucial considerations of the real and imaginary roles of women in society that Paredes decried so powerfully in his postwar journalism in Japan proved harder for him to maintain in Texas. Those who have followed him into the domain of borderlands studies are bound to share in some of those limitations, but they are equally obliged to transcend them to the extent that the new historical conditions of the postmodern and transnational eras require.

As a consequence of those obligations, and in response to the question of whether I am attempting a study of Paredes's life and work or whether I am extending the project that Paredes initiated, I maintain that it is possible and necessary to do both. The first option is that of traditional theory, which seeks to extend the critiques of post-Enlightenment modern traditions. The second option is in line with the radical transformation of Adorno and Horkheimer's notion of critical theory, or Mignolo's idea of the decolonization of knowledge. Along the path of critical thinking, as Horkheimer describes it, "the identification . . . of men of critical mind with their society is marked by tension, and the tension characterizes all the concepts of the critical way of thinking" (208). As I have attempted to show, this second path is the one that Paredes's own thinking cut, especially after his transformative experiences in Asia, which put his own identification with his border society into productive critical tension and produced a critical way of thinking. The idea of a special kind of border knowledge grounded on the topoi of the transnational imaginary of Greater Mexico came to fruition as a result of the tensions produced by his critical transitions from Texas to Japan and back again.

Américo Paredes was an exceptional man, but his greatness emerged less from uniquely heroic personal characteristics than from what he did working under exceptional historical circumstances. That working out produced an extraordinary insight, decades ahead of its time, namely, that the transnational is not only a structure of abstract ideas and ideology. It is also an experience of *transit*, *transition*, and *transitoriness* from one lived experience in a particular historical place into the experience of a different geosocial structure and its altered social and emotional space. In experiencing that transitoriness, we also experience the ways that specific forms of local ideology interact with the social environment of a particular cultural geography. In these transnational social and cultural spaces, we live the complex mix of ideas and locales resulting in the visceral emotional experience of the process of possible political change and social transformation within a variable cultural milieu that provides an incomparable opportunity of attacking the future with a new key. Greater Mexico thus became a figure for what America was coming to be—not a nationality but a *trans-nationality*, a weaving back and forth of innumerable threads of all sizes and colors, across conceptual boundaries whose colors bleed and shade into each other. All of which makes these sites also trans-sentimental locales.

What is so startling in all of this is the discovery that Paredes more than anticipated postmodern, cross-disciplinary, transnational social criticisms and their complementary analytical formations and discursive strategies. Writing from the borderlands of the prewar era, from Tokyo and China in the postwar period, and from Greater Mexico in the 1950s, Paredes *created* an aesthetics sustained by historical critique and fired by his understanding of the workings of social imaginaries. In Paredes's literary and journalistic writings, insight into a new configuration of national and ethnic identity was emerging that was neither fixed, immutable, and essential nor simply vague, dispersed, and undecidable. In the lived experience of the postwar, transnational borderlands, its phenomenology was coherent even if not stable, performative even if not essential. Its symbolic correlative took the shape of folklore, song, poetry, legend, and other verbal arts that required discursive performance and produced the imaginary effect of an experientially shared sense of self. These processes of subject formation were most sharply perceivable in the reciprocity of the dialogic situation. Paredes saw these processes figured by performers and listeners of song, in the art of storytelling, and in the entire panoply of the metalogues of the vernacular arts recounting the lore of the past and its originary relation to the future in the present. However, they could also be perceived in the contours of the symbolic cartography of social forms and in what Roberto Schwarz has elegantly termed "the most modest matters of everyday life" (31). The vernacular arts of the everyday allowed him to conceive of alternative modernities with a difference, questioning universalizing idioms of freedom, historicizing the contexts of ideas, localizing and pluralizing the subjective experiences of modernity. Like a latter-day alchemist, Américo Paredes was learning to transmute the dross of everyday life into gold, revealing the poetry hidden behind the most appalling contrasts of social modernity.

Walter Benjamin contends that the most basic function of the storyteller is to provide "counsel" for a community. "After all," Benjamin remarks, "counsel is less an answer to a question than a proposal concerning the continuation of a story which is in the process of unfold-ing. . . . Counsel woven into the fabric of real life [*gelebten Lebens*] is wisdom" ("The Storyteller" 145–46). His words suggest one final point of resonance with Paredes. As the consummate storyteller that he was, Paredes attempted in his literary and his scholarly writings to seek counsel from the modest matters of the everyday in the most traditional of senses, as a continuation of a story in the process of un-folding. For this reason, in describing his first major scholarly work, Paredes also advanced the related sense of providing "counsel": "I was writing a *brief*," he contended. "I was being an *advocate* for my people." To write this brief and provide this counsel, he would first have to be able to tell a story.

As he turned from his own literary works to the study of the forms and social aesthetics of the transnational imaginary, he sought a sub-ject suitable for fashioning "the raw material of experience . . . in a solid, useful, and unique way" (Benjamin, "The Storyteller" 162). It is not surprising, therefore, that as he began his scholarly career, Américo Paredes settled on a "useful" doctoral dissertation topic that focused on the arts of traditional storytelling represented by the ex-emplary performance situation of the paradigmatic *corrido* of border conflict, "El corrido de Gregorio Cortez." For it was there, in the most localized of vernacular forms and everyday life, that he found a way to access and activate the workings of the transnational imaginary in the borderlands of culture.

1 Memory Is All That Matters

1 For a review of the voluminous literature on the concept of borders, border theory, and borderlands studies, see Alvarez, who cites over two hundred entries in his review. An excellent discussion of the distinction between the notion of borderlands as employed by the protégé of Frederick Jackson Turner, Herbert Eugene Bolton, and its use by scholars like Patricia Nelson Limerick and José David Saldívar is the work of Jeremy Adelman and Stephen Aron. See also Gutiérrez-Jones and Saldivar-Hull, as well as the excellent collection of essays by Truett and Young. On the relationship between borderlands theory and globalization, see Sadowski-Smith.

2 For examples of the new postnationalist American studies, see Moya and Saldívar; Kaplan; Brannon, Greene, and National Council of Teachers of English; Giles; Reynolds and Hutner; Pease; Rowe; and Pérez Firmat, *Do the Americas Have a Common Literature?*. An excellent new model for American literary historiography that takes into account the "transamerican origins of Latino writing" is Gruesz. Further, the historian Devra Weber demonstrates that the discussion of the transnational nature of American society is not a recent development. Weber cites an essay by Randolph Bourne in which Bourne urges the historically prescient recognition that dual citizenship is "the rudimentary form of that 'international citizenship' to which we . . . aspire" (Bourne 94). Discussions of the postnational character of the contemporary world are the focus of the essays in Dear, Leclerc and Berelowitz.

3 See Bazant 1–5. See also Herzog.

4 Throughout his study of this title, Gamio uses the metaphor of the metallurgic forging of bronze and iron to describe the art and labor of nation building.

5 Early Mexican constitutions moved to broaden the base of citizenship by abolishing race and caste as criteria of inclusion while simultaneously restricting access to public office and the public sphere to independent and literate male property owners. An excellent discussion of the evolution of citizenship in Mexico is Lomnitz 306–7. See also Moon and Davidson.

6 See also Lomnitz 315–17.

7 See Habermas, *Structural Transformation*: "The bourgeois public

sphere may be conceived above all as the sphere of private people coming together as a public; they soon claimed the public sphere regulated from above against the public authorities themselves, to engage them in a debate over the general rules governing relations in the basically privatized but publicly relevant sphere of commodity exchange and social labor. The medium of this political confrontation was peculiar and without historical precedent: people's public use of their reason" (27). Habermas's description of an eighteenth-century historical phenomenon is applicable to the processes of enlightened liberalism that partially governed the construction of modern Mexico.

8 Negt and Kluge extend Habermas's analysis of the public sphere from its origins in the eighteenth and nineteenth centuries to twentieth-century conditions (Negt and Kluge 1–2).

9 Lomnitz points out that Ignacio López Rayón's attempt at a Mexican constitution in 1811 referred to Mexicans as an "American people," and to loyal Mexicans as "Americans" (305).

10 For a discussion of the relationship between popular nationalism and gender identity, see also Alonso.

11 See Truett and Young 1–32. Truett and Young point out that "struggles to delimit and define national and ethnic identity in the [United States–Mexico] borderlands exposed the incoherency of the imagined bounded space" of both nations (2).

12 Young argues that Garza's rebellion at the end of the nineteenth century formed part of a century-long struggle of borderlands peoples to maintain their autonomy in the face of two powerful and encroaching nation-states.

13 The provisions of an act of the Mexican Congress on October 23, 1835, established a strong centralized government. The installation of this centralist republic resulted in the maturation of a political and military conflict in the northern settlements, culminating in the independence of Texas as a new republic. See Aboites Aguilar 49. See also Santa Anna's version of these events in Castañeda et al. 8–49.

14 On the making of a "US-Mexican" literary citizen-subject in the post-1848 borderlands, see Coronado 1–47. Coronado's emphasis on what he terms the "colonized" status of the lettered elite of the region makes him at times undervalue the importance of resistance and opposition among the dispossessed and disenfranchised sectors of the former Mexican population, but his argument about the emergence of "competing modernities" in the guise of colonialism is powerfully illuminating.

15 For the full text of the treaty as ratified by the United States, see ap-

pendix 2 in Griswold del Castillo. See especially the text of articles 8 and 9 of the Treaty of Guadalupe Hidalgo on the citizenship and rights of property. For the original text of these articles before they were amended by the US Senate, see Holden and Zolov, "Treaty of Guadalupe Hidalgo" 31–33.

16   See the excellent discussions of Bourke and Dobie in Limón, *Dancing with the Devil*. On Jovita González, see Cotera, "Native Speakers." Also on González's critical relationship to Bourke, see Cotera, "Refiguring."

17   A US Army officer as well as an anthropologist, Bourke documented the cultural practices of the border with an imperialist's eye. His analogies between the Rio Grande borderlands region and Egypt and the Congo underscore the colonial and racist nature of the projected Americanization of the border. See Bourke, "American Congo."

18   González writes that before meeting Dobie, "the legends and stories of the border were interesting, so I thought, just to me. However, he made me see their importance and encouraged me to write them, which I did" (xii).

19   Limón discusses the contradictory position that González occupies as a member of the upper-class Mexican families who distinguished themselves from both Anglo-Americans and the dark-skinned *peones* who labored for them.

20   Gonzalez's master's thesis is one of the earliest documents of this revisionary history. It offers a dramatically different social and political vision of the region than that of her mentor Dobie. See Cotera's illuminating analysis of the complex relationship between González and Dobie in her PhD dissertation, "Native Speakers" 253–328. During this same era, Walter Prescott Webb, one of the most respected historians of his day, was writing that "without disparagement it may be said that there is a cruel streak in the Mexican nature, or so the history of Texas would lead one to believe. This cruelty may be a heritage from the Spanish of the Inquisition; it may, and doubtless should, be attributed partly to the Indian blood. Among the common class, ignorance and superstition prevail, making the rabble susceptible to the evil influence of designing leaders" (14). José David Saldívar discusses the movie versions of Webb's "southern white supremacist orientation" history in "Chicano Border Narratives" 169.

21   See my works cited for a full listing of Paredes's literary works.

22   Paredes's notion of Greater Mexico has been taken up as an analytical category by Limón, *Mexican Ballads*. See also Limón, *American Encounters*. Also in this genealogy of thought is Alonzo. A richer elaboration of it can be found in Calderón. In my own use of the concept of Greater Mexico, I wish to emphasize Paredes's contribution to the literature of globalization, transnationalism, and the repositioning of citizenship in borderland spaces.

23   This and other variants of "El corrido de Gregorio Cortez" are from Paredes, *"With His Pistol in His Hand"* 151–74.

24   This is the sense in which Arjun Appadurai speaks of the "work of the imagination" within public culture (13–14).

25   For a full discussion of modernity as a multiple experience, see Taylor, "Two Theories of Modernity." Against what he terms "acultural" theories of modernity that conceive of modernity arising (as a singular phenomenon) from the transformations that any traditional culture could undergo as a result of culture-neutral social changes, Taylor argues for the countervailing import of "cultural" theories of modernity. These culture-specific explanations for the rise of alternative modernities (in the plural) allow us to recognize that transitions to modernity taking place in different cultural contexts "will produce different results that reflect their divergent starting points" (182).

26   These articles were written for the *Brownsville Herald*. See, for example, Paredes, "Old Grammar School."

27   Of this work from the 1930s, poetry and nonfiction prose appeared in the *Brownsville Herald* and in the "Los lunes literarios" ("Literary Mondays") section of *La Prensa de San Antonio* in English and Spanish. Paredes published one volume of poetry in Spanish, Paredes Manzano, *Cantos de adolescencia*.

28   Américo Paredes, interview by the author, March 3, 1995. Austin, Texas.

29   "X" designated the radio call sign of all stations south of the border. For an excellent selection of music from the outlaw border radio stations period, see the audio CD "Los Super 7: Heard It on the X." For a history of Spanish-language radio in the United States during the civil rights era, see Gutiérrez and Reina Schement, who employ the concept of *internal colonialism* in their study of the history of Spanish-language radio.

30   Agustín Lara (1896?–1970); on Lara's musical career and its influence on the development of Mexican popular music and mass media, see Aura. See also A. Lara 16. This volume includes an excellent selection of Lara's songs on CD.

31   The organizers of the Golden Gate International Exposition commissioned Diego Rivera to paint a large-scale fresco to be exhibited for the duration of the fair. Rivera's design was based on his syncretic mestizo vision of what he called "Pan-American Unity— *Unión de la expresión artística del norte y sur de este continente*," a majestic synthesis of history, religion, art, politics, and the technology of the Americas. The ten panels of the mural are now on permanent display in the campus theater of the City College of San Francisco. See the excellent discussion of this mural in Hedrick (155–56).

32   The first twentieth-century wave of Latino culture and music popularity in the United States occurred during the 1930s, followed by a second one in the 1950s, and a third in the 1980s and 1990s. On the effects of these patterns of cultural transmission on the so-called Latinization of the United States, see the excellent discussions by Aparicio and Chávez-Silverman; Pérez Firmat, *Life on the Hyphen: The Cuban-American Way*; and Flores.

33   Américo Paredes, personal communications with the author, July 1992. Austin, Texas.

34   A contemporary of Benjamin, Kracauer wrote "The Mass Ornament," the essay cited here, in 1927 when he was the cultural correspondent for the *Frankfurter Zeitung* at the height of the artistic revolutions in Berlin during the years of the Weimar Republic. In his essays from the period, Kracauer offers an astonishing anticipation of Theodor W. Adorno and Max Horkheimer's notion of the dialectic of enlightenment, but with a more positive view of the possibilities of mass culture when used in the service of the community as a whole.

35   Consuelo "Chelo" Silva (1922–88). Américo Paredes, Jr., interview by the author, April 29, 2005. See Del Toro, Strachwitz, and Nicolopulos. See also Nicolopulos and Strachwitz, who note that "during the late 1950s [Silva] was probably the bestselling female Hispanic recording artist on either side of the border."

36   A few months before Paredes was to meet Amelia Nagamine in the offices of the American Red Cross in Tokyo, he writes in his "Far East Notebook" on July 15, 1947: "Suddenly remember that I am still married. Must see the consul soon . . ." Américo Paredes Papers box 8, folder 12.

37   Ideal Records was launched in 1946 by Armando Marroquín of Alice, Texas, to cater to the growing transborder musical market in the postwar era. Working outside the domain of the formalized culture industry, Marroquín and his wife pressed their records in the kitchen of their home in the early days of the label. See the history of Ideal Records at www.lib.utexas.edu/benson/border/arhoolie2/raices.html. Accessed August 2004.

38   For an excellent discussion of the construction of theories of citizenship, see Kymlicka and Norman 355–69. On the particular meaning of American citizenship, see Shklar, who argues that citizenship in America "has been overwhelmingly a demand for inclusion in the polity, an effort to break down excluding barriers to recognition, rather than an aspiration to civic participation" (3).

39   Soldier and statesman Hideki Tojo served as prime minister of Japan during most of World War II (1941–44) and was subsequently tried and executed for war crimes by the Allied powers and their military tribunal for the Far East.

40 In my research in the Hoover Library at Stanford University, the general libraries at the University of California–Berkeley, at the American History Center at the University of Texas–Austin, and at the Benson Latin American Collection at the University of Texas–Austin, where the Américo Paredes Papers are housed, I have collected seventy-one articles from *Pacific Stars and Stripes* and *El Universal* from the period 1946–47. In addition, the archives contain fourteen typed reports, essays, and sketches depicting Paredes's experiences in revolutionary China from November 1946 to March 1947 covering war relief activities for the American Red Cross.

41 Paredes, personal communication with the author, December 1993.

42 Paredes, interviews by the author, July 5–6, 1990, Austin, Texas.

43 The contemporary historiography of the region is beginning to pursue these relationships. See, for example, Truett and Young.

44 See, for example, Espinosa.

45 In a similar vein, see Bakhtin, *Problems of Dostoevsky's Poetics* 110.

46 See "Historical Bloc" in Gramsci, *Selections* 360. See "Heteroglossia" in Bakhtin, "Discourse in the Novel" 270–73.

47 Paredes is citing Flower.

48 Gramsci argued that folklore should not be conceived of as something *pittoresco* (picturesque), but should be conceived of as "concezione del mondo e della vita" (a conception of the world and life). For this reason, he claims, there is a strict relationship between folklore and *senso comune* (common sense), which is nothing less than *il folklore filosofico* (philosophical folklore). See "Osservazioni" 215.

49 In a conversation with me on September 5, 1985, on the history of modern folklore studies, Paredes referred to the term *clases subalternas*, from the work of folklorist Luigi Maria Lombardi Satriani. The study of folklore as an expression of the *clases subalternas* was a position with which he claimed to be in basic sympathy. Paredes was well aware that Lombardi Satriani was working from a Marxist and Gramscian model of the folk.

50 On the shifting relationship between citizenship and nationality, see Wiener; Bader; and Sassen.

51 Paredes's concerns with the fates of racialized, classed, and gendered individuals in the processes of social interactions in the realm of the historical correspond to Jacques Lacan's schema of the Imaginary, the Symbolic, and the Real as Fredric Jameson has defined those terms in the essay "Imaginary and Symbolic in Lacan." See also Parker et al.

52 The translation is mine. See also, E. Pérez.

53 This is one way of understanding the semantic shifts performed by the formal aspects of song, narrative, the vernacular arts, and other symbolic genres. V. N. Volosinov's related term is *sociological poetics*: "A poet uses metaphor in order to regroup values and not for the sake of a linguistic exercise" (116).

54 See also, Taylor's discussion of the social imaginary in "Two Theories" 188–92.

55 On the "language of citizenship," see Held, "Between State and Civil Society" 24. Wiener distinguishes between the "language of citizenship" as a "theory" from the "discourse of citizenship" as a "practice" (553).

2 Life in the Borderlands

1 Américo Paredes, interview with the author, March 2, 1995. Austin, Texas.

2 See Paredes, "Mi tía Pilar." Another sketch, "Mr. White," was published posthumously.

3 Additional autobiographical details from this period appear in Calderón and López-Morín. An earlier biographical sketch is offered by Limón, "Américo Paredes." The only biography of Paredes currently available is the short booklet by Rebecca Thatcher Murcia.

4 With the aid of Alicia Schmidt Camacho, my research assistant and a graduate student in the Program in Modern Thought and Literature at Stanford University at the time, I recorded almost twelve hours of conversation during four three-hour sessions of conversation in 1995. The tapes of the interview were later transcribed by Marcial González, also a research assistant and a graduate student in the Program in Modern Thought and Literature at the time. The tapes and transcriptions are in my personal collection. A second round of extended interviews followed on November 6–10, 1998, when I accompanied Paredes on a trip to Brownsville and south Texas, occasioned by Paredes's desire to visit friends and family in Brownsville and my own planned visit to the area. Additional conversations with Paredes continued by telephone and regular mail from the time that we returned from south Texas to the weeks before his death in 1999. These notes, transcripts, and original letters are likewise part of my personal collection. I draw here also from various personal correspondences, journalistic first-person writings, and unpublished biographical sketches archived in the Américo Paredes Papers. Paredes's sons, Alan and Vincent, also provided additional biographical information about their father and their mother, Amelia Nagamine, in August 2004. Finally, Américo Paredes Jr. graciously shared information about his father and his mother, Chelo Silva, on April 29, 2005.

5 Paredes, "The Undying Love."

6 The *décima*, not unlike the French *dizaine*, is an exquisitely complex

Spanish Golden Age poetic verse form, often used as a mode for oral performance. As its name suggests, the *décima* is a tight ten-line composition of octosyllables in which lines five and six are joined by enjambment while lines six to ten mirror the substance of lines one to five. There are numerous rhyme schemes, but the mirror *décima* uses the characteristic pattern, *a b b a a c c d d c*. "This is scarcely a form one would expect to find among the folk," notes Paredes, "yet the *décima* for centuries has been an important folksong type among all peoples of Spanish culture." Paredes, "The Décima," 235.

7 See Rosaldo, *Culture and Truth*. In characterizing *"With His Pistol in His Hand,"* Rosaldo emphasizes that Paredes "uses a nostalgic poetic mode to depict his Garden of Eden. . . . If taken literally, Paredes's view of the frontier social order seems both pre-feminist and as implausible as a classic ethnography written and read in accord with classic norms. How could any human society . . . function without inconsistencies and contradiction? Did patriarchal authority engender neither resentment nor dissent? Read as poetic vision, however, the account of primordial south Texas-Mexican society establishes the terms of verbally constructing the warrior hero as a figure of resistance. It enables Paredes to develop a conception of manhood rhetorically endowed with the mythic capacity to combat Anglo-Texan anti-Mexican prejudice" (151).

8 In 1891, Catarino Erasmo Garza (1859–95), a journalist and political activist, led a band of rebels out of south Texas across the Rio Grande, declaring a rebellion against the dictatorship of Porfirio Díaz. On the history of Garza's revolution, see Pierce; Paredes, *A Texas-Mexican Cancionero*; and E. Young, *Catarino Garza's Revolution*.

9 Lorenzo Paredes (1904–2003) was the last surviving of the Paredes siblings.

10 James Babbage Wells Jr., (1850–1923), known in south Texas as Judge Jim Wells, was a longtime Democratic boss of south Texas who settled in Brownsville, Texas, in 1878. With the support of the powerful ranchers of south Texas, "Wells defended sometimes suspect land claims, arranged low property tax valuations, and lobbied for the deployment of Texas Rangers and federal troops to provide protection against cattle rustling and border raids. He relied on the ranchers to mobilize their Hispanic workers and tenants for elections. . . . He welcomed the participation of prominent Mexican ranchers and businessmen in his political organization and local government, and he provided modest, informal welfare support for some of his loyal but impoverished constituents in the tradition of the Mexican *patrón* and big city boss. In this he epitomized the contemporary style of Caucasian relations with Hispanic Texans. Ranchers and border-town businessmen also bene-

fited from Wells's efforts to promote the extension of railroad construction to the lower Rio Grande Valley. The resulting boom in irrigation and vegetable and fruit farming not only transformed the regional economy and attracted thousands of new settlers but ultimately proved to be Wells's political and economic undoing. Exhibiting both a progressive commitment to honest, efficient government and an aversion to Hispanic participation in politics, the new settlers eventually turned against Democratic boss rule, and Wells's machine collapsed in 1920. . . . Despite his political astuteness and record of accomplishment, Wells could not survive the changing demographic structure in the region, the rising tide of racial hatred between Caucasians and Hispanics following the Mexican border raids of 1915 and 1916, and his loss of favor at the state level." *Handbook of Texas Online*, s.v. "Wells, James Babbage, Jr."

11 Mifflin Kenedy, (1818–95), rancher, shipowner, businessman, railroad builder, was among the first Texas ranchers to fence his lands. *Handbook of Texas Online*, s.v. "Kenedy, Mifflin."

12 Emma Tenayuca and Homer Brooks explain that under provisions of treaties from 1848, the Texas Constitution allowed noncitizen Mexican residents to vote until 1921, when the constitution was amended and the right to vote was rescinded. See Tenayuca and Brooks.

13 Juventino Rosas (1868–94). Frequently misattributed, Paredes here confuses the popular Mexican waltz "Sobre las olas" with "Lara's Theme," by Maurice Jarre, from the film *Doctor Zhivago* (1965).

14 At the time of this interview, Paredes was preparing this vignette about his Tía Pilar for eventual publication. He showed me his working manuscript, which I later used in the transcription of this interview.

15 Paredes first mentioned this story from his childhood to me in a conversation of July 1991. At the time, he mentioned that this vignette was one of a set of pieces he had been composing as parts of an autobiography. The manuscript of the sketch is available in box 13, folder 3 of the Américo Paredes Papers. It was subsequently published posthumously as "Mr. White," *Reflexiones* 3–6.

16 Garza Griego was the editor of the Matamoros newspaper *El Mañana de Matamoros* (no date); Sabas Klahn (1915–92) was a friend and intellectual colleague of Paredes's. Guálinto Gómez is the name of Paredes's hero in the novel *George Washington Gómez*. The "Diccionario moderno mundial" includes the following entries: "heroe, matón 'par excellente'; communismo, doctrina de lo tuyo is mío y lo mío es mío; fascismo, doctrina de lo mío es mío y no hay nada tuyo ni siquiera de mentiritas; atrocidades, todas las acciones del enemigo" (hero, killer "par excellence"; communism, a doctrine in which what is yours is mine and what is mine is mine; fascism, a doc-

trine in which what is mine is mine and there is nothing that is yours, not even in make-believe; atrocities, all of the enemies' actions). Circa 1940; my translation. See box 12, folder 1, Américo Paredes Papers.

17 Surveying issues of *La Prensa* for 1935 and 1936, one finds numerous examples of poetry by Manuel de Góngora, Sor Juana Inés de la Cruz, Ramón Valle Inclán, Luis Guillermo Govea, Miguel de Unamuno, Federico García Lorca, and Jorge Guillén, all of whom figure prominently in Paredes's cast of poetic influences. See *"Lunes literarios de La Prensa."*

18 César Augusto Sandino (1893–1934); "Nicaraguan revolutionary fighter and popular guerilla leader fought against the Somoza dictatorship and U.S. interventions in Central America." *Encyclopaedia Britannica Online,* search.eb.com/eb/article-9065475 (accessed August 8, 2005). Lázaro Cárdenas (1895–1970), president of Mexico (1934–40), noted for his attempts to complete the radical reforms of the revolution of 1910. He distributed land, made loans available to peasants, organized workers' and peasants' confederations, and expropriated and nationalized foreign-owned industries. His presidency represented "the last great reforming phase of the Mexican Revolution" Knight 245. Emma Tenayuca (1916–99) was a lifelong labor activist and secretary of the Communist Party of Texas during the 1930s.

19 Ricardo and Enrique Flores Magón, anarcho-syndicalists and editors of the journal *Regeneración*, influenced the peasant revolutionism of Emiliano Zapata and of revolutionaries on the US side of the border. See Sandos.

20 Hart Stilwell (1902–75) was a writer, reporter, and newspaper editor of some regional fame.

21 Paredes first described his wartime life to me in a conversation of July 1991.

22 Paredes first described his initial duties in occupied Japan to me in a letter of December 13, 1992. In the August 5, 1946, issue of *Stars and Stripes*, Paredes and de la Croix collaborated on a cartoon feature for the daily column, "The Inquiring Reporter." This daily feature column was normally done as a straight piece of reporting on issues of concern to GIs, accompanied by photographs of the soldiers interviewed. Here Paredes and de la Croix are enjoying themselves at the expense of the serious reporting of *Pacific Stars and Stripes*.

23 Here and in correspondence of December 13, 1992, Paredes identifies himself as the political editor for *Stars and Stripes*. The masthead for the entire run of 1946 of *Pacific Stars and Stripes* does not indicate a particular position of political editor; Paredes did, however, write all of the major political articles and reports, often on page 1, during the time that he was on the staff of the newspaper.

24 Barnard Rubin returned to the United States to write reviews and articles for progressive publications such as *Masses and Mainstream* (October 1949) and the *Daily Worker* (August 9, 1950).

25 Later, I realized that Paredes was here recalling scenes described in articles he wrote for the Mexico City daily *El Universal*. The bylines of three of these articles read "E. Paredes." This is incorrect; the articles were written by Américo Paredes. See Paredes, "Desde Tokio (11 de julio)"; and Paredes, "Desde Tokio (25 de julio)." I have been able to locate nine other columns published in *El Universal* with the date lines "Desde Tokio" and "Desde China" in the Américo Paredes Papers at the University of Texas at Austin. The rest of these other articles are all correctly attributed to Américo Paredes. Box 11, folder 9, of the Américo Paredes Papers contains correspondence between Paredes and Miguel Lanz Duret, president and general managing editor of *El Universal*. One letter of note from Paredes requests that payment for a proposed series of articles "Desde Tokio" be sent to his elder brother Eliseo, a resident of Matamoros, Tamaulipas. Perhaps this explains how the "E. Paredes" attribution was made for three of the published columns. My thanks to Christian Kelleher and his staff at the Américo Paredes Papers, for his assistance with these questions.

26 *Pacific Stars and Stripes*, May 4, 1946. Reprinted in edited form in *Pacific Stars and Stripes* 6–7. *Pacific Stars and Stripes* began publishing in Tokyo with volume 1, number 1 on October 3, 1945.

27 Paredes first mentioned this incident to me in a letter of December 13, 1992.

28 Paredes first mentioned this abandoned project to me in a personal correspondence of December 13, 1992. The notes for this abandoned project can be found in the Américo Paredes Papers, box 11, folder 11.

29 "Si Tokio es una ciudad moribunda, Shanghai es una ciudad enferma, una ciudad consumida por una fiebre de actividad artificial e insalubre" (If Tokyo is a defunct city, Shanghai is a very ill city, consumed by feverish and insalubrious activity). Paredes, "Desde China, Shanghai." Paredes was remembering an incident he described in personal correspondence to Horst de la Croix, October 28, 1946, preserved in the Américo Paredes Papers, box 20, folder 2.

30 Horst de la Croix (1915–92) and Paredes corresponded from October 28, 1946, to February 14, 1992, eight days before de la Croix's death. In a letter of May 2, 1991, Paredes says to de la Croix that he considers him "my only real friend." Of this forty-six years' friendship, Paredes writes, "Because though we came from such different backgrounds we have had very much in common and some very good memories to treasure. The fact that our friendship has continued all these years in spite of the fact that circum-

stances have kept us from seeing each other frequently since we left Japan—
that says something about our friendship." Paredes, personal correspondence
to Horst de la Croix, Américo Paredes Papers, box 20, folder 2. After the
war, de la Croix received a PhD in art history at the University of California
at Berkeley and then joined the faculty of San José State University, where
he taught until his retirement. He was the editor and author of two books.
See Gardner and de la Croix.

31 These scenes are described more fully in Paredes, personal correspondence to Horst de la Croix, October 28, 1946, Américo Paredes Papers, box
20, folder 2.

32 Paredes, personal correspondence to Horst de la Croix, October 28,
1946, Américo Paredes Papers, box 20, folder 2.

33 These scenes were fresher in Paredes's memory than they otherwise
might have been at the time of my interview with him in 1995 because in
December 1990 de la Croix had returned to Paredes the letters he had received from him in Japan describing some of these events. See De la Croix
to Paredes, September 11, 1989; Paredes to De la Croix, October 21, 1989; De
la Croix to Paredes, December 12, 1990; and Paredes to De la Croix, May 2,
1991, Américo Paredes Papers, box 20, folder 2. Paredes referred to these
letters numerous times in personal conversation with me from 1991 to 1995.

34 Paredes kept meticulous typed and handwritten notebooks that detailed his experiences in the Far East. This information concerning how
he met Amelia Nagamine is described in the entry for Wednesday, September 29, 1948, "Far East Notebook no. 1," box 8, folder 12, Américo Paredes Papers. My thanks to Alan and Vincent Paredes, sons of Américo and
Amelia, who confirmed these and other details during an interview in Austin,
Texas, on August 28, 2004.

35 Stith Thompson was dean of American folkloristics at the time; Frank
Harper Wardlaw (1913–1989) served as the founding director of the Univer-
sity of Texas Press from 1950–1974. For examples of Thompson's work see
S. Thompson, *Narrative Motif-Analysis*; and S. Thompson, *The Folktale*.

36 Bourke, too, gives *chapparejos* as meaning "goat- or sheepskin over-
trousers." Bourke, "The American Congo," 604. Dobie probably learned
this mistaken derivation directly from Bourke. Santamaría gives the correct
Mexican Spanish word *chaparreras* as meaning "goatskin or cowhide over-
trousers."

37 Américo Paredes, letter to Sharon Reynolds, n. d. Paredes gave me a
copy of this letter for my personal records on November 8, 1992.

38 See Sandos. Also see MacLachlan.

39 See Campa; Sánchez; and Galarza.

40 Paredes Manzano, *Cantos*.

41 See Castañeda et al.

42 Ampudia was replaced by Arista as commander of the Division of the North, the Mexican force facing the American general Zachary Taylor along the Rio Grande in 1846. Robinson 23–24.

43 Ignacio Manuel Altamirano (1834–93); Amado Nervo (1870–1919); Manuel Gutiérrez Nájera (1859–95).

44 This joke is a variant of "The Two Psychiatrists" joke collected in Paredes, *Folktales of Mexico* 164–65.

45 In his Far East Notebook #2 dated December 1948–October 1949, Paredes in typically meticulous fashion keeps an exhaustive list "of the books I have read" during that period in order: "1) to study my true interests and my tastes and so be able to arrive at a better evaluation of myself, my capabilities, my real ambitions and desires; 2) to guide my future studies; 3) as reference, in case I remember a quote, a passage, a set of facts and forget where it came from." Américo Paredes Papers, box 8, folder 13. Among the forty plus works that he cites, are Zolá, *Nana*; Tolstoi, *Anna Karenina*; John Hersey, *Hiroshima*; Mariano Azuela, *Los de abajo*; Sinclair Lewis, *Main Street*; Eugene O'Neil (*sic*), *The Ice Man Cometh*; Isak Dinesen, "Seven Gothic Tales"; and W. E. B. Du Bois's "Porgy" published by Du Bois under the pseudonym of DuBose Heyward.

46 Vasconcelos. See also Gamio, *Mexican Immigration to the United States*, 128–29. In his consequential account of immigration in the 1930s, Gamio notes the "curious" attitudes of "Mexicans who are American citizens" toward new Mexican immigrants who "call these recent immigrants *cholos* or *chicanos*." The immigrant, in turn, "considers the American of Mexican origin as a man without a country. . . . The American of Mexican origin is known as a *pocho*" (129). Santamaría notes that "cholo, chola" derives from the caste term designating the product of the mixing of white and indigenous persons, a mestizo/a or a criollo/a and, by extension, someone of base origins. Today, however, the colloquial equivalent means a "homey," someone from the "hood." In "Tres faces del Pocho" (1936) Paredes had explored the possibility of a "pocho" aesthetic as a prelude to a "proto-chicano" cultural form.

47 Bourke, *On the Border with Crook*. See also Bourke, "The American Congo," *Scribner's*.

48 "*Susto,*" a Mexican American folk illness, "is the loss of the spirit or soul due to a sudden shock," Sandoval 78. This shock loosens the soul from the body. Healing requires the luring of the soul back into the body by means of herbs and rituals. See also Castro.

49   Paredes refers to this "many-layered" notion of social conflict in *Uncle Remus con Chile* 14.

3   Checkerboard of Consciousness

1   Even though the last decade has seen a growth of interest in James, many considerations of postcolonial theory, subaltern studies, and globalization continue to underestimate the importance of James for an understanding of the present development of the area of the decolonization of knowledge. The absence of James in American studies appears especially striking. On the special meaning of *humanity* for James, see Bogues 69–93. Bogues notes that the questions of humanism and of the meaning of humanity are for James inseparable from the possibilities of human emancipation and are therefore central to the project of decolonizing and shifting the geography of knowledge. Attempting to construct a new basis for humanism different from that of the European Renaissance, James and other radical anticolonial thinkers shifted the terms of the discussion to freedom and to "how we think of ourselves as humans" (Bogues 118–19). Concerning James's argument about the contradictions of Enlightenment thought in relation to the imperial world, see also Gilroy 46–58. See also Mustapha.

2   The epistemological and political implications of how the past is conceived in relation to the future is especially evident in James's 1938 masterpiece of cultural analysis *The Black Jacobins*. See D. Scott.

3   On the radical nature of James's theoretical turn as a historian, see Bogues 69–71.

4   The first chapter of Jameson's *Postmodernism*, from which this statement is taken, first appeared in the *New Left Review* as "Postmodernism; Or, the Cultural Logic of Late Capitalism."

5   See Fukuyama. The collapse of socialism was an event so prodigious in scope that the social theorist Robin Blackburn speculated that it might have proved "sufficiently comprehensive to eliminate [communism] as an alternative to capitalism and to compromise the very idea of socialism" (5). This is surely what Fukuyama meant by his claim that in the wake of the worldwide victory of the liberal democratic revolution, Western civilization had truly reached "the end of history."

6   This is the term that Spivak employs to examine the construction of subjectivity (3–32). See also Carby.

7   On the aesthetics of Mexican American border *corridos*, see Paredes, *"With His Pistol in His Hand"*; Limón, *Mexican Ballads*; R. Saldívar, *Chicano*

Narrative; and R. Saldívar, "Transnational Migrations." On the historical development of the form, see McDowell; G. Saldívar, *Historia de la música*; and V. Mendoza.

8 For a full discussion of this history of conflict, see Montejano, *Anglos and Mexicans*.

9 See Sandos.

10 This is reprinted in Paredes, *Texas-Mexican Cancionero* 71; translation mine.

11 For a more detailed discussion of the corrido as a socially symbolic form, see my discussion in *Chicano Narrative* 30–42.

12 See R. Flores, "The Corrido." Flores discusses how "Los sediciosos" is a watershed in the form of the classic *corrido* genre and anticipates forms and practices of later Chicano and Chicana narratives.

13 The verse line of the song, "los que van a pagarla [la mecha encendida]," may be translated as "those who will pay for it," or as "those who will extinguish [the lit match]." For an excellent reading of "Los sediciosos" and of the social context that gives it life, see R. Flores, "The Corrido."

14 An interesting counterpoint to Paredes's narrative is Hart Stilwell's 1945 novel *Border City*. Stilwell's novel chronicles the same region in the same historical era from an Old Left perspective. As Paredes told me during conversations in July 1991, Paredes, who worked as a newspaper reporter under Stilwell, the editor of the *Brownsville Herald* at the time, appears as a minor character in Stilwell's novel. *George Washington Gómez* was written and completed, although not circulated for publication, during the period that Paredes worked as a newspaper reporter in Brownsville, Texas, from 1935–40. I first saw the text of the novel in manuscript copy in 1986. The novel was accepted for publication in 1990 with Paredes's stipulation that it be published exactly as he had left it in 1940. Américo Paredes, interviews by the author, July 1990.

15 For related readings of this primal naming scene, see J. Saldívar, "Américo Paredes and Decolonization" 297–98. See also H. Pérez.

16 "El corrido de Jacinto Treviño," a classic example of the *corrido* in the heroic mode of border conflict, tells the story of a violent confrontation between the representatives of the old Texas Mexican and the new Anglo Texan power structures. Since the outcome of the struggle is preordained, the ends of the struggle are less important than the fact of its occurrence and the manner in which the Texas Mexican figure enacts it. Feliciano sings verses from this song periodically to punctuate his own private resistance to cultural change. For the text and an analysis of this *corrido*, see Paredes, *Texas-Mexican Cancionero* 32, 69–70.

17 The viciousness of the Texas Rangers with regard to the violent suppression of Mexican American civil liberties is well documented in both nineteenth-century sources by Anglo historians and by twentieth-century Chicano and Chicana revisionist historians. See Oates; Samora, Bernal, and Peña; Anzaldua; and Montejano, *Anglos and Mexicans*. The myth of the Texas Ranger as the lone source of civilized order was a product of the jingoist histories written by J. Frank Dobie and Walter Prescott Webb and consolidated by Hollywood in numerous early to mid-twentieth-century Westerns set in the borderlands. For discussions of the cinematic representation of the Texas Ranger, see Wright; J. Saldívar, "Chicano Border Narratives" 169–70; and Slotkin.

18 In "The Ideology of Difference," Jameson cautions against the "pseudodialectical" nature of postmodern versions of difference. Jameson, *Postmodernism* 340–41. I make a complementary argument in *Chicano Narrative* 215–18.

19 This is the difference of the dialectical system that I described as "the dialectics of difference" in *Chicano Narrative* 4, 83, 216–18. Its kinship with Bakhtin's notion of dialogism consists precisely in its rejection of the reifying abstractions of orthodox dialectics and their recourse to synthesis. Against dialectics in that synthetic mode, Bakhtin announces: "Dialogue and dialectics. Take a dialogue and remove the voices (the portioning of voices), remove the intonations (emotional and individualizing ones), carve out abstract concepts and judgments from living words and responses, cram everything into one abstract consciousness—and that's how you get dialectics" ("From Notes Made" 147). For this reason, Bakhtin imagines dialogics replacing "a reified model of the world" (Morson and Emerson 57).

20 Stevens was working on "Notes toward a Supreme Fiction" in the months immediately before and after American entry into World War II in 1941.

21 Benjamin makes this point in greater detail in the section on mirrors of the work translated as *The Arcades Project* ("Mirrors" 537).

22 See Gramsci, *Selections* 323 on the role of folklore in bolstering identity. See also Gramsci, "Philosophy." What Gramsci refers to here as "common sense," and as "folklore" in other places, does not mean "false consciousness." While common sense can contribute to a people's subordination by making the current situation seem natural and immutable, Gramsci argues that it can also contain elements of truth. As Forgacs points out, "It is contradictory—it contains elements of truth as well as elements of misrepresentation—and it is upon these contradictions that leverage may be obtained in a 'struggle of political hegemonies'" (Forgacs 421).

23 According to Bakhtin, this is one kind of restrictiveness that speech

genres impose on the semantic heteroglossia of any particular utterance. See "The Problem of Speech Genres." See also Holquist 64–65.

24 This is how Gramsci conceives of folklore in its relation to language. See "Osservazioni" 215–18. See also Femia 44–45. Femia points out that with his training in linguistics and awareness of its latest discoveries, Gramsci understood that "every culture discloses and guides its system of values and its general cognitions in its language" (Femia 44).

25 Holquist points out that the notion of the self in Bakhtin is a dialogical one made up of the sorting out of these ratios and proportions. See Holquist 29–30.

26 On the concept of the subject-effect, see Spivak, "Subaltern Studies" 12. Spivak expands and revises her original argument and links the notion of the subaltern to Gramsci's and Raymond Williams's idea of the emergent aspects of resistance to hegemony in *A Critique of Postcolonial Reason*. The most interesting use of the category of the subaltern in relation to nineteenth-century Mexican American writers is to be found in Sánchez and Pita.

27 "Black Roses" (1936), Américo Paredes Papers, box 7, folders 18–19. The manuscript includes variants of the foreword. The manuscript's title alludes to Amado Nervo's *Perlas negras* (1916).

28 On the philosophy of identity, see Jameson, *Late Marxism* 11–12.

29 See also Jameson's discussion of this passage in Jameson, *Late Marxism* 19–24. I use Jameson's corrected translation of this passage.

30 Kymlicka and Norman identify the legal and economic forms of subjectivity in "citizenship theory" as "citizenship-as-legal-status" and "citizenship-as-desirable activity." Both ideas concern the nature of participation in a political community (Kymlicka and Norman 353).

31 See also Jameson, "Modernism and Imperialism."

32 Mandel contends that multinational capitalism is the latest, purest state of classical capitalism. See Mandel 118.

33 See Montejano, *Anglos and Mexicans*; Gutiérrez, *Walls and Mirrors*; and Foley on changing modes of production in the Southwest after 1848 and their relation to changing social structures.

34 On the production of whiteness as a historical process in early twentieth-century Texas and the Southwest, see Foley.

35 Negt and Kluge point out that in social practice, the public sphere may include both the social and the personal; something that is a purely private matter can be a matter of great public interest. See the chapter entitled "The Workings of Fantasy as a Form of Authentic Experience" in their *Public Sphere and Experience*, 32–38. On the "mutual infiltration of public and private spheres," see also Habermas, *Structural Transformation* 141–51.

36 On the concept of articulation, see Hall, "On Postmodernism." Hall defines articulation as a metaphor used "to indicate relations of linkage and effectivity between different levels" of material relations, structures, and concepts in "Race, Articulation and Societies Structured in Dominance" 325. See also Paveltich and Backus 130–35. On the relationship between gender, sexuality, and the concepts of nationalism and citizenship, see Parker et al; Miller; and especially the incisive work of C. Mohanty.

37   The *corrido* as a genre of political critique constantly renews itself. In the aftermath of the great Mexican labor diasporas of the 1980s and 1990s, for instance, an entire corpus of new *corridos* emerged to document and analyze the effects of global economic shifts on the lives of individual men and women. See my discussion of this different form of contemporary *corridos* in "Transnational Migrations." See also Herrera-Sobek; and McKenna.

38   For a full discussion of this question, see Saldivar-Hull. See also Padilla 38–40.

39   This is the definition of the bildungsroman that Benjamin offers in the essay "The Storyteller" 146–47.

40   According to Frantz Fanon in *Black Skin, White Masks*, this is a classic instance of the experience of the assimilated middle classes under racist colonialism.

41   Américo Paredes Papers, Box 8, folder 14. See also Paredes's remarks concerning how the novel might have ended if he had followed out his original design for the protagonist's life.

42   While Paredes's novel is situated solidly within the modernist tradition, it nevertheless consistently tests the frontiers of modernism, especially as the economic modernization of the borderlands begins to shift into another stage of development at mid-century. On Paredes's modernism in relation to the social and cultural development of the borderlands, see Schedler.

4   Transnational Modernisms

1   For an account of Paredes's seminal influence, see J. Saldívar, "Chicano Border Narratives" 170.

2   The problematic of border writing is a topic unto itself. See Hicks. See also Fusco. For different perspectives on the border and the Mexican postmodern, see Rouse; and Bartra. There is also an excellent discussion of the problematics of border culture in Fox. Of recent critiques of the postmodern in relation to border studies, the most compelling is that of M. González.

3   I am relying here on the excellent formulations of the question of modernism in the visual arts by Drucker. See also Bell. Important recent discus-

sions of modernism and modernity occur in Jameson, *Postmodernism* 302–13; and Jameson, *A Singular Modernity*. In contrast to Jameson's modernity regarded in the singular is the analysis offered by Taylor, "Two Theories."

4   The literature on modernism is vast, but following are the key texts for an understanding of the relationship between the extension of Western modernization worldwide and the ascendancy of cultural modernism. The works that I am most indebted to in this study are Horkheimer and Adorno; Horkheimer; Benjamin, *Charles Baudelaire*; Lukács, *History and Class Consciousness*; Williams, *Marxism and Literature*; DeMan; Derrida; Hall, "On Postmodernism"; Said, *Culture and Imperialism*; Eagleton, "Capitalism"; and Jameson, *A Singular Modernity*. On modernity in relation to the Americas, see Dussel.

5   See Drucker; Hutcheon; Felski; Butler; Sedgwick; and especially, Spivak, *Critique of Postcolonial Reason*.

6   On transculturation, see also Rosaldo, foreword; and Beverley 41–64.

7   The category of the *counterculture of modernity* is taken from Gilroy 36–40.

8   Gregory Bateson employs the term *metalogue* to describe expressions of discourse whose formal qualities embody their conceptual intent. See Bateson. I find it here appropriate to Paredes's intention to disrupt the assumed symmetries of both American and Mexican national identities and their distinct forms of modernity.

9   In addition to the works cited earlier on the new American studies and the work of Corse, see as examples the contemporary versions of these questions in Tompkins; Bellah, *Habits of the Heart*; and Scheckel. On the romantic origins of cultural nationalism, see Trumpener.

10   In personal correspondence of April 1994, Paredes pointed out to me that in the years since he had first written this poem in 1934, it had passed into the realm of oral poetry and had become part of the vernacular political discourse of south Texas. Without his knowledge, "The Mexico-Texan" was first circulated at various political rallies and meetings in manuscript form, and then later was published as an anonymous piece in the League of United Latin American Citizens newsletter. Still later, in 1960, the poem was collected as a piece of folk composition by anthropology students from the University of Texas doing fieldwork in south Texas.

11   See also the discussion in Kennedy 469–70; and in Foner 221–36.

12   As early as March 1929, Roosevelt had already claimed that "modern social conditions have progressed to a point where such demands [as basic human rights] can no longer be regarded other than as matters of an absolute right." Qtd. in Greer 14.

13 The cataclysm of World War II was imperial to the extent that it resulted from the clash of nations involved in the grab for portions of Africa, Asia, South Asia, and the Asian Pacific during the eighteenth and nineteenth centuries.

14 In commemoration of the fiftieth anniversary of the 1943 *Saturday Evening Post* issues that published Norman Rockwell's paintings and four accompanying essays, Stuart Murray and James McCabe edited a volume that includes the Rockwell paintings accompanied by five new essays. Laurie Norton Moffatt explains that these essays were intended to reflect on "the relevance and meaning of these freedoms in today's society and today's world conditions." Foreword in Murray and McCabe x.

15 In chapter 8, book 4 of *The Social Contract*, Rousseau outlines the requirements of civil religion: belief in the existence of God, the life to come, the reward of the just and punishment of sinners, the sanctity of the social contract and the law, and the denial of intolerance. See "Du contract social" 468–69. See also Rousseau, *The Social Contract* 185–86. The argument for the importation of Rousseau's notion of civil religion into an American context is made by Bellah, "Civil Religion" 172–76.

16 Rockwell himself was later not pleased with these last two paintings, writing that *Freedom from Want* represented "overabundance, the table was so loaded down with food," while *Freedom from Fear* was based "on a rather smug idea." Qtd. in Murray and McCabe 51.

17 See also, Olson on the "visual rhetoric" of Rockwell's icons. The original issues of the *Saturday Evening Post* that I consulted in the Stanford University archives are in mint condition except for the fact that three of the illustrations have been carefully cut from the bound volume. Only the illustration of the Thanksgiving feast represented in *Freedom from Want* remains in the collection.

18 See Tarkington; Durant; Bulosan, "Freedom from Want"; and Bénet.

19 See the illuminating discussion of this episode in Bulosan's life in Foner 227.

20 The autobiography that Bulosan was writing at the time would turn out to be one of the first great expressions of postwar ethnic identity. See Bulosan, *America Is in the Heart*.

21 I cite the *Saturday Evening Post* version. All four of the essays are reprinted in Murray and McCabe 125–37.

22 See also Walzer's discussion of the problem of citizenship in a chapter of this title in his *Obligations*, 205–7.

23 Concerning the claims of Roosevelt's Four Freedoms that "freedom from want" meant that "rich nations would help poor nations rather than

exploit them" and that "freedom from fear" meant that "powerful nations would not commit acts of physical aggression against weaker ones," Paredes comments dryly in a footnote to his poem, "Some people were skeptical" (*Between Two Worlds* 139 n. 6). Translations of the Spanish are my own.

24 Américo Paredes, personal communication with the author, March 15, 1995.

25 A strikingly similar position concerning the nature of cultural imposition and Americanization had been voiced earlier in the century when "America" was on the verge of entering the earlier world war. See Bourne 89–91. Bourne questioned what would be the course of American nationalism in the coming age of cosmopolitanism and argues for dual citizenship as the rudimentary form of an intellectual internationalism to which he aspired (94). "America is coming to be, not a nationality, but a trans-nationality, a weaving back and forth, with the other lands, of many threads of all sizes and colors" (96).

26 On the integration of the citizen-subject in Rousseau, a radical alternative to Locke's liberal model of the propertied citizen, see the excellent discussion by Langan 32–33.

27 *Alma* (soul) is a feminine noun in Spanish, requiring the corresponding feminine ending of the adjectival modifier *pocha*. On the derivation and meaning of the Mexicanism *pocho/a*, Santamaría notes that it is "a name designating the North American descendents of Mexicans"; the word apparently also suggests "someone of limited abilities," "stupid" and can refer to the "corrupted Castilian tongue, mixture of English and poor Spanish, spoken by North American descendents of Mexican origin" (872). Paredes activates all valences of the term and converts their pejorative quality into honorifics.

28 Federico de Onís once suggested that the life of Peruvian poet José Santos Chocano (1875–1934) "would have been an excellent subject for a novel" (Qtd. in Florit and Jiménez 131). Celebrated in the early part of the twentieth century for his attempts to synthesize in poetry the history and culture of Latin America, Chocano, like other figures that Paredes admired and emulated during the 1930s, was an aesthetic and political revolutionary. He joined the forces of the Mexican insurgent Pancho Villa during the Mexican Revolution and remained an active revolutionary throughout his life. His best-known work from this period was a book of verse titled *Alma América*. See Florit and Jiménez (131–37). As in the case of many other poets of his era, the influence and presence of Walt Whitman as a poet of the Americas is also inescapably evident.

29 See, for example, Chocano's poem, "La canción del camino" (The Song of the Road), from *Fiat lux* in Florit and Jiménez 136–37.

30 The selectivity with which freedom was available to these other Americans would be severely tested soon, when of the approximately nine thousand enemy alien nationals taken into custody under the Alien Enemies Act of 1798 after the attack on Pearl Harbor on December 7, 1941, 1 of every 923 were Italian nationals, 1 of every 80 were German nationals, and 1 of every 8 were Japanese nationals. See Stone 285.

5 Modernist Vernacular Intellectuals

1 A similar argument concerning the nature of an African American vernacular aesthetic is proposed in Baker.

2 See also García. The preface to the Calvin Horn edition of Sánchez's *Forgotten People* was written, not in 1940 as García suggests (255), but in 1967.

3 Concerning the invention of the Southwest as a Spanish colonial rather than a Mexican entity, see the excellent discussion in Calderón 1–27. See also the interview with Paredes, which also addresses this matter (Calderón and López-Morín). In his own work on folklore, Paredes was later to deride what he called the "Hispanophile" view of the history of the "Spanish" Southwest. In its extreme form, Paredes argued, this view held that "Mexican American folklore . . . is almost totally Spanish-Peninsular, in other words—in its origins, having come directly from Spain to the parts of the United States where it is found today" ("Folklore of Groups" 4). Mexican folklore in this view is unlike "Spanish American" (that is, White European versus mestizo Mexican) folklore since "the latter is mixed with indigenous elements which have diluted its grace and elegance" (4), while the Spanish American kind remains purely peninsular in origin. A less extreme version of this view still held, according to Paredes, that "the Spanish folklore of the United States is thus superior to that of Mexico, not only because it is *criollo* (Spanish-American) with impeccable colonial credentials, but also because it represents survivals of ancient and valuable European forms" (4). Paredes cites Aurelio Espinosa as a proponent of this latter view. Paredes's own view was historical, transnational, and material.

4 On the mediation between morality and politics, see Negt and Kluge 9–10. See also Habermas, *Structural Transformation* 102–17.

5 Emma Tenayuca (1916–99); see her autobiographical essay titled "I Saw Those Women Herded and Taken into Jail." This essay is a reprint of her address to the National Association of Chicana and Chicano Studies (formerly

National Association for Chicano Studies) in Austin, Texas, 1984. Paredes in several places has stated that Emma Tenayuca was one of his heroes as he was reaching maturity in south Texas.

6   Borders of Modernity

1   *Pocho* is a term of opprobrium used by Mexicans to refer to Mexican Americans. In accepting the award by the Mexican government of La Orden Mexicana del Aguila Azteca (Mexican Order of the Aztec Eagle) in 1991, Paredes cited José Vasconcelos as the originator of the term in his work *La tormenta*. I refer to a copy of the speech in my personal collection. As is evident in this poem, and as he said to me in a conversation of September 19, 1985, "I prided myself in being a *pocho*."

2   On Guillén, see the excellent discussions of Kutzinski, *Against the American Grain*; Kutzinksi, *Nicolás Guillén*; Pérez Firmat, *Cuban Condition*; Pérez Firmat, "Nicolás Guillén"; and Schmidt Camacho. The book version of this latter work is *Migrant Dreams: Development and Subalternity in the Mexico-U.S. Borderlands* (New York: New York University Press, 2005). Here as elsewhere, I am deeply indebted to the insightful commentary of each of these scholars.

3   For discussions of the history of Mexican music, see Campos. See also G. Saldívar, *Historia de la música*.

4   Pérez Firmat, "Nicolás Guillén" 323. See also the excellent discussion in J. D. Saldívar, "Américo Paredes" 305–7.

5   The transformations, however, are not always what one would wish. Writing a year after he first wrote "Paso Doble," Paredes returns to the heroic Hispanic scene of "Paso Doble" only to undercut it. In an English-language verse titled "If You Let Me Kiss Your Lips," he writes now as "a belated traveler, his sense gone awhirl," as "a poet [with] a muse starved and thin," whose "spavined . . . Pegasus" and "lyre made of tin" speak of latter-day falls from grace (*Between Two Worlds* 20).

6   See Habermas, "Modernity" 251 on modernity and the rejection of normalization. Habermas's full analysis of the problem of modernity occurs in Habermas, *Philosophical Discourse*.

7   Paredes's footnote in *Between Two Worlds* points out that "The Rio Grande" was first published in a local newspaper, the (Harlingen) *Valley Morning Star*, in October 1934. This is "odd in retrospect," he claims, "since Harlingen at the time was extremely racist" (139 n. 1.) "El Río Bravo" is dated July 21, 1936, in *Cantos de adolescencia*. See the original publication of "El

Río Bravo" in *La Prensa de San Antonio*. Fittingly, Paredes's son Vincent read "The Rio Grande" as a eulogy for his father at the memorial held for Paredes at the University of Texas at Austin on May 23, 1999.

8 See Santamaría 151. *Bravo* can also mean "courageous" or "stormy." Hot, spicy *chile picante* can be said to be *bravo*.

9 On the trading center of Bagdad, see Pierce 41, 54–55. Pierce notes that Bagdad, Tamaulipas, Mexico, had existed as a settlement at the mouth of the Rio Grande as early as 1780. During the nineteenth century, it served as the port of entry for all goods destined for Mexico through Matamoros. It reached its high mark, however, during the American Civil War and the French imperial invasion of Mexico, from 1862 to 1866. During this epoch, Bagdad was a truly binational town, boasting a "conglomerate citizenship" (55) of Mexicans and Americans and "served as an outlet for Confederate cotton" (Paredes, "Folklore and History" 67). Bourke, too, describes it as "a commercial metropolis, frequented by the traders of Havre, Liverpool, and Hamburg" ("American Congo" 592–94). As if in proleptic emulation of a scene of magical realism from one of Gabriel García Márquez's novels, the historical Bagdad was wiped from the face of the earth in a hurricane of 1874 as if by a biblical wind and was never rebuilt. The Mexican version of this history is offered in G. Saldívar, *Historia compendiada*.

10 Paredes is here clearly playing with the etymological qualities of the term *peon* (pedestrian, foot soldier) as defined by Santamaría.

11 See the excellent discussion of the relationship between poetry, music, and memory in P. Anderson.

12 On the Kantian bridging of the object and the idea in relation to modernity, see Jameson, *A Singular Modernity* 46–47.

13 Baudelaire's essay first appeared in *Le Figaro* of November 26 and 29 and December 3 of 1863. References are to this translation of Baudelaire's essay; additional reference is to "Le peintre de la vie moderne" in the Pléiade edition, 1152–92.

14 I refer here to the original text because most English translations render "le transitoire" incorrectly as "the ephemeral" rather than as "the transitory" in Baudelaire's formula for modernity. Baudelaire wishes to emphasize the "transitional" rather than the "ephemeral" quality of modernity. See Baudelaire, "Painter" 12; Pléiade 1163.

15 The "transmodern," claims Dussel, embraces both "modernity and its alterity" by denying the innocence of modernity and affirming the reason of the victims of modernity (137).

16 See the elegant discussion of the mestizo origins of high modernism by Hedrick. On the recasting of modernism in a New World context to better represent the postcolonial experience of modernity, see also Pollard.

7 Bilingual Aesthetics

1 Composed in 1935, this poem was first published in the *Southwest Review* (Autumn 1964): 306.

2 See also the discussion of McCarthy in Moya and Saldívar 14–16.

3 I first presented a version of this chapter at the conference "Bilingual Aesthetics" organized by Doris Sommer at Harvard University. For an elaboration of some of the themes of that seminal conference, see Sommer, *Bilingual Aesthetics*.

4 "El corrido del hijo desobediente" is one of the most widely known of Mexican ballads. This version of the *corrido* combines the versions of the song performed by Américo Paredes as transcribed in Limón, *Mexican Ballads*; the version paraphrased in Paredes's novel, *The Shadow*; other variants of the song, including my transcript of the verses from a 1921 recording; and the version collected in Kuri-Aldana and Martínez 446–47. Limón notes that Paredes informed him in personal correspondence that "El corrido del hijo desobediente" was his favorite *corrido*. The Archive of Recorded Sound at Braun Music Library, Stanford University, has one of the earliest recorded versions of the song. Aurora Perez, operations manager and archivist there, helped me locate a pristine copy of a seventy-eight RPM recording of the *corrido* by Martin y Malena con Mariachi, recorded April 7, 1921. The classic Mexican movie, *Flor silvestre* (1943), directed by Emilio "El Indio" Fernández (1904–86), the greatest filmmaker of the Golden Age of Mexican cinema, and starring the luminous Dolores del Río and macho par excellence Pedro Armendáriz, includes a scene in which *guitarreros* perform the *corrido* with exquisite emotive flair. Julia Tuñón comments that *Flor silvestre* tells "the unhappy love story of a couple from different social classes who face the opposition of [the hero's] wealthy *hacienda*-owning parents at a time of Revolutionary violence and confusion. This romance alludes to the conflictual encounter between tradition and the modern values implied by the desire for equality that [the hero] discovers in Revolutionary ideas" (182). In Paredes's poem and in his rendition of the ballad, the focus is on violence, confusion, and contradiction in a time of revolutionary change rather than on irresolvable romantic woes.

5 Variants of the *corrido* use the words *desgraciado* (wretched) and *desdichado* (ill-fated) interchangeably. Even if we choose as the preferred reading of the song *desgraciado* instead of *desdichado*, a similar case can be made concerning the ambiguity, indeed contradictory nature, of the word. The crucial issue here is the use of the verb *fue* (he was), rather than the alternate form, *era* as the operative modal. The first possibility implies passive force—

Felipe was disgraced/ill-fated (by something/someone); the second denotes continuity of condition — Felipe was disgraced/ill-fated (as a state of being).

6   See my discussion of this theme in *Chicano Narrative* 36–38.

7   For a more complete discussion of the *corrido* as a "socially symbolic act," see my discussions under the headings "The Folk Base of Chicano Narrative" and "Paredes, Villarreal, and the Dialectics of History" in *Chicano Narrative* 26–73.

8   See Luke 2:34, where Christ is described as "a sign that is rejected" (Jerusalem Bible); "a sign which shall be spoken against" (King James Version); or "signum cui contradicetur" (Biblia Vulgata). In the later poem "Tres faces del pocho," Paredes's narrator sings to Mexico "un himno extraño / . . . para que sepas bien lo desdichado / que pueden ser los hijos de tus hijos" (an odd hymn / so that you may know the wretched (contradiction) / that the children of your children can be), *Between Two Worlds* 40.

9   The phrase is Hobsbawm's from his classic study of the relationship between modernity and tradition, *The Invention of Tradition*. See Hobsbawm and Ranger 54. On Mexican masculinity, see Irwin, who describes the shifting constructions of masculinity in the early twentieth century.

10   This is not to say that other kinds of *corridos* might arise to serve the function of symbolic action and vernacular critique that the *corrido* of border conflict had formerly performed. For discussions of the function of the *corrido* in the contemporary period, see Herrera-Sobek; and J. Saldívar, *Border Matters*. See also my discussion of the transnational theme and the contemporary function of the *corrido* in "Transnational Migrations." On critical vernacular culture, see also Kymlicka, *Politics in the Vernacular*.

11   As one of the anonymous readers of this book for Duke University Press points out, García Lorca's beautiful poem, "La guitarra" from *Poema del cante jondo* (1931), about the yearning for "cosas lejanas" (faraway things) may be part of the intertextual *red* or *redil* of "Guitarreros." García Lorca's poem links the image of the guitar with yet another "transfixed heart," that of the Virgin of Sorrows, pierced by swords. See the lovely illustration of the Virgin of Sorrows and her pierced heart adorning the title page of García Lorca's "Poema del canto jondo" 92.

12   The contrapuntal subtext to Paredes's line about "malas mujeres" is certainly Lydia Mendoza's protofeminist recording of the classic tango, "Mal hombre" ("Evil Man"), first recorded in 1934: "Mal hombre / tan ruin es tu alma que no tiene nombre, / eres un canalla, eres un malvado, / eres un mal hombre" (Evil man, / your soul is so vile it has no name, / you are despicable, you are evil, / you are an evil man). See Mendoza 19–21.

13   Arnold wrote the "Stanzas from the Grande Chartreuse" (285) some-

time between 1851 and 1855, probably mainly in 1852. Another of Arnold's poems, "The River," roughly from this same period, is also noteworthy in relation to Paredes. It is probably more than coincidence that Paredes's river poems echo Arnold's when he speaks of his soul seeking "immunity from my control" as it "wander[s] round the world" (Arnold, "The River" 232).

14   For a discussion of the changing role of the Chicano warrior hero under the impact of feminism, see Rosaldo, *Culture and Truth* 150–66.

15   Fredric Jameson made this point in a lecture titled "Aesthetic Autonomy in the Age of Capitalism," delivered at Stanford University on January 26, 1998. The lecture has been published in *A Singular Modernity* 42–55.

16   See also Gagnier's exceptionally insightful account of Kant's ethical aesthetics in *The Insatiability of Human Wants* 124–25.

17   See *Critique of Judgment*, First Book, Analytic of the Beautiful, Part VI. "The beautiful is that which, apart from concepts, is represented as the Object of a Universal delight" 292.

18   I follow and am deeply indebted here to the illuminating discussion of Smith, Shaftesbury, Hume, Burke and the Kantian imaginary in Eagleton, *Ideology* 31–66. Also on Kant's aesthetic, see Jameson, *A Singular Modernity* 175–76. And see Robert Kaufman's wonderfully suggestive idea that Kant "began and executed much of his critical project—the *Third Critique* most obviously" from the impasses into which intellectual rigor had led him and was fully aware that these impasses "corresponded to the structure of the real." In "Red Kant" 688–89.

19   Jameson discusses "cognitive mapping" in several places, most notably in "Cognitive Mapping." See also the concluding chapter of his *Postmodernism* 409–13. Jameson's proposition there is that the stages of capitalism, from its classical market form to that of monopoly capitalism in the stage of imperialism to the moment of late capitalism and the multinational network "generate a type of space unique to it." The conceptual spaces that Jameson refers to are not literal terrains but "are all the result of discontinuous expansion of quantum leaps in the enlargement of capital," especially in its "penetration and colonization of hitherto uncommodified areas" (410).

8   Border Subjects, Transnational Sites

1   See the fine discussion of Gramsci's cultural criticism in Crehan 101.

2   See Montejano, "Frustrated Apartheid" 133.

3   On the influence of anarchist thought in the early twentieth century borderlands, see Sandos 72–73.

4 For a discussion of the possible authenticity of the "Plan de San Diego," see Harris and Sadler 385.

5 See Harris and Sadler 386.

6 See the discussion of the *corrido* of "Los sediciosos," in Paredes, *Texas-Mexican Cancionero*; and in R. Saldívar, *Chicano Narrative* 30–31.

7 See Harris and Sadler 390–92; and Sandos 108–10. See also Pierce 114–15; and for the Mexican historical version of these incidents, G. Saldívar, *Historia compendiada*.

8 Gramsci, "War of Position and War of Manoeuvre" 229–30; See also Hall, "Gramsci's Relevance." Here, as in my discussion of *George Washington Gómez*, I am much indebted to Hall's arguments in this essay, especially in regard to the seven specific points he makes concerning the applicability of Gramsci for the contemporary study of race and ethnicity. Hall argues that Gramsci brings "a distinctive theoretical perspective to bear on the seminal theoretical and analytic problems which define the field" (435).

9 For the publication history and a related close reading of "The Hammon and the Beans" and "Over the Waves Is Out," see my *Chicano Narrative* 48–60. Here I elaborate my earlier readings of these stories by situating them in the context of Paredes's transnational experiences before and after World War II.

10 Homi Bhabha makes a related argument about the difference between colonizer and colonized as "almost the same but not quite." See "Of Mimicry and Men."

11 It is easy to overread this scene sentimentally as one reader does who claims that with her mimicry "Chonita claims ownership over Anglo discourse as she creates a hybrid voice that turns Anglo discourse against itself to expose it as an ideology of conspicuous (over)consumption." This "claim of ownership" is not validated by the text in either discursive or material terms. See Alemán 57.

12 See Paredes's comments earlier in this book: "In my early years, Mark Twain and Charles Dickens were authors that most influenced me. I read many others of course in high school and junior college, mostly writers in English and Spanish before 1920." The Dickensian influence is also visible in the metonymic relationships Paredes establishes between characters and settings, but it is one I do not pursue here.

13 "Over the Waves Is Out" and "The Hammon and the Beans" are the only stories from the collection to have been previously published. "Over the Waves Is Out" was written in China in 1946 and published in 1953. "The Hammon and the Beans" was written in 1939 but published in 1963.

14 Juventino Rosas (1868–94), the Mexican composer of "Sobre las olas"

("Over the Waves"), a waltz that has become familiar internationally, is the composer to whom the story refers.

15 For a selection of Posada's prints, see Posada. See also the excellent discussion in Posada et al.

16 See also Zamora and Smith.

17 The unpublished collection included two episodes drawn from the manuscript of the novel *George Washington Gómez*. Paredes won five hundred dollars in books for his efforts.

18 See also my discussion in *Chicano Narrative* 74–90.

19 See Pierce 26–27. See also Robinson 23.

20 The site of the first encounter of the US-Mexican war was Palo Alto, Texas, located on "an extensive prairie 9 miles north of Brownsville, just west of Loma Alta," (Pierce 26–27). See also Robinson 23.

21 See Paredes, "Problem of Identity" 22–23, and, Paredes, "United States, Mexico" 227–29, respectively, for discussions of the phallocentric value of the image of the mounted man with his pistol in hand.

22 On the particular version of Gramsci's theories of subalternity in a Latin American context see Rodríguez. See also Moreiras; and Beverley.

9 Idioms of Race, Nation, and Identity

1 I cite here Paredes's translation of the essay, a shorter version of his original Spanish-language text.

2 Raymond Williams explores with rare beauty life in a "border country" in his novels dealing with the history of Welsh nationalism. See Williams, *Border Country*; and Williams, *People of the Black Mountains*.

3 On the globalization of literary studies, see Livingston. See also Baucom; and Jay.

4 In this regard, Paredes's work anticipates and provides historical perspective to current discussions of multicultural citizenships. See, for instance, Kymlicka, *Multicultural Citizenship*; Kymlicka, *Politics in the Vernacular*; and Miller. On the history of the concept of citizenship in early Spanish America, see Herzog 43–64; Lomnitz; and Escalante.

5 Kymlicka makes very useful distinctions among the terms *multinational, polyethnic, multiculturalism*, and *cultural pluralism* in the context of citizenship. See Kymlicka, *Multicultural Citizenship* 11–26.

6 Paredes continues by noting that in *The Flavor of Texas*, J. Frank Dobie "defends the Mexican by switching stereotypes, from treacherous knife-stabber to kindly Uncle Remus" (*Uncle Remus con Chile* 11).

7 In *War without Mercy*, John W. Dower describes how simian imagery was part of the prevalent Allied propaganda effort to dehumanize the Japanese. The epithet Mex, of course, had already carried a similar dehumanizing valence in other American imperial wars.

8 On the conflict between Roosevelt and MacArthur and Truman and MacArthur, see Schaller 20.

9 In a column appearing in *El Universal* on June 11, 1946, Paredes writes about the "young Japanese women [who] offer themselves for a box of field rations or a bar of chocolate. The people call them '*chocoreto no mumume*' — the chocolate girls." My translation. See also Américo Paredes Papers, box 11, folder 13, which contains the notes for a story to be called "Yamamoto Was Her Name."

10 "Le Sage ne rit qu'en tremblant" (The Sage laughs only in fear and trembling) (976), says Baudelaire, and later, "Il faut ajouter qu'un des signes très-particuliers du comique absolu es de s'ignorer lui-même" (I should add that one of the most distinctive signs of the absolute comic is that it remains unaware of itself) (992) ("De l'essence du rire" 976, 992).

11 On the democratic spirit of laughter, humor, and irony, see Bakhtin, "Forms of Time" 236–42.

12 In personal correspondence of December 13, 1992, Paredes notes: "Based on an experience to a young friend of [Amelia's] family. He was not half Mexican but had been born in Mexico. Like many Nisei, he was caught in Japan by the war. It was a crucifix he was wearing on a chain around his neck when he was digging his own grave along with other members of his platoon. There were plenty of 'war crimes' committed by U. S. forces long before Vietnam and My Lai. Yet we executed the Japanese leaders as war criminals because Japanese soldiers also committed the same kind of atrocities."

13 On the history of Asian migration to Mexico in general and the characteristics of Japanese migration in particular see Ota Mishima.

14 As political editor for *Stars and Stripes*, Paredes covered the first few months of the Far East war crimes trials after the war in the Pacific. At one point during the trial, Paredes was granted an exclusive interview with Hideki Tojo at Sugamo prison. Américo Paredes, personal correspondence with the author, December 13, 1992. See also Paredes's account given in chapter 2 of this book.

15 Utagawa Hiroshige (1797–1858) is generally regarded as one of the two greatest landscape artists in Japanese printmaking. See the beautiful selection of Hiroshige prints in Forrer.

16 The town is based on the actual lovely seaside resort town of Atami. Américo Paredes, telephone conversation with the author, August 18, 1993.

17   *Picadero*, derived from *picar* (to prick), suggests various puns in Spanish, including *pícaro* (the traditional knavish adventurers of Spanish fiction), *picador* (the horseman who pricks the bull's neck muscles in the bullfight to prepare it for the fall), and *picardía* (the Mexican oral lore of pungent wordplay). It also carries sexual connotations.

18   Américo Paredes, personal correspondence with the author, February 7, 1992. In traditional Mexican folktales about the village of San Fernando, the official dolt at issue in the story is usually the "mayor" or some other governmental bureaucrat who misapprehends words because of his ignorance. Here, of course, the fool is not a Mexican public official but an Anglo-American one at the Brownsville-Matamoros border bridge. See the folktale "The Mayor of San Fernando" collected in Paredes, *Folktales of Mexico* 42–43, 208–9.

19   See the line "So many mounted Rangers against one lone Mexican!" from "El corrido de Gregorio Cortez."

20   On the film careers and cultural significance of Cantinflas and Tin Tan, see also Medina de la Serna 167. See also the very useful review of Mexican cinema by A. Scott. One of Germán Valdés's early successful films was the 1945 hit *El hijo desobediente*, directed by Humberto Gómez Landero. Of the two Johnny Picadero stories, Paredes would later write, "Also included [in the collection] are two attempts at humor that may or may not fly in Chicanolandia these days of political correctness." Américo Paredes, personal correspondence with the author, February 7, 1992.

21   See A. Sánchez. See also Medina de la Serna 167.

22   On the aesthetic imaginary in the experiences of Mexican nationals who served in the US Army during World War II, see Paredes, *Uncle Remus con Chile* 146–47, 75–76.

10   Occupation-Era Writings

1   On the end of the war in the Pacific, see Dower, *Embracing Defeat* 36, 40.

2   On the Japanese attitudes toward the American occupation, see Schaller 3.

3   See Rubinfien, Phillips, and Dower 13.

4   Dower explains the nature of the Allied participation in the decision making procedures of the occupation.

5   Ehrlich discusses the occupation in relation to the films produced during the era.

6 Yamanashi writes: "The phrase 'Occupation era' sounds odd to me, brought up as I was entirely in the postwar period. Japanese people usually call this time 'confusion era' or 'just after the war'" (23).

7 The first of Paredes's published materials from Japan that I have been able to locate dates from December 30, 1945, at the Eleventh Replacement Depot near Nagoya, Japan. Private Américo Paredes is listed as the editor of the camp newsletter. In an article for *El Universal* dated July 26, 1947, Paredes wrote that he landed in Japan "a few weeks after the first Allied forces disembarked in Japan." His "Notes for Reference Crossing over from U.S. to Japan" give the date of November 18, 1945, for arrival in Nagoya aboard the Liberty troopship SS *Cape Victory*. Américo Paredes Papers, box 7, folder 16.

8 The byline in the Mexico City *El Universal* lists Paredes as "Cabo del Ejército Norteamericano" (corporal in the US Army) from September 4, 1946, until May 12, 1947, when he begins to be identified as "Sargento." I have not been able to verify the promotion.

9 An article in *Stars and Stripes* from February 11, 1946, covering the dismissal of Rubin and Pettus notes that Rubin had been a union official in Waterbury, Connecticut, before the war and had fought in the International Brigade in the Spanish civil war. He had acknowledged "a four year membership in the Communist Party." This and all of the following citations and illustrations from *Pacific Stars and Stripes* are reprinted with permission from *Stars and Stripes*, a Department of Defense publication. © 2003 *Stars and Stripes*.

10 See *Stars and Stripes*, February 11, 1946, and the following daily numbers for March 1946. Rubin had been with *Pacific Stars and Stripes* since the publication of its first edition in Tokyo on October 3, 1945, using the requisitioned space of the English-language *Japan Times*.

11 See also Harootunian x.

12 See *Stars and Stripes*, April 8, 1946; *Stars and Stripes*, May 2, 1946; *Stars and Stripes*, May 21, 1946; and *Stars and Stripes*, June 25, 1946.

13 See *Stars and Stripes*, May 2, 1945; and *Stars and Stripes*, June 21, 1946.

14 Phrases from Paredes's *Stars and Stripes* July 21, 1946, article, "Rebirth of the Ginza," are repeated verbatim in Spanish in the "Desde Tokio" column of *El Universal* of August 11, 1946, (date line July 25, 1946) under the signature of "E. Paredes."

15 Translations from the articles in *El Universal* here and following are my own.

16 Molasky documents how "the occupation has been remembered, recreated, and disseminated" in Japanese literature (1). This literature represents the mirror image of Paredes's literary and nonfiction writings. My thanks to Christopher D. Scott for pointing out this valuable source to me.

17   These volumes of pictorial works by Japanese and American photographers offer an unparalleled visual record of the period covered by Paredes's dispatches from occupied Japan. My sincerest thanks to Etsuko Maruyama, lecturer at Keio University in Tokyo, and Christopher Scott of Stanford University for providing translations of the captions to this and other photographs from these publications.

18   This and two other columns from *El Universal* to which I refer are signed by "E. Paredes." Box 11, folder 9 of the Américo Paredes Papers contains the drafts of the articles Paredes wrote for the "Desde Tokio" and "Desde China" columns in 1946 and 1947. Also in this folder is correspondence between Paredes and Miguel Lanz Duret, president and general manager of *El Universal*, including a letter from Paredes requesting that his payment be sent to his brother Eliseo, very likely the source for the "E. Paredes" byline. My sincere gratitude to Christian Kelleher, director of the Américo Paredes Papers, for his generous assistance in determining the authorship of these *El Universal* columns.

19   See the excellent discussion in Molasky 1. I am greatly indebted to this invaluable discussion for helping me situate Paredes's discussion of the Ginza and the sex industry.

20   For an extended discussion of the evolving cultural interactions during the occupation period, see Dower, *Embracing Defeat* 122, 32–38.

21   Besides performing dozens of Latin favorites during a long career, María Mendez Grever (1885–1951) wrote many of her own hits, including "Cuando vuelva a tu lado," "Júrame," "Te quiero dijiste," and "Ya no me quieres." Later in the 1950s, both Pérez Prado and Stan Getz recorded "Lamento gitano" in a jazzed-up mambo beat.

22   This is the first issue of *Stars and Stripes* listing Paredes's name on the masthead.

23   For a full discussion of the paradoxes of the Japanese postwar film industry, see Ehrlich 45–46.

24   These are the 1947 hits made popular by the performer Shizuko Kasagi. See text and illustration in *Asahi* 164. The Japanese postal system issued a stamp commemorating "Ringo-no-Uta" and postwar popular culture on November 24, 1998.

25   On the role of Mexican armed forces in the Pacific during World War II, see Knight 302–5.

26   See Paredes, "Miss Stateside." Although no byline accompanies this story, it closely parallels the description of the event by Paredes in *El Universal* on July 12, 1946, and it is thus very likely that Paredes was the reporter for *Stars and Stripes*.

27   See Harries and Harries 105.

28 See also *Pacific Stars and Stripes* 6–7. Paredes's article appears in this volume in edited form as one of the representative pieces commemorating the anniversary of the first forty years of the publication of *Pacific Stars and Stripes*.

29 Paredes first mentioned this incident to me in a letter of December 13, 1992, and then again in an interview on March 2–3, 1995. See Paredes's full account of this incident in chapter 2.

30 For a full discussion of Okawa's career, see Harries and Harries 136.

31 As Paredes was later to write about the Japanese general Tomobumi Yamashita, the commander of Japanese forces in the Philippines also executed as a war criminal in 1946, "It may be that our armed forces were more interested in eliminating a symbol than in executing a 'war criminal.'" Paredes, "Yamashita" 161.

32 See Hill 100, 117.

33 See Igarashi 11–12.

34 Harootunian makes this argument about "history's actuality" in Japan's encounter with modernity. See Harootunian 372–80.

35 See the chapter entitled "Folkism and the Spectre of Fascism" in Harootunian 399–414. Harootunian argues that in interwar Japan, "the privileging of the folk could not help but supply fascism with its most powerful trope, an object of fantasy and political desire, and thus could not, itself, avoid complicity with the 'gathering' of fascism" (400). A contemporary account of the relationship between race and nationalism that Paredes had read in 1948 is Fairchild.

36 See the "Far East Notebooks," numbers 1, 2, 3, Américo Paredes Papers, box 8, folders 12, 13, 14. Two other features on the Ainu in *Stars and Stripes* that Paredes would have seen are Friedman; and "The Ainu."

11 Imaginary Functioning of Institutions

1 The article quotes Mike Masaoka, the national Japanese American Citizens League Anti-Discrimination Committee legislative director, who comments that the new law "will give GI's in Japan and Korea the same right to happiness that any American has stationed anywhere else in the world" and that he was "grateful and pleased" that "Congress has seen fit to eliminate discriminatory racial laws for servicemen in the Orient."

2 See chapter 2, page 140.

3 Américo Paredes, personal correspondence with the author, August 19, 1994. Paredes added, "I have dug up the various re-writes I did on *The*

Shadow, a short novel that won me a $500 prize back in 1955 or '56. . . . And, as I may have told you, I am thinking of doing a series of semi-autobiographical sketches. Nothing may come of it; I don't know how much energy I can summon—and how many other problems face Amelia and me. But writing a few other things is good therapy, and I may do so."

4   See chapter 2, page 70.

5   See Gilly, *La revolución interrumpida* 60–63. On the conditions leading up to the Mexican Revolution, see Gilly's definitive discussion in the chapter titled "1910."

6   See also Balibar, "Propositions." An insightful commentary on Balibar and Paredes's *The Shadow* is offered by Schmidt Camacho. I am greatly indebted to Alicia Schmidt Camacho for numerous discussions on Paredes's *The Shadow* in relation to Mexican labor history during the course of the writing of her dissertation.

7   The fictional Mexican city of Morelos represented in the novel is the imaginary counterpart of the equally fictional American Jonesville-on-the-Grande, both corresponding to the real border cities of Matamoros, Tamaulipas, and Brownsville, Texas. See Américo Paredes Papers, box 12, folder 12, which contains Paredes's notes for an unfinished novel, *The River Man*, where he makes this identification.

8   Rulfo's novel *Pedro Páramo* (1955) and his short story collection about the Mexican Revolution, *El llano en llamas* (1953) are exactly contemporaneous with Paredes's novel and are about strikingly similar themes dealing with postrevolutionary Mexico.

9   See Gilly, *La revolución interrumpida* 356. On the construction of a uniquely *norteño* (northern) Mexican border identity from the possibilities of multiple regional alternatives, see Aboites Aguilar 13–30.

10   See Schmidt Camacho 41–65. Schmidt Camacho provides an excellent reading of "the friction between the 'modern' and the 'traditional' in the process of post-revolutionary state-formation and development" in *The Shadow*. Lomnitz notes that although the postrevolutionary governments "upheld the ideal of the private farmer in the 1920s and thought it a much more desirable goal than that of the communitarian peasant, the task of building up the state was more important to them than that of establishing the citizen" (309).

11   See the remarkably informative essay by Womack 127.

12   See Meyer 202.

13   On the processes by which "a people" formulates its aspirations for reform and social revolution in the act of nation building, see Balibar, "Nation Form" 93.

14 Two Saint Anthonys are celebrated in the Christian calendar. The allusion to the temptations of the flesh as orchestrated by the devil clearly identifies the referent here as Saint Antony of Egypt (251–356), the most appropriate point of reference for Paredes's narrative. Saint Antony of Egypt is the subject of numerous classical paintings including one by Breughel, which in turn inspired Flaubert's *La tentation de Saint-Antoine* (1874). In all of these representations, the devil takes the shape of a seductive woman to tempt Saint Anthony. See *La tentation de Saint-Antoine* in Flaubert 23–268. Flaubert's Antoine magnificently represents the frailty of human desire and links them, as Paredes does here, to the processes of modernity and modernization. In Flaubert, Eros and Thanatos, the principles of pleasurable modernity, haunt the holy man and attempt to seduce him into a world-historical rupture with the past. Saint Antony of Padua (1195–1231), an early leader of the Franciscan order, whose members established many of the colonial fort missions of Spanish America, is the other, less satisfactory, alternative reference. On the two Saint Anthonys, see A. Butler 20–21, 86–87.

15 I cite both the 1983 translation and the 1971 Spanish-language editions of Gilly's distinguished book since each represents different stages in Gilly's thinking and includes different revisions, epilogues, and afterwords.

16 See Paredes's discussion of these specific *corridos* in *Texas-Mexican Cancionero*. See also Paredes, *"With His Pistol in His Hand"* 148.

17 See Santamaría 335. *Cuitlacoche* is the indigenous Aztec name for a Mexican Indian trufflelike morsel, an edible corn fungus, *Ustilago maidis*. Santamaría observes that a secondary and vulgar meaning of *cuitla*, from Aztec *cuitlatl*, is "excrement," or more exactly, "shit," particularly "chicken shit." *Cuitlacoche*, then, regarded as the excrement of the corn because of its color and odor, is the metaphoric waste product of the corn. Traveling in central and southern Mexico, I have seen the alternate form, *huitlacoche*, for this unusual delicacy.

18 See Jordan. For a discussion of the role of belief in the supernatural as a way of creating communities of identity, see also Castro 216. For a useful list of ingredients and recipes for dealing with the malady, see Sandoval 78–79.

19 For a different reading of the significance of the ghost, see Alonzo.

20 As a child in Brownsville, Texas, I witnessed a ritual *barrida* performed in just this manner in my home as part of an enactment of the ritual to cure a lingering case of malignant *susto*. More recently, traveling in Oaxaca in the summer of 2004, I experienced a *barrida* as part of an indigenous Temezcal cleansing ceremony.

21 Jameson makes this argument concerning the status of the supernatural as an oppositional belief system. See Jameson, *Political Unconscious* 85–87.

22 See also Benjamin, "Calderón's."

23 Womack makes this point about the course of the Mexican Revolution in general. See Womack 128.

24 These are the kinds of questions posed by political theorists and sociologists such as Sassen 9–12; Wiener 529; and Bader 780–83.

25 On the question of Mexican labor migration within the contemporary period, see Rouse. See also, Gutiérrez, "Migration"; and Weber.

26 See also Miller.

27 See G. Thompson 1, 8. On the concept of cultural citizenship, see Rosaldo, "Cultural Citizenship"; and, on multicultural citizenship, see Kymlicka, *Multicultural Citizenship* 17–19; and Kymlicka, *Politics in the Vernacular* 317–26.

28 The term differentiated citizenship is Marion Young's; she develops this distinctive version of citizenship in "Polity and Group Difference" 258. For a related version of the "new" citizenship, see Chantal Mouffe, *Dimensions of Radical Democracy*.

Aboites Aguilar, Luis. *Norte precario: Poblamiento y colonización en México, 1760–1940*. Mexico City: Colegio de México, Centro de Estudios Históricos, 1995.

Adelman, Jeremy, and Stephen Aron. "From Borderlands to Borders: Empires, Nation-States, and the Peoples in North American History." *American Historical Review* 104.3 (1999): 814–41.

Adorno, Theodor. *Minima Moralia: Reflections from Damaged Life*. Trans. E. F. N. Jephcott. London: New Left Books, 1974.

———. *Negative Dialectics*. 1966. Trans. E. B. Ashton. New York: Continuum, 1973.

"The Ainu." *Pacific Stars and Stripes*, July 14, 1946.

Alarcón, Norma. "Traddutora, Traditora: A Paradigmatic Figure of Chicana Feminism." *Cultural Critique* 13 (1989): 57–87.

Alemán, Jesse. "Chicano Novelistic Discourse: Dialogizing the *Corrido* Critical Paradigm." *MELUS* 23.1 (1998): 49–64.

Alonso, Ana María. *Thread of Blood: Colonialism, Revolution, and Gender on Mexico's Northern Frontier*. Tucson: University of Arizona Press, 1995.

Alonzo, Juan J. "Américo Paredes's *The Shadow*: Social and Subjective Transformation in Greater Mexico." *Aztlan* 27.1 (2002): 27–57.

Altamirano, Ignacio Manuel. *Obras completas*. Mexico City: Secretaría de Educación Pública Departamento de Divulgación, 1949.

Althusser, Louis. "Ideology and Ideological State Apparatuses: (Notes toward an Investigation)." Trans. Ben Brewster. *Lenin and Philosophy and Other Essays*. New York and London: Monthly Review Press, 1971. 127–86.

Alvarez, Robert R., Jr. "The Mexican-U.S. Border: The Making of an Anthropology of Borderlands." *Annual Review of Anthropology* 24 (1995): 447–70.

Anderson, Benedict. *Imagined Communities: Reflections on the Origin and Spread of Nationalism*. Rev. ed. London: Verso, 1991.

Anderson, Paul Allen. *Deep River: Music and Memory in Harlem Renaissance Thought*. Durham, NC: Duke University Press, 2001.

Anzaldúa, Gloria. *Borderlands/La Frontera: The New Mestiza*. San Francisco: Spinsters/Aunt Lute, 1987.

Aparicio, Frances R., and Susana Chávez-Silverman, eds. *Tropicalizations: Transcultural Representations of Latinidad*. Hanover, NH: University Press of New England, 1997.

Appadurai, Arjun. *Modernity at Large: Cultural Dimensions of Globalization*. Minneapolis: University of Minnesota Press, 1996.

Arendt, Hannah. *The Human Condition*. Chicago: University of Chicago Press, 1958.

Arnold, Matthew. *The Poems of Matthew Arnold*. Ed. Kenneth Allott. London: Longmans, 1965.

Arteaga, Alfred. "Beasts and Jagged Strokes of Color: The Poetics of Hybridization on the US-Mexican Border." *Bakhtin: Carnival, and Other Subjects*. Ed. David Shepherd. Amsterdam: Rodopi, 1993. 277–93.

Asahi rekishi shashin raiburari: Senso to shomin, 1940–49. Vol. 4. Ed. Rekishi shashin kanko iinkai. Tokyo: Asahi Shinbunsha, 1995.

Aura, Alejandro. *La hora intima de Agustín Lara*. Mexico City: Cal y Arena, 1990.

Bader, Viet. "The Cultural Conditions of Transnational Citizenship: On the Interpenetration of Political and Ethnic Cultures." *Political Theory* 25.6 (1997): 771–813.

Baker, Houston, Jr. *Blues, Ideology, and Afro-American Literature: A Vernacular Theory*. Chicago: University of Chicago Press, 1984.

Bakhtin, M. M. "The *Bildungsroman*." 1934–38. Trans. Vern W. McGee. *Speech Genres and Other Late Essays*. Ed. Caryl Emerson and Michael Holquist. Austin: University of Texas Press, 1986. 10–59.

———. "Discourse in the Novel." 1934–35. Trans. Caryl Emerson and Michael Holquist. *The Dialogic Imagination: Four Essays*. Ed. Holquist. Austin: University of Texas Press, 1981. 259–422.

———. "Forms of Time and of the Chronotope in the Novel: Notes toward a Historical Poetics." 1937–38. Trans. Caryl Emerson and Michael Holquist. *The Dialogic Imagination: Four Essays*. Ed. Holquist. Austin: University of Texas Press, 1981. 84–258.

———. "From Notes Made in 1970–71." Trans. Vern W. McGee. *Speech Genres and Other Late Essays*. Ed. Caryl Emerson and Michael Holquist. Austin: University of Texas Press, 1986. 132–58.

———. "The Problem of Speech Genres." 1952–53. Trans. Vern W. McGee. *Speech Genres and Other Late Essays*. Ed. Caryl Emerson and Michael Holquist. Austin: University of Texas Press, 1986. 60–102.

———. *Problems of Dostoevsky's Poetics*. 1963. Ed. and trans. Caryl Emerson. Minneapolis: University of Minnesota Press, 1984.

Balibar, Etienne. "The Nation Form: History and Ideology." Trans. Balibar and Chris Turner. *Race, Nation, Class: Ambiguous Identities*. Ed. Balibar and Immanuel Wallerstein. London: Verso, 1991. 86–106.

———. "Propositions on Citizenship." *Ethics* 98 (1988): 723–30.

Bartra, Roger. *Blood, Ink, and Culture: Miseries and Splendors of the Post-Mexican Condition*. Trans. Mark Alan Healey. Durham, NC: Duke University Press, 2002.

Bateson, Gregory. "Why Do Things Get in a Muddle?" *Steps to an Ecology of Mind*. New York: Ballantine, 1972. 3–8.

Baucom, Ian. "Globalit, Inc.; Or, the Cultural Logic of Global Literary Studies." *PMLA* 116.1 (2001): 158–72.

Baudelaire, Charles. "De l'essence du rire." 1857. *Baudelaire: Œuvres complètes*. Ed. Claude Pichois. Paris: Editions Gallimard, 1961. 975–93.

———. "The Painter of Modern Life." 1863. *The Painter of Modern Life and Other Essays*. Ed. and trans. Jonathan Mayne. New York: Phaidon, 1995. 1–41.

———. "Le peintre de la vie moderne." 1863. *Baudelaire: Œuvres complètes*. Ed. Claude Pichois. Paris: Editions Gallimard, 1961. 1152–92.

Bauman, Richard. Introduction. *Folklore and Culture on the Texas Mexican-Border*. By Américo Paredes. Ed. Bauman. Austin: Center for Mexican American Studies, University of Texas at Austin 1993. ix–xxiii.

Bazant, Jan. "From Independence to the Liberal Republic, 1821–1867." *Mexico since Independence*. Ed. Leslie Bethell. New York: Cambridge University Press, 1991. 1–48.

Bell, Michael. "The Metaphysics of Modernism." *The Cambridge Companion to Modernism*. Ed. Michael Levenson. New York: Cambridge University Press, 1999. 9–32.

Bellah, Robert Neelly. "Civil Religion in America (1967)." *Beyond Belief: Essays on Religion in a Post-Traditionalist World*. Berkeley: University of California Press, 1970. 168–89.

———. *Habits of the Heart: Individualism and Commitment in American Life*. Berkeley: University of California Press, 1996.

Bénet, Stephen Vincent. "Freedom from Fear." *Saturday Evening Post*, March 13, 1943, 12.

Benjamin, Walter. "Calderón's *El mayor monstruo, Los celos* and Hebbel's *Herodes und Mariamne*: Comments on the Problem of Historical Drama." *Selected Writings*, vol. 1, *1913–1926*. Ed. Marcus Bullock and Michael W. Jennings. Cambridge, MA: Belknap, 1996. 363–86.

———. "Central Park." Trans. Edmund Jephcott et al. *Selected Writings*, vol. 4, *1938–1940*. Ed. Howard Eiland and Michael W. Jennings. Cambridge, MA: Belknap, 2003. 161–99.

———. *Charles Baudelaire: A Lyric Poet in the Era of High Capitalism*. London: New Left Books, 1973.

———. "Critique of Violence." *Selected Writings*, vol. 1, *1913–1926*. Ed. Marcus Bullock and Michael W. Jennings. Cambridge, MA: Belknap, 2000. 236–52.

———. "Eduard Fuchs, Collector and Historian." Trans. Howard Eiland et al. *Selected Writings*, vol. 3, *1935–1938*. Ed. Eiland and Michael W. Jennings. Cambridge, MA: Belknap, 2002. 260–302.

———. "Excavation and Memory." Trans. Rodney Livingstone et al. *Selected Writings*, vol. 2, *1927–1934*. Ed. Howard Eiland, Michael W. Jennings, and Gary Smith. Cambridge, MA: Belknap, 1999. 576.

———. "Mirrors." Trans. Howard Eiland and Kevin McLaughlin. *The Arcades Project*. Cambridge, MA: Belknap, 1999. 537–42.

———. "The Storyteller: Observations on the Works of Nikolai Leskov." Trans. Howard Eiland et al. *Selected Writings*, vol. 3, *1935–1938*. Ed. Eiland and Michael W. Jennings. Cambridge, MA: Belknap, 2002. 143–66.

———. "Theater and Radio: The Mutual Control of Their Educational Program." Trans. Rodney Livingstone et al. *Selected Writings*, vol. 2, *1927–1934*. Ed. Howard Eiland, Michael W. Jennings, and Gary Smith. Cambridge, MA: Belknap, 1999. 583–86.

———. "Theory of Remembrance." Trans. Howard Eiland et al. *Selected Writings*, vol. 4, *1938–1940*. Ed. Eiland and Michael W. Jennings. Cambridge, MA: Belknap, 2003. 139–312.

———. "Theses on the Philosophy of History." Trans. Harry Zohn. *Illuminations*. Ed. Hannah Arendt. New York: Harcourt Brace World, 1968. 253–64.

Beverley, John. *Subalternity and Representation: Arguments in Cultural Theory*. Durham, NC: Duke University Press, 1999.

Bhabha, Homi K. *Nation and Narration*. New York: Routledge, 1990.

———. "Of Mimicry and Men: The Ambivalence of Colonial Discourse." *The Location of Culture*. New York: Routledge, 1994. 85–92.

Bierhorst, John. *The Mythology of Mexico and Central America*. New York: William Morrow, 1990.

Blackburn, Robin. "Fin de Siècle: Socialism after the Crash." *New Left Review* 185 (1991): 5–66.

Bogues, Anthony. *Black Heretics, Black Prophets: Radical Political Intellectuals*. New York: Routledge, 2003.

Boltin, Herbert Eugene. *The Spanish Borderlands: A Chronicle of Old Florida and the Southwest*. New Haven: Yale University Press, 1921.

Bonfil Batalla, Guillermo. *México profundo: una civilización negada*. Mexico City: Grijalbo, 1987.

Bourke, John Gregory. "The American Congo." *Scribner's*, May, 1894, 590–610.

———. *On the Border with Crook.* New York: Scribner's Sons, 1892.

Bourne, Randolph. "Trans-national America." *Atlantic Monthly* 1916, 86–97.

Brannon, Lil, Brenda M. Greene, and the National Council of Teachers of English. *Rethinking American Literature.* Urbana, IL: National Council of Teachers of English, 1997.

Bulosan, Carlos. *America Is in the Heart: A Personal History.* New York: Harcourt Brace, 1946.

———. "Freedom from Want." *Saturday Evening Post*, March 6, 1943, 12.

Bürger, Peter. *Theory of the Avant-Garde.* Trans. Michael Shaw. Minneapolis: University of Minnesota Press, 1984.

Butler, Alban. *Lives of the Saints.* 1883. Ed. James Bentley. New York: Gallery Books, 1990.

Butler, Judith. *Gender Trouble: Feminism and the Subversion of Identity.* New York: Routledge, 1990.

Calderón, Héctor. *Narratives of Greater Mexico: Essays on Chicano Literary History, Genre, and Borders.* Austin: University of Texas Press, 2004.

Calderón, Héctor, and José Rósbel López-Morín. "Interview with Américo Paredes." *Nepantla* 1.1 (2000): 197–228.

Campa, Arthur Leon. *Spanish Folk-Poetry in New Mexico.* Albuquerque: University of New Mexico Press, 1946.

Campos, Rubén M. *El folklore y la música mexicana: Investigación acerca de la cultura musical en México (1525–1925).* 1928. Mexico City: Consejo Nacional para la Cultura y las Artes, 1991.

Carby, Hazel. "Proletarian or Revolutionary Literature: C. L. R. James and the Politics of the Trinidadian Renaissance." *South Atlantic Quarterly* 87.1 (1988): 39–52.

Castañeda, Carlos E., et al. *The Mexican Side of the Texan Revolution [1836].* Dallas: P. L. Turner, 1928.

Castañeda Shular, Antonia, Tomás Ybarra Frausto, and Joseph Sommers, comps. *Literatura chicana: Texto y contexto/ Chicano Literature: Text and Context.* Englewood Cliffs, NJ: Prentice-Hall, 1972.

Castro, Rafaela G. "Susto." *Chicano Folklore: A Guide to the Folktales, Traditions, Rituals, and Religious Practices of Mexican Americans.* New York: Oxford University Press, 2001. 216.

Chase, Cida S. "Américo Paredes." *Dictionary of Literary Biography.* Ed. Francisco A. Lomelí and Carl R. Shirley. Detroit: Gale Group, 1999. 182–93.

Coronado, Raúl, Jr. "Competing American Colonial Modernities: Politics, Publishing, and the Making of a U.S.-Mexican Literary Culture, 1836–1939." PhD diss. Stanford University, 2004.

Corse, Sarah M. *Nationalism and Literature: The Politics of Culture in Canada and the United States*. Cambridge: Cambridge University Press, 1997.

Cotera, María Eugenia. "Native Speakers: Locating Early Expressions of U.S. Third World Feminist Discourse; A Comparative Analysis of the Autoethnographic and Literary Writing of Ella Cara Deloria and Jovita Gonzalez." PhD diss. Stanford University, 2000.

―――. "Refiguring 'the American Congo': Jovita González, John Gregory Bourke, and the Battle over Ethno-historical Representations of the Texas Mexican Border." *Western American Literature* 25.1 (2000): 75–94.

Crehan, Kate. *Gramsci, Culture, and Anthropology*. Berkeley: University of California Press, 2002.

Dear, Michael, and Gustavo Leclerc, eds. *Postborder City: Cultural Spaces of Bajalta California*. New York: Routledge, 2003.

De la Croix, Horst. *Military Considerations in City Planning: Fortifications*. New York: Braziller, 1972.

DeLaura, David J. *Hebrew and Hellene in Victorian England: Newman, Arnold, and Pater*. Austin: University of Texas Press, 1969.

Del Toro, Leticia, Chris Strachwitz, and James Nicolopulos. CD liner notes. *Chelo Silva: La reina tejana del bolero*. El Cerrito, CA: Arhoolie Records, 1995.

DeMan, Paul. *Blindness and Insight: Essays in the Rhetoric of Contemporary Criticism*. Minneapolis: University of Minnesota Press, 1983.

Derrida, Jacques. *Specters of Marx: The State of the Debt, the Work of Mourning, and the New International*. Trans. Peggy Kamuf. New York: Routledge, 1994.

Dower, John W. "Contested Ground: Shomei Tomatsu and the Search for Identity in Postwar Japan." *Shomei Tomatsu: Skin of the Nation*. Ed. Leo Rubinfien, Sandra S. Phillips, and Dower. San Francisco: San Francisco Museum of Modern Art, 2004. 58–77.

―――. *Embracing Defeat: Japan in the Wake of World War II*. New York: Norton, 1999.

―――. *War without Mercy: Race and Power in the Pacific War*. New York: Pantheon, 1986.

Drucker, Johanna. *Theorizing Modernism: Visual Art and the Critical Tradition*. New York: Columbia University Press, 1994.

Durant, Will. "Freedom of Worship." *Saturday Evening Post*, February 27, 1943, 12.

Dussel, Enrique. *The Invention of the Americas: Eclipse of "the Other" and the Myth of Modernity*. Trans. Michael D. Barber. New York: Continuum, 1995.

Eagleton, Terry. "Capitalism, Modernism, and Postmodernism." *Against the Grain: Selected Essays*. London: Verso, 1986. 131–47.

———. *The Ideology of the Aesthetic*. Oxford: Blackwell, 1990.

Echevarría, Roberto González. "Threats in Calderón: Life Is a Dream, 1, 303–08." *Yale French Studies* 69 (1985): 180–91.

Ehrlich, Linda C. "Erasing and Refocusing: Two Films of the Occupation." *The Confusion Era: Art and Culture of Japan during the Allied Occupation, 1945–1952*. Ed. Mark Sandler. Washington, DC: Arthur M. Sackler Gallery, Smithsonian Institution, 1997. 39–51.

Eliot, T. S. "The Metaphysical Poets." *Selected Essays*. New ed. New York: Harcourt Brace, 1950. 241–50.

Escalante Gonzalbo, Fernando. *Ciudadanos imaginarios: Memorial de los afanes y desventuras de la virtud y apología del vicio triunfante en la República Mexicana tratado de moral pública*. Mexico City: Centro de Estudios Sociológicos, El Colegio de México, 1992.

Espinosa, Aurelio M. "Comparative Notes on New Mexican and Mexican Spanish Folktales." *Journal of American Folklore* 27 (1914): 211–31.

Fairchild, Henry Pratt. *Race and Nationality as Factors in American Life*. New York: Ronald Press, 1947.

Fanon, Frantz. *Black Skin, White Masks*. Trans. Charles Lam Markmann. 1967. New York: Grove Weidenfeld, 1998.

———. *The Wretched of the Earth*. Trans. Constance Farrington. New York: Grove, 1963.

Felski, Rita. *The Gender of Modernity*. Cambridge, MA: Harvard University Press, 1995.

Femia, Joseph V. *Gramsci's Political Thought: Hegemony, Consciousness, and the Revolutionary Process*. Oxford: Clarendon, 1981.

Flaubert, Gustave. *Œuvres complètes*. Paris: Seuil, 1964.

Flores, Juan. *From Bomba to Hip-Hop: Puerto Rican Culture and Latino Identity*. New York: Columbia University Press, 2000.

Flores, Juan, and George Yúdice. "Living Borders/Buscando América: Languages of Latino Self-Formation." *Social Text* 8.2 (1990): 57–84.

Flores, Richard R. "Aesthetic Process and Cultural Citizenship: The Membering of a Social Body in San Antonio." *Latino Cultural Citizenship: Claiming Identity, Space, and Rights*. Ed. William V. Flores and Rina Benmayor. Boston: Beacon, 1997. 124–51.

———. "The Corrido and the Emergence of Texas-Mexican Social Identity." *Journal of American Folklore* 105.416 (1992): 166–82.

Florit, Eugenio, and José Olivio Jiménez. "Chocano, José Santos." *La poesía hispanoamericana desde el modernismo*. Ed. Florit and Jiménez. New York: Appleton-Century-Crofts, 1968. 131–37.

Flower, Robin. *The Western Island; Or, the Great Basket*. Oxford: Clarendon, 1944.

Foley, Neil. *The White Scourge: Mexicans, Blacks, and Poor Whites in Texas Cotton Culture*. Berkeley: University of California Press, 1997.

Foner, Eric. *The Story of American Freedom*. New York: Norton, 1998.

Forgacs, David, ed. *The Antonio Gramsci Reader: Selected Writings, 1916–1935*. New York: New York University Press, 2000.

Forrer, Matthi, ed. *Hiroshige: Prints and Drawings*. New York: Prestel, 1997.

Foucault, Michel. *History of Sexuality*, vol. 1, *An Introduction*. Trans. Robert Harley. New York: Pantheon, 1978.

Fowler, Gene, and Bill Crawford. *Border Radio: Quacks, Yodelers, Pitchmen, Psychics, and Other Amazing Broadcasters of the American Airwaves*. Rev. ed. Austin: University of Texas Press, 2002.

Fox, Claire F. *The Fence and the River: Culture and Politics at the U.S.-Mexico Border*. Minneapolis: University of Minnesota Press, 1999.

Fregoso, Rosa Linda. *The Bronze Screen: Chicana and Chicano Film Culture*. Minneapolis: University of Minnesota Press, 1993.

Friedman, Robert. "The Ainu." *Pacific Stars and Stripes*, January 6, 1946.

Fukuyama, Francis. *The End of History and the Last Man*. New York: Free Press, 1993.

Fusco, Coco. "Interview with Guillermo Gómez-Peña and Emily Hicks." *Third Text* 7 (1989): 53–76.

Gagnier, Regenia. "A Critique of Practical Aesthetics." *Aesthetics and Ideology*. Ed. George Levine. New Brunswick, NJ: Rutgers University Press, 1994. 264–82.

———. *The Insatiability of Human Wants: Economics and Aesthetics in Market Society*. Chicago: University of Chicago Press, 2000.

Galarza, Ernesto. *Merchants of Labor: The Mexican Bracero Story: An Account of the Managed Migration of Mexican Farm Workers in California, 1942–1960*. Charlotte, CA: McNally and Loftin, 1964.

Gamio, Manuel. *Forjando patria (pro nacionalismo)*. Mexico City: Porrúa Hermanos, 1916.

———. *Mexican Immigration to the United States: A Study of Human Migration and Adjustment*. Chicago: University of Chicago Press, 1930.

Gaonkar, Dilip Parameshwar. "On Alternative Modernities." *Alternative Modernities*. Ed. Gaonkar. Durham, NC: Duke University Press, 2001. 1–23.

García, Mario T. *Mexican Americans: Leadership, Identity, and Ideology, 1930–1960*. New Haven, CT: Yale University Press, 1989.

García Canclini, Néstor. *Consumers and Citizens: Globalization and Multicultural Conflicts*. Trans. George Yúdice. Minneapolis: University of Minnesota Press, 2001.

———. *La globalización imaginada*. Buenos Aires: Editorial Paidós, SAICF, 1999.

———. *Hybrid Cultures: Strategies for Entering and Leaving Modernity*. Trans. Christopher Chiappari and Silvia L. López Chiappari. Minneapolis: University of Minnesota Press, 1995.

———. "Rewriting Cultural Studies in the Borderlands." Trans. Chelo Alvarez. *Postborder City: Cultural Spaces of Bajalta California*. Ed. Michael Dear and Gustavo Leclerc. New York: Routledge, 2003. 277–85.

———. *Transforming Modernity: Popular Culture in Mexico*. Trans. Lidia Lozano. Austin: University of Texas Press, 1993.

García Lorca, Federico. *Collected Poems: Bilingual Edition*. Trans. Catherine Brown et al. Ed. Christopher Maurer. New York: Farrar, Straus and Giroux, 2002.

———. *Gypsy Ballads*. Ed. and trans. Robert G. Harvard. Warminster, UK: Aris and Phillips, 1990.

Gardner, Helen. *Art through the Ages*. 9th ed. Rev. Horst de La Croix and Richard G. Tansey. San Diego: Harcourt Brace Jovanovich, 1991.

Giles, Paul. *Virtual Americas: Transnational Fictions and the Transatlantic Imaginary*. Durham, NC: Duke University Press, 2002.

Gilly, Adolfo. *The Mexican Revolution/La revolución interrumpida*. Trans. Patrick Camiller. Exp. and rev. ed. London: New Left Books, 1983.

———. *La revolución interrumpida: México, 1910–1920; La guerra campesina por la tierra y el poder*. Mexico City: Ediciones El Caballito, 1971.

Gilroy, Paul. *The Black Atlantic: Modernity and Double Consciousness*. Cambridge, MA: Harvard University Press, 1993.

González, Jovita. "Jovita González: Early Life and Education." *Dew on the Thorn*. Ed. José E. Limón. Houston: Arte Público Press, 1997. xi–xxviii.

———. "Social Life in Cameron, Starr, and Zapata Counties." MA thesis. University of Texas, 1930.

González, Marcial R. "The Postmodern Turn in Chicana/o Cultural Studies: Toward a Dialectical Criticism." Ph D diss. Stanford University, 2000.

Gramsci, Antonio. "Integral Journalism." *The Antonio Gramsci Reader: Selected Writings, 1916–1935*. Ed. David Forgacs. New York: New York University Press, 2000. 383–84.

———. "Observations on Folklore." *The Antonio Gramsci Reader: Selected Writings, 1916–1935*. Ed. David Forgacs. New York: New York University Press, 2000. 360–62.

———. "Osservazioni sul folclore." *Letteratura e vita nazionale: Quaderni del carcere*. Vol. 5. 6th ed. Turin: Giulio Einaudi, 1966. 215–21.

———. "Philosophy, Common Sense, Language, and Folklore." *The An-*

tonio Gramsci Reader: Selected Writings, 1916–1935. Ed. David Forgacs. New York: New York University Press, 2000. 323–62.

———. *Selections from the Prison Notebooks of Antonio Gramsci*. Ed. and trans. Quintin Hoare and Geoffrey Nowell Smith. New York: International Publishers, 1971.

———. "War of Position and War of Manoeuvre." *The Antonio Gramsci Reader: Selected Writings, 1916–1935*. Ed. David Forgacs. New York: New York University Press, 2000. 225–30.

Greer, Thomas H. *What Roosevelt Thought: The Social and Political Ideas of Franklin D. Roosevelt*. East Lansing: Michigan State University Press, 1958.

Griswold del Castillo, Richard. *The Treaty of Guadalupe Hidalgo: A Legacy of Conflict*. Norman: University of Oklahoma Press, 1990.

Gruesz, Kirsten Silva. *Ambassadors of Culture: The Transamerican Origins of Latino Writing*. Princeton, NJ: Princeton University Press, 2002.

Guillén, Nicolás. "*Balada de los dos abuelos*, from *West Indies, Ltd.* (1934)." *Callaloo* 10.2 (1987): 184–88.

Gutiérrez, David G. "Migration, Emergent Ethnicity, and the 'Third Space': The Shifting Politics of Nationalism in Greater Mexico." *Journal of American History* 86.2 (1999): 481–517.

———. *Walls and Mirrors: Mexican Americans, Mexican Immigrants, and the Politics of Ethnicity*. Berkeley: University of California Press, 1995.

Gutiérrez, Félix, and Jorge Reina Schement. *Spanish-Language Radio in the Southwestern United States*. Austin: Center for Mexican American Studies, University of Texas at Austin, 1979.

Gutiérrez Nájera, Manuel. *Poesías completas*. Mexico City: Editorial Porrúa, 1953.

Gutiérrez-Jones, Carl Scott. *Rethinking the Borderlands: Between Chicano Culture and Legal Discourse*. Berkeley: University of California Press, 1995.

Habermas, Jürgen. "Modernity—an Incomplete Project." Trans. Seyla Ben-Habib. *The Anti-aesthetic: Essays on Postmodern Culture*. Ed. Hal Foster. Port Townsend, WA: Bay, 1983. 3–15.

———. *The Philosophical Discourse of Modernity: Twelve Lectures*. Trans. Frederick G. Lawrence. Cambridge, MA: MIT Press, 1987.

———. *The Structural Transformation of the Public Sphere: An Inquiry into a Category of Bourgeois Society*. Trans. Thomas Burger, with the assistance of Frederick Lawrence. Cambridge, MA: MIT Press, 1989.

Hall, Stuart. "Cultural Identity and Diaspora." *Identity: Community, Culture, Difference*. Ed. Jonathan Rutherford. London: Lawrence and Wishart, 1990. 222–37.

———. "Gramsci's Relevance for the Study of Race and Ethnicity (1986)." *Stuart Hall: Critical Dialogues in Cultural Studies*. Ed. David Morley and Kuan-Hsing Chen. New York: Routledge, 1996. 411–40.

———. "On Postmodernism and Articulation: An Interview (1986)." *Stuart Hall: Critical Dialogues in Cultural Studies*. Ed. David Morley and Kuan-Hsing Chen. New York: Routledge, 1996. 131–50.

———. "Race, Articulation, and Societies Structured in Dominance." *Sociological Theories: Race and Colonialism*. Paris: Unesco, 1980, 305–45.

Hallam, Arthur Henry. "On Some of the Characteristics of Modern Poetry, and on the Lyrical Poems of Alfred Tennyson (1831)." *The Writings of Arthur Hallam*. Ed. Thomas Hubbard Vail Motter. New York: Modern Language Association of America, 1943. 182–98.

Hamilton, Edith. *Mythology*. Boston: Back Bay Books, 1998.

Handbook of Texas Online, s.v. "Kenedy, Mifflin," http://www.tsha.utexas .edu/handbook/online/articles/KK/fke23.html (accessed September 2, 2003).

Handbook of Texas Online, s.v. "Wells, James Babbage, Jr.," http://www.tsha .utexas.edu/handbook/online/articles/WW/fwe22.html (accessed September 2, 2003).

Harootunian, Harry D. *Overcome by Modernity: History, Culture, and Community in Interwar Japan*. Princeton, NJ: Princeton University Press, 2000.

Harries, Meirion, and Susie Harries. *Sheathing the Sword: The Demilitarisation of Japan*. London: Hamilton, 1987.

Harris, Charles H., III, and Louis R. Sadler. "The Plan of San Diego and the Mexican-United States War Crisis of 1916: A Reexamination." *Hispanic American Historical Review* 58.3 (1978): 385–92.

Hedrick, Tace. *Mestizo Modernism: Race, Nation, and Identity in Latin American Culture, 1900–1940*. New Brunswick, NJ: Rutgers University Press, 2003.

Heidegger, Martin. *Nietzsche*, vol.1, *The Will to Power as Art*. Trans. David Farrell Krell. San Francisco: Harper and Row, 1979.

Held, David. "Between State and Civil Society: Citizenship." *Citizenship*. Ed. Geoff Andrews. London: Lawrence and Wisehart, 1991. 24.

———. *Democracy and the Global Order: From the Modern State to Cosmopolitan Governance*. London: Polity, 1999.

Herrera-Sobek, María. *The Mexican Corrido: A Feminist Analysis*. Bloomington: Indiana University Press, 1990.

Herzog, Tamar. *Defining Nations: Immigrants and Citizens in Early Modern Spain and Spanish America*. New Haven: Yale University Press, 2003.

Hibbs, Ben. "Bulosan." *Saturday Evening Post*, March 6, 1942, 4.

Hicks, Emily. *Border Writing: The Multidimensional Text*. Minneapolis: University of Minnesota Press, 1991.

Hill, Patricia. "Picturing Progress in the Era of Westward Expansion." *The West as America: Reinterpreting Images of the Frontier, 1820–1920*. Ed. William H. Truettner. Washington, DC: Smithsonian Institution Press, 1991. 97–147.

Hobsbawm, Eric. *The Age of Empire, 1875–1914*. New York: Vintage, 1989.

Hobsbawm, Eric, and Terence Ranger, eds. *The Invention of Tradition*. Cambridge: Cambridge University Press, 1983.

Hogeland, William. "The Inventors of Commercial Country Music." *New York Times*, August 1, 2004.

Holden, Robert H., and Eric Zolov, eds. "Texas, Mexico, and Manifest Destiny." *Latin America and the United States: A Documentary History*. New York: Oxford University Press, 2000. 21–23.

———. "The Treaty of Guadalupe Hidalgo." *Latin America and the United States: A Documentary History*. New York: Oxford University Press, 2000. 31–33.

Holquist, Michael. *Dialogism: Bakhtin and His World*. 2d ed. London: Routledge, 2002.

Horkheimer, Max. *Critical Theory: Selected Essays*. Trans. Matthew J. O'Connell et al. New York: Continuum, 1972.

Horkheimer, Max, and Theodor W. Adorno. *Dialectic of Enlightenment*. New York: Continuum, 1969.

Hughes, Langston. *The Collected Poems of Langston Hughes*. Ed. Arnold Rampersad and David E. Roessel. New York: Vintage, 1994.

Hutcheon, Linda. *The Politics of Postmodernism*. London: Routledge, 1989.

Igarashi, Yoshikuni. *Bodies of Memory: Narratives of War in Postwar Japanese Culture, 1945–1970*. Princeton, NJ: Princeton University Press, 2000.

Irwin, Robert McKee. *Mexican Masculinities*. Minneapolis: University of Minnesota Press, 2003.

James, C. L. R. *The Black Jacobins: Toussaint L'Ouverture and the San Domingo Revolution*. 2d rev. ed. New York: Vintage, 1963. 28–40.

———. "Dialectical Materialism and the Fate of Humanity." 1947. *The C. L. R. James Reader*. Ed. Anna Crimshaw. Oxford: Blackwell, 1992. 153–81.

———. "Why Negroes Should Oppose the War." 1940. *Fighting Racism in World War II*. Ed. Fred Stanton. New York: Monad, 1980.

Jameson, Fredric. "Cognitive Mapping." *Marxism and the Interpretation of Culture*. Ed. Cary Nelson and Lawrence Grossberg. Urbana: University of Illinois Press, 1988. 347–57.

————. "Imaginary and Symbolic in Lacan." 1977. *The Ideologies of Theory: Essays 1971–1986.* Vol. 1. Minneapolis: University of Minnesota Press, 1988. 75–115.

————. *Late Marxism: Adorno; Or, the Persistence of the Dialectic.* London: Verso, 1990.

————. "Modernism and Imperialism." *Nationalism, Colonialism, and Literature.* Ed. Seamus Deane. Minneapolis: University of Minnesota Press, 1990. 43–66.

————. "On Negt and Kluge." *October* 46 (1988): 152–77.

————. *The Political Unconscious: Narrative as a Socially Symbolic Act.* Ithaca, NY: Cornell University Press, 1981.

————. "Postmodernism; Or, the Cultural Logic of Late Capitalism." *New Left Review* 146 (1984): 53–92.

————. *Postmodernism; Or, the Cultural Logic of Late Capitalism.* Durham, NC: Duke University Press, 1991.

————. *A Singular Modernity: Essay on the Ontology of the Present.* London: Verso, 2002.

"Japan-U.S. Marriage Regulations Clarified." *Nippon Times,* September 14, 1950.

Jay, Paul. "Beyond Discipline? Globalization and the Future of English." *PMLA* 116.1 (2001): 32–47.

Johnson, Richard. "What Is Cultural Studies Anyway?" *Social Text* 16 (1986): 38–80.

Jordan, Rosan A. "Ethnic Identity and the Lore of the Supernatural." *Journal of American Folklore* 88.350 (1975): 370–82.

Joseph, G. M., and Timothy J. Henderson. *The Mexico Reader: History, Culture, Politics.* Durham, NC: Duke University Press, 2002.

Joyce, James. *Finnegans Wake.* New York: Viking Press, 1939.

Kant, Immanuel, and Carl J. Friedrich. *Critique of Judgment.* 1790. *The Philosophy of Kant's Moral and Political Writings.* New York: Modern Library, 1993.

Kanzaki, Kyoshi. "A Cageless Zoo: Ueno, Once Cultural Center of Tokyo, Has Turned into Hotbed of Vices." *Japan Review* 12.3 (1949): 1–14.

Kaplan, Amy. *The Anarchy of Empire in the Making of U.S. Culture.* Cambridge, MA: Harvard University Press, 2002.

Kaufman, Robert. "Negatively Capable Dialectics: Keats, Vendler, Adorno, and the Theory of the Avant-Garde." *Critical Inquiry* 27 (2001): 354–84.

————. "Red Kant; Or, the Persistence of the Third Critique in Adorno and Jameson." *Critical Inquiry* 26 (2000): 682–724.

Kennedy, David M. *Freedom from Fear: The American People in Depression and War, 1929–1945.* New York: Oxford University Press, 1999.

Knight, Alan. "The Rise and Fall of Cardenismo, c. 1930–c. 1946." *Mexico since Independence*. Ed. Leslie Bethell. New York: Cambridge University Press, 1991. 241–320.

Knox, Bernard. Introduction. *The Iliad*. By Homer. Trans. Robert Fagles. New York: Viking, 1990. 3–64.

Kracauer, Siegfried. *The Mass Ornament: Weimar Essays*. Trans. Thomas Y. Levin. Cambridge, MA: Harvard University Press, 1995.

Kuri-Aldana, Mario, and Vicente Mendoza Martínez. *Cancionero popular mexicano*. 2 vols. Mexico City: Consejo Nacional para la Cultura y las Artes, 2001.

Kutzinski, Vera M. *Against the American Grain: Myth and History in William Carlos Williams, Jay Wright, and Nicolás Guillén*. Baltimore, MD: Johns Hopkins University Press, 1987.

———, ed. *Nicolás Guillén*. Spec. issue of *Callaloo* 10.2 (1987).

Kymlicka, Will. *Multicultural Citizenship: A Liberal Theory of Minority Rights*. Oxford: Clarendon, 1995.

———. *Politics in the Vernacular: Nationalism, Multiculturalism, and Citizenship*. Oxford: Oxford University Press, 2001.

Kymlicka, Will, and Wayne Norman. "Return of the Citizen: A Survey of Recent Work on Citizenship Theory." *Ethics* 104 (1994): 352–81.

LaCapra, Dominick. *History and Memory after Auschwitz*. Ithaca, NY: Cornell University Press, 1998.

Langan, Celeste. *Romantic Vagrancy: Wordsworth and the Simulation of Freedom*. Cambridge: Cambridge University Press, 1995.

Lara, Agustín. *Agustín Lara: Cien años, cien canciones*. Ed. Mario Arturo Ramos. Mexico City: Oceano, 2000.

Lara, Luis Fernando. *Diccionario básico de español de México*. Mexico City: Colegio de Mexico, 1986.

Lewis, Tracy Hammond. *Along the Rio Grande*. New York: Lewis Publishing, 1916.

Lewis-Smith, Paul. *Calderón de la Barca: La vida es sueño*. London: Grant and Cutler, 1998.

Limerick, Patricia Nelson. *The Legacy of Conquest: The Unbroken Past of the American West*. New York: Norton, 1987.

Limón, José E. *American Encounters: Greater Mexico, the United States, and the Erotics of Culture*. Boston: Beacon, 1998.

———. "Américo Paredes: A Man from the Border." *Revista Chicano-Riqueña* 8.3 (1980): 1–5.

———. *Dancing with the Devil: Society and Cultural Poetics in Mexican-American South Texas*. Madison: University of Wisconsin Press, 1994.

————. *Mexican Ballads, Chicano Poems: History and Influence in Mexican-American Social Poetry*. Berkeley: University of California Press, 1992.

Livingston, Robert Eric. "Global Knowledges: Agency and Place in Literary Studies." *PMLA* 116.1 (2001): 145–72.

Locke, Alain, ed. *The New Negro*. 1925. New York: Atheneum, 1968.

Locke, John. *The Second Treatise of Government*. 1690. Ed. Thomas P. Peardon. Upper Saddle River, NJ: Prentice-Hall, 1997.

Lombardi Satriani, Luigi Maria. *Apropriación y destrucción de la cultura de las clases subalternas*. Mexico City. 1978.

Lomnitz, Claudio. "Modes of Citizenship in Mexico." *Alternative Modernities*. Ed. Dilip Parameshwar Goankar. Durham, NC: Duke University Press, 2001. 298–326.

Los Super 7. *Heard It on the X*. CD. Telarc, 2005.

Lowe, Sarah M. *Frida Kahlo*. New York: Universe Publishing, 1991.

Lukács, Georg. *The Historical Novel*. Trans. Hannah Mitchell and Stanley Mitchell. Lincoln: University of Nebraska Press, 1983.

————. *History and Class Consciousness: Studies in Marxist Dialectics*. Cambridge, MA: MIT Press, 1971.

"Lunes literarios de La Prensa: Producciones selectas antiguas y modernas." *La Prensa de San Antonio* 1935, 1936 (newspaper section that appeared every Monday).

MacLachlan, Colin M. *Anarchism and the Mexican Revolution: The Political Trials of Ricardo Flores Magón in the United States*. Berkeley: University of California Press, 1991.

Mailer, Norman. *The Naked and the Dead*. New York: Rinehart, 1948.

————. Interview with Terry Gross. *Fresh Air*. National Public Radio. WHYY, Philadelphia. January 31, 2003.

Mandel, Ernest. *Late Capitalism*. London: Verso, 1978.

Martin y Malena con Mariachi. *El hijo desobediente*. Seventy-eight rpm recording. Peerless Label, April 7, 1921.

McCarthy, Cormac. *All the Pretty Horses*. New York: Knopf, 1992.

————. *Cities of the Plain*. New York: Knopf, 1998.

————. *The Crossing*. New York: Knopf, 1994.

McDowell, John Holmes. "The Corrido of Greater Mexico as Discourse, Music, and Event." *"And Other Neighborly Names": Social Process and Cultural Image in Texas Folklore*. Ed. Richard Bauman and Roger D. Abrahams. Austin: University of Texas Press, 1981. 44–75.

McKenna, Teresa. "On Chicano Poetry and the Political Age: Corridos as Social Drama." *Criticism in the Borderlands: Studies in Chicano Literature, Culture, and Ideology*. Ed. Héctor Calderón and José David Saldívar. Durham, NC: Duke University Press, 1991. 181–202.

Medina de la Serna, Rafael. "Sorrows and Glories of Comedy." *Mexican Cinema*. Ed. Paulo Antonio Paranagua. London: British Film Institute, 1995. 163–77.

Mendoza, Lydia. *Lydia Mendoza: A Family Autobiography*. Eds. Chris Strachwitz and James Nicolopulos. Houston: Arte Público Press, 1993.

Mendoza, Vicente T., ed. *El corrido mexicano: Antología*. Mexico City: Fondo de Cultura Económica, 1954.

Meyer, Jean. "Revolution and Reconstruction in the 1920s." *Mexico since Independence*. Ed. Leslie Bethell. New York: Cambridge University Press, 1991. 201–40.

Mignolo, Walter D. *Local Histories/Global Designs: Coloniality, Subaltern Knowledges, and Border Thinking*. Princeton, NJ: Princeton University Press, 2000.

Miller, David. *Citizenship and National Identity*. Cambridge, UK: Polity, 2000.

Mohanty, Chandra Talpade. *Feminism without Borders: Decolonizing Theory, Practicing Solidarity*. Durham, NC: Duke University Press, 2003.

Mohanty, Satya P. *Literary Theory and the Claims of History: Postmodernism, Objectivity, Multicultural Politics*. Ithaca, NY: Cornell University Press, 1997.

Molasky, Michael S. *The American Occupation of Japan and Okinawa: Literature and Memory*. London: Routledge, 1999.

Montejano, David. *Anglos and Mexicans in the Making of Texas, 1836–1986*. Austin: University of Texas Press, 1987.

———. "Frustrated Apartheid: Race, Repression, and Capitalist Agriculture in South Texas, 1920–1930." *The World-System of Capitalism: Past and Present*. Ed. Walter L. Goldfrank. Beverly Hills, CA: Sage, 1979.

Moon, Michael, and Cathy N. Davidson. *Subjects and Citizens: Nation, Race, and Gender from Oroonoko to Anita Hill*. Durham, NC: Duke University Press, 1995.

Moreiras, Alberto. "A Storm Blowing from Paradise: Negative Globality and Critical Regionalism." *The Latin American Subaltern Studies Reader*. Ed. Ileana Rodríguez. Durham, NC: Duke University Press, 2001. 81–107.

Moretti, Franco. *The Way of the World: The Bildungsroman in European Culture*. Trans. Albert Sbragia. London: Verso, 2000.

Morford, Mark P. O., and Robert J. Lenardon. *Classical Mythology*. 7th ed. New York: Oxford University Press, 2003.

Morson, Gary Saul, and Caryl Emerson. *Mikhail Bakhtin: Creation of a Prosaics*. Stanford, CA: Stanford University Press, 1990.

Mouffe, Chantal. *Dimensions of Radical Democracy: Pluralism, Citizenship, Community*. London: Verso, 1992.

Moya, Paula, and Ramón Saldívar, eds. "Fictions of the Trans-American Imaginary." Spec. issue of *Modern Fiction Studies* 49.1 (2003).

Murcia, Rebecca Thatcher. *Americo Paredes*. Hockessin, DE: Mitchell Lane Publishers, 2004.

Murray, Stuart, and James McCabe, eds. *Norman Rockwell's Four Freedoms: Images That Inspire a Nation*. Stockbridge, MA: Berkshire House, 2003.

Mustapha, Abdul-Karim. "Questions of Strategy as an Abstract Minimum: Subalternity and Us." *The Latin American Subaltern Studies Reader*. Ed. Ileana Rodríguez. Durham, NC: Duke University Press, 2001. 211–24.

Nairn, Tom. "The Modern Janus." *The Break-Up of Britain: Crisis and Neo-nationalism*. 2d ed. London: Verso, 1981. 329–63.

Negt, Oskar, and Alexander Kluge. *Public Sphere and Experience: Toward an Analysis of the Bourgeois and Proletarian Public Sphere*. Trans. Peter Labanyi, Jamie Daniel, and Assenka Oksiloff. Minneapolis: University of Minnesota Press, 1993.

Nervo, Amado. *Perlas negras, místicas, las voces*. París, Mexico: C. Bouret, 1916.

Nicolopulos, James, and Chris Strachwitz. CD liner notes. *Tejano Roots: The Women (1946–1970)*. El Cerrito, CA: Arhoolie Records, 1991.

Nora, Pierre. "The Return of the Event." 1974. Trans. Arthur Goldhammer. *Histories: French Constructions of the Past*. Ed. Jacques Revel and Lynn Hunt. New York: New Press, 1995. 427–36.

Oates, Stephen B. "Los Diablos Tejanos: The Texas Rangers." *The Mexican War: Changing Interpretations*. Ed. Odie B. Faulk and Joseph A. Stout Jr. Chicago: Sage Books, 1973. 120–36.

Olson, Lester C. "Portraits in Praise of a People: A Rhetorical Analysis of Norman Rockwell's Icons in Roosevelt's 'Four Freedoms' Campaign." *Quarterly Journal of Speech* 69 (1983): 15–24.

Ortiz, Fernando. *Cuban Counterpoint: Tobacco and Sugar*. Trans. Harriet de Onís. Durham, NC: Duke University Press, 1995.

Ota Mishima, María Elena. "Características sociales y económicas de los migrantes japoneses en México." *Destino México: Un estudio de las migraciones asiáticas a México, siglos XIX y XX*. Ed. Ota Mishima, et al. Mexico City: El Colegio de México Centro de Estudios de Asia y Africa, 1997. 55–84.

Padilla, Genaro. *My History, Not Yours: The Formation of Mexican American Autobiography*. Madison: University of Wisconsin Press, 1993.

Pacific Stars and Stripes: The First 40 Years, 1945–1985. Novato, CA: Presidio, 1985.

Paredes, Américo. *Américo Paredes Papers, 1886–1999*. Benson Latin American Collection, General Libraries, University of Texas at Austin.

———. *Between Two Worlds*. Houston: Arte Público Press, 1991.

———. "The Décima on the Texas-Mexican Border: Folksong as an Adjunct to Legend." 1966. *Folklore and Culture on the Texas-Mexican Border*. Ed. Richard Bauman. Austin: Center for Mexican American Studies, University of Texas at Austin, 1993. 235–46.

———. "Desde China, Shanghai." *El Universal*, November 17, 1946.

———. "Desde Tokio (11 de julio)." *El Universal*, July 11, 1946.

———. "Desde Tokio (25 de julio)." *El Universal*, August 11, 1946.

———. "Desde Tokio: Era mi primera noche (28 de mayo)." *El Universal*, May 28, 1946.

———. "Estados Unidos, México y el machismo," *Journal of Inter-American Studies* 9 (1967): 65–84.

———. "The Folk Base of Chicano Literature." *Modern Chicano Writers: A Collection of Critical Essays*. Ed. Joseph Sommers and Tomás Ybarra-Frausto. Englewood Cliffs, NJ: Prentice-Hall, 1979. 4–17.

———. *Folklore and Culture on the Texas-Mexican Border*. Ed. Richard Bauman. Austin: Center for Mexican American Studies, University of Texas at Austin, 1993.

———. "Folklore and History." *Singers and Storytellers*. Ed. Mody Boatright, Wilson M. Hudson, and Allen Maxwell. Dallas: Southern Methodist University Press, 1961. 58–68.

———. "Folklore, *lo Mexicano*, and Proverbs." *Aztlan* 13.1–2 (1982): 1–11.

———. "The Folklore of Groups of Mexican Origin in the United States." 1979. *Folklore and Culture on the Texas-Mexican Border*. Ed. Richard Bauman. Austin: Center for Mexican American Studies, University of Texas at Austin, 1993. 3–18.

———. *Folktales of Mexico*. Chicago: University of Chicago Press, 1970.

———. *George Washington Gómez: A Mexicotexan Novel*. Houston: Arte Público Press, 1990.

———. "The Hammon and the Beans." *Texas Observer*, April 18, 1963.

———. *The Hammon and the Beans and Other Stories*. Houston: Arte Público Press, 1994.

———. "Jorge Isidoro Sánchez Y Sánchez (1906–1972)." *Humanidad: Essays in Honor of George I. Sánchez*. Ed. Paredes. Los Angeles: Chicano Studies Center Publications, 1977. 120–26.

———. "The Mexican Corrido: Its Rise and Fall." 1958. *Folklore and Culture on the Texas-Mexican Border*. Ed. Richard Bauman. Austin: Center for Mexican American Studies, University of Texas at Austin, 1993. 129–41.

———. "Miss Stateside: Fifteen Fair Femmes Fluttering as Forthcoming Finals Focused." *Pacific Stars and Stripes*, May 12, 1946.

———. "Mi tía Pilar." *Reflexiones: New Directions in Mexican American*

Studies. Ed. Yolanda C. Padilla. Austin: Center for Mexican American Studies, 1998. 147–51.

———. "Mr. White." *Reflexiones: New Directions in Mexican American Studies*. Ed. Richard R. Flores. Austin: Center for Mexican American Studies, 1999. 3–6.

———. "Old Grammar School Influenced Brownsville's Life: Many a Successful Career Launched in Old Educational Center Here." *Brownsville Herald*, December 6, 1942.

———. "On Ethnographic Work among Minority Groups: A Folklorist's Perspective." 1977. *Folklore and Culture on the Texas-Mexican Border*. Ed. Richard Bauman. Austin: Center for Mexican American Studies, University of Texas at Austin, 1993. 73–110.

———. "On Gringo, Greaser, and Other Neighborly Names." *Singers and Storytellers*. Ed. Mody C. Boatright, Wilson M. Hudson, and Allen Maxwell. Dallas: Southern Methodist University Press, 1961. 285–90.

———. "Over the Waves Is Out." *New Mexico Review* 23.2 (1953): 177–87.

———. "The Problem of Identity in a Changing Culture." 1978. *Folklore and Culture on the Texas-Mexican Border*. Ed. Richard Bauman. Austin: Center for Mexican American Studies, University of Texas at Austin, 1993. 19–47.

———. "The Problem of Identity in a Changing Culture: Popular Expressions of Culture Conflict along the Lower Rio Grande Border." *Views across the Border: The U.S. and Mexico*. Ed. Stanley R. Ross. Albuquerque: University of New Mexico Press, 1978. 68–94.

———. *The Shadow*. Houston: Arte Público Press, 1998.

———. "Some Aspects of Folk Poetry." 1964. *Folklore and Culture on the Texas-Mexican Border*. Ed. Richard Bauman. Austin: Center for Mexican American Studies, University of Texas at Austin, 1993. 113–28.

———. *A Texas-Mexican Cancionero: Folksongs of the Lower Border*. Urbana: University of Illinois Press, 1976.

———. *Uncle Remus con Chile*. Houston: Arte Público Press, 1993.

———. "The Undying Love of 'El Indio' Córdova: Décimas and Oral History in a Border Family." 1987. *Folklore and Culture on the Texas-Mexican Border*. Ed. Richard Bauman. Austin: Center for Mexican American Studies, University of Texas at Austin, 1993. 247–61.

———. "The United States, Mexico, and *Machismo*." 1971. Trans. Marcy Steen. *Folklore and Culture on the Texas-Mexican Border*. Ed. Richard Bauman. Austin: Center for Mexican American Studies, University of Texas at Austin, 1993. 215–34.

———. *"With His Pistol in His Hand": A Border Ballad and Its Hero*. Austin: University of Texas Press, 1958.

———. "Yamashita, Zapata, and the Arthurian Legend." *Western Folklore* 36.2 (1977): 160–63.

Paredes Manzano, Américo. "Black Roses (1936)." Unpublished poetry manuscript. Américo Paredes Papers, 1886–1999. Benson Latin American Collection, General Libraries, University of Texas at Austin.

———. *Cantos de adolescencia.* San Antonio: Librería Española, 1937.

———. "El Río Bravo." *La Prensa de San Antonio,* December 14, 1936.

Parker, Andrew, et al., eds. *Nationalisms and Sexualities.* New York: Routledge, 1992.

Paveltich, Joanna, and Margot Gayle Backus. "With His Pistol in Her Hand: Rearticulating Corrido Narrative in Helena Maria Viramontes' 'Neighbors.'" *Cultural Critique* 27 (1994): 127–52.

Pease, Donald E., ed. *National Identities and Post-Americanist Narratives.* Durham, NC: Duke University Press, 1994.

Pérez, Emma. *The Decolonial Imaginary: Writing Chicanas into History.* Bloomington: Indiana University Press, 1999.

Pérez, Héctor. "Voicing Resistance on the Border: A Reading of Américo Paredes's *George Washington Gomez.*" MELUS 23.1 (1998): 27–48.

Pérez Firmat, Gustavo. *The Cuban Condition: Translation and Identity in Modern Cuban Literature.* Cambridge: Cambridge University Press, 1989.

———. *Do the Americas Have a Common Literature?* Durham, NC: Duke University Press, 1990.

———. *Life on the Hyphen: The Cuban-American Way.* Austin: University of Texas Press, 1994.

———. "Nicolás Guillén between the *Son* and the Sonnet." *Callaloo* 10.2 (1987): 318–28.

Pérez-Torres, Rafael. *Movements in Chicano Poetry: Against Myths, against Margins.* Cambridge: Cambridge University Press, 1995.

Pierce, Frank Cushman. *A Brief History of the Lower Rio Grande Valley.* Menasha, WI: George Banta, 1917.

Pollard, Charles W. *New World Modernisms: T. S. Eliot, Derek Walcott, and Kamau Brathwaite.* Charlottesville: University of Virginia Press, 2004.

Posada, José Guadalupe. *Posada's Popular Mexican Prints: 273 Cuts.* Comp. Roberto Berdecio and Stanley Appelbaum. New York: Dover, 1972.

Posada, José Guadalupe, et al. *Monografía: Las obras de José Guadalupe Posada, grabador mexicano, con introducción de Diego Rivera.* Mexico City: Ediciones Toledo, 1991.

Pratt, Mary Louise. *Imperial Eyes: Travel Writing and Transculturation.* London: Routledge, 1992.

"President Signs New GI Bride Bill." *Nippon Times,* September 14, 1950.

Reynolds, Larry J., and Gordon Hutner, eds. *National Imaginaries, American Identities: The Cultural Work of American Iconography*. Princeton, NJ: Princeton University Press, 2000.

Richie, Donald. "The Occupied Arts." *The Confusion Era: Art and Culture of Japan during the Allied Occupation, 1945–1952*. Ed. Mark Sandler. Washington, DC: Arthur M. Sackler Gallery, Smithsonian Institution, 1997. 11–22.

Rivera, Tomás. *Y no se lo tragó la tierra/ And the Earth Did Not Part*. First ed. Berkeley: Quinto Sol, 1971.

Robinson, Charles M. *Texas and the Mexican War: A History and a Guide*. Austin: Texas State Historical Association, 2004.

Rockwell, Norman, and Thomas Rockwell. *Norman Rockwell: My Adventures as an Illustrator, as Told to Thomas Rockwell*. Garden City, NY: Doubleday, 1960.

Rodríguez, Ileana. "Reading Subalterns across Texts, Disciplines, and Theories: From Representation to Recognition." *The Latin American Subaltern Studies Reader*. Ed. Rodríguez. Durham, NC: Duke University Press, 2001. 1–32.

Roosevelt, Franklin Delano. "Annual Message to the Congress, January 3, 1940." *War—and Aid to Democracies, 1940*. Vol. 9 of *The Public Papers and Addresses of Franklin D. Roosevelt*. New York: Macmillan, 1941.

———. "Annual Message to the Congress, January 6, 1941." *War—and Aid to Democracies, 1940*. Vol. 9 of *The Public Papers and Addresses of Franklin D. Roosevelt*. New York: Macmillan, 1941.

Rosaldo, Renato. "Cultural Citizenship, Inequality, and Multiculturalism." *Latino Cultural Citizenship: Claiming Identity, Space, and Rights*. Ed. William V. Flores and Rina Benmayor. Boston: Beacon, 1997. 27–38.

———. *Culture and Truth: The Remaking of Social Analysis*. Boston: Beacon, 1989.

———. Foreword. Néstor García Canclini. *Hybrid Cultures: Strategies for Entering and Leaving Modernity*. Minneapolis: University of Minnesota Press, 1995. xi–xvii.

Rosaldo, Renato, and William V. Flores. "Identity, Conflict, and Evolving Latino Communities: Cultural Citizenship in San Jose, California." *Latino Cultural Citizenship: Claiming Identity, Space, and Rights*. Ed. Flores and Rina Benmayor. Boston: Beacon, 1997. 57–96.

Rouse, Roger. "Mexican Migration and the Social Space of Postmodernism." *Diaspora* 1 (1991): 8–23.

Rousseau, Jean-Jacques. "Du contract social." 1767. *Oeuvres complètes*. Ed. Bernard Gagnebin and Marcel Raymond. Paris: Gallimard, 1964. 3:351–470.

————. *The Social Contract.* Trans. Maurice Cranston. Harmondsworth, UK: Penguin, 1968.

Rowe, John Carlos, ed. *Post-nationalist American Studies.* Berkeley: University of California Press, 2000.

Rubinfien, Leo, Sandra S. Phillips, and John W. Dower, eds. *Shomei Tomatsu: Skin of the Nation.* San Francisco: San Francisco Museum of Modern Art, 2004.

Ruiz, Vicki L. *From out of the Shadows: Mexican American Women in Twentieth-Century America.* New York: Oxford University Press, 1998.

Sadowski-Smith, Claudia. *Globalization on the Line: Culture, Capital, and Citizenship at U.S. Borders.* New York: Palgrave, 2002.

Said, Edward W. *Culture and Imperialism.* New York: Knopf, 1993.

————. "Reflections on American 'Left' Literary Criticism." *The World, the Text, and the Critic.* Cambridge, MA: Harvard University Press, 1983. 158–77.

Saldívar, Gabriel. *Historia compendiada de Tamaulipas.* Ciudad Victoria, Mexico: Gobierno del Estado de Tamaulipas, Dirección General de Educación y Cultura, 1988.

————. *Historia de la música.* Mexico City: Ediciones Gernika, 1987.

Saldívar, José David. "Américo Paredes and Decolonization." *Cultures of United States Imperialism.* Ed. Amy Kaplan and Donald E. Pease. Durham, NC: Duke University Press, 1993. 292–311.

————. *Border Matters: Remapping American Cultural Studies.* Berkeley: University of California Press, 1997.

————. "Chicano Border Narratives as Cultural Critique." *Criticism in the Borderlands: Studies in Chicano Literature, Culture, and Ideology.* Ed. Héctor Calderón and Saldívar. Durham, NC: Duke University Press, 1991. 167–80.

————. *The Dialectics of Our America: Genealogy, Cultural Critique, and Literary History.* Durham, NC: Duke University Press, 1991.

Saldívar, Ramón. *Chicano Narrative: The Dialectics of Difference.* Madison: University of Wisconsin Press, 1990.

————. "Transnational Migrations and Border Identities: The Case for a Postnational Aesthetics." *South Atlantic Quarterly* 98 (1999): 217–30.

Saldivar-Hull, Sonia. *Feminism on the Border: Chicana Gender Politics and Literature.* Berkeley: University of California Press, 2000.

Samora, Julian, Joe Bernal, and Albert Peña. *Gunpowder Justice: A Reassessment of the Texas Rangers.* Notre Dame, IN: University of Notre Dame Press, 1979.

Sánchez, Alberto Ruy, ed. *Artes de México: Revisión del cine méxicano.* 3d ed. Vol. 10. Mexico City: Artes de México y del Mundo, 1990.

Sánchez, George I. *Forgotten People: A Study of New Mexicans*. Albuquerque: Calvin Horn Publications and University of New Mexico Press, 1940.

Sánchez, Rosaura, and Beatrice Pita. Introduction. *The Squatter and the Don*. By Amparo Ruiz de Burton. Houston: Arte Público Press, 1992.

Sandos, James A. *Rebellion in the Borderlands: Anarchism and the Plan of San Diego, 1904–1923*. Norman: University of Oklahoma Press, 1992.

Sandoval, Annette. "Susto." *Homegrown Healing: Traditional Home Remedies from Mexico*. New York: Berkley Books, 1998. 78–79.

Santamaría, Francisco. *Diccionario de mejicanismos*. 3d ed. Mexico City: Editorial Porrua, 1978.

Sassen, Saskia. "The Repositioning of Citizenship: Emergent Subjects and Spaces for Politics." *Berkeley Journal of Sociology* 46 (2002): 4–26.

Schaller, Michael. *The American Occupation of Japan: The Origins of the Cold War in Asia*. New York: Oxford University Press, 1985.

Scheckel, Susan. *The Insistence of the Indian: Race and Nationalism in Nineteenth-Century American Culture*. Princeton, NJ: Princeton University Press, 1998.

Schedler, Christopher. "Inscribing Mexican-American Modernism in América Paredes' *George Washington Gómez*." *Texas Studies in Literature and Language* 42.2 (2000): 154–76.

Schmidt Camacho, Alicia R. "Migrant Subjects: Race, Labor and Insurgency in the Mexico-U.S. Borderlands." PhD diss. Stanford University, 2000.

Schwarz, Roberto. *Misplaced Ideas: Essays on Brazilian Culture*. Ed. and trans. John Gleason. London: Verso, 1992.

Scott, A. O. "A Different Mexican Revolution." *New York Times*, June 27, 2004.

Scott, David. *Conscripts of Modernity: The Tragedy of Colonial Enlightenment*. Durham, NC: Duke University Press, 2004.

Sedgwick, Eve Kosofsky. *Epistemology of the Closet*. Berkeley: University of California Press, 1990.

Shklar, Judith N. *American Citizenship: The Quest for Inclusion*. Cambridge, MA: Harvard University Press, 1991.

Slotkin, Richard. *Gunfighter Nation: The Myth of the Frontier in Twentieth-Century America*. Norman: University of Oklahoma Press, 1998.

Smith, Adam. *The Theory of Moral Sentiments*. 1759. Cambridge: Cambridge University Press, 2002.

Soja, Edward. W. *Postmodern Geographies: The Reassertion of Space in Critical Social Theory*. London: Verso, 1989.

Sommer, Doris. *Bilingual Aesthetics: A New Sentimental Education*. Durham, NC: Duke University Press, 2004.

————. *Foundational Fictions: The National Romances of Latin America.* Berkeley: University of California Press, 1991.

Spaulding, Robert M. "CCD Censorship of Japan's Daily Press." *The Occupation of Japan: Arts and Culture.* Ed. Thomas W. Burkman. Norfolk, VA: General Douglas MacArthur Foundation, 1988. 1–16.

Spivak, Gayatri Chakravorty. *A Critique of Postcolonial Reason: Toward a History of the Vanishing Present.* Cambridge, MA: Harvard University Press, 1999.

————. "In a Word, Interview: With Ellen Rooney." *Differences* 2 (1990): 124–56.

————. "Subaltern Studies: Deconstructing Historiography." *Selected Subaltern Studies.* Ed. Ranajit Guha and Spivak. New York: Oxford University Press, 1988. 3–32.

Stalin, Joseph. *Marxism and the National and Colonial Question: A Collection of Articles and Speeches.* Ed. A. Fineberg. New York: International Publishers, 1934.

Stevens, Wallace. *Collected Poems.* New York: Knopf, 1954.

————. "Notes Toward a Supreme Fiction." *Collected Poems.* 1975 ed. New York: Knopf, 1954. 380–408.

Stilwell, Hart. *Border City.* New York: Doubleday, Doran, 1945.

Stone, Geoffrey R. *Perilous Times: Free Speech in Wartime from the Sedition Act of 1798 to the War on Terrorism.* New York: Norton, 2004.

Tarkington, Booth. "Freedom of Speech." *Saturday Evening Post,* February 20, 1943, 12.

Taylor, Charles. *Modern Social Imaginaries.* Durham, NC: Duke University Press, 2004.

————. "Two Theories of Modernity." *Alternative Modernities.* Ed. Dilip Parameshwar Gaonkar. Durham, NC: Duke University Press, 2001. 172–96.

Tenayuca, Emma. "I Saw Those Women Herded and Taken into Jail." 1984. *La Voz de Esperanza* 12.7 (1999): 4–5, 8–9.

————. "Living History: Emma Tenayuca Tells Her Story." *Texas Observer,* October 28, 1983.

Tenayuca, Emma, and Homer Brooks. "The Mexican Question in the Southwest." *Communist* 18.3 (1939): 257–68.

Tennyson, Alfred Lord. *Poetry. Tennyson's Poetry: Authoritative Texts, Contexts, Criticism.* Ed. Robert W. Hill. 2nd ed. New York: W. W. Norton, 1999.

Thompson, E. P. "Folklore, Anthropology, and Social History." *Indian Historical Review* 3.2 (1978): 247–66.

Thompson, Ginger. "Mexico's Migrants Profit from Dollars Sent Home." *New York Times*, February 23, 2005.

Thompson, Stith. *The Folktale*. New York: Dryden, 1946.

———. *Narrative Motif-Analysis as a Folklore Method*. Helsinki: Suomalainen Teideakatemia, 1955.

Tompkins, Jane P. *Sensational Designs: The Cultural Work of American Fiction, 1790–1860*. New York: Oxford University Press, 1985.

Trotsky, Leon. *The History of the Russian Revolution*. 1919. London: V. Gollancz, 1932.

Truett, Samuel, and Elliott Young, eds. *Continental Crossroads: Remapping U.S.-Mexico Borderlands History*. Durham, NC: Duke University Press, 2004.

Trumpener, Katie. *Bardic Nationalism: The Romantic Novel and the British Empire*. Princeton, NJ: Princeton University Press, 1997.

Tuñón, Julia. "Emilio Fernández: A Look behind the Bars." Trans. Ana Lopez. *Mexican Cinema*. Ed. Paulo Antonio Paranagua. London: British Film Institute, 1995. 179–92.

Twain, Mark. *Adventures of Huckleberry Finn*. New York: Random House, 1996.

Vasconcelos, José. *La raza cósmica: Misión de la raza iberoamericana*. Paris: Agencia mundial de librería, 1920.

Volosinov, V. N. "Discourse in Life and Discourse in Art (Concerning Sociological Poetics) 1926." Trans. I. R. Titunik. *Freudianism: A Marxist Critique*. Ed. Neal H. Bruss. New York: Academic Press, 1976. 93–116.

Walzer, Michael. *Obligations: Essays on Disobedience, War, and Citizenship*. Cambridge, MA: Harvard University Press, 1970.

"War Crimes: Road Show." *Time*, May 20, 1946, 24.

Webb, Walter Prescott. *The Texas Rangers: A Century of Frontier Defense*. Boston: Houghton Mifflin, 1935.

Weber, Devra. "Historical Perspectives on Mexican Transnationalism: With Notes from Angumcutiro." *Social Justice* 26.3 (1999): 39–58.

Westbrook, Robert B. "Fighting for the American Family: Private Interests and Political Obligation in World War II." *The Power of Culture: Critical Essays in American History*. Ed. Richard Wightman Fox and T. J. Jackson Lears. Chicago: University of Chicago Press, 1993. 195–221.

White, Hayden. *The Content of the Form: Narrative Discourse and Historical Representation*. Baltimore, MD: Johns Hopkins University Press, 1987.

———. *Figural Realism: Studies in the Mimesis Effect*. Baltimore, MD: Johns Hopkins University Press, 1999.

Wiener, Antje. "Making Sense of the New Geography of Citizenship: Fragmented Citizenship in the European Union." *Theory and Society* 26 (1997): 529–60.

Williams, Raymond. *Border Country, a Novel.* London: Chatto & Windus, 1960.

———. *The Fight for Manod.* London: Chatto and Windus, 1979.

———. *Marxism and Literature.* Oxford: Oxford University Press, 1977.

———. *People of the Black Mountains.* London: Chatto and Windus, 1989.

———. *Second Generation: A Novel.* New York: Horizon, 1964.

Womack, John. "The Mexican Revolution, 1910–1920." *Mexico since Independence.* Ed. Leslie Bethell. New York: Cambridge University Press, 1991. 125–200.

Wordsworth, William, et al. *The Prelude 1799, 1805, 1950: Authoritative Texts, Contexts, and Reception, Recent Critical Essays.* New York: Norton, 1979.

Wright, Will. *Sixguns and Society: A Structural Study of the Western.* Berkeley: University of California Press, 1975.

Yamanashi, Emiko, and Thomas Rimer. "Painting in the Time of 'Heavy Hands.'" *The Confusion Era: Art and Culture of Japan during the Allied Occupation, 1945–1952.* Ed. Mark Sandler. Washington, DC: Arthur M. Sackler Gallery, Smithsonian Institution, 1997. 23–37.

Young, Elliott. *Catarino Garza's Revolution on the Texas-Mexico Border.* Durham, NC: Duke University Press, 2004.

Young, Iris Marion. "Polity and Group Difference: A Critique of the Ideal of Universal Citizenship." *Ethics* 99 (1989): 250–74.

Young, Robert. *White Mythologies: Writing History and the West.* New York: Routledge, 1990.

Zamora, Martha, and Marilyn S. Smith. *Frida Kahlo: The Brush of Anguish.* San Francisco: Chronicle, 1990.

RAMÓN SALDÍVAR

is Hoagland Family Professor of Humanities

and Sciences and Milligan Family University

Fellow in Undergraduate Education in the

Departments of English and Comparative

Literature at Stanford University.

Library of Congress Cataloging-in-Publication Data
Saldívar, Ramón.
The borderlands of culture : Américo Paredes and
the transnational imaginary / Ramón Saldívar.
p. cm. — (New Americanists)
Includes bibliographical references and index.
ISBN 0-8223-3776-2 (alk. paper)
ISBN 0-8223-3789-4 (pbk. : alk. paper)
I. Paredes, Américo. 2. American literature—Mexican
American authors—History and criticism. 3. Mexican
American authors—Biography. 4. Mexican Americans—
Intellectual life. 5. American literature—Mexican-Ameri-
can Border Region—History and criticism. 6. Mexican-
American Border Region—In literature. 7. Mexican-
American Border Region—Intellectual life.
8. Transnationalism. I. Title. II. Series.
PS3531.A525Z88 2006
813'.54—dc22   2005031720